ARCHAEOLOGICAL HISTORY
OF THE
ANCIENT MIDDLE EAST

ARCHAEOLOGICAL HISTORY OF THE ANCIENT MIDDLE EAST

Jack Finegan

Westview Press • Boulder, Colorado
Dawson • Folkestone, England

Copyright © 1979 by Westview Press, Inc.

Published in 1979 in the United States of America by
   Westview Press, Inc.
   5500 Central Avenue
   Boulder, Colorado 80301
   Frederick A. Praeger, Publisher

Published in 1979 in Great Britain by
   Wm. Dawson and Sons, Ltd.
   Cannon House
   Folkestone
   Kent CT19 5EE

Library of Congress Catalog Card Number: 77-29258
ISBN (U.S.): 0-89158-164-2
ISBN (U.K.): 0-7129-0880-3

Printed and bound in the United States of America

CONTENTS

PART ONE
MESOPOTAMIA AND RELATED AREAS

PART TWO
EGYPT AND RELATED AREAS

TABLES

ILLUSTRATIONS

PREFACE

The purpose of this book is to give a connected account of what happened in the ancient Middle East, primarily on the basis of the records and monuments that have been recovered through the work of modern archaeology. The Middle East is defined as extending from the western border of Egypt (20° E) to the eastern border of Iran (60° E), and the ancient period in this area is considered to begin with settled human life and to continue to the time of Alexander the Great. In this area and this time, the great river valleys of the Tigris and Euphrates and of the Nile provided the natural determinants of the lands the Greeks called ἡ Μεσοποταμία ("Mesopotamia"), and ἡ Αἴγυπτος ("Egypt"). These lands in turn were inevitably related to adjacent regions of western Asia and Africa: Mesopotamia, to Arabia on the south, the Iranian plateau on the east, and Asia Minor on the west; Egypt, to Nubia on the south, Libya on the west, and Sinai on the east; and both Mesopotamia and Egypt, to Palestine/Syria/Lebanon, as the bridge between the two.

In archaeology it has been customary to designate the successive periods of human life in terms of the materials chiefly employed at the time. In Palestine, which is more or less in the center of the whole area under consideration, a tabulation of these periods and their approximate dates (doubtless debatable in details but widely accepted as a substantially correct overall outline) is as follows:

Paleolithic Age, before 10,000 B.C.E.
Mesolithic Age, 10,000–7000 B.C.E.
Neolithic Age, 7000–4500 B.C.E.
Chalcolithic Age, 4500–3100 B.C.E.
Early Bronze Age, 3100–2100 B.C.E.
Middle Bronze Age, 2100–1500 B.C.E.

xxiii

Late Bronze Age, 1500-1200 B.C.E.
Early Iron Age, 1200-900 B.C.E.
Middle Iron Age, 900-600 B.C.E.
Late Iron Age, 600-330 B.C.E.

As a common, but only very general, frame of reference, this outline is superimposed upon our table of contents both for Mesopotamia and for Egypt. Within these ages, the point at which history "begins" is usually equated with the point at which writing appears. As far as is now known, writing began in Mesopotamia, in particular in Sumer, at about the middle of the fourth millennium and was found in a similar but different form in Egypt at a slightly later time; therefore, the idea may have spread from one land to the other. Although our history begins at this point, the text provides a historical viewpoint by briefly tracing development in Mesopotamia and in Egypt in the prehistoric period.

In the long expanses of prehistoric time, human beings moved from the nomadic existence of the Paleolithic and Mesolithic Ages—hunting and gathering to obtain food, while residing in caves and temporary camp sites—to the relatively permanent settlements of the Neolithic Age, associated with the growing of plants and the domestication of animals (the "neolithic revolution"), and to the cities of the Chalcolithic and Early Bronze Ages (the "urban revolution").[1] It is these cities—Kish, Uruk, and Jemdet Nasr in Mesopotamia—and that aspect of city life we call civilization (from Latin *civis*, "citizen," *civitas*, "city") that spawned the first written documents and gave birth to history, as we define it. The very earliest documents, however, are either undeciphered or limited in the amount of information they offer; therefore, they are sometimes said to represent a period that was Protoliterate and Protohistoric (3500-2900). In the ensuing Early Dynastic period (beginning in 2900), written records are more numerous and correlation with surviving monuments is more possible. At this point, therefore, we enter the first fully historical period in Mesopotamia.[2] In Egypt the period before the Early Dynastic period is more commonly called the Predynastic period (before 3100) and stretches on back into prehistoric times. In Part 1, the sequence of events in Mesopotamia in the prehistoric and protohistoric periods is dealt with in some detail. In Part 2 the corresponding periods in Egypt are outlined much more briefly, because the available evidence for the times and stages of the "neolithic revolution" is relatively scanty.[3]

The nature of the evidence in the prehistoric and historic periods is, of course, such that the dates given for early times are rather broad approximations while in later times they attain much greater precision. In general the relative precision intended for the dates will be evident from the context, and thus I have not repeatedly prefixed them with *circa*. Moreover, because the dates are naturally B.C.E. I have not felt it necessary to repeat that notation throughout. Any date from C.E. times has been clearly identified.

In Mesopotamia the chronology follows Porada and Hallo in the earlier periods, Brinkman from the Third Dynasty of Ur onward, and Parker and Dubberstein for Nabopolassar and onward. In Egypt the chronology follows *The Cambridge Ancient History* (CAH³) and Simpson in the earlier periods, Hornung for the New Kingdom, Kitchen for the Third Intermediate period and the Kushite and Saite dynasties, and Kienitz and von Beckerath for the balance of the Late Dynastic period.

Specific references to ancient sources and modern studies are in the notes. They are intended to make it possible for interested readers to pursue further all significant points and they are also an expression of my indebtedness to others.

ARCHAEOLOGICAL HISTORY
OF THE
ANCIENT MIDDLE EAST

PART ONE
MESOPOTAMIA
AND RELATED AREAS

1. PREHISTORIC (10,000-3500) AND PROTOHISTORIC (3500-2900) PERIODS

Shanidar, Karim Shahir, and Tell Mlefaat

Archaeological periods in the large area of western Asia of which Mesopotamia is the focal point are exhibited in the strata of the Shanidar cave, a large cavern on the edge of the Zagros mountains in northeastern Iraq.[1] In 13.5 meters of accumulated habitation debris, Layer D is Middle Paleolithic (Mousterian) with stone implements and Neanderthal type skeletal remains; Layer C Upper Paleolithic (here called Baradostian from Baradost mountain); Layer B Mesolithic with characteristic microliths, and charcoal from the bottom of the layer dated by Carbon 14 to 10,000 years before the present era; and Layer A Neolithic, historic, and modern (since Kurdish shepherds still inhabit the cave in the winter).[2] Between the cave-dweller life illustrated at Shanidar and the first permanently established villages, links are seen at Karim Shahir (200 kilometers southeast of Shanidar and 75 kilometers northeast of Kirkuk), where a sort of pebble pavement and microlithic flints suggest a camp site;[3] and at Tell Mlefaat (35 kilometers northeast of Mosul), where a pebble-floored pit with a hearth at one end, and many microliths, represent a slightly more permanent residence.[4]

NEOLITHIC AGE (7000-4500)

Jarmo

Relatively permanent settlement is attested at Qalat Jarmo (eight kilometers southwest of Karim Shahir), where mud-walled houses of several rooms each, flint sickles, clay statuettes of presumably

3

domesticated animals, and clay figures of the mother goddess type have been found. As yet, no pottery has been discovered in the lowest ten occupation levels. In an inhabited area about 90 by 140 meters in extent (more than three acres), an estimate allows for an original fifty houses and a population of 300 persons.[5] Carbon 14 determinations center at about 6570 B.C.E., with a tolerance of 500 years on either side and with an assumed duration for the site of up to 400 years.[6] Here in this pre-pottery Neolithic community, "village life had begun in earnest, and with it, the germs of the economic, political, social and moral orders which were to blossom into the earliest civilization."[7]

After Jarmo, successive periods are commonly designated by the names of the "type sites," where distinctive assemblages of cultural materials, particularly pottery, are found first or most fully. According to present knowledge these are Hassuna (including a Samarra phase), Halaf, Ubaid (including Eridu and Hajji Muhammad phases), Uruk, and Jemdet Nasr.[8] With respect to geographical distribution, the Hassuna and Halaf cultures are represented in the north, the Ubaid in both the south and the north, the Uruk in the south (contemporaneously with Gawra in the north), and the Jemdet Nasr in the south. As to the date of the periods, Hassuna and Samarra occupy most of the sixth millennium; Halaf in the north and the Eridu phase of Ubaid (i.e., Ubaid 1) in the south begin before 5000; the Hajji Muhammad phase (Ubaid 2) begins about 4900, Ubaid 3 about 4300, Ubaid 4 about 3900, Uruk about 3500, and Jemdet Nasr about 3100.[9] At about 2900 we enter the Early Dynastic period. In the Hassuna period, no metal has been found in situ: in these terms, we are still in the Neolithic Age. Copper was used in the north in the Halaf and Ubaid periods, and in the south for the first time in the Uruk period, signaling the Chalcolithic Age.[10] In Jemdet Nasr sites, bronze is found, and we enter the Bronze Age. The first written documents are found in the Uruk and the Jemdet Nasr periods (at Kish, Uruk, and Jemdet Nasr), so these two periods are grouped as the Protoliterate or the Protohistoric period. With the Early Dynastic period we enter the first fully historical times in Mesopotamia.[11]

Hassuna

Tell Hassuna (thirty-five kilometers south of Mosul) exhibits three successive camp sites in Level Ia, associated with stone axes and coarse archaic unpainted pottery and, in Levels Ib-VI, adobe buildings together with archaic painted pottery developing into the standard Hassuna ware, painted or incised (or both) in geometric patterns. Flint-toothed sickles, sunken clay grain storage bins, flat rubbing-stones for grinding flour, and

5

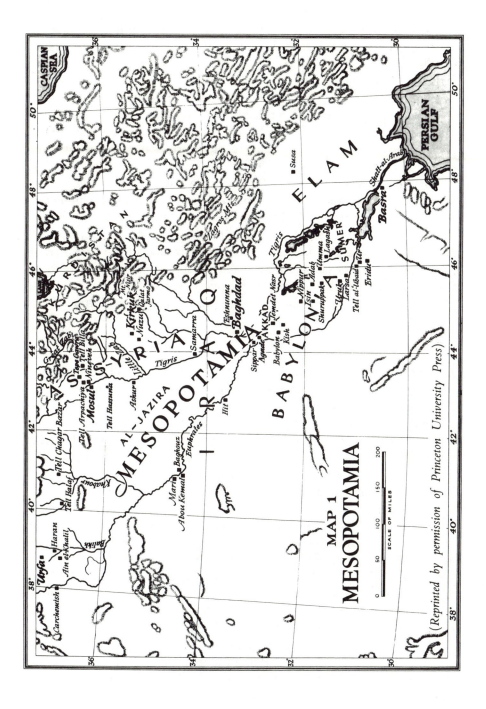

CASPIAN SEA

PERSIAN GULF

E L A M

• Susa

Tigris

Shatt-al-Arab

Basra•

S U M E R

Tigris Mts.

Lagash•
Umma•
Adab•
•Nippur
Isin• Shuruppak•
•Tell al-'Ubaid
Eridu•
Tello•
Larsa•
Uruk•

Z A G R O S

Kirkuk•
Nuzu•Qalat•
Jarmo•

Eshnunna•
•Baghdad
•Tepe Gawra •Tell Billa
Mosul• Nineveh•
Aššur•

•Tell Arpachiya
Tell Halaf•

S Y R I A

Tepe Gawra

Great Zab

Little Zab

Samarra•

Tigris

AKKAD•
Agade• •Tell Asmar
Babylon• •Tutub-Nasr
Kish•
Sippar•

B A B Y L O N

I R A Q

A L - J A Z I R A

M E S O P O T A M I A

Tell Hassuna

Hit•

•Tell Chagar Bazar

Khabour

Mari• •Baghouz
Abou Kemal•

Euphrates

Carchemish•

Urfa• •Haran
Ain el-Khalil•

Balikh

MAP 1
MESOPOTAMIA

SCALE OF MILES
0   50   100   150   200

(Reprinted by permission of Princeton University Press)

clay baking ovens represent agricultural and culinary practices. Bones of evidently domesticated animals include the ox, ass, and sheep. Infant burials were made in pottery jars, and other jars, perhaps for food and water, were sometimes placed nearby. Other objects are beads, amulets, and mother goddess figurines. The lowest Hassuna level, and the appearance of pottery in it, probably date not long after 6000.[12] Other Mesopotamian sites with levels approximately contemporary with Hassuna and including coarse early pottery are Matarrah (twenty-five kilometers south of Kirkuk);[13] Telul ath-Thalathat (twenty-five kilometers west of Mosul), Level XVI;[14] Nineveh (just across the Tigris from Mosul), the strata called Ninevite 1 and 2;[15] Tell Arpachiya (six kilometers north of Nineveh);[16] and Tell Chagar Bazar (in the area drained by the Khabur river), Level 15.[17] Also at Tell ej-Judeideh in the Plain of Antioch in Syria, the pottery of Level XIV is similar to that of the first level at Nineveh;[18] and at Jericho in Palestine the oldest pottery in Layer IX (above the pre-pottery levels) is comparable with that of Judeideh XIV and Hassuna I—perhaps even slightly more primitive than the latter.[19]

Samarra

At Samarra (on the Tigris 100 kilometers north of Baghdad), under much later Islamic ruins, badly preserved graves in a layer of debris less than two meters thick, resting on virgin soil, contained an abundance of painted pottery, comparable to standard Hassuna ware but of such excellence in manufacture and decoration as to constitute a special phase of the Hassuna period.[20] Similar ware has also been found at Baghouz (on the Middle Euphrates just inside the border of Syria),[21] and at Tell Shimshara (north of Jarmo, above the village of Dokan on the Little Zab River).[22]

The evidences of the Hassuna/Samarra culture thus extend from the Tigris to the Mediterranean and reveal a village life whose most characteristic marks are its pottery and its houses built of clay. The domestication of animals and the practice of agriculture provide the economic basis of the life of the society. Figurines and amulets attest religious and magical practices, and the burial of the dead with objects accompanying them suggests belief in an afterlife. Lacking metal, the culture was still on the Neolithic level. Artistically, the high point is represented in the Samarran pottery. In Level V at Hassuna, in which there is much of this fine pottery, Carbon 14 dates have been obtained prior to 5000 years B.C.E. All together, the Hassuna/Samarra period may have extended over most of the time between 6000 and 5000.[23]

CHALCOLITHIC AGE (4500-3100)

Halaf

Tell Halaf (on the Khabur River in Syria, just south of the border with Turkey) gives its name to the Halaf period. The pottery, found in a thick stratum under the palace of a later Aramean ruler, is beautifully painted and is considered the finest, both technically and artistically, of all the handmade wares of ancient Mesopotamia. It is characteristically thin, covered with a smooth cream or buff slip, and decorated with polychrome designs in black and orange-red paint. It was evidently fired at an intense heat, giving it an almost porcelainlike finish. Many of the decorative designs are geometrical, but bird, animal, and human representations also appear.[24]

Other sites with Halaf-type pottery are Carchemish (on the Euphrates more than 160 kilometers west of Tell Halaf), Tell Chagar Bazar (80 kilometers to the east), and Tell Hassuna, Tell Arpachiya, and Tepe Gawra (280 kilometers to the east in the vicinity of Mosul). Several of these sites have already entered the picture as representing the Hassuna period; it is the higher levels in the mounds that represent the Halaf period—namely, at Tell Chagar Bazar Levels 15-6, at Tell Hassuna Levels VI-X, and at Tell Arpachiya Levels 10-6 (TT 10-6).[25] At Tepe Gawra (25 kilometers northeast of Mosul and 4 kilometers northeast of Khorsabad), the oldest pottery was found in Area A at the southeast foot of the mound, at the Northeast Base, and in Stratum XX. As at Tell Halaf, the wares are usually thin and hard, having been fired at high temperature. In Stratum XVI, closed underground kilns were found of the sort that would have made possible the necessary temperature control.[26]

At Tell Arpachiya, the Halaf pottery can be divided into three phases: early, from outside the mound; middle, from TT 10-7; and late, from TT 6.[27] Decoration includes oxhead (bucranium) and cross designs, the latter appearing also on stone pendants, which were probably used as stamp seals and were thus the forerunners of the cylinder seals later so characteristic of Mesopotamia.[28] In architecture, ten structures built on circular stone foundations and probably completed in adobe as round domed buildings (something like the "beehive tombs" of Mycenae and the "beehive dwellings" of today in northern Iraq and northern Syria) were probably some kind of shrine.[29]

The Halaf culture extended from the Euphrates and Khabur regions of Syria to the Mosul region of Iraq; in date it probably began before 5000 and lasted to around 4300. The first sun-dried bricks in Mesopotamia appear in the north in this period around 5000, and are used in the south in the Ubaid period. The first burned bricks are found in Uruk Level III around 3100-3000.[30] Some copper and lead are found in the context of Halaf sites; in this period, therefore, we have moved into the Chalcolithic Age.

Ubaid

Tell al-Ubaid (six kilometers northwest of the more famous site of Ur) gives its name to the Ubaid period, but two earlier phases of the period are recognized at Tell Abu Shahrain and Qalat Hajji Muhammad, and other Ubaid materials are found at other sites in the south (Ur, in levels beneath the "flood" deposit; Warka, in Levels XVIII-XV in the Eanna precinct; Tell el-Oheimir) and in the north (Tell Hassuna, Levels XI-XIII; Tell Arpachiya, TT 5-1; Tepe Gawra, Levels XIX-XII).[31] At the southern sites the Ubaid materials usually rest on virgin soil, so the people who lived there were probably the first permanent settlers in the region. Previously Lower Mesopotamia was presumably too swampy for anything more than some sort of marsh-dwellers' existence, and the use of reeds for buildings in the Ubaid period shows the continuation of a marshy state (as has been to a considerable extent true ever since), but sickles and mortars also show that there must have been cultivable land, too.

Both coarse and fine pottery are found at Tell al-Ubaid. Most vessels were handmade, some turned on a slow wheel (tournette). A creamy white clay, when fired, turned to a dull green. Painted decoration was in geometrical designs in black or brownish red. Houses were usually built of reeds plastered with mud, but some building was done with bricks of mud dried in the sun. The mud-plastered walls were sometimes decorated with mosaics of slender pencillike cones of baked clay, the ends left plain or painted red or black. This usage provided almost waterproof protection and permanent decoration and was practiced for centuries in Mesopotamia.[32]

Hajji Muhammad and Eridu

Qalat Hajji Muhammad (fifty-five kilometers up the Euphrates from Ubaid near the larger and more famous site of Uruk) has pottery that appears to be an early variety of Ubaid ware.[33] Tell Abu Shahrain (twenty kilometers southeast of Tell al-Ubaid) is identified as the ancient city of Eridu, center of the god Enki, deity of the subterranean waters and of wisdom, and site of the first antediluvian kingship according to the Sumerian King List. On the main mound are the ruins of a staged temple tower (ziggurat) of Amar-Sin (2046-2038), third king of the Third Dynasty of Ur, and under a corner of it is a series of eighteen prehistoric mud-brick temples, one succeeding the other. In the strata distinguished by these temples, in the lowest levels, 18-15, the pottery has some reminiscences of Samarra and Halaf, but is made of local clay and is commonly called Eridu ware; in the next levels, 14-12, the ware is more like that at Hajji Muhammad; beginning in part in Level 12 and continuing up through Level 8, it is like that characteristically found at classical Ubaid sites; in Levels 7-6 it is late forms of the same (above that, Levels 5-1 belong to the Uruk and Jemdet Nasr periods). Since there appears to be a continuous development here, four phases of the entire Ubaid period are recognized: Ubaid 1 (Eridu ware), before 5000; Ubaid 2 (Hajji Muhammad ware), 4900-4300; Ubaid 3 (classical Ubaid ware), 4300-3900; Ubaid 4 (late Ubaid ware), 3900-3500.[34] On the whole, taking the pottery as the hallmark of the period, the Ubaid ware is not as excellent as that of the Halaf period, the clay being less good and the painted decoration less imaginative.

Like the round structures of the Halaf period at Tell Arpachiya, which were probably the earliest structures in northern Mesopotamia to have been erected for religious purposes, these eighteen temples at Eridu (identified as such by offering tables, altars, ashes, and remains of sacrifices—in one case fish bones in a pottery vessel, perhaps a sacrifice to Enki, the water god of the city) are the earliest shrines in southern Mesopotamia. In the more developed examples, Temples 11-6 of the classical and late Ubaid phases, the plan is that of a long nave with altar at one end and offering table at the other and with smaller rooms and niches on both long sides, essentially the standard form of the Sumerian temples of the succeeding Uruk period. On the outside are shallow buttresses and niches, and the orientation is with the corners of the buildings to the cardinal points of the compass, these also being standard features in almost all subsequent Mesopotamian shrine architecture. On the northwest side of Tell Abu Shahrain, a cemetery of one thousand graves dates by its pottery to the late Ubaid period, contemporary with Temples 7-6. The graves are oblong boxes built of sun-dried bricks. Pottery accompanies the dead; in one grave the skeleton of a dog lay directly upon that of a young boy. In another grave was a terra-cotta model of a boat, with socket for the mast amidships, and hooked ornaments at prow and stern, much like sailing craft still used on the Lower Euphrates.[35]

In the north, Tepe Gawra is among the sites with occupation levels (XIX-XII) of the Ubaid period. In Stratum XX, chiefly Halaf-type pottery is found; in the levels above, Ubaid ware predominates; in Stratum XI, painting itself as a means of decorating pottery is for a time almost completely discarded or forgotten, and only quite different wares are found. Seal pendants like those of the Halaf period at Tell Arpachiya are found, but also many other stamp seals of various forms—flat button, lentoid, and hemispheroidal. The decoration is in linear patterns, probably derived from the seal pendants, but also with other designs including animal and human figures. In public architecture three large temples of Stratum XIII (about 4000), built of sun-dried mud brick, plastered and painted, enclosed three sides of a large court and formed an imposing acropolis. The construction must have required the combined efforts of a large community and attests the social and religious development of the Ubaid period.[36]

Uruk

Uruk, type site of the period subsequent to the Ubaid period and the biblical Erech (Gen. 10:10; Ezra 4:9), is now known as Warka (sixty kilometers up the Euphrates from Ur and on the east side of the river). The most ancient precinct in the middle of the site was called Eanna ("House of Heaven") after its temple, which was dedicated to An (Anu, Anna), the god of heaven, and to Inanna ("Lady of Heaven"). In the excavations at Warka,[37] a sounding was carried down in this precinct to a depth of more than eighteen meters, to or near virgin soil, and revealed eighteen distinguishable levels of occupation. Levels XVIII-XV, amounting to almost half the depth, contain Ubaid-type pottery; in Levels XIV-IV this gives way to very different pottery, brick-red to plum-red wares, and black and gray vessels that were baked in a kiln smothered down to make the smoke penetrate and color the clay. This new pottery, the mark of the Ubaid period, was made on a genuine spinning potter's wheel, was often slipped and burnished, but was left unpainted. On the whole it is hardly elegant, and the invention of the fast wheel may have been responsible for the decadence of the art. On the basis of the stratification, the Uruk period divides into three phases: Early (Levels XIV-IX, 3500-3400), Middle (Levels VIII-VI, 3400-3300), and Late (Levels V-IV, 3300-3100). Above, in Level III (3100-3000), the pottery is comparable to that at Jemdet Nasr.[38]

It is in the Uruk period that the first written records are found. The oldest example, according to present knowledge, is on a small limestone tablet discovered at Tell el-Oheimir (twenty kilometers east of Babylon), the ancient Kish, the city of the first postdiluvian kingship according to the Sumerian King List.[39] On both sides of the tablet, arranged in areas marked off by straight lines, are small pictures of various objects, recognizable among which are a human head, hand, foot, and a threshing sledge. These

Left—FIGURE 1. One Side of the Pictographic Tablet from Kish. *(Ashmolean Museum, Oxford)* *Right—FIGURE 2.* Other Side of the Pictographic Tablet from Kish. *(Ashmolean Museum, Oxford)*

are presumably pictographs—i.e., pictures intended to convey ideas—and other marks on the tablet are thought to be numerals. The date is probably around 3500, at the point of transition from the Ubaid to the Uruk period. The text, although undecipherable, is the earliest known from Mesopotamia.[40]

At Warka no fewer than five or six hundred inscribed clay tablets, or fragments thereof, were found, the majority in Level IV (3200-3100) and some in Level III (3100-3000) contemporary with Jemdet Nasr. In all, it is the earliest large collection of written documents known. Both pictograms and arbitrary signs appear, together with numerals and impressions of cylinder seals, the last presumably to identify the persons involved in whatever transactions are recorded. Although not fully translatable, some tablets note such and such a number of sheep or goats and record the giving—presumably as wages—of bread and beer for a day to a number of individuals whose names are listed. The documents are therefore probably memorandums relating to economic activities in the temples. That the writing probably already represents the Sumerian language will be noted below.[41]

In architecture the Eanna precinct contains a series of temples and related buildings extending from Level VII to Level III, some of whose particular features lead to their designation by the excavators as the Limestone Temple, the Red Temple, the Pillar Temple, and the Labyrinth. Not far away in the area of the Anu temple itself—which the excavators call the Anu ziggurat—the archaeological sounding penetrated levels designated by the letters *A* to *G,* with a yet lower level called *X.* Here a succession of temple structures was finally embodied in a monumental

FIGURE 3. Ziggurat and Eanna Precinct at Uruk. (*State Antiquities Organization, Baghdad, Republic of Iraq*)

platform, forty-two by forty-six meters in extent, rising more than fifteen meters above the plain, with the White Temple on the summit. In the entire development—with superimposed levels, approach stairway and ramp, and temple on top—the essential form of the ziggurat was reached. Of these monumental stepped towers, so characteristic of Mesopotamian temple architecture, the locations of more than thirty are now known.[42]

As at Tepe Gawra in the Ubaid period, so here at Warka stamp seals and their impressions are found (e.g., in Eanna Level XII), but now cylinder seals and their impressions also appear (in Eanna Level V and upward and in the Anu ziggurat Levels D and C and upward). Engraved in intaglio, as the cylinders were rolled across soft clay, they left an image standing out in relief. Small as the scale of the work had to be, the design and execution of the seals found here and at other sites of the Uruk period are excellent: fine and elaborate scenes show plants, animals, monsters, human figures, heraldic groups, and hunting, battle, and ritual occasions.[43]

Sculpture on a larger scale is also found at Warka. In Eanna Level IV was a gray alabaster statuette of a bearded, muscular man, the eyes made of shell, the pupils of lapis lazuli.[44] Among a mass of small objects in a room in Eanna Level III, probably collected from an earlier time and deriving from the Uruk period proper, was a beautiful alabaster vase, about one

FIGURE 4.   Alabaser Vase from Uruk. (*State Antiquities Organization, Baghdad, Republic of Iraq*)

meter in height, sculptured in panels of low relief. A robed female figure stands in front of two tall standards, each a bundle of reeds with curved top. Since at least later the standards are known as a symbol of Inanna, the standing figure is probably the goddess or possibly her priestess. Naked priests advance with offerings of fruit, and behind the first, where a figure is now missing, there evidently came an important personage, perhaps the king, since the next man bears up his long-tasseled belt. No doubt a religious ceremony is in progress, perhaps even the spring festival of the New Year (Sumerian *zagmuk,* Akkadian *akitu*), in which, according to later Mesopotamian texts, the god of fertility, who had been absent in the winter season, was brought back and reunited in sacred marriage with the goddess of fertility, the roles of the deities being enacted by the king and the priestess of the goddess.[45]

Gawra

In the north the period approximately contemporaneous with the Uruk period in the south exhibits different characteristics and customarily receives a different designation, namely, the Gawra period, from the already mentioned Tepe Gawra. This period is defined more exactly as comprising Levels XIA-VIIIB at Tepe Gawra and those levels at other sites that have comparable material.[46] In the levels just mentioned at Tepe Gawra, the pottery is no longer painted as it was in the preceding Ubaid-period levels, but is decorated with incised or impressed marks and punctures, and even with modeled figures; the most common designs are geometric, and human and animal figures are highly stylized. Many stamp seals and their impressions are found, but no cylinder seals. A series of six temples occupies the levels in question. Tombs are sunk in the ground and roofed with matting, wood, mud bricks, or slabs of stone.[47]

EARLY BRONZE AGE (3100-2100)

Jemdet Nasr

Jemdet Nasr (twenty-five kilometers northeast of Babylon) is the type site for the last period in the long sequence of periods prior to the Early Dynastic. The Jemdet Nasr period may begin about 3100, and the Early Dynastic about 2900. The distinctive pottery first found here and, afterward, at other sites in southern Mesopotamia, is a wheel-turned painted ware, with geometrical and naturalistic designs in black and red and often on a deep red ground.[48] Cylinder seals are numerous but, as compared with the earlier ones of the Uruk period, more limited in design, coarser, and more careless in execution, presumably having been made in larger numbers for more common use.[49] Metal was now used more extensively, and the appearance of bronze in Jemdet Nasr sites signals the Bronze Age in Mesopotamia.[50]

In several different rooms of a large mud-brick building, probably a temple, on the tell at Jemdet Nasr, and in association with painted pottery and cylinder seals of the Jemdet Nasr period, were found groups of inscribed clay tablets, 194 in all. In Eanna Level III at Warka, tablets of the same type were also found. The writing is semipictographic, somewhat more advanced than that of the Uruk period. Like the earlier Uruk tablets, the greater number of the Jemdet Nasr tablets appear to be economic texts but some are word lists, perhaps used in schools.[51] As will be noted below, the language is surely Sumerian.

Sculpture in stone is prominent in the Jemdet Nasr period, and excellent examples come from Eanna Level III at Warka: a woman's head of noble appearance in white marble;[52] a black basalt stela, the first monument of this type known, with a double scene of man combating lion, the man once armed with spear and again with bow and arrow;[53] and a limestone ewer, with a circle of alternating lions and bulls, each lion rearing up to clutch the bull ahead with his claws.[54]

Other sites in the south with strata of the Jemdet Nasr period include Tell el-Oheimir (Kish),[55] Tell Fara, and Tell Asmar, the last two founded in the Jemdet Nasr period and, like Kish, important in the subsequent Early Dynastic period. Tell Fara (150 kilometers down the Mesopotamian valley from Jemdet Nasr in the direction of Warka) is identified with ancient Shuruppak and exhibits Jemdet Nasr pottery, seals, and stone vases.[56] Many written texts were also found, but these are later, in about the twenty-fifth century, in the Early Dynastic period.[57] Tell Asmar (80 kilometers north of Jemdet Nasr and 50 kilometers northeast of Baghdad, in the region of the Diyala River) is the ancient Eshunnna. Here, too, Jemdet Nasr pottery is witness to the first settlement; and the Earliest Shrine, a little sanctuary built of small, irregular bricks, belongs to the same period.[58]

In the north the period approximately contemporary with the Jemdet Nasr period in the south has its distinctive characteristics. It is sometimes called Ninevite and defined as comprising most or all of Level 5 at Nineveh and levels with analogous materials at other sites. The pottery—Ninevite 5 ware—consists of plain, incised, and heavily painted vessels, and many cylinder seals are found too, apparently now for the first time having become known in the north.[59] Tell Brak (on the headwaters of the Khabur River in northeastern Syria) also has pottery up through the Halaf, Ubaid, Gawra, and Ninevite periods. Four Eye Temples on the tell, the first from

FIGURE 5. Marble Head of Lady from Uruk. (*State Antiquities Organization, Baghdad, Republic of Iraq*)

the Gawra period, the next three from the Ninevite period, preserved thousands of small black or white alabaster images with flat body and long neck surmounted by a pair of large staring eyes, perhaps conventionalized idols of a mother goddess, with eyes made prominent to emphasize the all-seeing nature of the deity.[60]

Sumerians, Ubaidians, and Semites

According to the evidence just surveyed, in the Uruk and Jemdet Nasr periods new types of pottery appeared, the fast potter's wheel was used, the stamp seal was succeeded by the cylinder seal, sacred architecture developed in the direction of the ziggurat, sculpture was done in stone, and, most importantly, written records are found, composed probably in the Sumerian language. Therefore a new people may have come into Lower Mesopotamia at this time, i.e., in the second half of the fourth millennium, and they are probably to be identified as the Sumerians, who are relatively well known as the dominant people in the ensuing Early Dynastic period.[61] Yet there are also lines of continuity from earlier times—as seen, for example, in the distinctive form of temple found already in the Ubaid period and continuing into the Uruk and later periods. Moreover, the earliest pictographs, on the tablet from Kish, come probably from about the point of transition from the Ubaid to the Uruk periods; so, although the earliest records of any extent are Sumerian, the Sumerians might have adapted and developed a system of writing that was already in existence.[62]

In their later literature, the Sumerians refer to a sacred land called Dilmun, "where the sun rises,"[63] and this suggests that they themselves came from somewhere in the East. Dilmun has been variously identified with southern Iran, the Indus valley, or the island of Bahrain in the Persian Gulf.[64] Assyrian references to Dilmun as "in the midst of the sea of the rising sun," and "in the midst of the Lower Sea" (i.e., the Persian Gulf, in contrast with Tyre, "in the midst of the Upper Sea," i.e., the Mediterranean) can favor the identification with Bahrain.[65] Excavations on the island have shown that at least by 2000, Bahrain was in contact both with the Sumerians in Mesopotamia and with the cities of the Indus valley.[66]

In the Sumerian language itself, certain non-Sumerian "substrate" words are preserved. These include geographical names, e.g., the names of the Tigris and Euphrates rivers (*idiglat* and *buranun* in cuneiform) and of many of the oldest cities (Eridu, Uruk, Ur, Lagash, Larsa, etc.), and the names of various kinds of workers, e.g., *engar* for plowman, *naggar* for carpenter, *tibira* for metalworker, etc. These may come from the earlier people who founded the first towns and developed the first civilized activities in Lower Mesopotamia, in other words, the people responsible for the earliest materials of the Ubaid period. Hence these otherwise unknown people are sometimes called Ubaidians or Proto-Euphrateans.[67]

Similarly, linguistic evidence also points to the early presence of Semitic people in Mesopotamia. Some of the words just cited are also found in the Semitic languages—e.g., with the same meaning of carpenter or woodworker, the word *naggar* appears in almost identical form in Hebrew, Aramaic, and Arabic. Some of the deities in the Sumerican pantheon are the equivalent of Semitic deities, e.g., the Sumerian Enki is the Semitic Ea, and Inanna is Ishtar. Since the Sumerian names are descriptive epithets ("earth lord," "lady of heaven"), these deities may have been originally Semitic and given the new designations by the Sumerians.[68] Furthermore, in the First Dynasty of Kish, the first dynasty after the flood in the Sumerian King List, several kings have Semitic names (Kalibum or "Dog," Qalumun or "Lamb," Zuqaqip or "Scorpion"); in the Third Dynasty of Kish, a Sumerian queen, Ku-Baba, gave her son a Semitic name, Puzur-Sin, and he gave his son a Sumerian name, Ur-Zababa, but the son in turn chose a Semitic vizier named Sharrum-kin. Thus it may be theorized that Ubaidians and Semites were the first people in Lower Mesopotamia and that when the Sumerians came, they joined rather peaceably with their predecessors in the more advanced civilization that then developed. Seen in this light, the struggles that did ensue between the city-states may be explained as mainly political and determined by social and economic factors, not as racial strife.[69]

By way of distinction, however, the title King of Sumer and Akkad is found in the inscriptions of some of the early rulers, and as early as 1869 Jules Oppert deduced correctly that Akkad applied to the Semitic people and Sumer to the non-Semitic. Geographically, the name *Sumer* applies to the lower part of Lower Mesopotamia, and *Akkad* to the upper part, where the plain is narrower (south of Baghdad).[70] Linguistically, the speech of the Sumerians is the Sumerian language,[71] that of the Semites in Akkad is Akkadian.[72] Technically stated, the Sumerian language is agglutinative, but Semitic, like Indo-European, is inflected.

With respect to writing, a painted representation such as that of the naturalistic or stylized oxhead (bucranium) on the Halaf pottery at Tell Arpachiya was a work of art but could be combined with pictures of other objects to convey a series of ideas and thus constitute writing by pictographs. Such pictures appear on the tablet from Kish around 3500. On the Uruk tablets (Level IV, 3200-3100) an ox is represented by the old bucranium design—the outline of an oxhead with two curved lines for the horns—and a cow is signified by the same design without the horns; but a sheep is indicated by the arbitrary, or at least conventionalized, sign of a circle with a cross in it, an advance in the character of writing.[73] In a further advance, in the Jemdet Nasr period tablets (Uruk Level III, 3100-3000), a sign stands not only for an object and the word that is the name of that object, but also for the same-sounding word even when the word expresses a different idea. Thus, the sign has phonetic, rather than ideographic, value. For example, the sign of an arrow depicts that object, called *ti,* and also stands for "life," sounded as *ti;* and two wavy lines picture a stream of water, called *a,* and also stand for the same-sounding word, which means "in."[74]

With respect to language, the Kish tablet does not provide enough material to make a determination possible. The Uruk IV tablets, however, contain two signs that are later well known as symbols of deities among the Sumerians. One is the curved-top bundle of reeds of Inanna, also seen on the alabaster vase in Eanna Level III. The other is a star, usually with eight points, the sign for *dingir,* "god," and *an,* "heaven," and thus the name of the heaven god An, the highest deity of the Sumerians. The tablets also employ a numerical system based upon sixty (as well as a less-used decimal system), and the sexagesimal count was characteristic of the Sumerians. In the Jemdet Nasr period tablets, the names of other Sumerian deities— Enlil, Enki, and Utu—are found, and the name of Enlil occurs frequently with the arrow sign (*ti*), expressing the wish, "May Enlil grant life," a characteristically Sumerian expression. The word *Kidnun* also appears with such frequency and in such position as probably to be the name of the ancient city at Jemdet Nasr. So the Jemdet Nasr (Uruk III) texts surely, and the preceding Uruk IV documents in all probability, represent the Sumerian language.[75] This language continued in use, and the Sumerian people continued to be an important factor in Mesopotamian life, down into the second millennium, until about the First Dynasty of Babylon, when the language was no longer used and the people ceased to exist as political entity.

The method of writing that was developed was also of long-lasting significance. From an early time, small pictures such as the bucranium design at Tell Arpachiya were painted on pottery, and the small signs on the document from Kish were cut into a limestone tablet. But soon, as in the tablets from Warka and Jemdet Nasr, clay was used most widely. As to the instruments, painting was done with some kind of brush, incised signs were cut into stone with a sharp instrument, and a pointed instrument was drawn through clay like a pen even in the tablets of the Jemdet Nasr period.

The last method pushed the clay into ridges, however, and blurred the signs. In the tablets of the Early Dynastic period from Tell Fara, signs were produced by a reed, cut at the end into a triangular prism and pushed directly into the clay.[76] This resulted in the wedge-shaped writing known as cuneiform (Latin *cuneus,* "wedge"), the script that was ultimately employed not only for the Sumerian language but also for Akkadian (Babylonian and Assyrian), Elamite, Hittite, Hurrian, Ugaritic, and Old Persian (although in Ugaritic and Old Persian, the forms of the signs may be independent local creations).[77]

In addition to sites already mentioned, Sumerian texts have been discovered in especially large numbers at Telloh (65 kilometers north of Ur), the local name of which is a contracted form of the Arabic Tell el-Loh, meaning the Mound of Tablets;[78] and at Nuffar, ancient Nippur (160 kilometers south of Baghdad), city of the god Enlil and, judging from its surviving materials, a major cultural center of all ancient Sumer.[79] In all, the known Sumerian writings include myths and epics (commonly but not too clearly distinguished as respectively more concerned with the gods or more with human beings), historiography, legal texts, letters, hymns, prayers, and wisdom compositions. The poetic form of parallelism is often used, and proverbial sayings are often couplets, with synonymous or antithetical meaning of the two lines.[80] Much of the Sumerian literature was also translated or adapted in Akkadian and thus was of influence for a very long time.

Sumerian Religious Ideas

The Sumerian literature does not provide a systematic statement of philosophy or theology, but allows the recognition that the Sumerians believed in a flat disklike earth, a vaulted sky or heaven above, a realm in between roughly corresponding to the atmosphere, and a boundless sea surrounding the whole. The sky or heaven was *an,* the earth *ki,* and the atmosphere *lil,* a word with the approximate meanings of air, wind, breath, and spirit. With heaven and earth as its main components, the entire universe was *an-ki,* "heaven-earth." In control of this universe was a pantheon of anthropomorphic, but invisible and immortal, beings, the gods, who functioned as an assembly. The words *en,* "lord," *in* and *nin,* "lady," are often components of their names. Four deities appear as the most important: An (Anu, Anna), the sky or heaven god, with main center at Uruk, where the Eanna was his "house;" Enlil, the air lord, with Nippur as his city and the Ekur as his house; Enki (also known as Nudimmud and, in Akkadian, as Ea), the earth lord, in charge of the *abzu* (Akkadian *apsu*), the

FIGURE 6. Excavations in the Tell of Nippur. (*State Antiquities Organization, Baghdad, Republic of Iraq*)

abyss of sweet water under the earth, god of wisdom and civilization, with center at Eridu; and Ninhursag (also Nintu, Ninmah), the exalted lady, mother goddess and mother of all living things. In addition, Urash is wife of Anu; Nammu is mother of Enki; Shulpae is husband of Ninhursag. Ninlil (later identified with Sud, tutelary goddess of Shuruppak) is wife of Enlil, and they are the parents of Nanna (Nannar), the moon god, known in Semitic as Sin. Nanna's wife is Ningal, and their important center in Lower Mesopotamia was the temple called Ekishnugal in Ur. The children of Nanna and Ningal are Utu, the sun god, with centers at Sippar and Larsa and widely known in the Semitic world as Shamash; and Inanna, the lady of heaven, goddess of love and war, identified with the planet Venus and known in the Semitic world as Ishtar. Yet others are Ninurta, warrior god of the stormy south wind, often associated with the Akkadian Adad, god of the thunder; Dumuzi (Tammuz, Ezek. 8:14), shepherd god and husband of Inanna; Ereshkigal, older sister and enemy of Inanna, and queen of the netherworld; Nergal, king of the netherworld, and Ninisinna, daughter of Anu and queen of Isin, his wife; and Namtar, fate, the netherworld demon responsible for death. There is also mention of the Anunnaki, children of Anu, who participate in the heavenly assemblies and of whom seven are judges of the dead. Yet another group, also unnamed individually, are the Igigi.

Sumerian Ideas of Early Events

In their conceptions of early happenings, the Sumerians encompassed the creation of the universe and of human beings, the development of civilization, the displeasure of the gods with humankind, the flood, and the confusion of tongues, together with lists of kings both before and after the flood. Many parts of the same scheme of events are also found in the Akkadian literature: notably, the creation, the development of civilization and the disturbance of the gods by humankind, and the flood, in the Epic of Atrahasis; the creation in the Epic of Marduk; and the flood in the Epic of Gilgamesh. The same literary pattern appears in the first eleven chapters of the book of Genesis, where there are both specific similarities (e.g., in the acount of the flood) and fundamental differences (e.g., in the account of creation), so that the supposition of a common ancient tradition, at least in part, seems likely.[81]

Creation

On a Sumerian tablet preserved in the Louvre, a cosmogonic list of fifteen pairs of deities begins with Enmesharra and Ninmesharra, something like "lord of the being of the universe" and "lady of the being of the universe," and comes down to Enanna and Ninanna, "sky lord" and "sky lady," and to Enki and Ninki, "earth lord" and "earth lady." At this point heaven and earth were still united (*an-ki*), but a Sumerian work known as Gilgamesh, Enkidu, and the Nether World tells how An carried off heaven and Enlil carried off earth; thus they were separated. After this, the name of humanity was "fixed," i.e., the creation of humankind was determined and decreed. Yet another Sumerian work known as the Myth of the Pickax relates that at a place in Nippur called Duranki ("bond of heaven and earth"), Enlil repaired the gash caused by the separation of heaven and earth, then brought into existence the pickax as a tool of agriculture and building, and drove his own golden pickax in the ground at Duranki in a particular spot called Uzumua. At Uzumua—the name means the "place where flesh sprouted forth"—the first human beings broke up through the ground, just like plants sprouting through the crust of the earth. A Sumerian Enki and Ninhursag text presents a different picture of the origin of humankind. Here the gods are complaining of the difficulty of obtaining their daily bread, and Nammu suggests to her son Enki the fashioning of servants of the gods. Enki, in turn, declares that the creature whose name his mother has "uttered" exists, and humankind was forthwith fashioned out of the clay that is over the abyss. In the two statements (in Gilgamesh, Enkidu, and the Nether World, and in Enki and Ninhursag) that the name of the created being was "fixed" and "uttered," it appears that creation took place by the speaking of a word, as if in analogy with the pronouncement of a command by a human being, and so we have an intimation of the doctrine of the creative power of the divine word, a doctrine that became widespread in the ancient Middle East.[82]

Sumerian Flood Story

A broken Sumerian tablet from Nippur, preserved in the University Museum of the University of Pennsylvania, relates further that after An, Enlil, and Ninhursag had created the black-headed people (as the Sumerians called themselves), animals multiplied on the plains, kingship came down from heaven, five ruling cities were founded, and each city (*uru* in Sumerian, *alu* in Akkadian) was placed under a tutelary deity.[83] Later a certain king named Ziusudra ("life of long days," in Akkadian called Atrahasis, "exceeding wise," and Utnapishtim, "he has found life") is advised by some deity that a storm will sweep over the capitals and destroy humankind. Ziusudra, however, together with some other persons and animals rode out the storm in a great boat, afterward made grateful sacrifices to the gods, and was himself given life as if he were a god and transferred to live in the sunrise land of Dilmun.[84]

W hether only harmless animals were saved from the flood is not stated, but the Sumerian text known as Enmerkar and the Lord of Aratta describes an idyllic state of an unidentified time when there were no harmful beasts and consequently no fear and no terror. Then this work mentions the four districts into which the Sumerians divided the world, namely, Shubur and Hamazi to the east (roughly corresponding to Iran), Sumer to the south, Uri to the north (Akkad), and Martu to the west. The people of all these districts, an additional fragmentary tablet of the same text says, spoke to the god Enlil "in one tongue," but the god Enki for some reason "changed the speech in their mouths," evidently producing a confusion of tongues in place of the one speech that had previously prevailed.[85]

Sumerian King List

The flood tablet from Nippur names five antediluvian cities and their tutelary deities, and the same five cities and their kings are listed at the outset of the text known from its opening words (as was customary) as *nam-lugal* ("kingship") and now commonly called the Sumerian King List.[86] This text begins with the statement, "When kingship was lowered from heaven the kingship was in Eridu," and then continues with the several dynasties. The information these two sources give about these cities and their deities and rulers is shown in Table 1.

TABLE 1. ANTEDILUVIAN DYNASTIES IN THE SUMERIAN KING LIST

City	Deity	King	Years of Reign
1. Eridu (Tell Abu Shahrain)	Nudimmud (Enki)	1. Alulim	28,800
		2. Alalgar	36,000
2. Badtibira (Tell el-Madain,	Inanna (?)	3. Enmenlu-Anna	43,200
between Uruk and Telloh)[a]		4. Enmengal-Anna	28,800
		5. divine Dumuzi,	
		a shepherd	36,000
3. Larak (Tell el-Wilaya, eighty	Pabilsag	6. Ensipazi-Anna	28,800
kilometers north of Uruk)[b]			
4. Sippar (Abu Habba, thirty kilo-	Utu	7. Enmendur-Anna	21,000
meters southwest of Baghdad)			
5. Shuruppak (Tell Fara)	Sud (Ninlil)	8. Ubar-Tutu	18,600
			241,200

a   Vaughn E. Crawford in *Iraq* 22 (1960):197-199.
b   Salim al-Alusi in *Sumer* 15 (1959):43-55.

Alulim of Eridu, first king in the list, was evidently of great reputation, for a late Assyrian text (if correctly restored) wishes the monarch Ashurbanipal "the years of Alulim."[87] Enmendur-Anna of Sippar, seventh king in the list, is also known from a text in the library of Ashurbanipal, where he is called Enmenduranki and it is said that he was summoned into the assembly of the gods, especially including the sun god, tutelary deity of his city of Sippar. There he was taught oil-divination and liver-divination as well as secrets of astrology and mathematics, which knowledge he passed on, so that every diviner is really descended from him.[88] As for Ubar-Tutu ("friend of the god Tutu"), king of Shuruppak and last king of the entire antediluvian series, his son Ziusudra (Utnapishtim) is the hero of the story of the flood.[89]

Berossos

A later form of the same list of antediluvian kings is preserved by Berossos, a priest in Babylon who dedicated a *Babylonian History* (Βαβυλωνικά, Χαλδαϊκά), written in Greek, to Antiochus I Soter (281-260).[90] The names have undergone changes but are still usually recognizable as derived from the Sumerian. Thus Enmendur-Anna (Enmenduranki) has become Euedoranchos, and Ubar-Tutu is Otiartes. The latter is preceded by Amenpsinos and followed by Xisuthros (Ziusudra), making ten kings in all. The lengths of reign come to a larger total (Table 2).[91]

TABLE 2. ANTEDILUVIAN DYNASTIES IN BEROSSOS

King	Years of Reign
1. Aloros	36,000
2. Alaparos	10,800
3. Almelon	46,800
4. Ammenon	43,200
5. Amegalaros	64,800
6. Daonos	36,000
7. Euedoranchos	64,800
8. Amenpsinos	36,000
9. Otiartes	28,800
10. Xisuthros	64,800
	432,000

Flood

At this point in the Sumerian King List, the scribe sums up the record and states the event that put an end to the period: "These are five cities, eight kings ruled them for 241,000 years. Then the Flood swept over the land." After that, kingship was lowered again from heaven—this time first in Kish, then in other places—and the list goes on with the further cities and kings. In the postdiluvian portion of the list, the names of kings are recognizable who are known from other sources too and, although clothed in legend, are probably historical, e.g., Enmebaragisi and Agga in the First Dynasty of Ur, and others. Ziusudra himself may, of course, be a historical personage, too. Thus Mesopotamian tradition justifies the notion that the times before the flood were prehistoric and protohistoric, and the times after the flood historic.

The flood account itself may also have some basis in fact: strata of clay apparently laid down by large inundations have been discovered in excavations at Ur (Tell al-Muqayyar, formerly on the Euphrates, which now flows fifteen kilometers to the east at Nasiriya), toward the end of the Ubaid period;[92] at Uruk between Level II (the end of the Jemdet Nasr period) and Level I (Early Dynastic);[93] at Tell Fara (ancient Shuruppak, fifty kilometers north of Uruk), between the Jemdet Nasr and Early Dynastic layers;[94] and at Kish, with several lesser inundations at about the same time as those at Uruk and Shuruppak, and another larger one somewhat later in the Early Dynastic period.[95] Since in Sumerian tradition

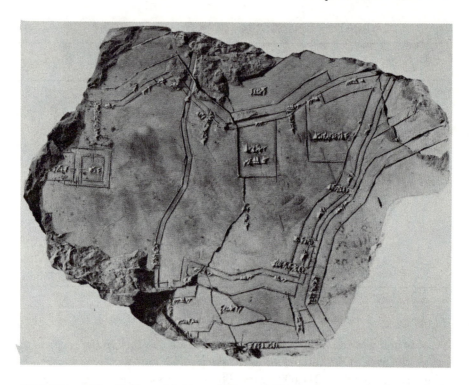

FIGURE 7. Clay Tablet with Map of Nippur (thirteenth century). The rectangle of the Ziggurat (Ekur) is at the extreme right, to the left thereof the canal in the midst of the city, and at the extreme left the Euphrates River paralleled by the city wall with several gates. (*Hilprecht-Sammlung Vorderasiatischer Altertümer, Freidrich-Schiller-Universität, Jena*)

Shuruppak was the last ruling city before the flood, and Kish the first thereafter, it was presumably the inundation attested at Shuruppak between the Jemdet Nasr and Early Dynastic periods (and at Uruk and Kish at about the same time) that was the historic flood so long remembered. The date was about 2900.[96]

2. EARLY DYNASTIC PERIOD
(2900-2371)

The information provided in the Sumerian King List for the period after the flood and before the Dynasty of Akkad, i.e., for the Early Dynastic period, is summarized in Table 3.[1] In this period each of the cities was probably the center of a city-state of the same name (but in the second millennium the residence of the king was usually the capital of a larger kingdom of a different name), and the cities chosen for inclusion in the King List were probably thought to exercise rule, at least for a time, over the whole of Sumer.[2] In fact, however, some kings' names are contemporaneous, which shows that there was overlapping of the dynasties rather than strict succession. The total number of years, more than 30,000 altogether, is of course excessive. However, sharply reduced and therefore more possibly historical dates appear in the First Dynasty of Ur and in many dynasties thereafter.

Tell Asmar and Khafajah

For the chronology of the Early Dynastic period, stratification is especially significant at two sites in the region of the Diyala River—Tell Asmar (ancient Eshnunna, fifty kilometers northeast of Baghdad) and Khafajah (ancient Tutub, twenty kilometers northeast of Baghdad).[3] At Tell Asmar the so-called Abu Temple was founded in the form of the Earliest Shrine in the Jemdet Nasr period, and at Khafajah the first five building phases of the Temple of Sin (Sin I-V) are assigned to the same period. Above that, at both sites, a new and distinctive kind of planoconvex brick appears,[4] and the higher building levels are assigned to three phases of the Early Dynastic period, with dates, as follows: Abu Archaic Shrine IV-I and Sin Temple VI-VII, Early Dynastic I (abbreviated ED I), 2900-2750; Abu Square Temple III-I and Sin Temple VIII-IX, Early Dynastic II (ED II), 2750-

TABLE 3. EARLY DYNASTIC PERIOD IN THE SUMERIAN KING LIST

Name of Dynasty	Number of Kings	Years of Reign
1. First Dynasty of Kish	23	24,510
2. First Dynasty of Eanna (i.e., Uruk)	12	2,310
3. First Dynasty of Ur	4	177
4. Dynasty of Awan	3	356
5. Second Dynasty of Kish	8	3,195
6. Dynasty of Hamazi	1	360
7. Second Dynasty of Uruk	3	187
8. Second Dynasty of Ur	4	116
9. Dynasty of Adab	1	90
10. Dynasty of Mari	6	136
11. Third Dynasty of Kish	1 (queen)	100
12. Dynasty of Akshak	6	99
13. Fourth Dynasty of Kish	7	491
14. Third Dynasty of Uruk	1	25

2600; Abu Single Shrine III-I and Sin Temple X, Early Dynastic III (ED III), 2600-2371 (with the subdivisions ED IIIa, 2600-2500; ED IIIb, 2500-2371).[5]

In the Square Temple at Tell Asmar (ED II), a remarkable hoard of a dozen statues was found beneath the floor where they had perhaps been hidden after being taken out of service.[6] Each figure holds a cup in clasped hands; two stand out for large size and very large eyes, one male (seventy centimeters high, with full black beard, wearing a fringed kilt) and one female (shorter, wearing a long cloak). The latter two may be the king and queen, leading the others in worship; or they may be deities sharing communion with their worshippers, perhaps Abu (whose name was found on an inscribed copper vessel in the temple—hence the name the Abu Temple) and his consort. In the Sumerian work known as Enki and Ninhursag, Abu is called "the king of the plants" and thus may have been a god of vegetation and fertility.[7] These are the oldest known Sumerian cult statues and at the same time representations of "the black-headed people," the Sumerians themselves.

In the Sin Temple Level IX (end of ED II) at Khafajah were other statues, less archaic, more realistic. One is inscribed with the name of a certain Urkisal, who is identified as a priest of Sin (Nanna, the moon god)—hence the name of the Sin Temple.[8] Not far away is the so-called

Temple Oval (ED II and III), a large oval-shaped precinct of more than 8,000 square meters, surrounded by heavy double walls, with a sanctuary on an elevated platform at one end. Similar ovals have been found in the temple of Ninhursag at Tell al-Ubaid and at Tell el-Hiba, and the form seems to be unique to the Early Dynastic period.[9]

In an area southeast of the Abu Temple at Tell Asmar and in an area between the Sin Temple and the Temple Oval at Khafajah, many private houses of the Early Dynastic period were excavated. In general they were built of unbaked bricks, with small rooms around a central open court, and the several houses set closely together in contiguous blocks. Burials were made under the floors. The lanes leading to the houses were often no more than one meter wide; main streets, such as those in the vicinity of the temples, were three to five meters wide.[10] Based upon the extent of the ruins at Tell Asmar and Khafajah and certain other sites, it is estimated that the population of the typical city-state in the Early Dynastic period varied from 10,000 to 20,000.[11]

First Dynasty of Kish

In the Sumerian King List the first dynasty after the flood is the first that was centered at Kish. Among the individual kings of this dynasty, Etana was of special fame. In addition to the usual statistical information, the King List describes him as "a shepherd, he who ascended to heaven and who consolidated all countries." The story to which this reference alludes is pictured on cylinder seals of the Old Akkadian period[12] and told in Old Babylonian and Assyrian texts.[13] Etana, being without a son, desired to obtain "the plant of birth" and, directed by Shamash, rescued a wounded eagle, which carried him into the heavens. From a height that the sea could no longer be distinguished, he plunged back earthward. There the text breaks off, but the mission must have been somehow successful, for the King List credits him with a long reign and names the son, Balih, by whom he was succeeded. On the seals Etana's dogs and other shepherds gaze upward as he rises on the back of the eagle.[14]

The last two kings of the dynasty were Enmebaragesi and his son Agga. A fragment of an inscription with a part of the name of Enmebaragesi was found at Khafajah,[15] and a more complete inscription with his name and title as king (*lugal*) is in the Iraq Museum in Baghdad.[16] The Khafajah inscription was in the Temple Oval Level I, contemporary with Sin Temple Level VIII (ED II), so Enmebaragesi may be dated about 2700.

Both Enmebaragesi and Agga appear in a Sumerian document known as the Tummal Inscription. The Tummal was a precinct in Nippur, not located archaeologically but consecrated to Enlil and Ninlil and no doubt containing their temples. According to the document, Enmebaragesi built the house of Enlil, and Agga made the Tummal preeminent. Continuing in a stylized pattern, the text goes on to say that the Tummal fell into ruin for the first time; then Mesannepadda (founder of the First Dynasty of Ur) built the house of Enlil, and Meskiagnunna, his son, made the Tummal preeminent. The Tummal fell into ruin a second time, then Gilgamesh (fifth king of the First Dynasty of Uruk) built the house of Enlil, and Ur-lugal, his son, made the Tummal preeminent; and so on.[17] In another Sumerian work known as Gilgamesh and Agga, Gilgamesh of Uruk has received some sort of threat from Agga of Kish. Gilgamesh consults "the convened assembly of the elders," and they advise submission; but he consults "the convened assembly of the men" (probably those who bear arms), and they say to fight for independence, which pleases him.[18] Incidentally, the two assemblies appear to reflect a sort of primitive democracy in ancient Mesopotamia.[19] So Mesannepadda and his son Meskiagnunna of Ur preceded Gilgamesh of Uruk in control of Nippur, but they followed Agga of Kish, who was himself a contemporary of Gilgamesh. Thus they must all have been to some extent contemporaries; that is, the end of the First Dynasty of Kish (of which Agga was the last king), the middle of the First Dynasty of Uruk (of which Gilgamesh was the fifth king), and the beginning of the First Dynasty of Ur (of which Messannepadda was the first king)—all to some extent overlapped.

First Dynasty of Uruk

The second dynasty after the flood, in the Sumerian King List, was centered in Eanna, i.e., the temple precinct of Anu and Inanna at Uruk. The first several rulers were Meskiaggasher, son of the sun god Utu and himself both high priest and king; his son Enmerkar, the builder of Uruk; Lugalbanda a shepherd; the god Dumuzi a fisherman; and the divine Gilgamesh. Enmerkar and Lugalbanda appear in a number of other Sumerian texts (Enmerkar and the Lord of Aratta, Lugalbanda and Enmerkar, etc.), particularly in connection with military or trade relationships with Aratta, a place across the mountains of Anshan, evidently in Iran.[20] Gilgamesh, the contemporary of Agga of Kish, as we have just seen, was one of the most famous personages in all of ancient Mesopotamia, figuring in many Sumerian epics (Gilgamesh and Agga, Gilgamesh and the Land of the Living, Gilgamesh, Enkidu, and the Nether World, etc.).[21] These and other materials were translated and enlarged in Akkadian, and so, eventually, the great Epic of Gilgamesh was produced.[22]

In the epic he is credited with building the wall of "ramparted Uruk"—
and, in partial exploration of the Uruk city wall, it was found to be made
mainly of the planoconvex bricks characteristic of the Early Dynastic
period.[23]

First Dynasty of Ur

In the First Dynasty of Ur, the Sumerian King List names four kings—
Mesannepadda, Meskiagnanna, Elulu, and Balulu. In the excavation of Ur,
the cemetery area was found in what had once been the rubbish heap of the
ancient city, in whose lowest levels was evidence of the flood of the Ubaid
period. From the objects discovered therein, the cemetery is assigned to the
Early Dynastic period, the earliest graves to ED II, the "royal tombs"
probably to ED IIIa, and two overlying strata of rubbish (identified as SIS
1-2) to ED IIIb.[24]

In the rubbish strata (ED IIIb) were found a seal impression with the
name of Mesannepadda and the title "king (*lugal*) of Kish," and a lapis lazuli
cylinder with the name of "the lady (*nin*) Nintur, wife of Mesannepadda."
These are probably the founder of the dynasty and his queen.[25] As for the
designation "king of Kish," we have already seen other evidence that
Mesannepadda probably did follow Agga in control of Kish, and the title
may have carried the connotation of wider ruler in Sumer and Akkad, but
hardly of the whole of the land, since Mesannepadda was also
approximately contemporary with Gilgamesh of Uruk. The name of
Mesannepadda king of Ur was also found in an early Dynastic III palace at
Mari on a lapis lazuli bead, which he dedicated to a deity named Gal, when
G[an]su(d) was king of Mera.[26] Mera (a name found also in the prologue of
the Code of Hammurabi)[27] must be Mari; Gansu(d) is probably the same as
Ansu(d), a name on other inscriptions of Mari, and probably the same as the
first king of the Dynasty of Mari, the tenth dynasty after the flood in the
Sumerian King List. If these correspondences are correct, Mesannepadda, founder of the First Dynasty of Ur, was contemporary with the founder
of the Dynasty of Mari.

Several inscriptions found at Ur and Tell al-Ubaid tell us that
Mesannepadda had a son named A-annepadda, who was also a king of Ur
and builder of a temple for Ninhursag at Ubaid.[28] The son's name is
therefore almost certainly to be restored in the King List after the name of
the father (the similarity of names no doubt having led to accidental
omission), and the eighty years attributed in the King List to
Mesannepadda may likewise no doubt be distributed between the two.

Meskiagnanna, third king in the dynasty (if the foregoing restoration is
correct), is also known from the Tummal Inscription. As for Elulu, his

successor, there is possible mention of his name in an inscription on a broken clay cone, perhaps from Warka, in the British Museum.[29] Balulu, the last king in the list, remains otherwise unknown.

The finding of the inscriptions of Mesannepadda and Nintur in the rubbish strata (ED IIIb) can suggest that the burial places of the dynasty were in this region. But if so, they have long since been destroyed and lost. In the lower levels of the cemetery area (ED II-IIIa), however, about two thousand common graves were excavated and sixteen much more elaborate tombs. Of the latter, two (PG/800 and PG/1054) were intact, and these and even the others, although plundered long ago, preserved rich contents. The ordinary common grave consisted of a rectangular shaft, from 1.5 to nearly 4 meters deep, with the body of the deceased laid at the bottom, wrapped in matting or enclosed in a coffin, lying in the attitude of sleep, and accompanied by personal belongings and vessels for food and drink.[30] The sixteen relatively elaborate tombs were built of brick or stone, the main personages therein were accompanied in many cases by the bodies of others, apparently the victims of human sacrifice, and by an abundance of objects including gold vessels and jewelry of the most exquisite artistry (e.g., a gold helmet in the form of a wig with the locks of hair hammered up in relief, an inlaid "standard" with scenes of war and peace, beautiful lyres of gold and silver, and much more).[31] On cylinder seals in the tombs were the names of Meskalamdug with the title "king" (*lugal*), Akalamdug with the title "king of Ur," Abargi with no title, and Shubad with the title "lady" (*nin*). On other vessels was the name of another Meskalamdug with the title "hero of the good land."[32]

These titles, the richness of the contents of the tombs, and the apparent concomitant sacrifice of attendants make it probable that royal persons were buried here.[33] Human sacrifice of this sort is possibly reflected in the Sumerian text known as the Death of Gilgamesh (where Gilgamesh presents offerings in the netherworld on behalf of his family and retinue, who may have accompanied him thither) and is perhaps also attested in the Third Dynasty of Ur. But it otherwise does not appear to be known in Mesopotamia.[34] Since Akalamdug is called "king of Ur," and since the dynasties chosen for inclusion in the Sumerian King List may have been those that established some wider authority in Lower Mesopotamia, the personages of the tombs may have been only local rulers and, for that reason, not included in the King List. Since these tombs were under the rubbish strata in which was found the seal of Mesannepadda, their occupants—perhaps constituting a "Kalam" dynasty—may presumably be placed at a time just prior to the First Dynasty of Ur, of which Mesannepadda was the founder.

One more king possibly connected with the First Dynasty of Ur is Enshakushanna. His father's name was Elilina, possibly to be identified with Elulu, next to the last king in this dynasty in the King List, but he himself might have ruled in another city. The item of particular interest within his reign is an inscription that dates a year with the formula, "Year when Enshakushanna fought with Kish."[35] This is the first known example of the Sumerian practice of giving to each year an official name in terms of some important political or religious event. The formula consists of the word "year" (*mu*) and then a concise statement of the memorable event. Obviously, the event had already taken place and thus, as known in later examples, an event of the preceding year was normally the name of the present year. Lacking an event of sufficient importance to provide a name, the formula began with "year following" (*mu ussa*) and stated that this was the year following the year that had such and such a year name. Once it was determined, the name of the year was announced by official proclamation and in the course of time, lists of successive year-names were compiled.[36] These would provide basic data for larger-scale listings, such as the Sumerian King List. Not until the Kassite period, nearly a thousand years later, did the method of dating by the numbered "year of reign" (*bal* in Sumerian, *palu* in Akkadian) of the king come into general use in Mesopotamia.

First Dynasty of Lagash

After the First Dynasty of Ur and before Sargon of Akkad, the Sumerian King List records eleven more dynasties. Of these, except for the last, the Third Dynasty of Uruk, little is known. Within the Early Dynastic period, however, there was a dynasty that the King List does not mention, presumably because of its local character, which is nevertheless relatively well known from its own inscriptions and monuments. This is commonly called the First Dynasty of Lagash. Many of the records of its rulers have been found at and around Telloh, with which site Lagash was therefore previously identified; now identification with Tell el-Hiba (twenty-four kilometers to the southeast) appears more probable. From the records, the rulers—who used the title "governor" (*ensi* in Sumerian, *ishakku* in Akkadian)—were Ur-Nanshe, Akurgal, Eannatum, Enannatum I, Entemena, Enannatum II, Enetarzi, Lugalanda, and Urukagina.[37]

Ur-Nanshe tells how, as ruler of Lagash, he built the house of Ningirsu tutelary god of Lagash, the house of Nanshe goddess of Lagash (especially concerned with ethical standards and also with the interpretation of dreams), and a building called the Ibgal, presumably also a temple. He also

FIGURE 8.   Alabaster Relief Tablet of Ur-Nanshe Relating to the Erection of a Temple, from Telloh. In the upper register, the king carries a basket of bricks in the presence of his daughter and four sons; in the lower register, he is seated at the consecration ceremony, together with two officials (behind and in front of him) and three more of his sons. (*Cliché des Musées Nationaux, Paris*)

speaks of "the ships of Dilmun," which brought wood as tribute from foreign lands. On a stela from Telloh, Ur-Nanshe carries a basket of mud to make the first brick of a temple and in a second scene, sits with cup in hand to celebrate the completion of the work, in each case being accompanied by members of his family. On another such monument, he again appears on one side with family members, and, on the other side, a seated goddess wears a crown and holds a palm branch.[38]

   Both Eannatum and Enannatum (I) are named in texts found at Tell el-Hiba. On the southwest edge of the mound was a large temple oval, built of planoconvex bricks, much like the ovals at Khafajah and Tell al-Ubaid. In Level I (probably ED IIIb) were foundation deposits consisting of inscribed stones and copper figurines. The figurines represent a horned male deity

FIGURE 9. Fragment of the Stela of the Vultures of Eannatum, from Telloh. In the upper register, the king goes at the head of his helmeted, spear-carrying soldiers, who march over the bodies of conquered enemies; in the lower register, Eannatum is in his war chariot. On another fragment, Ningirsu, chief god of Eannatum, holds a great net filled with the bodies of slain enemies, and on yet another fragment, vultures carry off the limbs of the slain, hence the name of the monument. (*Cliché des Musées Nationaux, Paris*)

with hands clasped in front of his chest, presumably in a gesture of prayer. On the stones Enannatum says that he built the Ibgal and the Eanna for the goddess Inanna, and put the figurines in place "so that his god, Shulutula, might pray forever to Inanna in the Ibgal for the well-being of Enannatum . . . the governor of Lagash." The divine praying figure is, therefore, the personal god of Enannatum, named Shulutula, making supplication to Inanna on behalf of the governor, and the oval itself is the Ibgal of Inanna, apparently located in a larger area called the Eanna. Presumably this is the same Ibgal that Ur-Nanshe, as ruler of Lagash, also built, and the discovery of the structure here goes far to establish the identification of Tell el-Hiba with Lagash.[39]

Texts of Eannatum, Enannatum I, and also of Entemena tell of long-continued boundary disputes between Lagash and Umma (Tell Jokha, twenty-four kilometers southwest of Tell el-Hiba). At an earlier time, a king of Kish named Mesilim—possibly to be identified with Mesannepadda, king of Ur, who also bore the title king of Kish[40]—had erected a stela to mark the border between the two city-states. The people of Umma later invaded Lagash and removed the stela, then Eannatum fought against them and replaced the boundary marker. This victory is commemorated on the Stela of the Vultures, preserved in fragments.[41] Eannatum goes ahead of his soldiers, one time on foot, again in a chariot, and vultures carry away heads and limbs of the enemy from the field of slaughter. A symbolical statement of the same events shows an imposing bearded figure, holding a mace in his right hand and in his left, an emblem and a large net, containing naked captives. The large figure is no doubt Ningirsu, god of Lagash, who is named prominently in the text of the stela. The emblem of Ningirsu consists of a lion-headed eagle, here grasping two lions in its claws, and is probably to be identified with the divine bird, Imdugud, the embodiment of the storm clouds, which is spoken of by Gudea, a later governor of Lagash, as being by the side of Ningirsu.[42] The same lion-headed eagle also appears four times, now grasping two lions, then two goats, again a pair of lions, and yet again a pair of oxen, on a beautiful silver vase of Entemena from Telloh.[43]

Urukagina, last member of the dynasty, found the common people of Lagash suffering from the greed of their own officials and instituted remarkable reforms. Texts found at Telloh, which appear to have come contemporary historian, tell how he removed the parasitical officials, reduced or eliminated the contributions required from the people, and stopped the exploitation of the poor by the rich. So he "established the freedom" of the citizens of Lagash, and the word *freedom* (*amargi*), it has been observed, occurs here for the first time in recorded history.[44]

Third Dynasty of Uruk

In the fourteenth and last of the dynasties that the Sumerian King List places after the flood and before Sargon of Akkad, namely, the Third

Dynasty of Uruk, only one king is listed—Lugalzagesi. In contemporary documents he is met first as governor of Umma and, in this position, as conqueror of Lagash, the conquest coming no doubt as the climax of the long rivalry between the two city-states. The text that describes this event is written from the point of view of Lagash and expresses such strong support of Urukagina of Lagash, the defeated ruler, that the author may be the same historian who praises Urukagina for the reforms he carried out for his people. Lagash was overwhelmed and plundered by Lugalzagesi, and some twenty of its temples and other public buildings were burned. It was not the sin of Urukagina that led to this disaster, but the sin of Lugalzagesi and of his personal deity, Nidaba (goddess of writing and of accounts). "As for Lugalzagesi, governor of Umma, may his goddess Nidaba bear the responsibility for that sin."[45]

Beyond the overthrow of Lagash, Lugalzagesi made wide additional conquests. In a long text on a vase from Nippur—a vessel of the type he mentions as used by himself to bring food offerings and to pour out libations to Enlil—Lugalzagesi claims not only the kingship of "the land" (i.e., Sumer), but also the submission of all the people "from the Lower Sea, along the Tigris [and] Euphrates, to the Upper Sea," and he prays for the permanence of his reign.[46] If he did in fact, as this claims, exercise some kind of dominion from the Persian Gulf to the Mediterranean, the rule of Lugalzagesi already foreshadowed the empire of Sargon of Akkad.

3. OLD AKKADIAN (2371-2230) AND POST-AKKADIAN (2230-2112) PERIODS

Dynasty of Akkad

The Sumerian King List describes the transition from the Third Dynasty of Uruk to the Dynasty of Akkad in the usual fashion, by saying that Uruk was defeated and its kingship carried off to Akkad, then lists the kings and their lengths of reign. The first five and the most important of these are shown, with their probable dates, in Table 4.

The capital city of Akkad has not been located but was probably somewhere in the vicinity of the later Babylon; at any rate, the region of Akkad was the narrow northern plain of Lower Mesopotamia,[1] the people were the Akkadians, and their speech the East Semitic language called Akkadian.[2] From Akkad as their base, these Semitic-speaking kings established their control of all of Lower Mesopotamia and of a much wider realm as well, and numerous Old Akkadian sources, both royal inscriptions and other texts, survive to attest their rule.[3] Foreshadowed by the appearance of some Semitic names in several earlier dynasties and by the proto-empire of Lugalzagesi, the transition was now fulfilled from Sumerian to Semitic rule and from city-state and kingdom to empire. Yet the continuity of Mesopotamian civilization persisted: in spite of differences in language and political control, fundamental ideas in religion, art, government, and law remained the same and provided strongly unifying factors.[4]

Sargon of Akkad

At the point where the Sumerian King List introduces Sargon, the text is not entirely clear, and it appears to be said that either he or his father was a gardener. The so-called Legend of Sargon, available only in New Babylonian and New Assyrian fragments, elaborates the account to the

TABLE 4. DYNASTY OF AKKAD

Name	Years of Reign	Date
1. Sargon	56	2371–2316
2. Rimush	9	2315–2307
3. Manishtushu	15	2306–2292
4. Naram-Sin	37	2291–2255
5. Sharkalisharri	25	2254–2230

effect that his father was unknown, that his mother was a "changeling" (presumably referring to some kind of alteration in social, religious, or national status), that she put him in the river in a basket of rushes (cf. Exod. 2:1-10),[5] and that Akki, a drawer of water, lifted him out, reared him as his son, and made him his gardener.[6] The King List says further that Sargon served as cupbearer to Ur-Zababa and that he was the king of Akkad who built Akkad. Ur-Zababa appears in the King List as the second king of the Fourth Dynasty of Kish, being the son of the first king of that dynasty, Puzur-Sin, who was himself the son of Ku-Bau, the queen and only ruler in the Third Dynasty of Kish. Ur-Zababa was also famous, according to a later text, for having given his name to a musical instrument.[7] Evidently Sargon broke away from the service of Ur-Zababa, was somehow able to establish his own kingship, and build his own capital city, meanwhile assuming the name by which we know him, Sargon, meaning "the legitimate king."[8]

The Legend of Sargon describes his conquests in broad terms, to the effect that he not only ruled the black-headed people but also scaled the upper and lower ranges, circled the sea lands three times, and captured Dilmun. The mountains were perhaps in the northeast and northwest, Dilmun in the Persian Gulf, and the sea lands the so-called Sealand kingdom on the Gulf.[9] Other texts make it possible to follow Sargon's conquests in more exact detail. From Akkad he marched against Uruk and overthrew the powerful Lugalzagesi, who claimed the kingship of the land, i.e., of Sumer. A historical inscription, probably written soon after the time of the Dynasty of Akkad, describes the victory: "Sargon, king of Akkad . . . defeated Uruk and tore down its wall; in the battle with the inhabitants of Uruk he was victorious. Lugalzagesi, king of Uruk, he captured in this battle, he brought him in a dog collar to the gate of Enlil."[10]

The gate of Enlil would have been at Nippur, the special city of Enlil, and the presentation at that place of the captured Lugalzagesi to the chief god of the Sumerians showed that the rule had now passed to Sargon. With respect to Sumerian religious tradition, Sargon also installed his own daughter, Enheduanna, as high priestess of the moon god at Ur. On a carved disk from Ur, she wears a long flounced robe and conducts an offering ceremony,[11] yet she was also devoted to Inanna and wrote in Sumerian a long hymn in exaltation of this goddess.[12]

After establishing himself firmly in Sumer and Akkad, Sargon moved against Amurru in the west, Elam in the east, and Subartu in the north. The same historical inscription just quoted makes him victorious in thirty-four campaigns. He went to Tutul (Hit, on the Euphrates, 200 kilometers above Babylon),[13] prayed there to Dagan, chief god of the western Semites (well known in the Ras Shamra texts and among the Philistines, Judg. 16:23, etc.). Dagan gave him the Upper Region, including Mari (another 200 kilometers up the Euphrates) and other cities, and as far as the Cedar Forest (the Amanus and Lebanon) and the Silver Mountain (the Taurus). He caused ships from Tilmun (Dilmun) and other places to moor at Akkad; thus he controlled the shipping of the Persian Gulf. Another inscription calls him "the subjugator of Elam;"[14] a chronicle, in a late Babylonian copy, and two omen texts mention his wars in Subartu.[15] A stela, showing his soldiers taking captives, was found at Susa; a magnificent bronze head, found in a rubbish heap at Nineveh, is thought to be Sargon himself.[16] Old Akkadian tablets found at Gasur (Yorgan Tepe, 20 kilometers southwest of Kirkuk, the later Nuzi of the Hurrians) show the commercial activities of this one small city extending over considerable portions of this far-flung empire of Sargon.[17]

Rimush and Manishtushu, the younger and older sons respectively of Sargon, and his successors in turn, faced revolts. Rimush fought against Kaku, king of Ur, and the warriors of many cities of Sumer; Manistushu speaks of rebellion by all the countries his father had left him.[18] Across the Lower Sea, Manishtushu made an expedition in ships;[19] in the north, he left an inscription at Ashur and is said by Shamshi-Adad I to have built a temple at Nineveh.[20] Eventually both sons died in revolts at home. Omen texts describe Rimush as the one "whom his servants killed with their tablets" (clay tablets used as weapons?) and Manishtushu as the one "whom his palace killed."[21]

Naram-Sin

Naram-Sin, son of Manishtushu and grandson of Sargon, emulated his famous grandfather in conquests and went beyond him in the titles he assumed: "The divine Naram-Sin, the mighty, the god of Akkad, king of

FIGURE 10.   Bronze Head of Akkadian King, Believed to Be Sargon of
Akkad, from Nineveh. (*State Antiquities Organization, Baghdad, Republic of Iraq*)

the four quarters.''[22] For the first time in Mesopotamia, the determinative of divinity is found with the name of a king; the custom was followed by all kings of the Third Dynasty of Ur except the first, by the kings of Isin, and by a few others. But otherwise, in contrast with Egypt, it did not prevail here.[23] Likewise, the claim to universal dominion—expressed in the words *king of the four quarters* is new. Shulgi and following kings of the Third Dynasty of Ur made the same claim.

Like Sargon, Naram-Sin marched to the Cedar Mountain and into Asia Minor. An inscription at Ur tells of his conquest of the Cedar Mountain— explicitly identified with the Amanus—and makes acknowledgement to the gods Nergal and Dagan for what he did.[24] Among various places on the expedition to the Cedar Mountain, this text mentions Ebla. Ebla is now identified with Tell Mardikh in North Syria (halfway between Hama and Aleppo), where a library of 15,000 cuneiform tablets has been brought to light. Most of these are written in the Sumerian script but in a language (now called Eblaite) that is a dialect of West Semitic and that is related to biblical Hebrew. A number of syllabaries provide bilingual vocabularies in Sumerian and Eblaite. The texts reveal Ebla as a city of 260,000 inhabitants and the center of a kingdom that controlled much of Syria and Palestine and flourished around 2400-2250, i.e., until it was destroyed by Naram-Sin. The written materials reportedly include a law code, the oldest so far found, with the regulations formulated in the standard form of case law ("If, then"); a treaty between Ebla and Ashur, probably the oldest international treaty extant; an account of the creation of the world; and an account of the flood, said to be closer to the previously known Mesopotamian flood stories than to the biblical account. The chief god at Ebla was Dagan. The king had the Sumerian title *en,* for which the Eblaite vocabularies give *malik* as the equivalent. The names of six of the kings are preserved; one is Ebrum (*eb-uru-um*), linguistically similar to Eber, eponymous ancestor of the Hebrews (Gen. 10:21) and to Hebrew (*ᶜibri*).[25]

An inscription at Larsa asserts that Naram-Sin marched to Talkhadum (in Anatolia).[26] Doubtless to protect the route to the northwest, he built a large fortresslike palace at the ancient site of Tell Brak, where the mud bricks are stamped with his name.[27] In the north he left an inscription at Nineveh;[28] in the east he set up statues with his name at Susa.[29] There in the Zagros, he also fought with the Lullubi and celebrated the campaign with a very impressive Victory Stela, discovered at Susa, on which, wearing the horned helmet of a god, he strides inexorably up the mountain as his enemies fall beneath his feet.[30]

Although Naram-Sin thus exercised power from Anatolia to Susa, formidable foes were already appearing upon the periphery of the empire.

Certain texts refer to an apparently barbarous people, called the Umman-Manda, who seem to have come from Anatolia or beyond and swept along the northern border of Akkad in his time.[31] A Sumerian composition known as the Curse of Akkad (probably composed a century or two after Naram-Sin and preserved on tablets of the eighteenth century) tells of the invasion of the Gutians, a people from the mountains to the east or north.[32] Originally, it is said, Enlil gave Sargon the rule of Akkad, Inanna dwelt in her shrine in the city, and all was prosperity. During the reign of Naram-Sin, however, the gods for some reason withdrew their favor and the city suffered. At first, Naram-Sin accepted the reversal of fortune humbly, but then defied the word of Enlil, marched against Nippur, and destroyed the Ekur, the sacred precinct of Enlil. Thereupon Enlil brought Gutium down from the mountain, and this uncontrollable people covered the earth in vast numbers like locusts. Communications were disrupted, cities struck down, agriculture ruined, and famine and death prevailed. Finally some of the great gods uttered a curse upon Akkad, evidently to the end that this city might suffer a worse fate than it had inflicted upon Nippur. Thus would Enlil be satisfied and the rest of the land be saved. So Akkad became an uninhabitable ruin. "On its canalboat towpaths . . . no one walks among the wild goats and darting snakes. . . . Akkad is destroyed."[33]

It is hardly probable that all of this disaster was fulfilled in the time of Naram-Sin, although in the foregoing text he was blamed for the whole matter. Rather, he was followed on the throne by his son Sharkalisharri, who was able to rebuilt the Ekur, a work upon which there is considerable emphasis in his inscriptions.[34] A year in the reign of Sharkalisharri is also named a "Year when he undertook a campaign against Gutium,"[35] which presumably reflects a countermilitary action of some success. But the pressure of the Gutians is unmistakable and is illustrated, for example, in a letter from a farm owner of the time of Sharkalisharri to his representative insisting that the latter proceed with cultivation in spite of the danger and, if the Gutians attack, bring the cattle into town for security.[36]

Another year name in the reign of Sharkalisharri is "Year when Sharkalisharri overcame Martu in Basar,"[37] which points to danger in the west. Basar is identified with Gebel Bishri, a low mountain range between Palmyra and the Euphrates,[38] and Martu (Akkadian Amurru) designates both the land and the people in that region, the originally nomadic people known in the *Bible* as the Amorites (Gen. 10:16, etc.).[39]

Post-Akkadian (Gutian) Period

Like Rimush and Manishtushu, Sharkalisharri evidently died by assassination, for an omen text speaks of him, too, as one "whom his servants killed with their tablets."[40] After him, the Sumerian King List asks, "Who was king? Who was not king?" and names four kings—Igigi, Nanum, Imi, and Elulu—who together reigned only three years. It then names two more—Dudu and Shudurul—with longer reigns of twenty-one and fifteen years, respectively, but of whom little is known. In the next mentioned Fourth Dynasty of Uruk, five kings are listed as reigning for thirty years, but of them also little is known. Then the King List names "the Gutium hordes" and credits them with twenty-one kings. But it does not have all of their names and gives the length of their period as either ninety-one or one hundred twenty-four years, according to various texts. It is evident that after Sharkalisharri, anarchy and Gutian domination prevailed, and the time, usually put at somewhat over a century, down to the Third Dynasty of Ur, may be called the Post-Akkadian or Gutian period (2230-2112). In a text copied at Babylon in the third century but probably composed after the death of Sharkalisharri and during the domination of the Gutians, the state of affairs is reflected in a lament in which the women of various towns are said to be weeping, and then a series of summonses is issued to mourn for a certain number of the same towns. Both Uruk and Akkad are prominent in the list.[41]

It is possible to see, however, that even in this time Sumerian civilization persisted. At Lagash, prominent already in the Early Dynastic period, a certain Lugalushumgal is known from seals of Naram-Sin and Sharkalisharri as governor of Lagash. Sometime afterward, Ur-Bau, Gudea, Ur-Ningirsu, Ugme, Urgar, and Nammahani appear in the same position.[42] In order, these governors probably ruled in the sequence just given, and Nammahani, at the end of the list, was slain by Ur-Nammu, founder of the Third Dynasty of Ur, as the latter claims.[43] In family relationships, Gudea, Urgar, and Nammahani were sons-in-law of Ur-Bau, Ur-Ningirsu was son of Gudea, and Ugme was grandson. Of them all, the best known is Gudea, many of whose statues and inscriptions were found at Telloh.[44] The statues represent a turban-wearing, clean-shaven, grave, and kindly man. The inscriptions present the Sumerian language in its classic form, even as the Code of Hammurabi is the classic in Akkadian.

Also at Uruk, the line of local rulers must have persisted. The Sumerian King List follows the period of "the Gutium hordes" with the Fifth Dynasty of Uruk, in which there was only one king, Utuhegal, who reigned for seven and one-half years and who was evidently considered the deliverer of the land from the Gutians. A text, probably inscribed originally on a stela in Uruk and available in two later copies, describes Gutium as "the dragon of the mountains" and tells how Enlil and Inanna

FIGURE 11. Standing Statue of Gudea, from Telloh. (*Cliché des Musées Nationaux, Paris*)

chose Utuhegal for his mission. He marched forth against the Gutians, defeated and captured their king, Tirigan (whose name is probably also to be read in the damaged text of the King List as the last Gutian king), and brought the sovereignty of Sumer back into his own hands.[45] This important event is also recalled in the omen texts, in one of which it is said the Tirigan "died amidst his army."[46] But Utuhegal himself apparently drowned at the end of his relatively brief reign, for a text says that "the river bore his corpse away."[47]

4. NEW SUMERIAN PERIOD (2112-2004)

Third Dynasty of Ur

The Gutian invasion marked the collapse of the Akkadian empire, but the Gutians were driven out, and, under a Third Dynasty of Ur, a renaissance of Sumerian culture ensued. In this dynasty, five kings reigned for a total of 100 years. Their names and lengths of reign (from the Sumerian King List) and probable dates are shown in Table 5.[1]

Ur-Nammu

Ur-Nammu appears first in an inscription of Utuhegal, found at Ur, as governor of Ur and apparently involved in work on the sacred area of the city called Ekishshirgal.[2] At least after the death of Utuhegal, he made himself king of Ur and, in about his fourth year, assumed the inclusive new title of "king of Sumer and Akkad"—although he did not use the more universal "king of the four regions," nor the divine determinative, both of which had been employed by Naram-Sin and would be used by his own successors.[3] As to the military conquest by which he attained this position, we know only his claim (noted above) to have killed Nammahani, last in the series of governors at Lagash that included the famous Gudea. But building inscriptions of Ur-Nammu have been found not only at Ur but also at Uruk, Nippur, Eridu, and Larsa, so he held sway in all these places and bestowed the benefactions of his architectural activities upon them.[4]

At Nippur, as the Tummal Inscription states, he built (i.e., rebuilt) the Ekur, the ancient temple of Enlil, which Naram-Sin had destroyed and Sharkalisharri had reconstructed. The excavated levels of the temple belonging to this period exhibit great massiveness and solidity.[5] A Nippur inscription reads: "Ur-Nammu, king of Ur, king of Sumer and Akkad,

TABLE 5. THIRD DYNASTY OF UR

Name	Years of Reign	Date
1. Ur-Nammu	18	2112–2095
2. Shulgi, the son of Ur-Nammu	48	2094–2047
3. Amar-Sin, the son of Shulgi	9	2046–2038
4. Shu-Sin, the son of Amar-Sin	9	2037–2029
(an incorrect statement, for another text shows that Shu-Sin, like Amar-Sin, was a son of Shulgi[a])		
5. Ibbi-Sin, the son of Shu-Sin	25[b]	2028–2004

a   A poem addressed to the king, probably composed by a priestess, calls him "my divine Shu-Sin . . . my son of Shulgi." ANET, p. 496.

b   In some texts this length of reign is 24 years and the dynasty is given 108 years total.

who built the temple of Enlil."[6] At Uruk, Ur-Nammu built the ziggurat of Inanna in the Eanna precinct.[7] At Ur, he built his mightiest known monument, the ziggurat of Nanna the moon god.[8] The best preserved of all the monuments of this type in Mesopotamia, the ziggurat was more than sixty by forty-five meters at the base. It rose in the form of a stepped pyramid in three stages; it was approached by three converging staircases, and it probably had the shrine of the moon god on the summit. The lowest stage alone is well preserved, fifteen meters high, and the total height was probably between twenty and twenty-five meters. A solid mass of brickwork, the core is of unbaked mud brick, the facing of baked brick 2.5 meters in thickness and set in bitumen.[9] Weep holes in the exterior make it likely that the terraces were planted with trees and irrigated; thus the whole was like a great mountain with green upon its cliffs.[10]

That there was an archaic ziggurat here is suggested by bricks characteristic of the Jemdet Nasr period. Then planoconvex bricks of the succeeding Early Dynastic period indicate rebuilding at that time. But the bulk of the existing structure is from Ur-Nammu, whose name and title are stamped on the bricks. Finally, Nabonidus of Babylon (556-539) restored the monument and left cuneiform cylinders to attest his work. On these he states that Ur-Nammu built the ziggurat but did not complete it and that his son Shulgi finished it. Then Nabonidus concludes with a prayer for his own son Belshazzar.[11] A stela—partially reconstructed from fragments found at Ur—shows Ur-Nammu being commissioned by Nanna for the task and setting forth with the instruments of a builder on his shoulder.[12]

FIGURE 12.   Main Stairway of the Ziggurat at Ur. (*Jack Finegan*)

Ur-Nammu also promulgated a code of laws, which has been found on a tablet from Nippur and on fragments from Ur. After the law code reportedly found at Ebla, the code of Ur-Nammu is the oldest presently known.[13] As in the time of Urukagina, various officials were making excessive exactions of those subject to them, and Ur-Nammu acted to establish equity or justice (Sumerian *nigsisa,* Akkadian *misharum*) in the land. Such action was apparently customary by a king at the beginning or in the course of his reign, and a law code might incorporate some of the provisions set forth in such connection. So it came to pass by what Ur-Nammu did that "the orphan was not delivered up to the wealthy man; the widow was not delivered up to the mighty man; the man of one shekel was not delivered up to the man of one mina."[14] Specific regulations deal with sexual offenses,[15] physical injuries, and the bearing of witness in a lawsuit. On the last subject: "If a man came forward as a witness, but refused to testify under oath, he must make good as much as was involved in that lawsuit" (par. 26). As in the Ebla code, this is also the format of casuistic law, each regulation dealing with a specific case and describing both the offending action and the consequent penalty—the normal form of almost all ancient law thereafter throughout the entire Middle East. The chief exception is an unqualified, apodictic form of expression found in some stipulations in the Hittite treaties and in a considerable number of biblical commands (Exod. 20:2-17, etc.).[16]

FIGURE 13. Law Code of Ur-Nammu, Two Fragments of a Single Tablet from Ur—U. 7739 obv., U. 7740 obv. (*E. Sollberger, Keeper, Department of Western Asiatic Antiquities, the British Museum*)

Last Kings of Ur

After the pattern of Naram-Sin, all the last kings of Ur, from Shulgi to Ibbi-Sin, claimed to be "divine" and to rule the "four quarters."[17] Shulgi, it has already been noted, completed the ziggurat of Nanna at Ur, and according to the Tummal Inscription, he "made preeminent" that shrine of Ninlil at Nippur,[18] where figurines of both Ur-Nammu and Shulgi have been discovered in foundation boxes.[19] According to texts from several sites, Shulgi himself was probably honored as a god with temples and offerings, both within his own lifetime and afterward.[20] At Ur adjacent to the royal cemetery already described, he built with bricks bearing his own stamp a mausoleum, probably for his father, Ur-Nammu. On either end of the mausoleum were added similar buildings, probably Shulgi's tomb built by Amar-Sin and Amar-Sin's tomb built by Shu-Sin. Two burial chambers were under each building, probably one for the king, one for other persons. The fact that both were permanently closed at the same time suggests the possibility of human sacrifice. In the building above, evidence of offerings also suggests that the kings were worshiped as gods after their death.[21]

Bricks with the name of Amar-Sin show that he was the builder, as already mentioned, of the ziggurat on the summit of the main mound at Eridu. At Nippur, he was "the lifter up of the head of the temple of Enlil"; therefore, he was evidently a builder there, too.[22] In the north and east, his governor, named Zariqum, ruled first at Ashur and later at Susa.[23] As to Amar-Sin's end, several omen texts say that a shoe was fitted to his foot and that he "died from the 'bite' of the shoe," presumably therefore from an infected foot.[24]

Shu-Sin faced dangers in the east and the west. Inscriptions speak of his fighting in the land Zabshali and the lands of the Su, which were perhaps in the vicinity of Susa.[25] The name of his fourth year was "Year when the wall of Martu was built," and the name of the wall was Muriq Tidnum, "that which keeps Tidnum at a distance." Martu designates the Amorite land and people, whom Sharkalisharri had already confronted, and Tidnum is evidently another name for these western tribes and their lands. According to to one text, the wall was some 275 kilometers long, and it probably ran across the country somewhere northwest of modern Baghdad.[26]

Despite such defenses, the dangers around the edges of the kingdom mounted to the point of disaster for the Sumerians in the time of Ibbi-Sin. At first he claimed victories in both the west and the east. There was a "Year when the Martu, a storm-power, which from ancient times did not know cities, made submission to him"; other date formulas mark successful campaigns against Susa and against the land of Anshan.[27] But even nature seemed hostile, for there was a year when "a great flood by the will of the gods devastated the bounds of heaven and earth."[28] In the meantime, the kingdom was being diminished by the rise of independent rulers at various places.

At Eshnunna (Tell Asmar), a certain Ituria was an evidently loyal governor under Shu-Sin and Ibbi-Sin. His son Illushuilia at first called himself the servant of the divine Ibbi-Sin but soon abandoned reference to Ibbi-Sin and called himself instead the servant of Tishpak, the city god of Eshnunna (the same as the Hurrian Teshub). He thus had probably become an independent ruler. Among his successors were Kirikiri, whose name is probably Elamite, and the latter's son Bilalama, both of whom were probably in some sense vassals of the king of Elam.[29]

From Mari, a non-Sumerian (perhaps a Semitic Akkadian) named Ishbi-Irra came into the service of Ibbi-Sin and later wrote to him to report that the Martu had entered the interior of the country and taken one by one all of the great fortresses. He suggested that he himself, therefore, be put in charge of the defenses of Isin (unexcavated Ishan Bahriyat, thirty kilometers south of Nippur)[30] and of Nippur.[31] Once so installed, Ishbi-Irra soon made himself independent and sought to take over the kingship of Sumer. Ibbi-Sin wrote to Puzur-Numushda, his governor at Kazallu (an unidentified place): "Now did Enlil give the kingship to a worthless man, to Ishbi-Irra, who is not of Sumerian seed. . . . Ishbi-Irra, the man of Mari, will tear down the foundations of Ur, will measure out Sumer."[32] Comparison of year names suggests that Ishbi-Irra began to issue his own date formulas about the twelfth year of Ibbi-Sin's twenty-four-year or twenty-five-year reign, and therefore became independent at about that time.[33] At about the same time or perhaps even slightly earlier, at Larsa (Senkereh, southeast of Warka and twenty kilometers north of the Euphrates),[34] a man with an Amorite name, a certain Naplanum, made himself the ruler.[35]

Already in the first half of his reign, then, Ibbi-Sin's kingdom was much reduced by the rise of these independent rulers at Eshnunna (the Elamite Kirikiri and those who followed him), Isin (the man of Mari, Ishbi-Irra, and his successors), and Larsa (the Amorite Naplanum and his successors). All three of these kingdoms would continue after his own fall. In fact, tablets with dates later than the fifth or sixth year of Ibbi-Sin have not been found anywhere except at Ur—so, for all practical purposes, the once-large kingdom of the Third Dynasty of Ur was even that early reduced to substantially only the city-state of Ur itself.[36]

The final blow came with the fall of Ur. That blow was delivered by the Elamites and the Su, who stormed down out of their hills, sacked the capital city, and carried off Ibbi-Sin captive to Anshan. A long Sumerian lamentation, on more than thirty tablets and fragments found for the most part at Nippur and Ur,[37] recalls the earlier enemies—the Gutians from the east and the Tidnum people, the Amorites, from the west—and narrates in sad detail the final downfall at the hands of the Su people and the Elamites. The deities Nanna and Ningal his wife departed from the city, and the people were so hard beset by weapons without and famine within that they flung open the gates to the attackers. Ur was shattered like a potter's vessel, and "in its midst there was uttered nothing but laments and dirges." So the destruction remained in historical remembrance as a classical picture of national downfall. In the excavation of Ur, in fact, every building of the Third Dynasty bore the marks of violent overthrow.[38] Later kings rebuilt many of the monuments, but Ur was never again of great importance. The Sumerians themselves gradually disappeared from the scene of military and political affairs in Mesopotamia, although their influence in literature and thought continued to be felt for a long time.

5. OLD BABYLONIAN PERIOD (2004-1595)

With the fall of the Third Dynasty of Ur and its once very extensive kingdom, and with the rise of the several new dynasties at Eshnunna, Isin, and Larsa, there ensued an intermediate time of disunity in Mesopotamia. Out of this disunity was eventually built the large kingdom whose greatest king was Hammurabi.[1]

Isin and Larsa

The Sumerian King List marks the transition point succinctly: "Ur was defeated, and its kingship was carried off to Isin." Then, as its final section, it lists the members of the Dynasty of Isin. That this is the final section makes it probable that the King List was completed at the time to which it here extends, but also suggests that the Dynasty of Isin was thought of as continuing and concluding the Sumerian tradition. Although Ishbi-Irra, founder of the dynasty, was a non-Sumerian from Mari, perhaps a Semitic Akkadian, he and his successors, the kings of Isin, used the Sumerian language in their official inscriptions, rebuilt Ur, took the old titles, "king of Ur" and "king of Sumer and Akkad," and encouraged the copying and composition of works of Sumerian literature, for a great many of the known Sumerian texts, especially from Nippur, come from this period. Approximately contemporary with the Dynasty of Isin were the dynasty at Larsa, founded by the Amorite Naplanum, and the dynasty at Eshnunna, in which the Elamite Kirikiri was prominent.

For the kings of Isin, there are three texts of the Sumerian King List,[2] and two copies of an independent list;[3] the latter, omitting one king who reigned for only six months, lists fifteen rulers with a total of 224 years. For the kings of Larsa, there is a single table,[4] listing fourteen kings with a total of 263 or 264 years. For the rulers of Eshnunna, there is no known king list,

TABLE 6. DYNASTIES OF ISIN AND LARSA

| | Dynasty of Isin | | | Dynasty of Larsa | | |
Name	Years of Reign	Date		Name	Years of Reign	Date
1. Ishbi-Irra	33	2017–1985		1. Naplanum	21	2025–2005
2. Shu-ilishu	10	1984–1975		2. Emizum	28	2004–1977
3. Iddin-Dagan	21	1974–1954		3. Samium	35	1976–1942
4. Ishme-Dagan	19	1953–1935		4. Zabaia	9	1941–1933
5. Lipit-Ishtar	11	1934–1924		5. Gungunum	27	1932–1906
6. Ur-Ninurta	28	1923–1896		6. Abisare	11	1905–1895
7. Bur-Sin	22	1895–1874		7. Sumuil	29	1894–1866
8. Lipit-Enlil	5	1873–1869		8. Nur-Adad	16	1865–1850
9. Irra-imitti	8	1868–1861		9. Sin-iddinam	7	1849–1843
10. Enlil-bani	24	1860–1837		10. Sin-eribam	2	1842–1841
11. Zambiia	3	1836–1834		11. Sin-iqisham	5	1840–1836
12. Iter-pisha	3	1833–1831		12. Silli-Adad	1	1835
13. Urdukuga	3	1830–1828		13. Warad-Sin	12	1834–1823
14. Sin-magir	11	1827–1817		14. Rim-Sin	60[b]	1822–1763
15. Damiq-ilishu	23[a]	1816–1794				

a   This list actually gives only four years for Damiq-ilishu and was probably written in, say, that king's fifth year. His full length of reign—twenty-three years—is derived from one of the texts of the Sumerian King List. Kraus in JCS 3 (1949):13.

b   This list actually gives 61 years for Rim-Sin, but other correlations suggest 60. Edzard, *Die "Zweite Zwischenzeit" Babyloniens*, p. 22. The figures given in the table total 263 years; if Rim-Sin is given 61 years the total is 264.

but other sources of the usual sort provide some of the names, including not only Kirikiri and Bilalama but also Naram-Sin, Dadusha, and Ibalpiel II.[5] The dynasties of Isin and Larsa are shown in Table 6.

From other sources, especially year names of some of the kings, various synchronisms can be established. For example, the name of Rim-Sin's thirtieth year reads in full, "With the exalted weapon of Anu, Enlil, and Enki, the true shepherd Rim-Sin conquered the royal city of Isin and its entire population, as many as belonged to it, and granted the sparing of life to its numerous inhabitants, and made his royal name famous for all times"; or, in abbreviated form, "He conquered Isin." Since this refers to an event of Rim-Sin's preceding year and of the last year of the last king of Isin, the twenty-ninth year of Rim-Sin is to be equated with the twenty-third year of Damiq-ilishu.[6]

Law Codes of Eshnunna and Lipit-Ishtar

With respect to the kingdom of Eshnunna, tablets found at Tell Abu Harmal (ancient Shaduppum, on the southern outskirts of Baghdad) and written in the Akkadian language, contain some sixty paragraphs of a law code issued by some ruler, who acknowledges that Tishpak gave him the kingship over Eshnunna and goes on to enunciate legislation, stated in casuistic form, on such subjects as the price of commodities, the hire of wagons and boats, the wages of laborers, marriage, divorce and adultery, assault and battery, and responsibility for an ox that gores a man, a mad dog that bites a man, and a boat that is sunk by the negligence of the boatman.[7] At Isin, the rulers from Ishme-Dagan and Lipit-Ishtar on use the same language as Ur-Nammu and regularly affirm that they have established "equity" or "justice." A date formula of Lipit-Ishtar, found at Ur, reads, "Year when Lipit-Ishtar established justice in Sumer and Akkad." This probably took place at the beginning of his reign, since other inscriptions also refer back to "when he had established justice in Sumer and Akkad."[8] From the same king, a law code is available, written in the Sumerian language (although Lipit-Ishtar was a king of an Amorite dynasty); it is found on tablets, most of which were excavated at Nippur. Framed by a prologue and epilogue, the legal text proper, of which less than half is preserved, contains some thirty-eight regulations of the same sort already found in the codes of Ur-Nammu and of the kingdom of Eshnunna.[9]

First Dynasty of Babylon

In the time when these kingdoms of Isin, Larsa, and Eshnunna were the most prominent powers in Mesopotamia, other rulers, mainly Amorites, were managing also to establish themselves at various points. This was true at Kazallu, Sippar, Uruk, Kish, Marad (Wannah-es-Saadun, fifty kilometers south of Kish), and other towns,[10] and, most importantly, at Babylon (fifteen kilometers northwest of Kish). Of this last place, the oldest name was *Ka-dingir* ("gate of god") in Sumerian. This was translated into Akkadian as *Bab-ilu,* with the same meaning, and texts of the New Babylonian period (around 600) have both *Bab-ilu* and also *Bab-ilani* ("gate of the gods"), hence both the Hebrew *Babel* (Gen. 10:10; 11:9) and the Greek and English *Babylon.*[11]

The first reference to Babylon is a date formula of Sharkalisharri, who states that he built a temple there.[12] From then until the time of Hammurabi, the history of Babylon is mostly derived from date formulas of various kings. Under Shulgi and Amar-Sin, for example, we hear of governors of Babylon and thus learn that at that time the city was under the sway of the Third Dynasty of Ur. For the First Dynasty of Babylon, there are not only date formulas of all the kings,[13] but also two later king lists,

TABLE 7. FIRST DYNASTY OF BABYLON

Name	Years of Reign	Date
1. Sumuabum	14	1894–1881
2. Sumulael	36	1880–1845
3. Sabium	14	1844–1831
4. Apil-Sin	18	1830–1813
5. Sin-muballit	20	1812–1793
6. Hammurabi	43	1792–1750
7. Samsuiluna	38	1749–1712
8. Abieshuh	28	1711–1684
9. Ammiditana	37	1683–1647
10. Ammisaduqa	21	1646–1626
11. Samsuditana	31	1625–1595

Babylonian King List A and Babylonian King List B, preserved fragmentarily on two tablets in the British Museum.[14] From these sources eleven kings, reigning for 300 years (according to the date formulas, or 305 according to King List B), may be listed, with probable dates, as shown in Table 7.

The names of these rulers indicate West Semitic or Amorite origin, and a tablet in the British Museum from the reign of Ammisaduqa (fourth successor of Hammurabi) confirms this when it lists twenty-eight names, of which the last nine are the series from Sumuabum to Ammiditana, and then identifies them all as "the dynasty of the Martu."[15]

The first year of Sumuabum was named after his building of the great wall of Babylon (a proper undertaking for the first year of a new king); the fourth for the construction of the temple of Ninisinna, tutelary goddess of Isin; the fifth for the building of the temple of Nanna, moon god of Ur; the eighth for the installation of a cedar door in the Nanna temple; and the thirteenth for a conquest of Kazallu. Similarly, the year names of Sumulael refer to various walls, buildings, and battles, and also to the digging of several canals. Several of his texts also use the familiar phrase to say that he "established justice." Under Sabium, Apil-Sin, and Sin-muballit, the year names are of similar character and also show the continued expansion of the kingdom of Babylon until it extended at least from Sippar (where half a dozen of the date formulas of Apil-Sin have been found) to Marad (where Sin-muballit built a wall), i.e., for more than 100 kilometers along the Euphrates valley.[16]

In the meantime, Rim-Sin of Larsa "conquered Isin," as commemorated in his thirtieth year name quoted above, and put an end to the Isin dynasty. With this and certain other conquests, Rim-Sin was now the sole ruler of all southern Mesopotamia and therewith the chief obstacle to the further expansion of the kingdom of Babylon. At this point in the First Dynasty of Babylon—according to the other relevant synchronisms and correlations out of which the chronology is reconstructed—Sin-muballit was in the next-to-last year of his twenty-year reign. The next king of Babylon was Hammurabi, who in the prologue of his well-known Code of Laws speaks of himself as son and heir (one word in Babylonian) of Sin-muballit.

Hammurabi

According to the date formulas of Hammurabi,[17] he was engaged in several successful military campaigns in the earlier years of his reign but made his major conquests only in the later years. The seventh year name declared: "Uruk and Isin were conquered;" the tenth said that the city and inhabitants of Malgia were crushed, and so on. This tenth year name also dates the record of a legal action in Babylon involving a person of probable Assyrian origin, and in this the usual oath-formula names both Hammurabi and Shamshi-Adad. Thus, an important synchronism shows that this king of Assyria, Shamshi-Adad I (1813-1781), was still on the throne in the ninth year of Hammurabi (1784).[18]

Except for the warlike examples already cited and a few more, for nearly thirty years the date formulas of Hammurabi's reign celebrate chiefly such events as the building of temples, the making of images and appurtenances of the gods, the construction of walls, and the digging of canals. But in his twenty-ninth year (according to the thirtieth year name), Hammurabi was attacked by a coalition in which the main forces were those of Elam, Subartu, Gutium, and Eshnunna; these he defeated and thereby "made firm the foundations of Sumer and Akkad." The next year he himself moved against Rim-Sin, overthrew this last king of the Dynasty of Larsa, and made this important city his own southern administrative capital. The year after that he again faced a coalition of some of the same enemies as before, defeated the army of Eshnunna, Subartu,and Gutium, and advanced along the Tigris as far as the frontier of Subartu.[19] Thus in the battles of three successive years—his own twenty-ninth, thirtieth, and thirty-first years of reign (1764, 1763, 1762)—Hammurabi established his supremacy in all of southern and central Mesopotamia.

On the Middle Euphrates, however, and athwart the route to the Mediterranean, was Mari, the city from which Ishbi-Irra had come. Hammurabi proceeded against this objective, too, in his thirty-second year (1761). First, however, according to the description of that year in his thirty-third year name, he dug the canal called "Hammurabi is abundance for the people," thus providing "permanent water of plenty" for Nippur, Eridu, Ur, Larsa, Uruk, and Isin. He also reorganized Sumer and Akkad from what he calls a state of confusion, literally of "scattering." Then, according to the same year name, he overthrew Mari and another city named Malgi and, "by a friendly agreement," made them listen to his orders. But the "friendly agreement," whatever it was, was evidently not lasting, for only two years later (1759) he returned and destroyed the walls of both cities. Finally, in his thirty-sixth to thirty-eighth years (1757-1755), he vanquished the army of Subartu, destroyed Eshnunna with a flood (probably artificially engineered), and "smote upon the head the totality of his enemies up to the land Subartu."[20] Not without some right the king described himself in the prologue of his law code as "the sun of Babylon, who causes light to go forth over the lands of Sumer and Akkad, the king who has made the four quarters of the world subservient."

Mari and Alalakh

Mari (Tell Hariri on the Middle Euphrates, ten kilometers north of Abu Kemal and within the territory of Syria) was founded in the Jemdet Nasr period at the end of the fourth millennium, flourished in the first half of the third millennium contemporary with the Early Dynastic period and prior to its capture by Sargon of Akkad, and reached its greatest height in the first third of the second millennium contemporary with the First Dynasty of Babylon and up to the time when Hammurabi destroyed the city.[21]

In this time of the First Dynasty of Babylon, Amorite kings ruled in Mari, of whom the names of three in a direct line of descent are known, namely, Iagitlim, Iakhdunlim, and Zimrilim. In a handsome dedication inscription for the temple of Shamash (called the Temple of the Splendor of Heaven and Earth) at Mari, written in Akkadian,[22] Iakhdunlim calls himself son of Iagitlim, and king of Mari and of the country of Khana (i.e., the region of the Middle Euphrates).[23] There are also date formulas for nine years of his reign.[24] Iakhdunlim probably lost his life in a palace revolt, perhaps instigated from without, and the Assyrian Shamshi-Adad I (1813-1781) occupied Mari. Iakhdunlim's son, Zimrilim, took refuge with the king of Halab (Aleppo) in the land of Iamkhad.[25] The younger son of Shamshi-Adad I, Iasmakh-Adad, was then placed in control of Mari, and, for this period of Assyrian rule, there are four year names and seventeen names of eponyms according to the Assyrian manner of dating.[26] But upon the death of Shamshi-Adad I, Zimrilim, probably with the help of Aleppo (where he had married the daughter of the king, Iarimlim), regained the throne (which was rightfully his) in Mari, and for his reign thirty-two year

FIGURE 14. Investiture Perhaps of Zimrilim, Wall Painting from Mari. (*Cliché des Musées Nationaux, Paris*)

names are known.[27] Of these year names, one records his going to the aid of Babylon, another his journeying to Iamkhad, and yet others to fighting against various enemies, including the *bini iamina* ("the sons of the south"), evidently nomadic raiders.[28] Then, however, he lost his kingdom to Hammurabi (1761 and 1759).

The palace of these rulers at Mari was a very large structure, eight acres in extent, with 300 rooms, corridors, and courts. But it bore the marks of two destructions in close succession, no doubt corresponding to the two times when Mari fell to the Babylonian king (1761 and 1759).[29] Some of the mural paintings with which the palace was adorned still survived at the time of excavation, including a picture of the king (perhaps Zimrilim himself) receiving from Ishtar the staff and ring that were the emblems of his authority.[30] The palace also still preserved royal archives in the form of more than 20,000 cuneiform tablets, almost all in the Babylonian language and largely belonging to the reign of Zimrilim. These include administrative and economic documents, political and diplomatic communications, and a few literary and religious compositions.[31]

The diplomatic correspondence touches upon events in the reigns of

Zimrilim, of Iasmakh-Adad and Shamshi-Adad I of Assyria, of Iarimlim and Hammurabi (son and successor of Iarimlim) of Aleppo, and of Hammurabi of Babylon. The correlations thereby provided have much to do with the fixing of the chronology of this period. Similar historical and chronological importance also attaches to cuneiform tablets found at Alalakh (Tell Atchana, on the road from Aleppo to Antioch and the Mediterranean). In Level IV of the excavations, the tablets were of the fifteenth century, when Alalakh was largely populated by Hurrians; in Level VII, they were of the time of the First Dynasty of Babylon and contain reference to rulers and events of the period.[32]

In respect to religion, one Mari text lists the number of sheep sacrificed to no fewer than twenty-five deities, including Dagan the god of the region, Itur-Mer the god of the city, Igi-Kur a local god (after whom one month of the Mari calendar was named, as was the case with Dagan, too), and many of the great gods of Sumer and Akkad.[33] In a Mari letter, a representative of Zimrilim named Ibalel reports the making of peace between two tribes on which occasion he "caused the foal of an ass to be slaughtered."[34] In several Mari texts, the utterances of prophets and prophetesses—both private persons and cult officials—are recorded.[35] In some cases, revelations have come in dreams; again there is reference to apparently ecstatic experience.[36] Like biblical prophecies, the messages of these prophets may foretell doom, convey reassurance, or contain ethical exhortation; on occasion, they are addressed directly to the king. In one of his letters, an emissary of Zimrilim named Itur-Asdu tells of a man who went into the temple of Dagan at Terqa,[37] to whom the god gave a message to be delivered to Zimrilim;[38] in another case, a prophet writes directly to Zimrilim and begins, "This is what Shamash, the lord of the land, has said."[39] Yet another correspondent reports to the same king: "A man's wife came to me . . . and spoke to me on the news about Babylon as follows: 'Dagan sent me. Write to your lord. He is not to worry, nor is he ever to worry!' "[40] A parallel to a biblical manner of speech occurs in a letter in which the king of Qatna (Tell el-Mishrifeh in Syria, south of Hama) uses in an oath formula the phrase, "the god of my father";[41] and in a letter in which an appeal is made to Hammurabi (probably the son and successor of Iarimlim at Aleppo), "by the name of Adad, lord of Halab and the god of your father"[42]—the comparison being with the patriarchal manner of speech, in which personal worship is directed by children and children's children in successive generations to the deity "of your father" (Gen. 26:24; 28:13), "of my father" (Gen. 31:5), and "of their father" (Gen. 31:53).

Law Code of Hammurabi

Hammurabi of Babylon was not only a successful military commander but also a strong administrator and notable lawgiver. Of his capital city of Babylon, relatively little remains to be seen, both because the levels of his time are mostly under the level of the ground water and because the city was almost entirely reconstructed in the sixth century by Nabopolassar and Nebuchadnezzar II. In one quarter, however, dwelling houses of the period of Hammurabi have been unearthed, and the area is marked by the planned way in which the streets are laid out in regular straight lines intersecting at approximately right angles.[43] The letters of Hammurabi illustrate the close attention he gave to all the details of his realm and the terse clarity with which he issued his instructions.[44] As for Hammurabi's well-known code of laws,[45] with its nearly three hundred paragraphs of provisions touching commercial, social, and domestic life, and the relations of the *awilum* or noble, the *mushkenum* or commoner, and the *wardum* or slave,[46] it is evident that it draws upon a legal heritage already reflected in the Sumerian code of Ur-Nammu, the Akkadian laws of Eshnunna,[47] and the Sumerian code of Lipit-Ishtar, even as it is also related at not a few points to the later laws of Israel.[48]

Written Documents

A great many written documents remain from the Old Babylonian period. Not only official correspondence but also many private letters have been found, and show that a considerable part of the population was literate.[49] Works properly designated as scientific come into view, particularly in mathematics and astronomy.[50] Major epics, deriving in essential content from Sumerian times and dealing, like their Sumerian prototypes, with topics from creation to the flood, were reedited.

Epic of Atrahasis. The Epic of Atrahasis, known originally as *Enuma ilu awelum* ("When the gods like men," the opening words of the work), is found in its most nearly complete edition on three tablets, probably from Sippar (Abu Habba), in the colophons of which it is stated that the text was written by a scribe named Ku-Aya in the reign of Ammisaduqa (fourth successor of Hammurabi) and that the work totaled 1,245 lines.[51] In addition, there are some other Old Babylonian fragments and fairly extensive fragments of a late Assyrian version, the latter all from the seventh-century library of Ashurbanipal at Nineveh.[52] Altogether, the work tells of the making of humankind out of clay to serve the gods, the development of cities and the troubling of the gods by humanity, and the

coming of the flood in which the hero—the Sumerian Ziusudra and
Akkadian Utnapishtim—is called by the title Atrahasis, "exceeding wise."

Epic of Gilgamesh. The Akkadian Epic of Gilgamesh, *Sha nagba imuru*
("He who saw everything"), has been found in an Old Babylonian
fragment from probably around the time of Hammurabi,[53] in its most
complete form in texts from the library of Ashurbanipal,[54] in a cuneiform
tablet with forty lines of text in the debris of the excavation at Megiddo,[55]
and in a Hittite translation in the archives of Boghazköy.[56] As copied in the
seventh century, the work filled twelve large tablets, each of about three
hundred lines, except for the twelfth, added later and containing only
about half as many lines. The hero is the famous king of the First Dynasty of
Uruk, and the epic begins with a brief summary of his remarkable career,
then goes on to narrate these things in detail: he knew all things, he
brought a report about the time before the flood, he went on a long journey
(to try to obtain immortality, as we learn later in the work), he recorded
his labor on a stone stela, and he built the walls of Uruk and of its sanctuary
Eanna. The climax of the account comes when, in bewilderment at the
death of his friend Enkidu, with whom he has shared many adventures,
Gilgamesh sets out to seek the secret of lasting life. He comes at last to the
immortal survivor of the flood (the Sumerian Ziusudra, here in Akkadian
called both Utnapishtim and Atrahasis) and hears from him the story of
that cataclysmic event.[57] As related here, the narrative of the flood shows
both similarities in general and differences in detail in comparison with the
account in Gen. 6:5-9:17, so that a relationship is definitely indicated, but
perhaps in the form of mutual dependence upon a common ancient
tradition rather than of direct borrowing of the one from the other.[58]

Epic of Marduk. The Epic of Marduk, *Enuma elish* ("When on high"), also
often called the Epic of Creation, was found first on tablets and fragments
from the library of Ashurbanipal at Nineveh; other portions were
discovered at the city of Ashur and date from around 1000, and yet others
have come from Kish, Uruk, and elsewhere, dating in the sixth century and
later.[59] In all, the epic occupies seven tablets and about one thousand lines.
In its main intent, the account shows the supremacy of Marduk, god of
Babylon, over all the other Babylonian gods, which makes the composition
likely in the time of Hammurabi, when Babylon rose to political
supremacy and Marduk became the national god.

The epic begins with only two divine principles in existence, the
mythical personalities Apsu (the Sumerian *abzu,* the primeval abyss of
sweet water beneath the earth) and Tiamat (the primeval ocean of salt
water). They became the father and mother of the gods. When the
behavior of the gods became annoying, Apsu intended to destroy them, but

the god Ea perceived the plan and was able to fetter and slay Apsu. Then the real hero of the myth comes forward—Marduk, city god of Babylon, son of Ea and Damkina, with Sarpanit as his own consort. Marduk challenges Tiamat, and a fierce battle ensues. In the struggle, Marduk holds lightning before his face and looses the hurricane against his enemy; he is himself therefore probably a storm god.[60] Having slain his antagonist, Marduk divides the body of Tiamat and sets up half thereof as sky. Then he established the earth, poetically called Esharra and apparently thought of as a canopy over the Apsu, and caused the three great gods to occupy their places—Anu in the sky, Enlil in the air and on the surface of the earth, and Ea in the sweet waters beneath the earth.[61] Marduk also established the constellations, three for each of the twelve months of the year, and caused the moon to shine to signify the days and, waxing and waning, to mark the months. Thereafter out of the blood of Kingu, leader of the hosts of Tiamat and blamed for instigating her revolt, humankind was fashioned. The service of the gods was then laid upon humanity, and the Anunnaki themselves labored to construct Esagila ("house of the uplifted head"), the great temple complex of Marduk at Babylon, which included the ziggurat Etemenanki ("house of the foundation of heaven and earth"), the biblical "tower of Babel" (Gen. 11:1-9). Finally, the gods joined in a festive banquet and sang the praises of Marduk, upon whom they conferred fifty names, representing the power and attributes of the various deities, and thus "made his way supreme."

> Let the wise and the knowing discuss the fifty names together,
> Let the father recite them and impart them to his son.[62]

As an account of creation, the Epic of Marduk bears comparison with the creation account in Gen. 1:1-2:3, and certain common Mesopotamian elements may be embodied in each, although the differences between them are so great as to make any direct borrowing unlikely.[63] Both refer to a watery chaos at the beginning,[64] and in both the same happenings take place in the same order, namely, the creation of the firmament, of dry land, of the luminaries,[65] and of humankind.[66]

Habiru

In the time of the First Dynasty of Babylon, people called Habiru are known in Mesopotamia. A text from Babylon mentions the issue of clothing to Habiru soldiers, a letter to Zimrilim of Mari speaks of two thousand Habiru soldiers, and another tablet from Mari refers to thirty Habiru who have come from a district north of Babylonia.[67] Many other texts, dating mostly from the eighteenth to the twelfth centuries and coming from many places mostly on the borders of Babylonia and Assyria, also mention the Habiru. Often described as foreigners, they also several times have fixed places of abode; they find employment not only as soldiers by also as workers of many sorts; they voluntarily enter into labor contracts; and some attain to high positions in government.[68] Habiru are also mentioned frequently in the Amarna Letters, where they appear as marauding raiders in Syria and Palestine. The related form ʿApiru is found in Egyptian texts, and a similar form in cuneiform texts from Ras Shamra.[69] A possible etymology derives the term from a root meaning to "pass" or "cross" and suggests passing from place to place, i.e., being a nomad,[70] or crossing a boundary, i.e., being an immigrant, an outsider, a person away from his homeland.[71] Since not all the Habiru were nomads, the latter is more probable. The same word also corresponds very closely with "Hebrew," and in the Bible this term occurs first in Gen. 14:13, where it is applied to "Abram the Hebrew," and where the Septuagint translates with δ περάτης "the passer," "the one from across." The biblical Hebrews were assuredly not coextensive with the Habiru/ʿApiru, but as far as the designation goes, were probably among them and like them in that they, too, left their original land and dwelt in another land.

Haran and Aram

Abram or Abraham is described as coming from Ur of the Chaldeans (Gen. 11:31, etc.) and from "across the river," i.e., from beyond the Euphrates (Josh. 24:2f.). He and Isaac and Jacob—all of them the biblical "patriarchs"[72]—also had close connections with Haran (Gen. 11:31), Aram-naharaim (Gen. 24:10), and Paddan-aram (Gen. 28:2). The Chaldeans (Kashdu in Babylonian, Kaldu in Assyrian) were a Semitic people, an Aramean tribe, who probably settled in southern Babylonia about the end of the second millennium and later established the Chaldean or New Babylonian empire. The reference to Ur as "of the Chaldeans" may, therefore, point to the well-known city of that name (Tell al-Muqayyar) in Lower Mesopotamia, although it is also possible that there was another city of the same name in the northwest, perhaps at Urfa or vicinity, and that the latter is intended.[73] The other places were in northwestern Mesopotamia. Haran (on the Balikh river ninety-five kilometers west of Tell Halaf) is mentioned frequently in the cuneiform sources, including the Mari letters, and appears as a flourishing city in the nineteenth and eighteenth centuries; the name may derive from Assyrian *harranu* ("road" or "route"), appropriate to a natural stopping place on the major caravan route between the upper reaches of the Tigris and the

Euphrates.[74] In his time, Nabonidus (555-539) of Babylon not only rebuilt the ziggurat at Ur, where his daughter was a priestess of Sin (Nanna), but also rebuilt the temple of Sin, called Ehulhul, in Haran, where his mother was a strong devotee and perhaps priestess of the same moon deity.[75] In the great mosque at Haran, a building of the twelfth century of the present era, reused stelas of Nabonidus have been found, so the ancient moon temple may have been here beneath the present mosque. Thus the ancient city of Haran may lie beneath the present city.[76]

Aram-naharaim may mean "Aram of the two rivers" and is translated as Mesopotamia in the Septuagint; several Targums render it as "Aram which is on the Euphrates," suggesting that it was most particularly the land within the great bend of the Euphrates.[77] As for Paddan-aram, the name occurs already in an inscription of Naram-Sin, and the first part may derive from Assyrian *padanu* (like *harranu,* "road" or "route"). Therefore, this was the "route of Aram" and was presumably the original home of the Arameans.[78]

As to a journey from Ur to Haran and the west, a northern route is described in an itinerary that probably comes from the time of Rim-Sin of Larsa, contemporary of Hammurabi. A round trip, probably a royal or military expedition, was made from Larsa, not far from Ur, up the Euphrates to Babylon and Sippar, up the Tigris to Ashur and beyond, then across the headwaters of the Khabur to Haran and on to Emar in Syria, at the bottom of the great bend of the Euphrates. Judging from the days of march and the distances involved, the trip was made at a speed of twenty-five to thirty kilometers per day; with stops and layovers, the outbound journey took 87 days, the return 107 days.[79] A direct route, attested in several other texts, followed the Euphrates all the way to Mari, whence one could go westward across the desert to Qatna or continue along the Euphrates to the Khabur and the Balikh, and up the Balikh to Haran.[80]

Since Abraham's grandson Jacob became Israel and the ancestor of the Israelites (Gen. 32:28, 32; 35:10f., 22-26) and since his brother Nahor was the ancestor of the Arameans (Gen. 22:20-24; 25:20), the Israelites and the Arameans are represented as closely related, and the biblical patriarchs may be considered members of the Aramean (or proto-Aramean) branch of the Semitic family of peoples (cf. the confession in Deut. 26:5, "A wandering Aramean was my father").[81] When Jacob and Laban the Aramean made a covenant and swore by "the God of Abraham and the God of Nahor, the God of their father" (Gen. 31:53), it is suggested that the Israelites and the Arameans also shared a common background in religion. And, as has already been noted, the concept of "the god of the fathers" is attested in the Mari letters; it will also be found in the Cappadocian tablets (see page 88), likewise dating in the early part of the second millennium.[82]

Nuzi

Social and legal practices reflected in the patriarchal narratives are also comparable to those attested in tablets from Nuzi.[83] Known in the third millennium and the Old Akkadian period as Gasur, with a predominantly Semitic population, this place became in the second millennium a provincial center of the Hurrians and was called Nuzi.[84] The Hurrians probably came into Mesopotamia from the north in the second half of the third millennium and were an important ethnic element throughout the Middle East in the second millennium.[85] They are the biblical Horites.[86] The thousands of Nuzi tablets here referred to were written by Hurrian scribes in the Babylonian language but with occasional employment of native Hurrian words.[87] The bulk of the tablets date in the fifteenth century, i.e., just after the Old Babylonian period, but they record transactions of all kinds in which the prevailing customs were no doubt of long standing. Customs comparable to those in the patriarchal narratives are seen in the areas of adoption (Gen. 15:2-4), marriage (Gen. 16:1f.; 21:11; 30:1-3), inheritance and household gods (Gen. 31:34), and other matters.[88]

Abraham

In general, then, the biblical accounts concerning the patriarchs—their travels, customs, and religious beliefs—fit well with what is known of Mesopotamia in the Middle Bronze Age and the first half of the second millennium. In Palestine, the situation was also in agreement with the presuppositions of the biblical accounts, for Canaan was generally free of outside domination and not the place where Egyptians, Hittites, and Hyksos struggled for power and influence as they did in the Late Bronze Age. From evidence in Palestine, particularly in the Negeb, where Abraham is described as journeying (Gen. 12:9, 13:1, 3) and dwelling (Gen. 20:1, 24:62), it may be possible to narrow this time span further to Middle Bronze I, approximately 2000 to 1800. At this time, according to the pottery, there was settled life there—as there had not been for a thousand years before nor for eight hundred years afterward.[89] As for biblical chronology itself, it can be understood to place the life and work of Abraham at about the same time, say in the late twentieth or early nineteenth century.[90] If this is correct, he left Mesopotamia in the intermediate time of disunity after the disastrous fall of the Third Dynasty of Ur and before the rise of the First Dynasty of Babylon, of which the greatest king was Hammurabi.

Successors of Hammurabi

After Hammurabi, the First Dynasty of Babylon endured through five more rulers. In the ninth year name of Samsuiluna, son and first successor of Hammurabi, and again in an uncertainly sequenced date formula of his son Abieshuh, there is mention of the "Kassite army," against which presumably these kings had to fight in the years indicated—a portent of the future, for the Kassites were later to rule Babylon during a long, if little known, period in Mesopotamian history. Again in the thirty-seventh year name of Ammiditana, the next king, he says that "he destroyed the wall of Dur, which the people of Damiq-ilishu built." This probably refers to the king of this name in the First Dynasty of the Sealand.[91]

As for Ammisaduqa, the next king, in addition to texts already mentioned from his reign (genealogy of the Hammurabi dynasty, copy of the Atrahasis Epic), another document is of interest as illustrating the proclamation of justice (*misharum*) at the beginning of a reign or afterward (as was done by Ur-Nammu and other previous kings). This document is the actual text of such an act of reform as promulgated by Ammisaduqa. It provides that various debts and obligations shall be remitted, persons forced into slavery because of their debts be given freedom, etc., "because the king has instituted the *misharum* in the land."[92] From the reign of Ammisaduqa come also the so-called Venus tablets, a collection of omen texts in which are recorded observations about the disappearance and reappearance of the planet Venus and the portents these phenomena were believed to provide. Together with the synchronistic data provided by texts of the sort mentioned above, particularly those from Mari and Alalakh, the astronomical data from the Venus tablets are important for the chronology of the First Dynasty of Babylon, especially for the pivotal forty-three year reign of Hammurabi of Babylon.[93]

After Ammisaduqa, there was one more king in the dynasty, Samsuditana, and date formulas are available for many of the years of his thirty-one-year reign.[94] Then Babylon was taken by the Hittites (1595). A later Babylonian chronicle describes the final disaster tersely: "Against Samsuditana the men of Hatti marched, against the land of Akkad."[95] A Hittite text, cited on page 94, records the action as done by Murshilish I and says that he carried captives and booty to Hattusha, the Hittite capital in Asia Minor. The conquest was, however, a raid rather than a permanent occupation. It was others, notably the Kassites, who succeeded thereafter to a long period of rule in Babylonia.

6. MIDDLE BABYLONIAN PERIOD (1595-626)

After the destruction of Babylon by the Hittites (1595), a series of further dynasties arose there and elsewhere in Lower Mesopotamia, the sequence of which extends down to a so-called Ninth Dynasty of Babylon. These dynasties span a period of nearly one thousand years, prior to the Chaldean Dynasty and the beginning of the New Babylonian period (626), and comprise a Middle Babylonian period. Babylonian King Lists A and B, already cited for the First Dynasty of Babylon; the so-called Synchronistic Chronicle, a likewise fragmentary document written by an Assyrian scribe in the seventh century, in which Assyrian and Babylonian kings are listed side by side; and other chronicles and inscriptions—all provide limited materials for the partially known history of these dynasties.[1]

LATE BRONZE AGE (1500-1200)

First Dynasty of the Sealand (Second Dynasty of Babylon)

After the First Dynasty of Babylon, the Babylonian King Lists A and B continue with a series of ten or eleven kings who ruled at an otherwise unknown capital called Urukug. Judging from their place in the lists, these kings formed a Second Dynasty of Babylon; from a later attested title of one of the kings, this was the First Dynasty of the Sealand.[2] The "sea lands" were "circled" already by Sargon of Akkad, so presumably there was a kingdom there, somewhere in the vicinity of the Persian Gulf, already in his time. In the present series, the first three kings are Ilimailum (so in King List B, abbreviated as Ilima in King List A), Ittiilinibi (Ittili), and Damiq-ilishu (Damiq-ili). The last of these (who took the name of the last king of the Dynasty of Isin) was mentioned by Ammiditana, third from the last king of the First Dynasty of Babylon, so the two dynasties evidently overlapped, but this new dynasty evidently eventually came to rule Babylon, too. The occurrence of the universal term *ilu* ("god") in the names of the first several kings has been thought to reflect an approach to henotheism or monotheism. But the name of the last king in the series is Eagamil, whose name refers to Ea, the well-known deity of the subterranean waters in the Mesopotamian pantheon. Moreover, the Sealand town of Dur (*duru,* "fortified city") or Dur Ea was named for the same god and contained a temple in his honor; and again in the Second Dynasty of the Sealand, there was a king (Eamukinzeri) whose name contained the name of the god. So Ea was prominent at least in the later history of the Sealand.[3]

Kassite Dynasty (Third Dynasty of Babylon)

After the First Dynasty of the Sealand, the Babylonian King List B breaks off, but King List A and the Synchronistic Chronicle continue. The next dynasty in their lists may, therefore, be called the Third Dynasty of Babylon, but is better known as the Kassite Dynasty. The Kassites are probably to be recognized as a Caucasian people, at home in the region of the Zagros mountains, and with an Indo-European ruling element. As noted above, Samsuiluna and Abieshuh of the First Dynasty of Babylon already spoke of the Kassite army and probably had to fight against the same. The Kassite penetration at this time was evidently a part of the pressure of advancing Indo-European peoples, which was felt all along the northern boundary of the Fertile Crescent from here in the east to the Hittites in the west. The eponymous god of the Kassites was Kashshu, which was probably the name of their homeland, too. Other deities were Harbe, whom in Babylonia they identified with Enlil, and Shipak, whom they equated with Marduk. Their Indo-European connections are shown by other deities in their pantheon, for example, Shuriash, who was identified with the Babylonian Shamash but was unmistakably the same as the Hindu Surya (and the Greek Helios); and Maruttash, who was equated with Ninurta in Babylon but was probably originally the same as Marut in India. Like other Indo-Europeans, also, the Kassites employed the horse and, indeed, considered it a divine symbol, and it became common in Babylonia only after their entry.[4]

Samsuiluna and Abieshuh probably repelled successfully any actual invasion by the Kassites, but the latter seem to have continued to make a peaceful penetration of the country, since for almost 150 years Kassite names appear in Babylonian business documents as laborers, harvesters, and handlers of horses. Finally, although it was the Hittites who actually overthrew the First Dynasty of Babylon, and although the First Dynasty of the Sealand evidently continued to hold the lower part of Mesopotamia for a considerable time, the Kassites established a dynasty that ruled in Babylon for half a millennium and endured in fact longer than any other in the history of the land. This long continuance points to relatively stable conditions under their rule, and their adoption of Sumero-Akkadian deities as just mentioned is one indication of the fact that they continued the ancient traditions of the land.

For the Kassite period, in addition to the Babylonian King List A and the Synchronistic Chronicle, there are many inscriptions of many of the Kassite kings, recovered at various sites. There is also the so-called Synchronistic History, preserved on fragments in the British Museum. It is probably the first part of an agreement between Assyria and Babylonia, written from the Assyrian point of view, on the limits of their respective territories, and it cites scattered items in the relations of the two countries, beginning with the Assyrian king Ashur-bel-nisheshu (1419-1411) and his contemporary, the Kassite king Karaindash. Since the record extends on down into the early eighth century it is relevant not only to the Kassite period but also to later times.[5]

According to the Babylonian King List A, the Kassite Dynasty consisted of thirty-six kings who ruled for 576 years and nine months. Only some of the names are shown in Table 8, and only for the later names does the evidence allow the assignment of approximate dates.[6]

Certain of the royal sources of the Kassite period state that Agum (probably the second king of this name and the tenth ruler in Table 8) brought back the god Marduk and his wife Sarpanit to the Esagila temple in Babylon after the god had lived away for twenty-four years. This is probably a reference to the time when Murshilish and the Hittites conquered Babylon (1595) and carried off the statues of its chief deities.[7] If this is correct, Agum II would have been ruling in Babylon around 1570, and Gandash and the other early kings at the beginning of the dynasty would have been contemporary with the later kings of the First Dynasty of Babylon.

After Agum II, the next kings were Burnaburiash I, his sons Kashtiliashu III and Ulamburiash, and Agum III, son of Kashtiliashu III. In the Synchronistic History (1. 5-7), we learn that Puzur-Ashur (III) and Burnaburiash (I), king of Karduniash (as Babylonia was called in this time), made a treaty fixing their common boundaries.[8] In a Babylonian Chronicle, we hear that Ulamburiash defeated Eagamil, king of the Sealand, and in a building inscription, Ulamburiash takes the title of king of the Sealand for himself.[9] This sounds as if the Sealand Dynasty (Second

TABLE 8. KASSITE DYNASTY

Name	Years of Reign	Date
1. Gandash	16	
10. Agum II		
11. Burnaburiash I		
12. Kashtiliashu III		
13. Ulamburiash		
14. Agum III		
15. Kadashman-Harbe I		
16. Karaindash		
17. Kurigalzu I		
18. Kadashman-Enlil I		
19. Burnaburiash II	29	1375–1347
22. Kurigalzu II	22	1345–1324
28. Kashtiliashu IV	8	1242–1235
32. Adad-shuma-usur	30	1218–1189
33. Melishipak	15	1188–1174
34. Marduk-apal-iddina (Merodach-Baladan) I	13	1173–1161
35. Zababa-shuma-iddina	1	1160
36. Enlil-nadin-ahi	3	1159–1157

Dynasty of Babylon) came to an end at this time, yet the Babylonian Chronicle also states that Agum (III), son of Kashtiliashu, attacked the Sealand, captured the city Dur Ea, and destroyed the temple of Ea.[10]

A further important series of Kassite kings is composed of Kadashman-Harbe I, Karaindash, Kurigalzu I, Kadashman-Enlil I, Burnaburiash II, and— skipping two kings of lesser significance—Kurigalzu II, all of whom are represented in various texts. In the Synchronistic History (1. 1-4), we read the Karaindash, king of Karduniash and Ashur-bel-nisheshu (1419-1411), king of Assyria made a covenant with regard to boundaries fixed beforetime; here again, as in the case of Burnaburiash I and Puzur-Ashur III, we see the basic division of Mesopotamia into the two parts of Babylonia and Assyria, as continued long thereafter.[11]

Numerous inscriptions contain the name of Kurigalzu, but unless the father's name is also given (Kurigalzu I was son of Kadashman-Harbe I,

Kurigalzu II son of Burnaburiash), it is not always possible to determine which of the two kings of this name is meant.[12] These inscriptions have been found at Ur, Nippur, Aqar Quf, and other places. Aqar Quf (between the Tigris and Euphrates, thirty-two kilometers west of Baghdad) was the ancient Dur Kurigalzu, i.e., the fortified city of Kurigalzu, and was probably founded by the first king of this name as the Kassite capital. The same name found in the later strata of the site probably refers to Kurigalzu II.[13] At Aqar Quf, the ziggurat, greatly eroded, but still standing to a height of nearly sixty meters above the plain and approached by a great triple stairway, is even in its ruins a very striking example of this type of structure in Mesopotamia. There was also a large palace, with wall paintings, and temples dedicated to Enlil, Ninlil, and Ninurta. In the temple of Enlil, called Eugal ("house of the great lord"), were large inscribed fragments of a more than life-sized statue of Kurigalzu, probably Kurigalzu I.[14] The text is in Sumerian, even though Semitic Akkadian was generally used in this period, and it deals with the duties and powers of some of the Sumerian gods and goddesses, and with their cult rites, all of which shows how the Kassites were continuing the ancient traditions of the land.

As for Kadashman-Enlil I and his son Burnaburiash II, the Amarna Letters (nos. 1-5, 6-11, 14) preserve their correspondence with Amunhotep III and Amunhotep IV (Akhenaten) in Egypt.[15] There is a friendly relationship and even a firm alliance between the two lands, cemented by marriages and rich wedding presents. But quite in accord with what the Amarna Letters otherwise reveal about the disturbed conditions in the Asiatic territories of Egypt, Burnaburiash II complains to Amunhotep IV (in Letter no. 8) that Babylonian merchants have been robbed and murdered in the land of Kinahhi (Canaan), and he calls upon the Egyptian king to make amends for, he says, "Kinahhi is thy land."

In the time of Kurigalzu II, there was battle with Enlil-nirari (1329-1320) of Assyria in which, according to the Synchronistic History (1. 18-23), the latter was victorious and some new division of territory was made.[16] Then, in the time of Kashtiliash IV, both the Elamites and the Assyrians attacked. The king of Elam was Untash-Gal, known from many Elamite inscriptions as a great builder at Susa and also at a city called by his own name, Dur Untash (now Choga Zambil, thirty-two kilometers southeast of Susa).[17] At the latter site, Untash-Gal erected a palace, temples, and a tremendous ziggurat, dedicated to Inshushinak, the chief Elamite deity, which is still probably the most impressive of all the ziggurats in the entire Middle East. The war with the Kassite king is attested in an Akkadian inscription in which Untash-Gal says that he took away by force (the statue of) the god Immira, who was the personal protector of Kashtiliash, and placed this in Susa, where the Elamite gods could thenceforward keep watch over him. This language must mean that a military victory was won.[18]

The Assyrian king who attacked the Kassites was Tukulti-Ninurta I (1244-1208), one of whose inscriptions tells how he defeated and captured Kashtiliash and brought him, stripped and bound, before his own national god Ashur.[19] A Babylonian chronicle records the same event, describes the depradations of the conqueror including the destruction of the wall of Babylon, indicates that the Assyrians continued their rule for seven years until the Babylonian nobles revolted and restored the national dynasty, and takes satisfaction in the final downfall of Tukulti-Ninurta himself.[20] In this account, the defeated Kashtiliash was brought before Ninurta, the Assyrian war god, and the Babylonian Marduk was removed from his abode and carried off to Assyria.[21]

After the interregnum in the Kassite dynasty due to the defeat of Kashtiliash IV and the seven years of Assyrian rule, fourteen more kings held the throne for shorter or longer periods of time, the more important of whom are listed in the latter part of Table 8. Then the former enemies—the Assyrians and the Elamites—returned to accomplish the final overthrow. This time it was the Assyrians who did the lesser damage and the Elamites who occupied Babylon. The Assyrian Ashur-dan I (1179-1134) took territory on the Lower Zab river away from Zababa-shuma-iddina. The Elamite Shutruk-Nahhunte replaced Zababa-shuma-iddina with his own son Kutir-Nahhunte and carried off spoils to Susa, which included the Victory Stela of Naram-Sin and the Code of Hammurabi. For three years longer, Enlil-nadin-ahi resisted Elamite rule, but Kutir-Nahhunte crushed him too, then returned to Susa to succeed his father. Babylon was no longer the capital, and Kutir-Nahhunte even took the image of Marduk off to Elam, as earlier it had been taken away by the Hittites and by the Assyrians.[22]

It has already been mentioned that in the Kassite period the system of designating each year by a name was generally superseded by the method of numbering the regnal years of the king. In the year in which the king died, up to the point of his death the year was still one of his regnal years, numbered in the sequence already established. At the point of his death and of the succession of his successor, the year was called "the year of the beginning of the kingship of _____," and the latter portion of the year was the "accession year" (*mu-sag-namlugal-ak* in Sumerian, *resh sharruti* in Akkadian, *reshiyt malkut* in Hebrew) of the new king. Then the first numbered regnal year of the new king began with the beginning of the next calendar year. From the Kassite period onward, this system prevailed among the Babylonians and was also used in Assyria and Persia.[23]

EARLY IRON AGE (1200-900)

Second Dynasty of Isin (Fourth Dynasty of Babylon)

Although the Elamites overthrew the last of the Kassite kings, they did not themselves maintain a hold on Babylonia. New rulers arose there who, as natives of Isin, established the Second Dynasty of Isin (1156-1025), also called the Dynasty Pa-she (a word probably the equivalent of Isin) and, in the continuing sequence, the Fourth Dynasty of Babylon. The Babylonian King List A credits the dynasty with eleven kings, who ruled for 132 years and six months, and the so-called Babylonian King List C lists the first seven kings of the series, with their several lengths of reign clearly preserved.[24] As in the reigns of certain of the Kassite kings, so in the case of several kings of the Second Dynasty of Isin, synchronisms with certain kings of Assyria continue to provide a relatively firm basis for the chronology.[25] Of the kings, mention may be made of the fourth, Nabu-kudurri-usur ("Nabu protects the boundary") or Nebuchadnezzar I (1124-1103), who invaded Elam and brought back to Babylon the image of Marduk from its captivity in the foreign land;[26] and the sixth, Marduk-nadin-ahhe (1098-1081), who was involved in hostilities with Tiglath-pileser I (1115-1077) of Assyria.[27]

Second Dynasty of the Sealand, the Dynasty of Bazu, and the Elamite Dynasty (Fifth, Sixth, and Seventh Dynasties of Babylon)

In the Babylonian King List A, the fifth group of kings (three kings—Simbarshipak, Eamukinzeri, and Kashshunadinahi—who together reigned for twenty-one years and five months) is identified as a dynasty of the Sealand, hence was a Second Dynasty of the Sealand (1024-1004). The sixth group also consists of three kings, who together reigned for twenty years and three months. This was the Dynasty of Bazu (1003-984), perhaps the place of that name (probably east of the Tigris), which Esarhaddon (680-669), attacked and described as a district afar off, a desert stretch of salt earth, a thirsty region.[28] The seventh dynasty comprised only the six-year rule of one king, Marbiti-apla-usur, a man probably of Elamite descent. It is thus known as the Elamite Dynasty (983-978).[29]

MIDDLE IRON AGE (900-600)

Dynasty of E (Eighth Dynasty of Babylon)

The eighth group of kings, called the Dynasty of E (977-732), was evidently stronger than its several predecessors, for it consisted of a relatively long series of some twenty-two rulers. The first was Nabu-mukinapli (977-942), whom the Synchronistic Chronicle shows as a contemporary of Tiglath-pileser II (967-935). At the time Assyria was relatively weak, and the Aramean tribes were reaching their greatest power. A Babylonian Chronicle states that in the time of Nabu-mukinapli, "the Arameans became hostile," and Babylon was so cut off that for several years it was not even possible to celebrate the customary New Year festival, which involved processions in which Bel (Marduk) was taken out of the city and Nabu brought from Borsippa to Babylon.[30] Among the Aramean tribes were probably the Kaldu, or Chaldeans, who were later to emerge as a separate entity and to establish the Chaldean Dynasty, which ruled Babylon in one of its most famous periods.

Nabonassar and the Babylonian Calendar

In the Dynasty of E, the twentieth king was Nabunasir (747-734), known in Greek as Nabonassar. From a fragment of Berossos preserved by Syncellus (11a), it appears that a reform of Babylonian chronology was instituted under this king.[31] Already with the Sumerians, the day began at sunset, the month began at the first sighting of the crescent new moon in the evening sky, and the year began in the spring and consisted of months whose names varied in different cities and were usually derived from agricultural activities or religious festivals.[32] As established by observation, the lunar month varied between 29 and 30 days, and twelve months of an average 29½ days each made a year of 354 days, short of the year observable from the agricultural seasons or determined by the annual course of the sun. Upon occasion, therefore, additional months were inserted, and the name of such an extra twelfth month has been found, for example, at Nippur. For practical purposes, a simplified, schematic calendar with twelve months of 30 days each was used. It is attested in business documents and even in astronomical texts, where it expressed future dates in round numbers, which could be made more precise by later observation.[33] But on the basis of what must have been centuries of observation, which were climaxed perhaps in the reign of Nabonassar, it was recognized that 235 lunar months have almost exactly the same number of days as nineteen solar years: therefore, in addition to the 228 months in nineteen twelve-month years, it was necessary to insert seven extra months in order to reconcile (almost exactly)[34] the lunar and solar years in that period. Many such inserted months are mentioned in the later cuneiform sources, and the system of intercalation appears to have reached its standardized form in the fourth century. In standardized form, the year still began in the spring, and New Year's Day, the first day of the first month, fell in late March or early April. The twelve months were called Nisanu, Aiaru, Simanu, Duzu, Abu, Ululu, Tashritu, Arahsamnu, Kislimu, Tebetu, Shabatu, and Addaru, and the standard intercalary months were a second Ululu (August/September), or a second Addaru (February/March). With knowledge of the standard points of intercalation and with astronomical calculation of the new moons, tables now restate Babylonian dates in terms of the Julian calendar from 626 B.C.E. to the year 75 C.E. with a probable error of not more than one day.[35] So prestigious was the Babylonian civilization, and so precise was this arrangement of the divisions of time, that the Babylonian calendar was adopted by the Assyrians, Jews, Persians (and the Achaemenians made it official in the entire Persian empire), Seleucids (who used Macedonian names for the months), and Parthians.[36] Finally, it may be noted, in the famous *Almagest* of Ptolemy, the chronological table of kings known as the Canon, which extends to Antoninus Pius (138-161), begins with Nabonassar.[37]

Ninth Dynasty of Babylon

As known from the Babylonian King List A, the Synchronistic Chronicle, and other sources, the Ninth Dynasty of Babylon comprised sixteen rulers, and not a few of these kings were monarchs of Assyria, ruling also in Babylon (Table 9).

The first king, Nabu-mukinzeri (abbreviated as Ukinzer and Kinzer), was an Aramean, and the first use of Aramean appears in his reign in an explanatory note added to a text in Babylonian cuneiform, the latter still being the legal language in business documents.[38] Tiglath-pileser III (744-727) of Assyria tells how he devastated the land of Kinzer and himself took over the rule of Babylon, where, on New Year's Day, he "grasped the hands of Marduk" (evidently a literal gesture in front of the statue of the god to signify that the new king was his man and ruled in accordance with his will).[39] In Babylonia, the Assyrian king was known as Pulu or Pul (2 Kings 15:19; 1 Chron. 5:26). His successor, Shalmaneser V (726-722), continued to rule Babylonia, where he was known as Ululaia, of the dynasty of Baltil (perhaps a name of the innermost part of the city of Ashur). At the point where Shalmaneser V was succeeded by Sargon II

TABLE 9. NINTH DYNASTY OF BABYLON

Name	Years of Reign	Date
1. Nabu-mukinzeri	3	731–729
2. Pulu (Tiglath-pileser III)	2	728–727
3. Ululaia (Shalmaneser V)	5	726–722
4. Merodach-Baladan II	12	721–710
5. Sargon II	5	709–705
6. Sennacherib	2	704–703
7. Marduk-zakirshumi II	1 month	703
8. Merodach-Baladan II	9 months	703
9. Bel-ibni	3	702–700
10. Ashur-nadinshumi	6	699–694
11. Nergal-ushezib	1	693
12. Mushezib-Marduk	4	692–689
13. Sennacherib	8	688–681
14. Esarhaddon	12	680–669
15. Shamash-shumukin	21	668–648
16. Kandalanu	21	647–627
Assyrian interregnum	1	626

(721-705) in Assyria, Merodach-Baladan II took the throne of Babylon and ruled for twelve years (2 Kings 20:12; Isa. 39:1).[40] Tiglath-pileser III calls Merodach-Baladan II the son of Iakina, king of the Sealand. Sargon II speaks of him bitterly for his rebellion, calls him king of Kaldu (Chaldea), "whose settlements are situated on the secluded shore of the sea of the east [the Persian Gulf]," says he was assisted by Humbanigash, king of Elam, and tells how he himself defeated him and caused him to flee in his own twelfth year of reign and himself took the hand of Marduk in Babylon.[41]

Sennacherib (704-681) also controlled Babylon, but only for two years, after which, as the Synchronistic Chronicle reports, "the inhabitants of Akkad revolted."[42] Marduk-zakirshumi II (with the same name as a king of the Dynasty of E, and himself a former official of Merodach-Baladan II)[43] and Merodach-Baladan II (who had taken refuge in Elam) now reigned briefly, but the latter, even though supported by the armies of Elam, was defeated in battle in the plain of Kish and fled, as Sennacherib relates, into the swamps and marshes to save his life.[44]

Bel-ibni, next in the list, was probably a member of the family of Merodach-Baladan II. Sennacherib calls him a scion of Shuanna (the sacred precinct of Babylon) who had grown up in his own palace "like a little dog"; therefore Sennacherib probably thought that Bel-ibni would rule satisfactorily on his (Sennacherib's) behalf. When that failed, Sennacherib sent his own firstborn son, Ashur-nadinshumi, but rebellions came again, and the king's son lost his life. Two Chaldeans followed, Nergal-ushezib (whom Sennacherib calls Shuzubu) and Mushezig-Marduk; then Sennacherib moved in and destroyed Babylon completely (689).[45]

Now the Assyrian kings again ruled Babylon directly, Sennacherib for the remaining eight years of his reign and Esarhaddon (680-669) for the twelve years of his. The latter reversed the policy of his father and rebuilt the city.[46] In the rebuilt Babylon, Esarhaddon was followed by his son, Shamash-shumukin (Shamash-shum for short). But at the time a younger son, Ashurbanipal (668-627), took the throne in Assyria, and, in due time, the older brother revolted against the younger. Thereupon Ashurbanipal called him "my evil brother Shamash-shumukin" and marched against him and the allies who had been attracted by "the rebellious propaganda of Akkad."[47] In the wars that ensued, Shamash-shumukin perished, and a Chaldean named Kandalanu was installed as the last king of the Ninth Dynasty of Babylon. He, too, finally rebelled and died, and there was an interregnum on the eve of the establishment of the Chaldean Dynasty.[48]

7. HITTITES

In the period of almost one thousand years between the fall of the dynasty in which Hammurabi had been the most famous king and the end of the last Babylonian dynasty before the Chaldeans, it was the Sealand kings, the Kassites, and others noted above who played the chief role in the rule of Babylonia. But it was an invasion of the Hittites that overthrew the First Dynasty of Babylon (1595), and it was the Assyrians who dominated Babylonia during much of the Ninth Dynasty of Babylon and both destroyed and rebuilt the city within that time. Therefore, the Hittites and the Assyrians are to be considered further in this chapter and the next.

Early Anatolia

The center of the Hittites was in Anatolia, roughly equivalent to Asia Minor (a term not used by the classical geographers, and first found in Orosius in the fifth century). Here temporary human settlement is attested at a Mesolithic rock-shelter at Beldibi (on the Mediterranean coast fifty kilometers southwest of Antalya), where microlithic implements probably go back into the ninth millennium.[1] Permanent settlement is found at Hacilar (also in the southwest, twenty-six kilometers southwest of Burdur), where there was a small aceramic agricultural village of the Neolithic period around 7000,[2] and at Çatal Hüyük (fifty-two kilometers southeast of Konya), where there was a great city, still of the Neolithic period but with pottery, which occupied an area of thirty-two acres and flourished around 6700-5700.[3]

Old Assyrian Period

In the Old Akkadian period, as noted above, Sargon of Akkad marched as

far as the Silver Mountain (the Taurus), and a bilingual inscription of
Hattushilish I (in the Hittite Old Kingdom, around 1650) probably refers
to the fact that Sargon had come across the Euphrates. Therefore,
historical traditions appear to have been handed down in Anatolia from at
least Old Akkadian times.[4] Later, at about 1900, Assyrian trading colonies
were established in Anatolia and are represented by thousands of
cuneiform tablets, written in Old Assyrian, found at Boghazköy (ancient
Hattusha, 160 kilometers east of Ankara in the great bend of the Halys
River), Alishar Hüyük (probably ancient Ankuwa, 80 kilometers southeast
of Boghazköy), and most notably at Kültepe (ancient Kanesh, south of the
Halys River near Kayseri). Commonly known as the Cappadocian tablets
(since this part of central Asia Minor was called Cappadocia in the
Hellenistic period), these are mainly business documents and show that the
Assyrian traders were bringing in by caravan large quantities of metals,
textiles, and other goods, and sending back to Assyria large amounts of
silver and gold in payment.[5] At Kültepe, the houses and workshops of the
Assyrian merchants have been found at the foot of the mound proper of the
ancient city, and the texts refer to this settlement as *karum Kanesh* (*karum* is
literally "port," or administrative center).[6]

Since two copies of an inscription of the early Assyrian king Erishum I
were found at Kültepe, and since the same king speaks in an inscription at
Ashur of establishing the freedom of movement of silver, gold, copper,
lead, wheat, and wool, it seems likely that he had to do with the
establishment of these Assyrian commercial relations with Anatolia; and
the occurrence of the names of his successors Ikunum and Sharrum-ken
(Sargon I) at Kültepe also suggests that they were likewise so involved.[7]
Additional slightly later Kültepe texts attest to the presence of the
Assyrians also in the time when Iasmakh-Adad, younger son of Shamshi-
Adad I (1813-1781), was ruling at Mari.

In the documents of the Assyrian traders, the names of native princes are
found, who evidently continued to rule in their several city-states. In a
number of cases the names could be Indo-European, so these could have
been Hittites already present here in central Asia Minor before 1900. There
are Hurrian and Amorite names in the tablets as well.[8] Among the possibly
Indo-European names are those of Pitkhana and his son Anitta, and the
same names are found in Hittite texts (as Pitkhanash and Anittash) at
Boghazköy, where we learn that they were kings of a city called Kushshar
(conjecturally located 100 kilometers southeast of Kültepe, not far from
Kumanni),[9] that Pitkhana captured Nesha (i.e., Kanesh), and that Anitta
destroyed Hattusha and other places.[10] In a large burned building on the
mound proper at Kültepe was a dagger inscribed "palace of Anitta, the

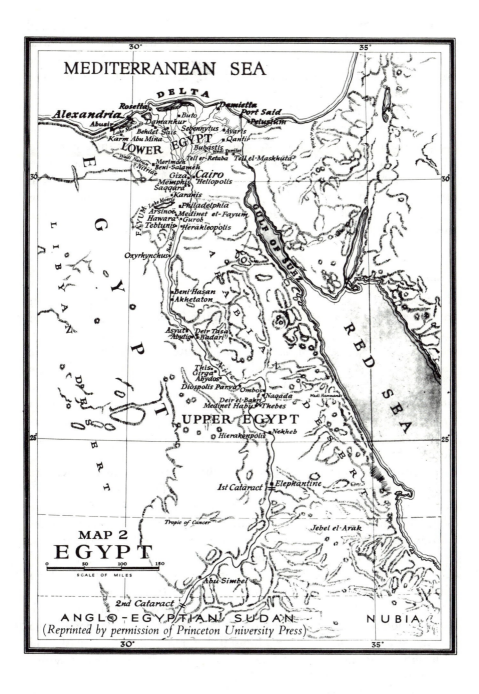

MEDITERRANEAN SEA

DELTA

Alexandria
Rosetta
Damietta
Port Said
Pelusium
Abusir
Damanhur
Buto
Sebennytus
Lake Mareotis
Behdet Sais
Avaris
Karm Abu Mina
Qantir
LOWER EGYPT
Bubastis
Wadi Natrun
Tell er-Retaba
Tell el-Maskhuta
Merimden
Beni-Salameh
Nitriae
Giza
Cairo
Heliopolis
Memphis
Saqqara
Karanis
Lake Moeris
Arsinoe
Philadelphia
FAYUM
Hawara
Medinet el-Fayum
Tebtunis
Gurob
Herakleopolis

LIBYA

EGYPT

Oxyrhynchus

Beni Hasan
Akhetaton

Asyut
Deir Tasa
Abutig
Badari

This
Girga
Abydos
Diospolis Parva
Ombos
Deir el-Bahri
Naqada
Wadi Hammamat
Medinet Habu
Thebes

UPPER EGYPT

Hierakonpolis
Nekheb

LIBYAN DESERT

ARABIAN DESERT

GULF OF SUEZ

RED SEA

1st Cataract
Elephantine

Tropic of Cancer

Jebel el-Arak

MAP 2
EGYPT

0   50   100   150
SCALE OF MILES

Abu Simbel

2nd Cataract

ANGLO-EGYPTIAN SUDAN   NUBIA

(Reprinted by permission of Princeton University Press)

ruler," so he probably ruled here in the city his father had captured earlier.[11] Over the burned building was another large building with central hall (*megaron*). It contained typical Hittite objects and continued in use down to the end of the main Hittite period around 1200. Thus Kültepe illustrates altogether a historical continuity from the Old Assyrian traders to the unmistakably recognizable Hittites.[12]

Among the Assyrians and the Amorites (i.e., the Semitic peoples) in the Cappadocian tablets we hear not only of the usual gods such as Ashur, Ishtar, and Adad, but also find cases in which each family or clan has its own deity, which was in a special way its own protector, and this one was often referred to as "the god of your father," "the god of our father," or "the god of our fathers," a usage comparable to that already noted at Mari and in biblical examples.[13]

Hittite Old Kingdom

A consecutive account of unmistakably Hittite history first becomes possible at a point somewhat later than Anitta, on the basis of Hittite texts and monuments discovered at many places, most notably at Boghazköy, which these texts establish as the main Hittite capital Hattusha.[14] The Boghazköy texts are in a half-dozen different languages. Here and elsewhere the Hittite language—closely related to the Indo-European family of languages—is written both in cuneiform script (no doubt borrowed from Mesopotamia) and also in hieroglyphic signs (which seem to have no relation to the pictographs of the early Sumerians or to the hieroglyphs of Egypt).[15]

The history is commonly divided into three periods, with approximate dates as follows: Old Kingdom (Labarnash to Telepinush), 1700-1500; Middle Kingdom (Alluwamnash to Tudhaliash III), 1500-1450; Empire (Shuppiluliumash I to Shuppiluliumash II), 1450-1200. Two main sources provide basic materials—for the first period the so-called Proclamation of Telepinush, and for all three periods the Hittite lists of offerings for royal ancestors.[16] In the long preamble to the proclamation, Telepinush, last king of the Old Kingdom, contrasts the strength of the Hittites in an earlier time when they were a united people with their weakness due to internal strife in the period just before he himself took the throne. In this connection, he lists the kings who had preceded himself, beginning with Labarnash, and with eight names in all down to and including himself. These kings, with a few probable dates, are listed in Table 10.

"Formerly Labarnash was great king," says Telepinush as he begins the preamble of his proclamation, and he goes on to relate that the land was

TABLE 10. HITTITE OLD KINGDOM

Name	Date
1. Labarnash	
2. Hattushilish I	destroyed Alalakh, 1650
3. Murshilish I	destroyed Babylon, 1595
4. Hantilish I	
5. Zidantash I	
6. Ammunash	
7. Huzziyash I	
8. Telepinush	around 1520

then small but united, and Labarnash successful in campaigns that apparently carried the frontiers of Hittite rule to the Mediterranean. Labarnash was plainly a famous king, for many later Hittite rulers took his name in addition to their own, as a sort of title. The same was true with respect to his queen, Tawannannash, whose name was assumed by later queens.

For Hattushilish I, bilingual records in Hittite and Akkadian are also available, and in these, he is called the man of Kushshar—presumably indicating the origin of his family in the town where Anitta had ruled—and the king of Hattusha.[17] Since the name Hattushilish also means the man of Hattusha, it may be surmised that it was he who transferred the Hittite capital to the previously destroyed Hattusha.[18] In the same bilingual text, Hattushilish I says that in his second year he marched against Alkhalikha (Alalakh). This action may probably be equated with the destruction of Level VII at Tell Atchana (Alalakh), which, on various grounds, may be dated about 1650.[19] In other years, Hattushilish I marched against the land Arzawa in western Asia Minor and the land Hanigalbat, which was Hurrian territory, and crossed the Euphrates (Mala in Hittite, Purattu in Akkadian) to overcome the country of Hashshu (in which connection, according to a probable emendation of the text, he compares his accomplishment with the exploit of Sargon of Akkad, who crossed the same river). From various conquered places he brought back gold, silver, and other booty and "filled Hattusha." Concluding the campaign of a given year, he says, "Then I came home to Hattusha." The city was plainly his residence and capital.

Concerning Murshilish I, the Proclamation of Telepinush says that he destroyed Aleppo, then "he went to Babylon, and destroyed Babylon, and defeated the Hurrians, and carried captives and possessions of Babylon to Hattusha." This is the Hittite record of the event, told more briefly in the Babylonian Chronicle (quoted above), which, although it did not result in permanent occupation of the famous Babylonian capital by the Hittites, brought the First Dynasty of Babylon to a close (1595).

Despite his accomplishments, Murshilish I became the victim of conspiracy, and the Hittite Old Kingdom fell increasingly into turmoil at home and weakness abroad. As Telepinush tells the melancholy story, the sister of Murshilish I was married to a cupbearer named Hantilish; the latter plotted with his son-in-law Zidantash, and they killed Murshilish. When Hantilish himself was old and "about to become a god" (a usual manner of expression in the Hittite documents for death), Zidantash killed members of his family and became king. Then the son of Zidantash, named Ammunash, became his enemy and killed Zidantash, his father. So violent deeds led to more deeds of violence, and this bitter chain of events continued until the time of Telepinush. The gods, however, avenged the ceaseless bloodshed. Already in the time of Ammunash, agriculture did not prosper at home, many countries abroad became hostile, and Hittite military power was ineffectual. Finally, perhaps around 1520, Telepinush came to the throne and called an assembly at Hattusha to establish a state of affairs in which royal assassinations would no longer be the order of the day, and the kingdom could again be strong. To that end he promulgated the regulations that make up the main body of his proclamation.[20]

Hittite Middle Kingdom and Kingdom of Mitanni

Despite the valiant effort of Telepinush to strengthen the state, there ensued in the Middle Kingdom a time of relative obscurity and weakness, approximately the first half of the fifteenth century. From the offering lists, the kings who appear to belong here were those in Table 11.

In this time other peoples increased in power, particularly the Hurrians, even though Murshilish I had fought successfully against them at the same time that he destroyed Aleppo and Babylon. Now what had probably been several Hurrian states scattered across northern Mesopotamia and Syria were brought together in the kingdom of Mitanni. The geographical center of this kingdom was in the region of the Upper Khabur river, and was probably more or less the same as Hanigalbat, against which Hattushilish I had marched at an even earlier time. Here, probably contemporary with the first successors of Telepinush, a certain Saustatar ruled in a capital called Washshukkanni and is even recorded to have taken from Ashur a door of silver and gold and set it up in his palace at home.[21]

TABLE 11. HITTITE MIDDLE KINGDOM

Name
1. Alluwamnash
2. Hantilish II
3. Zidantash II
4. Huzziyash II

Although the population of Mitanni was predominantly Hurrian, the names of several of the later kings, including Tushratta and his son Mattiwaza, probably indicate that they were of Indo-European origin.[22] Like Kadashman-Enlil I and Burnaburiash II of the Kassite Dynasty in Babylon, Tushratta was in correspondence—preserved in the Amarna Letters (nos. 17-29)—with Amunhotep III and Amunhotep IV (Akhenaten). The subject matter is largely the royal marriages that sealed the friendship of Mitanni and Egypt. In one letter (no. 23), received in Egypt, according to a hieratic notation at the end, in the thirty-sixth year of Amunhotep III, Tushratta tells of sending Ishtar of Nineveh to Egypt. Since this was near the end of the reign of the Egyptian king, the latter may have been ill and the statue sent with the hope of bringing healing. To this point Mitanni was apparently accorded full respect by Egypt, but after the death of Amunhotep III, Tushratta asks Tiy, widow of Amunhotep III and mother of Amunhotep IV, to send richer gifts. Thus the standing of Mitanni would appear then to have been on the decline (Amarna Letter no. 26). Likewise, over against the Hittites, at an early date Tushratta won some victory against them, for in one of his earliest letters (no. 17) to Amunhotep III, he says that he has sent gifts to the Egyptian king "of the booty of the land of Hatti." But later the Hittite sources show that the situation was different.

Hittite Empire

Shuppiluliumash I

The kings of the Hittite Empire are listed in Table 12, with family relationships and some dates.[23] Up to the sixth king, Shuppiluliumash I, the Hittite state was still hard pressed by enemies and relatively insignificant. In two texts from Boghazköy, Hattushilish III, grandson of

TABLE 12. HITTITE EMPIRE

Name	Date
1. Tudhaliash II	
2. Arnuwandash I, son of Tudhaliash II	
3. Tudhaliash III, son of Arnuwandash	
4. Hattushilish II, brother of Tudhaliash III	
5. Tudhaliash the younger, son of Tudhaliash III	
6. Shuppiluliumash I, son of Hattushilish II	
7. Arnuwandash II, son of Shuppiluliumash I	
8. Murshilish II, son of Shuppiluliumash I	first year, 1344
9. Muwatallish, son of Murshilish II	battle of Qadesh, 1286
10. Murshilish III (Urhi-Teshub), son of Muwatallish	
11. Hattushilish III, brother of Muwatallish	treaty with Ramses II, 1270
12. Tudhaliash IV, son of Hattushilish III	
13. Arnuwandash III, son of Tudhaliash IV	
14. Shuppiluliumash II, brother of Arnuwandash III	

Shuppiluliumash I and the eleventh king, describes the prior state of affairs and the accomplishment of his grandfather: "Formerly the Hatti-lands were utterly ravaged by foes from outside. . . . But when my grandfather Shuppiluliumash . . . ascended the throne . . . he expelled the foes from the Hatti-lands and restored to order the Hatti-land and resettled the Hatti-land."[24] The same texts also tell us that Shuppiluliumash I campaigned successfully in the Hurrian lands, made the Mala (the Euphrates) his border, and installed his own sons as kings, Telepinush in Aleppo and Piyashilish in Carchemish. On another side, he fixed the Hittite boundary at the land of Qadesh (on the Orontes River) and at the land of Amurru.

With respect to the Hurrian lands, details are provided in a long treaty, preserved in two versions and several copies, between Shuppiluliumash I and Mattiwaza, son of Tushratta.[25] Like other Hittite treaties, this consists of three parts—a historical introduction, the provisions of the treaty proper, and a list of the deities called upon to serve as witnesses of the agreement. In the introduction, Shuppiluliumash I recalls that he made a treaty with Artatama, king of Hurri, then Tushratta, king of Mitanni, threatened him. So Shuppiluliumash I crossed the Euphrates and invaded the country of Isuwa (between the Upper Euphrates and Tigris),[26] then descended upon Washshukkanni, the capital of Mitanni, where he found that Tushratta had already departed rather than staying to fight. In the ensuing turmoil, however, Tushratta was killed by an unnamed son of his, and his son Mattiwaza became king with the help of Shuppiluliumash I, also receiving a daughter of Shuppiluliumash as wife. Following this historical introduction, the treaty proper spells out the resulting boundaries between the Hittites and Mitanni, then both Hittite and Hurrian deities are listed as witnesses. And, we are told, duplicate copies of the text were deposited before the Hittite sun goddess of Arinna (a holy city within a day's journey from Hattusha, but unlocated) and before Teshub, the storm god of the Hurrians.

Amurru, the Amorite land in North Syria, was probably at this time smaller than the Martu of Babylonian times, but it was still the natural border region between the Hittite realm and Egypt. Here Shuppiluliumash I concluded a treaty with a king of Amurru named Aziru.[27] The latter is also well known from the Amarna Letters (nos. 156-162), in which he protests his loyalty to Egypt. But in the present treaty, Shuppiluliumash I says that Aziru "parted from the gate of Egypt and became subservient to the Sun, the king of Hatti land," and expresses his great pleasure over this allegiance.

Shuppiluliumash I was also himself in correspondence with Egypt. When Amunhotep IV (Akhenaten) became king, Shuppiluliumash wrote (Amarna Letter no. 41) and expressed the wish for good mutual friendship. From a long but very fragmentary biographical work known as the Deeds of Shuppiluliumash, composed by his son Murshilish II, we learn of a further incident.[28] At this juncture Tutankhamun (here called Niphururia)[29] has died, and his widowed queen (here called Dahamunzu, probably representing the Egyptian title "king's wife" but perhaps taken in the Hatti land for a proper name)[30] writes to ask for a son of Shuppiluliumash I to become her husband. Shuppiluliumash I sends a messenger to Egypt to investigate, the queen writes again to reproach him for distrust and delay, he does at last send a son, named Zannanzash. But the latter is slain on the way by the Egyptians, perhaps by Horemheb, the general who commanded the Egyptian troops in Palestine and who not long afterward took the Egyptian throne for himself.

The sequel is told in the Deeds of Shuppiluliumash and more fully in the so-called Plague Prayers of Murshilish II.[31] In response to the murder of Zannanzash, the Hittite king sent another son, Arnuwandash II, to attack the Egyptians in Amqa, which was Egyptian territory (probably the Beqa valley between the Lebanon and the Anti-Lebanon mountains). The Hittites won the battle, but with the prisoners whom they brought back there came plague as well. When Murshilish II wrote, it had raged for twenty years, in his father's days, in his brother's days, and in his own.

Murshilish II believed that the Hattian storm god had allowed
Shuppiluliumash I to prevail over the Egyptians, but he also felt that the
god was somehow offended, so he made confession, offerings, and prayers
for deliverance from the terrible plague: "It is only too true that a man is
sinful. My father sinned. . . . But I have not sinned. . . . However . . . the
father's sin falls upon the son. . . . Let not the good perish with the wicked!"
(cf. Jer. 31:29f.; Ezek. 18:2–4). The ravages of the plague in the household
of Shuppiluliumash I are also attested in a prayer of one of his children
named Kantuzilish: "Life is bound up with death. . . . Man cannot live for
ever. . . . Now I cry for mercy. . . . [Thou], my god, [art father and mother]
to me; [beside thee there is no fa]ther or mother for me."[32]

Murshilish II

The accession and successive years of reign of Murshilish II are recorded in
a work known as the Annals of Murshilish, an early example of the year-
by-year form of record well known in later annals of Assyrian and
Babylonian kings.[33] Here the transition from one year to the next is marked
by the words, "And that I did in one year. In the next year. . . . " Murshilish
II tells us that when his father Shuppiluliumash I died, his brother
Arnuwandash II took the throne but also became sick himself—all of this
perhaps from the same great plague—and was attacked by many enemy
lands, but that he himself in the endeavors of ten years thoroughly
reestablished Hittite ascendancy in Asia Minor and Syria. To secure the
more and more critical border with Egypt, he also made a treaty with
Tuppi-Teshub, king of Amurru, grandson of Aziru, with whom
Shuppiluliumash I had made a similar treaty for a similar purpose.[34] In the
spring of the tenth year of Murshilish II another text mentions an omen of
the sun, perhaps a reference to a solar eclipse of March 13, 1335, which
would provide a fixed date and place the first year of the king in 1344.[35]

Muwatallish

Under Muwatallish came the major confronation with Egypt. With the
rise of the Nineteenth Dynasty, Egypt renewed its Asiatic aspirations, and
Seti I (1304–1290) marched into Syria. The record of the campaign at
Karnak shows the fortress of Qadesh on the Orontes and names both the
land of Qadesh and the land of Amor.[36] Thus Qadesh and at least a portion
of the land of Amurru were evidently brought under Egyptian sway. This
is confirmed for Amurru in a treaty between Tudhaliash IV and a king of
Amurru named Ishtar-muwash, which states that when Muwatallish
became king, the people of Amurru deserted him and went over to the king
of Egypt.[37] Then Ramses II also pushed northward, and in his fifth year

(1286), a great battle was fought at Qadesh. According to the records of the Egyptian king, Muwatallish brought together very large forces not only from the Hatti land but also from allied lands as far away as Arzawa in the west and Mitanni in the east.[38] In an autobiographical work, Hattushilish III, brother of Muwatallish, tells that he brought troops from the regions he then governed,[39] and in another text describes the outcome briefly: "At the time that my brother took the field against the king of the land of Egypt and the country of Amurru, and when he then had defeated the king of the land of Egypt and the country of Amurru, he returned to the country Apa. When my brother Muwatallish had also defeated Apa, he returned to the Hatti land."[40] Apa, mentioned also in the Amarna Letters (Abe, Ube),[41] is probably the district around Damascus, especially to the north, so Muwatallish evidently went after the Egyptians that far, and Qadesh and Amurru were no doubt recovered for the Hittites.

Hattushilish III

When Muwatallish died without leaving a queen's son to succeed him, he was followed on the throne by the son of a royal concubine (in accordance with the regulations established long before by Telepinush), whose name was Murshilish (III), and in Hurrian Urhi-Teshub. In his autobiographical account (cited just above), Hattushilish III, brother of Muwatallish and uncle of the new king, says that he supported him at first but, when Urhi-Teshub attacked him, he saw him exiled "across the sea" (probably to Cyprus [Alashiya], with other evidence suggesting that he went on to Egypt), and Hattushilish III himself became king.[42] The queen of Hattushilish III was Pudu-Heba, daughter of a priest and herself, by her name, a devotee of the goddess Hebat, wife of the Hurrian storm god Teshub and worshiped in the Hurrian lands of the Lebanon mountains. In a prayer on a Boghazköy tablet, Pudu-Heba addressed the Hittite sun goddess: "O sun goddess of Arinna, queen of all the countries! In the Hatti country thou bearest the name of the sun goddess of Arinna; but in the land which thou madest the cedar land thou bearest the name Hebat."[43]

The major event in the reign of Hattushilish III was the conclusion of a treaty of nonaggression and mutual assistance with Ramses II of Egypt, copies of which have been found both at Boghazköy and in Egypt.[44] The Egyptian copy gives the date as the twenty-first year of Ramses II (1270), sixteen years after the battle of Qadesh (1286). The original text was engraved on a silver tablet, brought by Hittite ambassadors to Ramses II at his city of Per-Ramses. On the tablet were seals showing Hattushilish III with the Hittite storm god (called Seth in the Egyptian text, he being also a storm god and the nearest equivalent among the Egyptian deities), and

Pudu-Heba with the Hittite sun goddess of Arinna (called by the name of the Egyptian sun god Re in the Egyptian text). Long after, in the thirty-fourth year of the Egyptian pharaoh (1257), Hattushilish III gave a daughter in marriage to Ramses II. In Egypt she was called "Maatnefrure ["She who sees the beauty of Re," the name of the last hour of the night], daughter of the chief of Kheta [i.e., the Hatti land]," and she is represented alongside Ramses II at Abu Simbel and Tanis.[45]

In the time just discussed, Adad-nirari I (1307-1275) was on the throne of Assyria. We learn of events in his long reign chiefly from his numerous building inscriptions.[46] In Hanigalbat, as the Assyrians continued to call what had been the kingdom of Mitanni, the rulers were Shattuara and then his son Wasashatta (presumably descendants and successors of Mattiwaza, with whom Shuppiluliumash I made a treaty). In two campaigns, Adad-nirari I conquered them both. His conquests included Washshukkanni, the old capital of Mitanni, and the district of Haran up to Carchemish on the bank of the Euphrates. This whole territory he incorporated into Assyria. It is a reasonable surmise that, on the one hand, the preoccupation of the Hittites with their struggle with Egypt gave Adad-nirari I his opportunity to move to the west and, on the other hand, the extension of the Assyrian presence to the Euphrates provided a strong reason for Hattushilish III to negotiate his treaty with Ramses II.[47]

In its closing days, the Hittite empire was beset from both the east and the west. Tudhaliash IV must have been largely contemporary with Shalmaneser I (1274-1245) of Assyria, and the latter tells of moving against Hanigalbat, conquering another king named Shattuara, and slaughtering his allies, an army of Hittites and Ahlami (i.e., Arameans).[48] Again it was probably in the time of Arnuwandash III that Tukulti-Ninurta I (1244-1208) of Assyria says that he carried off a large number of Hittites "from the other side of the Euphrates."[49] On the other hand, Merneptah (1224-1204) of Egypt, probably also a contemporary, says that he sent grain in ships, presumably on some occasion of famine, "to keep alive that land of Kheta [the Hatti land]."[50] Finally, with the reign of Shuppiluliumash II, the empire reached its end. Such records of this king as were found in the archives at Boghazköy were the latest datable items there. About 1200, the city was violently destroyed and burned.[51] The destroyers must have been the so-called Peoples of the Sea. Soon after 1200, Ramses III tells of their invasion of the whole eastern Mediterranean, an invasion that then threatened Egypt as well. Of the more northern lands over which they had swept, he says: "Not one stood before their hands from Kheta [the Hatti land] on. . . . Carchemish, Arzawa, and Alashiya [Cyprus] were wasted."[52]

Later Hittites and Arameans

After the fall of the Hittite empire, western Anatolia was dominated by other peoples. Herodotus (7. 73) tells of the Phrygians, who came into the region from Europe, and Assyrian records speak of the Mushki (probably the same as the Phrygians) and of Tabal,[53] these two names probably corresponding with Meshech and Tubal, sons of Japheth, in Gen. 10:2 (cf. Ezek. 27:13; 32:26). Farther east were a number of smaller kingdoms and city-states in which the traditions of Hittite culture were perpetuated, to which the designation of New Hittite is sometimes given. After the fall of Hattusha, the first Assyrian king to come into these areas was Tiglath-pileser I (1115-1077); and he speaks of proceeding against the city of Milid of great Hatti, against Carchemish in the land of Hatti, and of receiving the submission of a king of great Hatti.[54] Thus the ancient name of Hatti was still in use and, in fact, in the form Hatay is still given to the province of Antioch. Archaeological discoveries also reveal the continuation of Hittite culture at such sites as Til-Barsip (Tell Ahmar) on the Upper Euphrates,[55] Hamath on the Orontes, and Zinjirli, Sakje-gözü, and the district of Kummuhu (classical Commagene) in southeast Asia Minor.[56] Biblical references to "the kings of the Hittites" in the time of Solomon (1 Kings 10:29; 2 Chron. 1:17) and of the divided kingdom (2 Kings 7:6) will presumably be to rulers of some of these small kingdoms. It may also be remembered that the Hittites' Ahimelech (1 Sam. 26:6) and Uriah (2 Sam. 11:3, etc.) served under David, and that among Solomon's many foreign women were Hittite women (1 Kings 11:1).

Biblical references to Aram and the Arameans in northwestern Mesopotamia have been noted (above) already in the time of Abraham, and, in cuneiform sources, the Arameans are first plainly mentioned by this name in the reign of Tiglath-pileser I (1115-1077) and appear to have reached their greatest prominence in the next two centuries (the eleventh and tenth).[57] In North Syria, the Arameans were undoubtedly in conflict with the later Hittites and are known, for example, to have overthrown New Hittite dynasties at Zinjirli and Tell Ahmar.[58] Among other places, the Arameans had a capital at the ancient, long-abandoned site of Tell Halaf, known at this time in Assyrian records as Guzana.[59] In the time of David there were Aramean kingdoms, against which he fought (2 Sam. 10:6, 8). These included Aram-Zobah (Ps. 60 title), which was in the Beqa, and Aram-Beth-Rehob (cf. Judg. 18:28; 1 Sam. 14:47 LXX) and Aram-Maacah (1 Chron. 19:6), which were in the vicinity of Mount Hermon.[60] Of the several Aramean centers, the most important was at Damascus (called Aram–Damascus in 2 Sam. 8:6), and this city became the capital of the most inclusive Aramean kingdom, known as Syria. Contemporary with the kings of Judah and Israel, the kings of Syria play an important role in biblical history (e.g., 1 Kings 15:18; 2 Kings 13:3), and Damascus is often excoriated by the prophets and its coming destruction foretold (Amos 1:3-5; Isa. 17:1-3; Jer. 49:23-27). As prophetic utterance (Isa. 10:5-11) also indicated, the destruction of Damascus, Hamath, Carchemish, and other cities came from the side of Assyria, and this was in fact the power before which the New Hittite and Armaean kingdoms alike fell in the course of the eighth century. Yet Hittite cultural influence continued into the first century of the present era in the kingdom of Commagene,[61] and the language of the Arameans—the West Semitic dialect (or group of dialects) known as Aramaic—was used in Babylonia, became an official language of the Assyrian (cf. 2 Kings 18:26) and Persian empires, and was the common speech of the whole Middle East until the Arab invasion of the seventh century C.E.[62]

8. ASSYRIANS

Early Assyrian Kings

The homeland of the Assyrians was the triangle formed by the Tigris and the Little Zab rivers and the Zagros Mountains. The national god was Ashur, and this was also the name of the city-state that gave its name to the country and the empire. The site of Ashur (Qalat Sharqat, 100 kilometers south of Mosul)[1] was occupied from the early part of the third millennium, and the city is first mentioned in literary sources in texts of the Old Akkadian period from Nuzi.[2] In the Old Akkadian period, Sargon of Akkad and Naram-Sin came as conquerors but were later remembered with admiration as rulers of wide empire, so that two Assyrian kings used the name of Sargon and one the name of Naram-Sin.

The outline of Assyrian history is provided by a King List, of which three main copies are available,[3] and by lists of *limmu*s or eponyms, i.e., high officials (usually the king himself in his first or second regnal year) chosen to give their name to the year.[4] Under Bur-Sagale, *limmu* in the tenth year of Ashur-dan III (772-755), the eponym lists mention an eclipse of the sun in the month Simanu (May/June); this is identified with a solar eclipse of June 15, 763, so a fixed point is provided in the chronology.[5] The early form of the Assyrian calendar is not well known, but the Babylonian calendar was probably introduced toward the end of the twelfth century, perhaps in the reign of Tiglath-pileser I (1115-1077).

The Assyrian King List begins with a certain Tudija and provides a continuous sequence to Shalmaneser V as the 109th king, and the remaining known kings bring the total to 117. At the end of the first seventeen names, a note says, "Total of seventeen kings who dwelt in tents," which must mean that these were desert sheikhs and presumably the ancestors of the nomadic tribes that made up the Assyrian nation. Some of the names are the same as some in the British Museum tablet that traces the ancestry of the First Dynasty of Babylon back to Amorite tribes, so there was some common background.[6] The next to the last of the seventeen is Ushpia. In inscriptions marking their own rebuilding of the temple of Ashur in the city of Ashur, Shalmaneser I (1274-1245) and Esarhaddon (680-669) mention Ushpia as the first builder of that temple. In his time, therefore, the nomadic period was evidently coming to an end.[7]

The second section of the King List is summarized with the note, "Total of ten kings who are ancestors." The names are given in genealogical order, beginning with the last king of the group, Aminu son of Ila-kabkabi, and going on back to overlap with Apiashal son of Ushpia and last of the first seventeen kings. The third section begins with Sulili son of Aminu and contains six names, ending with Ilushuma. An obscure notation at the end says their *limmus* are "eaten up," presumably meaning that the eponym lists of their reigns were in some way destroyed. The second king in this group is Kikkia. In his day, Ashur-rim-nisheshu (1410-1403) rebuilt the city wall of Ashur and gave credit to those who had built it before himself, first of all naming Kikkia, then Ikunum, Sargon (I), Puzur-Ashur (II), and Ashur-nirari (I).[8]

At the point of the thirty-third king and following, the listings are fuller, giving the name of the king, the name of his father, the length of his reign, and, sometimes, a brief statement of historical events. In the compilation of the years of reign, the year in which a king dies and his successor comes to the throne is still counted as the former ruler's last year and only the accession year of the new king, and the first full regnal year of the new king is the first full calendar year after his accession.

With their lengths of reign where preserved, the thirty-third to thirty-ninth kings are: Erishum I son of Ilushuma (forty years), Ikunum son of Erishum, Sargon I son of Ikunum, Puzur-Ashur II son of Sargon I, Naram-Sin son of Puzur-Ashur II, Erishum II son of Naram-Sin, and Shamshi-Adad I son of Ila-kabkabi (thirty years). Of these kings, as has already been noted, Erishum, Ikunum, and Sargon I had connections with the Assyrian trading colonies in Anatolia around 1900; Shamshi-Adad I (1813-1781) had connections at a slightly later date. Likewise, Ikunum, Sargon I, and Puzur-Ashur II were builders of the city wall of Ashur, as seen in the just-quoted inscription of Ashur-rim-nisheshu.

Shamshi-Adad I

For Shamshi-Adad I, the otherwise limited data in the King List are supplemented by a historical passage. Shamshi-Adad I was the son of Ila-kabkabi, who cannot be the earlier king of that name (who appears in the

King List as the twenty-fifth ruler and father of Aminu), but is probably the Ila-kabkabi who appears in the Mari letters as ruling some unnamed place contemporaneously with Iagitlim, king of Mari. From the information given, we gather that when Ila-kabkabi died, Naram-Sin seized his territory, and Shamshi-Adad fled to Karduniash (Babylonia). Later he came back, seized Ekallate (the royal city not far south of Ashur), and after three more years, came on to Ashur and took the throne away from Naram-Sin's son, Erishum II. As king of Assyria, Shamshi-Adad I was contemporary with Sin-muballit (1812-1793) and Hammurabi of Babylon (1792-1750), and appears in the documents of Babylon and Mari as well as those of Assyria. According to the tenth year name of Hammurabi (already cited), Shamshi-Adad I was still on the throne in the ninth year (1784) of the Babylonian king. This and other relationships lead to the conclusion that he died in or about the twelfth year of Hammurabi (1781). With a reign of thirty-three years, according to the King List, Shamshi-Adad I may be dated 1813-1781.

In his own inscriptions, Shamshi-Adad I calls Ashur "my city," says he rebuilt in it the temple of Enlil that Erishum (I) son of Ilushuma had built, and claims to have erected a stela in Lebanon on the shore of the Great Sea (the Mediterranean).[9] From history already recounted, we know he placed his son Iasmakh-Adad as ruler of Mari and put another son, Ishme-Dagan, in charge of Ekallate. In due time Ishme-Dagan succeeded his father and appears in the King List as the fortieth ruler, credited with forty years of reign, perhaps overlapping his father. In the thirty-sixth and thirty-eighth years of Hammurabi (1757 and 1755), the Babylonian king defeated enemies "as far as the country of Subartu";[10] and since Subartu is the northland, this could include Assyria and mean that reverses were suffered within the reign of Ishme-Dagan I. At any rate, disturbed conditions must have ensued, for the King List places after Ishme-Dagan I a certain Ashur-dugal, who was "the son of a nobody [i.e., not of royal descent], without right to the throne," and apparently adds that during his lifetime six more kings, also sons of nobodies, ruled in periods of less than one year each (i.e., each did not rule beyond his accession year).

Assyrian Kingdom

After the "sons of nobodies," the throne was taken by Adasi, forty-seventh ruler in the King List, and he was followed by five more kings in direct line of descent, until the lineal succession was again broken by "Lullaja son of a nobody." In the Synchronistic Chronicle, Adasi is contemporary with Damiq-ilishu of the First Dynasty of the Sealand,[11] and may perhaps be dated around 1700. In spite of any interruption in lineal descent, Adasi was considered the founder of the dynasty to which all subsequent Assyrian rulers belonged, and we may call the period from Adasi up to but not including Tiglath-pileser I (1115-1077, eighty-seventh king in the King List and first king of the Assyrian empire) the period of the Assyrian kingdom. A thousand years later, Esarhaddon (680-669) said on a stela at Zinjirli that he himself, son of Sennacherib and (grand)son of Sargon (II), was of the line of Belu-bani, son of Adasi, "who established the kingdom of Assyria . . . and ended the servitude of the city of Ashur."[12]

At the point of the sixty-first ruler in the King List, we meet Puzur-Ashur III, who signed an agreement with the Kassite Burnaburiash I on the division of Mesopotamia between Assyria and Babylonia (probably somewhat before 1500). Although similar territorial agreements were also made later (e.g., the other one already noted between Ashur-bel-nisheshu [sixty-ninth Assyrian king, 1419-1411] and Karaindash of Babylonia), the relations between the two countries were not lastingly stabilized. Strife recurred again and again. From the side of Assyria and in the time of the Assyrian kingdom, a high point was reached when Tukulti-Ninurta I (seventy-eighth king, 1244-1208) vanquished Kashtiliash and established Assyrian rule in Babylon for an interregnum of seven years in the Kassite Dynasty. In commemoration of the victory, the Assyrian king built a new city, Kar-Tukulti-Ninurta (Tulul el-Aqir, across the Tigris from Ashur), where fragments of wall paintings have been found in the ruins of the palace.[13] Finally, Ashur-dan I (eighty-third king, 1179-1134) was associated with the Elamite Shutruk-Nahhunte in the complete overthrow of the Kassite Dynasty.

Egypt pushed farthest toward Assyria when, in his twenty-third year (1468), Thutmose III fought at Megiddo, marched on into Lebanon and, in the tribute list of his next year, claimed that "the chief of Ashur" brought him lapis lazuli, Assyrian vessels, and other objects.[14] But when Ashur-uballit I (seventy-third king, 1365-1330) sent gifts to Amunhotep IV (Akhenaten), he spoke as an equal "brother" and expected "much gold" in return (Amarna Letters nos. 15-16).

Greater pressure came from the Hittites in the west and the kingdom of Mitanni in between; as already noted, Saustatar, ruling Mitanni in the first half of the fifteenth century, took from Ashur a door of silver and gold and set it up in his palace at Washshukkanni. The power of the Hittites and of Mitanni was to diminish, however, and Ashur-uballit I was later remembered as the one "who destroyed the armies of the widespreading Subarians, who enlarged boundary and frontier."[15] Thus, he may have

FIGURE 15.   Altar of Tukulti-Ninurta I from the Temple of Ishtar at Ashur, the King Shown Twice as a Worshiper before the Altar of the Fire God Nusku. (*Vorderasiatisches Museum, Staatliche Museen zu Berlin, Deutsche Demokratische Republik*)

expanded the area of Assyrian domination to the north and also to the west, although there were still wars to fight with Hanigalbat, the state that arose thereafter in more or less the same area as Mitanni. Certainly, Ashur-uballit I was one of the rulers who by conquest and political strategy began to make the kingdom of Assyria into the empire it eventually became.

Life in the kingdom is reflected in the so-called Middle Assyrian Laws, copies of which were found at Qalat Sharqat. The tablets date from the time of Tiglath-pileser I, but the laws they contain probably go back to as early as the fifteenth century. The Babylonian code, or a closely similar body of laws, was still evidently the law of the land, but where this was inadequate to Assyrian requirements and customs, amendments and further regulations were necessary, and these are represented by these laws.[16] An Assyrian text of this time is also found in a collection of dream-omens from Susa, showing how dreams were interpreted as indications of events to come.[17]

Assyrian Empire

Tiglath-pileser I

Tiglath-pileser I (eighty-seventh king in the Assyrian King List, 1115-1077) came to the throne when the old balance of power in the Middle East was destroyed with the fall of the Hittite empire, the decline of Egypt after the New Kingdom, and the existence of a multiplicity of minor New Hittite and Aramean kingdoms. Thus the opportunity was at hand for Assyria to take its place in international affairs as the dominant power. That opportunity was seized by the new king. Now also, for the first time in Assyrian history, detailed annals with year-by-year records of the king's reign are available.[18]

Annals of the first five years of the reign of Tiglath-pileser I are found on clay prisms from the foundations of the temple of Anu and Adad in Ashur. In summary of the year-by-year record, the king claims to have conquered forty-two lands from beyond the Lower Zab to the farther side of the Euphrates (which he crossed in vessels made of skins) and to the land of Hatti and the Upper Sea of the West.[19] Characteristic of the record, and of all later Assyrian military records, is the emphasis upon the frightfulness of the proceeding: "The corpses of their warriors I hurled down in the destructive battle like the storm god. Their blood I caused to flow in the valleys and on the high places of the mountains. I cut off their heads and outside their cities, like heaps of grain, I piled them up."[20] Characteristic also both in these annals and in the other inscriptions that are available for the later years of his reign is the record of building and also the claim of valor on the part of the king in the hunting of wild bulls, elephants, and lions, and even in the killing of a "sea horse" as he sailed upon the Mediterranean.[21]

The successors of Tiglath-pileser I through nearly a dozen reigns have left relatively few inscriptions and were probably hard pressed by enemies on many sides. It was in the time of Tiglath-pileser II (97th king, 967-935) and his contemporary Nabu-mukinapli (977-942) of the Eighth Dynasty of Babylon that a Babylonian text says that "the Arameans became hostile." Their pressure was no doubt directed against Assyria as well as Babylonia. Only with Adad-nirari II (99th king, 911-891) and his son Tukulti-Ninurta II (100th king, 890-884) are annals available again, and they record campaigns in many directions.[22]

With Ashurnasirpal II, son of Tukulti-Ninurta II and 101st ruler in the King List, the series of kings begins who brought the Assyrian empire to its height, ruled over it at its greatest extent, and then saw it fall swiftly to destruction (Table 13).

TABLE 13. KINGS IN THE ASSYRIAN EMPIRE

Name	Years of Reign	Date
101. Ashurnasirpal II	25	883–859
102. Shalmaneser III	35	858–824
103. Shamshi-Adad V	13	823–811
104. Adad-nirari III	28	810–783
105. Shalmaneser IV	10	782–773
106. Ashur-dan III	18	772–755
107. Ashur-nirari V	10	754–745
108. Tiglath-pileser III	18	744–727
109. Shalmaneser V	5	726–722
110. Sargon II	17	721–705
111. Sennacherib	24	704–681
112. Esarhaddon	12	680–669
113. Ashurbanipal	42	668–627
114. Ashur-etililani		
115. Sin-shumlishir		
116. Sin-sharishkun		
117. Ashur-uballit II	3	611–609

Ashurnasirpal II

Like his predecessors, Ashurnasirpal II records his military conquests, conducted with the utmost ferocity, his building activities, and other undertakings, in extensive annals.[23] Like Tukulti-Ninurta I, who built a new capital at Kar-Tukulti-Ninurta across the Tigris on the east bank from Ashur, Ashurnasirpal II also established himself in a new capital city, namely, at Kalah (the modern Nimrud, on the east side of the Tigris eighty kilometers above Ashur and Kar-Tukulti-Ninurta and above where the Great Zab flows in). The present name preserves the remembrance of Nimrod, who, according to Gen. 10:8-12, built Calah, Nineveh, and certain other Assyrian cities and, as a "mighty man" and a "mighty hunter," was a proper prototype of the Assyrian kings with their boasts of prowess in war and hunting. Excavation at Kalah[24] has indicated occupation of the site as early as 3000 and has uncovered the palace of Ashurnasirpal II, guarded by colossal winged man-headed lions and other hybrid creatures[25] and adorned with sculptured wall reliefs.[26] It has also uncovered another palace with bricks bearing the name of Shalmaneser III, son and successor of Ashurnasirpal II, and with clay tablets in the nature of

FIGURE 16.   Ashurnasirpal II on the Lion Hunt, Relief from Nimrud (Kalah). (*Trustees of the British Museum*)

FIGURE 17.   Eagle-Headed Winged Geniuses with Palm Tree, Relief from Nimrud (sap is scraped from the holy tree and used to anoint the Assyrian king, to protect him from danger). (*Trustees of the British Museum*)

administrative records, mostly from the reign of Tiglath-pileser III.[27] In a small temple near the first palace was a half-life-size, standing statue of Ashurnasirpal II, holding battle mace and curved scepter and making the impression of an implacable, ruthless ruler.[28] The inscription on the statue claims conquest of the whole region from the Tigris to Mount Lebanon and the Great Sea. Other Kalah inscriptions speak also of the Nairi lands in the north and give Urartu as the northern boundary of the conquests of Ashurnasirpal II.[29]

Shalmaneser III

For the reign of Shalmaneser III, there are available several successive editions of relatively complete annals, as well as some shorter and fragmentary inscriptions. A type of eponym list known as the Eponym Chronicle (listing the major military and occasionally civil or religious event of each year) begins in the middle of his reign and extends to the first years of Sennacherib.[30] In his first year, recorded fully in the Monolith Inscription and summarized briefly on the Black Obelisk, Shalmaneser III crossed the Euphrates at its flood (i.e., in the spring, the customary time to launch a military campaign), advanced to the shore of the sea of the setting sun, climbed Mount Amanus, and cut cedar and cypress wood.[31] In subsequent years he continued, for the most part, the thrust toward the west. In his sixth year, which was the year of the eponym Daian-Ashur (853/852), he again set forth in the spring and, no doubt in the summer, fought a great battle at the strategic site of Qarqar on the Orontes River in Syria, against a formidable coalition of twelve Aramean and other kings.[32] In the list of opposing allied leaders Hadadezer of Damascus is named first, then Irhuleni of Hamath, and then "Ahab the Israelite." Ahab is in command of 2,000 chariots and 10,000 soldiers and, in chariotry, has the largest force, Hadadezer being credited with 1,200 and Irhuleni with 700. Shalmaneser III claims victory in the battle, but this may be more boast than fact, for he avoided Syria in the next several years, then fought further battles there in the west before finally, in his eighteenth year (841/840), receiving submission and tribute from his enemies.

According to the record of the eighteenth year in the annals, Shalmaneser III smashed the army of Hazael of Damascus in front of Mount Lebanon, proceeded to Mount Hauran, went on to a mountain called Baalirasi, set up his royal image, and received the tribute of a certain Baalima-Anzeri of the Tyrians, and of Jehu the son of Omri.[33] Hazael of Damascus is well known in biblical references (1 Kings 19:15; 2 Kings 8:7ff., etc.). Mount Hauran is the district east of the Jordan River and the Sea of Galilee and north of the Yarmuk River, still called by the same

FIGURE 18.   Bronze Relief on the Gates of Shalmaneser III at Balawat, showing tribute brought ashore to the king from the island city of Tyre. (*Trustees of the British Museum*)

name (el-Hauran). The mountain Baalirasi is, from its name, associated with the Syrian-Canaanite god Baal; in the annals it is also described as "the head (land) of the sea, the entrance of the Tyre land"; therefore, it is probably Mount Carmel, well known (1 Kings 18:19–40) for its associations with Baal. Shalmaneser III must therefore have moved directly across northern Israel, thus making the first Assyrian invasion of Israel. In his day the prophet Hosea anticipates the complete destruction of his country by the Assyrians and says it will take place even "as Shalman destroyed Beth-arbel on the day of battle" (Hos. 10:14). Shalman must be Shalmaneser III, and Beth-arbel is probably Arbela (modern Irbid, in the district of Pella in Transjordan), a site occupied in Iron I and II (1200–600).[34] Thus Hosea is referring to the place where the Assyrian army for the first time entered Israelite territory.[35]

On his Black Obelisk, Shalmaneser III pictures the receiving of tribute from five different regions, and in one register Jehu is shown bowing upon hands and knees before the Assyrian king as his countrymen bring forward the tribute.[36] The designation of Jehu in the annals and on the Black Obelisk as the son of Omri simply means that the name of Omri was still associated with the rule of Israel. Actually Jehu had put an end to the house of Ahab the son of Omri (2 Kings 9) and not only reversed previous policy when he paid tribute to Shalmaneser III, but also emulated Assyrian custom (noted already above in the case of Tiglath-pileser I) when he piled up the heads of the seventy slain sons of Ahab in two heaps at the gate of Jezreel (2 Kings 10:8).[37]

Til Barsip (Tell Ahmar, on the left bank of the Euphrates, forty kilometers below Carchemish and, like the latter, commanding an important crossing of the river) was at this point the chief town of an Aramean state known as Bit Adini. According to various passages in his annals, Shalmaneser III took Til Barsip from its king, built a palace for his royal residence, and called the city by his own name, Kar-Shalmaneser.[38] The palace continued in use until the time of Ashurbanipal and within this time, largely in the eighth century, was decorated with brightly colored wall paintings, spread over more than 120 meters of walls. This is the most extensive display of such Assyrian art ever found. The largest single composition shows Tiglath-pileser III, with his officials, giving audience to a group of foreigners; other scenes show the lion hunt, winged man-headed bulls, and other subjects.[39] Together with his father Ashurnasirpal II, Shalmaneser III is the only other Assyrian king represented in extant statues in the round, and, of him, four statues have been found at Nimrud and Qalat Sharqat and placed in museums in Baghdad, Istanbul, Berlin, and London (the British Museum). Two statues are standing but broken; two are seated but headless. The appearance in the standing statues is much like that of Ashurnasirpal II, and the conception of the Assyrian ruler is being continued and standardized in terms of an imposing and unrelenting figure, devoid of any compassionate human feeling.[40]

Like Ashurnasirpal II before him, Shalmaneser III frequently mentions the northern Nairi lands and the kingdom of Urartu. At the beginning of his kingship, he penetrated "steep mountains, which like the blade of an iron dagger push their summits up into the heavens," smote the armies of the Nairi land, stormed a royal Urartian city named Sugunia, and descended to the sea of Nairi to wash his weapons. As late as his twenty-seventh year, he sent his commander (*tartanu*, cf. 2 Kings 18:17) against Urartu and against a king named Sarduri.[41] Plainly now a formidable antagonist of Assyria, Urartu was also the object of campaigns by later Assyrian rulers—e.g., Shamshi-Adad V, whose officer (*rabshakeh*, cf. 2 Kings 18:17) took two hundred cities from a ruler named Ushpina; Tiglath-

pileser III, who besieged a king named Sarduri in his city Turushpa; and
Sargon II, who fought against Ursa of Turushpa.[42]

The sea of Nairi is Lake Van, and the oldest Urartian sites have been
found in the vicinity of the lake. They date from the third quarter of the
ninth century, the very time of Shalmaneser III. The capital city of
Turushpa was on a great crag overlooking the lake near the present city of
Van, and the site preserved texts of Sarduri (probably the first king of this
name, mentioned by Shalmaneser III) in cuneiform Assyrian, suggesting
cultural dependence upon Assyria in spite of military opposition. It also
preserved texts of Ishpuini (the Ushpina of Shamshi-Adad V) in both
Assyrian and Urartian.[43]

Adad-nirari III

Shamshi-Adad V succeeded his father Shalmaneser III, but only after
putting down a serious revolt led by another son.[44] Shamshi-Adad V's
queen was Sammuramat, and their son was Adad-nirari III, the next ruler
in the Assyrian King List.[45] The latter king speaks, in a stela found at Sabaa
(a tell on the border between Iraq and Syria north of the Euphrates), of
ordering an advance against Palashtu (Palestine) in his fifth year of reign,
when he took his seat on the royal throne.[46] From this it may be supposed
that he assumed the actual functions of a ruling king only in his fifth official
year; as to the one who might have ruled for him in the earlier time, it is a
reasonable surmise that it was his mother Sammuramat, in whom we may
recognize the famous queen known to the Greeks as Semiramis (Herodotus
1. 184; Diodorus 2. 4-20).[47] Another stela found at Tell al-Rimah (eighty
kilometers west of Mosul), which is undated but may well be later, tells of
a western campaign on which Adad-nirari III took tribute from, among
others, Iaasu the Samaritan. This must be Joash (Jehoash), son of Jehoahaz
and grandson of Jehu (2 Kings 13:1, 10), king of Israel in 798-782 as
reckoned from the relatively well fixed date of the beginning of the reign
of Jehu. The name Samaria occurs here for the first time in contrast with
the usual Assyrian designation of the land of Israel by the name of Omri,
and can suggest that Joash was ruling at the time over a relatively limited
territory around the city of Samaria. This can accord with the record that
his father Jehoahaz had lost much territory to the Syrians, which he himself
later recovered (2 Kings 13:3, 7, 25).[48]

Tiglath-pileser III

Three sons of Adad-nirari III provided the next three kings of Assyria. But
relatively little is known of them, and Assyria was evidently in a period of

decline. The first of the three was Shalmaneser IV. The second was Ashur-dan III, in whose tenth year and in the eponymy of Bur-Sagale the solar eclipse took place that can be identified with the known solar eclipse of June 15, 763, and is thus important for Assyrian chronology. The third was Ashur-nirari V, who made a campaign in his second year against Arpad (Tell Rifaat, forty kilometers northwest of Aleppo) and made the ruler, Matiilu, his vassal through a treaty, which has been preserved in an Akkadian text. In another treaty, however, probably made not long afterward and preserved in three Aramaic copies on stelas at Sefire (a small village twenty-five kilometers southeast of Aleppo), the same king (called Matiel in Aramaic) entered into a different agreement with the ruler of another kingdom, an agreement solemnized with this curse should the other ruler be unfaithful: "May Arpad become a mound to be the home of the gazelle and the fox and the hare and the wildcat and the owl and . . . the magpie!" (cf. Isa. 34:13-15; Zeph. 2:14f.).[49]

Then Tiglath-pileser III took the throne, but whether as a usurper or as the son of Ashur-nirari V (as one form of the King List says) is not certain. At any rate, he took the year in which his predecessor died as his own first regnal year rather than his accession year. In that manner of reckoning, he had nineteen years of reign (745-727) rather than eighteen.[50] In the Eponym Chronicle, the chief event of each year of his reign is stated very briefly. In the king's Annals, which were carved upon slabs in his palace at Kalah (Nimrud), there is a fuller narrative, but the slabs were later removed by Esarhaddon and used in another palace in the same city. Therefore, the texts have been recovered in a fragmentary and disarranged state, making the determination of dates difficult.[51]

According to the Eponym Chronicle, Tiglath-pileser III took the throne on the thirteenth day of Aiaru (April/May), and since this was only the second month of the new year, there was perhaps a semblance of justification for calling the whole year his own first year of reign. In his third year (743), when he was himself the eponym, Tiglath-pileser III was in Arpad (as the Eponym Chronicle tells), and, probably at this time, he received tribute (as is recorded in the Annals, but without a date) from, among others, Azariah (Uzziah) of Judah and Menahem of Samaria (the latter event is also recorded in 2 Kings 15:19, where the Assyrian king is called Pul, the name by which Tiglath-pileser III was known in Babylon).[52] In his thirteenth and fourteenth years (733 and 732), Tiglath-pileser III fought against Damascus (according to the Eponym Chronicle) and, in the climax of this endeavor (732), overthrew Rezin of Damascus, deported to Assyria the people of Israel, and received tribute from Jehoahaz (Ahaz), these events being told in the Annals and another historical text, and corresponding with biblical record (2 Kings 15:29f.; 16:9f; 1 Chron. 5:26).[53] Like Shalmaneser III, Tiglath-pileser III thought of Israel in connection with the house of Omri and said about *Bit Humria* that he carried off to Assyria all its inhabitants and their possessions, while in Israel they overthrew their king Pekah, and he placed Hoshea as king over them.

The main capital of Tiglath-pileser III was at Kalah (Nimrud), and important sculptures of his have been recovered there.[54] The wall paintings at Til Barsip, in which he is prominently portrayed, have already been mentioned. He also built a palace at Arslan Tash (the ancient Hadattu, meaning "New Town" in Aramaic), intended, no doubt, like other provincial residences of the Assyrian kings, as a starting point for campaigns and a reminder to the area of the power of the empire. At Arslan Tash, both stone sculptures and ivory carvings have been recovered. On a relief stela, a storm god, perhaps Adad, stands on the back of a bull and holds lightning bolts in each hand. On an ivory inlay piece for furniture, an Aramaic inscription states that this was made for Hazael; since Shalmaneser III fought against Hazael of Damascus, the inlaid furniture could have been part of the booty, later placed in the palace of Tiglath-pileser III at Haddattu.[55]

Shalmaneser V

Shalmaneser V, son and successor of Tiglath-pileser III, ruled, as his father had done, in Babylonia as well as Assyria. Assyrian records of his reign are scanty,[56] but a Babylonian chronicle (B.M. 92502) provides important information.[57] At the point of present interest, this chronicle states (1. 27-31), as the noteworthy event in the reign of Shalmaneser V, that the city of Shamarain was destroyed. It goes on to say that Shalmaneser died in his fifth year, in the month of Tebetu (December/January), and that on the twelfth day of that month (probably December 20, 722, or January 18, 721), his successor Sargon (II) took the throne of Assyria. Since the city of Shamarain is surely Samaria, this must be the cuneiform record of the fall of the capital of northern Israel in the ninth year of Hoshea (723/722), narrated more fully in 2 Kings 17:1-6.[58]

Sargon II

Sargon (Sharrukin) II, according to one text brother of Shalmaneser V,[59] made his capital successively at Ashur (Qalat Sharqat), Kalah (Nimrud), and Nineveh, and then finally at a city named after himself Dur-Sharrukin (sixteen kilometers northeast of Nineveh; the ruin was later ascribed to the Sassanid hero Khosroes and called Khorsabad). According to the dimensions stated in Sargon's own texts and confirmed by excavations, the

FIGURE 19.   Winged Human-Headed Bull from Dur-Sharrukin (Khorsabad).
(Cliché des Musées Nationaux, Paris)

Left—FIGURE 20. Sargon II Carrying a Sacrificial Ibex, Relief from Dur-Sharrukin. *(Cliché des Musées Nationaux, Paris) Right—FIGURE 21.* Figure, Perhaps Gilgamesh, Holding a Lion Cub, Relief from Dur-Sharrukin. *(Cliché des Musées Nationaux, Paris)*

circumference of the walls of Dur-Sharrukin was more than 8,000 meters. On a fifteen-meter-high terrace on the northwest side, and partly projecting outside the wall, was the palace, a great complex of rooms and courts, and beside the palace at its southwest corner was the temple precinct with its high ziggurat.[60]

The extant texts of Sargon II are numerous. But they differ as to which events are assigned to which regnal years, and pose a particular problem in the earliest part of his reign.[61] According to the earliest and generally most reliable text, the so-called Ashur Charter, the military expeditions of Sargon II began in his second regnal year (720/719); therefore, he was no doubt occupied with the securing of his throne and the performing of tasks at home in his accession year and his first regnal year.[62] But in the late Khorsabad Annals and Display Inscriptions, he claims that in the beginning of his reign (presumably meaning already in his accession year, or at least in his first regnal year) he captured Samaria, carried off 27,290 people from it, and resettled the city.[63] In view of the contradiction between the early and the late sources, the late claim to have taken Samaria (which was actually taken by Shalmaneser V) may be explained as an attempt to glorify his reign by showing that his military successes began already at its outset, something that was all the more indicated because of the assumption that the great kings made expeditions every year.[64] As for the expedition of the second regnal year, the Khorsabad Annals and Display Inscriptions record that at that time Sargon II overcame a certain Yaubidi of Hamath and allies in a battle near Qarqar, went on to capture Hanno king of Gaza, and to drive off Sibe (or Ree), the Egyptian army commander who came out against him from his city of Rapihu (Raphia, Tell Rifah, near the sea, thirty-two kilometers southwest of Gaza). This was the farthest toward Egypt that the Assyrians had yet come.[65] On the way back, Sargon II might well have had to do with Samaria, perhaps with matters of deportation and resettlement, since again in his seventh year he settled some Arabs there.[66]

In all, Sargon II conducted many expeditions, many of which are illustrated in the relief carvings that adorn his great palace at Dur-Sharrukin.[67] In these, Sargon II is pictured as the same kind of implacable Assyrian monarch already seen in the statues of Ashurnasirpal II and Shalmaneser III. His soldiers are likewise portrayed as the powerful and completely confident representatives of the overwhelming military might of Assyria.

Sennacherib

In contrast with the picture presented by Sargon II of incessant military activity in every year of his reign, the records of Sennacherib report only eight campaigns by the king in twenty-four years of rule, and texts having to do with building and administrative activities are proportionately more numerous.[68] Evidently, the empire was substantially established in the extent to which military action was undertaken to carry it, and more attention could be given to other matters.

In building, Sennacherib did much at Nineveh (on the east bank of the Tigris, across from Mosul). It was already previously a royal residence and administrative center, but now, under himself and his successors Esarhaddon and Ashurbanipal, it was the main capital. Sennacherib himself planned the fortifications of Nineveh, gave the city a system of waterworks, restored its temples, and built for himself a great palace, the walls of which were adorned for more than 3,000 meters with sculptured slabs.[69]

FIGURE 22. Tigris Boat and Fishermen on the Tigris River, Relief from the Palace of Sennacherib at Nineveh (Quyunjik). (*Trustees of the British Museum*)

In his campaigns, he first accomplished the defeat of Merodach-Baladan of Babylon.[70] In the second, he moved against the Kassites and even received tribute from the distant Medes.[71] And in the third, he went against the Hittite land here, as frequently in the late Assyrian inscriptions, meaning Syria.[72] On the coast, he took Sidon, Ushu (the old mainland settlement opposite the island of Tyre), and Akko, then faced harder opposition in the south. In the plain of Altaqu (probably the Eltekeh of Josh. 19:44; 21:23), he overcame Palestinian forces assisted by Egyptian and Ethiopian chariotry and bowmen, then besieged Jerusalem and Hezekiah the Jew, who was a participant in the resistance to Assyria. The biblical record of the same events (2 Kings 18:13-19:37; 2 Chron. 32:1-22; Isa. 36:1-37:38) names Tirhakah king of Ethiopia as the leader of the Egyptians, dates the Assyrian invasion in the fourteenth year of Hezekiah (702/701), and tells of the deliverance of Jerusalem from the siege. Tirhakah is the Ethiopian Taharqa, who probably led the Egyptian and Ethiopian forces against Sennacherib and himself in fact came to the throne of Egypt only a few years later; the sequence of events in the reign of Sennacherib places the third campaign most probably in 701 and the siege of Jerusalem in the summer of 701, in agreement with the biblical chronology. As to the deliverance of Jerusalem, it is noticeable that Sennacherib makes no claim to have taken the city.[73]

Esarhaddon

Sennacherib's oldest son, Ashur-nadinshumi, perished at Babylon, as we have seen, and among the other sons the king designated the youngest, Esarhaddon, as his successor. This led to revolt by the other brothers, including the assassination of Sennacherib, but Esarhaddon won the contest and sat down joyfully, as he says in a historical text, upon the throne of his father in Nineveh.[74] The mother of Esarhaddon was a younger wife of Sennacherib named Naqia ("the Pure One" in West Semitic, rendered in Assyrian as "Zakutu"), and in the relevant texts, she is called first the queen consort of Sennacherib and then the queen mother of Esarhaddon. There is little doubt that she maneuvered to see that her son obtained the throne.[75] Apparently she herself also exercised actual rule in southeast Babylonia, with an administrative center at a city called Lahira, and she was probably involved in the rebuilding of Babylon by Esarhaddon after its destruction by Sennacherib. When again an older son of Esarhaddon named Shamash-shumukin became king of Babylon, but a younger son, Ashurbanipal, obtained the greater prize of the kingship of Assyria, for which Shamash-shumukin fought against him to his own disaster, we may suppose that Naqia was again active in gaining preferment for a favorite grandson. To the Greeks, there were two famous queens, Semiramis and Nitocris, said to have lived five generations apart (Herodotus 1. 184), which points to Naqia as Nitocris.[76] Interestingly enough, Sennacherib claims to have destroyed Babylon by flooding the entire site,[77] and Herodotus (1. 185-187) says that in her building work at Babylon, Nitocris constructed the embankments of the river and made an artificial lake a long way above the city.

As to the most important campaigns of Esarhaddon, we learn in the Babylonian Chronicle (B.M. 92502, IV) that in the seventh year of his reign (674/673) the Assyrian army was defeated in a bloody battle in Egypt (an event understandably omitted in the Esarhaddon Chronicle). We learn in both the Babylonian Chronicle and the Esarhaddon Chronicle (B.M. 25091) that in his tenth year (671/670), the army marched against Egypt, this time successfully: Memphis was conquered, its king escaped indeed, but his son was captured, and many prisoners and much booty were taken.[78] The Egyptian king who escaped was Taharqa (690-664), and the son who was captured was Ushanahuru; both are named on a victory stela set up by Esarhaddon at Zinjirli in northern Syria.[79]

Once again in his twelfth year (669), Esarhaddon marched toward Egypt. The Esarhaddon Chronicle states concisely in its record of that year what happened: "The king of Assyria went to Egypt. He fell sick on the way and died in the month of Arahsamnu [October/November], the tenth

day. For twelve years Esarhaddon was king of Assyria. Both his sons,
Shamash-shumukin in Babylonia, Ashurbanipal in Assyria, sat down upon
the throne.''[80]

Ashurbanipal

Ashurbanipal was called Osnappar in Ezra 4:10, and Sardanapallus by the
Greeks, and there are numerous texts from his reign.[81] These record nine
military campaigns. In his first campaign (667/666), Ashurbanipal marched
against Egypt and Ethiopia, where Taharqa had reasserted himself and
taken up residence in Memphis, the city that Esarhaddon had conquered
and incorporated into Assyrian territory. At Memphis, Ashurbanipal won
a great battle, and Taharqa fled to Ni, i.e., Thebes. This city, too,
Ashurbanipal seized, and Taharqa, overcome with terror in some place
where he had taken refuge, was never heard of again. So Ashurbanipal
records the campaign.[82]

In Egypt, Taharqa was succeeded by Tanutamun (664-656), and he too
asserted himself against the Assyrians. Thereupon, in a second campaign
(664/663), Ashurbanipal returned and conquered both Memphis and
Thebes. Tanutamun (whom the Assyrian text calls Urdamane) fled to a
place called Kipkipi, and Ashurbanipal carried the rich booty of Thebes
back to Nineveh.[83]

In all, nine military campaigns in forty-two years of reign are relatively
few, and the texts also tell much of the administrative and building
activities of Ashurbanipal, of his personal interest in study and hunting, and
of other matters. As a youth he learned the wisdom of Nabu (the god of
writing), read the beautiful clay tablets from Sumer and the obscure
Akkadian writing, which is hard to master, and took pleasure in
deciphering inscriptions on stone stelas from before the flood. He also
learned to shoot the bow, to ride, and to drive, as well as to know the ways
of royal decorum.[84] To assemble a great library, he sent scribes throughout
Assyria and Babylonia with authority to copy and translate writings they
found, and tens of thousands of clay tablets were brought together and
placed in his palace at Nineveh. As rediscovered in modern times, these
texts contain epics, historical, scientific, religious, and magical literature,
official dispatches and archives, business documents, letters, and other
materials.[85] In the royal palace were also the magnificent sculptured
reliefs, especially depicting the lion hunts of Ashurbanipal, which, with
their close attention to animal forms, their impressive realism, and
unmistakable atmosphere of the excitement of the chase, represent the
climax of Assyrian art.[86] Yet with Assyria thus apparently at the height of

FIGURE 23.   Ashurbanipal on the Lion Hunt, Relief from Nineveh. (*Trustees of the British Museum*)

FIGURE 24.   Horse's Head, Relief from Ninevah. (*Trustees of the British Museum*)

FIGURE 25.   Ashurbanipal Carrying a Basket of Earth or Bricks for the Building of the Esagila Temple of Marduk in Babylon, a Stela from Babylon. (*Trustees of the British Museum*)

its power and glory under Ashurbanipal, decline was at hand and the end
was surprisingly near.

Fall of Nineveh

In the fifteen years between the end of the reign of Ashurbanipal in 627 and
the fall of Nineveh in 612, three evidently undistinguished and relatively
obscure rulers occupied the throne—Ashur-etililani, Sin-shumlishir, and
Sin-sharishkun. Then the long line of Assyrian kings came to an end with
its 117th member, Ashur-uballit II, who for another three years maintained
a vestige of Assyrian power in the west.

In the scanty Assyrian records of the time, Ashur-etililani calls himself
the son of Ashurbanipal and the (grand)son of Esarhaddon, and speaks of
Sin-shumlishir as a general who helped him obtain the throne, which
suggests disturbances at the death of Ashurbanipal and military assistance
to enable the son to come to the throne.[87] In a fragmentary King List from
Uruk, Sin-shumlishir and Sin-sharishkun are both named as rulers of
Babylon for one year (626) prior to Nabopolassar, so their reigns appear to
have overlapped; perhaps each ruled only a part of the empire.[88] Like
Ashur-etililani, Sin-sharishkun also calls himself the son of Ashurbanipal
and the (grand)son of Esarhaddon, and expresses the hope for future kings
who would be his sons.[89] But this was not to be. His rule ended with the fall
of Nineveh in 612 (as will be further narrated below). Ashur-uballit II
(611-609), who held out in the west for a little while longer, was not a
descendant in the royal line but only an Assyrian noble.[90]

9. NEW BABYLONIAN PERIOD
(626-539)

As the Assyrian empire approached its end, two new empires were arising: in Babylonia that of the Chaldeans, in Iran that of the Medes and Persians. In the end, it was the Chaldeans and the Medes who combined their efforts in the final overthrow of Nineveh. The Chaldeans, called "an ancient nation" in Jer. 5:15, were Aramean tribes who appeared in Lower Mesopotamia around 1000 and later. They stirred up disaffection against Assyrian rule of Babylonia, and in the course of the Ninth Dynasty of Babylon, several of their chiefs, including Merodach-Baladan II and Kandalanu, ruled Babylon. After Kandalanu, the aforementioned Uruk King List shows the Assyrian kings Sin-shumlishir and Sin-sharishkun ruling in Babylon for one year, then continues with Nabopolassar and the other kings of the Chaldean or New Babylonian Dynasty.[1] The same source gives incomplete lengths of reign for these kings; there are many exact dates in the New Babylonian Chronicles, and altogether we have the listing of rulers shown in Table 14.[2]

Nabopolassar

Specific evidence of descent is lacking, but it seems likely that Nabu-apalusur (Nabopolassar in Greek) was a member of the same line or lines of Sealand kings or governors of whom the contemporary Assyrian kings speak (Iakina, his son Merodach-Baladan II, and his son Naid-Marduk; Nabu-kudurri-usur [Nebuchadnezzar] and his son Belibni).[3] Like some of these Sealand kings, Nabopolassar moved from that position to the rule of all of Babylonia. The struggles by which he did so are intimated in the New Babylonian Chronicles. The Chronicle of Years (B.M. 86379) states, "After Kandalanu, in the accession year of Nabopolassar, there were rebellions in Assyria and Akkad. The war continued and there were

TABLE 14. CHALDEAN DYNASTY

Name	Years of Reign	Date
1. Nabopolassar	21	625–605
2. Nebuchadnezzar II	43	604–562
3. Evil-Merodach	2	561–560
4. Neriglissar	4	559–556
5. Labashi-Marduk	3 months	556
6. Nabonidus	17	555–539

perpetual battles."[4] The chronicle that records the accession of Nabopolassar (B.M. 25127) says that "for one year there was no king in the land" (presumably the year 626, in which the Uruk King List shows Sin-shumlishir and Sin-sharishkun as rulers of Babylon), then relates that Nabopolassar defeated the Assyrians in the battle for Babylon and took the throne there: "On the twenty-sixth day of Arahsamnu [November 23, 626], Nabopolassar sat upon the throne in Babylon. This was the 'beginning of reign' of Nabopolassar."[5]

In this (B.M. 25127) and succeeding Babylonian chronicles (B.M. 21901, 22047), it is possible to follow events in most of the years of reign of Nabopolassar. In his tenth year (616/615), the king of Akkad (as the chronicles now call Nabopolassar) defeated an Assyrian force south of Haran, even though an Egyptian army endeavored to assist them. In the eleventh year (615/614), Nabopolassar unsuccessfully besieged Ashur, and a new foe of Assyria appeared when "the Mede came down upon the territory of Arrapha [modern Kirkuk]." In the next year (614/613), the Median king—Cyaxares II—captured Ashur, and Nabopolassar and he established an alliance. Then or later, the alliance was confirmed by a royal wedding, for Berossos tells us that Amytis, daughter of Cyaxares' son Astyages, was married to Nebuchadnezzar II, son of Nabopolassar.[6] In the fourteenth year of Nabopolassar (612/611), the king of Akkad and Cyaxares, the king of the Umman-manda (a name now perhaps inclusive of the Medes and the Scythians),[7] besieged Nineveh from Simanu (May/June) to Abu (July/August), and then the city was captured (612). The defeated king was Sin-sharishkun, and the once proud city was turned into a mound of ruins.[8] Diodorus (2. 27) adds the information that Nineveh (which he calls Ninus) finally fell only when the river (which he calls the Euphrates instead of the Tigris) rose to an unusual height and broke down a long stretch of the city's walls and that, at this juncture, Sardanapallus (as he calls Sin-sharishkun) burned himself to death in his palace. The destruction described by Zephaniah (2:13-15) and Nahum came to pass, and the fate the Assyrians had visited upon Thebes was returned in full upon Nineveh (Nah. 3:8f.).[9]

Later in the same fourteenth year of Nabopolassar (612/611), as the same chronicle (B.M. 21901) goes on to record, one more king of Assyria sat on his throne in Haran. The name of this king is missing at this point in the text. But it occurs twice in the balance of the chronicle—Ashur-uballit. Perhaps an officer of Sin-sharishkun, he took the name of the seventy-third king in the Assyrian King List. He is thus Ashur-uballit II.

Now in his own fifteenth and sixteenth years (611/610, 610/609), Nabopolassar "marched above victoriously in Assyria" (i.e., presumably here in the northwest where the remnant of the Assyrian empire was established). Ashur-uballit II abandoned Haran and withdrew west of the Euphrates. In the seventeenth year of Nabopolassar in the month Duzu (June/July 609), "a great Egyptian army" came to help Ashur-uballit II try to recapture Haran, but evidently the attempt failed, for the attackers "retired" and Ashur-uballit II disappeared from the scene.[10] The Egyptian army was undoubtedly the force of Pharaoh Necho II (610-595), which King Josiah of Judah tried unsuccessfully to resist as it passed through Palestine on its way north (2 Kings 23:29f.; 2 Chron. 35:20-24).[11]

In the next several years (B.M. 22047), the Egyptians continued their resistance in the northwest, and we hear for the first time of the oldest son of Nabopolassar, the crown prince Nebuchadnezzar (II), who marches in the field with his father.[12]

LATE IRON AGE (600-330)

Nebuchadnezzar II

In the twenty-first year of Nabopolassar (605/604), as the record continues in the next of the chronicles (B.M. 21946),[13] the king of Akkad stayed in his own land (probably for reasons of age and health, as Berossos implies in his account of these events),[14] and Nebuchadnezzar commanded the Babylonian troops in a decisive defeat of the Egyptian army at Carchemish and a complete conquest of the whole area of the Hatti country. But in the meantime Nabopolassar died, and Nebuchadnezzar returned to Babylon to ascend the throne on the first day of the month Ululu (September 7, 605).[15] On the first day of Nisan in the following spring, he "took the hands of Bel and the son of Bel [i.e., of Marduk and Nabu]"[16] and celebrated the New Year festival. Thus began his first full year of reign (604/603). In this first regnal year, he went back to the West, and all the kings of the Hatti land (presumably including Jehoiakim of Judah [cf. 2 Kings 24:1]) brought him tribute. He was in the same region in his second and third years as well. In the fourth year (601/600), he marched to Egypt, where each side inflicted havoc on the other and he and his troops "turned back and returned to Babylon." This virtual defeat may have encouraged the rebellion of Jehoiakim against Nebuchadnezzar after he had been his servant for three years (2 Kings 24:1). In the next year, the king of Akkad stayed in his own land and assembled his chariots and horses in great numbers. Then in the sixth and seventh years he marched again to the Hatti land. His purpose now undoubtedly included punishment of the defection of Judah and reestablishment of his control there. In the seventh year on the second day of the month Addaru (March 16, 597), Nebuchadnezzar II seized the city of Judah (Jerusalem), captured the king, appointed a new king, took tribute, and sent captives to Babylon. According to the biblical record, the captured king of Judah was Jehoiachin, the young king who succeeded his father Jehoiakim for three months (or three months and ten days) before he was taken away to Babylon (2 Kings 24:8-16; 2 Chron. 36:9-10). The newly appointed king was Jehoiachin's uncle (or brother) Mattanish, whose name was changed to Zedekiah (2 Kings 24:17; 2 Chron. 36:10).[17]

Even though he was installed in the kingship of Judah as a vassal of Nebuchadnezzar II, Zedekiah also rebelled. The Babylonian king came back to take Jerusalem a second time, destroy it thoroughly, and carry its people and its blinded king into exile (2 Kings 25:1-12; Jer. 39:1-10; 52:4-16; 2 Chron. 36:17-21). The chronicle (B.M. 21946) that records the first fall of Jerusalem (597) reports several further expeditions of Nebuchadnezzar II to the Hatti land but comes to an end with his eleventh year. Thus it does not extend far enough to cover the second taking of Jerusalem. But the biblical record dates the fall of the city on the ninth day of the fourth month in the nineteenth year of Nebuchadnezzar (July 18, 586).[18]

Babylon

Many of the inscriptions of Nebuchadnezzar II deal with his extensive building operations, and the extant remains of Babylon are for the most part from his period.[19] It was also the city as it took shape in this time that is described by Herodotus (1. 178-187), who visited Babylon in about 460; Diodorus (2. 7-10); Strabo (16. 1, 5f.); and Berossos (quoted by Josephus, *Against Apion* 1. secs. 139-141; *Ant.* 10. 11. 1. secs. 224-226), who lived there as a priest of Marduk. After Alexander the Great, who died at Babylon in 323, the city's place in history was taken by Seleucia on the Tigris (Tell

FIGURE 26.   Southern Palace of Nebuchadnezzar II at Babylon. (*Jack Finegan*)

FIGURE 27.   Foundations of the Hanging Gardens at Babylon. (*Jack Finegan*)

FIGURE 28.   Ishtar Gate, Reconstructed in Berlin. (*Vorderasiatisches Museum, Staatliche Museen zu Berlin, Deutsche Demokratische Republik*)

FIGURE 29.   Enameled Brick Bull on the Ishtar Gate (replica), Babylon. (*Jack Finegan*)

FIGURE 30.   Enameled Brick Dragon on the Ishtar Gate (replica), Babylon. (*Jack Finegan*)

FIGURE 31.   Enameled Brick Lion from the Processional Way, Babylon. (*The Metropolitan Museum of Art, Fletcher Fund, 1931*)

Umair), the new capital founded in 312 by Seleucus I Nicator on the west bank of that river forty kilometers below modern Baghdad; and by Ctesiphon, the metropolis of the Arsacids and the Sassanians on the opposite bank.[20] Thereafter Babylon sank into ruins, was plundered through the centuries for building materials, and is now represented by a series of mounds known as Babil (preserving the ancient name), Qasr, Merkes, and others, and a depression called es-Sakhn.

The city was laid out in a great square, surrounded by outer and inner city walls and cut through in the center by the Euphrates River. The Babil mound at the north encloses the ruins of the summer palace of Nebuchadnezzar II. The Qasr ("castle") was the citadel, a complex of fortifications and buildings including the main palace and perhaps the famous hanging gardens. The Ishtar Gate, with enameled bricks showing bulls (symbol of the storm god Adad) and serpent-headed dragons (emblem of Marduk), gave access to the processional street, with marching lions (associated with Ishtar). This led to the sacred area in which were the ziggurat Etemenanki ("house of the foundation of heaven and earth"), now the sunken area called es-Sakhn ("the pan"), and the Marduk temple Esagila ("house of the uplifted head"), found under the mound of Amran ibn-Ali. To the east, the Merkes mounds represent what was a large inner-city residential area.

At Borsippa (Birs Nimrud, sixteen kilometers south of Babylon), the main center of the god Nabu, Nebuchadnezzar II rebuilt the ziggurat Eurmeiminanki ("house of the seven leaders of heaven and earth," i.e., the sun, moon, and five planets), the ruins of which are still very impressive, and the temple of Nabu called Ezida. It was from here that Nabu was brought to Babylon to share with Marduk, his father in the annual festival of the New Year, and Nebuchadnezzar II proudly called himself "the preserver of Esagila and Ezida."[21]

Nabonidus and Belshazzar

The Chaldean empire was also to fall; decline came rapidly, and the salient events are described concisely by Berossos (quoted by Josephus, *Against Apion* 1. secs. 147-153). The son and successor of Nebuchadnezzar II was Amel-Marduk, who—says Berossos—was arbitrary and licentious. After a short reign, Amel-Marduk was assassinated by his sister's husband. The latter was Nergal-sharusur (in Greek Neriglissar), probably the Nergal-sharezer who was the Rabmag[22] among the chief officers of the king of Babylon at the final fall of Jerusalem (Jer. 39:3, 13). He was therefore a high military commander as well as the son-in-law of Nebuchadnezzar II

and in a strategic position to take the throne. In a fragmentary chronicle
(B.M. 25124), a campaign in his third year of reign is recorded in which he
went against a certain Appuashu, king of Pirindu, a country in Cilicia in
Asia Minor.[23]

The son of Neriglissar, Labashi-marduk (Laborosoardoch), came to the
throne as "a mere boy"—Berossos relates—and reigned for only three
months (according to the Uruk King list; Berossos says nine months) before
he was murdered by conspirators.[24]

After the murder of Laborosoardoch, the conspirators held a meeting—
Berossos continues—and, by common consent, conferred the kingship
upon Nabonnedus (Nabonidus, Babylonian Nabunaid), who was a
Babylonian and "one of their gang." This uncomplimentary introduction
of the new king probably betrays the same kind of hostility to Nabonidus
that is also recognizable in the so-called Verse Account of Nabonidus (see
page 132). In both cases, it probably reflects the prejudice of the priesthood
of Marduk at Babylon. In other texts, however, Nabonidus says that he
was raised to the sovereignty of the land by Marduk, and, like
Nebuchadnezzar II, he calls himself the preserver of Esagila [the temple of
Marduk at Babylon] and Ezida [the temple of Nabu at Borsippa]; his own
name, Nabunaid, means "The god Nabu has exalted the king."[25]
Nevertheless, in fact, Nabonidus seems to have directed his real devotion
to the moon god (Nanna, Sin), and this was probably responsible for the
animosity of the priests of Marduk.

As for the entire reign of Nabonidus, Berossos says that in his reign the
walls of Babylon on the river were splendidly built with baked brick and
bitumen, then goes on immediately to tell that in the king's seventeenth
year, Cyrus the Persian took Babylon, besieged Nabonidus in Borsippa
whither he fled, and, upon his surrender, sent him off to Carmania (a
district on the Persian Gulf), where he remained until he died.[26] The
Nabonidus Chronicle (B.M. 35382) extends from the accession year of
Nabonidus to his seventeenth and last year, but there are many gaps in the
text.[27] In the seventh, ninth, tenth, and eleventh years, it is stated that the
king stayed in Tema, and the crown prince, the officials, and the army
were in Akkad. In each of these years, the king did not come to Babylon for
the ceremonies of the month of Nisanu, Nabu did not come to Babylon
(i.e., from Borsippa), Bel did not go out (i.e., from Esagila in procession),
and the festival of the New Year was omitted.

Tema, where Nabonidus spent these and probably other years, is
undoubtedly the oasis of that name in northwest Arabia (cf. Isa. 21:13f.),
800 kilometers southwest of Babylon. Along with Ur and Haran, it was a
center of the worship of the moon god (Nanna, Sin).[28] At Ur, Nabonidus

rebuilt the ziggurat and installed his daughter as priestess of Sin; at Haran, he restored the temple of Sin, called Ehulhul, and there his mother Adad-guppi was a devotee of the moon god. On two of four stelas found at Haran (and Eski-Haran, just east of the city), Nabonidus is shown before the circle and superimposed crescent of Sin, the sun disk of Shamash, and the seven-pointed star of Ishtar. In the text, he says that Sin called him to the kingship but that the citizens of Babylon and other cities of Babylonia "devoured one another like dogs," with resultant disease and famine (all this evidently meaning revolt), and the moon god caused him to go away to Arabia for ten years. And on the other two stelas, Adad-guppi tells of her long life of 104 years, spent in remarkably good health and in devotion to the moon god.[29]

The so-called Verse Account of Nabonidus, preserved on a damaged tablet in the British Museum (B.M. 38299),[30] speaks of Cyrus in connection with the fall of Babylon and blames the Babylonian king (who can only be Nabonidus, although the name is not preserved) for the happening. The purpose of this account was apparently to reconcile the people of Babylonia to their loss of independence by showing how evil was the rule of their last king. That king "thought out something worthless." He made an image of the moon god and proposed to make for the god a temple called Ehulhul. He declared that he would omit all festivals and cause the festival of the New Year to cease. Then he went away to Tema and, in his absence, entrusted the kingship to his oldest son. In another text (B.M. 38299), Cyrus himself is represented as calling his defeated predecessor on the throne of Babylon "a defective one" or "a weak one," using a term that probably implied mental defect and even insanity.[31]

If, however, such defamatory accounts concerning Nabonidus represent the hostility of the priests of Marduk at Babylon, who were threatened by what he did, it is possible that he should in fact be recognized as a reformer who attempted to revive the ancient cult of Sin (Nanna), with its emphasis on the worship of the one god seen in the moon. He may even have tried to move his capital to Tema in accordance with that worship, his actions in these regards bearing some similarity to those of Amunhotep IV (Akhenaten) in Egypt, who resisted the priests of his time, moved his capital to Amarna, and directed his devotion to the one god seen in the sun to the exclusion of the many deities worshipped in the land.[32]

So, in the extended absence of Nabonidus from Babylon during much of his reign, the actual rule was exercised by his oldest son, the crown prince. The name of this son is known from various texts—Bel-sharusur (Belshazzar). In the fifth year of Nabonidus, for example, a business document records a loan of money from a certain Nabu-mukinahi, "the scribe of Belshazzar, the son of the king." In the seventh year, an astrological report of a certain Shumukin reads, "I have observed the Great Star [Venus] and I shall study this with regard to a favorable interpretation for my lord Nabonidus, king of Babylon, as well as to my lord Belshazzar, the son of the king."[33] This is the Belshazzar who appears in Dan. 5; 7:1; 8:1 as, in effect, the last Chaldean king of Babylon.[34]

Fall of Babylon

In the seventeenth regnal year of Nabonidus, Babylon fell to Cyrus the Persian.[35] The Nabonidus Chronicle (B.M. 35382) gives exact dates: in the month of Tashritu on the fourteenth day (October 10, 539), the Persian forces took Sippar; on the sixteenth day (October 12), they entered Babylon without battle; and in the month of Arahsamnu on the third day (October 29), Cyrus himself came into the city. The Persian record is preserved on the Cyrus Cylinder, an inscribed clay barrel in the British Museum (B.M. 90920).[36] This declares that Marduk chose Cyrus to take Babylon, that in Babylon Cyrus received the submission and tribute of all the kings of the entire world, that he benefited the inhabitants of Babylon by lifting their yoke and restoring their "dilapidated housing," and that he returned many exiles in Babylon to their former habitations and resettled the images of their gods in their former sanctuaries, which had long been in ruins. Congruently therewith, 2 Chron. 36:22f. and Ezra 1:1-4 quote an edict of Cyrus allowing the Jewish exiles to return to their homeland and rebuild the house of the Lord in Jerusalem.[37] This permission was no doubt an important part of the reason for the description of Cyrus in Isa. 44:28; 45:1, 13 as the shepherd and the anointed of the Lord.

10. PERSIAN PERIOD (539-330)

The homeland of the Persian empire was the western and larger part of the Iranian plateau, which stretches from the Mesopotamian valley on the west to the Indus valley on the east, and from the Caspian Sea in the north to the Persian Gulf in the south. Surrounded by mountain ranges, it is a high and arid land, with a waterless salt desert in the center. Nevertheless, the trade route from Central Asia to the West ran through the region, and human settlements arose at an early date.

Early Iran

For example, important sites of the fifth and fourth millenniums are at Tepe Yahya in southeastern Iran (near the present village of Baghin), where artistic motifs on the artifacts are akin to those of the Indus valley on the one hand and of Mesopotamia on the other,[1] and at Tepe Sialk on the western side of the central desert (240 kilometers south of Teheran).[2] Important sites of the third and second millenniums are at Tureng Tepe[3] and Tepe Hissar[4] in the northeastern province of Gurgan; at Tepe Giyan in the Nehavend valley of eastern Luristan (100 kilometers south of Hamadan)[5] and other sites in central western Iran;[6] and at Yanik Tepe (32 kilometers southwest of Tabriz)[7] and other sites in Azerbaijan and around Lake Urmia (Reza̔ iyeh) in the northwest.[8]

Elam

In southwestern Iran, the famous site of Susa (200 kilometers north of the head of the Persian Gulf) and the surrounding sites of Susiana are in the region later known as Elam. The early cultures are designated as Susiana a to e, and Susiana e is equated with Susa A or Susa I, the lowest level of the main mound of Susa proper. In comparison with Mesopotamia, Susiana *a* probably belongs to the Hassuna period (sixth millennium), and Susiana *e* or Susa I, at the end of this sequence, is contemporary with the end of the Ubaid and the beginning of the Uruk period (around 3500).[9] Later, in the Early Dynastic period of Mesopotamia, we hear of the kingdom of Elam in this region. Enmebaragesi of the First Dynasty of Kish (around 2700) is described in the Sumerian King List as "he who smote the weapons of the land Elam," and, from then on for a long time, Elam and Mesopotamia were involved in a pattern of both interrelationship and antagonism.[10]

Aryans

By the beginning of the first millennium, there is evidence that a new people came into Iran. For example, there is a distinctive change in burial custom at Tepe Sialk at this time. In the early town, graves were dug under the floors of houses or between houses, and in Cemetery A (as it is called) at the end of the second millennium there were simple tombs. But in Cemetery B, in the tenth, ninth, and beginning of the eighth centuries, tombs were built up with a mound of earth and protected with heavy slabs of stone or terra-cotta, angled against each other to form a gable roof. This can reflect a northern type of roof in the "house" provided for the deceased, in contrast with the normally flat roofs of the Middle East, and can suggest the arrival of newcomers from northern lands. Likewise, the pottery in these tombs is a new type in every way, including color and decoration. The handle or spout of the vessel is often in the form of an animal or bird, and the painted designs include ibex, horse, roaring lion, and warrior-hunter, as well as many geometric motifs. Copper and bronze are still employed, but iron has also come into general use. Thus, from at least around 1000 and onward, we are in the Iron Age in Iran, and a new northern people have entered the area, presumably the Aryans or Iranians (at this point, perhaps the Proto-Iranians), from whom in due course, the land took its name.[11]

Painted pottery of the sort found at Tepe Sialk represents the major art of the Iranian plateau in the first two centuries of the first millennium, but in the ninth and eighth centuries fine work in bronze, silver, and gold is also found at sites considered successors to Sialk, in particular at Khurvin (80 kilometers northwest of Teheran), Hasanlu (near the southwestern shore of Lake Urmia), and Amlash (135 kilometers northwest of Teheran).[12]

In the ninth century, the Iranians are also moving into the light of history, as their two most famous tribes—the Medes and the Persians—appear in the written records of Assyria. At this time the Assyrian empire was expanding into western Iran, and Shalmaneser III mentions Parsua (the land of the Persians) in the record of the campaign of his sixteenth year (843/842), and both Parsua and Madai (the land of the Medes) in the record of the campaign of his twenty-fourth year (835/834).[13] Later, we also hear of the Parthava, the future Parthians, settled around the Caspian Gates, and of the Bactrians and the Arachosians in northern and southern Afghanistan, respectively. These in all make up the five great Iranian tribes.[14]

Medes

The Medes are mentioned by every Assyrian king from Shalmaneser III to Ashurbanipal. From the Assyrian point of view, they are "the powerful Medes of the east," whose land is "on the border of the salt desert" and "on the edge of Mount Bikni [Mount Demavend]." Thus they occupied much of northwestern Iran.[15] Their capital was at Hagmatana ("place of assembly," Greek Ecbatana, modern Hamadan) at the foot of Mount Elvend, the dominant natural feature of the whole Zagros region. Their kings, with lengths of reign and probable dates, are listed in Table 15.[16]

Herodotus (1. 96-101) attributes the foundation of Ecbatana to "a clever man" named Deioces, the son of Phraortes, who united the nomadic Median tribes (among the tribes he names the Magi) into one nation and ruled them for fifty-three years. Deioces is probably the Daiaukku whom Sargon II, in a text of his seventh year (715/714), names as governor of the Manneans (an indigenous people around the southern shore of Lake Urmia) and says he deported to the land of Hamath. Again, in a text of his ninth year (713/712), Sargon II calls the Median land Bit-Daiaukku, "the house of Deioces was Phraortes (evidently named for his grandfather), who of the ruling dynasty of the Medes.[17] Diodorus (2. 32. 2f.), however, says the founder of the universal empire of the Medes was Cyaxares, who became king in the second year of the seventeenth Olympiad (711/710) and who may be the Uksatar who gave tribute to Sargon II in the eighth year of the latter (714/713).[18] Therefore, Deioces may have been succeeded by Cyaxares I within the fifty-three years assigned by Herodotus to himself alone.

Still following Herodotus (2. 102), we are told that the son and successor of Deioces was Phraortes (evidently named for his grandfather), who subjugated the Persians but perished on a campaign against the Assyrians after having ruled for twenty-two years. In turn (Herodotus 1. 103-107; 4. 1) Cyaxares II, son and successor of Phraortes, renewed the Median attack upon Assyria and laid siege to Ninus (Nineveh). At this juncture, the Scythians, who had driven the Cimmerians out of Europe and pursued

TABLE 15. KINGS OF THE MEDES

Name	Years of Reign	Date
1. Deioces ⎱	53	728–713
2. Cyaxares I ⎰		712–675
3. Phraortes	22	674–653
4. Cyaxares II	40	652–613
5. Arbaces	28	612–585
6. Astyages	35	584–550

them in their flight, came into the Median country and ruled Asia for twenty-eight years, during which time they went at least as far as Palestine. Then the Medes reasserted themselves and took Nineveh, and Cyaxares died after a reign of forty years. From the Nabopolassar Chronicle (B.M. 21901), in which Cyaxares II is called the king of the Umman-manda (a name perhaps inclusive of both the Medes and the Scythians), we have already learned that it was by the combined efforts of Cyaxares II and Nabopolassar of Babylon that Nineveh fell (612).[19]

In the fall of Nineveh and the overthrow of the Assyrian empire, Diodorus (2. 24-28) gives a leading role to a Median general named Arbaces and says that he was made king afterward. Presumably he is the Arphaxad who ruled over the Medes in Ecbatana, against whom Nebuchadnezzar II made war in his own twelfth year (593/592), according to the Book of Judith (1:1ff.). Herodotus (1. 107-130), however, goes on directly from the reign of Cyaxares II to that of his son Astyages, and to the story of Cyrus, son of Astyages' daughter Mandane, who took the kingdom from Astyages after Astyages had reigned for thirty-five years and joined it with the kingdom of the Persians. This event the Nabonidus Chronicle (B.M. 35382) reports in the sixth year of Nabonidus (550/549), stating that Ishtumegu (Astyages) marched against Cyrus, but that his own army revolted and turned him over to Cyrus, and that Cyrus seized his royal residence at Agamtanu (Ecbatana) and thus became master of the Medes as well as the Persians.[20]

Persians

Like the land of the Medes (Madai), the land of the Persians (Parsa, Parsu, Parsua, Parsuash, Parsumash) is mentioned many times in the Assyrian texts. From Shalmaneser III to Sargon II, the references point to a location in the northwestern Zagros and the vicinity of Lake Urmia; from Sennacherib to Ashurbanipal, the references suggest the southwest, in the neighborhood of Elam; but the center of the Achaemenian Persians was in the south in the area bounded by the Persian Gulf on the south and west, corresponding with the present province of Fars. This situation is variously explained by supposing that in the course of time the Persian tribes migrated from the northwest to the southwest and south or, on the other hand, that there were three groups of Persians in the three regions at about the same time and that Assyrian attention was simply directed to one or another of the western areas at one time or another.[21]

Early Achaemenians

In the Cyrus Cylinder, Cyrus calls himself the king of Anshan, the son of Cambyses, grandson of Cyrus, and descendant of Teispes, each of these predecessors also being called king of Anshan.[22] In the Bisitun inscription, Darius I names his ancestors in a line running back through Hystaspes, Arsames, Ariaramnes, and Teispes to Achaemenes. For this reason, Darius explains, "we are called Achaemenians," and he says further that "in two series we are nine kings." Moreover, he speaks of Cambyses as the son of Cyrus and a member of "our family" and a king. But of his own father, Hystaspes, Darius indicates only that he was a governor of Parthia and Hyrcania and does not call him king.[23] These data make possible the listing of the two lines of Achaemenians in Table 16.

Cyrus II

According to the cuneiform evidence, the death of Cyrus II (fighting on the northern frontier) was probably reported in Babylon in August 530. Herodotus (1. 214) states that he reigned for twenty-nine years. Therefore, the beginning of the reign of Cyrus as king of Anshan may be placed in 559; the beginning of his world rule was October 12, 539, when Babylon fell to him.[24]

In 559, when Cyrus II comes on the scene, the major powers that had divided among themselves substantially the entire western part of the Middle East were Media, Lydia, Chaldea, and Egypt. Cyrus himself was in a position of subservience to the Medes. As to his own kingdom, the title he uses in the Cyrus Cylinder for himself and his predecessors (Teispes, Cyrus I, Cambyses I) is that of king of Anshan, which is also the title given to him in the Nabonidus Chronicle (B.M. 35382) in the record of the sixth year of Nabonidus (550/549).[25] But in the ninth year of Nabonidus (547/546), the Nabonidus Chronicle calls Cyrus the king of Persia (Parsu).

TABLE 16. EARLY ACHAEMENIANS

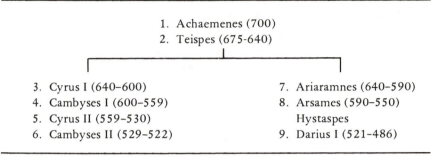

3. Cyrus I (640–600)	7. Ariaramnes (640–590)
4. Cambyses I (600–559)	8. Arsames (590–550)
5. Cyrus II (559–530)	Hystaspes
6. Cambyses II (529–522)	9. Darius I (521–486)

By or shortly before this time, therefore, Cyrus II has incorporated the Persian land properly so called (Parsa, Parsu, etc.) in his realm, the whole being approximately equivalent to the modern province of Fars in southern Iran.[26] It is a reasonable suppposition that even as Cyrus I, Cambyses I, and he himself had ruled in Anshan, so the kings in the other line also descended from Teispes—namely, Ariaramnes and Arsames—had ruled in Parsa, and that then Cyrus II had either displaced Arsames or, after his death, claimed the kingdom for himself, leaving Hystaspes only a lesser position elsewhere.[27] This supposition is substantiated by two inscriptions found on gold tablets at Hamadan. In one, Ariaramnes calls himself son of Teispes and grandson of Achaemenes, and king of Parsa, and says that "this country Parsa which I hold" was bestowed upon him by the great god Ahuramazda"; in the other, Arsames similarly names himself son of Ariaramnes and king of Parsa and makes acknowledgement for his realm to Ahuramazda. By their linguistic characteristics, the inscriptions are thought to have been written not earlier than the time of Artaxerxes II (404-359), and the tablets were perhaps set up at that time to identify small portraits or other monuments of the royal ancestors. Nevertheless, the texts can contain correct historical information.[28]

As to the conquest by Cyrus II of the other major world powers, Herodotus (1. 125-130) proceeds immediately to the story with respect to Media. Cyrus, he relates, assembled the Persian tribes and persuaded them to revolt against the Medes. There were many of these tribes, the most prominent being that of the Pasargadae, to which the royal house of the Achaemenians belonged. Astyages, the Median king, recognized the new danger to his rule and summoned Cyrus to Ecbatana, but Cyrus sent back word that Astyages would see him sooner than he desired. After that two battles were fought, and in the second of these, Astyages was captured but treated by Cyrus with magnanimity. From the Nabonidus Chronicle, the date was the sixth year of Nabonidus (550/549). Ecbatana was now a capital in a united Iran, and Parsa became the first ranking satrapy, Media the second, and Elam the third. The sovereignty of the Persians was established, but the Medes had equal honor with them; and foreigners spoke of either "the Persians and the Medes" (Esther 1:19) or "the Medes and Persians" (Dan. 5:28, etc.). "The Mede" was a single term for both.[29]

In the west, the Median empire stretched to the Halys River in Asia Minor, where the kingdom of Lydia began. There, as Herodotus (1. 77-90) relates, the famously rich Lydian king, Croesus, was in alliance with Amasis king of Egypt and with Labynetus (i.e., Nabonidus) king of Babylon. Cyrus besieged Croesus in his capital city of Sardis, took him prisoner, spared his life, and made Lydia a satrapy of the empire. The Nabonidus Chronicle puts the action against Lydia in the ninth year of Nabonidus (547/546). Herodotus also narrates the conquest of Chaldea (1. 178ff.), and we have already taken note of the information on the same subject in the Cyrus Cylinder and the Nabonidus Chronicle, with the date of October 12, 539, for the fall of Babylon. Of the major powers, Egypt remained, but the conquest of that land was to wait for Cambyses II, son of Cyrus II.

Although Herodotus tells of the conquests of Cyrus in the west in detail, he does not provide comparable information about what Cyrus may have done in the east; in that respect, direct cuneiform sources are lacking, too. Nevertheless, it is certain that Cyrus II campaigned in the east and northeast, too, and incorporated large territories in that area into the Persian empire. Xenophon (*Cyropaedia* 1. 1. 4) says that Cyrus started out with a little band of Persians; became by their own consent leader of the Medes and the Hyrcanians; then conquered Syria, Assyria, Arabia, Cappadocia, Phrygia, Lydia, Caria, Phoenicia, and Babylonia; and ruled over Bactria, India, and Cilicia, and "very many other nations." Herodotus (3. 88) says that the whole of Asia that was made subject to Darius I was subdued first by Cyrus and by Cambyses after him. Since the major effort of the short reign of Cambyses II was against Egypt, most of the other conquests in Asia, which created the empire to which Darius I succeeded, must have been by Cyrus II. In the Bisitun inscription, Darius I lists the provinces of his empire and, as far as the east and northeast are concerned, names not only Hyrcania and Bactria as mentioned by Xenophon, but also Parthia, Drangiana, Aria, Chorasmia, Sogdiana, Gandara, Scythia, Sattagydia, Arachosia, and Maka. He also indicates that his own father, Hystaspes, was governor of Parthia and Hyrcania. Sogdiana was the land between the Oxus (Amu Darya) and the Iaxartes (Syr Darya) rivers, and in connection with the march of Alexander the

Great through these regions, we hear of a city called Cyra or Cyropolis, which was on the Iaxartes and was the last city founded by Cyrus (Strabo, 11. 4; Arrian, *Anabasis* 4. 3. 1). Strabo also says that the Iaxartes was the boundary of the Persian empire. Therefore, it is uncertain whether Cyrus II also ruled over India, as Xenophon states; at most, this would have meant the region of the Indus River.

As to when Cyrus II carried out these conquests in the east and northeast, clear evidence is lacking, but it might have been relatively early, perhaps between the conquest of Lydia (547/546) and the taking of Babylon (539).[30] Xenophon's remark that Cyrus became leader of both the Medes and the Hyrcanians by their own consent can suggest that at least Hyrcania (extending east of the Caspian Sea to the Oxus) was early a part of his realm. After the fall of Babylon, he also fought against the Massagetae, a people whom Herodotus (1. 201-215) desribes as like the Scythians and living beyond the Araxes (the modern Aras, which flows into the Caspian Sea from the west). But these he did not conquer—in battle against them, he was killed (530).

Zarathustra. Cyrus II's incorporation of the eastern and northeastern regions into his empire was probably significant for the spread of Zarathustrianism in Persia, because the prophet Zarathustra probably lived and worked in that area and in the time shortly before and extending into the early years of the reign of Cyrus. As to the area, according to Ammianus Marcellinus (23. 6. 32), Zarathustra was a Bactrian; and according to the Zoroastrian *Vendidad* (1. SBE 4, p. 5), the realm of his royal convert, the Kayanian king Vishtaspa, was in "the Airyanam Vaejo [the expanse of the Aryans], by the good river Daitya [the Oxus]," a region to be equated approximately with Chorasmia (east of the Caspian Sea and on the Oxus, the modern Khorezm district in the Uzbek SSR).[31] As to the time of Zarathustra, the Pahlavi *Bundahish* (34. 7f. SBE 5, pp. 150f.) gives the years of reign of several kings from "the coming of the religion" in the reign of Kai Vishtasp (the conversion of Vishtaspa by Zarathustra) through the reign of Darai son of Darai (Darius III Codomannus, the last Persian king) as totaling 258 years, and the Muslim chronographer al-Biruni (1000) counts 258 years from the appearing of Zarathustra to the beginning of the era of Alexander. The figure of 258 years may well rest upon genuine historic remembrance. In Persia, the era of Alexander was no doubt reckoned from his sack of Persepolis and the death of Darius III in the spring of 330 (in Babylon the first regnal year of Alexander was counted as beginning on Nisanu 1, April 3, 330); therefore, the year in which Zarathustra came forward and successfully converted Vishtaspa was 588.[32] At this point the prophet was said to have been forty-two years

Left—FIGURE 32. Winged Genius at Pasargadae. *(Jack Finegan) Right—*
FIGURE 33. Column (with stork's nest on top) of the Audience Palace of Cyrus II
at Pasargadae. *(Jack Finegan)*

of age, and seventy-seven years old when he died (*Dinkard* 7. 4. 63f.; 5. 1,
SBE 47, pp. 64f., 73f.). Therefore, his life was 630-553. Since Bactria and
Chorasmia were among the regions brought under his sway by Cyrus II,
perhaps even relatively early in his reign, Cyrus II might have there
obtained personal acquaintance with Zarathustrian teachings. At any rate,
the inclusion of these regions in the empire must have facilitated the
spread of those teachings to the west.[33]

Pasargadae. As a member of the tribe of the Pasargadae, Cyrus built his
own capital in the tribal homeland, in the district of Parse (Fars). The city

itself was called Pasargadae. The site (now Tall-i Nokhodi) is in the large plain of Murghab on the Polvar River (160 kilometers northeast of Shiraz). The construction probably took place soon after the conquest of Lydia, and the work was probably executed by architects from there. The buildings are laid out according to an apparently unified plan, over a distance of 2 kilometers from north to south. At the north on a natural hill is a stone terrace known locally as the Takht-i-Madar-i-Sulaiman ("throne of the mother of Solomon"), perhaps intended as the platform of an elevated palace enclosure like the later terrace at Persepolis. Some distance to the south was a group of scattered individual palaces and pavilions, set amid gardens and surrounded by a masonry wall some four meters thick. The columns of the buildings were of stone, the walls of sun-dried mud brick.[34] On some of the columns is the inscription in Akkadian, Elamite, and Old Persian, "I, Cyrus, the king, the Achaemenian."[35] At a doorway, a four-winged figure wearing a long robe and Egyptian-type crown (*atef*) has survived, probably a guardian genius, perhaps with the facial features of an earthly king, perhaps even of Cyrus himself.[36]

Between the palaces and the terrace at the north, and still within the limits of the walled palace area, is one remaining tall wall of a square stone tower, known locally as the Zendan-i-Sulaiman ("prison of Solomon"); and in a secluded area 1,600 meters to the northwest of the tower are two open-air limestone altars, which stand about 8 meters apart. The tower was evidently originally almost identical in shape and size with the Kaabah-i-Zardusht at Naqsh-i-Rustam, not far from which are also two open-air altars. The Naqsh-i-Rustam tower is directly in front of the tomb of Darius I and no doubt the work of that king; here at Pasargadae, a fragmentary inscription on a stone from the tower is probably from Darius I and appears to say that Cyrus II built this tower.[37] Since Zarathustra established the use of fire altars for the worship under the open sky of the god of light named Ahuramazda ("Wise Lord"), the two altars may be understood as intended for such purpose; the tower may also be understood as a "place of fire" (*atashgah*) where the sacred fire was always guarded and kept pure.[38]

Southwest of the palace area at Pasargadae, at a distance of some 1,300 meters and adjacent to the present village of Madar-i-Sulaiman, is a large stone-built tomb, known locally as the Mechhed-i-Madar-Sulaiman ("grave of the mother of Solomon"). Standing on a platform of six steps, a plain rectangular chamber is entered by a low doorway and surmounted by a gable roof made of five very large slabs of stone. The steep slope of the roof is reminiscent of the same feature in the tombs of Tepe Sialk (Cemetery B) and, as there, suggests a northern type of house. In all

FIGURE 34. Tomb of Cyrus II at Pasargadae. (*Jack Finegan*)

probability, this impressively simple structure is the tomb of Cyrus II, described by Arrian (*Anabasis* 6. 29. 5) and Plutarch (*Alexander* 69. 2).[39]

Cambyses II

Cambyses II, son and successor of Cyrus II, accomplished the major task yet remaining for the establishment of Persian rule in the entire Middle East, namely the subjugation of Egypt. The campaign was in his own fifth year, in the spring of 525, when Amasis had been succeeded by his son Psammenitus (Psamtik III) as king of Egypt. As Herodotus (3. 10-16, 27-37, 61-67) relates, Cambyses marched across the desert with the help of the Arabians in the supply of water, routed the Egyptians at the Pelusiac mouth of the Nile, captured Memphis, and took the Egyptian king captive. At first, he dealt mildy with Psamtik III, but afterward performed many acts of madness against the Egyptian people and their religion; and Herodotus explains that he was afflicted from birth with the "sacred" disease (presumably epilepsy) and was diseased of mind as well. Within his own family, Cambyses II was responsible for the murder of his own brother Bardiya, also known as Smerdis. When the people did not know of the murder, a Magian named Gaumata pretended to be Bardiya/Smerdis and raised a rebellion. Cambyses II left Egypt for Persia but, in Syria, accidentally wounded himself with his own sword and soon died. He had reigned for seven years and five months. He left behind him no children at all.

Darius I

With the death of Cambyses II, the ruling line of Cyrus II came to an end, and it was Darius I in the other Achaemenian line who came forward to rescue the empire from the breakup that threatened. His own record of events is preserved in the famous carving and trilingual (Akkadian, Elamite, Old Persian) inscription on the rock above the village of Bisitun (thirty kilometers east of Kermanshah), placed where it would be seen by all travelers on the ancient caravan route between Ecbatana and Babylon.[40] As the record states, with exact dates, on the ninth day of the month Garmapada (Duzu), Gaumata, a Magian, impersonating Bardiya, seized the kingdom (July 1, 552). On the tenth day of Bagayadish (Tashritu), Darius I killed Gaumata and his chief followers in Media and thus himself became king (September 29, 552). Other challengers arose but were overcome. Indintu-Bel of Babylon claimed to be Nebuchadnezzar (III) son of Nabonidus, but was defeated on December 18, 522; Araka of Armenia established himself at Babylon as Nebuchadnezzar (IV) son of Nabonidus, but was defeated on November 27, 521. In all, nine kings were conquered in one and the same year after Darius I became king. In a second year, he killed Atamaita in Elam and in a third year, captured Skunkha in Scythia. In the relief sculptures, Darius I receives the submission of the first nine rebels, from Gaumata to Araka; the figure of Skunkha appears to have been added a little later.[41] With the suppression of the rebellions, Darius I was able to claim the rule of Persia, Elam, Babylonia, Assyria, Arabia, Egypt, those who are beside the sea, Sardis, Ionia, Media, Armenia, Cappadocia, Parthia, Drangiana, Aria, Chorasmia, Bactria, Sogdiana, Gandara, Scythia, Sattagydia, Arachosia, and Maka—a total of twenty-three provinces or satrapies.[42]

As he describes these happenings in the Bisitun inscription, Darius I says that it was "the Lie" that had "waxed great in the country" and had made the provinces rebellious, and for all of his own accomplishments he gives frequent and full acknowledgement to Ahuramazda. Likewise, in the relief panel he stands with one foot on the prostrate form of Gaumata and with bow grasped in left hand, but he raises his right hand toward an altar on which a fire is burning, while there hovers overhead an anthropomorphic figure (with feathered lower part) arising out of a winged disk, plainly the symbol of Ahuramazda, the god to whom he expresses his devotion.[43] Since the concept of the antagonistic spirit known as the Lie (*Druj*) is well known in Zarathustrianism along with the doctrine of Ahuramazda, Darius I appears as surely an adherent of the teachings of Zarathustra.[44]

Darius I also redug the Nile–Red Sea canal,[45] erected a new capital at Persepolis (fifty kilometers south of Pasargadae), to which Xerxes I and Artaxerxes I also made major contributions; and engaged in the Greco-Persian wars, in which, during his reign, the Persian armies suffered defeat at Marathon (491) and, a few years after his death, the Persian fleet was beaten at Salamis (480).[46]

When he died, probably in November 486, Darius I was buried in a rock-hewn tomb at Naqsh-i-Rustam ("pictures of Rustam," a legendary Persian hero), provided with sculptured reliefs and trilingual inscriptions as at Bisitun.[47] At this place (ten kilometers northeast of Persepolis), the great cliffs may have been sacred from an early time, for the remains of Elamite bas-reliefs are still to be seen. The tomb is high in the cliff, with a cruciform facade twenty-two meters high, but its inner chamber has a gabled roof like the tomb of Cyrus II and the tombs of Sialk (Cemetery B). In the sculptured relief panel at the top, the representatives of thirty nations support the platform on which the king stands, and he himself faces a fire altar, while the emblem of Ahuramazda floats overhead. In the accompanying inscription, Darius I names the thirty nations of his realm and declares his opposition to the Lie and his devotion to Ahuramazda.

Directly in front of the tomb of Darius I is a tall, square stone tower, known locally as the Kaabah-i-Zardusht ("square building of Zoroaster") a virtually intact example of the type of building found in ruins at Pasargadae. The tower is about twelve meters in height, with a stairway on one side, three rows of blind windows on the other three sides, and an inner chamber in the upper part. The position in front of the tomb of Darius I and the multitoothed chisel marks on the masonry (such as appear first on the other free-standing monuments of Darius I and his successors), support the attribution of the monument to Darius I. Nearby, cut in the rock, almost two meters high, are two open-air altars. As at Pasargadae, the tower was probably a place for the permanent keeping of the sacred fire of Ahuramazda, and the altars the place of worship in the open air.[48]

Later Achaemenians

In succession to Darius I, the line of Achaemenian kings continued to the end of the dynasty as shown in Table 17.

TABLE 17. LATER ACHAEMENIANS

Name	Date
1. Xerxes I	485–465
2. Artaxerxes I Longimanus	464–424
3. Darius II	423–405
4. Artaxerxes II Memnon	404–359
5. Artaxerxes III Ochus	358–338
6. Arses	337–336
7. Darius III Codomannus	335–330

Xerxes I

It was the original intention of Darius I that he should be succeeded by his oldest son Artobazanes, born to him by a wife who was the daughter of Gobryas, his spear bearer.[49] But then he selected instead the oldest of the four sons born to him by Atossa, a daughter of Cyrus II (Herodotus 7. 2f.). As Xerxes I himself says, in an inscription at Persepolis: "Other sons of Darius there were, but Ahuramazda desired it so: Darius my father made me the greatest after himself."[50]

In a longer Persepolis inscription, Xerxes I lists thirty-two nations over which he was king. But he also speaks of "commotion" in one of these countries and says that he destroyed the sanctuary of the false gods (Old Persian *daivas*), that where previously the false gods were worshiped, there he reverently worshiped Ahuramazda and *arta*.[51] The false gods are the *daevas* of the Avesta, the old Aryan gods opposed by Zarathustra as the enemies of Ahuramazda; *arta* is the Avestan Asha, divine law, cosmic order, and truth, the opposite of the Druj, the Lie, involving deceit, falsehood, and untruth.[52] Thus, at the accession of Xerxes I, revolts were probably led by priests of old religions, which the tolerant Achaemenians had allowed to persist. Along with suppression of revolt, Xerxes I also destroyed certain of their temples and put the worship of Ahuramazda in their place.

In the wars with the Greeks, Xerxes I plundered the Acropolis at Athens but afterward saw his fleet destroyed at Salamis (480) and his armies defeated at Plataea (479) and elsewhere. Understandably, these defeats do not figure in his own inscriptions, but Herodotus (7-9) gives a detailed account. In his later years Xerxes I was involved in harem intrigues (Herodotus 9. 108ff.) and finally was murdered by his vizier Artabanus.[53]

FIGURE 35. Kaabah-i-Zardusht at Naqsh-i-Rustam. (*Jack Finegan*)

Artaxerxes I

Xerxes I was succeeded by his son Artaxerxes I Longimanus, so surnamed because his right hand was longer than his left. He avenged the murder of his father by slaying Artabanus, but, in general, his administration was mild and in favor with his subjects. He was remembered as preeminent among the kings of Persia for his gentleness and magnanimity (Diodorus 11. 69. 6; 71. 1f.; Plutarch, *Artaxerxes* 1). There was further conflict with the Greeks, but in a peace agreement in 449, Athens gave up claim to Cyprus and Egypt and the Persians gave up the west coast of Asia Minor.[54] In a

FIGURE 36. Tomb of Artaxerxes I at Naqsh-i-Rustam. (*Jack Finegan*)

FIGURE 37.   All Lands Gateway of Xerxes I at Persepolis. (*Jack Finegan*)

Persepolis inscription, Artaxerxes I credits his kingship and work to the favor of the great god Ahuramazda, "who created this earth, who created yonder sky, who created man, who created happiness for man."[55]

Persepolis. Darius I, Xerxes I, and Artaxerxes I were all involved in the building of the great Persian capital at Persepolis. The site is on a spur of the Kuh-i-Rahmat ("mountain of mercy"), overlooking the vast plain of Marv Dasht. Diodorus (17. 71. 306) mentions three walls at Persepolis and speaks of the richness of the buildings in the palace area. There was in fact a triple fortification system, with one row of walls and towers running over the crest of the mountain. The chief buildings were erected upon a stone terrace platform 12 meters high and 500 by 300 meters in area. According to the excavations and inscriptions, Darius I built the platform, the monumental stairway, the Triple Portal, and his own palace and also began the Treasury and the large columned hall called the Apadana. Xerxes I finished the Apadana, erected the All Lands gateway, his own palace, and the Harem, and began the Throne Hall (the Hall of One Hundred Columns). Artaxerxes I completed the Throne Hall, began work on an unfinished portico in front of it, and may also have constructed a private palace.[56]

The walls of the buildings were of sun-dried mud brick on stone foundations. Tall stone columns were surmounted with capitals consisting of the foreparts (protomas) of two animals joined in the middle. Doorways and staircases were adorned with sculptured reliefs. On the sides of the Apadana stairway, representatives from throughout the empire bring their gifts to the king, the entire scene probably being the annual ceremony at the New Year festival each spring. Where a lion is attacking a bull, there is probably a representation of the constellations of Leo and Taurus, known already to the Sumerians and shown here in a configuration symbolic of the spring equinox and the beginning of the New Year.[57] Elsewhere the king sits upon his throne on a platform supported by the representatives of the nations, sits before two fire altars, stands beneath a sunshade, or fights with fearsome animals. Ranks of Persian and Median guards and dignitaries also appear. Overhead, repeatedly, is the symbol of Ahuramazda, and the inscriptions of the kings declare that it was by the favor of Ahuramazda that they built these buildings.[58]

In his description of Persepolis, Diodorus (17. 71. 7) also speaks of the graves of the kings that were in the royal hill east of the royal terrace. In fact three tombs much like those at Naqsh-i-Rustam are cut into the rock face of the Kuh-i-Rahmat. Although they lack the names of their owners, they are provisionally assigned to Artaxerxes II, Artaxerxes III, and Darius III.[59]

Top—FIGURE 38. East Portico of the Apadana of Darius I at Persepolis. *(Jack Finegan)* *Left—FIGURE 39.* Persian Guard on the East Stairway of the Apadana, Persepolis. *(Jack Finegan)* *Right—FIGURE 40.* East Portico of the Tripylon, Darius I Enthroned, Xerxes I behind Him, Ahuramazda Symbol Overhead, Persepolis. *(Jack Finegan)*

Top—FIGURE 41. Lion Capital at Persepolis. *(Jack Finegan)* *Middle—FIGURE 42.* Griffin Capital at Persepolis. *(Jack Finegan)* *Bottom—FIGURE 43.* Bull's Head on the Tripylon, Persepolis. *(Jack Finegan)*

Ecbatana and Susa. Even with the building of Pasargadae by Cyrus II and of Persepolis by Darius I and his successors, the more ancient cities of Ecbatana and Susa remained as two of the four main capitals of the Persian empire. By reason of their respective locations, Ecbatana was a summer residence, Susa a winter capital.

Ecbatana, the former Median capital, founded in the eighth century by Deioces according to Herodotus, is described by the same author (1. 98) as surrounded by seven circular walls, each higher than the last, the first five painted in white, black, purple, blue, and orange, and the last two coated with silver and gold. Polybius (*Histories* 10. 27. 3-10) says more simply that the citadel was strongly fortified, that the palace area was seven stadia in circumference, and that in the palaces the woodwork was of cedar and cypress, plated with either silver or gold. The book of Judith (1:2-4) also describes the powerful walls and gates of Ecbatana, and Ezra 6:2 indicates that the archives of the Persian empire were preserved there. Ecbatana is the modern Hamadan, and large mounds of the ancient city are visible, but excavation is lacking. Inscriptions have been found at Hamadan of Darius I, Xerxes I, and Artaxerxes II, as well as of Ariaramnes and Arsames.[60]

Susa, capital of the Elamite kingdom from the third millennium (and called Shushan in Neh. 1:1; Esther 1:2, etc.; Dan. 8:2), became a part of the Achaemenian empire when Cyrus II took Babylon (539) and all its provinces. The greatest monument of Persian Susa is the royal palace, begun by Darius I and enlarged and further beautified by the later kings.[61] An inscription of Darius I, his longest inscription after those at Bisitun and Naqsh-i-Rustam, tells of the materials and artisans brought from many parts of the empire for the construction.[62] Most notable are the colored glazed bricks, which show lions, lion-griffins, winged bulls, and the spearmen of the guard. These probably come from the reign of Artaxerxes II Memnon.[63]

Artaxerxes II Memnon

When Artaxerxes I and his queen Damaspis both died on the same day at the end of 424 or very early in 423, their son Xerxes II was recognized at least in Susa (but probably not in Babylonia) as king. But after only forty-five days of reign, Xerxes II was murdered and probably buried together with his father and mother in the tomb to the left of the tomb of Darius I at Naqsh-i-Rustam.[64] The murderer of Xerxes II was Sogdianus, son of Artaxerxes I and a Babylonian concubine named Alogune. He, too, was soon put aside, and a son of Artaxerxes I and another Babylonian concubine named Cosmartidene took the throne. This son was named

FIGURE 44. Hall of Ninety-Nine Columns, Persepolis. (*Jack Finegan*)

FIGURE 45. Symbol of Ahurmazda on the Palace of Xerxes I, Persepolis. (*Jack Finegan*)

FIGURE 46. Enameled Bricks Showing the Spearmen of the Guard, from Susa. (*Cliché des Musées Nationaux, Paris*)

Ochus and reigned as Darius II, sometimes being called Darius II Ochus or, on account of his origin, Darius II Nothus. In Babylonia he was recognized as king by February 423, but during his reign he faced almost continuous disturbances in his realm, including outright rebellions in Media and Egypt.[65]

The wife of Darius II was his own sister Parysatis, and their oldest son Arsicas succeeded his father and reigned as Artaxerxes II, a name to which the Greeks added Memnon (the "mindful"). For seventeen years, a Greek physician Ctesias, from Cnidus in Asia Minor, served as court physician under Artaxerxes II and, professedly from the royal records, wrote the *Persica,* a history of Assyria and Persia, of which fragments are preserved by Diodorus (1. 32. 4), Plutarch (*Artaxerxes*), and other ancient writers.[66] In these sources we learn of revolts in Cyprus, Egypt, and elsewhere, and of further wars with Greece, in the reign of Artaxerxes II. We also learn of the unsuccessful challenge to his rule by his brother, Cyrus the Younger (d. 401), also a son of Darius II and Parysatis.[67] In his own inscriptions, Artaxerxes II speaks for the most part about his building activities, and he also prays for protection to Ahuramazda, Anahita, and Mithra.[68]

Darius III Codomannus

When Artaxerxes III Ochus, son and successor of Artaxerxes II, came to the throne, the empire was still imperiled by many revolts. He devoted most of his reign to the suppression of these and the reestablishment of the unity of the realm, notably including the reconquest of Egypt, where, as Diodorus (17. 46. 2ff.; 51. 2) relates, he ruthlessly plundered the shrines and demolished the walls of the most important cities. Diodorus (17. 5-6) also states concisely the ensuing course of events. Artaxerxes III Ochus was hated for his savage disposition and harsh oppression of his subjects, and was poisoned by his general Bagoas. Bagoas also killed the older sons of Artaxerxes III and placed the youngest son, Arses, on the throne, thinking that he could control him easily because he was barely of age. When it became known, however, that Arses intended to punish Bagoas for his crimes, Bagoas killed Arses and his children while Arses was still only in the third year of his reign. Thus no one was left in the direct line of descent to claim the throne, and Bagoas gave it to Darius III Codamannus, descended from a brother of Artaxerxes II. When Bagoas undertook to eliminate this new king too, Darius III compelled him to take his own poison. Thus Diodorus introduces the last of the Achaemenian house, the man whom fate had selected, he says, to be the antagonist of Alexander.

Coming of Alexander

In the "many and great struggles for the supremacy," as Diodorus (17. 6. 3ff.) calls them, in which Darius III and Alexander III the Great opposed each other, Alexander defeated the Persians at the river Granicus (334), on the plain of Issus (333), and then again, after his intervening expedition to Egypt, at Gaugamela near Arbela beyond the Tigris (October 331). As Diodorus (17. 64ff.) and Plutarch (*Alexander* 37-43) tell the further story, at Babylon the people surrendered the city, and Alexander sacrificed to Marduk. Susa had already surrendered to one of his generals, and Alexander went there, then (in January 330) proceeded over the mountains to Pasargadae and Persepolis. At each place treasures were collected, and at Persepolis, with three thousand of his soldiers occupying the royal terrace, Alexander put the torch to the palace of Xerxes I, reciprocating the plundering of the Acropolis at Athens and at the same time marking with symbolic, if wanton, action the end of the rule of the Achaemenians. Meanwhile, Darius III was fleeing eastward across the desert. Alexander pursued him through Rhagae and, some 320 kilometers beyond, to the vicinity of the later capital of Parthia, Hecatompylos, the "Hundred-gated" city near present Damghan. There Alexander found him, either dead or at the point of death, the victim of Bessus, the satrap of Bactria. Alexander ordered a royal funeral, and the body was returned (May 330) to the mother at Persepolis, where one of the tombs to the east of the royal terrace probably became the last resting place of the last of the rulers of the Persian empire. In Babylonian chronology, Alexander was recognized after Gaugamela (October 331), and his first regnal year was reckoned from the ensuing New Year's Day, Nisanu 1, April 3, 330.[69] It was the beginning of a new era.

PART TWO
EGYPT AND RELATED AREAS

11. PREHISTORIC (10,000-45000) AND PREDYNASTIC (4500-3100) PERIODS

MESOLITHIC AGE (10,000-7000)

Sebil

As in Mesopotamia, so too in Egypt the evidences of human cultures are found already in the Paleolithic and Mesolithic ages. In the Middle Paleolithic, stone implements of Mousterian type (as in Shanidar Level D in Iraq) are widely found on the terraces of the desert overlooking the Nile valley. In the Upper Paleolithic, there were camp sites around what was once a lake in the plain of Kom Ombo (below Aswan east of the Nile near Gebel es-Silsileh).[1] Here the culture is called Sebilian (from the present-day village of Sebil in the Kom Ombo plain), and the same name is applied to similar evidences as far away as the Fayum, where there was at that time a much larger lake than now. At first, the Sebilian implements are typically Mousterian, but they evolve into fine microliths such as are generally characteristic of the Mesolithic Age (as in Level B at Shanidar).[2]

NEOLITHIC AGE (7000-4500)

Deir Tasa

In the Neolithic Age, human settlements moved generally closer to the Nile. Important sites of the Upper Neolithic are at Merimdeh (near Beni-Salameh, on the edge of the desert eighty kilometers northwest of Cairo in the direction of Wadi Natrun), in the Fayum, and at Deir Tasa (in the plain east of the Nile opposite Abutig, thirty-two kilometers south of Asyut). At Merimdeh, the people lived in reed huts, made rude, undecorated pottery by hand, and buried the dead beneath the houses of the living. In contrast with that primitive custom, at Deir Tasa the deceased were interred in cemeteries at the edge of the desert. These burials were in shallow pits in which the body, covered with skins, matting, or cloth, lay in a contracted

164

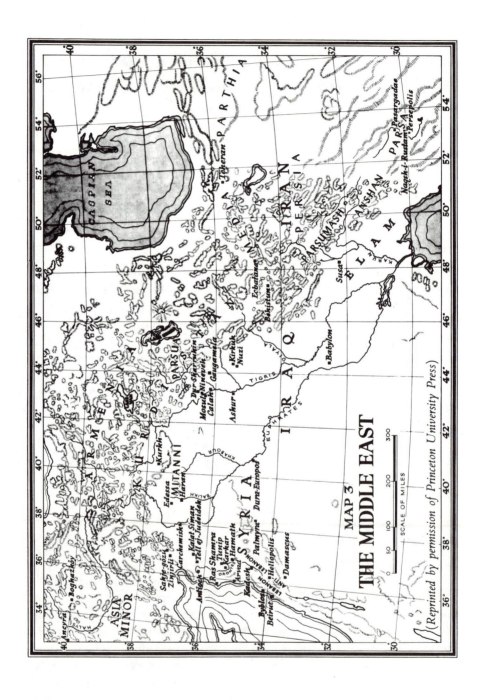

MAP 3

THE MIDDLE EAST

SCALE OF MILES

0 50 100 200 300

(*Reprinted by permission of Princeton University Press*)

position on the side and was accompanied by pottery vessels with food and drink, alabaster and limestone palettes on which eye-paint and face-paint were ground, items of jewelry of bone, ivory, and shell, and stone implements of various kinds. This type of burial remained normal throughout the balance of prehistoric time in Egypt and continued in use for common people long thereafter. This burial location also remained standard as the kings and nobles later placed their mastabas, pyramids, and rock-hewn tombs on the plateaus and in the hills on the edge of the desert beside the river valley. Likewise, the placing of many materials with the dead attests ideas of the life beyond such as continue throughout Egyptian history.[3]

CHALCOLITHIC AGE (4500-3100)

Although it is still within the Prehistoric period, it is customary to speak of a Predynastic period in the later part of the development that leads up to the first historical dynasty of Egypt. In this period, three stages are recognized and designated by the names Badarian, Amratian (Naqada I), and Gerzean (Naqada II).

Badari

The Badarian culture takes its name from the village of el-Badari (six kilometers south of Deir Tasa) and is represented by settlements and cemeteries in that vicinity and also at other sites in Upper Egypt and Nubia. Although the Badarian culture is not in all ways clearly separable from the preceding Tasian, there was no metal in the Tasian materials— but some copper is now found in the Badarian sites. Most characteristic of the Badarians is very excellent pottery. At its best the wares are extremely thin, in many cases decorated with rippled grooves, and colored black, brown, and red. Other objects are ivory spoons and combs, slate palettes for eye-paint, and jewelry made of shells, stones, and softer materials covered with a vitreous glaze, often in the greenish blue color so favored in all Egyptian art. Burial of the dead was like that of the Tasians, and the evident care with which the face of the deceased was turned toward the setting sun suggests that thought of the life beyond was in some way associated with the West.[4]

Amreh (Naqada I)

The Amratian culture derives its name from the village of el-Amreh (ten

FIGURE 47.   Decorated Predynastic Vases Showing Boats with Cabins. (*The Metropolitan Museum of Art*)

kilometers southeast of the royal tombs of Abydos). Materials like those found here were also uncovered near Naqada (on the west side of the Nile, opposite the mouth of Wadi Hammamat, not far below Luxor)—hence the alternative designation. Other sites with similar materials are found elsewhere in Upper Egypt and Nubia. The pottery includes a dark red ware with blackened tops and interiors, and a red ware ornamented with geometrical designs in white paint. Vases were made of stone, and a stone disk with a very sharp edge was used for a macehead. Clay models of boats were found at el-Amreh, and a painting on the interior of a bowl shows boat construction with bundles of papyrus lashed together. In the graves, clay figurines of animals were presumably intended to guarantee that the deceased would not be lacking such possessions in the afterlife; female figurines may have represented wives or servants or, in some cases, perhaps a goddess.[5]

Gerzeh (Naqada II)

The Gerzean culture takes its name from the village of Gerzeh (on the eastern edge of the Fayum) and is also designated as Naqada II from the later materials at this site. Other representative sites are found elsewhere in Lower Egypt, Upper Egypt, and Nubia.[6] The potter's wheel was now in use, and pottery elaborately decorated with red-line designs may be reminiscent of the wheel-turned polychrome ware of Jemdet Nasr in Mesopotamia.[7] In addition to patterns of lines, there are representations of antelopes, flamingos, ibexes, and occasional human figures. Also shown are large boats, probably of papyrus construction, with many oars and two cabins. Usually affixed to one cabin is a standard with an emblem, and it may be supposed that this cabin is a shrine and the emblem the symbol of a god or goddess. In at least some cases, these emblems are recognizably the same as symbols used later to designate towns or territories as well as the deities worshiped there. These territories were called nomes by the Greeks, and eventually there were twenty-two of these in Upper Egypt and twenty in Lower Egypt, each with its own name, distinctive sign, principal city, and chief god or goddess.[8]

Other aspects of the Gerzean culture include many more stone vessels, increased use of copper, and the making of the glazed frit ware known as faience (earthenware glazed with powdered quartz, fired at a high temperature). The stone-disk macehead of the Amratian period is largely replaced by a mace with a pear-shaped head. The pottery model of a house found at el-Amreh suggests a building of wattle and mud, with wood-framed door and windows. Graves are larger and more nearly rectangular, a side ledge may provide place for funerary offerings, there is roofing with wood or matting, and the same materials are sometimes used to line the interior, a custom that presumably led to the wooden paneling and the wooden coffins of dynastic tombs.

At Hierakonpolis (the Egyptian Nekhen, the present Kom el-Ahmar, on the west bank of the Nile seventeen kilometers northwest of Edfu), a yet more elaborate tomb of late Gerzean date[9] has walls and floor of bricks covered with plaster and whitewashed. The walls are decorated with paintings—the first example of the tomb murals ever afterward so important in Egyptian art and funerary practice. In style and subject matter, the paintings are similar to the painting on the decorated pottery of the Gerzean period. The main mural depicts five ships of the same type as on the pottery, but another one of a very different kind, probably Mesopotamian in type. The five ships are headed south and are colored red, white, and green, and their crew have red skins; the other ship is headed north and its one passenger is black. Scattered around the scene are hunters with quarry, two pairs of fighting men, a conqueror brandishing a mace with pear-shaped head over prisoners bound in a row, and a man standing between two wild animals, which rise up against him on either side, again a Mesopotamian motif. In interpretation of the main scene, it may be that at this time Hierakonpolis marked the southern limit of Upper Egypt and controlled entry into Nubia (as was the case later in the Old Kingdom at Elephantine and the First Cataract) and that what is shown is some successful confrontation by a ruler of Hierakonpolis of some incursion from the south.[10]

With respect to the Badarian, Amratian (Naqada I), and Gerzean (Naqada II) phases of the Predynastic period, layers representing these cultures have been found in plain stratification in this order in an excavation near the village of el-Hammamiya (ten kilometers southeast of el-Badari), so the temporal sequence of all three cultures is confirmed.[11] Although the three phases are recognizably distinct, it was at the same time essentially the same civilization in process of development, as seen in such already mentioned features as the type of burials and the use of palettes of stone for the grinding of eye-paint. As also noted, there is evidence of outside influence from the Asiatic side, at least by the time of the Gerzean phase. Altogether in the Gerzean pottery, late Uruk, Jemdet Nasr, and Early Dynastic influence from Mesopotamia is believed recognizable, as well as influence from Palestine.[12] Several cylinder seals found in late Gerzean graves are of Jemdet Nasr style and presumably imports from Mesopotamia; others may have been made in Egypt after Mesopotamian models.[13] On a carved ivory knife handle from Gebel el-Araq (near the mouth of Wadi Hammamat), there are Mesopotamian-type ships and the Mesopotamian motif of a man with two lions rising up on either side of him, even as in the Hierakonpolis tomb painting already mentioned.[14]

The route by which Asiatic influence reached Egypt could presumably have been overland across Palestine and Sinai, the way so much used in later history. Or it could have been by sea around the Arabian peninsula, up the Red Sea, and then through the Wadi Hammamat, which penetrates the desert hills and opens into the Nile valley at Koptos below Thebes. The prominence of the Mesopotamian-type ships among the items of evidence mentioned above, and the fact that many of the items of evidence are from such sites as Naqada and Gebel el-Araq, which are in the neighborhood of the mouth of Wadi Hammamat, may make the latter alternative the more likely at this point.[15]

King Scorpion

The relative elaborateness of the decorated tomb at Hierakonpolis suggests that this was the burial place of a very prominent person, perhaps an early king of Upper Egypt. The actual name of an early king is found on a large pear-shaped ceremonial limestone macehead, found in fragments in the temple precinct at Hierakonpolis.[16] As restored, the macehead is twenty-three centimeters high and carved in relief in three superimposed horizontal registers.[17] The king appears in the main middle register. He

Top—FIGURE 48. Gebel el-Araq Flint Knife with Carved Ivory Handle, Side with Ships. *(Cliché des Musées Nationaux, Paris) Bottom—FIGURE 49.* Gebel el-Araq Knife, Side with Man between Two Lions, and Perforated Boss for Carrying. *(Cliché des Musées Nationaux, Paris)*

wears a tunic fastened over his left shoulder, a bull's tail fastened at the waist as an attribute of royalty, and, on his head a tall helmetlike crown, from this time on well known as the White Crown of Upper Egypt. He stands on the edge of some water, presumably the bank of the Nile; in the lower register, the same river curves around an island on which two men are engaged in agricultural work. With two fanbearers behind him, the king holds a hoe, and in front of him, another person extends a basket to receive the soil dug up. This may represent an agricultural ceremony in which the ruler began the cultivation of the soil in a new season of planting after the Nile receded, and an official received the first basketful of silt. Above and in front of the king are a seven-pointed star and a scorpion. The scorpion is probably the hieroglyph of the king's name, so he is King Scorpion; the star may indicate his celestial nature as a god and probably as the representative of the sky god Horus, as the king certainly was in later Egyptian history.

In the upper register are two processions of standards, and, like the standards on the boats on the Gerzean pottery, they are surmounted by emblems. Among these are what are later known as the emblem of the god Min, a symbol provisionally identified as two of the conical fossils known

FIGURE 50.   Relief on the Macehead of King Scorpion. (*Ashmolean Museum, Oxford*)

as belemnites, and the emblem of the god Seth, a strange animal, variously identified in its numerous occurrences as a pig or donkey but most often looking more like a greyhound, with long stiff tail, thin muzzle, and straight pointed ears, perhaps a composite, imaginary creature. Min was the ithyphallic deity (equated by the Greeks with Pan), worshiped at the Egyptian Gebitou (Greek Koptos) at the mouth of the Wadi Hammamat, and was the patron of the caravan route through that great desert valley to the Red Sea.[18] Seth was the famous opponent of Osiris and Horus, and was identified by the Greeks with Typhon. The Pyramid Texts (secs. 204a, 370b) of the Fifth and Sixth dynasties describe Seth as dwelling in Ombos (Nubet), name him "the Ombite" or "He of Ombos," and call him the "lord of the land of the South" (i.e., Upper Egypt).[19] So the standards probably stand for various Upper Egyptian territories or nomes. Furthermore, there is a rope hanging from each of the standards. In the one procession, each rope is tied around the neck of a lapwing (a plover). In the other procession facing in the opposite direction (of which only one complete standard is preserved), the rope is attached to a bow. Since in hieroglyphs the lapwing stands for "common folk," the bow for "foreign people," and in later literature the "Nine Bows" for the traditional enemies of Egypt on its borders, the entire monument may be interpreted to say that King Scorpion led some of the nomes of Upper Egypt in victory over some of the Egyptian populace, probably inhabitants of Lower Egypt, and over some foreigners, probably living on the edges of the Delta, and then afterward devoted himself to works in the improvement of his country, especially in agriculture. Presumably the capital of King Scorpion was at Hierakonpolis, where his great macehead was uncovered, but his name has also been found in the area where ancient Thinis is thought to have been located—near Girga, north of Abydos—and it is possible that the seat of government was shifted thither in the course of his reign.[20]

Hierakonpolis and Buto

Since the Greeks called the Egyptian city of Nekhen by the name of Hierakonpolis ("city of the falcon"), it is probable that it was an ancient center of the worship of the sky god Horus, whose form as a falcon is well known and who was considered to be embodied in the reigning king. In the Pyramid Texts, the god is called "Horus of Nekhen" (secs. 295a-b, 296a, 1293d, 2011d), and the Horus king is "the bull of Nekhen" (sec. 276a). Across the Nile from Nekhen at the present el-Kab was the ancient Egyptian town of Nekheb (the Greek Eileithyiaspolis), the center of the worship of the vulture goddess Nekhbet. In the Pyramid Texts (secs. 729, 2003), Nekhbet is identified with the White Crown of Upper Egypt and described as the mother of the deceased king after his rebirth in the afterlife, in which capacity she is called "the great wild cow who dwells in Nekheb." It was in the latter capacity that the Greeks equated Nekhbet with Eileithyia, their own goddess of childbirth. As the protective goddess of Upper Egypt, Nekhbet was represented in hieroglyphic writing in

FIGURE 51. Water Lily at the Egyptian Museum, Cairo. (*Jack Finegan*)

FIGURE 52. Papyrus at the Egyptian Museum, Cairo. (*Jack Finegan*)

FIGURE 53.   White Crown of Upper Egypt, Portrait Head of a King, in the
Egyptian Museum, Cairo. (*Jack Finegan*)

Right—FIGURE 54. Hieroglyphic Signs for the Two Titles, "King of Upper and Lower Egypt" (plant of the South and bee of the North), and the "Two Goddesses" (vulture goddess Nekhbet of Upper Egypt and cobra [uraeus] goddess Wadjet of Lower Egypt), Relief from Hurbeit. *(The Metropolitan Museum of Art, Rogers Fund, 1911)* *Left—FIGURE 55.* Red Crown of Lower Egypt, Portrait of a King, from Hurbeit in the Delta. *(The Metropolitan Museum of Art, Rogers Fund, 1911)*

connection with the sign for a plant evidently typical of Upper Egypt, usually identified as a lily or sedge.

In respect to Lower Egypt, the Pyramid Texts speak of "the kings of Lower Egypt who were in Pe" (sec. 1488b) and represent the deceased king as arriving in the other world and declaring, "I have come from Pe" (secs. 570, 697a). In several references to Pe there is also mention of Horus (secs. 1242, 2190, 2250), so he was evidently worshiped in Lower as well as in Upper Egypt. Apparently close by Pe was another place called Dep, of which the Pyramid Texts also speak frequently. Here the chief deity was the cobra goddess Wadjet, called in the Pyramid Texts "Wadjet in Dep" (sec. 1671a). She was identified with the Red Crown of Lower Egypt and, in hieroglyphic writing, was often represented in connection with the papyrus plant of the Delta marshes. The name of Wadjet was later pronounced as Edjo and reproduced in Greek as Uto (and equated with the Greek goddess Leto). So eventually Pe and Dep were together called Per-Wadjet, "the house of Edjo (Uto)." From this came the Greek name of the entire city, Buto. Buto was in the Lower Egyptian Nome VI ("Mountain

Bull"), and Herodotus (2. 155f.) describes it as a great city on the Sebennytic arm of the Nile.[21] He also relates the legend of how Typhon (Seth), having murdered Osiris, sought for the son of Osiris, the child Horus; but Horus was kept safe by his mother Isis and by Leto (Wadjet) on a floating island near Buto called Chemmis. Buto is identified with Tell el-Farain ("mound of the pharaohs," twelve kilometers northeast of Dissuq and ninety-five kilometers east of Alexandria), and a nearby village of Ibtou still preserves the ancient name of Buto.[22]

In the Pyramid Texts, Pe plainly stands for Lower Egypt as Nekhen does for Upper Egypt, and the two are balanced with each other, as are also the cobra goddess Wadjet of Dep (beside Pe) and the vulture goddess of Nekhbet of Nekheb (across the river from Nekhen). Upon the ascension of the deceased king to heaven, it is declared that "the Mistress of Dep [i.e., Wadjet] rejoices, and she who dwells in Nekheb [i.e., Nekhbet] is glad" (sec. 1107b). The king says, "I have not forgotten my mother the White Crown . . . dwelling in Nekheb" and goes on to salute Wadjet, "O Red Crown, O Lady of the lands of Dep, O my mother" (secs. 910a-b, 911a-b). The Pyramid Texts (e.g., sec. 904) also speak frequently of the "Souls of Pe" and the "Souls of Nekhen," probably meaning the deceased kings of Lower and Upper Egypt who have become immortal, deified spirits. The texts also employ the title "Souls of On [Heliopolis]" probably as a collective designation of both, since Heliopolis was a very ancient religious center and, as such, presumably the legendary cradle of the entire royal house. The collectivity of the royal ancestors is probably also meant by the name "Followers of Horus" (secs. 26f., 897a, 921a), since the god Horus was worshiped at both Hierakonpolis and Buto.[23]

So in the early times still reflected in the Pyramid Texts, there were two kingdoms of Upper Egypt and Lower Egypt, with their chief centers and deities as just indicated. In some of the Pyramid Texts (e.g., secs. 725d, 1107b), Buto is mentioned first ahead of Hierakonpolis, which may reflect an early situation in which the Lower Kingdom was more important than the Upper. The probable incursion of King Scorpion of Upper Egypt into Lower Egypt suggested by his great macehead suggests, however, that at this time Upper Egypt was the stronger. The next monument found at Hierakonpolis—namely, the palette of Narmer, perhaps the immediate successor of Scorpion—quite plainly records the conquest of the north by the south. As a result, all Egypt was unified and the Dynastic period began. But in the united country, the remembrance of the two kingdoms always persisted, and many elements from the two were always preserved and balanced in the way observed in the Pyramid Texts.

12. EARLY DYNASTIC PERIOD, FIRST AND SECOND DYNASTIES (3100-2686)

Narmer

The monument of Narmer, mentioned in Chapter 11, is a slate palette such as the Egyptians had long used for the grinding of eye-paint. But it is an object of large size, sixty-four centimeters in height, surely a memorial of victory and probably a votive offering in the temple at Hierakonpolis, in the precinct of which it was found.[1] On either side at the top are two heads of Hathor, shown with human face and the ears and horns of a cow, and the name of the king. The king's name is written within a rectangle at the bottom of which is a design of recessed paneling, probably representing the facade of the king's palace. The whole arrangement is well known on later monuments and is called the *serekh* (literally the "proclaimer"). The name is made up of two signs, a catfish (*n'r*) abundant in the Nile River, and a chisel (*mr*) familiar in everyday life, thus giving the name Narmer.

On the verso in the main register is the tall figure of the king, wearing the White Crown of Upper Egypt and raising a mace with pear-shaped head over an enemy chieftain in a pose much like that of the conqueror brandishing a mace over prisoners in the decorated tomb at Hierakonpolis. In front of the king a falcon holds a rope attached to a man's head, which head is connected with a rectangle out of which grow six stylized plants, probably papyrus representing the Delta. The import of the pictures seems plain: the falcon god Horus, embodied in the king, conquers his enemies of the papyrus country.

On the recto in the first register, the king, now wearing the Red Crown of Lower Egypt and preceded by four standard bearers with the emblems of kingship,[2] inspects two rows of decapitated enemies. In the second and largest register are two fantastic animals. They have the paws and heads of lions or panthers, but extremely elongated necks, and the necks are

Left—FIGURE 56. Cast of Slate Palette of King Narmer, Verso, the King Smiting his Enemy. *(Oriental Institute, University of Chicago)* *Right—FIGURE 57.* Cast of Slate Palette of King Narmer, Recto, Animals with Intertwined Necks. *(Oriental Institute, University of Chicago)*

intertwined to make the circular pan of the palette for the grinding of the eye-paint. In Mesopotamian art, very similar animals with intertwined necks appear on seals of the Uruk and Jemdet Nasr periods, so Mesopotamian influence in Egypt is again indicated.[3] The message of the entire palette thus far seems clear: Narmer king of Upper Egypt has conquered Lower Egypt and united the two lands; he now wears both the White Crown and the Red Crown; the two lands are bound together like the symbolic animals with the intertwined necks.

In the bottom registers of the palette on either side are additional scenes. On the verso are two fallen or fleeing enemies; on the recto, the king in the guise of a bull tramples an enemy underfoot and demolishes what may be an oval-shaped fortified city with a sloping-sided tower inside it. On the verso, the first enemy is accompanied by a recessed rectangle, which is probably a fortified city, the second by a sign that can be a semi-circular enclosure with two long walls spreading out from it. The former could be a city in western Palestine, where there were certainly fortified cities from this time onward; the latter could be one of the ancient rock-walled enclosures of comparable shape found in great numbers in Jordan and reasonably explained as "sheepfolds" (cf. Gen. 49:14; Judg.

5:16). If this interpretation is correct, Narmer may even have penetrated Palestine. There appears to be confirmation of such an invasion in the finding of the *serekh* design and the stylized catfish sign, which is the first element of Narmer's name, on potsherds at Tell el-Erani and Tel Arad in Israel.[4]

On the Narmer palette, a small complex of pictures (the head, six plants, and falcon) evidently conveys a meaning in symbols and is something more than just a pictorial representation. Several signs provide the name of the king and perhaps of some other persons—thus there are here found some of the oldest known examples of Egyptian writing. Since writing was already known in Mesopotamia in the Uruk period, the invention of writing in Egypt, along with other features already noticed, may have been due to Mesopotamian stimulus. Nevertheless, the system developed in Egypt was and always remained distinctively Egyptian. Because in later times the Egyptian writing was used largely for "sacred" inscriptions "carved" on temple walls, the Greeks called it hieroglyphic. In the system the small pictures that are the hieroglyphs may either denote what they portray or may suggest something else, the name of which has a similar sound (as when the catfish and the chisel give the name of Narmer). Moreover, in time, twenty-four of the hieroglyphs were used for consonant sounds, and thus a sort of alphabet was provided. Found here at the beginning of the history of united Egypt and still occurring, at least in isolated examples, as late as in the third century C.E., hieroglyphic writing was in use for more than three thousand years. In the Middle Kingdom and thereafter, however, hieroglyphic was written in a cursive form in which the original pictures were so modified as to be hardly recognizable. As it was the usual script employed by the Egyptian priests, the Greeks called it hieratic. Yet again, by around 700, an even more rapidly written form of hieratic came into use. As it was the common writing of everyday life, the Greeks called this demotic or "popular."[5]

As to the name of the king, written in a *serekh* design on the Narmer palette, on other monuments the *serekh* is often surmounted by a falcon (as is true of the *serekh* with the catfish sign at Tel Arad); this is the so-called Horus name of the ruler. In its developed form, at least from the Fifth Dynasty on, the royal nomenclature comprised five titles, which the king assumed on his accession day, and five names distributed in association with the titles.[6] The first title was Horus, meaning that the king was the embodiment of the falcon god, and the accompanying name was the Horus name, written in the *serekh*. The second title was Two Ladies (*nebty*), also translatable as He of the Two Goddesses, and this identified the king with the vulture goddess Nekhbet of Upper Egypt and the cobra goddess

Wadjet of Lower Egypt. The third title was Horus of Gold, and the Golden Horus name went with this. The fourth title was He of the Sedge and the Bee (*insibya*). Since sedge and bee were symbols of the two parts of the land, respectively, this title designated the ruler as the King of Upper and Lower Egypt. With this title went the throne name (*prenomen*), given at accession. The fifth title was Son of Re, and with this went the personal name of the king (*nomen*), given at birth, or, at any rate, his family name. From the Old Kingdom onward, the throne and personal names were emphasized by being written within an oval frame (*cartouche*). This was later used for queens, princes, and princesses as well.

As for the title *Pharaoh* (Gen. 12:15, etc.), this is the Egyptian *per-o,* meaning "great house" (written with the hieroglyphic signs for a house and a wooden column, the latter also meaning "great"). Originally the term referred to the palace itself; with Thutmose III in the Eighteenth Dynasty and onward, it was used for the king himself; and with one of the Sheshonqs in the Twenty-second Dynasty and onward, it was employed as a title preceding the proper name (as Pharaoh Hophra, Jer. 44:30; Pharaoh Neco, Jer. 46:2; 2 Kings 23:29, etc.). Following the name of the king and also following various terms connected with royalty such as Great House are often found the hieroglyphs for life (the *ankh,* originally perhaps a sandal strap),[7] prosperity (a fire-drill), and health (a folded cloth, probably a handkerchief). Together (♀⚒) they constituted the exclamatory interjection, "May he live, prosper, and be healthy!" (in translation conveniently abbreviated "l. p. h.").

Palermo Stone

The macehead of Scorpion and the palette of Narmer are evidently contemporary memorials, but later king lists, annals, and historiographic writings also provide important information. Of these the first is the fragmentary Palermo Stone.[8] In small compartments in the first row of carvings on this monument are seated figures, each holding a flail as a royal appurtenance, wearing the Red Crown, and accompanied by signs that are presumably names although unidentifiable. Judging from the crowns, these are king of Lower Egypt, and if a preceding lost portion of the stone showed kings of Upper Egypt, there were provided lists of the predynastic kings of both kingdoms. In the rows that follow, the king's name and that of his mother are written in the horizontal space above the row. The rows themselves are divided into yearly compartments, in each of which is the record of some outstanding event or events of the year. In a small section at the bottom of each compartment are signs for cubits, palms, and fingers, probably measures of the height of the inundation of the Nile in the given year.[9] Above the second and third rows, the kings' names are not preserved, but we are probably in the First Dynasty. Above the fourth row (at the left), the king sits on a throne, holds the flail, and wears the double crown combining the White Crown of Upper Egypt and the Red Crown of Lower Egypt. His Horus name, written in a rectangle surmounted by a falcon, is Nynetjer, otherwise known as a king of the Second Dynasty. In the sixth and last row on the front of the stone, the yearly compartments are much larger and contain more items of information. The accompanying king's name is that of Snefru, first king of the Fourth Dynasty. On the back of the stone, in less good condition, are the names of Shepseskaf, a late king of the Fourth Dynasty, and of Userkaf, Sahure, and Neferirkare, the first three kings of the Fifth Dynasty.

At the dividing point between reigns, there are indications of time: crescent moons for months and the circle of the sun together with straight lines for the number of days. Thus at the end of the reign of the preceding king (whose name is lost), four months and 24 days are shown; at the beginning of the reign of Shepseskaf, there are seven months and 11 days. This agrees with the otherwise known Egyptian calendar year of twelve months of 30 days each (plus 5 additional days, or 365 days in all) and means that in the calendar year in question, the preceding king died at the end of four months and 24 days and Shepseskaf began to reign in the last seven months and 11 days of the same year.

At each point where a new reign begins on the Palermo Stone, there are, in addition to the signs for months and days, hieroglyphs that read "Union of the Two Lands" and "Circuit of the Wall." In two instances, these are preceded by "Rising of the King of Upper Egypt" and "Rising of the King of Lower Egypt." The union of the two lands is signified by the knotting together of the papyrus and the sedge around a symbol of union, the circuit of the wall was a procession around the White Wall at Memphis, and the rising (like the sun) of the king was his appearing at the time of his accession. These ceremonial events at the enthronement of a new king provided the name of his first year; later years were named by important events such as "smiting of the nomads." Along with the naming of individual years and the counting of the years of the reign of the king, under King Nynetjer of the Second Dynasty we come upon an item, "Fourth occurrence of the numbering," and similar references recur in every second year. Under a later king of the same dynasty, this is called a "numbering of gold and lands"; and, under Userkaf of the Fifth Dynasty, we hear of a "numbering of large cattle" and also of the "year after the seventh numbering." Therefore, there was a biennial census of cattle and other property. The year when it was taken for such-and-such a time, and the year thereafter, provided a way of keeping track of successive years. Among the several festivals named on the Palermo Stone is the Heb Sed. This Sed festival or jubilee was, as far as possible, held at least once in the reign of every king, sometimes after thirty years, sometimes after a lesser interval. It was intended to renew the potency and authority of the king, and it was associated with the raising of the Djed pillar, a column, perhaps originally of papyrus stems, connected with Osiris and symbolizing rebirth and resurrection.[10]

Egyptian Calendar

As noted above, the calendar reflected in the Palermo Stone notations of days, months, and years is understandable as consisting of twelve months of thirty days each (modified by the addition of 5 days to make a year of 365 days). Back of this calendar probably lay a very early system of reckoning time in which the beginning of the month was determined by the sighting of the new moon. This system, in fact, continued in use for a long time, for in all periods of Egyptian history, the dates of many religious festivals were determined in relation to the new moon and in terms of the lunar month.[11] In the early lunar calendar, at least some of the month names referred to agricultural events—e.g., "Swelling of Emmer," and "Harvest"—and there must have been some way of adjusting the calendar to keep the months in a measure of harmony with the seasons.[12] The year itself was also related to agriculture and to the all-important annual inundation of the Nile. It was divided into three seasons: (1) Akhet or "Inundation" (written in hieroglyphics as a pool with lotus flowers), starting when the Nile began to rise (at Memphis about the third week in July); (2) Peroyet or "Coming Forth," when the fields emerged again from the water and crops were planted and grew; and (3) Shomu or "Deficiency," when the crops were reaped and the water was low, before the next inundation. By a simple process of recording and averaging, over a period of some length, the intervals between inundations, it could probably have been ascertained that the year was approximately 365 days in length,[13] and astronomical observations could eventually provide a more precise result. At Memphis in the early third millennium, the summer solstice fell about July 14-16 and the heliacal rising of Sirius (Egyptian Sopdu, Greek Sothis) on July 17-19— i.e., in the approximate period of the annual inundation of the Nile and could have provided points from which to count. They would have given a year of about 365¼ days.[14] That such a reckoning was made relatively early is suggested by a text, probably of the First Dynasty, which is perhaps to be translated as saying, "Sothis, the opener of the year; the inundation";[15] in the Twelfth Dynasty and later, at any rate, there are several texts that record the heliacal rising of Sothis in terms of the civil calendar.

For practical purposes, a calendar year of twelve months of thirty days each was used and is reflected, for example, in a record where the daily income of a temple is stated for purposes of calculation as 1/360 of the annual revenue. But, for greater accuracy, five additional days were placed at the end of the year and before the beginning of the new year. The Egyptians called these "the five days upon the year" or "the five days added to the year"; the Greeks named them "epagomenal days." Plutarch (*Isis and Osiris* 12) relates the legend that they were invented by Thoth and explains that the five days were observed by the Egyptians as the birthdays of the five deities—Osiris, Horus, Seth, Isis, and Nephthys. When (in the Persian period) the months were given names from the feasts with which they were connected, it was appropriate that the first month of the year was named for the same Thoth, ibis-headed lunar deity, scribe of the gods, inventor of numbers, and measurer of time.

In relation to the astronomical year of approximately 365¼ days, however, the 365-day year was still about one quarter-day short. Assuming that at the outset the first day coincided with the day of the heliacal rising of Sirius, in the next year the calendar would start one-quarter day early. In four years it would begin one full day early, at which time the heliacal rising of Sirius, which should mark the first day of the calendar year, would fall one day late on the second day of the first month. After eight years, there would be a discrepancy of two days, and so on. In 1,460 years (4 x 365) the beginning of the calendar year would have moved all the way around the cycle to coincide once again with the rising. This period of 1,460 years is called a *Sothic cycle*. In view of this problem the Egyptian civil year (*annus civilis*) is also sometimes called the *annus vagus* or *Wandeljahr*, i.e., the "wandering year." Perhaps reflecting the discrepancies involved, a papyrus of about the Twentieth Dynasty says, "Winter is come in summer, the months are reversed, the hours in confusion."[16]

As for the regnal year of the king, this normally began with the New Year's day of the civil calendar, i.e., with the first day of the first month (Thoth) of the Akhet ("Inundation") season; exceptionally, however, in the Eighteenth through the Twentieth Dynasty each regnal year was counted from accession day to accession day. Thus here a factual system was used in which there was no attempt to bring the regnal year and the calendar year into harmony with each other. In contrast with the accession-year system of Mesopotamia, it was the usual custom in Egypt to count the fractional portion of a calendar year in which a king's reign began as already his first regnal year, the ensuing full calendar year as his second regnal year, and so on. In the case of a coregency, the junior member began to count his own regnal years immediately upon taking his position, and while the coregency continued, regnal years were cited in double form, so that, for example, in the Twelfth Dynasty, Year 30 of Amunemhet I corresponded with Year 10 of Sesostris I, and so on.[17]

King Lists

In addition to the list of kings and the yearly records extending into the Fifth Dynasty provided by the Palermo Stone, other lists of kings are: (1) the Table of Abydos, inscribed on the walls of the temples of Seti I and of Ramses II at Abydos in Upper Egypt; it lists in hieroglyphics the names of seventy-six of the ancestors of these Nineteenth Dynasty kings;[18] (2) the Table of Saqqara, found in the tomb of a scribe named Thunery at Saqqara; it preserves in hieroglyphics the names of about fifty earlier kings honored by Ramses II;[19] (3) the Turin Canon of Kings, a papyrus in some fifty fragments now in the Museum of Turin; it is written in hieratic script, probably dates from the reign of Ramses II, and begins the history of Egypt with the reputed rule of gods and demigods, then gives a long list of kings' names beginning with Menes.[20]

Manetho

Materials such as these preserved on the Palermo Stone and in the Abydos, Saqqara, and Turin king lists were doubtlessly available to the ancient Egyptian writer of history, Manetho. His home was in Sebennytus (ancient Tjeb-neter, modern Samannud) in the Delta, and he became high priest in Heliopolis (On), the famous city of the sun. He served under Ptolemy II Philadelphus (285-246), thus was approximately contemporary with Berossos of Babylon, who wrote under Antiochus I Soter (281-260). Like Berossos, Manetho wrote in Greek, and several works are attributed to him, of which the chief is his *Egyptian History* (Αἰγυπτιακά). Like the *Babylonian History* of Berossos, this survives only in fragments, the text of which is often corrupt.[21]

According to Eusebius (in the Armenian version of his *Chronicle*), Manetho's *Egyptian History* was composed in three books dealing with (1) the gods, (2) the demigods, the spirits of the dead, and (3) the mortal kings. The gods were (1) Hephaistos (Ptah), the god of Memphis and creator of the world, represented in art in the form of a man wrapped in a robe like a mummy and holding a tall sceptor in his two hands; (2) Helios (Re), the sun god; (3) Sosis (Shu), a human-headed god who symbolized the atmosphere and the divine, life-giving breath; (4) Chronos (Geb), also human-headed, who personified the earth, and he and his wife, the sky goddess Nut, were the parents of Osiris, Isis, Nephthys, and Seth; (5) Osiris; (6) Typhon (Seth); and (7) Horus. In the Turin Canon, the list is the same to this point, but goes on with (8) Thoth and (9) Maat, the daughter of Re and goddess of truth and justice, who wore on her head the ostrich feather, which was the weight of truth placed in the balance for weighing the heart of the deceased in the last judgment.

After the gods, Manetho lists with various individual names the demigods, or spirits of the dead, and the Turin Canon speaks of the "Followers of Horus" or "Spirits who were Followers of Horus." Since these are mentioned in these two sources before the kings of the historical dynasties are listed, they may be understood as the last predynastic kings, the same as the "Followers of Horus" in the Pyramid Texts, who, after their decease, were the "spirits" and the "souls" of Pe and of Nekhen.

In succession to the gods and the demigods, Manetho goes on to the "mortal kings" and devotes the balance of his work to these historical rulers. To each group of kings in a given time and place he gives the name of a "dynasty" and, in some instances but not all, designates one king as the son of another. In at least some cases and perhaps in many, therefore, the dynasty was a family group. In all, Manetho listed thirty such dynasties. To these was added later, perhaps from materials derived from Manetho, a thirty-first dynasty consisting of Persian kings who ruled Egypt just before the land was conquered by Alexander the Great in 332.

As to the names of the kings in the various sources and periods, in the first three dynasties the Horus name was prominent, although sometimes accompanied or replaced by the name that went with the Two Ladies (*nebty*) title, or by the name that went with the He of the Sedge and the Bee (*insibya*) title and became the throne name (*prenomen*). In the Fourth Dynasty and onward, the personal name (*nomen*) became much more important, and Manetho often prefers this.

First and Second Dynasties

The essential outline of the First and Second dynasties provided by Manetho (according to Africanus) is reproduced in Table 18.

Menes

Menes, according to Manetho the first king of the first historical dynasty, is also named (Meni) in the same position in the Table of Abydos and the Turin Canon. He was known likewise to Herodotus (Min, 2. 99), Diodorus

TABLE 18. *FIRST AND SECOND DYNASTIES ACCORDING TO MANETHO*

First Dynasty (3100–2890)

---

1. Menes the Thinite. He was carried off by a hippopotamus and perished.
2. Athothis. He built the palace at Memphis, and his anatomical works are extant, for he was a physician.
3. Kenkenes
4. Uenephes. He erected the pyramids near Kochome.
5. Usaphais
6. Miebis
7. Semempses
8. Bieneches

Second Dynasty (2890–2686)

---

1. Boethos. In his reign a chasm opened at Bubastis, and many perished.
2. Kaiechos. In his reign the bulls—Apis at Memphis and Mnevis at Heliopolis—and the Mendesian goat were worshiped as gods.
3. Binothris. In his reign it was decided that women might hold the kingly office.
4. Tlas
5. Sethenes
6. Chaires
7. Nephercheres
8. Sesochris
9. Cheneres

(Menas, 1. 45. 1), and Pliny (Menes, *Nat. Hist.* 7. 193). The Two Ladies (*nebty*) name of a king Men (the hieroglyphic sign of a draughtboard read phonetically as *mn*) also occurs on various monuments and is probably this same ruler.[22] The historical position of this king, named Men/Meni/Menes, would seem to be in close agreement with the historical position of the king named Narmer. On his own palette (according to probable interpretation), Narmer appears as the one who united the two kingdoms of Upper and Lower Egypt and perhaps even pushed as far abroad as Palestine. Here, in Manetho and other sources, Menes is the founder of the dynastic rule of the united land, and in the version of Manetho given by Eusebius and transmitted by Syncellus, it is even stated that Menes "made a foreign expedition and won renown." Since Narmer is a Horus name and Menes probably one of the other royal names, perhaps the personal name (which Manetho often prefers), the two can be one and the same king.

As to the date of the rise of the First Dynasty, and of Menes if he were indeed its founder: of three records in terms of the civil calendar of the heliacal rising of Sothis in the period of the Middle Kingdom, the earliest is on a papyrus fragment of a temple register from Lahun (a city at the entrance to the Fayum, built by Sesostris II of the Twelfth Dynasty). The date is Year 7, Month 8, Day 16, probably in the reign of Sesostris III; astronomical calculation places the point between 1876 and 1864, probably in 1872. Counting backward from this point with the aid of figures in the Turin Canon, records on the Palermo Stone, and other reckonings, we arrive at the approximate date of 3100 for the beginning of the Early Dynastic period, with the First Dynasty in 3100-2890 and the Second Dynasty in 2890-2686.[23] In comparison with Mesopotamia, this means that the Early Dynastic period in Egypt was approximately contemporary with the end of Level IV at Uruk (3100), with Jemdet Nasr and Level III at Uruk (3100-3000), and with Early Dynastic I (3000-2900) and most of Early Dynastic II (2900-2600).

First and Second Dynasty Sites

Abydos

With respect to places, Manetho describes Menes and his successors in the first two dynasties by the adjective Thinite, presumably implying a proper noun Thinis (or possibly This, as a Greek nominative) corresponding to Egyptian Tjeni and Coptic Tin, and meaning that these kings ruled in a city of this name or that they came from there ancestrally. The unlocated site of Thinis is supposed to have been in the vicinity of modern Girga (twenty kilometers north of Abydos), west of the Nile, in Upper Egyptian Nome VIII ("Great Land"), and discoveries at Abydos (Egyptian Abdu, eleven kilometers southwest of el-Balyana) confirm connections of the early dynastic kings with this area. In the ruins at Abydos are three sectors. In the northern is the temple of Khentamentiou (local wild dog god of the dead, called "First of the Westerners," later equated with Osiris), dating in its earliest form from the First Dynasty, and two mud brick "forts" of the Second Dynasty. In the central sector are necropolises, of which the outlying one in the area known as Umm el-Qaab ("mother of pots") is of chief interest at the present point. In the southern sector are a temple and cenotaph of Seti I and a temple of Ramses II.[24] Although plundered and destroyed in antiquity, there are a dozen large tombs at Umm el-Qaab, surrounded by hundreds of subsidiary graves. In general the burials are like those of the late Predynastic period but are gradually becoming more

FIGURE 58. Stela of King Djet (First Dynasty), from Abydos. The king's name, which is a serpent, is inscribed within the *serekh* frame, representing the royal palace, and this is surmounted by the falcon of the god Horus. (*Cliché des Musées Nationaux, Paris*)

elaborate. The large tombs are subterranean chambers, built of wood and protected by walls of brick, originally roofed with wood and covered above ground with a mound of sand or gravel held in place by brick walls. The subsidiary burials were in some cases apparently made at the time when the main personage was entombed; therefore, they may represent human sacrifices as in the royal tombs at Ur. On the other hand, many members of the family and the court no doubt desired to be buried in proximity to their king, perhaps to remain under his protection in the life beyond, and many of the subsidiary graves may be so accounted for. If the custom of human sacrifice did exist in the First Dynasty, there is little evidence for it in Egypt in later times.[25]

On stelas that once stood in pairs in front of each large tomb, and on objects still remaining in the tombs, were the names of ten kings and one queen. The names of the kings are normally Horus names, written in the *serekh* with the falcon on top, although occasionally the animal of Seth appears instead of the falcon of Horus. Another name is sometimes found too, introduced or followed by the *insibya* or the *nebty* title. Eight kings are thought to belong to the First Dynasty, corresponding with the like number of kings listed by Manetho in the First Dynasty, and two kings are believed to belong to the Second Dynasty, in which Manetho lists nine rulers (see Table 18). The first name is that of Narmer, already equated in probability with Menes, and there is some evidence for other equations (Aha/Athothis, Anedjib/Miebis). The queen was Merneith, and she was probably the wife of Djet. The Horus (and Seth) names are shown in Table 19 in their generally accepted sequence.[26]

Northwest of the Umm el-Qaab necropolis, adjacent to the Khentamentiou/Osiris temple, on a hill called Shunet el-Zebib, are the two aforementioned "forts." They are dated by clay jar sealings and other objects found in them to the reigns of Peribsen and Khasekhemwy (Second Dynasty). They are built of sun-dried brick on a rectangular plan, with recessed paneled exterior walls, the same architectural feature apparently represented in the palace facade in the *serekh* design and also widely found in other Egyptian buildings of this time and onward. For the appearance in Egypt at this time of monumental brick architecture, with such recesses as exterior ornamentation of the walls, it is probable that Mesopotamian influence is to be recognized.[27] These buildings were also surrounded by rows of small brick-lined graves, presumably subsidiary burials as at the royal tombs. Two groups of graves, surrounding the very scanty remains of yet other rectangular structures, belong to the reigns of Djer and Djet (First Dynasty). All of these "forts" may have been some sort of "funerary palaces," associated with memory of the spirits of the deceased kings and those buried with them.[28]

TABLE 19. FIRST AND SECOND DYNASTY KINGS AT ABYDOS (UMM EL-QAAB)

First Dynasty

---

1. Narmer
2. Aha
3. Djer
4. Djet
5. Den
6. Anedjib
7. Semerkhet
8. Qaa

Second Dynasty

Peribsen (Seth Name)
Khasekhemwy (Horus Name and Seth Name)

Memphis

Concerning the second king in his First Dynasty list, Athothis, Manetho says that he built the palace at Memphis and that he was a physician with extant anatomical works. Although Athothis may well have erected the palace at Memphis, it is the first king in the same list, Menes, who is credited, at least by the classical writers, with the original foundation of this city. Herodotus (2. 99) relates that Min, first king of Egypt, built a dam to divert the Nile and, on the site so gained, founded Memphis, dug a lake outside the city to the north and west, and, in the city, built a temple of Hephaistos (Ptah). Diodorus (1. 50. 3–5) names Ouchoreus as the founder, and, if this is a slight variant of ὀχυρός ("firm," "lasting"), it can be a translation of Menes (understood as related to μένω, "remain"). Diodorus also emphasizes the strategic location of Memphis, "at the gates of the Delta," where it controlled commerce with Upper Egypt. Strabo (17. 1. 31f.) likewise describes Memphis as near the Delta and near Babylon (the Roman encampment, the ruins of which are in Old Cairo) and speaks especially of the Memphis temples. One temple is that of the bull Apis, who is the same as Osiris; another is the Hephaisteion; and there is also a Sarapium "in a place so very sandy that dunes of sand are heaped up by the winds." Ptah (Hephaistos) was the chief god of Memphis, the Apis bull a manifestation of this god. In time, the latter was combined with Osiris to emerge as Osiris-Apis, i.e., Serapis, a great god of both the Egyptians and the Greeks in the kingdom of the Ptolemies. The Serapeum at Memphis was the burial place of the Apis bulls and the sanctuary of this deity.[29]

The original Egyptian name of Memphis was White Wall (*ineb hedj*), sometimes abbreviated to Wall or Walls, and used also as the name of Lower Egyptian Nome I, in which this was the chief residence city. In later times when the city was larger, White Wall was still the name of its third quarter, which was evidently fortified especially strongly (Thucydides 1. 104. 2). In the Sixth Dynasty, the pyramid of Pepy I at nearby Saqqara was called Mennefer-Pepy ("Pepy is enduring in beauty"). This name, abbreviated as Mennefer and pronounced successively as Menfer and Memfer, gave rise to the Greek name Memphis, which still survives as the name Memfi of a small village a few kilometers south of the pyramids of Giza.[30] As the city of the god Ptah, in the New Kingdom and later Memphis was called *Hekaptah*, the "House of the Ka of Ptah" (e.g., in the Amarna Letters, no. 84, l. 37, Hikuptah), and this name is supposed to have given rise by extension to the Greek name for the whole land Ἄιγυπτος, Latin *Aegyptus*, English *Egypt*. The Egyptians themselves, however, called their country the Black (*Kemi*), meaning the cultivable valley of the Nile in contrast to the Red (*Dsrt*), which was the desert on either side. They also called Lower Egypt *To-mehu* ("the land under water") and Upper Egypt *To-shemau* ("the land above the water") and spoke of all Egypt as the Two Lands (*Tawy*) and of Memphis as the Life of the Two Lands (*Ankh-tawy*).

The site of ancient Memphis is twenty kilometers south of Old Cairo and near the apex of the Delta, as the classical authors observed. The few remains of the city lie in a plain west of the Nile and at the foot of the Saqqara plateau. On the west is the present village of Mit Rahineh; southeast of the village is the rectangular temple precinct of Ptah with propylaea on the east, west, and south sides; to the north is a depression representing the lake mentioned by Herodotus; and yet to the north of this are vestiges of a fortress and palace and of a temple of Neith. Just outside the southern propylaea of the precinct of Ptah are two fallen colossal statues of Ramses II, to the northeast is a temple of Merneptah, to the northwest is a building where the Apis bull was probably housed, and on the south are the remains of a temple of Apis and a temple of Siamun (Twenty-first Dynasty).[31]

Saqqara

Of the First Dynasty king whom he names Uenephes, Manetho says that he built the pyramids at Kochome. Kochome is probably a Greek rendering of Egyptian "black bull" (*k'-km*) and thus contains an allusion to the sacred Apis, worshiped at Memphis and buried on the desert plateau to the west.

There on the edge of the desert is a vast burial ground, in ancient times called by the general names of the Necropolis or the West. It is now customary to designate five sectors therein, from north to south, by the names of the present villages nearest at hand: (1) Abu Roash, eight kilometers northwest of the Great Pyramids of Giza; (2) Giza; (3) Abusir; (4) Saqqara; and (5) Dahshur, ten kilometers south of Saqqara. The Saqqara area is that most directly opposite Memphis to the west. It stretches from north to south for seven kilometers, and from east to west for 500 to 1,500 meters, and contains burial monuments extending through many Egyptian dynasties and into Ptolemaic and Coptic times. Near the northern end of this area is the cemetery of the Apis bulls, known as the Serapeum, which makes it probable that Manetho's Kochome, referring to the "black bull," is to be identified with Saqqara. The latter name, however, is believed to derive from Sokar, an ancient god of the dead at home in the desert near Memphis and later associated with Ptah and Osiris (Sokar is pictured as a mummified falcon or falcon-headed man and is often shown as a falcon riding in a boat). He is mentioned frequently in the Pyramid Texts,[32] and the Feast of Sokar is listed several times on the Palermo Stone. At least as known in terms of the later calendar, this feast began on the twenty-sixth day of the fourth and last month (Choiak) of the Inundation season. Accompanied by the god, herds were driven around Memphis as if beginning the season of ploughing, and along with this agricultural ritual, the king's Circuit of the Wall took place. Mythologically speaking, the cutting up of the earth was in preparation for the interment of Osiris, which took place on the thirtieth day of the same month. Then the Djed pillar, symbolic of resurrection, was set up, and on the immediately ensuing first day of the first month (Tybi) of the season of Coming Forth, the coronation of the king was celebrated, since he was Horus succeeding his father, Osiris, on the throne. One may surmise that at least the nucleus of these ceremonies went back to the time when Memphis was first made the capital of united Egypt.

At Saqqara the Early Dynastic cemetery begins in the northern region near Abusir and extends to the neighborhood of the Step Pyramid of Djoser. Here there are some fifteen very large mastabas—flat-topped rectangular tombs (forty to sixty meters in length, fifteen to thirty meters in width), built of sun-dried mud brick, with deeply recessed exterior walls, and burial chambers at the bottom of a deep vertical shaft.[33] Interior walls are covered with painted relief scenes of everyday life. Alongside several of these tombs are brick enclosures for the boat in which the deceased would journey in the afterlife, and there are also many smaller subsidiary graves in the area. In the tombs were found the names of six of the same kings as at Abydos (Aha, Djer, Djet, Den, Anedjib, Qaa), of two queens (Merneith and Herneith), and of other personages. No royal stelas were found such as marked the individual tombs at Abydos, and these impressive tombs at Saqqara may have been only the burial places of very important officials of the time.[34]

Bubastis and Heliopolis

In his record of the Second Dynasty, Manetho mentions two more cities— Bubastis and Heliopolis. Bubastis (Tell Basta, two kilometers southeast of Zagazig) was the Egyptian Baset or Per-Baste ("House of Bastet," Hebrew Pi-beseth [Ezek. 30:17]), the city of the lion-headed (or cat-headed) goddess Bastet, and residence city of Lower Egyptian Nome XVIII ("Upper Royal Child"). Herodotus (2. 59f., 67, 137f.) identifies Bastet with Demeter, says her temple was on an island in the midst of the city, with a view down into it from all around as the surrounding city was raised. He describes her festival as the chief of all the solemn assemblies held by the Egyptians. There, too, dead cats, sacred to Bastet, were embalmed and buried. The ruins of the temple lie now in a rectangular depression, where the beds of the canals by which it was surrounded are still traceable. Best preserved is a colonnaded hall of Osorkon II (Twenty-second Dynasty), but there are also inscribed blocks with the names of other kings back to Khufu and Khafre of the Fourth Dynasty and Teti of the First Dynasty.[35]

Heliopolis, so called by the Greeks as the well-known (e.g., Herodotus 2. 59) center of the worship of the sun (Re, Atum, Khepri, Harakhte, Aten), was the Egyptian Onou (Hebrew On), the residence city of Lower Egyptian Nome XIII ("Hearty Sovereign").[36] In the Pyramid Texts, Heliopolis is mentioned frequently.[37] There we hear of a "double palace of the Souls of On" (sec. 1262b), which may mean that the ancient palace (or perhaps shrine, or both combined) of the king of Upper Egypt and that of the king of Lower Egypt were combined, either actually or ideally, in Heliopolis.[38] Another passage mentions "the two pillars of the great palace" (sec. 524d). These are designated with a word (written as a column with a tenon at the top) that is an element in the name of On. Thus, this was the "pillar city."

Strabo (17. 1. 27, 29) describes Heliopolis as greatly damaged by Cambyses and, in his own time, entirely deserted. But he also mentions the temple of Helios and the ox Mnevis in a sanctuary. He speaks, too, of the reputation of the priests of Heliopolis in ancient times for their knowledge of philosophy and astronomy and states that both Plato and Plato's comrade, the Greek astronomer Eudoxus of Cnidus, studied there. Today the site is found at Tell el-Hisn (three kilometers north of the village of Matariyah, itself ten kilometers northeast of Cairo), but of the once great and famous city, after Thebes and Memphis the third of importance in ancient Egypt, relatively little remains to be seen.

In the Twelfth Dynasty, to commemorate the thirtieth year of his reign, Sesostris I erected two obelisks in front of the temple at Heliopolis. Of these, one was destroyed in the twelfth century, but the other still stands, a shaft of red granite (twenty meters high), with an inscription calling the king "beloved of the Souls of On" and mentioning his Sed festival. In the Eighteenth Dynasty, Thutmose III erected two obelisks with pyramidions of electrum.[39] These were taken to Alexandria by Augustus in the year 22 B.C.E., then again in the nineteenth century carried away and placed, one on the Thames embankment in London, the other in Central Park, New York City. In the Nineteenth Dynasty, Seti I put up a plain obelisk, and his son, Ramses II, "beautified" it.[40] This was taken to Rome by Augustus in the year 10 B.C.E. to stand in the Circus Maximus, and it is now in the Piazza del Popolo. To the west of the still-standing obelisk of Sesostris I, some granite blocks remain from the ancient temple, with inscriptions of Ramses II; in one scene he is offering wine to Atum. Elsewhere in the vicinity, other fragments bear the cartouches of both Thutmose III and Ramses II. In the Twentieth Dynasty, Ramses III built or rebuilt the three main temples, which were dedicated to Re, Atum, and Horus, respectively. These and other benefactions were recorded at his death by his son, Ramses IV, in the lengthy Papyrus Harris I (B.M. 10053).[41] This source calls the Heliopolitan high priest the Great Seer, and mentions more than twelve thousand priests and other persons who were attached to the several temples. When the Kushite Piankhy (Twenty-fifth Dynasty) conquered Egypt, he went to Heliopolis to be recognized as king by the sun god. He records on a stela that he worshiped at the Sand Hill, beheld his father Re in the glorius house of the Benben, together with the morning bark of Re and the evening bark of Atum, then entered into the house of Atum, "following the image of his father, Atum-Khepri the Great, of Heliopolis."[42] In the Twenty-sixth Dynasty, Psamtik II erected an inscribed obelisk at Heliopolis. It was taken to Rome by Augustus at the same time as the obelisk of Seti I and put up in the Campus Martius (Pliny, *Nat. Hist.* 36. 14f., 72f.), but it is now in the Piazza di Montecitorio.

Egyptian Religious Ideas

Heliopolitan Theology

As represented in the Pyramid Texts, the solar theology of Heliopolis used several names for different aspects of the one god manifest in the sun. Re, equated with Helios in Greek and represented by the solar disk, is the most general and frequent name and can designate the sun, especially in the middle of the day. Atum is the evening sun and the sole creator, and is usually depicted as a living man, wearing the combined crowns of the Two Lands and holding in his hands the *ankh* sign ("life") and the *was* scepter ("power"). Khepri is the morning sun, thought of as a scarab-beetle and also portrayed as a man with a beetle in place of the head. Harakhte ("Horus of the Horizon," called Harmakhis by the Greeks) is the sun as connected with the sky god and falcon god Horus, and is pictured as a falcon or falcon-headed man with a sun disk on the head, flying or moving in a boat across the heavens. Hyphenated forms are Re-Atum, Atum-Khepri, and Re-Harakhte, and in other places and times Re was also correlated with other deities, e.g., with the ram-headed potter-creator Khnum (worshiped at Elephantine) as Khnum-Re, with the crocodile god Sobek (worshiped in the Fayum) as Sobek-Re, and with the Theban Amun (shown as a man or with a ram's head) as Amun-Re. There was also a word that generally signified the actual heavenly body, the orb of the sun (*itn*), usually rendered as the Aten or translated as the Sun Disk. This occurs for the first time on a scarab of Thutmose IV, where it is said that the Aten goes before the king in battle and brings the inhabitants of foreign lands under his rule.

At Heliopolis, the sun god was also considered to be incarnate in, or heralded by, the Mnevis bull. Like the Apis bull at Memphis, the Mnevis bull was also in time identified with Osiris and known as Osiris-Mnevis, but it always remained much less prominent than Osiris-Apis/Serapis. As for the Mendesian goat, mentioned by Manetho in the same passage with the Apis and Mnevis, this was a sacred ram worshiped at Mendes, the residence city of Lower Egyptian Nome XVI ("Dolphin") and center of the Twenty-ninth Dynasty.[43]

The teaching enunciated at Heliopolis emphasized the role of Atum (or Re-Atum, or Atum-Khepri) as the creator of all things. In the creation, it was quite universally believed in ancient Egypt, there first emerged out of the waters of chaos a Primeval Hill, which was probably represented in the sun temple at Heliopolis by the place called the Sand Hill or the High Sand. Associated with the hill was a stone called the Benben (*bnbn*) and with it a bird called the Ben-bird (*bnw*), originally the heron but later the phoenix (Herodotus 2. 73). Using yet another word of related etymology (*wbn*, which means both "to arise" and "to shine"), and thus allowing for a whole series of plays on words, a Pyramid Text (sec. 1652a-b) embodies this whole complex of ideas in an address to the sun god:

O   Atum-Khepri,   thou   wast   on   high   on   the   Primeval   Hill;

thou didst arise or shine forth as the Ben-bird of the Benben-
stone in the Ben-house [i.e., the Benben temple] in On [Heliopolis].[44]

Since the hieroglyphic sign for the hill looks like a step pyramid, it is
probable that the later architectural form of the step pyramid, and of the
true pyramid derived from it, were representations of the Primeval Hill
and thus stand for the creative power of the sun.[45] Likewise, the
hieroglyphic sign for the Benben-stone in the Pyramid Texts shows a
tapering, somewhat conical shape, and it is a reasonable surmise that at
Heliopolis, the "pillar city," this stone was held aloft on a pillar or column;
at any rate in the case of the obelisks, which are so prominent in all later
Egyptian temple architecture, the pyramidion at the top, often covered
with copper or gold, is called by a name (*bnbnt*) etymologically related to
Benben. Therefore, like the pyramids, the obelisk too, usually standing
appropriately in an open court and reflecting from its shining top the rays
of the sun, must have been intended to glorify the sun god and to point to
his creative power.

As the work of creation is reflected in the Pyramid Texts and narrated in
the Bremner-Rhind Papyrus (B.M. 10188, dated about 310 B.C.E., but
embodying early materials), Atum produced Shu and Tefnut, they became
the parents of Geb and Nut, and these two brought forth Osiris, Horus,
Seth, Isis, and Nephthys.[46] Shu is the god of the atmosphere (represented as
a man with a feather on his head); Tefnut is the goddess of moisture (a
woman with a solar disk on her head, often with the head of a lioness); Geb
is the earth god (a man wearing the *atef* crown, a continuation of the White
Crown of Upper Egypt, often with a small sun disk on top, and the double-
feather crown, which has an upright ostrich feather on either side, often
with the addition of a horizontal pair of ram's horns at the base); and Nut is
the sky (a woman with her feet on the eastern horizon, her body curving
above the earth to make the vault of heaven, and her arms hanging down to
the level of the setting sun).

As for the five well-known remaining deities, they were supposed to
have been born by Nut on the five successive epagomenal days of the year
(cf. Diodorus 1. 13. 4, where Nut is Rhea and Geb is Cronos). Leaving aside
Horus, more often considered to be the son of Osiris and Isis, we have nine
deities in all: (1) Atum-Re, (2) Shu and (3) Tefnut, (4) Geb and (5) Nut, (6)
Osiris and (7) Isis, and (8) Seth and (9) Nephthys, the pairs being both
brother and sister and husband and wife (cf. Diodorus 1. 27. 1). The entire
number constitutes the Great Ennead, which is in Heliopolis (Pyramid
Texts secs. 1655a–b, cf. 167a–177a, 1521).

In the Bremner-Rhind Papyrus (27. 2f.), we also learn that (in some way
not here explained) the Eye of the sun god came to be missing from his

body and that (with a play on the words *rmw* "tears" and *rmt* "men") the tears shed over this loss brought humankind into being. When the missing Eye was returned, it was angry because the sun god had made another in its place. Therefore, the sun god advanced the wrathful Eye to a place on his forehead, i.e., he made it the uraeus. "So I promoted it in my face, and when it exercised governance over this entire land, its wrath died away."

Memphite Theology

The incomplete extant text of a work known as the Memphite Theology is preserved on the Shabaka Stone in the British Museum (no. 498), an inscription copied by order of Shabaka (Twenty-fifth Dynasty) from a papyrus or leather roll in the temple of Ptah at Memphis.[47] Of his ancient source the king says, "My majesty had found it as a work of the ancestors. It had been devoured by worms. It was unknown from beginning to end." It reflects the time when Memphis became the capital of the Two Lands and Ptah, as the god of Memphis, took first place in the divine realm.

In the badly damaged first section of the work, Ptah is called Ta-Tjenen, "the Risen Land," no doubt referring to the belief that creation began with the emergence of the Primeval Hill out of the waters of chaos. Here this Risen Land is at one and the same time Ptah himself, the earth in general, and the land of Egypt in particular. In the second section, Horus and Seth were quarreling, and conflict prevailed in the universe and the state. Geb intervened and made Seth king of Upper Egypt and Horus king of Lower Egypt. Then he changed his mind and gave the whole country to Horus. Thus, the Two Lands were united in the White Wall nome.

The third and fourth sections of the document are badly damaged. After that, the fifth section sets forth at length the sole creatorship of Ptah. In explicit contrast with the manner of creation by Atum, it is here affirmed that everything came into being out of the heart and by the tongue of Ptah, for the heart is that which causes every thought to come forth, and the tongue is that which puts into effective utterance what the heart thinks. "All the divine order really came into being through what the heart thought and the tongue commanded."[48] Ptah was in fact the creator of Atum himself and of all the gods, and thus his own Ennead was completed (Ptah, Atum-Re, Shu, Geb, Osiris, Seth, Horus, Thoth, and Maat, according to Manetho and the Turin Canon). He himself also provided the images in which the deities might appear, because their statues are made of wood and stone and clay, and these materials come from the earth, which is one with Ptah himself. So Ptah, having made everything, "was satisfied" or "rested,"[49] and "all the gods as well as their *ka*'s gathered themselves to him, content and associated with the lord of the Two Lands."[50] Finally the sixth section of this document speaks of Memphis as the place were Isis and Nephthys rescued Osiris from drowning in the river. Since Osiris represents revitalizing force, this explains the position of Memphis as not only the capital but also the veritable granary of Egypt.

Osirian Theology

As has been seen, Osiris and the deities associated with him appear prominently already in the texts from which we learn of the Heliopolitan and Memphite theologies. In contrast with solar theology, the Osirian system itself had aspects of an agricultural and fertility cult, and some passages in the Pyramid Texts express hostility to this system, e.g., an utterance (secs. 1267-1273) intended to protect the tomb of the king against the "evil coming" of Osiris, Horus, Seth, Isis, Nephthys, and others. But both systems of religious thought had to do with death and the life beyond; therefore, they naturally met and mingled. Both were also concerned with the king, but in somewhat different ways; the solar cult affirmed his celestial immortality, but the Osirian system equated the deceased king with Osiris restored to life and ruling in the underworld, and recognized the living king as the son Horus. In the long run, also, the Osirian cult became more and more a religion of the people, not just of the king, and offered its promises concerning the afterlife to all.

In the Pyramid Texts (secs. 182a, 614a), Osiris is called "dweller in Andjet," a district in the eastern Delta, where his city was Djedu (probably taking its name from the Djed pillar) or Per-Osiris ("House of Osiris"), out of which the Greeks made Busiris (Arabic Abusir, on the left bank of the Nile, five kilometers south of Sebennytus). In Upper Egypt, he was also closely connected with Abydos. In the story reported by Plutarch (*Isis and Osiris*), he was treacherously slain by his brother Seth (Typhon) and cast into the sea, but his body was recovered and restored to life by his devoted wife Isis and her sister Nephthys. As the god who passed through death to live again as king and judge of the dead, he is associated with many natural phenomena that are characterized by diminishing or disappearing and then increasing and coming again, e.g., the renewed growth of vegetation, the annual inundation of the Nile, the waxing and waning of the moon, and the setting and rising of the stars, especially of the constellation Orion. Osiris's titles were Onnophris ("the one who is good") and Khentamentiou ("First of the Westerners," borrowed from the wild dog god of the desert cemeteries). In art he is a man with a long narrow beard, shrouded in a tight-fitting garment like a mummy, and wearing the White Crown of Upper Egypt. He may stand, holding crook (*heqa*), scepter (*was*), and flail (*nekhekhw*), or lie upon his bier, naked or mummified and sometimes ithyphallic.

As sister and wife of Osiris, Isis became the most notable of all the Egyptian goddesses. When she recovered the body of Osiris and roused him again, she received the seed of the deceased and became the mother of Horus, whom she reared alone in the marshes near Buto. On the monuments, she holds a papyrus scepter and wears a vulture headdress with solar disk and pair of horns, and perhaps also the hieroglyphic sign for "seat," which gives the sound of her name. Other favored representations show her with the pair of wings with which she fanned the breath of life into Osiris, or with the child Horus on her lap.

Nephthys also wears upon her head the symbol of her name, interpreted as "lady of the house" and consisting of the plan of a rectangular building with a wickerwork basket on top. In art the two sisters often stand at the head and foot of the funeral bier of Osiris. In a Pyramid Text (secs. 1280f.), they weep together for their brother and are compared with the kite, which utters shrill and plaintive cries as it circles overhead. Nephthys was sister-wife of Seth and mother of Anubis, but, according to Plutarch (*Isis and Osiris* 12. 38), who identifies Nephthys with Aphrodite, the father was Osiris rather than Seth.[51]

Horus, perhaps originally the name of several different gods but eventually intermingled beyond disentangling, was best known as the falcon god of the sky and as the son of Osiris and Isis. As the small Harpocrates ("Horus the child"), he is an infant putting his finger toward his mouth in a childish gesture. As the rightful heir to the terrestrial kingdom of his father, he grows up to fight against Seth (whose life he finally spares) and to claim that kingdom. Among many places of worship, at Edfu on the probable site of a much more ancient temple a great sanctuary of Horus was built in Ptolemaic times. It is today considered the best preserved ancient temple in the world.[52] In the story of Horus, which is inscribed on the walls, Horus is sometimes confused with and sometimes differentiated from the sun god Re or Re-Harakhte, and we hear of both Horus of Behdet and Horus the son of Osiris and Isis, these two appearing sometimes as different gods and sometimes as merged in each other.[53] Among other events narrated is one where Horus of Behdet is traveling with Re or Re-Harakhte in his bark. When enemies plot against the sun god, Horus flies up to heaven as the great Winged Disk to contend against them. When the foes descend into the water and become crocodiles and hippopotamuses, Horus assumes the form of the Winged Disk on the prow of the bark, Nekhbet and Wadjet are with him as two uraei to terrify the enemies; and Horus and his followers attack them with harpoons while Seth disappears into the ground in the form of a roaring serpent. Then Re-

Harakhte commands Thoth: "Thou shalt make this Winged Disk in every place in which I have rested, in the places of the gods in Upper Egypt, in the places of the gods in Lower Egypt." So, the comment that follows explains, "As for the Winged Disk which is on the shrines of all the gods and goddesses of Upper and Lower Egypt, and on their chapels likewise, it is Horus of Behdet."[54] Thus it is well understandable that the winged sun disk is prominent in the symbolism of the reliefs at Edfu as well as at many other places.

As for Seth, it has already been noted that his strange greyhoundlike animal is on the macehead of King Scorpion and that the Pyramid Texts place him at Ombos (Nubet) in Upper Egypt. Perhaps surprisingly in view of the character later ascribed to him, in the Pyramid Texts he is generally the friend and helper of the dead, and he and Horus are found cooperating in assisting the deceased to ascend the "ladder" (perhaps the rays of the sun) that reaches up to heaven (secs. 390a-b, 971a-e). In the Bremner-Rhind Papyrus, where the sun is opposed every night by the dragon Apophis, it is Seth who stands in the prow of the bark of Re and repulses this demon. In his most familiar role, Seth is brother and murderer of Osiris and enemy of Horus. Plutarch (*Isis and Osiris* 41, 49, 62) says that his name means "overpowering." Thus he personifies the element of conflict and strife in the universe and was naturally equated by the Greeks with Typhon, who was associated with volcanic forces and dangerous winds. Seth was also known as "lord of the foreign lands," and, as the "red god," he was the deity of the uninhabitable desert (the Red Land)—in contrast with Osiris, who was associated with the fertile valley (the Black Land).

Seth was also worshiped in Lower Egypt as well as in Upper Egypt from an early time. In the Second Dynasty Peribsen writes his name under the sign of the Seth-animal, as we have noted above, and also in his inscriptions names a city (probably the Greek Sethroe), somewhere in the northeastern Delta between Tanis and Pelusium. If Seth was at home in that region in that time, he may have been a local god of that name who was later combined with "the Ombite" of Upper Egypt.[55]

Finally, as to the cultural as well as religious level attained in the Early Dynastic period, at least in the upper levels of society, Diodorus (1. 45. 1) remarks that Menas "taught the people to worship gods and offer sacrifices, and also to supply themselves with tables and couches and to use costly bedding and, in a word, introduced luxury and an extravagant manner of life." In fact, in place of the flint implements, rough mats, pottery jars and dishes, and paste and shell ornaments of the Prehistoric and Predynastic periods, the Egyptians were now using tools and weapons of copper and bronze, fine furniture of wood and ivory, dishes of metal and stone, and jewelry of gold and semiprecious stones. From First Dynasty tombs at Abydos and Saqqara, for example, come ivory legs for beds or stools and game boards, excellently carved as the fore and hind legs of bulls; a slate dish, probably patterned after a metal prototype, with edge and compartments so made as to form the two hieroglyphic signs *ka* ("spirit") and *ankh* ("life") (these items are now in the Metropolitan Museum of Art in New York City); and armbands of gold, lapis lazuli, and turquoise, one of alternating gold and turquoise pieces that are falcon-surmounted *serekh*-frames with the name of the Horus Djer (now in the Egyptian Museum in Cairo). Other examples of Early Dynastic art are a powerful alabaster statue of a seated baboon, inscribed with the name of Narmer (in the Berlin Museum); and a seated limestone tomb statuette of a woman, probably of the Second Dynasty (in the Metropolitan Museum of Art), exhibiting like other later examples of the same sort an air of permanence and eternity.[56]

13. OLD KINGDOM, THIRD TO SIXTH DYNASTIES (2686-2181)

It was on the foundations laid in the Early Dynastic period that the splendid civilization of the Egyptian Old Kingdom or Pyramid Age arose. The date was approximately contemporary with the also remarkable Early Dynastic III (2600-2371) and Old Akkadian or Sargonic (2371-2230) as well as Gutian (2230-2112) periods in Mesopotamia.[1]

Third Dynasty

Manetho (Africanus) describes the Third Dynasty as consisting of nine Memphite kings. But he gives details only about the first two—namely, Necherophes, in whose reign the Libyans revolted against Egypt; and Tosorthros, in whose reign lived a person (whose name is missing) who is credited with the reputation of Asklepios because of medical skill, with the invention of building with hewn stone, and with giving attention to writing.

From the Turin Canon and the monuments, the Third Dynasty kings may be listed as in Table 20.[2] Of these kings, the first two are named on clay jar-stoppers from Third Dynasty mastabas at Beit Khallaf (twenty kilometers north of Abydos). In one example (from Tomb K2), the Horus name Sanakhte is accompanied by a second name, probably to be restored as [Neb]ka; the latter name is enclosed in a cartouche, the first occurrence of a cartouche in the writing of a king's name. In another inscription (from Tomb K1), the name of Neterirykhet is accompanied with that of a certain Nymaathap as "mother of the king of Upper and Lower Egypt."[3] The first three kings of the dynasty are also represented in rock carvings and inscriptions at Magharah ("Caves") in Sinai, where the Egyptians were

TABLE 20. THIRD DYNASTY (2686-2613)

Horus Name	Personal Name
Sanakhte	Nebka
Neterirykhet	Djoser
Sekhemkhet	Djoser Teti
Khaba	
	Nebkare
	Huni

probably now mining in the great cliffs for turquoise. Here each king is shown raising his mace above a kneeling Bedouin chieftain, in the fashion already familiar from the decorated tomb at Hierakonpolis and the palette of Narmer.⁴

Djoser and Imhotep

Between the names of the Third Dynasty kings in Manetho and on the monuments, the most unmistakable equation is that of Tosorthros with Neterirykhet/Djoser—the most famous king of this dynasty.⁵ The person associated with him and famed in medicine, building, and writing, whose name is missing in Manetho, was Imhotep (Imuthes in Greek), who is known from other texts. In the so-called Famine Stela (a text of the Ptolemaic period on the island of Sehel in the Nile south of Elephantine Island, at the foot of the First Cataract), we are told that there was a seven-year period in the reign of the Horus Neterirykhet, King Djoser, when the Nile failed to rise and the land was in lack of food (cf. Gen. 41:27ff.). The king appealed to Imhotep, his minister and priest (in this text called the Ibis and the Chief Lector Priest) and, being told that the Nile came from two caverns at Elephantine where Khnum was the lord of the cataract region, made a grant of land to the temple of Khnum so that the god might become favorable and the Nile rise again.⁶

In medicine Imhotep must have been preceded by others such as Athothis of the First Dynasty. But, as Manetho indicates, it was Imhotep who was identified with Asklepios, the Greek god of healing. In Oxyrhynchus Papyrus 1381 (early second century C.E.), it is related that Nectanebo II (Thirtieth Dynasty) ordered a priest Nechautis to investigate an ancient scroll in the temple of Imhotep, probably at Memphis. Nechautis proposed to publish this document in Greek, but actually went

FIGURE 59.   Head of King Djoser in the Egyptian Museum, Cairo. (*Jack Finegan*)

forward with the work only after both he and his mother were miraculously cured of illness by the god. According to the ancient document, Imhotep was worshiped as a god already by King Mencheres (i.e., Menkaure of the Fourth Dynasty). Whether or not Imhotep was actually deified this early, he certainly was later, and the same text calls him both "the son of Ptah, Imuthes" (ll. 201f.) and "Asklepios son of Hephaistos" (ll. 228f.).[7]

As to the activity of Imhotep in the field of writing, in a composition known as a Song of the Harper (preserved in Papyrus Harris 500 in the British Museum, dating around 1300, and in even earlier copies in tombs at Saqqara and Thebes), Imhotep and Hordedef (a son of Khufu of the Fourth Dynasty) are named as the two traditional wise persons of Egypt. Here the mention of them is intended to illustrate the transitoriness of life, for the text asks, "What are their places now? Their walls are broken apart, and their places are not—as though they had never been!"[8] But another papyrus of about the same date (Papyrus Chester Beatty IV, in the British Museum) is concerned to encourage diligence in study and observes that the names of learned scribes of the past are still known because of the books they wrote. Some eight persons of such reputation are then listed, and the first two names are the same as the two in the Song of the Harper. "Is there anyone here like Hordedef? Is there another like Imhotep? . . . Though they are gone and their names are forgotten, it is writing that makes them remembered."[9]

As to building, Imhotep was hardly the first to work with hewn stone, as Manetho asserts, for already in the tomb of Khasekhemwy, last king of the Second Dynasty, at Abydos the central chamber was constructed of stone.[10] But Imhotep was plainly of great fame in this regard and surely deservedly so, for he was almost certainly the architect of the Step Pyramid of Djoser. In the columned hall that gives access to the precinct of this pyramid at Saqqara was found the base of a statue of Djoser, on which was the name of Imhotep with titles including these: First One under the King, High Priest of Heliopolis, Chief Sculptor, and Chief Carpenter.[11]

The precinct of the Step Pyramid is surrounded by a wall of limestone originally 10.4 meters high and extending 277 meters from east to west and 545 meters from north to south. In the wall are thirteen simulated gates and one real gateway, which opens into a long hall of stone columns. Within the precinct are several courts and buildings. The pyramid itself may have been constructed first as a large mastaba but, in its final form, rose in steps like superimposed mastabas to a probable height of 60 meters on a base about 140 meters from east to west and 118 meters from north to south. Underneath, at the bottom of a vertical shaft nearly 28 meters deep, was the tomb chamber of the king. On the north side of the pyramid are the remains of a temple and, beside it, a small chamber (called the *serdab,* the word used for a living room in the lower level of modern homes in the Middle East), in which was found an almost life-sized, seated limestone statue of Djoser (now in the Cairo Museum). The king wears a long robe, a beard now partly broken away, and a cloth headdress (*nemes*) over a long wig. In the person of his statue, the king could look through small openings into the adjacent temple where, presumably, the rites of the funerary cult were conducted.

In general, the architecture of the buildings around the Step Pyramid reproduces the kind of structures that had for the most part previously been made in Egypt, structures of wood, reeds, and sun-dried brick. But now the building material was chiefly limestone. Since Greek architecture also put earlier forms of wooden buildings into stone, there is some feeling here

FIGURE 60. Step Pyramid at Saqqara. (*Jack Finegan*)

FIGURE 61. Papyrus Wall at the Step Pyramid. (*Jack Finegan*)

in the structures around the Step Pyramid of what is found later in classical Greek style. But such beautiful and characteristic features of the entire complex as the Cobra Wall and the Papyrus Wall are certainly typically Egyptian motifs.[12]

West of the Step Pyramid of Djoser is the Unfinished Step Pyramid, with only a lower stage and part of a second stage rising to a present height of about seven meters. Running up to it and still in place are construction ramps of rubble. In subterranean galleries and the burial chamber were found stone vases, gold bracelets, and jar-stoppers with the name of the Horus Sekhemkhet, probably the successor of Neterirykhet/Djoser.[13] At Zawiet el-Aryan (between Giza and Abusir), the name of Khaba, probably the successor of Sekhemkhet, was found on bowls in the cemetery surrounding the Layer Pyramid (where layers of masonry were added to the core of the superstructure, and the intention was probably to build a step pyramid);[14] and the name of Nebkare, probably a yet later king of the same dynasty, was found in association with another unfinished pyramid. At Medum (eighty-eight kilometers south of Cairo, on the west side of the Nile beside the Fayum), the Truncated Pyramid may have been built in its original stepped form by Huni, last king of the Third Dynasty, although its final form encased as a true pyramid is probably due to Snefru, first king of the Fourth Dynasty, whose name occurs in graffiti in buildings associated with the pyramid.[15]

Fourth Dynasty

Manetho (Africanus) says that the Fourth Dynasty consisted of eight Memphite kings, "belonging to a different line." Table 21 shows in their probable correlations the names in Manetho, the personal names in the King Lists, the Horus names on the monuments, the names in Herodotus (2. 124, 127, 129) and Diodorus (1. 63f.), and the lengths of reign in the Turin Canon or (with a question mark) as otherwise estimated. The personal name (*nomen*) is now regularly written in a cartouche and is more important than the Horus name.

Snefru

The founder of the Fourth Dynasty, Nebmaat ("master of justice") Snefru, was born in Upper Egyptian Nome XVI ("Oryx"), which, therefore, was also known as Menat-Snefru ("Nurse of Snefru"). When he came to the throne, a certain Kagemni was made overseer of the residence city and vizier, and a work known as the Instruction addressed to Kagemni (Papyrus Prisse in the Bibliothèque Nationale in Paris) describes the

TABLE 21. FOURTH DYNASTY (2613-2494)

Manetho	Personal Name	Horus Name	Herodotus	Diodorus	Years of Reign
Soris	Snefru	Nebmaat			24
Suphis (I)	Khufu	Medjedu	Cheops	Chemmis	23
	Redjedef	Kheper			8
Suphis (II)	Khafre	Userib	Chephren	Chabryes	25 (?)
	Baufre (?)				
Mencheres	Menkaure	Kaykhet	Mycerinus	Mencherinus	18 or 28
Ratoises					
Bicheris					
Sebercheres	Shepseskaf	Shepsesykhet			4
Thampthis	Dedefptah (?)				2

transition by saying that Huni, king of Upper and Lower Egypt (last king of the Third Dynasty) died and that Snefru was exalted as king in the entire land, at which time Kagemni was put in his new position.[16]

Snefru was married to a princess named Hetepheres (I), and their son was Khufu, the next king and builder of the Great Pyramid at Giza. In front of the east side of the Great Pyramid, at the bottom of a thirty-meter-deep shaft, was found an intact cache of the tomb furniture and the empty alabaster sarcophagus of Queen Hetepheres. It appears that Hetepheres was originally buried at another place, perhaps Dahshur. Then her tomb was robbed. When Khufu learned of it, he ordered everything remaining transferred to the new hiding place, perhaps without realizing that the body of his mother had already been removed from its almost intact sarcophagus.[17]

The record of five years of the reign of Snefru is preserved on the Palermo Stone. In the second of these years is recorded the "hacking up of the land of the Nubians" and the bringing of 7,000 prisoners and 200,000 cattle. There is some evidence for incursions into Nubia already by Aha in the First Dynasty and by Khasekhemwy in the Second Dynasty, but the conquest by Snefru was apparently on such a scale as to amount to the real subjugation, probably for the first time, of that land by the Egyptians.[18] In the same year is also recorded the "bringing of 40 ships filled with cedarwood," which must describe the return of a sea expedition to Lebanon, and it is of interest that well-preserved cedar beams are found in the burial chamber of Snefru's Bent Pyramid at Dahshur.[19] In the same year and the next, we also hear of the building of ships of cedarwood and of *meru*-wood (also from a coniferous tree) of a length of 100 cubits (fifty-two meters).[20] Again in the last year of Snefru, on the Palermo Stone we read that the southern and northern gates of the king's palace were made of cedarwood, for which reason the palace front was called the Double Gate.

In his foreign affairs, Snefru also went into Sinai, where at Magharah, like the kings of the Third Dynasty, he is shown in the pose of smiting a nomad, and with the inscription, "Snefru, the great god. . . . Subjugating foreign countries."[21] Although the earlier kings had probably already been seeking the turquoise of Sinai, Snefru was afterward (in Middle Kingdom inscriptions) thought of as the real founder of Egyptian mining in the area, and as a god of the region.

At Medum (fifty-eight kilometers south of Saqqara, near the Fayum), Snefru probably gave true pyramid form to what was previously a step pyramid of King Huni of the Third Dynasty. This pyramid is 144 meters square at the base, 92 meters high, and the smooth sides have an angle of 51° 52'. The upper portion of the pyramid is stripped away, however, and a tremendous pile of debris surrounds the structure at is base, leading to the plausible suggestion of a major building collapse in the final stage of attempted construction. At Dahshur (ten kilometers south of Saqqara), Snefru built two more large pyramids. Of these the southern is the Bent Pyramid. Built of local limestone with a relatively intact casing of fine white limestone, it rises on a base 189 meters square to a height of 101 meters. The lower sides slope up to a height of 49 meters at an angle of 54° 31', then change for the rest of the way to the summit to the less steep angle of 43° 21'. The Northern Pyramid (1.6 kilometers north of the Bent Pyramid) is 220 meters square at the base, 99 meters high, and has sides rising smoothly at the same angle all the way to the top, slightly more than 43°. Again it is an interesting speculation that the disaster at the Medum pyramid led to the alteration of plan to a less steep angle in the Bent Pyramid when it was still at less than half of its height, and to the adoption of the same, more moderate angle in the entire slope of the Northern Pyramid. On both pyramids at Dahshur are quarry marks with the name of Snefru, and a text of King Pepy I (Sixth Dynasty) in a temple near the northern monument speaks of the "two pyramid towns of Snefru." So both great structures are certainly to be attributed to him.[22] At the Medum pyramid and also at the Bent Pyramid at Dahshur, there is a complete pyramid complex of subsidiary structures, and the extensive layouts, the first such known, became the accepted model for later pyramid builders.[23]

Khufu

Like his father before him, Khufu, son of Snefru and Hetepheres, was born in the Oryx Nome, which then became known also as Menat-Khufwy ("Nurse of Khufu"). There the ram god Khnum was prominent, and the full name of this son was Khnum-khufwy ("Khnum protects me"), shortened to Khufwy or Khufu, and rendered as Suphis (I) by Manetho but more usually as Cheops by the Greeks. His Horus name Medjedu ("he who commands") was appropriate to a ruler who had such control over his country as to be able to accomplish the enormous work of the construction of the Great Pyramid at Giza.[24] Of him Manetho (Africanus) writes, "He reared the Great Pyramid, which Herodotus says was built by Cheops"; and Herodotus himself, who visited the monument personally (around 450), describes the Great Pyramid at some length (2. 124f.).[25]

As it now stands, the Great Pyramid measures 227 meters on each side of the base and is 137 meters high. Originally, it was 230 meters on each side and 146 meters high, and the angle of the sides was 51° 50', a slope as steep as at Medum, but with which the builders had evidently now learned to cope. The orientation of the pyramid was so precise that, according to modern measurement, the north and south sides are only 2' 28" and 1' 57" south of west, respectively, and the east and west sides 5' 30" and 2' 30" west of north. Thus, the errors were only very small fractions of one degree. The core of the pile is of large blocks of local limestone, and the outer casing was of the finer white limestone from Tura, a few blocks of which still remain at the base of the north side. In the entire pyramid are an estimated 2,300,000 blocks of stone, each weighing on the average two and one-half tons, with some reaching a maximum of fifteen tons. The entrance to the interior was near the center of the north face, about 20 meters above the ground; the lower hole, which now gives access, was broken in by the Caliph Mamun in the ninth century. Inside there are both descending and ascending passageways and several chambers, of which the highest, built entirely of granite and containing a rectangular granite sarcophagus, was presumably the final resting place of the king.

On the east was a mortuary temple, and a causeway led up from the valley temple, the latter probably now lost under the present village of Nazlet el-Samman. Three subsidiary pyramids on the east were probably for the wives of Khufu, and both to the east and west were many mastabas for the king's son and other members of the court. Five boat pits have been found: one parallel to the upper end of the causeway, two along the east side of the pyramid, and two on the south side with the boats still in them.[26]

As to the personal appearance of Khufu, no stone statues are known, only an ivory statuette from a store-chamber at Abydos.[27] Small as it is, the portrait conveys an impression of the energy and will of the builder of the greatest of the pyramids. In Magharah in Sinai, Khufu is shown in the conventional pose of the king who protects the Egyptian mines against enemy nomads.[28]

FIGURE 62. Great Pyramid at Giza from Exit of Second Pyramid (with jet aircraft overhead). (*Jack Finegan*)

FIGURE 63. Stone Blocks of the Great Pyramid. (*Jack Finegan*)

FIGURE 64. Ivory Statuette of King Khufu (Cheops), from Abydos. (*The Egypt Exploration Society, London*)

The oldest surviving son and successor of Khufu was Redjedef (also read in reverse order as Djedefre), perhaps the Ratoises of Manetho, and the first Egyptian king to call himself the "son of [the sun god] Re." His pyramid, perhaps left unfinished, is at Abu Roash (nine kilometers north of Giza), near the boundary between Lower Egyptian Nome I ("White Wall") and Nome II ("Thigh"). As it stands the pyramid is about 100 meters square at the base and 12 meters high. On the east face, several blocks of red granite are still in place, so a granite casing was at least begun.

In the debris in a large boat pit on the east side were found three handsome heads of Redjedef, broken from their statues. These are in the Cairo Museum and the Louvre.[29]

Khafre

Redjedef was succeeded by another son of Khufu, whose name may have originally been Rekhaef. But the name was later read in the reverse order and is commonly rendered as Khafre.[30] Like his predecessor, he called himself "son of Re," and he built a temple for the sun god near Bubastis in the eastern Delta.[31] For his own burial monument, he built the Second Pyramid at Giza. In its original dimensions, this spectacular monument was 215.5 meters square at the base, 143.5 meters high, and had a steep slope of 53° 10'. At the base a portion of red Aswan granite casing is preserved, and Herodotus (2. 127) evidently refers to this when he says that the lowest layer of the pyramid of Chephren is of "variegated Ethiopian stone." At the apex, for somewhat less than the upper one-fourth of the slope, the original casing is also in place, and here it is of fine white Tura limestone, now weathered to shades of brown. In the valley temple, near the village of Nazlet el-Samman, were places for twenty-three statues of the king, and in a well in the entryway was found one magnificent diorite statue, which is now in the Cairo Museum. Khafre, seated, wears the royal headcloth (*nemes*) and a ceremonial beard, and the falcon Horus stands on the back of the throne and spreads his wings protectingly at the back of the king's head.

On the northwest side of the valley temple and directly in front of the Second Pyramid is the famous monument that, among classical authors, only Pliny (*Nat. Hist.* 36. 17. 77) mentions and calls in Latin *sphinx*. The term may be derived from an Egyptian phrase meaning "living image of the god"; in Egyptian texts, the monument is most commonly called Horemakhet ("Horus in the horizon") or Hor-akhty (Harakhte, Greek Harmakhis, "Horus of the horizon"). Therefore, the Sphinx was probably seen as a representation of the sun god and/or of the king who, in death, was united with him. The monument was sculptured out of a spur of natural rock and later repaired with additional blocks of stone. It is more than twenty meters high and fifty-seven meters long and faces the rising sun. The body is that of a crouching lion; the head wears the *nemes* headdress and the uraeus of the king, and may be an idealized portrait of Khafre.[32]

Menkaure

In the fragments of the Turin Canon, there appears to be space for a king between Khafre and Menkaure. This king is perhaps to be equated with the

FIGURE 65. King Khafre (Chephren) Protected by the Horus Falcon. (*Library of the Egyptian Museum, Cairo*)

Bicheris of Manetho, although his Egyptian name is not known, and he probably held the throne for only a short time.[33] Menkaure (Mycerinus) was a son of Khafre and the builder of the Third Pyramid, the southernmost and smallest of the three main Giza pyramids.[34] This pyramid is about 108.5 meters square at the base and was originally 66.5 meters high, with an angle of the sides of 51°. The lower courses of the exterior were cased with red granite from Aswan, to which Herodotus (2. 134) again refers as "Ethiopian stone," and the upper courses were faced with white limestone from Tura.

The entire pyramid complex of Menkaure was completed only by his successor, Shepseskaf, and that for the most part in mud brick. In a storeroom of the valley temple, several beautiful sculptures in slate were found; these are now in the Cairo Museum and the Boston Museum of Fine

FIGURE 66.   Sphinx and Second Pyramid at Giza. (*Jack Finegan*)

FIGURE 67.   Valley Temple of the Second Pyramid. (*Jack Finegan*)

FIGURE 68. King Menkaure (Mycerinus) in the Egyptian Museum, Cairo. (*Jack Finegan*)

Arts. In a sculpture twice life size, Menkaure stands with his chief queen, Khamerernebty II, oldest daughter of Khafre, the queen with her arm around the king. In several triadic groups, the king is associated with Hathor, identified by her usual symbol of horns and disk on her head, and with another goddess, identified as one of the nome deities by the nome sign on her head. In some examples, the two goddesses stand respectfully slightly behind the king but reach around him from either side to clasp his arms in the affectionate gesture that otherwise, in Egyptian sculpture, is used among members of the same family.[35]

For himself, Shepseskaf built a sort of rectangular mastaba with a rounded top and vertical ends, which is in the southern area at Saqqara and is known as the Mastabat Faraun.[36] Finally, according to Manetho, the Fourth Dynasty came to an end with Thampthis. As a guess, he might correspond with an otherwise unrecorded ruler with the Egyptian name Dedefptah.[37]

FIGURE 69.   Triad of Mycerinus with Hathor and the Goddess of Upper Egyptian
Nome XVII ("Dog"). (*Library of the Egyptian Museum, Cairo*)

Fifth Dynasty

For the Fifth Dynasty, Manetho (Africanus) lists nine names and says that these kings were from Elephantine, a statement that is not otherwise supported and may be incorrect. The names are for the most part recognizable as equivalent to the names known from the king lists and the monuments, as shown in Table 22, where known or probable lengths of reign are also given from the king lists.

In the Westcar Papyrus (probably written in the Hyksos period, now in the Berlin Museum), a popular story is related about the origin of the line of kings of the Fifth Dynasty. Long before, a magician named Djedi prophesied to King Khufu that his dynasty would endure only through the reigns of his son Khafre and his grandson Menkaure (evidently only the names of the builders of the major pyramids were spoken of in popular tradition) and would be superseded by a new house of kings to be born as the offspring of the sun god Re and of the wife, named Ruddedet, of a priest of Re serving in one of the sanctuaries of the sun in Lower Egypt. In due time, it came to pass that Ruddedet brought forth three sons, and Isis and Nephthys, together with Meskhenet (the goddess of birth), Heket (a frog goddess associated with birth), and Khnum (the potter-creator), assisted at the triple birth. As each infant is born, Isis makes a pronouncement that involves a word play on the child's name, and we recognize that the triplets are none other then Userkaf, Sahure, and Neferirkare Kakai, the first three kings of the Fifth Dynasty.[38]

That the three kings are represented as sons of the sun god undoubtedly reflects the fact that they were devotees of Re and that the priesthood of Heliopolis and the cult of the sun were increasingly important in this time. The adoption of the title "son of Re" by Redjedef and Khafre in the preceding dynasty already signaled a tendency in this direction. The same designation now becomes a regular part of the royal titulary, and many of the kings bear names compounded with the name of Re. Also on the Palermo Stone as far as it extends with Fifth Dynasty kings, namely, with Userkaf, Sahure, and Neferirkare Kakai, the records are largely concerning gifts of land and offerings to Re, to Hathor who was closely associated with the sun god, and to "the spirits of Heliopolis." Also in connection with each of these kings, there is mention of a sun temple and, in one case, of a sun boat.

In general, as far as the monuments are concerned, the kings of the Fifth Dynasty build much smaller pyramids than their predecessors in the Fourth Dynasty, and most of these are found in the vicinity of Abusir, between Saqqara and Giza. Most distinctively, however, they also built sun temples,

TABLE 22. FIFTH DYNASTY (2492–2345)

Manetho	Personal Name	Horus Name	Years of Reign
1. Usercheres	Userkaf	Irmaat	7
2. Sephres	Sahure	Nebkhau	14
3. Nephercheres	Neferirkare Kakai	Userkhau	10
4. Sisires	Shepseskare Isi	Sekhemkhau	7
5. Cheres	Neferefre	Neferkhau	7 (?)
6. Rathures	Neuserre	Isetibtowy	[3] 1
7. Mencheres	·Menkauhor Akauhor	Menkhau	8
8. Tancheres	Djedkare Isesi	Djedkhau	39 (?)
9. Onnus	Unis	Wadjtowy	30

and from the Palermo Stone and other texts, the names of at least six of these are known. Two have been identified and excavated—one built by Userkaf at Abusir, and the other constucted by Neuserre at Abu Gurob. Judging from these examples, the general layout of a sun temple was similar to the pyramid complex, with a valley temple and a causeway leading up to the west, but, in place of the pyramid itself, there was a mastabalike platform, surmounted by a large pillar or obelisk, standing under the open sky. Since the High Sand and the Benben stone were chief features of the great, but long lost, temple of the sun at Heliopolis, it may be supposed that the architectural features of the platform and the obelisk in the Fifth Dynasty sun temples were in imitation of what existed at Heliopolis.[39]

The relatively modest pyramid complex of Userkaf lies about 200 meters beyond the northeast corner of the enclosure of the Step Pyramid of Djoser at Saqqara. From it have come a great granite head of Userkaf, three times life size, the earliest example (except for the Sphinx) of sculpture in excess of life size, and fragments of fine reliefs showing water birds in the papyrus marshes and other scenes. All of these materials are now in the Cairo Museum. The sun temple of Userkaf at Abusir is very badly destroyed but reveals four building periods from Userkaf to Neuserre and onward. Several small limestone tablets record work on the structure; in one a hieroglyphic sign for the sun temple appears to show a platform with an obelisk on top, agreeing with our understanding of the essential features of a sun temple.[40] On the Palermo Stone, Userkaf is credited with the donation of "two oxen, two geese every day" for his sun temple.

Of the next five kings of the Fifth Dynasty, four built pyramids at Abusir, namely, Sahure, Neferirkare, Neferefre, and Neuserre. The best preserved of these pyramids is that of Sahure.[41] Painted reliefs from the mortuary temple on the east side of the pyramid, now in the Cairo Museum, show the king's victory over Asiatics and Libyans, and the departure and return, with cargo and a number of Asiatics, of twelve seagoing ships, probably the record of an expedition to Lebanon, such as was already made by Snefru. On the Palermo Stone, in the reign of Sahure there is mention of commerce with the malachite country, presumably Sinai,[42] and with Punt, probably the Somali coast, from which latter place myrrh and electrum were brought back.

Neferirkare built the largest of the four pyramids at Abusir; Neferefre did little more than begin his; and Neuserre erected one that was relatively small but constructed a large and impressive sun temple at Abu Gurob (1.5 kilometers north of Abusir). In the sun temple of Neuserre, fine painted reliefs were placed inside the corridor around the court and inside the ramp at the base of the obelisk. The scenes in the ramp depict the Sed festival; those in the corridor show the seasons of the Egyptian year. A woman carrying upon her head a basin with stalks of lotus is identified in the accompanying inscription as Akhet ("Inundation"); a second figure was probably included originally to represent Peroyet ("Coming Forth"); a man carrying upon his head a sheaf of ripened grain is identified as Shomu ("Deficiency"). Smaller figures represent the nomes of Upper and Lower Egypt and also provide personifications of the Nile, of grain, and of other subjects. All of these are bringing their offerings to Re, and the entire composition is an orderly presentation of the agricultural year and an expression of praise to the sun, upon which the Two Lands depended for their prosperity.[43]

Of Menkauhor, relatively few monuments are known. Djedkare is represented by his unexcavated pyramid on the edge of the southern plateau at Saqqara, known from its commanding position as el-Shawwaf ("the Sentinel"), and his name also occurs in a fragmentary administrative papyrus found in the funerary temple of Neferirkare at Abusir. The fragments, presumably dating from his time near the end of the Fifth Dynasty, are judged the oldest known written papyri.[44] Under Djedkare, there served as vizier Ptahhotep, who was considered one of the famous wise men of ancient Egypt along with Imhotep, Hordedef, and others. His mastaba is at Saqqara, and the Papyrus Prisse of the Bibliothèque Nationale, which contains the Instruction addressed to Kagemni, preserves a similar work in his name (probably also a pseudepigraph of the Sixth Dynasty) known as the Instruction of Ptahhotep.[45]

FIGURE 70. Pyramid Texts in the Pyramid of Unis. (*Library of the Egyptian Museum, Cairo*)

Pyramid Texts

The pyramid of Unis, last king of the Fifth Dynasty, is southwest of the Step Pyramid of Djoser at Saqqara and thus diagonally opposite across that precinct from the pyramid of Userkaf, the founder of the dynasty. Inside, the walls of the inner end of the main passageway, of the antechamber, and of the burial chamber contain hieroglyphic texts, cut into the stone and filled with blue paint, the earliest example of the Pyramid Texts. In all, such texts are found also in the pyramids of the Sixth Dynasty kings Teti, Pepy I, Merenre I, and Pepy II, and in the pyramids of two queens (each named Meryreankhnes) of Pepy I and of three queens (Neith, Iput II, Udjebten) of Pepy II; in the pyramid of the Eighth Dynasty king Kakare Ibi (all of the foregoing at Saqqara); and in the tomb of a Twelfth Dynasty official named Senusertankh at Lisht. Although first available in these pyramids, the texts plainly include materials of earlier date and in various passages reflect conditions in earlier dynasties and even prior to the union

TABLE 23. SIXTH DYNASTY (2345–2181)

Manetho	Personal Name	Horus Name	Years of Reign
Othoes	Teti	Seheteptowy	12
	Userkare		1 (?)
Phios (I)	Meryre Pepy I	Merytowy	49
Methusuphis	Merenre Antiemsaf I	Ankhkhau	14
Phiops (II)	Neferkare Pepy II	Netjerkhau	94 (?)[a]
Menthesuphis	Merenre Antiemsaf II		1
	Netjerykare		
Nitocris	Nitokerti		2 (?)

a This figure for the long reign of Pepy II is based upon the statement of Manetho (Africanus) that he began to reign at the age of six and continued until his hundredth year. In a small alabaster statue in the Brooklyn Museum, he is seated on the lap of his mother, already wearing the royal headcloth *(nemes)* with the uraeus on his forehead.

of Upper and Lower Egypt. Thus, they have already been cited many times in our foregoing account. Before they were inscribed in the pyramids, the same materials were no doubt written on papyrus and potsherds and, before that, even transmitted orally; even as found in the pyramids, they represent the oldest phase of the Egyptian language now available.[46] In form, the utterances are often couplets, displaying parallelism in the arrangement of words and thought. In main theme, they are concerned with the resurrection of the deceased king. They envision and intend to assist his awakening in the tomb, his ascent to the sky, and his acceptance among the immortal gods. In modified form, materials from the Pyramid Texts are also found in the Coffin Texts of the Middle Kingdom and in the Book of the Dead in the New Kingdom, where the concept of the resurrection applies to others as well as the king.

Sixth Dynasty

For the Sixth Dynasty, Manetho (Africanus) gives six names and says that these rulers were Memphites. The names and the names from the king lists and monuments, with probable years of reign, are shown in Table 23.

Of these kings, Teti, Pepy I, Merenre I, and Pepy II have already been mentioned as the builders of Saqqara pyramids in which Pyramid Texts are found, and the pyramid of Pepy I (Mennefer-Pepy) also gave its name to Memphis. In general, these pyramids, and the adjacent pyramids of some of

FIGURE 71.   Mastabas of Mereruka (left) and Kagemni (right) at Saqqara. (*Jack Finegan*)

FIGURE 72.   Tomb Statue of Mereruka. (*Jack Finegan*)

FIGURE 73. Fishing, Relief in the Mastaba of Kagemni. (*Robert H. Schertle*)

FIGURE 74. Birds, Relief in the Mastaba of Kagemni. (*Robert H. Schertle*)

FIGURE 75. Donkeys at the Watering Trough, Relief in the Mastaba of Ti. (*Library of the Egyptian Museum, Cairo*)

their queens, followed the traditions of their predecessors, but were less well constructed and are now in relatively poor condition. At the same time, the mastabas of other officials are more numerous and finer than before. The centralized power of the king is apparently weakening, and the importance of the nobles is increasing.

A notable mastaba is that of Mereruka, vizier of King Teti, in which are fine painted reliefs with scenes of animals, hunting, offering bearers, and other subjects.[47] A remarkable official was Uni, who served under Teti, Pepy I, and Merenre I. The inscription on a large block of limestone from his mastaba at Abydos, now in the Cairo Museum, narrates his career.[48] Under Teti, he held only minor office. Under Pepy I, he was made a judge and conducted an inquiry against one of the king's wives. He also led five military campaigns against "the Asiatics and Sand-Dwellers." The "sand-dwellers" might be taken for nomads in Sinai, but the text mentions their orchards, vineyards, and buildings; therefore, it may be that Uni's army went into Palestine. On one of the campaigns, the troops were transported by ship, and Uni "made a landing at the rear of the heights of the mountain range on the north of the land of the Sand-Dwellers," perhaps a reference to the Carmel range. Under Merenre I, Uni became governor of the South.[49] In this position he went to Elephantine and on to Ibhet (in the Abu Simbel area) to obtain a sarcophagus and granite for his queen's pyramid. He also went to the alabaster quarry at Hatnub (in the eastern desert twenty kilometers from the later Akhetaten) to bring back an offering table of that substance. For transport of these materials, he used cargo boats, one built of acacia wood and sixty cubits in length. On another expedition, he dug five canals for navigation at the First Cataract. Merenre I himself also came to the First Cataract, received the homage of Nubian chiefs, and left inscriptions on the rocks to commemorate the event.[50]

Nitocris

Nitokerti ("Neith is excellent"), called Nitocris in Greek, was perhaps the sister, queen, and widow of Merenre Antiemsaf II, and was herself the last ruler of the Sixth Dynasty. Manetho, who said that it was determined already in the reign of Binothris (Second Dynasty) that women might hold the kingly office, describes Nitocris as noble, lovely, and of fair complexion. Herodotus (2. 100) speaks of only one Egyptian woman as ruler, namely, Nitocris, and states that she took the throne after her brother, who was the preceding king, was slain. She took revenge, he relates, by inviting those involved in the murder to a feast in a spacious underground chamber and then turning the river in upon them by a secret channel. This situation, where a woman takes the throne after the death of her brother as preceding king and then herself ends the dynasty, is paralleled at the end of the Twelfth Dynasty, when a woman named Sobknofru succeeds the preceding king, who was probably her brother or half-brother, Amunemhet IV, and herself ends the line and the period.

14. FIRST INTERMEDIATE PERIOD, SEVENTH TO TENTH DYNASTIES (2181-2040)

MIDDLE BRONZE AGE (2100-1500)

As the centralized authority of the Old Kingdom broke down, there ensued a time of disintegration and chaos when weak kings were unable to maintain a strong government, and many local rulers divided the country among themselves. This time, commonly called the First Intermediate period and considered as comprising Manetho's Seventh to Tenth dynasties, falls mostly within the New Sumerian period (2112-2004) in Mesopotamian history.[1]

Seventh and Eighth Dynasties

The kings of the Seventh and Eighth dynasties continued to rule at Memphis, Manetho (Africanus) says, but the ephemeral character of their sway is suggested by his statements about the duration of their reigns, namely, that in the Seventh Dynasty, seventy kings ruled for seventy days, and in the Eighth Dynasty twenty-seven kings reigned for 146 years. Although Manetho gives no individual names, other sources permit listing at least nine kings in the Seventh Dynasty within the dates 2181-2173, and six kings in the Eighth Dynasty within the years 2173-2160. Of these kings, one in the Eighth Dynasty, Kakare Ibi, is of interest for a small pyramid he built in the southern area at Saqarra. In it are Pyramid Texts, the latest of these texts thus far found in a royal tomb.

Ninth and Tenth Dynasties

Herakleopolis

The Ninth and Tenth Dynasties are located by Manetho at Herakleopolis.

The Egyptian name of the place was Nennesu, rendered as Hanes in Isa. 30:4 and preserved in Arabic as Ehnasiya el-Medina (130 kilometers south of Cairo, 16 kilometers west of Beni Souef, on the east bank of the Bahr Yusef, the main canal leading into the Fayum). The local deity was the ram-headed god Herishef, whom the Greeks called Harsaphes and identified with Herakles; hence the name Herakleopolis (Herakleopolis Magna in distinction from Herakleopolis Parva in the eastern Delta).[2] A tree of unidentified species called the Nar tree was honored here, too, and this was the residence city of Upper Egyptian Nome XX ("Upper Nar Tree").

Although Manetho (Africanus) says that there were nineteen kings in the Ninth Dynasty and a like number in the Tenth Dynasty, he gives only one personal name, that of the first king of the Ninth Dynasty, whom he called Achthoes. This corresponds with an Egyptian name that occurs frequently on Ninth and Tenth Dynasty monuments and is transcribed as Khety or Akhtoy.[3] The king of this name is probably the one who took the throne name of Meryibre, these two names being found together on several small monuments and on the rocks at the First Cataract.[4] Of Achthoes, Manetho says that he behaved more cruelly than his predecessors, wrought woes for the people of all Egypt, and afterward was smitten with madness and killed by a crocodile. Back of the reference to his cruelty may be the fact that he conquered some of the other local rulers and made his city of Herakleopolis the capital of a kingdom of some extent. From other sources, the names of half a dozen more kings of the two dynasties are known, two of them with this same personal name, so that in addition to Meryibre Akhtoy I, we know Nebkaure Akhtoy II in the Ninth Dynasty and Wahkare Akhtoy III in the Tenth Dynasty. Approximate dates are Ninth Dynasty 2160–2130 and Tenth Dynasty 2130–2040.

Although historical sources are relatively scanty in the First Intermediate period, several literary works appear to reflect the conditions of the time or explicitly place their account under a king of the period. In its extant form, the Admonitions of Ipuwer, on a fragmentary papyrus in the Leiden Museum (no. 344 recto), was probably copied in the Nineteenth or Twentieth Dynasty, but it gives a vivid picture of the kind of social disturbances and upset conditions that ensued upon the fall of the Old Kingdom. Government has broken down, law and order have collapsed, society is turned upside down, marauders are abroad, royal tombs are robbed, travelers are unsafe, suicide is frequent, commerce with Byblos is interrupted, and foreigners, probably Asiatics, have penetrated the Delta.[5]

In the Dispute between a Man and His Soul (Papyrus Berlin 3024), a person finds life so painful that he longs for death, although it is not entirely clear whether he is actually thinking of suicide (as was practiced by many in this time, according to the Admonitions of Ipuwer) or only hoping that a natural decease and traditional burial will come soon. At any event, death looks to him like homecoming after long absence in warfare or captivity.[6]

Three Berlin papyri (3023, 3025, 10499) and one in the British Museum (10274), probably copied in the Middle Kingdom, tell the story of the Eloquent Peasant, who, having been robbed and beaten by a subordinate official of the government, pleads so effectively for justice that he attracts the attention of King Nebkaure Akhtoy II (Ninth Dynasty) and obtains redress.[7]

Merikare

The Instruction addressed to King Merikare (Papyrus Leningrad 1116A in the Hermitage Museum and two other fragmentary papyri) may have been copied in the Eighteenth Dynasty, but the king appears as a member of the House of Akhtoy (ll. 142f.).[8] After the pattern of the Instruction of Prince Hordedef, the Instruction addressed to Kagemni, and the Instruction of Ptahhotep, the contents are the advice given to the king by his father—the father perhaps being Wahkare Akhtoy III (Tenth Dynasty) and Merikare belonging in the latter part of that dynasty. Along with advice on good behavior in personal life and kingly duties, the text touches upon wider affairs of state (ll. 69ff.). Merikare should not deal in an evil way with the Southland. This must refer to Thebes, from which center the Eleventh Dynasty would soon overcome and put an end to the Herakleopolitan kingdom. For the time being, however, granite was coming to Merikare "unhindered," so there was presently no unfriendly obstruction between Herakleopolis and the Aswan quarries. In the Northland, the situation was more perilous. The western region was, indeed, pacified, but the east abounded in bowmen, namely, Asiatics driven by harsh conditions in their homeland to press into the fertile Delta. Against this threat, there was a defensive district that stretched from Hebenu (in Middle Egypt)[9] to the Ways of Horus and to Kemwey (in the northeastern Delta).[10] In Djed-isut (Memphis), there are also ten thousand men and officials who have been in it since the time of the Residence (i.e., since the time when Memphis was the center or rule), and they form a "dike" (probably metaphorically rather than literally) as far as Herakleopolis. To further strengthen the Delta against the Asiatics, Merikare is himself urged to build buildings in the Northland.

Reference in this text to Djed-isut and the Residence (Memphis) makes it not unlikely that the Ninth and Tenth Dynasty kings, although ruling at

Herakleopolis, continued to place their tombs in the vicinity of Memphis as so many of the earlier kings had done. Merikare himself is instructed (ll. 78f.) not to despoil another's monument nor to build his tomb "out of ruins," but to quarry stone at Tura and construct his own tomb. Although his burial monument has not been discovered, it is well possible that he had a pyramid at Saqqara not far from the pyramid of Teti, for in the vicinity, sarcophagi identify their owners as priests in the service not only of that pyramid but also of the pyramid of Merikare, called the Abodes of Merikare Are Flourishing. The instruction also advises Merikare that the way to build a worthy "house of the West," i.e., a tomb, is by being upright in character and doing justice (ll. 127f.). It is taught that a person survives (literally, remains over) after death, that in the Beyond one's deeds are placed beside one in a heap (presumably to be weighed and judged), and that existence there is forever (ll. 55f.). As for the deity—presumably the sun god Re—he is regularly referred to in an almost monotheistic way simply as "god," and it is said that he hears when people weep, for he "knows every name" (ll. 131ff.)l.[11]

15. MIDDLE KINGDOM, ELEVENTH AND TWELFTH DYNASTIES (2133-1786)

Thebes

The Eleventh and Twelfth dynasties are described by Manetho as consisting respectively of sixteen and of seven kings of Diospolis. Diospolis was the "city of Zeus,"[1] corresponding with the local designation Newt-Amun, "city of Amun," also shortened to Newt, "city."[2] The Egyptian name of the city was the same as that of the nome (Upper Egyptian Nome IV) of which it was the capital, namely, Was ("Scepter," also Waset, Wese), and the Greeks called the city Thebes.[3] The site of the ancient city is on the Nile 674 kilometers south of Cairo, where there is a relatively wide plain beside the river on the east side and, on the other side, a line of very steep hills and cliffs on the edge of the western desert. The modern towns adjacent to the enormous ruins on the east side of the river have the Arabic names of Luxor ("castles") and Karnak ("fortress").[4]

As to the several deities worshiped at Thebes, the falcon-headed war god Montu was prominent from an early time in the whole region and had temples at the early towns of Hermonthis (now Erment) on the west bank of the Nile and Tod and Medamud on the east side, as well as later at Thebes. Although he was the patron of several kings of the Twelfth Dynasty, he was in the long run quite eclipsed by Amun. The origins of Amun are obscure, but he seems at least to have taken on some of the traits of Min, the deity worshiped at Koptos (forty-one kilometers north of Thebes) as the protector of the caravan route through Wadi Hammamat to the Red Sea. Min was represented as an ithyphallic figure, with two tall plumes on his head, and Amun was also pictured as a man with the same high feathers on his head, although he was sometimes given a ram's head.[5] The names of the two were also sometimes hyphenated as Min-Amun. A local goddess named Mut became the wife of Amun, and their son was

Khonsu, a moon god shown with a falcon's head surmounted by a lunar disk. The name of Amun, read as *amen,* meant "hidden" or "secret"; thus, he could be considered the Hidden One.[6] He was especially manifest in the wind and also in the breath and thus was the mysterious source of all life. Since the Thebans like all the Egyptians also recognized the life-giving power of the sun, it was not difficult to go on to the thought that the creative power of air and of sun were one and the same and thus to arrive at an identification of Amun and Re, in the form of Amun-Re, as the universal god. In one salutation, he is still immanent in nature: "Thine is what thou seest as light, what thou passest through as wind";[7] yet in another, he is the only creator of all that is:

Thou art the sole one, who made [all] that is,
[The] solitary sole [one], who made what exists. . . .
Who spends the night wakeful, while all are asleep,
Seeking benefit for his creatures. . . .
Hail to thee, Amun-Re, Lord of the Thrones of the Two Lands
Whose city loves his rising![8]

As to the place of Thebes in Egyptian history, in the Old Kingdom it was still only an insignificant village with some tombs in the western hills. But in the time now under consideration, local rulers were making it into an important center, and the Eleventh and Twelfth dynasties, which ruled here, may be considered as comprising the Middle Kingdom. The approximate dates are Eleventh Dynasty 2133-1991 and Twelfth Dynasty 1991-1786, and fall mostly within the New Sumerian (2112-2004) and Isin-Larsa (2025-1763) periods in Mesopotamia.[9]

Eleventh Dynasty

Manetho gives no names of individual kings in the Eleventh Dynasty, but from the king lists and monuments, at least those are known who are shown in Table 24. Although the sequential listing in Manetho would make it appear that the Eleventh Dynasty at Thebes followed the Tenth at Herakleopolis, the two were in fact probably largely contemporary. In the Instruction addressed to King Merikare, this ruler at Herakleopolis was concerned for his relations with the Southland, which was evidently the region of Thebes; and there is other evidence that Wahkare Akhtoy III, probably third king of the Tenth Dynasty and predecessor of Merikare, fought with the Horus Wahankh, King Inyotef II, third king of the Eleventh Dynasty.[10]

TABLE 24. ELEVENTH DYNASTY (2133-1991)

Horus Name	Throne and Personal Names
Tepia	Mentuhotep I
Sehertowy	Inyotef I
Wahankh	Inyotef II
Nakhtnebtepnefer	Inyotef III
Sankhibtowy	
Netjeryhedjet	Nebhepetre Mentuhotep II
Smatowy	
Sankhtowyef	Sankhkare Mentuhotep III
Nebtowy	Nebtowyre Mentuhotep IV

In what were thus evidently long struggles between the Eleventh Dynasty Theban rulers and the Tenth Dynasty kings at Herakleopolis a climax was reached—from the point of view of the former, a successful climax—with the long reign of Mentuhotep ("Montu is content") II (2060-2010). The progression of affairs is reflected in the succession of Horus names he assumed. He began to rule under the Horus name Sankhibtowy ("He who makes the heart of the Two Lands to live") and used this title, as inscriptions show, at least until his fourteenth year (2047). Sometime thereafter, he took the Horus name Netjeryhedjet ("Lord of the White Crown"), evidently showing his by then well-established rule of all of Upper Egypt. Finally, in the thirty-ninth year of his reign (2022), his Horus name appears as Smatowy ("Uniter of the Two Lands"). Between hi fourteenth and thirty-ninth years, therefore, say perhaps around 2040, he must have won a complete victory over Herakleopolis, i.e., probably over an unknown, but immediate, successor of King Merikare; he thus accomplished the reunion of Upper and Lower Egypt. Reflecting this accomplishment, an inscription in the Ramesseum in Western Thebes lists together the names of Menes of the First Dynasty, Nebhepetre (throne name of Mentuhotep II) of the Eleventh Dynasty, and Ahmose of the Eighteenth Dynasty, thus plainly intending to indicate the founders of what we know as the Old, Middle, and New kingdoms.[11]

In Western Thebes at Deir el-Bahri ("Northern [Coptic] Monastery"), Mentuhotep II erected an extraordinary monument, his tomb-temple called Glorious Are the Abodes of Nebhepetre. From the edge of cultivation beside the river, a causeway 1,200 meters long, walled but unroofed, led up to the site at the foot of the great cliffs on the edge of the

FIGURE 76. Head of a King, Wearing the Red Crown of Lower Egypt, with the Hand of a Divinity behind Him, from the Temple of Mentuhotep II at Deir el–Bahri. (*The Metropolitan Museum of Art, Gift of the Egyptian Exploration Fund, and Rogers Rund, 1906*)

desert. In a rectangular courtyard, a terraced ramp, with rows of trees on either side, approached a large platform surmounted by a pyramid or an altar, behind which was the mortuary temple partly cut back into the cliffs. From the courtyard, an underground passageway led down to a chamber under the platform in which was found a seated statue (now in the Cairo Museum) of the king, clothed in the short, close-fitting garment worn in the Sed festival. Another subterranean passageway led down from the courtyard behind the platform for more than 150 meters to the granite-lined burial chamber, deep under the cliffs. Here there was an alabaster sarcophagus, but when it was found in modern times, it was empty.[12]

Of the last king of the Eleventh Dynasty, Mentuhotep IV, the most

FIGURE 77. Funerary Boat of Meketre, Chancellor of Mentuhotep III, Modeled after Ancient Papyrus Boats, Preparing to Set Sail Upstream. (*The Metropolitan Museum of Art, Photograph by Egyptian Expedition*)

extensive record is on the rock walls of Wadi Hammamat, between Koptos and the Red Sea. Here, in a relief, the king offers a libation before the god Min of Koptos, the protector of the route, and a lengthy text records an expedition of ten thousand men sent to cut from the mountain the stone blocks that would form the sarcophagus of the king. The lid alone was about two meters wide, four meters long, and one meter thick, and it required three thousand sailors from the Delta to haul the sarcophagus overland to the Nile and then bring it up the river to Thebes. The leader of the expedition was an official named Amunemhet, called "the supervisor of everything in this whole land."[13]

Twelfth Dynasty

At this point, after Manetho (Africanus) has said that the Eleventh Dynasty consisted of sixteen kings of Diospolis (Thebes), he adds that "in succession to these, Ammenemes ruled for sixteen years," then goes on to list the seven kings who, he says, comprised the Twelfth Dynasty. From the similarity of the names and the eminence of the Amunemhet in the Wadi

TABLE 25. *TWELFTH DYNASTY (1991–1786)*

Manetho	Horus Name	Throne and Personal Names	Date
1. Ammenemes	Wehemmeswet	Sehetepibre Amunemhet I	1991–1962
2. Sesonchosis		Kheperkare Sesostris I	1971–1928
3. Ammanemes		Nubkaure Amunemhet II	1929–1895
4. Sesostris		Khakheperre Sesostris II	1897–1878
5. Lachares		Khakaure Sesostris III	1878–1843
6. Ameres		Nymare Amunemhet III	1842–1797
7. Ammenemes		Makherure Amunemhet IV	1798–1790
8. Scemiophris, his sister		Sobkkare Sobknofru	1789–1786

Hammamat inscription just cited, there can be little doubt that he and this Ammenemes (in Manetho's Greek) are one and the same person. Thus, it appears that after his service under Mentuhotep IV, he himself founded a new dynasty of Theban kings. Including him as the first, there were then eight kings in this Twelfth Dynasty, with probable reigns and overlapping coregencies, as listed in Table 25.

Amunemhet I

Upon his accession, Amunemhet I took the throne name Sehetepibre and also the Horus name Wehemmeswet. The latter name means "Repeater of Births," probably derived metaphorically from the monthly rebirth of the moon, and thus probably expressing the king's thought of himself as one who was beginning a new era. Likewise a text known as the Prophecy of Neferti (Papyrus Leningrad 1116B, copied in the Eighteenth Dynasty) was probably written in his reign or soon afterward and celebrates him as the great deliverer of Egypt.[14] Neferti, the prophet in this account and a priest of the cat goddess Bastet, declares to King Snefru (Fourth Dynasty) that the Old Kingdom will fall and chaos will ensue but that, in due time, order will be restored by a king whom he calls Ameny (a short form of Amunemhet). Neferti describes him as born in Upper Egypt, the son of a woman of To-Seti. The picture of the land in confusion is much like that in the Admonitions of Ipuwer: "Asiatics have come down into Egypt. . . . The land is diminished, but its administrators are many; bare, but its taxes are great." The future king, however, will be triumphant: "The Asiatics will fall to his sword, and the Libyans will fall to his flame. . . . There will be built the Wall of the Ruler . . . and the Asiatics will not be permitted to come down into Egypt that they might beg for water in the customary manner, in order to let their beasts drink. And justice will come into its place, while wrongdoing is driven out."

Itj-towy. The name To-Seti, used by Neferti for the place of origin of Amunemhet's mother, designated Upper Egyptian Nome I, of which Elephantine was the residence city. This name was also used for the Nile valley yet farther south to a limit that cannot be determined precisely, i.e., it included at least a part of Lower Nubia. Therefore, Amunemhet I may have been partly of Nubian descent. From his name, which means "Amun is in front," he was devoted to the god of Thebes, and Manetho calls him and his successors Diospolite kings. In spite of these Upper Egyptian and Theban associations, Amunemhet I evidently thought it desirable to rule from a point more strategically located with respect to the two parts of the entire country, and he built a new fortified palace city near the border between Upper and Lower Egypt. The name of this city was Itj-towy, signifying that "he has taken possession of the Two Lands." As various texts show, from his time onward throughout all of the Twelfth and Thirteenth dynasties and even later, Itj-towy was known as the Residence City and Thebes as the Southern City.[15]

The pyramid complex of Amunemhet I is a few hundred meters west of the present village of el-Lisht (near the Fayum, thirty kilometers south of Memphis and fifty kilometers south of Old Cairo), and the Residence City was no doubt in the immediate vicinity. This location was in Upper Egyptian Nome XXI ("Lower Palm Tree"), with Nome XXII ("Knives") across the Nile to the east, and the line of demarcation between these last nomes of Upper Egypt and the first nome of Lower Egypt ("White Wall") must have been not far north of Lisht. The exact line was marked by a locality appropriately known as Balance of the Two Lands, but just where this was is not known.

Story of Sinuhe. A work known as the Instruction of King Amunemhet I for His Son Sesostris I (in a number of copies dating from the Eighteenth to the Twentieth dynasties) purports to be the advice given by the aged king to his son, and may have been composed under Sesostris I.[16] It warns against having intimates and advises being on guard even when asleep, "because no one has adherents in the day of distress." Amunemhet I himself "gave to the destitute and brought up the orphan," but "it was he who ate my food that raised troops against me, and he to whom I had given my hands that created terror thereby." Then the text tells of a real or attempted assassination of the king when, in the evening after supper, he was lying upon his bed to rest.

The death of Amunemhet I, whether it transpired under these circumstances or later, provides the starting point for the Story of Sinuhe (in many texts from the late Twelfth to the Twenty-first Dynasty).[17] The

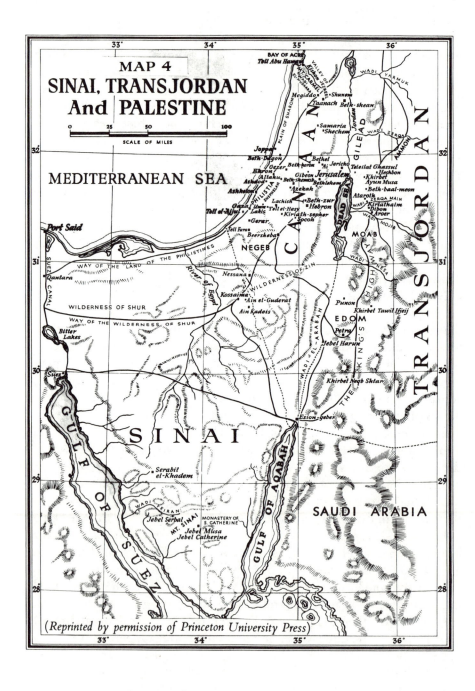

MAP 4
SINAI, TRANSJORDAN
And PALESTINE

SCALE OF MILES
0   25   50   100

MEDITERRANEAN SEA

(Reprinted by permission of Princeton University Press)

date was Year 30, Month 3 of Akhet ("Inundation"), Day 7, and "Sehetepibre was taken up to heaven and united with the sun disk."[18] The news was brought to Sesostris I, the king's oldest son and coregent, in the west where he was returning with an army from a campaign in Libya, and "the falcon flew away with his attendants, without letting his army know it," i.e., he evidently felt impelled to get back to the capital immediately to make his position secure before the word of his father's death became widely known. But other royal children with the army were also given the news, and Sinuhe, who was in the company, heard one of them speaking in such a way that he himself was terrified. "I being in the nearness of a conspiracy," says Sinuhe, and goes on to tell of his precipitate flight from Egypt, i.e., he was evidently involved in knowledge of some kind of royal conspiracy and thereby placed in such jeopardy that he felt he must flee the country forthwith. He avoided the Residence City, found a barge without a rudder and was blown by the wind across the Nile on it, proceeded east of the quarries in the height of the Mistress of the Red Mountain (Gebel el-Ahmar, "Red Mountain," northeast of Cairo, where red quartzite and brown sandstone were quarried), and reached the Wall of the Ruler. This wall, mentioned in the Prophecy of Neferti in connection with Amunemhet I, was evidently a line of fortresses along the northeastern frontier, and the present text describes it as "made to oppose the Asiatics and to crush the Sand-Crossers." Slipping past the wall by night, Sinuhe halted in the day at the Island of Kemwer ("Great Black," the Bitter Lakes),[19] where he almost perished of thirst but was rescued by an Asiatic sheikh. From there he set off for Byblos, approached Qedem (the East in general), and came to Upper Retenu (Palestine/Syria).[20] Here Sinuhe prospered and also became a commander of troops, either under or against personages who have the title "chief of foreign lands" (*heqa khoswe,* the term from which the name Hyksos was derived). In old age, he was invited by the king of Egypt to return to his homeland. So Sinuhe went back, no longer by surreptitious travel as long before, but apparently down the main coastal road, for he arrived openly and proudly at the Ways of Horus and proceeded by boat to the Residence City. There a pyramid-tomb of stone was constructed for him, and he remained under the favor of the king until the day of mooring had come, i.e., until the day of death.

Sesostris I

In foreign affairs, the Story of Sinuhe shows that there were independent rulers in Palestine/Syria at this time, with travel between there and Egypt freely possible. In Nubia, Sesostris I, himself perhaps partly of Nubian descent through his mother from To-Seti, extended Egyptian power. On a

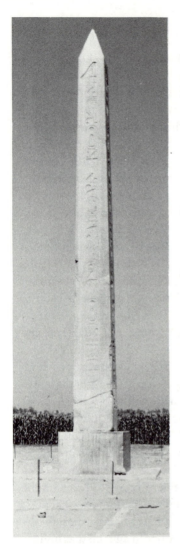
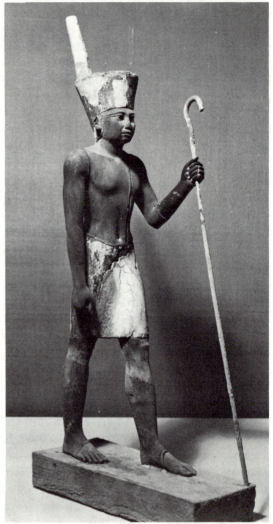

Left—FIGURE 78. Obelisk of Sesostris I at Heliopolis. *(Jack Finegan) Right—*
FIGURE 79. Wooden Statuette of Sesostris I Wearing the Red Crown of Lower
Egypt, from Lisht. (*The Museum of Art, Museum Excavations, 1913-14; Rogers Fund*
supplemented by Contribution of Edward S. Harkness)

stela dated in his eighteenth year and found at Buhen at the Second
Cataract, opposite the mouth of Wadi Halfa, the king stands before the
war god Montu and says, "I have brought for thee all countries which are
in Nubia," and ten captives symbolize ten localities that have been
conquered.[21] To solidify the conquest and establish a strong barrier against
the presumably formidable power of Kush to the south, Sesostris I built a
powerful fort at Buhen and probably at least began the whole series of

similar Egyptian forts (perhaps only completed by his successors, especially Sesostris III), which extends from below Elephantine to where the river narrows at Semna (sixty kilometers above Wadi Halfa).[22]

In Egypt monuments of Sesostris I are found all the way from Aswan to Alexandria. At Heliopolis, he rebuilt the sun temple, beginning in his third year (reckoned from his coregency with Amunemhet I). In his thirtieth year, to celebrate his Sed festival, he erected the two obelisks, already mentioned, of which one still stands.[23] On the occasion of the same jubilee festival, he constructed at Karnak a large limestone building, of which several pillars have been found, one with a standing statue of the king garbed as Osiris, nearly five meters high; and a beautiful small chapel, later torn down by Amunhotep III (Eighteenth Dynasty) and used for building material in the Third Pylon of the Karnak temple, but now recovered and rebuilt as the White Chapel (in the grounds on the north side of the First Court of the Karnak temple). At Lisht, he built his pyramid, two kilometers south of his father's,[24] and in the Fayum itself he was active as well.[25]

No doubt because of the impressive accomplishments of Sesostris I in both conquest and construction, and also because of similar achievements by the two other kings of the same name in the Twelfth Dynasty, especially Sesostris III, the name of Sesostris became in Greek tradition that of a legendary figure, hardly identifiable with any particular king and about whom many fabulous stories were told (e.g., by Herodotus 2. 102-110). As Diodorus (1. 53-58) tells the same stories, he calls the king Sesoosis, which may come from Sesesu, a short form of the name of Ramses II (Nineteenth Dynasty). Pliny (*Nat. Hist.* 36. 14. 71) also calls Ramses II Sesothis. Thus, traits from that famous king may have been woven into the same legend, too.

Unlike Amunemhet I and Sesostris I, who built their pyramids at Lisht, later rulers of the dynasty chose other places of burial. Amunemhet II, Sesostris III, and Amunemhet III built their pyramids at Dahshur; Sesostris II built a town and erected his pyramid at el-Lahun (Egyptian Rohenty, perhaps "mouth of the crocodile" or "gate of the canal"); and Amunemhet III built a pyramid (additional to his at Dahshur) at Hawara, both Lahun and Hawara being on the northeastern side of the Bahr Yusef, where this canal passes Gurob (on the southwestern side) and enters the Fayum through a break in the desert hills. A princess named Sithathoryunet, daughter of Sesostris II, sister of Sesostris III, and aunt of Amunemhet III, was buried in a tomb at Lahun near the pyramid of her father; her jewelry, recovered from that tomb, is the "treasure of Lahun," now largely in the Metropolitan Museum of Art. Other ladies of the royal court were buried at Dahshur near the pyramid of Sesostris III, and the "treasure of

FIGURE 80.   Relief Panel from the Throne of Sesostris I, Symbolizing the Unification of Upper and Lower Eygpt, from Tanis. (*Hirmer Fotoarchiv, Munich*)

Dahshur," similar to that of Lahun, is now for the most part in the Egyptian Museum in Cairo. The excellence of taste, beauty of design, and microscopic accuracy of execution in the materials witness to the elegance and refinement attained in the upper level of society in the Twelfth Dynasty.

Tomb of Khnumhotep II

In the Eleventh and up to the middle of the Twelfth Dynasty, at least some of the provincial governors in Egypt also had tombs of considerable magnificence. Of these there is a row of thirty-nine, cut in the cliffs on the east bank of the Nile at Beni Hasan (275 kilometers above Cairo). The site was in Upper Egyptian Nome XVI ("Oryx"), which included both banks of the Nile between the "Hare" nome (XV) on the south and the "Black Dog"nome (XVII) on the north. The tombs are generally entered through open porticoes with channeled columns left to support the architraves. Twelve tombs contain mural paintings on plaster-covered surfaces. In the tomb of Khnumhotep II, who served under Amunemhet II and Sesostris II, the paintings include a visit to Khnumhotep by thirty-seven Asiatic traders, whose leader is identified as a "chief of foreign lands" (the same title as in the Story of Sinuhe).[26]

Sesostris III and Amunemhet III

Sesostris III, great grandson of Sesostris I, emulated and surpassed the accomplishments of his illustrious ancestor. In the regions to the south of Egypt, he made a canal at the First Cataract—perhaps redigging or extending what Uni had already done under Merenre I (Sixth Dynasty)—and left a record on the rocks of the Island of Sehel.[27] He conducted several Nubian campaigns and set up stelas at Semna, above Wadi Halfa, to mark the southern boundary of his power.[28] He did more work on the series of forts begun by Sesostris I, and at least three of the forts at Semna are connected with his name.[29]

In the north, a small mortuary statue, found at Abydos, of Khusobek, a military commander under Sesostris III, mentions the taking of a place called Sekmem (perhaps biblical Shechem) in Retenu, the only record of any invasion of that region by any king of the Middle Kingdom.[30] There was evidently continued travel and trade, however, and the fragment of a statuette of an Egyptian named Thuthotep, found at Megiddo, probably belongs to this period.[31]

In Sinai, many inscriptions of Sesostris III and Amunemhet III show that Egyptian mining operations, begun long before, were continued and intensified, but no longer on the warlike basis represented in the Third and

Fourth Dynasty carvings in which the Egyptian king is characteristically shown in the act of smiting a kneeling Bedouin. Rather, among the personnel of the Egyptian expeditions are "Asiatics," "men of Retenu," and individuals with probably Semitic names, who may have been present to assist with relations with the inhabitants of the country;[32] and Amunemhet III is portrayed, not striking an enemy, but standing peacefully before Hathor (in Serabit el-Khadem) or before both Thoth and Hathor (in Wadi Magharah).[33]

Other Egyptian deities worshiped in Sinai, according to an inscription of the time of Amunemhet III in Wadi Magharah, were "Soped, lord of the east," and "Snefru, lord of the highlands."[34] In a Twelfth Dynasty inscription at Serabit el-Khadem, an Egyptian mining official credits Snefru with being his great predecessor in such work, and it was no doubt because Snefru was remembered as the most famous founder of mining in Sinai that he became a god of the area.[35] Soped appears already in the Pyramid Texts (secs. 148d, 456b-c, 480d, 994c-e) as a warlike god of the East and a smiter of the Asiatics. His center was at Per-Soped ("House of Soped"), residence city of Lower Egyptian Nome XX ("Soped"), at the site now called Saft el-Hineh (ten kilometers southeast of modern Zagazig), opposite the entrance to Wadi Tumilat, the chief route of travel eastward from the Delta to Sinai.[36]

Water Enterprises of Twelfth Dynasty Kings

Tale of the Shipwrecked Sailor. From the same ancient Egyptian inscriptions in Sinai, it is learned that the great mining expeditions of the Twelfth Dynasty utilized sea transportation on a relatively large scale, and a landing point from which to proceed inland to Wadi Magharah and Serabit el-Khadem may have been at Ras Abu Zenima on the east shore of the Gulf of Suez.[37] A Middle Kingdom papyrus in Moscow (Papyrus Leningrad 1115) contains a story within a story of a sea voyage "to the mining country"—in a very large ship (length 120 cubits, beam 40 cubits) with a crew of 120 weather-wise sailors—a voyage that ended in shipwreck on an island held by the ruler of Punt. By Punt, which they also called the Terraces of Incense, the Egyptians generally meant the African coast at the lower end of the Red Sea (modern Eritrea and Somaliland) and perhaps the land across on the other side of the straits of Bab el-Mandeb as well, so the island was probably somewhere in the Red Sea between Somaliland and South Arabia.[38] Eventually another ship came, and the shipwrecked narrator sailed northward to the Residence City, arriving there in two months.

Nile-Red Sea Canal. The story of the shipwrecked sailor appears to presuppose that it was possible for large Egyptian ships to pass back and forth between the Residence City (presumably Itj-towy near Lisht) and the Lower Red Sea, i.e., that there was water connection between the Nile and the Red Sea. In the Eighteenth Dynasty, moreover, Queen Hatshepsut sent a sea expedition to Punt, and the pictures in her temple at Deir el-Bahri appear to show the same ships both in the Red Sea and on the Nile.[39] Actually, originally the Red Sea probably extended northward where the Bitter Lakes and Lake Timsah remain, and a branch of the Nile probably flowed eastward through Wadi Tumilat to connect therewith. Passage this way may have been possible, at least in inundation time, in the Old Kingdom.[40] As the Red Sea receded, the water connection may have been deepened by hand, and eventually a genuine navigable canal was cut. Aristotle (*Meteorologica* 1. 14. 352b), Strabo (17. 1. 25-27), and Pliny (*Nat. Hist.* 6. 33. 165) attribute the origin of the canal to Sesostris, which presumably means that it was in existence in the Middle Kingdom.[41] Diodorus (1. 33. 9, 12) and Herodotus (2. 158; cf. 4. 39) say that the canal was begun by Necho II and continued or completed by Darius I, the latter obviously concerned for a route to Persia.[42] If the canal existed previously, these two would have done works of restoration. Of the work of Darius I, there is confirmation in the finding of the remnants of at least five granite stelas with his inscriptions along the route of the canal.[43]

The channel of the ancient canal is still traceable in parts of Wadi Tumilat, and its direction was frequently followed by the engineers of the freshwater canal constructed when the Suez Canal was built (1859-1869). In modern aerial photographs, soil markings have been discerned, and on the ground, artificial embankments have been found, which are believed to show that a portion of the ancient canal also came south from Pelusium some sixteen kilometers, veered across what is now the Suez Canal near Qantarah, and connected with the other portion of the canal near Ismailia. This would have provided connection from the Mediterranean at the Pelusiac mouth of the Nile, and the width of the canal—the embankments of which are as much as sixty meters apart—would also have made an effective barrier against potential invaders from the East.[44]

Fayum

Water-related enterprises of the Twelfth Dynasty kings are well attested for the Fayum. Until that time, much of the area had remained a swampland, used for fishing, hunting, and catching of waterfowl, and in the White Chapel of Sesostris I at Karnak, it is called a *pehou*, i.e., a reservoir that received the waters of the inundation and made them available for agriculture when there was need. Sesostris II probably made the first effort to control the waters with a dam near his pyramid at Lahun, and Amunemhet III probably reclaimed a considerable area for agriculture with a long curving dam that ran from Itsa (nine kilometers southwest of Medinet el-Fayum) and through Biahmu (seven kilometers north of Medinet el-Fayum). At Biahmu are the remains of two colossal, seated monolithic quartzite statues of Amunemhet III, elevated on limestone pedestals originally eighteen meters high and themselves originally eighteen meters in height. Located seventy meters apart on an east-west line corresponding to the course of the sun and, at that time, probably standing on the embankment of the lake and looking out over it to the north, these colossi were like the statues at the entrance to a temple. In similar way, they provided a monumental entrance to the fertile area behind them, which Amunemhet III had recovered from the waters. In its own way, this bringing out from the lake of dry land corresponded with the symbolic idea of the Fayum lake as the primeval ocean (personified as the god Nun), out of which all being originated. Likewise, from this entrance one went on the shortest and most direct way to Shedet (Krokodilopolis), which stood in local mythology for the place where the Primeval Hill first arose out of the waters and the sun god took his stand. In the classical tradition, it was Amunemhet III who was most of all remembered for his irrigation works in the Fayum, and down into Roman times he was himself the protective deity of the region.[45]

In connection with the Lake of Moeris, as they call the lake in the Fayum, Herodotus (2. 148), Diodorus (1. 61. 2), and Strabo (17. 1. 37) describe a "labyrinth," which was a maze of chambers both above ground and under the ground. They associate it with the burial place of an Egyptian king named Marrus, Mendes, or Imandes, by whom is probably meant Nymare Amunemhet III. In fact, to the south of the pyramid of this king at Hawara is a vast area of concrete foundation beds and limestone and granite chips, among which have been found the names of Amunemhet III and of his daughter Sobknofru. The extent of the structure that must have stood here was something like 305 by 244 meters, enough to hold the temples of Luxor and Karnak. This enormous building was probably the famous Labyrinth. In purpose, it may have served such functions as a palace, a mortuary temple, and a center of administration.[46]

Texts of the Middle Kingdom

Coffin Texts

Many works of literature belong to the Middle Kingdom, as has already been noted in citing the composition of didactic works (Prophecies of Neferti, Instruction of King Amunemhet I for His Son Sesostris I) and the copying (Eloquent Peasant) or composition (Story of Sinuhe, Tale of the Shipwrecked Sailor) of narratives and tales. In the area of religious compositions, the Coffin Texts must now be added. The Pyramid Texts of the Fifth and Sixth dynasties described a future life to be enjoyed by the king, but it does not have to be supposed that the lesser officials and ordinary people had no thought of afterlife; on the contrary, the grouping of many other graves around the royal pyramids was probably due, at least in part, to the desire of those buried there to enjoy the same destination in the hereafter as the king. Now, in the Middle Kingdom, many funerary texts are written in ink in cursive hieroglyphics on the interior surfaces of the large, rectangular wooden coffins, which are characteristic of the time and which generally belonged to persons other than the kings. In these materials there are excerpts from the Pyramid Texts, a whole new series of magical spells and incantations, and early forms of the writings that are found afterward on papyri of the New Kingdom and later periods, where they comprise the so-called Book of the Dead. Broadly speaking, all of these materials are Coffin Texts; strictly speaking, the term designates only the spells that are found neither in the Pyramid Texts nor in the Book of the Dead, but are peculiar to the coffins of the Eleventh and Twelfth Dynasties.[47]

As compared with the Pyramid Texts, in the new materials in the coffins and also on many tomb stelas of the Middle Kingdom, Osiris and the other figures associated with him are of increased prominence, doubtless because they were more attractive and comprehensible to the common people than the more sophisticated doctrines of the Heliopolitan and Memphite theologies. Thus for every person, the hope might be cherished of identification with Osiris after death, and therewith of justification and resurrection like his in the hereafter.[48] For example, in two coffins from Bersheh (Cairo no. 28083m; Berlin no. 14385) there are two versions of the Book of the Two Ways.[49] The "two ways" are those that lead by water and by land, respectively, to Rosetau, the gate to the underworld. They are not only named in the text but also pictured on the floors of the two coffins, where, along with boats and fantastic animals, a large rectangle contains two wavy lines, the upper blue, and the lower black. As the deceased journeys along, he reenacts various mythological experiences associated with Osiris and Re, and if he escapes the dangers that beset him and chooses the right way among the many that lead nowhere, he will come at last to the gates of the horizon and be with Osiris and Re forever.

Execration Texts

Although Amunemhet I built the Wall of the Ruler on the northeastern frontier to oppose the Asiatics, in the latter part of this dynasty and in the next, Asiatics were increasingly prominent in relation with Egypt and in possible threat to Egypt. Evidence that they were, upon occasion, seen as enemies appears in the so-called Execration Texts. These texts are written in hieratic script on small pottery bowls from Thebes (in the Berlin Museum) and on clay figurines of bound captives (in the Cairo and Brussels museums). The date is judged to be in the time of Sesostris III at the earliest and on into the Second Intermediate period. The inscriptions give the names of actual or potential enemies, and the objects were broken in what was evidently a magical ritual intended to break the power of these enemies, then buried near the tombs of the dead they were expected to protect. The inimical forces against which such protection was sought include general evils such as "every evil word . . . every evil plot"; Egyptians, both those named individually and also "all . . . who may rebel, who may plot, who may fight"; and foreigners, including Nubians, Libyans, and Asiatics. The Asiatics are the most prominent of all, and we hear of many places and rulers in Palestine and Syria.[50]

16. SECOND INTERMEDIATE PERIOD, THIRTEENTH TO SEVENTEENTH DYNASTIES (1786-1552)

According to Manetho (Africanus), the Thirteenth Dynasty was Theban, the Fourteenth Xoite, the Fifteenth and Sixteenth Hyksos, and the Seventeenth Hyksos and Theban. Together they comprise a Second Intermediate period, the dates of which fall in the Old Babylonian period (2004-1595) in Mesopotamian history.[1]

Thirteenth Dynasty

Manetho says that the Thirteenth Dynasty (1786-1633) consisted of sixty Diospolite (Theban) kings. The names of almost this many kings are in fact listed in the Turin Canon at this point (cols. 6-8), and not a few of these names appear on contemporary monuments. Although of Theban origin according to Manetho, the Thirteenth Dynasty kings maintained their center of government at Memphis and Itj-towy,[2] and at least some continued the tradition of building pyramids in this area.[3]

Three of the apparently most important kings of the dynasty, who are also relatively well known from contemporary monuments, are listed in the Turin Canon (col. 6, nos. 24, 25, 27), with lengths of reign preserved for the first two, namely, Sekhemre Sobkhotep III (three years), Khasekhemre Neferhotep I (eleven years), and Khaneferre Sobkhotep IV. In the reign of Sobkhotep III, there is evidence of the increasing presence of Asiatics in Egypt. A fragmentary papyrus in the Brooklyn Museum (no. 35.1446) is dated in the first and second years of this king and contains a list of ninety-five servants in the household of an Egyptian official in Upper Egypt. Of these nearly half are identified as Asiatics, either male or female, and nearly thirty names are plainly Semitic.[4] In the case of Neferhotep I, a stela from Abydos has to do with his making of a cult image of Osiris,[5] and the king's name is also on a fragmentary bas-relief found at Byblos on which a prince of Byblos named Yantin declares that he worships Re every day.[6] As for Khaneferre Sobkhotep IV, his throne name may be recognized in the King Chenephres of whom Artapanus (an Alexandrian Jew of the second century B.C.E.) says that he was "king of the regions above Memphis (for there were at that time many kings in Egypt)," a statement that well describes the situation at this time.[7]

Yet farther along in this portion of the Turin Canon (col. 7, no. 13) is a name preserved only in its last element, . . . *mose.* This may be the end of the personal name of Djedneferre Dudimose I, whose name occurs on a stela found at a temple of Hathor at Gebelein (on the west bank of the Nile thirty kilometers above Luxor). He, in turn, may possibly be the Tutimaios in whose reign, according to Manetho (Eusebius), the Hyksos mastered Egypt. A Djedhotepre Dudimose (II) is also named on a stela from Edfu, and he and a few remaining kings of the Thirteenth Dynasty would then have ruled only as vassals of the Hyksos.[8]

Fourteenth Dynasty

According to Manetho, the Fourteenth Dynasty (1786-1603) consisted of seventy-six Xoite kings. Strabo (17.1.19) says that Xois was in the interior of Lower Egypt, above the Sebennytic and Phatnitic mouths of the Nile, and was both an island and a city. Thus, it was evidently in the swamps of the central Delta. It is probably to be identified with the present Sakha, near Kafr esh-Sheikh (thirty-five kilometers north of Tanta), and belonged to Lower Egyptian Nome VI ("Mountain Bull"). Several names in the Turin Canon (cols. 8-9) may probably be assigned to the Fourteenth Dynasty, but scarcely any monuments of these rulers are known. In its own evidently restricted area, this dynasty was probably for the most part parallel with the Thirteenth Dynasty.

Already in the Twelfth and Thirteenth dynasties, indications have appeared of danger to Egypt from Asiatics and of the presence of Asiatics in the country. In the Turin Canon, where at least some kings in cols. 8-9 may belong to the Fourteenth Dynasty, the last name in col. 9 (no. 30) is Bebnem, probably an Asiatic name, suggesting that an Asiatic ruler has established himself somewhere in the Delta. Furthermore—if a particular fragment is correctly restored and placed—there were probably several more names, of which one survives, Khamudy, and then a summary statement (col. 10, no. 21): "[Total, Chiefs of] Foreign Lands, 6, they made 108 years."[9] Here is the same title found already in the Story of Sinuhe and in the Tomb of Khnumhotep II as the designation of chieftains of Palestine and Syria. At this point in the Turin Canon, some of these have evidently established themselves as rulers in Egypt.

Fifteenth Dynasty

These "chiefs of foreign lands" seem to have established themselves as rulers in Egypt at the beginning of the Fifteenth Dynasty, when, Manetho says, Egypt was taken by Shepherd Kings. In the version of Africanus, Manetho states that there were six of these foreign kings from Phoenicia, who seized Memphis, founded a town in the Sethroite nome, and subdued Egypt. Their names were Saites, Bnon, Pachnan, Staan, Archles, and Aphophis. In the version of Josephus, the invaders came in the reign of Tutimaios and are called Hyksos (explained as meaning "king-shepherds," and reportedly said by some to be Arabs). The names of the rulers are Salitis, Bnon, Apachnan, Apophis, Iannas, and Assis; the first of these, Salitis, rebuilt a city called Avaris.

The designation of these people as Hyksos is probably actually derived from *heqa khoswe,* the term meaning "chief of foreign lands," and applies properly to the rulers themselves. Other Egyptian references to these people usually describe them as Asiatics. They were probably predominantly Semitic Amorites (Canaanites), who are well known in Syria and Palestine in the Middle Bronze II period (1800–1500).[10] To what extent the Hyksos first made a peaceful penetration of Egypt is not entirely clear; at any rate, they were later remembered with hostility, and Manetho pictures them as taking Egypt by violence.[11] The number of six kings is the same as in the Turin Canon at this point. Manetho gives them a total of 284 years, the Turin Canon only 108. The smaller figure is no doubt the more likely, with dates for the Hyksos period perhaps 1660–1552.[12] A possible correlation of the names of the kings in the two versions of Manetho, respectively, and in other texts and monuments is given in Table 26.

A late genealogical table of priests of Memphis gives not only their ancestors but also the kings under whom these forebears served; in the time of the Hyksos, it names as a generation apart King Shalek, then Apophis, and then Ahmose (who expelled the Hyksos), and is ground for equating Shalek with Saites/Salitis.[13] Seuserenre Khyan, probably to be identified with Staan (Iannas), is named on cylinder seals and scarabs in Egypt and Palestine, and on other objects found as far away as Baghdad, Boghazköy, and Knossos, presumably attesting widespread Egyptian trade in the Hyksos period.[14] Aphophis (Apophis) appears in different texts with three different throne names (Aqenenre, Auserre, Nebkhepeshre), probably assumed at successive points during his long reign. This reign was the longest of any of the six kings (sixty-one years in Manetho, forty in the Turin Canon [col. 10, no. 19], the latter figure the more likely), and Apophis probably stands at the high point of the Hyksos period.[15] The name

TABLE 26. HYKSOS KINGS

Manetho		Other Texts and Monuments
Africanus	*Josephus*	
1. Saites	Salitis	Shalek
2. Bnon	Bnon	
3. Pachnan	Apachnan	
4. Staan	Iannas	Seuserenre Khyan
		Aqenenre
5. Aphophis	Apophis	Auserre $\Big\}$ Apophis
		Nebkhepeshre
6. Archles	Assis	Asehre Khamudy

of Asehre has been found on a small obelisk at Tanis (San el-Hagar) and probably corresponds with Archles (Assis); as probably the last king of the series, he should also correspond with the Khamudy who is the last "chief of foreign lands" in the Turin Canon.[16]

Of the foregoing names, at least Khyan and Khamudy are probably Semitic, as are the names of a ruler Jaqob-har and a chancellor Hur of the same period, found on scarabs throughout Egypt and in Lower Nubia. The distribution of the scarabs also suggests the widespread commercial and perhaps diplomatic relations of the Hyksos.[17] The Semitic background of the Hyksos is probably also recognizable in their devotion to the Egyptian god Seth (or Sutekh, as his name was by then mostly pronounced). For example, Papyrus Sallier I (a late Nineteenth Dynasty hieratic text in the British Museum, no. 10185) states that King Apophis "would not serve any god who was in the land [except] Seth" and that he built a temple and made daily sacrifices to Seth.[18] Conducive to this special regard for Seth were no doubt the title of Seth as "lord of the foreign lands" and his violent character, in which he was similar to the Semitic storm god Baal. At the same time, Apophis himself bears an Egyptian name, and his several throne names are all compounded with the name of the Egyptian sun god Re, as were many other Hyksos names. Thus, we gather that the Hyksos respected and adopted much in Egyptian religion and civilization. Their own contributions to Egypt probably included the horse-drawn chariot, widely known in western Asia in this time and probably introduced into Egypt in the Hyksos period; the compound bow; and new types of bronze daggers, swords, and other weapons. On the ebony and electrum handle of a bronze dagger found at Saqarra in the coffin of a man with the Semitic name of Abd, there appears not only the name of Nebkhepeshre Apophis but also the figure of another man with a probably Semitic name, Nehmen;

and the latter is shown with weapons of the type just mentioned. Thus, we may have an actual contemporary picture of one of the warriors of the Hyksos.[19]

Sixteenth and Seventeenth (Hyksos) Dynasties

Manetho (Africanus) speaks of the Sixteenth Dynasty as consisting of thirty-two Shepherd Kings and of the Seventeenth Dynasty as including both forty-three Shepherd Kings and also forty-three kings of Diospolis (Thebes). These large numbers of additional Shepherd Kings can probably be accounted for as the chiefs of smaller groups, largely contemporary with, and more or less under the leadership of, the central line of more prominent Fifteenth Dynasty Hyksos kings. As for the numerous kings of Thebes, who are also placed in the Seventeenth Dynasty, they were apparently a line of local rulers in Upper Egypt, who maintained or began resistance to the Hyksos and prepared the way for the Eighteenth Dynasty, which accomplished the full expulsion of the Hyksos.

Avaris

Manetho says (according to Africanus) that the Shepherd Kings founded a town in the Sethroite nome or (according to Josephus) that their first ruler, Salitis, found a city in the Saite nome, very favorably situated on the east of the Bubastite branch of the Nile, called Avaris and dedicated from earliest times to Typhon (i.e., the Egyptian god Seth), and rebuilt and fortified this place to guard his frontier. The name Avaris is to be recognized as a Greek rendering of the Egyptian Hatwaret, which occurs in the biography of Ahmose, a naval officer under the first kings of the Eighteenth Dynasty, as the name of the city where he fought on the canal when the Asiatics were driven out.[20] The fact that the Hyksos doubtless came in from the direction of Palestine/Syria and fortified this place to guard their frontier indicates that Avaris was located on the northeastern edge of the Delta. The Egyptian name is in agreement, being analyzed as connoting a fortified settlement with the determinative for a foreign land. Furthermore, Manetho (Josephus) says explicitly that Avaris was on the east of the Bubastite branch of the Nile. Judging from its name, this Nile branch certainly flowed past Bubastis (Tell Basta, two kilometers southeast of Zagazig); Ptolemy (*Geography* 4. 5) says unequivocally that the branch "which is called Bubasticus flows through the Pelusiacum mouth" and shows it (in his Third Map of Libya [Africa]) originating in the vicinity of Heliopolis and flowing into the sea at Pelusium (Tell Farama, thirty-two kilometers northeast of Qantarah and forty kilometers southeast of Port

Said). Thus the Bubastite branch of the Nile was identical with the Pelusiac, the easternmost Nile arm (as the Canopic was the western-most).[21] Accordingly, the Hyksos city of Avaris—until now not yet specifically located—is to be sought somewhere on the eastern border of the Delta, perhaps to the east of Qantir and on the way to Tjel/Sile.[22]

Israel

The strong Semitic presence in Egypt in the Second Intermediate period would seem to provide an appropriate background for the biblical narrative of the coming of the people of Israel to that land, and the biblical chronology can be understood to point to their arrival at about the time of the Hyksos domination.[23] Of interest in this connection is the fact that although the Egyptian capital had previously been at Memphis at the apex of the Delta, at Herakleopolis and Itj-towy (Lisht) near the Fayum, or at Thebes in Upper Egypt, the capital of the Hyksos (Avaris, east of the Bubastite/Pelusiac branch of the Nile) was in the easternmost part of the Delta. According to the biblical account, Jacob (Israel) and his party came from Beer-sheba (Gen. 46:5), entered Egypt in the land of Goshen, were met there by Joseph, who came out in his chariot (Gen. 46:28f.), and were allowed to dwell in the land of Goshen (Gen. 47:6).

The land of Goshen is almost certainly the Wadi Tumilat, the great valley that, as seen already in the Story of Sinuhe, provided a way of travel between the Delta and the wilderness.[24] Moreover, in Papyrus Anastasi VI (B.M. 10245, late Nineteenth Dynasty), a frontier official reports letting Bedouin tribes of Edom come in past the Fortress of Merneptah, which is in Tjeku, to the pools of Per-Atum to keep them and their cattle alive. The location is most probably the eastern end of Wadi Tumilat.[25] Tjeku will presumably be a general name for this region,[26] and Per-Atum ("House of Atum") will be the biblical Pithom (Exod. 1:11).[27] The fact that Joseph came out to meet his father in his chariot agrees wtih the supposition that he came from the court at Avaris to the land of Goshen in Wadi Tumilat, for this mode of transportation was appropriate for a relatively short overland journey; long journeys, on the other hand, were normally made by water wherever the numerous channels and canals of the Nile made this possible (as, e.g., in the return of Sinuhe from the Ways of Horus to the Residence City).

Seventeenth (Theban) Dynasty

Manetho gives no names of the numerous Diospolite or Theban kings he mentions along with the many Shepherd Kings in the Seventeenth

Dynasty. But some names that belong here are in the Turin Canon, and the tombs of several of the kings have been found at Thebes and their names found on coffins and other objects.[28]

Royal Tomb Robberies

Of interest in this connection and of value as sources in relation to some of the tombs of the Seventeenth Dynasty kings and of other kings and persons as well are several papyri that record tomb robberies carried out at Thebes in the time of the later Ramesside kings (Twentieth Dynasty).[29] At this time, under the king of all Egypt, Thebes as a whole was governed by a vizier; a mayor was in charge of the main city on the east side of the Nile, and a second mayor was in charge of the necropolis, called the West of Thebes, on the other side of the river. According to the Abbott Papyrus, in the sixteenth year of Ramses IX, Pesiur mayor of No (the city on the east side of the river) complained to the vizier Khaemwese that certain tombs had been plundered, for which his rival, Pewero, mayor of the West of Thebes, was responsible. The vizier thereupon appointed a commission which inspected ten royal tombs, four tombs of singing-women of the temples of Amun, and a number of private tombs. All of the tombs of the private persons had been violated. Two of the tombs of the singing-women had been plundered, and two were intact. One of the royal tombs had been broken into, and nine were intact. When the commission reported, Pewero handed in the names of the thieves, and they were seized, imprisoned, examined, and led to confess the crimes.

The condition of the royal tombs is stated carefully in the Abbott Papyrus, and they appear to be listed in the order in which they were visited, which has provided a clue for the identification of some of them in modern excavations. For the most part, they are located along the southeastern slope of the hill called Dira Abu'n-Naga between the Valley of the Tombs of the Kings and Deir el-Bahri, and they are constructed in the form of small, steep-sided pyramids of mud brick. The plundered royal tomb was that of the Thirteenth Dynasty King Sobkemsaf II and his queen Nubkhas, and immediately after this tomb the Abbott Papyrus lists the pyramids of King Seqenenre Tao, of another King Seqenenre Tao, "making in all two Kings Tao," and of King Wadjkheperre Kamose. Since the text clearly distinguishes the two Taos, the former may be called Seqenenre Tao I "the Elder." For Seqenenre Tao II, other inscriptions provide the distinguishing epithet of "the Brave." These two and Wadjkheperre Kamose are also otherwise known as the last three kings of the Seventeenth Dynasty and the immediate predecessors and ancestors of the first kings of the Eighteenth Dynasty.[30]

The sister and wife of Tao I was Queen Tetisheri, for whom their grandson Ahmose built a pyramid-chapel in the "sacred land" of Abydos. On a stela found there, Ahmose speaks of her to his own sister and wife, Nefertiri. The wife of Tao II was Queen Ahhotep I, and from the same inscription of Ahmose, we gather that they were also brother and sister, the children of Tao I and Tetisheri. The mummy (now missing) and jewelry of Ahhotep I were found in 1858 below the Dira Abu'n-Naga near the mouth of the Valley of the Kings; the mummy and coffin of Seqenenre Tao II were a part of the famous discovery made in 1881 in the royal cache near Deir el-Bahri. Seqenenre Tao II appears to have died at not more than the age of forty and that as a result of violence, for his mummy displays several terrible wounds in the head.[31] From evidence that will be noted momentarily, he was involved in conflict with the Hyksos, and the wounds may well have been received in the combat. As for the children of Seqenenre Tao II and Ahhotep I, five are known. Of these, King Wadjkheperre Kamose succeeded his father, fought against the Hyksos, and died shortly thereafter. King Nebpehtyre Ahmose succeeded his brother, completed the expulsion of the Hyksos, and founded the Eighteenth Dynasty. And Princess Ahmose Nefertiri married Kamose and Ahmose in succession. As already noted, the tomb of King Kamose was among those investigated and found intact by the commission under Ramses IX. Later the coffin and mummy of the king were removed and placed in a hole in the plain below the Dira Abu'n-Naga, where they were found in 1857, near where the body of Queen Ahhotep I was found in the following year.[32] The tomb of King Ahmose has never been found, but his mummy is one of those that were recovered and are now in the Cairo Museum.[33]

War against the Hyksos

In Papyrus Sallier I (B.M. 10185), there is a folk tale called the Contending of Apophis and Seqenenre, in which Apophis in Avaris (doubtless the Shepherd King named by Manetho) complains of the noise of the hippopotamuses kept by Seqenenre, ruler of the Southern City (i.e., Thebes), doubtless meaning Seqenenre Tao II. Although the text breaks off before the outcome of the matter is narrated, taken together with the epithet "the Brave" of Tao II and with the wounds in the head of his mummy, it is a reasonable surmise that there was armed conflict between the Theban king and the Hyksos ruler and that the former lost his life in this struggle.[34]

Certainly the son of Seqenenre Tao II, Wadjkheperre Kamose, conducted warfare with the Hyksos, for he recorded the conflict on a pair of stelas set up at Thebes.[35] From the text we learn that Kamose considered his position very unsatisfactory, because the Hyksos controlled much of the land (up the Nile as far as Cusae, a town forty kilometers south of Hermopolis) and because the Nubians to the south were evidently no longer under Egyptian rule either. So, in spite of the reluctance of his council of nobles, Kamose went north to attack the Asiatics. His forces were transported by ships on the Nile. At a point named Per-shaq, presumably a fortress, the horses of the enemy "were fled inside."[36] Farther along, Kamose captured a Hyksos fleet consisting of hundreds of ships of cedar, filled with gold, lapis lazuli, turquoise, "and all the good produce of Retenu." He also seized a letter from Auserre Apophis to the ruler of Kush asking the latter to come northward, presumably to render assistance to himself—which the interception of the missive no doubt forestalled even if assistance would have been given anyway. As the northernmost district conquered on his campaign, Kamose names the Nome of Cynopolis (Upper Egyptian Nome XVII, "Black Dog"), lying some eighty kilometers south of the entrance to the Fayum. From there he sailed home to Thebes claiming, with some exaggeration, to have "subdued the south and overthrown the north."

17. NEW KINGDOM, EIGHTEENTH DYNASTY (1552-1306)

With the final expulsion of the Hyksos by Ahmose, Egypt entered the period of its New Kingdom or empire, comprising the Eighteenth (1552-1306), Nineteenth (1306-1186), and Twentieth (1186-1070) dynasties. The Eighteenth Dynasty is sometimes called Thutmosid, the Nineteenth and Twentieth are Ramesside. In comparison with Mesopotamia, the New Kingdom falls in the Middle Babylonian period, which began in 1595, in particular in the time of the Kassite Dynasty (ending in 1157) and the Second Dynasty of Isin (1156-1025). It is also contemporary with the Hittite Middle Kingdom and Empire (1500-1200) and the Kingdom of Mitanni (fifteenth and fourteenth centuries).

Eighteenth Dynasty

As transmitted by Josephus, Africanus, and Eusebius, the lists of Manetho for the Eighteenth Dynasty exhibit considerable confusion. But in comparison with the names of the kings as shown from the other Egyptian records and monuments, the following equivalences appear to be recognizable: Tethmosis or Amosis (Ahmose), Amenophis (Amunhotep I), Amessis (Hatshepsut), Mephres (Menkheperre Thutmose III), Amenophis, "who was reputed to be Memnon and a speaking statue" (Amunhotep III), and Harmais (Horemheb). Table 27 gives the throne and personal names of the kings in commonly used transcriptions of the Egyptian names, with some alternative forms from the Greek of Manetho, and with probable dates.[1]

Ahmose and Expulsion of the Hyksos

The best contemporary account of the expulsion of the Hyksos by King

TABLE 27. EIGHTEENTH DYNASTY (1552-1306)

Name	Date
1. Nebpehtyre Ahmose (Amosis)	1552-1527
2. Djeserkare Amunhotep (Amenophis) I	1527-1506
3. Akheperkare Thutmose (Tuthmosis) I	1506-1494
4. Akheperenre Thutmose (Tuthmosis) II	1494-1490
5. Makare Hatshepsut	1490-1468
6. Menkheperre Thutmose (Tuthmosis) III	1490-1436
7. Akheprure Amunhotep (Amenophis) II	1438-1412
8. Menkheprure Thutmose (Tuthmosis) IV	1412-1402
9. Nebmare Amunhotep (Amenophis) III	1402-1364
10. Neferkheprure Amunhotep (Amenophis) IV, Akhenaten	1364-1347
11. Ankhkheprure Smenkhkare	1351-1348
12. Nebkheprure Tutankhamun	1347-1338
13. Kheperkheprure Ay	1338-1334
14. Djeserkheprure Horemheb	1334-1306

Ahmose is provided by the biography of one of his officers, also named Ahmose ("the Moon is Born").[2] It tells how he used to follow the excursions of King Ahmose in his chariot, indicating that the Egyptians, too, like the Hyksos, were now using the horse and chariot.[3] Then he was appointed to a ship and fought on the water at Avaris. Avaris was finally taken; then Sharuhen (probably Tell el-Far'ah in southern Palestine) was besieged for three years and taken. This evidently pushed the Hyksos beyond the point of being dangerous to Egypt, for Ahmose is next found accompanying his king on a campaign southward against the Nubians. Ahmose also continued to serve under Amunhotep I, with whom he went into Kush, and under Thutmose I, with whom he went both to Kush and to Retenu (Syria/Palestine) and as far as Naharin ("two rivers," probably Mesopotamia where the Euphrates makes its great bend westward). Thus, with the horse-drawn chariot as their own most effective instrument of war, the Egyptians were beginning to build an empire that would soon reach from the Fourth Cataract of the Nile to beyond the Euphrates.

Amunhotep I

In the case of Amunhotep I, son and successor of King Ahmose, his southernmost record is on the rocks at Semna, just above the Second Cataract. It names a certain Tjuroy as "king's son of the Southern Region," equivalent to viceroy of Nubia, and he is only one of a long line of officials through whom Egypt now administered that region.[4] From the biography of another nobleman, Ahmose-Pennekheb, we also hear of a campaign by Djeserkare (Amunhotep I) in Libya.[5]

Thutmose I

Thutmose I was probably the brother-in-law of his predecessor. That is, he was married to Ahmose, probably a younger sister of Amunhotep I and a daughter of King Ahmose and Queen Ahmose Nefertiri.[6] From the biographies of Ahmose and of Ahmose-Pennekheb, we learn of campaigns by Thutmose I to the Euphrates (as already noted) and in Kush.[7] The king's own inscription on the island of Tombos, just above the Third Cataract, shows how far his reach extended in that direction.[8] Moreover, an inscription at the First Cataract records the clearance of the canal at that place, dug earlier under Merenre (Sixth Dynasty) and Sesostris III (Twelfth Dynasty).[9]

Information on construction work by Thutmose I is provided in the biography of Ineni, an official who conducted many of the projects.[10] In the temple of Amun at Thebes, he erected a colonnaded hall (hypostyle), two pylons (the Fourth and Fifth), and two obelisks, one of which still stands while the other has fallen. To transport the great monoliths from the Aswan quarries, Ineni built a boat 120 cubits in length and 40 cubits in width. Thutmose I was the first to place his tomb in the famous Valley of the Tombs of the Kings in Western Thebes, and Ineni says of it, "I supervised the excavation of the cliff-tomb of his majesty alone, no one seeing and no one hearing," which suggests every possible precaution of secrecy.[11] In the Nineteenth Dynasty, Thutmose I was still being worshiped, and in a tomb of that date (no. 51) in the necropolis of Sheikh Abd el-Qurna belonging to Userhet, "chief priest of the royal *ka* of Thutmose," fine wall paintings show the priest making offerings and probably celebrating the anniversary of the king's burial with a large statue of the king in the place of his mummy and coffin.[12]

Thutmose II

Ineni also tells us what happened when Thutmose I died. The king went forth to heaven, he says, and "the hawk in the nest" appeared as the king of Upper and Lower Egypt, namely, Akheperenre (Thutmose II), i.e., the young king was the Horus-hawk who succeeded his father as Horus succeeded Osiris.[13] From other evidence it is known that when Thutmose I died, Hatshepsut was the only living child of himself and Queen Ahmose, and Thutmose II was the son of another mother, perhaps a younger sister of the queen, named Mutnefert. Therefore, presumably in order to

FIGURE 81.   Sail Boat on the Nile, Looking toward the West of Thebes. (*Jack Finegan*)

FIGURE 82.   Temple of Hatshepsut at Deir el-Bahri. (*Jack Finegan*)

strengthen his claim to the throne, Thutmose II was married to Hatshepsut, his half-sister.

Although an inscription at Aswan shows that Thutmose II crushed a rebellion in Kush,[14] and although a fragment from Hatshepsut's temple at Deir el-Bahri records an expedition on which he went as far as Upper Retenu (Syria),[15] his entire reign was evidently not long. He probably died while still relatively young.[16]

Hatshepsut

Referring to Thutmose II, Ineni continues his account by saying that this ruler also went forth to heaven and that his son stood in his place as king of the Two Lands. This son, not named by Ineni, is Menkheperre Thutmose III, and other evidence identifies him as the only son of Thutmose II, born to him by a member of his harem named Isis. He evidently came to the throne while still very young, and Ineni says that the sister (actually half-sister) and wife of Thutmose II, Hatshepsut, actually controlled the affairs of the country, and "Egypt was made to labor with bowed head for her."[17]

While still the queen of Thutmose II, Hatshepsut began a tomb for herself but never completed it. Inside, on the unfinished sarcophagus, are the titles that belonged to her at that stage of her career: "king's daughter, king's sister, wife of the god, great wife of the king . . . Hatshepsut."[18] Already in the second year of the reign of Thutmose III, however, Hatshepsut had herself proclaimed "king," and thereafter she is represented in some of her statues with the king's beard and is referred to in some inscriptions in the masculine.[19] After that she could also look forward to her own eventual burial in the fashion of the kings themselves. Accordingly, she constructed a vast mortuary temple at Deir el-Bahri north of, and partly patterned after, the smaller tomb-temple of Mentuhotep II (Eleventh Dynasty). Like the earlier temple, her temple was built up in terraces and colonnades ascending toward the great cliff. But in this case, the tomb (no. 20) was behind the cliff in the edge of the Valley of the Kings, and it was apparently the intention—not carried out—to connect it by a long corridor with the mortuary temple on the other side of the mountain.

On the walls of the temple are painted reliefs, notably on the middle colonnade a series on the north side about Hatshepsut's divine birth and establishment in the kingship. A series on the south concerns the sea expedition to Punt. Also on the south side of the lower colonnade, another series of reliefs records how barges brought the two great obelisks from Aswan to Thebes. Of these obelisks, only the summit portion of one is preserved at the Cairo Museum. But at Karnak one of a second pair of

Above—FIGURE 83. Statue of Hatshepsut as Osiris in Her Temple at Deir el-Bahri. *(Jack Finegan)* *Below—FIGURE 84.* Tree House in Punt, Relief in the Temple of Hatshepsut at Deir el-Bahri. *(Jack Finegan)*

FIGURE 85.   Hatshepsut as King, wearing False Beard and Atef Crown, Relief in Her Temple at Deir el-Bahri. (*Robert H. Schertle*)

FIGURE 86.   Fallen Obelisk of Hatshepsut at the Karnak Temple. (*Jack Finegan*)

Hatshepsut's obelisks still stands, and the upper portion of its companion lies nearby. The standing obelisk is the largest obelisk still in Egypt, is almost thirty meters high, contains 180 cubic yards of granite, and weighs an estimated 320,000 kilograms.

A famous person associated with Hatshepsut and evidently the overseer of many of her works was Senmut. In the Punt reliefs at Deir el-Bahri, he is called the "steward of Amun"; on the rocks at Aswan, an inscription says he conducted "the work of the two great obelisks" obtained there; and in several statues he holds, protectingly wrapped in a mantle, the queen's small daughter Nefrure. But he, too, apparently lost favor later in the reign.[20] For himself, Senmut prepared an earlier tomb at Qurna (no. 71), in modern times found almost totally ruined but with more than one thousand fragments of the sarcophagus in the tomb and vicinity;[21] and a later tomb under the forecourt of Hatshepsut's temple at Deir el-Bahri, left unfinished, but remarkable for its great astronomical ceiling and list of festivals of the various months.

In the twenty-second year of the reign of Thutmose III, Hatshepsut disappears from the records. She may simply have died, but later in the reign she was regarded with disfavor. Her figure and name were destroyed on many monuments throughout Egypt, and in many of the erased cartouches, her name was replaced by the name of Thutmose III or that of his father (Thutmose II) or his grandfather (Thutmose I).

Thutmose III

When at last Thutmose III reigned as pharaoh alone, he engaged in tremendous activities, both in conquest and in construction. He recorded all these on stelas and in inscriptions and annals on the walls of the temple of Amun at Thebes, carved there in recognition of the assistance of the god in his accomplishments.[22]

The first military campaign in Asia was the most important and is the most fully recorded. On the twenty-fifth day of the fourth and last month of the second season at almost the end of his regnal year 22, Thutmose III was at the border fortress of Tjel and led his army northward. On the fourth day of the first month of the ensuing third season, when the king's Year 23 (1468) had already begun, Gaza was reached. The march of 200 kilometers up the coast road had taken ten days, an average daily march of 20 kilometers. On the twenty-first day of the same month, the Egyptian forces were at Megiddo and fought successfully against a formidable coalition of Asiatics. After the capture of the city, the king marched on to southern Lebanon, where he built a fortress called "Menkheperre [Thutmose III] is the Binder of the Barbarians." In the second month of the first season in his same Year 23, the king was back in Thebes and celebrated the feast of Amun in gratitude for his victory. The entire campaign had taken approximately five months, probably late April to early October, within the limits of the dry season in Palestine/Syria.[23]

Further expeditions in the same direction were conducted by Thutmose III in sixteen summers in the next eighteen years, making a total of seventeen Asiatic campaigns. On the sixth campaign (Year 30), he captured Qadesh on the Orontes, long a center of resistance; on the eighth campaign (Year 33), he took Carchemish and crossed the Euphrates to set up a boundary tablet beside that of his grandfather Thutmose I; on the seventeenth and last campaign (not later than Year 42, when the king was probably over seventy years old), he again put down Qadesh together with Tunip and other allies from Naharin.[24]

With respect to the southern frontier, the Karnak annals record the regular receipt of tribute from Wawat and Kush. Moreover, a granite stela at the great rock of Gebel Barkal at the Fourth Cataract shows that before the end of the reign of Thutmose III, the Egyptians had moved this far into Kush and had founded the fortified town of Napata, which would later be the capital of an independent Ethiopian kingdom.[25] Thus the empire of Thutmose III extended from the Upper Euphrates to the Fourth Cataract of the Nile, and Egypt ruled a very large part of the ancient Middle East. In the north, there would be increasing contacts with the Hittites and, under Ramses II (Nineteenth Dynasty), a treaty with them. In the south, there was now for the first time regular contact with the African peoples whose natural home was above the Fourth Cataract; from this time onward, they appear frequently in Egyptian art.[26]

The inscriptions of Thutmose III also record his building works. At the temple of Amun in Thebes, he erected the Sixth Pylon, several gates and chapels, and four obelisks; and at Heliopolis, he erected two obelisks.[27] He also built a temple at Deir el-Bahri, in the ruins of which have been found portions of a statue and of reliefs representing himself.[28] His tomb is in the Valley of the Kings (no. 34), and his mummy, recovered from the royal cache near Deir el-Bahri, is in the Cairo Museum.[29] Between the mummy and a standing statue from Karnak in the Museum, there is a close resemblance, and the portrait head of the statue conveys an unmistakable impression of the vitality and strength of the great conqueror and builder.[30]

Many of the works of Thutmose III were supervised by his vizier, Rekhmire, whose tomb (no. 105) is near Qurna in Western Thebes and contains wall paintings and inscriptions depicting and narrating his career.[31] In one scene Rekhmire leans on his staff and inspects stonecutters, sculptors, brickmakers, and builders who toil before him. Among the makers and layers of bricks are Asiatic foreigners, and the accompanying inscription refers to the "captives brought by his majesty for the works of the temple of Amun." The bricklayers say, "He supplies us with bread, beer, and every good sort," and the taskmaster says to the builders, "The rod is in my hand, be not idle."[32] Other scenes show the arrival of foreign tribute—Asiatics come in with horses, and Kushites with cattle and a giraffe—the transport by boat of tomb furnishings, and the conduct of a funerary banquet with girl musicians playing harp, lute, and drum.

Amunhotep II

Thutmose III was followed on the throne by his son, Amunhotep II, who was probably already his coregent for a brief period.[33] In his youth, Amunhotep II was distinguished for his strength and athletic prowess, and a stela found near the Sphinx at Giza tells of his unparalleled exploits with the bow and arrow.[34] Other stelas found at Memphis, Karnak, Elephantine, and Amada in Nubia tell of events in his reign and speak of his mighty bow, which no one else could even draw. He campaigned several times in Retenu, and at Qadesh slew seven princes with his own mace and, afterward, hanged six of them on the wall at Thebes and one on the wall of Napata in Nubia. Finally he boasts—perhaps beyond the facts—that the princes of Naharin, Hatti, and Shanhar (i.e., Shinar, or Babylonia) proffered their submission.[35]

In a painted sandstone statue from Deir el-Bahri, Amunhotep II stands under the protection of the cow goddess, Hathor, a deity especially prominent in the Eighteenth Dynasty.[36] When his tomb (no. 35) was discovered in the Valley of the Kings in 1898, the royal mummy was intact; it is now in the Cairo Museum.[37] Tombs of some of his officials at Qurna contain excellent and naturalistic wall paintings. In the tomb of the royal scribe Weserhat (no. 56), for example, there is a hunting scene in the desert and a barbering scene in a garden. In the tomb of Djehuty (no. 45), a steward of the high priest of Amun, there is a scene in which the deceased man and a lady—identified in the accompanying inscription as his mother, but looking as young as himself—enjoy a fine repast in the afterlife.[38]

Thutmose IV

Thutmose IV was son of Amunhotep II and was himself married to a daughter of Artatama, king of Mitanni, perhaps in an alliance between Egypt and Mitanni against the rising power of the Hittites.[39] Egyptian power, however, still extended from the Upper Euphrates to Upper Nubia. Although preserved records of the military activities of Thutmose IV are relatively few, an attendant named Amunhotep tells on his own tomb stela of going with the king "on his expeditions in the south and north countries; going from Naharin [at the great bend of the Euphrates] to Karoy [the vicinity of Napata and Gebel Barkal near the Fourth Cataract] behind his majesty."[40] Likewise, a small scarab speaks of Menkheprure (Thutmose IV) as marching to Naharin and Karoy, with the Aten going before him to bring the inhabitants of foreign lands under his rule.[41]

The extensive ruins of the mortuary temple of Thutmose IV are in the West of Thebes south of the Ramesseum, and his tomb (no. 43) is in the Valley of the Kings. From the tomb come the body of a chariot (in the Cairo Museum) carved with realistic battle scenes, and wooden panels from a chair of state (in the Metropolitan Museum of Art and the Boston Museum of Fine Arts) showing the king as a sphinx smiting Nubian chieftains and also seated upon his throne with Thoth standing behind him with the symbols of "life" and "years." Wall paintings in private tombs reach probably their highest point of artistic excellence under Thutmose IV. With increasing naturalism, they present the happenings of everyday life, especially those that were important and pleasurable to the tomb owner, those that he hoped to relive in the life beyond. Outstanding examples at

Qurna are in the tombs of Nakht (no. 52), the scribe and astronomer (labor in the fields, harvesting and treading grapes, catching waterfowl in a net, plucking birds, a funerary banquet with girls playing harp, lute, and double flute); of Sobkhotep (no. 63), the "commander of the Lake of the South and of the Lake of Sobek" (jewelers at work, servants bringing offerings, Nubians bringing tribute, and bearded Syrians bringing tribute); of Menna (no. 69), the registrar of lands (transporting and treading wheat, sacrifice of an ox, men and girls bringing offerings, a large funerary boat, hunting and fishing in the marshes). There are also paintings in the British Museum from the no longer identifiable tomb of Nebamun (of the reign of Thutmose IV or of Amunhotep III), in which a superb fowling scene in the marshes is especially notable.[42]

Amunhotep III

Benefiting from the accomplishments of his predecessors, Amunhotep III, son and successor of Thutmose IV, ruled Egypt at the height of its power, prosperity, and cultural development. His chief queen, who appears prominently with him throughout his reign, was Tiy. The marriage is commemorated on at least a dozen scarabs, carved at the beginning of the reign, on which it is said of Tiy: "The name of her father is Yuya, the name of her mother is Thuyu. She is the wife of a mighty king, whose southern boundary is as far as Karoy and northern as far as Naharin."[43] From other inscriptions it is known that Yuya held a high military position and enjoyed the designation of "father of the god," meaning father-in-law of the pharaoh. The tomb of Yuya and Thuyu (no. 46) was found in 1905 in an isolated branch of the Valley of the Kings, still containing the two mummies and much of the tomb furnishings (now in the Cairo Museum).[44] It is surmised that the two were of Nubian origin.[45]

Queen Tiy herself is represented in a small, green schist head (in the Cairo Museum), which bears her name and was excavated in a temple at Serabit el-Khadem, where Amunhotep III did some work toward the end of his reign. As compared with earlier and more formal representations, this must be a relatively realistic portrait, and Tiy is of striking and even exotic appearance. In a tomb (no. 55) discovered in 1907 across a narrow valley from where the tomb of Tutankhamun was found fifteen years later were found various objects with the name of Queen Tiy and, with them, a small, uninscribed boxwood and ebony head (now in the Berlin Museum), which bears some resemblance to the green schist head of the queen. The uninscribed head has therefore been thought to be Queen Tiy also (or perhaps her daughter Sitamun). At any rate, it displays strongly Nubian characteristics and appears to confirm the Nubian background of the family.[46]

FIGURE 87. Fowling in the Marshes, Wall Painting in the Tomb of Menna in Western Thebes. (*Library of the Egyptian Museum, Cairo*)

Various inscriptions show that Amunhotep III and Queen Tiy were the parents of at least two sons—a certain Thutmose, who is named as the king's oldest son and a priest of Ptah, and Amunhotep IV (Akhenaten), who was next on the throne. This succession leads to the supposition that the older brother Thutmose died early. Amunhotep III and Queen Tiy also had at least four daughters—Sitamun, Isis, Henuttaunebu, and Nebetah.[47] Amunhotep III also married certain Asiatic princesses, doubtless for political reasons. The Amarna Letters contain his correspondence with Kadashman-Enlil I, Kassite king of the Third Dynasty of Babylon, about marriage with his sister and also his daughter (Letter 1); and with Tushratta, king of Mitanni, about marriage with his daughter (Letters 19, 22).

As to later family relationships, Amunhotep IV (Akhenaten) was followed for brief reigns in succession by Smenkhkare and Tutankhamun. Since Amunhotep IV is regularly portrayed with only daughters in his family, it is unlikely that these men were his sons. They may also have been sons of Amunhotep III and Queen Tiy, and younger brothers of Akhenaten.[48]

With respect to Amunhotep III as the probable father of Smenkhkare and Tutankhamun, there is no known monument of Smenkhkare to provide evidence. But there is an inscription of Tutankhamun on a granite lion (now in the British Museum), which he completed as a companion for another in a temple of Amunhotep III at Soleb in Nubia (below the Third Cataract); in the inscription he calls Amunhotep III "his father," and this statement may most naturally be taken literally.[49]

Above—FIGURE 88. Head of Queen Tiy, in Green Schist. (*Library of the Egyptian Museum, Cairo*) *Below—FIGURE 89.* Head of Queen Tiy (or possibly Sitamun), in Boxwood and Ivory. (*Ägyptisches Museum, Staatliche Museen Preussisches Kulturbesitz, Berlin, Bundesrepublik Deutschland*)

With respect to Queen Tiy as the probable mother of Smenkhkare and Tutankhamun, in the tomb of Tutankhamun (no. 62, discovered in 1922), in the so-called treasury room adjacent to the burial chamber, was found a small wooden coffin, less than one meter in length, which contained two yet smaller coffins. In one of the small containers was a solid gold squatting statuette of Amunhotep III, approximately five centimeters high. In the other was a locket in the form of a tiny anthropoid sarcophagus, which bore the title of Queen Tiy and contained several strands of her hair. Furthermore, in the tomb of Amunhotep II (no. 35, discovered in 1898) were three mummies, which had been stripped of their identifications by grave robbers. One of these is of special interest at the present point. The mummy is that of a woman, and the hair of her head has been proved—by electron probe of its chemical composition—to be identical with that of the hair of Queen Tiy in the locket from the tomb of Tutankhamun. Thus, the long-lost mummy of Queen Tiy has been found. Moreover, according to X-ray studies, the inherited features of the skull shape of this mummy belong logically at a point between Thuyu the mother of Queen Tiy, and Tutankhamun, and could not as reasonably have come from another ancestor or been passed on to another descendant.[50]

As to military activity on the part of Amunhotep III, there is relatively little evidence.[51] But there is no doubt about the magnitude of his building works. At Malkata south of Medinet Habu in Western Thebes, he built a vast residential complex with a south palace, a middle palace, a north palace, and, farthest to the north, a temple of Amun, as well as a harbor (the remains recognizable as Birket Habu ["Lake of Habu"]) and channel leading to the river.[52] Inscriptions on small objects found in the ruins name the king's palace "the House of Nebmare is the Splendor of the Aten"; and scarabs commemorate the making of a pleasure lake (perhaps the harbor just mentioned) for Queen Tiy, on which the king sailed in a barge named "the Splendor of the Aten."[53]

Two kilometers north of the palace complex at Malkata was the mortuary temple of Amunhotep III, the largest of all the funerary temples at Thebes. Little of the temple remains except the two enormous seated statues of the king (19.9 meters in height), which were in front of it and later became known as the Colossi of Memnon.[54] In the mortuary temple, Amunhotep III erected a large, black granite stela to record his works in honor of Amun, but Merneptah (Nineteenth Dynasty) later demolished the temple and reused its materials, including the stela in his own mortuary temple.[55]

At Karnak, Amunhotep III made additions to the temple of Amun, to the north built a temple of Montu the war god, and to the southwest may have

FIGURE 90.   Colossi of Amunhotep III in Western Thebes. (*Jack Finegan*)

begun the temple of Khonsu, son of Amun and Mut. At Luxor, he built major parts of the temple of Amun and, in one of the chambers, put on the walls scenes and inscriptions portraying his divine birth and his coronation by the gods, much like what was shown for Hatshepsut at Deir el-Bahri.[56] The Luxor and Karnak temples were already joined by an avenue of sphinxes; some of the sphinxes of Amunhotep III are still in place, and others were added later.[57]

In Nubia, Amunhotep III built for himself and Amun the temple we have already mentioned at Soleb (ninety kilometers north of the Third Cataract); a temple for Queen Tiy at Sedeinga (eight kilometers farther north); and probably a temple at Kawa (midway between the Third and Fourth cataracts, four kilometers south of Dongola, on the east bank of the river). Reflecting the prominence of the Aten already under Amunhotep III and especially under Amunhotep IV (Akhenaten), the last city was called Gematen ("Finding the Aten"). Even when Amun was again predominant, this name survived.[58]

The tomb of Amunhotep III (no. 22) was placed in a previously unoccupied western branch of the Valley of the Kings, and his mummy is in the Cairo Museum.[59] His likeness is seen in a magnificent head from a colossal sandstone statue, now in the British Museum; and he and Queen Tiy are seen in a colossal limestone seated group, with three small daughters standing in front of their throne, a work that is the largest statuary in the Cairo Museum.

FIGURE 91. Colossal Group Statue of Amunhotep III and Queen Tiy. (*Library of the Egyptian Museum, Cairo*)

Among the officials prominently associated with Amunhotep III was Amunhotep, the son of Hapu, also known simply as Hapu, who bore the titles of King's Scribe and Overseer of All Works of the King.[60] He was in charge of the erection of the Colossi of Memnon and was honored with a mortuary temple of his own to the south of that of Amunhotep III. He was also remembered as the author of proverbs and, in the Ptolemaic period, was a god of healing along with Imhotep, the two being shown together in a graffito in the Karnak temple. On two stelas (one in the British Museum, one in Cairo), we meet the twin brothers Suti and Hor (Seth and Horus), who were architects under Amunhotep III and Overseers of the Works of

Amun. In their inscriptions, Suti and Hor mention many deities but chiefly address themselves to the sun god, who is spoken of in syncretistic and universalistic terms and called the Aten as well as Amun, Re, and other names. In part, the text uses language also found in the Book of the Dead; in part, it anticipates phraseology in hymns to the Aten composed under Akhenaten. "Hail to thee, Aten of the daytime, creator of all and maker of their living! . . . He . . . who made himself and who beheld what he would make. The sole lord, who reaches the ends of the lands every day."[61]

Book of the Dead. As for the Book of the Dead, just mentioned, materials of the sort found already in the Pyramid Texts of the Old Kingdom and the Coffin Texts of the Middle Kingdom grew to be an even larger body of formulas and incantations designed to assist the deceased in the afterlife. In the New Kingdom, they were written out more or less fully in larger or smaller papyrus rolls (i.e., in the ordinary form of an Egyptian book) and placed in the tombs and with the mummies. It is these materials for which the collective modern name is the Book of the Dead. In Egyptian, the most common name was something like Formulas for Going Forth by Day; another name was the Chapter of Making Strong the Beatified Spirit. A great many of the manuscripts have been found. They extend down into the Ptolemaic period, are written in hieroglyphic, hieratic, and demotic script, and are illustrated with colored vignettes (in the New Kingdom) or line drawings (in the Late period).[62]

Book of What Is in the Underworld. Although the Book of the Dead recognized the possibility of the condemnation of the deceased and even presented a terrifying picture of the devourer of the dead, its main emphasis was upon acquittal and blessedness in the beyond. In a second category of funerary works found in the New Kingdom, however, the darker as well as brighter aspects of the world beyond are described and pictured, and much attention is given to the cosmography of the beyond and the punishment and destruction of the wicked in the lower world. These texts were known to the Egyptians under the collective designation of Amduat, which means literally, "that which is in the Dat," the Dat being the Underworld.[63]

Amunhotep IV (Akhenaten)

Whether in his first years of reign Amunhotep IV (Akhenaten) made his chief residence at Thebes or at Memphis is not certain. At any rate, he built extensively at Thebes and then built an entirely new capital, Akhetaten (Amarna). Materials from both Thebes and Akhetaten (stelas, statuary, temple and tomb reliefs, and other objects) provide information. According to year dates on vessels from Amarna, he reigned for seventeen years.[64]

Amunhotep IV and his wife, Queen Nefertiti, were the parents of six children, all daughters, namely, Meretaten, Meketaten, Ankhesenpaaten, Neferneferuaten, Neferneferure, and Setepenre.[65] In art, the increasing naturalism already evident under Amunhotep II, Thutmose IV, and Amunhotep III now applies to the king himself and his family and entourage. Earlier kings were seen in a conventionalized pose of august immobility, but Amunhotep IV is portrayed not only in this way but also in an informal and evidently entirely realistic way. In fact, the representation is such that it must be supposed that he suffered from some bodily abnormality.[66] As for the face of the king, e.g., in several colossal sandstone statues from his destroyed Aten temple at Karnak (in the Cairo Museum), it may suggest the nature of an idealist, an artist, and perhaps almost a fanatic. As for Queen Nefertiti, it is probably she who is represented in a famous painted limestone bust, which was discovered at Amarna in 1912 and placed in the Berlin Museum. In it the lady is shown with long slender neck and beautifully regular features, wearing a tall blue cap. The work is so excellent as to be thought the master portrait by a master sculptor, from which other copies would have been made.[67]

Furthermore, the daughters—as many as had been born at the time the picture was executed—are frequently shown with their parents in intimate family scenes. In the tomb prepared for the royal family (in a desert wadi eleven kilometers from the Amarna plain), one scene shows the king and queen weeping together over the dead body of Meketaten, so she evidently died before her parents. Some time after this, Nefertiti herself is no longer seen and was presumably deceased. Then Meretaten seems to have taken her place to some extent and also to have been married to Smenkhkare, who probably became coregent for the last few years of Amunhotep IV's reign. Ankhesenpaaten, according to some evidence, was eventually married to her father and bore him a daughter Ankhesenpaaten-tasherit (*tasherit* meaning "junior"). Afterward, at any rate, she became the queen of Tutankhaten and changed her name to Ankhesenamun when he changed his to Tutankhamun.[68] It was evidently she who, widowed by the early death of Tutankhamun, wrote to the Hittite king Shuppiluliumash I and asked him to send her one of his sons for a husband. But when, at last, he sent his son Zannanzash, the latter was murdered, perhaps by Horemheb, who soon replaced Ay on the Egyptian throne.

Atenism. It is in religion that the reign of Amunhotep IV (Akhenaten) is most remarkable. Already under Thutmose IV and Amunhotep III, the Aten or Sun Disk was increasingly prominent. But still there was a multiplicity of gods, and even the sun god continued to be known under various names and to be represented in various animal and human forms.

FIGURE 92. Nefertiti. (*Ägyptisches Museum, Staatliche Museen Preussiches Kulturbesitz, Berlin, Bundesrepublik Deutschland*)

FIGURE 93. Akhenaten and Nefertiti with Their Young Daughters, Sunken Relief from Amarna. (*Ägyptisches Museum, Staatliche Museen Preussisches Kulturbestiz, Berlin, Bundesrepublik Deutschland*)

Now with Amunhotep IV (Akhenaten), there was a genuine revolution of thought, and the Aten was presented as the one and only deity.[69] The new king began his reign with the same personal name as several of his predecessors in the same dynasty—Amunhotep ("Amun is content")—and took the throne name Neferkheprure ("Fair of forms like Re"). But early in his reign, he erected buildings for the Aten at Thebes. In the later reaction against the king and his religion, these buildings were pulled down. But the blocks from them were reused, notably by Horemheb in his new Second, Ninth, and Tenth pylons and in the foundations of the Hypostyle Hall at Karnak, and by Ramses II in his new shrine at Luxor, and many thousands of these blocks have been recovered. From their inscriptions, it is learned that by his fifth year Amunhotep IV had probably built at least eight buildings at Karnak, with names such as "the Sun Disk (Aten) is in the House of the Sun Disk." In the reliefs on the blocks, the most frequent scene is an offering rite in which the king and queen, or the queen and one or more of her daughters (most often the oldest, Meretaten), stand before a table and under the radiating rays of the Sun Disk.[70]

FIGURE 94. Akhenaten before the Aten, Princess Meretaten Shaking a Sistrum, Sunken Relief from Amarna. (*The Brooklyn Museum, Charles Edwin Wilbour Fund*)

FIGURE 95. Akhenaten, Sunken Relief on a Stone Block Recovered from One of His Temples at Thebes. (*Akhenaten Temple Project, University Museum, University of Pennsylvania*)

Akhetaten. After a few years, Amunhotep IV built a new capital. The site was on the east bank of the Nile 368 kilometers below Thebes in Upper Egyptian Nome XV ("Hare") and slightly more than halfway to Memphis. It is now known as Amarna.[71] Here the eastern cliffs of the river valley retreat to enclose a plain 5 kilometers wide and 13 kilometers long. To mark the boundaries, Amunhotep IV cut into the cliffs fourteen large stelas, from nearly four to as much as eight meters in height, eleven on the east side and three across the river, 20 kilometers away to the west.[72] Although none of the stelas is now completely intact, all were apparently of about the same design. As seen on the best preserved example (Stela "S" at the southeastern corner of the tract), there is a scene at the top with the king and queen raising their hands in adoration of the Sun Disk, from which long rays come down and terminate in hands, some holding the *ankh*. A text of greater or lesser length follows. Three stelas (on the east bank) appear to be earlier and, although the date is lost, probably belong to the king's Year 5; in eleven stelas the date is Year 6.[73] In the earlier stelas, the king tells how he found and marked the site, solemnly gave it to the Aten, and called it Akhetaten ("the Horizon of the Aten"); and for himself, he already uses the new name of Akhenaten ("Well Pleasing to the Aten").[74] He also speaks of his building projects for the new city, including Per-Aten ("House of the Aten"), Per-hai ("House of Rejoicing"), and apartments for himself and his queen. The whole area, within the landmarks, Akhenaten dedicates to the god manifest in the Sun Disk: "It belongs to my father, the Aten. . . . I have made it for the Aten, my father, forever and ever."

In spite of this hope for the long continuance of the new city, Akhetaten only endured as capital for something like fifteen years. Tutankhamun went back to Memphis and Thebes, and afterward, in the reaction against Akhenaten, like the Aten buildings at Thebes, Akhetaten was razed, perhaps by Horemheb. Nevertheless, modern excavation has recovered much of the plan of the city and of its major buildings.[75]

In the boundary stelas at Akhetaten, Akhenaten also speaks of planning a tomb for himself, Nefertiti, and Meretaten in the eastern mountain, and other tombs for his officials.[76] The royal tomb, already mentioned in connection with the relief scene in which the king and queen weep for Meketaten, was presumably the last resting place of the king, but his mummy evidently disappeared long ago. Of the tombs of the nobles, at least twenty-five are found in the limestone cliffs surrounding the Amarna plain, and they also contain many relief scenes of the royal family and their associates, as well as texts in praise of the Aten.

Of the Aten texts in the tombs of the officials, the longest was found in 1884 in the tomb of Ay (no. 25), but it has since been largely destroyed.[77] This "long hymn" is generally supposed to have been composed by Akhenaten himself, and the fact that the longest version of it was inscribed in the tomb of Ay may be appropriate to the fact that among other offices, Ay was private secretary to the king. In the hymn it is plainly affirmed that the deity who is manifest in the light of the Sun Disk is the only, universal, and beneficent god.[78]

Amarna Letters. In international affairs, the Amarna Letters show that the times were not favorable to Egypt.[79] In the north, Mitanni was an ally,

FIGURE 96. Akhenaten Offering to the Aten, Sunken Relief of the Amarna Period. (*Library of the Egyptian Museum, Cairo*)

but it was under pressure from the Hittites and desired from Egypt more than was forthcoming (Letter no. 26 from Tushratta to Queen Tiy). The Hittites expressed the wish for friendship (no. 41 from Shuppiluliumash I to Amunhotep IV), but this soon turned to enmity. In Babylonia, there was protest against the lack of security for their people in Asiatic territory supposedly under Egyptian control (no. 8 from Burnaburiash II to Amunhotep IV). Palestine/Syria had, in fact, been conquered in the expansion of Egyptian power concurrent with and subsequent to the expulsion of the Hyksos, but local rulers had been left in charge of their own territories, under Egyptian supervision. Many of these now appealed for help in the midst of various disturbances and especially against invading bands of Habiru (e.g., no. 74 and many others from Rib-Addi of Byblos to Amunhotep III and IV; no. 59 from the governor of Tunip in northern Syria to Amunhotep IV; nos. 285-289 from Abdi-Hiba of Jerusalem to Amunhotep IV). The distress expressed in the several appeals suggests that Akhenaten did not act with strength in such affairs, although in art there are representations of him in the traditional kingly pose of slaughtering the foe. In fact, his successor Tutankhamun says plainly in the Restoration Stela (below) that in the days of his predecessor, when the Egyptian army was sent to Palestine/Syria, it did not succeed at all. And so, after seventeen years, the reign of Akhenaten came to an end.

Smenkhkare and Tutankhamun

The brothers Smenkhkare and Tutankhamun succeeded Akhenaten in turn, and the first and older was probably already coregent with Akhenaten for a time. In several reliefs from Amarna, two kings are shown together who, although lacking positive identification, may well be Akhenaten and Smenkhkare in this coregency.[80] The reign of Smenkhkare by himself was evidently brief, and his mummy may be the one found in the Tomb of Tiy (no. 55) in the Valley of the Kings and assessed as that of a young man who died at the age of less than twenty-five.[81]

Tutankhamun was also only a youthful king. He probably came to the throne at the age of nine or ten and died by the age of eighteen or nineteen, as his mummy, found in his famous tomb (no. 62) in the Valley of the Kings indicates.[82] At the outset, his personal name appears as Tutankhaten, and he was probably still resident in Akhetaten.[83] His so-called Restoration Stela, found at Karnak, tells what happened soon afterward.[84] In the text, the date is missing but may have been the king's fourth regnal year, and the king's name appears as Nebkheprure Tutankhamun. Before Tutankhamun (i.e., under Akhenaten), it is stated, the temples of the gods and goddesses from Elephantine to the Delta were neglected. In consequence, the deities

FIGURE 97. In the Valley of the Kings, the Entrances to the Tombs of Tutankhamun (in the rectangle) and of Ramses VI (in the hillside). (*Jack Finegan*)

forsook the land, there was confusion at home, and the army was defeated abroad. Then Tutankhamun acceded to the throne, rebuilt the sanctuaries, and made fine images of Amun and Ptah; a goodly state of affairs came to pass. At the time of this restoration, Tutankhamun was in his palace in the estate of Akheperkare (Thutmose I), which, according to another inscription, was probably at Memphis, and the prominence of Ptah in the text also makes it possible that the stela itself originated at Memphis. The stela was set up, however, in the temple of Amun at Thebes, and in the relief scene, Tutankhamun is shown in the worship of Amun.[85] Therefore, both Memphis and Thebes were once again the major centers rather than Akhetaten.

Of the images of the deities that Tutankhamun made, there are examples in the temple of Amun at Karnak in two large statues, now reconstructed from broken pieces. One shows Amun with the face of the god carved in the likeness of the king. The other shows Amunet, the female principle corresponding to Amun, with her face probably carved originally in the likeness of Tutankhamun's queen, Ankhesenamun. In addition, on the inner walls of the portico at either end of the colonnade of Amunhotep III at Luxor, Tutankhamun depicted the Feast of Opet, in which Amun, Mut, and Khonsu were brought by boat from Karnak to Luxor and back again. Thus the new king provided a pictorial representation of the return of Amun to power after the time in which he was put aside by the devotees of the Aten.[86]

Under Tutankhamun, Nubia was administered by the viceroy Huy, whose tomb (no. 40) is in the necropolis of Kurnet-Murai in Western Thebes. Fine wall paintings in the tomb show Tutankhamun's assignment to Huy of territory from Nekhen to Napata, Huy's receipt of tribute from the north and the south, and Huy's return by sail to his post.[87]

For himself, Tutankhamun began a mortuary temple north of Medinet Habu, and two statues of the king (in the Cairo Museum) were found at this site. Both the temple and the statues, however, were later usurped by Ay and then by Horemheb. The relatively small tomb of the young king (no. 62) was broken into once or twice in antiquity, then covered by debris from the tomb of Ramses VI higher up the hill, and thus preserved relatively intact until its discovery in 1922.[88] The tomb consisted of a corridor, antechamber and annex, burial chamber, and adjacent "treasury" room. Only the burial chamber contains paintings: on the south wall, at the entrance from the antechamber, Tutankhamun between Anubis and the goddess of the west; on the west wall, at the head of the royal sarcophagus, four horizontal bands, the three lowest with baboons (the spirits of the first hour of the night in the realm through which the dead king must pass), the highest band showing the funeral procession; and on the north wall, opposite the entrance, Tutankhamun and his *ka* in the presence of Osiris and, again, Tutankhamun in the likeness of the mummified Osiris, with Ay in the costume of a living king and the leopard skin of a priest, performing the ceremony of "the opening of the mouth."[89] In the intact burial, the mummy of Tutankhamun was contained in a series of anthropoid coffins. The one closest to the body was solid gold with a portrait mask accurately representing the face of the king. The second coffin was of wood inlaid and plated with gold. The third was of gilt wood. And all were in a sarcophagus of red sandstone guarded at the four corners by the goddesses Isis, Nephthys, Neith, and Selkis.

Ay and Horemheb

After close association with Akhenaten and Tutankhamun, Ay took the throne for a short reign.[90] On a stela of his third year, Ay offers flowers to Hathor, and at Akhmim he built a rock-chapel to Min and other local gods—so he too, like Tutankhamun, abandoned worship of the Aten.[91] In his tomb (no. 23 in the western branch of the Valley of the Kings, wall paintings depict him and his wife Tiy; his granite sarcophagus, found smashed in the tomb, is reassembled in the Cairo Museum.

Above—FIGURE 98. Tutankhamun between Isis and Anubis, Wall Painting in the King's Tomb. *(Library of the Egyptian Museum, Cairo)* *Below—FIGURE 99.* Vignettes from the Book of the Dead, Wall Painting in the Tomb of Tutankhamun. *(Library of the Egyptian Museum, Cairo)*

Left—FIGURE 100. Tutankhamun and His Ka in the Presence of Osiris, Wall Painting in the Tomb of the King. (*Library of the Egyptian Museum, Cairo*) Right— FIGURE 101. King Ay Performing the Ceremony of "the Opening of the Mouth" for Tutankhamun (Tutankhamun in the guise of Osiris), Wall Painting in the Tomb of Tutankhamun. (*Library of the Egyptian Museum, Cairo*)

The successor of Ay was Horemheb ("Horus is in festival"). Information on his early career is provided by a seated, life-sized gray granite statue (in the Metropolitan Museum of Art) of himself as a royal scribe; in an account of his coronation on a statue (in the Turin Museum) in which he is seated beside his wife Mutnedjmet; and in reliefs (of which some fragments are scattered in six different museums) of a tomb he prepared for himself as a private individual south of the causeway of the pyramid of Unis at Saqqara.[92] Horemheb was a native of Hatnesut (Greek Alabastronpolis, modern Kom el-Ahmar, 105 kilometers north of Amarna on the east bank of the Nile) and, before his accession, was chief commander of the army, King's Deputy in the Whole Land, and Royal Scribe. In some of the reliefs from the Saqqara tomb (in the Leiden and Vienna museums), he acts as King's Deputy (although the reliefs were later altered to make him appear as king) as various groups of Asiatics present themselves, some of them refugees, whose town has been laid waste and whose countries are starving, who beg a home in Egypt, as they say, "after the manner of your fathers' fathers since the beginning."[93]

As king, Horemheb restored ruined temples from the Delta to Nubia and provided them with priests chosen (as a former general well might do) "from the pick of the army" (according to the coronation inscription on the Turin statue). He took steps to abolish graft and corruption among military and fiscal officials, particularly in connection with the collection of taxes (edicts recorded on a large stela set up adjacent to his Tenth Pylon at Karnak). In his sixteenth regnal year, he made a major campaign in Asia,

FIGURE 102.   Portrait Mask of Tutankhamun in Gold. (*Library of the Egyptian Museum, Cairo*)

on which he went on from Byblos as far as Carchemish (inscription on a stone bowl, probably from Memphis).[94]

In his position as king, Horemheb also abandoned his earlier tomb at Saqqara and made a new tomb for himself (no. 57) in the Valley of the Kings. Although this tomb was plundered in antiquity, its walls exhibit fine paintings, some never completed, and the king's magnificent sarcophagus of painted red granite is still in place. Of special interest also, on the walls of the burial chamber, are scenes and the text of a considerable portion of the Book of Gates, the oldest known example of that work.[95]

A private tomb of the time, that of Neferhotep (no. 50 at Qurna), a priest with the title of "the god's father of Amun," is of interest for its three examples of the Songs of the Harper. On the north wall of the passage from the outer hall to the inner shrine, Neferhotep is shown seated, with his wife beside him, at a table piled high with offerings of food, while a harper (whose figure is now destroyed) squats before them and sings to the accompaniment of his instrument the words that are carved above the group. Again, in the main hall of the tomb, there is a picture of the funerary banquet, together with two more songs of the harper. The priest in whose honor the harper sings is dead, and death is good, but it is also inevitable in the inexorable cycle of things. Therefore, the first song affirms, it is appropriate to seek worldly happiness as long as transitory life endures. But, in contrast with "those songs which are in the tombs of old," which deprecate the hereafter, the second song looks gladly away from the strife of this world toward the blessed peace of the beyond. "One says, 'Welcome, safe and sound!' to him who has reached the West." Furthermore, the third song says, the priest has served the gods in life, and the proper ritual has been performed at his burial; therefore, his survival in the hereafter is assured, and he is well received by the gods. Thus, in one tomb, three songs present three approaches to death and reflect love of life, fear of death, and confidence in immortality all at the same time.[96]

18. NEW KINGDOM, NINETEENTH AND TWENTIETH DYNASTIES (1306-1070)

Nineteenth Dynasty

The names and lengths of reign of the kings of the Nineteenth Dynasty as given by Manetho (according to Josephus, Africanus, and Eusebius) are listed in Table 28. In the Greek forms of Manetho, the Egyptian names are recognizable that are more commonly written as Ramses I, Seti I, Ramses II Meriamun ("beloved of Amun"), Amunmose, and Seti II. The son of Ramses II was Merneptah ("he whom Ptah loves"). By the time of Manetho, this name was probably pronounced as Meneptah and perhaps written in Greek as Menephtais, a form that could have degenerated into the Ammenephthes and Ammenephthis found in Africanus and Eusebius, and the Amenophis in Josephus. The wife and widow of Seti II was Queen Tawosre. After the death of Seti II she placed the boy Merneptah Siptah on the throne, probably acted as regent during his reign, and, upon his death, took the throne herself for some years. She is presumably the Thuoris in Manetho's list, and the possibly questionable status of Siptah may account for the omission of his name preceding hers. As for the lengths of the reigns, they vary considerably in the several lists. But the figures for the longest reign of the most important king, Ramses II Meriamun, may be understood as follows: the most exact figure of 66 years and 2 months in Josephus is rounded off to the lower figure of 66 years in Eusebius, and the 61 years in Africanus is a scribal error, which should be corrected to 66 because the stated total of 209 years for the dynasty requires this figure.[1]

In the more ancient Egyptian texts and monuments, the materials on the Nineteenth Dynasty are relatively abundant, and two items in particular bear on the chronology. On a stela from Abydos (in the Cairo Museum), Ramses IV of the Twentieth Dynasty offers a prayer that he might reign as long as did Ramses II, namely, sixty-seven years. Here, if Ramses II actually reigned sixty-six and a fraction years, the figure is rounded off to the next higher number.[2] In Papyrus Leiden 350, a new moon is recorded on

TABLE 28. NINETEENTH DYNASTY IN MANETHO

Josephus	Years	Months	Africanus	Years	Eusebius	Years
Ramesses	1	4				
			Sethos	51	Sethos	55
Harmesses Miamun	66	2	Rapsaces	61	Rampses	66
Amenophis	19	6	Ammenephthes	20	Ammenephthis	40
			Ramesses	60		
			Ammenemnes	5	Ammenemes	26
Sethos	10					
			Thuoris	7	Thuoris	7
				209		194

the twenty-seventh day of the sixth month in the fifty-second year of Ramses II, and the related calculations and considerations make it likely that his first regnal year was in either 1290 or 1279, most probably in 1290. In Table 29, the dates are congruent with this determination and follow in sequence from those of the Eighteenth Dynasty (Table 27).[3]

Ramses I

In a sculptured scene on the so-called Stela of the Year 400, found at Tanis, Ramses II is shown worshiping the god Seth. In the text that follows, he commemorates a visit to Tanis by his father Seti I ("Seth's man") in the "year 400" of Seth.[4] The god is spoken of as the father of the fathers of Ramses II, i.e., as the ancestor of this royal line, and the mention of the 400th year of Seth is equivalent to saying that the god had ruled at Tanis, as if he were a king, for 400 years. In the text, Seti I is obviously described in terms of his career before becoming king, for he is called Troop Commander, Overseer of the Fortress of Tjel/Sile, and other titles. In addition, the father of Seti I and the grandfather of Ramses II is named on the stela as Pa-Ramses ("the Ramses"), i.e., Ramses I, and he too is called Troop Commander, Overseer of the Fortress of Tjel/Sile, and other titles. Thus the visit of Seti I to Tanis was probably made before either he or his father was king, i.e., probably in the reign of Horemheb. At that time, therefore, both Ramses I and Seti I were military commanders in the northeastern Delta, and it was probably as a comrade of army days that Ramses I followed Horemheb on the throne, the latter presumably having no son of his own.

The only known date formula of Ramses I is on a stela he erected to commemorate work on a temple of Horus at Wadi Halfa. This mentions

TABLE 29. NINETEENTH DYNASTY (1306–1186)

Name	Date
1. Menpehtyre Ramses (Ramesses) I	1306–1304
2. Menmare Seti (Sethos) I	1304–1290
3. Usermare Ramses (Ramesses) II	1290–1224
4. Baenre Merneptah	1224–1204
5. Menmare Amunmose	1204–1200
6. Userkheprure Seti (Sethos) II	1200–1194
7. Akhenre-setepenre Merneptah (or Sekhaenre-setepenre Ramses) Siptah	1194–1188
8. Sitre-meryetamun Tawosre	1194–1186

only his second year, so he probably had only a brief reign and was probably already aged at the time of his accession.[5] Although he was at home in the northeastern Delta and although his dynasty either then or at least soon afterward had its center of rule in that district, Ramses I was buried in the Valley of the Kings at Western Thebes. His tomb (no. 16) is simple in plan but elaborately decorated, and his red granite sarcophagus is still in place.

Seti I

If Horemheb made at least one campaign into Asia, so too Seti I, as another king of army background, moved in that direction. His inscriptions speak of campaigns in Palestine and Syria, mentioning Pekanan ("the Canaan"), Retenu, and Qadesh.[6] All of this presumably means the successful reestablishment of Egyptian control of Palestine and Syria to a border somewhere in the vicinity of Qadesh on the Orontes, beyond which the Hittites maintained their formidable power. In the end, however, Seti I must have lost his more northerly conquests, because his son and successor, Ramses II, had to fight again at Qadesh.[7] To the west, also, the Libyans were a menace and evidently attempting to press into and settle in the Delta. The tribes here had long been known as the Tehenu, and Seti I speaks of "smiting the chiefs of Tehenu" and of taking prisoners "in the country of Tehenu."[8]

At home in Egypt, Seti I did much building. At Karnak, he constructed a considerable part of the hypostyle hall in the temple of Amun, although, like most of his building projects, this was unfinished at his death and was completed by Ramses II. Here the outside of the north wall and part of the east wall are covered with three rows of reliefs (now much weathered),

FIGURE 103. Statue of Seti I Wearing the *Nemes* Headdress and Offering to Osiris, from Abydos. (*The Metropolitan Museum of Art, Rogers Fund, 1922*)

which illustrate the wars of Seti I. The texts cited just above are from the inscriptions accompanying these pictures. Included in the reliefs is a veritable map of the ancient coastal road from Egypt to Palestine, the route on which Seti I marched, as have most of the land armies that have ever moved between Egypt and Palestine or Palestine and Egypt.[9]

At Abydos, ancient center of the worship of Osiris, Seti I built a large temple, finished by Ramses II, in which are two large courts, a hypostyle hall with seven doors, and, in the innermost area, seven sanctuaries dedicated to seven deities. In the center was the sanctuary of Amun, on the right the shrines of Re-Harakhte, Ptah, and Seti I himself, and on the left sanctuaries of Osiris, Isis, and Horus. In fine painted reliefs, Seti I is shown in the company of yet other gods—Thoth, Anubis, Mut, and many more. In a funerary scene, Isis stands at the head of the prostrate mummy of the king, and Horus at the feet, and they stretch their hands over him as they await his resurrection. Behind the temple, which is in the south sector of the ruins at Abydos, is a large, partly subterranean structure, perhaps a cenotaph, perhaps in its layout intended to represent the primeval hill that rose out of the waters at the creation of the world. When first found in modern times, it was thought to have been a symbolic tomb of Osiris, and is often called the Osireion.

In Western Thebes, Seti I constructed his mortuary temple at Qurna, and, as completed by Ramses II, it is one of the best preserved monuments of its type. The tomb of Seti I is in the Valley of the Kings (no. 17) and is probably the finest of all the royal tombs. The mummy of the king was recovered from the cache of royal mummies at Deir el-Bahri and is in the Cairo Museum.[10] Seti I also prepared a tomb (no. 38) for his mother, Queen Sitre, the wife of Ramses I, in a valley 1.5 kilometers southwest of his own tomb. This valley, now known as Wadi el-Biban el-Harmim ("Valley of the Tombs of the Queens"), contains altogether more than seventy tombs of wives and children of the Ramesside kings of the Nineteenth and Twentieth dynasties.

As the monuments of Seti I show, he recognized Amun the god of Thebes as the chief god and, like his father Ramses I, chose himself to be buried in the West of Thebes. This same Theban orientation prevailed also with the other Ramesside pharaohs. But at the same time, he and the others were especially interested in the northeastern Delta, both, it may be supposed, because the family was at home in that region and because the relationships with Asia were again of great importance. Accordingly, Seti I had a residence in the Delta and, under Ramses II, this became a great and famous capital.

FIGURE 104.   Isis and Horus Await the Resurrection of Seti I, Funerary Relief in the Temple of Seti I at Abydos. (*Library of the Egyptian Museum, Cairo*)

Ramses II

Ramses II was probably coregent with his father, Seti I, for a relatively short time, then succeeded him for his own long reign.[11] Ramses II was a builder on a very large scale, and his monuments contain a great many texts and reliefs that provide information concerning his reign. At the outset, he completed a number of projects his father had begun, and then did building of his own. At Abydos, he finished the temple of Seti I and inscribed in it his own longest record. This text states that he voyaged to Thebes in his first regnal year, then turned downstream to proceed to "the seat of might, Per-Ramses Meriamun Great of Victory." Before he had gone far, however, he turned off on a canal to Abydos (twelve kilometers west of the Nile) and there saw that Seti I's temple was unfinished and neglected. He therefore called his court together, announced his intention of completing his father's buildings, and, in the same connection, recalled how his father had made him his coregent while he was yet only a child.[12] At Abydos also, to

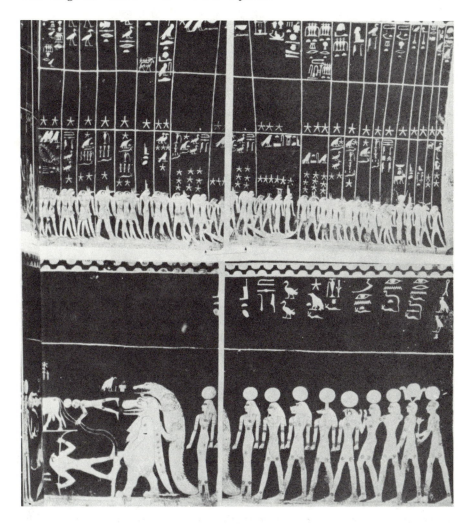

FIGURE 105.   Astronomical Ceiling in the Tomb of Seti I in Western Thebes.
(*Library of the Egyptian Museum, Cairo*)

the north of his father's temple, Ramses II built a temple for himself. At
Luxor, he completed the great colonnade begun by Amunhotep III and
added in front of it a large court with a massive pylon adorned with two
obelisks (one now in the Place de la Concorde in Paris) and six colossal
statues of himself.[13] At Karnak, he finished the great hypostyle hall of the
temple of Amun. In Western Thebes, he built his own very large mortuary
temple known as the Ramesseum.[14]

In Nubia, Ramses II built temples at Beit el-Wali, Gerf Hussein, Wadi,
es-Sebua, Derr, Abu Simbel, and Aksha, between the First and Second

FIGURE 106.   Hieroglyphs in the Tomb of Seti I. (*Robert H. Schertle*)

cataracts, and at Amara, above the Second Cataract.[15] Of these, the
temple of Ramses II at Abu Simbel is one of the largest rock-hewn
structures in the world, and the four seated statues of the king on the
exterior of the temple are each more than twenty meters in height and thus
larger than the Colossi of Memnon. Over the entrance to the interior is the
falcon-headed sun god Re-Harakhte, and, on the cornice over the colossal
statues, is a row of baboons who raise their arms in salute to the rising sun.
In the inner sanctuary are seated statues of Ptah, Amun, Ramses II, and
Re-Harakhte, and an inscription dedicates the temple to Re-Harakhte.
Close beside his own temple, Ramses II constructed a smaller temple for his
queen "Nerfertari, fair of face," and placed standing statues of himself and
of her on the exterior.[16]

   In the north, Ramses II also did much building, but climatic and
historical circumstances in the low-lying Delta, heavily populated and
often traversed by armies, have not been favorable for the preservation and
recovery of antiquities: much must be inaccessible beneath subsoil water

FIGURE 107. Avenue of Ram-Headed Sphinxes at the Entrance to the Karnak Temple, an Avenue that Once Extended from the Nile to the Temple. (*Jack Finegan*)

or under modern buildings, and much has been destroyed or carried off for use elsewhere. From his long inscription at Abydos and from the Blessing of Ptah on a stela in his temple at Abu Simbel, we know that Ramses II enlarged and endowed the ancient temple of Ptah at Memphis, and two colossal statues of the king still lie there. At Heliopolis (On), granite blocks lying west of the obelisk of Sesostris I bear inscriptions of Ramses II; in one carving, he offers a libation to Atum. In Wadi Tumilat, he did building work at Tell el-Maskhuta and Tell er-Retabeh.[17] Most importantly, he had a famous residence city, which bore his own name (Per-Ramses), in the northeastern Delta. This will be spoken of again below.

Concerning affairs abroad in the long reign of Ramses II, his records tell of military action in Nubia, Libya, and Asia, Asia being by far the most critical area. All three areas are represented in scenes and inscriptions of the great temple at Abu Simbel. In one scene, Ramses II presents African prisoners, identified as chiefs of Kush, to Amun, Mut, and Khonsu; in another, he smites Libyans; in yet another, he charges upon a Syrian city. In the temple at Beit el-Wali, the reliefs on the southern wall of the forecourt show war against the Nubians, and those on the northern wall depict wars

FIGURE 108.   Hypostyle Hall in the Temple at Karnak. (*Library of the Egyptian Museum, Cairo*)

FIGURE 109.   Overhead Beam in the Karnak Temple. (*Jack Finegan*)

FIGURE 110. Symbols of Upper Egypt (lily at the right) and Lower Egypt (papyrus at the left) on Columns in the Karnak Temple. (*Jack Finegan*)

FIGURE 111. Temple of Ramses II at Abu Simbel. (*Library of the Egyptian Museum, Cairo*)

against the Libyans and Asiatics.[18]

In Nubia, despite the record of warfare, the extensive building activity of Ramses II suggests relatively peaceful conditions, and the great monuments themselves may have been in part intended to impress the southern neighbors with the power of Egypt and thus to contribute to quiet in those regions. With respect to Libya, one of the inscriptions in the Beit el-Wali temple speaks of "the rebellious lands of Tehenu"; a hymn to the king in Papyrus Anastasi II (B.M. 10243, end of the thirteenth century) says, "Libya falls before [his] sword"; and in an inscription accompanying the Libyan scene in the Abu Simbel temple, Ramses II says that "he has settled the Tehenu on the heights, filling the strongholds, which he built, with the captivity of his mighty sword." The strongholds here mentioned may well be the line of six forts that Ramses II constructed, extending for 340 kilometers westward from Rhacotis (itself the chief frontier fortress in the northwestern Delta and later a suburb of Alexandria) to Apis (Egyptian Hut-ka, "House of the Bull," now Zawyet Um el-Rakham, "Hospice of the Mother of the Vultures"), west of modern Mersa Matruh.

FIGURE 112.   Temple of Queen Nefertari at Abu Simbel. (*Library of the Egyptian Museum, Cairo*)

FIGURE 113.   Fallen and Broken Statue of Ramses II at Memphis. (*Jack Finegan*)

From other references by Ramses II, we gather that there were three main Libyan tribes—the Tehenu in the desert west of the Delta, the Libu (from whom came the name of Libya) in the western desert and eastern Cyrenaica, and the Meshwesh in western Cyrenaica. He also mentions the Sherden with their ships of war, evidently a sea people somewhere in the western area.[19]

In Asia, Ramses II had to fight against the Hittites for many years. In his Year I (1290), he pushed northward as far as the Nahr el-Kalb ("Dog River") between Beirut and Byblos and left a stela that, although nearly illegible, at least provides this date.[20] In Year 5 (1286), he fought a major battle against the Hittite king Muwatallish at Qadesh.[21] In an idealized representation of the matter in the so-called Poem of Pentaur (the name of the copyist in the colophon in Papyrus Sallier III, British Museum), Ramses II "prepared his infantry, his chariotry, and the Sherden of his majesty's capturing," marched past Tjel/Sile, reached Ramses Meriamun in the Valley of the Cedar (evidently a town in the Lebanon named for himself), met the Hittites at Qadesh, and upon his return "arrived in peace in Egypt at Per-Ramses Great of Victory" to receive the welcome accorded a victorious conqueror. From other details in the Egyptian sources and from the Hittite records, we gather that, in fact, Ramses II was ambushed, probably fought with real bravery, but was rescued only by the timely arrival of a detachment of his army, which had come by a different route. He was fortunate to return to Egypt safely, and the Hittites came after the Egyptians as far as Damascus.

In subsequent years, Ramses II had to fight again and again in the regions from southern Palestine to northern Syria,[22] but eventually (in the Year 21

FIGURE 114. Head of Ramses II at Tanis. (*Jack Finegan*)

FIGURE 115.   Fallen and Broken Obelisk of Ramses II at Tanis. (*Jack Finegan*)

FIGURE 116.   Base of Obelisk at Tanis with the Name of Ramses II in the Cartouche. (*Jack Finegan*)

FIGURE 117.   Fragment of Winged Sun Disk at Tanis. (*Jack Finegan*)

of Ramses II [1270] and when Hattushilish III was king of the Hittites) a treaty of peace was concluded between the Egyptians and the Hittites, which included a mutual renunciation of invasion and provided for a joint defensive alliance against any other enemies. The original document embodying this treaty was engraved on a tablet of silver and brought by Hittite ambassadors to Ramses II at his city of Per-Ramses Meriamun.[23] Yet later (in Year 34 of Ramses II, 1257), the relations of Egypt and the Hittites were further cemented by the marriage of Ramses II and a daughter of Hattushilish III. The princess arrived, with a large delegation, at the city of Ramses Meriamun, and Ramses II found her "fair of face" and gave her the name of the King's Wife Maatnefrure ("She who sees the beauty of Re," the name of the last hour of the night). From then on, peace between the two lands was so stable that "if a man or a woman proceeded on their mission to Djahi [the Phoenician/Palestinian coast], they could reach the land of Hatti without fear around about their hearts, because of the greatness of the victories of his majesty."[24]

Per-Ramses. According to the texts cited above, when Ramses II voyaged downstream from Thebes in his first regnal year, his intended destination was "the seat of might," named Per-Ramses Meriamun Great of Victory. To the same city he returned from the battle of Qadesh, and to it came the Hittite ambassadors and the Hittite princess. Although the city was thus known by his own name as the House of Ramses Meriamun Great of Victory, the fact that it was the seat of power already in his first regnal year suggests that it was previously the royal residence. Therefore, it was probably established as such by Seti I. From the way the city figures in the relations with Asia, it is also suggested that it was in the part of Egypt toward Asia, i.e., in the northeastern Delta. This was also a natural location for the Ramesside family, which was at home in this region.

This obviously famous city is named and described in glowing terms in two poetical compositions extant in several papyrus copies.[25] According to these texts, the city was located between Djahi (the Phoenician/Palestinian coast) and Timuris (a Greek rendering of the Egyptian Ta-meri, "the beloved land," a name for Egypt), and was related to the Shi-Hor ("Waters of Horus") with its rushes and salt, and the reed-thicket with its papyrus. Thus again a northeastern Delta location is indicated.[26] The city is full of food and provisions, it is said, and those who dwell in it want for nothing. There are four temples in the four quarters of the city—the House of Amun in the west, the House of Seth (Sutekh) in the south, that of Astarte in the east (the direction appropriate to her as a Semitic goddess), and that of Buto (cobra goddess and protectress of the northern kingdom) in the north. The residence of the king is here, and the poet salutes him in his great city: "So dwell content of heart and free, without stirring from it, O Usermare Setepenre . . . Ramses Meriamun—life, prosperity, health!—thou god!" Per-Ramses is also presumably the city called Raamses, in the building of which the Israelites were constrained to labor, according to Exod. 1:11. If this is correct their oppression in Egypt is to be placed under Ramses II.[27]

Qantir, Khata^na, and Tanis. In the search for Per-Ramses, three sites come chiefly into consideration, namely, Qantir (ninety-five kilometers northeast of Cairo), Khata^na (two kilometers to the southwest of Qantir), and Tanis (eighteen kilometers north of Qantir). In terms of the ancient Nile river mouths, Qantir and Khata^na were probably somewhat to the west of the Bubastite/Pelusiac branch, and Tanis was on the Tanitic branch.[28]

At Qantir, excavation has established that there was a large palace begun, according to the inscriptions, by Seti I, enlarged by Ramses II, and used by later kings of the Nineteenth and Twentieth dynasties down to Ramses X, i.e., for a period of two hundred years.[29] This palace was decorated with tiles and statues of glazed faience, and a factory was also located where these and other objects of art were made.[30] Most importantly, for the identification of the site, eleven hieratic ostraca were found, five of which have the name Per-Ramses Meriamun, making it probable that this was that very residence city.[31]

At Khata^na, inscriptions have been found with names of rulers in the Twelfth Dynasty and of Seti I of the Nineteenth Dynasty.[32] Since the site is so near, the built-up area of Khata^na may well have merged with that of

Qantir, making it well possible that Qantir/Khataʿna should be considered a single city.[33]

The largest and most impressive remaining monuments of Ramses II, however, are found at Tanis, at the present village of San el-Hagar ("San of stone") on the Muwis Canal (the ancient Tanitic branch of the Nile).[34] It has already been noted on the Stela of the Year 400 that Seti I visited Tanis on the 400th anniversary of the worship of Seth at this place, so it was a very old religious center. As for Ramses II, there are more of his monuments here than anywhere else outside of Upper Egypt and Nubia, and they include huge obelisks and statues.[35] As excavated, the major area at the site appears to have been that of a very large temple, and this is appropriate to the long religious associations of the place. If Tanis was primarily a religious center and Qantir/Khataʿna primarily a residential center, the two areas should perhaps be considered as comprising the famous city of Per-Ramses.[36]

For the choice by Seti I and Ramses II of the Qantir/Khataʿna/Tanis region for the great residential, religious, and administrative center that Per-Ramses was, the location—farther from the wilderness and accordingly more protected than Avaris in its probable location east of the Bubastite/Pelusiac branch of the Nile, yet with ready access to the sea also through the Tanitic branch for the ships that voyaged to Syria—was appropriate. With Ramses II, the city came to bear his own name, and a larger area of the northeastern Delta, including Wadi Tumilat (where he also built at Tell el-Maskhuta and Tell er-Retabeh), was called "the land of Ramses" (Gen. 47:11).

After the establishment of lasting peace with the Hittites, it is probable that Ramses II could indeed fulfill the destiny wished for him by the author of the panegyric on Per-Ramses, that the king should "dwell content of heart and free, without stirring from" the great city. When he died in his sixty-seventh regnal year he must have been in his eighties, as so long a reign would surely require. He was buried in a tomb (no. 7) in the Valley of the Kings, which was pillaged already in antiquity and has been closed in modern times because of its dangerous condition. His mummy was recovered from the cache of royal mummies at Deir el-Bahri and placed in the Cairo Museum.[37]

Already a coregent with his father, Ramses II had a royal harem, and as king he was married to at least three wives whose names are known from many monuments. The first wife was Nefertari, who was evidently queen already in his first year and for whom he built the smaller temple at Abu Simbel. The second queen was Isinofre, to whom he was also probably married early in his reign, and it was one of her sons, Merneptah, who became the next pharaoh. The third queen was Maatnefrure, daughter of Hattushilish III of the Hatti land, to whom Ramses II was married in his thirty-fourth regnal year. The children of the king are named and pictured on many monuments, and a compilation from the various sources gives a total of at least seventy-nine sons and fifty-nine daughters.[38]

Merneptah

Records of the reign of Merneptah are found on numerous monuments, but many of these are ones he usurped from earlier kings.[39] At Memphis, he built a new palace adjacent to the great temple of Ptah (at the present village of Mit Rahineh); in the West of Thebes, he built a mortuary temple northwest of the mortuary temple of Amunhotep III and took from that structure most of the materials for his own. The tomb of Merneptah is in the Valley of the Kings (no. 8, ninety kilometers west of the tomb of Ramses II), and the king's great sarcophagus is still in place, its lid sculptured in red granite. The mummy of the king was found in a cache of several royal mummies in the tomb of Amunhotep II (no. 35) and is in the Cairo Museum.[40] It is judged to be that of a man of more than seventy years of age. The highest known date of Merneptah is regnal year 10, given in Papyrus Sallier I, and his whole reign was probably not much longer than that. He was probably already in his late fifties at the time of his succession to his long-lived father.

What was evidently the chief military engagement of the reign of Merneptah took place in his fifth regnal year (1220).[41] At this point, Libyan tribes made a serious invasion of the Delta. A fragmentary inscription on the Karnak temple appears to refer to the foreign invaders and states that they had pitched their "tents in front of Per-Berset and had made their habitation in the tract of Itj," apparently indicating some penetration even in the eastern Delta.[42] The coalition of tribes was led by a prince of the Libu named Mauroy, and the Karnak text says that he brought with him his wife and children, and had reached "the western boundary in the fields of Piyer." The family presence suggests the intention of the invaders to establish themselves in the land permanently. Encouraged by a dream in which Ptah extended a sword to him, Merneptah fought a great battle at the unidentified site of Piyer, and after six hours of conflict, the Egyptians were victorious. More than six thousand of the enemy were slain and more than nine thousand taken prisoner.

It was to celebrate this triumph that Merneptah placed his Hymn of Victory on the back of the large black granite stela he took from the mortuary temple of Amunhotep III. After describing the discomfiture of the Libyan chief and the joy felt in Egypt over the deliverance, the text celebrates the universality of Merneptah's triumph in poetic fashion and lists the opponents who have been overcome. In the first distich of the poem are the Nine Bows, the traditional term used inclusively for the enemies of Egypt on its borders. In the second distich, Libya, the land of the Hittites, and the land of Canaan are placed on a par with one another. In the third distich three Canaanite cities are correlated in a similar way. In the fourth distich, Israel and Hurru are balanced, and the name Israel occurs here for the only time in any known ancient Egyptian inscription. Hurru is the land of the Hurrians, the biblical Horites. Before the Hittite conquest, it included Syria; here it is essentially equivalent to Palestine.[43] Israel and Hurru (Palestine) are mentioned in parallelism, so Israel is evidently thought of as in Palestine, but the name of Israel is written with the determinative that means "people" rather than "land," so Israel is apparently pictured as hardly yet the settled possessors of the whole area.[44] Since the entire poetic passage is a grandiloquent declaration that Merneptah has smitten all of Egypt's enemies, and not any detailed description of marches and battles, it is not certain that Merneptah actually campaigned in Palestine. He hardly did so in the land of the Hittites, with whom peace presumably still prevailed; nevertheless, his title as "Binder of Gezer," in another inscription, may evidence at least a minor foray into Palestine on which he could have met Israelite tribes.[45]

EARLY IRON AGE (1200-900)

Amunmose and Seti II

In reliefs in the mortuary temple of Ramses III at Medinet Habu, in a procession of royal statues, Ramses II and Merneptah are followed only by Seti II before coming to Sethnakhte, the first king of the Twentieth Dynasty, and to his successor, Ramses III himself. This suggests that only Seti II was, at least later, considered a legitimate king in the last part of the Nineteenth Dynasty.[46] Other evidence indicates that several other persons were actually on the throne in this time, even if without full legitimacy and for relatively brief periods.

In Papyrus Salt (B.M. 10055), a chief workman named Peneb makes a complaint against a vizier named Amunmose to a person called Mose, and Mose removes the vizier from his office. Since a vizier ranked immediately under the king, only a king could have dismissed him. Of possible names that come into question, only that of Amunmose would appear to be indicated, and Mose may be recognized as an abbreviation or nickname of this name.[47] This name of Amunmose is found without a cartouche, so the person may have been a usurper on the throne. Yet a tomb of Amunmose is found in the Valley of the Kings (no. 10), which suggests royal standing.[48]

As for Seti II, his tomb (no. 15) is in the Valley of the Kings, and his mummy is in the Cairo Museum.[49] In what was an unusual honor for persons other than the king, the queen of Seti II, Tawosre, and his chancellor Bay, were also buried there in the Valley of the Kings (Tawosre no. 14, Bay no. 13).

Siptah and Tawosre

According to an ostracon from the Valley of the Kings (Cairo Museum no. 25515), Seti II died in the sixth year of his reign and he was succeeded by Siptah.[50] Information on the reign of Siptah is derived from graffiti in Nubia deriving from the king's viceroys in that region, particularly one viceroy named Seti.[51] This Seti was appointed to his post as "king's son of Kush" in the first year of Ramses Siptah and was still in office in the third year of Merneptah Siptah. Together with other evidence, this is recognized as showing that between his first and third years one and the same king simply changed his *nomen* from the one form to the other. The *prenomen* was changed, too, so that altogether he was first Sekhaenre-setepenre Ramses Siptah, and afterward Akhenre-setepenre Merneptah Siptah.[52] The tomb of Siptah (no. 47) is in the Valley of the Kings, and the sarcophagus is still in place.

In a badly damaged statue in the Munich Glyptothek (no. 122), the small figure of Akhenre-setepenre (i.e., Siptah) is seated upon the lap of a much larger figure that was intentionally destroyed. The surmise is that the larger figure was that of Queen Tawosre and that Siptah, presumably the son of Seti II and Tawosre, had been placed on the throne while still a boy and guided as king by Tawosre and the powerful chancellor Bay.[53] After the young king's death, Tawosre herself took the throne, with the throne name Sitre ("Daughter of Re"). In all, the role of Tawosre was something like that of Hatshepsut, and she also became the third example in Egyptian history (after Nitocris of the Sixth Dynasty and Sobknofru of the Twelfth Dynasty) of a woman who brings a dynasty to a close. She was buried in the Valley of the Kings (no. 14).[54]

Twentieth Dynasty

Of the Twentieth Dynasty, Manetho says that it consisted of twelve Diospolite kings, but gives no names. From the monuments, ten kings are listed as shown, with dates, in Table 30.[55] In Papyrus Harris I (B.M. 10053), the transition to the Twentieth Dynasty is described by Ramses III, who says that there was a preceding period of confusion under a Syrian prince

TABLE 30. TWENTIETH DYNASTY (1186–1070)

Name	Date
1. Userkhaure Sethnakhte	1186–1184
2. Usermare-meriamun Ramses III	1184–1153
3. Usermare-setepenamun (later Hikmare-setepenamun) Ramses IV	1153–1146
4. Usermare-sekheperenre Ramses V	1146–1142
5. Nebmare-meriamun Ramses VI	1142–1135
6. Usermare-meriamun-setepenre Ramses VII	1135–1129
7. Usermare-akhenamun Ramses VIII	1129–1127
8. Neferkare-setepenre Ramses IX	1127–1109
9. Khepermare-setepenre Ramses X	1109–1099
10. Menmare-setepenptah Ramses XI	1099–1070

(possibly named Irsu), after which order was brought to the land by his own father Sethnakhte. In turn Sethnakhte appointed him (Ramses III) to be crown prince, and Sethnakhte died "and rested in his eternal house west of Thebes."[56]

Ramses III

As king of Egypt, the son of Sethnakhte used both a *prenomen* and a *nomen* that were patterned after the names of Ramses II. He added to the throne name as a distinctive element the epithet Hikaon ("Ruler of Heliopolis"); thus, he was Usermare-meriamun Ramses Hikaon, or Ramses III. Information about his reign is provided both by the Harris Papyrus and by the monuments of the king himself.

According to Papyrus Harris I, Ramses III built a temple of Seth (Sutekh) at Per-Ramses, and a stela found at Memphis speaks of him as present in Per-Ramses and as making arrangements there for the worship of a statue of himself.[57] At least as far as building work is concerned, however, he directed his attention chiefly to the region of Thebes. According to the Harris Papyrus, he erected no fewer than five temples there, and at least three of these have been certainly identified, two at Karnak, and the third the king's mortuary temple at Medinet Habu on the western plain of Thebes. This last is the best preserved of all the royal buildings of its kind in Egypt.[58]

In historical respect, the reliefs and inscriptions of the mortuary temple at Medinet Habu are of special interest as documenting the great movements of peoples across and around the eastern Mediterranean, movements that, at this time, were threatening Egypt on the west and the north. Although Ramses III was able to repulse the invaders, and devotes much of the record at Medinet Habu to this accomplishment, a new time in history was actually being ushered in, in which his land would play a much less dominant role than in the older days, when Egypt had ruled so much of the East. In the pictures, large categories of foreign peoples are plainly distinguished in features and garb, and typical representations are recognizable of the Hittites, Syro-Palestinians, Africans, Libyans, and "peoples of the sea." Prominently included among the Sea Peoples are the Peleste, and it was some of these who settled on the Palestine coast and became the Philistines of the Bible.[59] As attested in the Medinet Habu records and Papyrus Harris I, the major campaigns of Ramses III were against the Libyans in his fifth year,[60] against a coalition of peoples from the north in his eighth year,[61] and against the Libyans again in his eleventh year.[62]

Papyrus Harris I also tells of peacetime activities of Ramses III including a notable sea expedition to Punt,[63] and describes society as secure and the land as "well satisfied" in his reign.[64] Nevertheless, the closing years of his reign were marked by unrest and internal decline in Egypt. As an indication of difficult economic conditions, a Turin Papyrus dated in the twenty-ninth year of Ramses III tells of strikes (the first such actions known in history) by the artisans who hewed and decorated the tombs of the pharaohs in the Theban necropolis.[65] Other papyri report an apparently unsuccessful palace conspiracy in which a wife of Ramses III named Tiy plotted to have the king assassinated and her son named Pentwere placed on the throne.[66]

For himself, Ramses III began a tomb at the site known as no. 3 in the Valley of the Kings. But he abandoned this and took instead the tomb (no. 11) begun by his father, Sethnakhte (who was actually buried in the tomb of Queen Tawosre, no. 14), and developed it into one of the largest and most elaborate of all the royal tombs. The mummy of the king, recovered from the cache at Deir el-Bahri, is in the Cairo Museum and is considered to be that of a man of about sixty-five years of age.[67]

With the relatively obscure reigns of Ramses IV-XI, the Twentieth Dynasty drew to a close.[68] With the possible exception of Ramses VIII, whose burial place has not been found, all of these kings had tombs in the Valley of the Kings, and the mummies of Ramses IV, V, and VI are in the Cairo Museum.[69] But even the tombs of kings were not safe in the midst of the evidently increasing disorder in the land, and we have already heard (Chapter 16) of the royal tomb robberies that took place in the reign of Ramses IX.

FIGURE 118. Hieroglyphs in the Tomb of Ramses VI in Western Thebes, with the King's Name in the Cartouche. (*Robert H. Schertle*)

Travels of Wenamun

Not only the erosion of pharaonic authority in Egypt but also the deterioration of Egyptian standing in the Asiatic regions are reflected in an account known as the Travels of Wenamun, preserved in the Golenischeff Papyrus.[70] Wenamun, an official of the temple of Amun at Thebes, is sent on a mission to Byblos and Syria to buy cedarwood for the ceremonial bark of Amun-Re. In the text, Wenamun mentions the pharaoh, probably Ramses XI, but speaks of a certain Herihor as his lord and master. The latter is evidently, for all practical purposes, the ruler of Upper Egypt. Wenamun goes to Djanet (Tanis) to board a ship for the Syrian sea. There he speaks of Nesbenebded and Tentamun, evidently a man and wife. They appear to have been, in effect, the rulers at that place. At Dor on the north coast of Palestine, Wenamun finds himself among the Tjeker people, and is robbed; at Byblos the king, Zakar-Baal, treats him with scant respect. He returns to Nesbenebded for more gold and silver, finally obtains the desired timber, but is driven by a contrary wind to Alashiya (Cyprus) where he almost loses his life. Only after these and other adventures and misadventures does he return to Egypt, where he tells his story in the first person. In the lands he has visited, the power and prestige of Egypt have sunk to a low point when an Egyptian envoy can be subjected to such humiliating treatment as he has experienced.

Herihor is known further from his addition of a hypostyle hall, forecourt, and pylon to the temple of Khonsu at Karnak (begun by Ramses III and continued by Ramses IV). In its reliefs and inscriptions, he appears as first prophet of Amun-Re and king's son of Kush. He even wears the double crown and uraeus; thus, at least within the confines of the temple, he indulged in some pretensions to royalty.[71] In the same temple, we also meet Herihor's wife, named Nodjme, and read a list of his numerous sons, of whom the first and presumably oldest is Piankhy. Later, but according to various indications while Ramses XI was still pharaoh, Piankhy himself appears (on a wall of a small temple between the Ninth and Tenth pylons of the temple of Amun at Karnak, and on a stela from Abydos, in Cairo) as first prophet of Amun-Re and king's son of Kush. Thus he has succeeded his presumably deceased father in the positions of high priest of Amun at Thebes and viceroy of Nubia.[72]

Nesbenebded, who appears in the Travels of Wenamun as in effect the ruler of Lower Egypt, even while Ramses XI was still actually the pharaoh, is recognizably the Smendes whom Manetho names as the first king of the Twenty-first Dynasty. Thus the shape of affairs in the ensuing period was already determined; the successors of Herihor and Piankhy constituted a line of powerful high priests of Amun at Thebes, and Smendes and those who followed him became the pharaohs of a new dynasty and ruled at Tanis.

19. THIRD INTERMEDIATE PERIOD, TWENTY-FIRST TO TWENTY-FOURTH DYNASTIES (1069-715)

As foreshadowed by the division of authority within Egypt and the loss of Egyptian control abroad in Asia and in Kush, and also as measured in comparison with the magnificent monuments of the Old, Middle, and New kingdoms, the period that now ensued in Egyptian history was relatively more confused and less impressive. It thus constitutes a Third Intermediate Period. In terms of Manetho's dynasties, the period comprises the Twenty-first Tanite dynasty and the Twenty-second, Twenty-third, and Twenty-fourth Libyan dynasties, also centered in the Delta. In terms of dates as presently established, the period extended from 1069 to 715, the terminal date being that of the end of the three Libyan dynasties with the conquest of Egypt by the Kushite Shabaka of the Twenty-fifth Dynasty.[1] In comparison with events in the lands to the north and east, the Third Intermediate Period was approximately contemporary with the Middle Babylonian dynasties from the "Fourth" (1156-1025) into the "Ninth" (731-626), with the Assyrian empire from just after Tiglath-pileser I (1115-1077) to Sargon II (721-705), and with the time of the Israelite judges and kings in Palestine to shortly after the fall of the northern kingdom (722).

Twenty-first Dynasty

From Manetho (Africanus) and the monuments, the kings of the Twenty-first Dynasty are listed, with dates, in Table 31.[2] From many scattered items of evidence, the high priests of Amun at Thebes are shown in Table 32 in approximate correlation with the kings with whom they were contemporary.[3]

Of the high priests, it is probable that Pinudjem I and Menkheperre, like

TABLE 31. TWENTY-FIRST DYNASTY (1069-945)

Manetho	Years of Reign	Egyptian Name	Date
1. Smendes	26	Hedjkheperre-setepenre Nesbenebded	1069–1043
2. Nephercheres	4	Neferkare-hikwast Amunemnisu	1043–1039
3. Psusennes I	46	Akheperre-setepenamun Psibkhaemne	1039–993
4. Amenophthis	9	Usermare-setepenamun Amunemope	993–984
5. Osochor	6	Akheperre-setepenre	984–978
6. Psinaches	[1] 9	Nutekheperre-setepenamun Siamun	978–959
7. Psusennes II	14	Titkheperure-setepenamun Psibkhaemne	959–945
	124		

Herihor before them, made some claim to kingship, and the last priest in the series, Psusennes, possibly became the Tanite king Psusennes II. Although for the most part the country was, in effect, divided between the high priests at Thebes and the kings at Tanis—and there must have been a measure of rivalry—on the whole the relationships appear to have been friendly, and the two lines were interrelated by marriage. Furthermore, although the god Sutekh (equated with the Asiatic Baal) and the Asiatic goddess Astarte had been prominently worshiped at Tanis under the Nineteenth Dynasty, now the triad of Amun, Mut, and Khonsu were the principal deities at Tanis as well as at Thebes.[4]

Psusennes I

Of the kings of the Twenty-first Dynasty, the best known is Psusennes I, because of the discovery of his intact tomb in the excavation of Tanis.[5] The mummy of the king was that of an old man, in agreement with the fact of his long reign. A second burial chamber in the tomb was for the sister and wife of Psusennes I, Queen Mutnodjme. But at some later time her mummy and funerary materials were removed, and the mummy and funerary equipment of King Amunemope were placed there, he having been buried at first in a separate tomb not far away. Several other mummies were also found in the tomb of Psusennes I. Presumably all of these placed there at a later time were so treated in order to protect them from the destruction that threatened other tombs. Meanwhile at Thebes, the royal burials were still in danger too, as they had been already in the Twentieth Dynasty, and the high priests of Amun were trying to rescue some of the royal remains. From dated hieratic notations on some of the mummies and coffins, it is learned that Pinudjem I "sent to reinter [literally, to repeat the burial of]"

TABLE 32. HIGH PRIESTS OF AMUN AT THEBES
AND CONTEMPORARY KINGS AT TANIS

King Smendes
Pinudjem I, son of Piankhy
Masahert, son of Pinudjem I
Menkheperre, son of Pinudjem I

King Amunemnisu
Menkheperre

King Psusennes I
Menkheperre
Smendes, son of Menkheperre

King Amunemope
Smendes
Pinudjem II, son of Menkheperre

King Osochor
Pinudjem II

King Siamun
Pinudjem II
Psusennes, son of Pinudjem II

King Psusennes II

the mummies of Amunhotep I and Thutmose II, made new wrappings for Seti I and Ramses III, and transferred the body of Ramses II to the tomb of Seti I.[6]

Because available Egyptian sources of the Twenty-first Dynasty give no detailed information about relations with Palestine and Syria, it may be assumed that the conditions encountered by Wenamun not long before continued to prevail, i.e., those areas were independent of Egyptian control, but there were associations in travel and trade. At this time, say broadly around 1000, Assyria was rising toward major power, but it was not yet making the devastating incursions into Syria and Palestine which began a century and a half later. In the region between Egypt and Assyria, therefore, conditions were favorable for the development of the several small kingdoms of Philistia, Phoenicia, Moab, Edom, and Israel, and such conflicts as they engaged in were with one another rather than with the greater powers on either side. According to biblical record, in fact, King Solomon was linked in marriage with the royal house in Egypt, and among all his many foreign wives, "the daugher of Pharaoh" is mentioned most

FIGURE 119.   Tomb of Psusennes I at Tanis. (*Jack Finegan*)

frequently (1 Kings 3:1; 7:8; 9:16, 24; 2 Chron. 8:11) and placed first in the list of these women (1 Kings 11:1).[7]

Instruction of Amunemope

An author who bears the same name as the fourth king of the Twenty-first Dynasty, and who possibly belongs to a time around 1000, wrote one of the most famous Egyptian books of wisdom, known as the Instruction of Amunemope.[8] In a way particularly reminiscent of Ptahhotep of the Fifth Dynasty, Amunemope offers adivce to his son on honesty, integrity, self-control, and kindliness. The ideal he holds up is that of the truly tranquil person, whom he contrasts with the hotheaded person in a figure of two trees (6:1-12). It is by reliance on god, he teaches, that this tranquility and, with it, freedom from overanxiety for the morrow, can be attained (19:11-17).[9]

Twenty-second Dynasty

Manetho (Africanus) states that the Twenty-second Dynasty consisted of nine Bubastite kings, of whom he gives three individual names—Sesonchis, Osorthon, and Takelothis, corresponding to the Egyptian names Sheshonq,

Osorkon, and Takelot. Many inscriptions of priests who served under the Twenty-second Dynasty are found on stelas from the Serapeum at Memphis, which commemorate the births and deaths of the sacred Apis bulls buried in that place. On one of these (in the Louvre, no. 278), a priest named Pasenhor records the interment of an Apis bull in the thirty-seventh year of a king named Akheperre Sheshonq.[10] Then the priest adds a prayer on behalf of himself and gives his own genealogy, running back through fifteen generations prior to himself. At the head of the list, in the first generation, he names "the Libyan, Buyuwawa." In the sixth generation, he names "the great chief Nimlot," son of Sheshonq and Mehtenweskhet and then, in the seventh to tenth generations, the kings Sheshonq (I), Osorkon (I), Takelot (I), and Osorkon (II). In conclusion he describes the entire line as "abiding . . . flourishing, in the temple of Harsaphes . . . one man the son of another man, without perishing, forever and ever . . . in Herakleopolis."[11] So a Libyan family had established itself at Hera-kleopolis, was there devoted to the worship of the main god of the city (the Egyptian Herishef, called Harsaphes by the Greeks and identified with Herakles), and was the family from which came the kings whom Manetho names as the kings of Bubastis in the Twenty-second Dynasty.[12] From the foregoing and other relevant sources, the kings of the Twenty-second Dynasty are listed, with dates, in Table 33.[13]

Sheshonq I

In the time of the Twenty-second Dynasty, the situation in Egypt was essentially feudal, with many local dynasts. There was neither a strongly centralized government at home nor a vigorous foreign policy abroad.[14] Nevertheless, before his reign was over, the founder of the dynasty, Sheshonq I, did considerable building at home and made at least one military campaign of importance outside of Egypt.

At Karnak, virtually no work had been done on the great temple of Amun since the close of the Nineteenth Dynasty, since the Tanite kings of the Twentieth Dynasty and the Theban high priests of the Twenty-first Dynasty had given their attention rather to the temple of Khonsu. Now Sheshonq I built a new colonnaded forecourt in the Amun temple west of the Second Pylon and the great hypostyle hall, with a triumphal gate that formed a westward extension of the south wall of the hypostyle hall.[15] On the triumphal gate (known as the Bubastite Gate), Sheshonq I and his son Iuput, high priest of Amun at Thebes, are depicted together with the gods, and on the south face of the Second Pylon between the gate and the south wall of the hypostyle hall is the record of a military campaign of the king, consisting of a large relief and a long inscription.[16] In the relief, Sheshonq I

TABLE 33. TWENTY-SECOND DYNASTY (945-715)

Name	Years of Reign	Date
1. Hedjkheperre-setepenre Sheshonq I	21	945–924
2. Sekhemkheperre-setepenre Osorkon I	35	924–889
Heqakheperre-setepenre Sheshonq II, coregent		890
3. Usermare-setepenamun Takelot I	15	889–874
4. Usermare-setepenamun Osorkon II	24	874–850
Hedjkheperre-setepenamun Harsiese, coregent		870–860
5. Hedjkheperre-setepenre Takelot II	25	850–825
6. Usermare-setepenre Sheshonq III	52	825–773
7. Usermare-setepenre Pimay	6	773–767
8. Akheperre-setepenre Sheshonq V	37	767–730
9. Akheperre-setepenamun Osorkon IV	15	730–715

stands at the right and the god Amun at the left, the latter leading by cords rows of Asiatic captives. The individual captives symbolize the towns that Sheshonq claims to have taken; in each case, the name of the place is enclosed in an oval, which represents a crenellated fortification and is marked out beneath the head and shoulders of the person. In the inscription, following the custom begun by Thutmose III and continued by many other kings of the Eighteenth and Nineteenth dynasties, a long list is given of the conquered places. Many are well-known biblical sites (Gaza, Arad, Aijalon, Beth-horon, Gibeon, Tirzah, Bethshan, Taanach, Megiddo, and others) and indicate a campaign that came up through the southern coastal plain of Palestine and the Negeb and into the central and northern parts of the country, i.e., it was an attack upon both the kingdom of Judah and the kingdom of Israel. This campaign must be the same as that described in 1 Kings 14:25f. and 2 Chron. 12:2-9, where the invading king is called Shishak, and the date is in the fifth year of Rehoboam (926/925). Since the previously united kingdom of Solomon had been broken apart under Rehoboam of Judah and Jeroboam I of Israel only a few years before, it was no doubt the weakness caused by this disruption that provided the favorable opportunity for the incursion by Sheshonq I. But the situation still did not allow the reestablishment of permanent Egyptian control in Palestine.[17]

MIDDLE IRON AGE (900-600)

Of Osorkon I and Takelot I little is known, but in the list of the kings of the dynasty, a Sheshonq II is provisionally inserted between them for a brief

FIGURE 120. Tomb of Sheshonq I at Tanis. (*Jack Finegan*)

coregency near the end of the reign of Osorkon I. The mummy of this previously unknown Sheshonq was found at Tanis, where, like the mummy of King Amunemope, it had been placed in the tomb of Psusennes I.[18] The tomb of Osorkon II was also found at Tanis. Like the tomb of Psusennes I, it was constructed of large stone blocks in relatively simple style, with several chambers within. In this tomb were the bodies of several other persons too, including King Takelot II.

Osorkon II

In the third year of the reign of Osorkon II, there was a very high inundation of the Nile, and an inscription of that date in the northwest corner of the hypostyle hall of the Luxor temple says, "All the temples of Thebes were like marshes."[19] In his twenty-second year, Osorkon II celebrated the Heb Sed, and in the great temple at Bubastis, he built a granite gateway between the two main halls of that temple and decorated the gateway with scenes of what took place on this occasion of the renewal of the kingship.[20]

Although he was no doubt the most important of the later kings of the Twenty-second Dynasty, Osorkon II was hardly in complete control of his whole country, especially because of the considerable independence still asserted at Thebes and in Upper Egypt. In particular, several monuments give the name of a certain Harsiese, who was not only high priest of Amun at Thebes but probably also claimed the title of king and was for a time coregent with Osorkon II.[21] No doubt because of such weakness internally, and because of the growing threat of westward advances by Assyria, the position of Egypt in international affairs was far different from what it once had been. No longer did Egypt extend the border of its empire to the Euphrates as in the days of Thutmose III, nor even make an invasion of Palestine as Sheshonq I had more recently done. Rather, from now on, whether by diplomatic maneuvers or by sharing in a limited way in military endeavors, Egypt tried to use or join with the states in Palestine/Syria in resistance to the increasing pressure from the east, that of Assyria and of the successors of Assyria too. For example, for the battle of Qarqar (853), which probably took place within the reign of Osorkon II, Shalmaneser III lists (in his Monolith Inscription) among the forces that opposed him "1,000 soldiers from Musri [Egypt]," a smaller contingent than the large forces from Damascus, Hamath, Israel, and elsewhere.[22]

In the reign of Takelot II, his son Osorkon was high priest of Amun at Thebes and left extensive annals, which constitute the longest inscription on the Bubastite Gate. In the entry for the fifteenth year of his father, there is further witness to dissension in Egypt: "Year 15 . . . the sky did not swallow the moon . . . a great convulsion broke out in this land. . . . There was warfare in the South and North."[23]

With respect to Sheshonq III, the Serapeum stela of a priest named Pediese records the birth of an Apis bull in Year 28 of Sheshonq III and the death of the animal at the age of twenty-six years in the second year of King Pimay; therefore, Sheshonq III reigned for fifty-two years, and Pimay was his successor.[24] The tomb of Sheshonq III has been found at Tanis and, like those of Psusennes I and Osorkon II, is also a relatively simple structure.

As already noted, the Serapeum stela of Pasenhor is dated in the thirty-seventh year of Sheshonq V; therefore, this king had a reign of at least this length.[25] It was probably toward the end of his reign—in 732—that Tiglath-pileser III of Assyria took Damascus and killed Rezin (2 Kings 16:5-10), then captured many cities of northern Israel and carried the people captive to Assyria (2 Kings 15:29; 1 Chron. 5:26). But it was now more than a century after Egyptian troops had joined the forces of Damascus, Israel, and other states to resist Shalmaneser III at Qarqar (853), and there is no sign that Sheshonq V made any move to assist the former allies.

Osorkon IV

A few years later, Hoshea, king of Israel, withheld tribute from Shalmaneser V and—obviously seeking help in this act of revolt—"sent messengers to So, king of Egypt" (2 Kings 17:4). But no help was forthcoming, and Samaria was captured and the Israelites carried away to Assyria (722). The name So is understandable as an abbreviation of Osorkon, and Osorkon IV is probably the Egyptian king to whom this appeal for help was made in vain. When Sargon II came as far as Raphia in his second regnal year (720), the army commander Sibe, who came out to meet him, was probably an officer under Osorkon IV.[26] Again four years later (716), Sargon II was at the Brook of Egypt (Wadi el-Arish, less than 225 kilometers from Bubastis) and says that "Shilkanni king of Musri [Egypt] . . . brought to me as his present twelve large horses of Musri, their like not to be found in this country [Assyria]." Shilkanni is probably an Assyrian rendering of Osorkon, so this too is probably Osorkon IV. With the Assyrian king so close, Osorkon IV tries with a rich gift—and apparently successfully—to dissuade him from coming any farther.[27]

Twenty-third Dynasty

Manetho (Africanus) describes the Twenty-third Dynasty as consisting of four Tanite kings—Petubates (Petubastis in Eusebius), Osorcho, Psammus, and Zet. The first of these is plainly the Egyptian Pedubast. His name occurs several times in Nile-level records at Karnak, and in one (no. 24), his Year 5 is equated with Year 12 of an unnamed pharaoh. In conjunction with other items of evidence, the likelihood is established that the latter was Sheshonq III of the Twenty-second Dynasty, and therewith the first year of Pedubast is indicated as 818.[28] From this point onward, then, the Twenty-third Dynasty was contemporary with the Twenty-second Dynasty. Since Tanis (along with Bubastis) was a main center of the Twenty-second Dynasty, the statement of Manetho that the Twenty-third Dynasty kings were Tanite can mean that they were an offshoot of the same family that ruled at Bubastis, as is also suggested by the identity of several of the names. Thus, there were probably now two Libyan dynasties in some measure of competition with each other. From the relevant and very complex records, the kings of the Twenty-third Dynasty, with lengths of reign and dates, are listed in Table 34.[29]

In the stela of Piankhy (see also pages 330, 334), the last of these kings,

TABLE 34. *TWENTY-THIRD DYNASTY (818–715)*

Name	Years of Reign	Date
1. Usermare-setepenamun Pedubast I[a]	25	818–793[b]
2. Usermare-setepenamun Iuput I	21	804–783[c]
3. Usermare-meriamun Sheshonq IV	6	783–777
4. Usermare-setepenamun Osorkon III	28	777–749
5. Usermare-setepenamun Takelot III	20	754–734[d]
6. Usermare-setepenamun Amunrud	3	734–731
7. (*prenomen* unknown) Iuput II	16	731–715

a This king is designated as Pedubast I to distinguish him from Pedubast II, who was probably a local king of Tanis mentioned by Ashurbanipal in the seve seventh century (ARAB 2, sec. 771), and from Pedubast III, a king of the Persian period (Kitchen, *The First Intermediate Period*, pp. 98, 396, 492).

b The twenty-five-year reign of Pedubast I is given in Manetho according to Eusebius. In Africanus the figure is forty years and there is a statement that "in his reign the Olympic festival was first celebrated." With accession in 818, a forty-year reign of Pedubast I would have extended to 778, close to the traditional date of the first Olympic festival in 776.

c For this coregency, see Nile-level text no. 26: "Year 16 of . . . Pedubast, which is Year 2 of . . . Iuput. ARE 4, sec. 794, no. 1(26).

d For this coregency, see Nile-level text no. 13: "Year 28 of King Osorkon [III] . . . which is Year 5 of his son Takelot [III]." Ibid., sec. 697, no. 13.

Iuput II, is located at Taremu (known to the Greeks as Leontopolis and identified with Tell Moqdam not far from Bubastis). Therefore, this may have been the residence city of this dynasty.[30] On Theban monuments, there is mention of the kings of the Twenty-second Dynasty up to Sheshonq III, but after that, all references to kings are to members of the Twenty-third Dynasty. Thus, from the accession of Pedubast I onward, Thebes appears to have given its loyalty to the Twenty-third Dynasty rather than the Twenty-second.[31]

Twenty-fourth Dynasty

In the Twenty-fourth Dynasty, Manetho names only the Saite king Bochchoris. This king is also mentioned by Diodorus (1. 45. 2; 79. 1–5; 94. 5) and Plutarch (*Isis and Osiris* 8), who name his father as Tnephachthus or Technatis. These two persons are identifiable with Wahkare Bakenranef and Shepsesre Tefnakht, who are named on various Egyptian monuments. In the Piankhy stela, Tefnakht is called "chief of the West," "chief of Me,"

TABLE 35. TWENTY-FOURTH DYNASTY (727–715)

Name	Date
Tefnakht, as Chief of the West	740–727
1. Shepsesre Tefnakht I[a]	727–720
2. Wahkare Bakenranef	720–715

a Tefnakht II appears later among the predecessors of the Twenty-sixth Dynasty; Tefnakht III was a chieftain in the time of Ashurbanipal. Kitchen, *The Third Intermediate Period*, p. 397.

and "chief of Sais," and on his own stelas uses similar titles as chief of the West, of the Me, and of the Libu. He also takes religious titles as "prophet of Neith [goddess of Sais]" and "prophet of Edjo [cobra goddess of Buto]," and later assumes royal titles too.[32]

As for Bakenranef, his name is found on a vase discovered, perhaps surprisingly, in an Etruscan tomb at the town of Tarquinia (100 kilometers northwest of Rome). On this vase, papyrus plants suggest the swamps of the Delta, and the king is seen in the company of deities, including the goddess Neith of Sais.[33]

Here, then, was yet another small Libyan dynasty ruling in the Delta, at Sais. From other evidence, including Serapeum inscriptions, the kings may be listed, with dates, as in Table 35.[34]

With authority in Egypt thus divided among at least three partially overlapping Libyan dynasties in the Delta, and doubtless among other local princes, as well as the high priests of Amun at Thebes, it is not surprising that opportunity was provided for the ensuing invasion from the south.[35] It was, however, largely the vigorous expansionist activity of Tefnakht, the "chief of the West," that provoked this invasion.

20. LATE DYNASTIC PERIOD, TWENTY-FIFTH TO THIRTY-FIRST DYNASTIES (716-332)

The Late Dynastic Period comprises the Twenty-fifth or Kushite Dynasty; the Twenty-sixth or Saite Dynasty; the Twenty-Seventh Dynasty, which was the first period of Persian rule; the Twenty-eighth to Thirtieth Dynasties, which originated in Sais, Mendes, and Sebennytus, respectively, in the Delta; and the Thirty-first Dynasty, which was the second and final period of Persian rule, terminated by the conquest of Alexander the Great. The time, from 716 to 332, was contemporary with that of the Assyrians from Sargon II to the end of their empire, of the Chaldeans in Babylonia, and of the Achaemenians in Persia. In Palestine the kingdom of Judah reached its end (586), and the exilic and post-exilic periods ensued.

Twenty-fifth (Kushite) Dynasty

Manetho (Africanus) says the the Twenty-fifth Dynasty comprised three Ethiopian kings—Sabacon, who took Bochchoris captive and burned him alive, Sebichos his son, and Tarcus. Greek writers used the name Ethiopia as equivalent to or including what the Egyptians called Kush (Upper Nubia and Sudan), and from monuments found at Napata and other sites in this area, as well as in Egypt, it is possible to ascertain the names and reconstruct the probable relationships of the members of the royal family here involved.[1] As thus known, the royal line begins with a chieftain named Alara and his brother Kashta. Kashta was followed in turn by an older son Piankhy and a younger son Shabaka. After Shabaka came two sons of Piankhy—Shabataka and Taharqa. Here it is clear that Shabaka, Shabataka, and Taharqa are the Sabacon, Sebichos, and Tarcus whom Manetho names. After Taharqa, the throne was occupied by a son of Shabataka named Tanutamun. This series of kings is shown, with probable lengths of reign and dates, in Table 36.[2]

TABLE 36. *TWENTY-FIFTH (KUSHITE) DYNASTY (716–656)*

Name	Years of Reign	Date
Alara	20	780–760
Maatre Kashta	13	760–747
Usermare Sneferre Piankhy[a]	31	747–716
1. Neferkare Shabaka	14	716–702
2. Djedkaure Shabataka	12	702–690
3. Nefertumkhure Taharqa	26	690–664
4. Bakare Tanutamun	8	664–656

a Of the two *prenomens* shown for Piankhy, Usermare was used first, Sneferre later, but the *nomen* was generally preferred.

As to Napata, this capital of the Kushite kings was below the Fourth Cataract, at the foot of the isolated, flat-topped rock, Gebel Barkal, anciently known as the Pure Mountain. In the vicinity are several temples and the royal tombs, both mastabas and pyramids. Judging from these remains, the Kushite kings were thoroughly Egyptianized, worshiping Amun, writing in hieroglyphics, and building monuments in the Egyptian style.[3]

Kashta and Piankhy

In earlier times, Egypt had entered Nubia to conquer and rule. Now with Egypt divided, the situation was reversed. A stela of Kashta found at Aswan is presumable evidence that his rule extended at least here to the border of Upper Egypt, and possibly even farther.[4] At any rate Piankhy, Kashta's son and successor, made an actual if temporary conquest of Egypt. This is recorded in detail on a large stela of pink granite discovered in the temple of Amun at Gebel Barkal (now in the Cairo Museum).[5] In a relief scene at the top, Piankhy stands before Amun and Mut, and four kings who have made submission to him are portrayed—Nemrot of Hermopolis, leading his horse, Osorkon IV (Twenty-second Dynasty) of Tanis and Bubastis, Iuput II (Twenty-third Dynasty) of Leontopolis, and Peftuabast of Herakleopolis. The text is dated in Year 21 of Piankhy and was presumably composed soon after the events it relates. The invasion may thus have taken place in the twentieth year, about 728. At that time, we learn, Tefnakht, the Libyan "chief of the West" (Twenty-fourth Dynasty), had launched an aggressive campaign of expansion, was in control of the West Delta as far as Memphis and even Itj-towy (Lisht), and was pushing on southward. At Herakleopolis (Ehnasiya el-Medina, 60 kilometers south of Lisht), the local ruler Peftuabast, son-in-law of King Amunrud (Twenty-third Dynasty), was resisting, but under siege. At Hermopolis (Ashmunein, 155 kilometers yet farther south), the local king, a man with the Libyan name of Nemrot, had been a vassal of Piankhy but now defected to Tefnakht.[6]

At this juncture Piankhy sent his troops northward and subsequently went to lead them in person.[7] Herakleopolis was delivered from the siege it had been under by the forces of Tefnakht, and Peftuabast welcomed Piankhy with much gratitude; Hermopolis was itself besieged by the Kushite forces, and Nemrot surrendered to Piankhy.[8] Many other places were taken by the Kushites, including Itj-towy, and Memphis, where a dramatic waterborne battle was fought. Tefnakht fled into the islands of the Delta swamps and sent a message of submission and took an oath of allegiance, and Piankhy, momentarily master of the Nile valley from Kush to the Delta, returned triumphantly to Napata.

Shabaka

Piankhy did not, however, maintain his position in Egypt proper, and Tefnakht shortly forgot his oath of allegiance and made himself king of much of Lower Egypt, to be succeeded somewhat later by his son Bakenranef (Twenty-fourth Dynasty). In Kush, meanwhile, Piankhy was succeeded by his younger brother Shabaka. Since Manetho says that he (Sabacon) killed Bakenranef (Bochchoris) and was the first king of the Twenty-fifth Dynasty, Shabaka must have reconquered Egypt and established the Kushite supremacy on a continuing basis. Since there is an inscription from the tomb of an Apis bull at Memphis with a date in Year 2 of Shabaka (715), he must have come at least that far by that time.[9]

As king of Egypt, Shabaka undertook at least some building projects. On the Fourth Pylon of the great temple at Karnak, an inscription states that he restored this "great and august gate."[10] At Medinet Habu, he began the second pylon in front of the temple of Thutmose III, a work that was completed by Taharqa. Also Shabaka's sister Amunirdis I was "god's wife of Amun" at Thebes, a position of political as well as religious importance, and her funerary temple was constructed at Medinet Habu (in front of the great temple of Ramses III).[11]

Shabataka and Taharqa

In the second year of Shabataka (701), nephew and successor of Shabaka, Sennacherib renewed the Assyrian thrust into Palestine, fought a great battle on the plain of Eltekeh near Ekron, captured Lachish, and besieged

Jerusalem. When Sargon II was in Palestine and thus dangerously close to Egypt, Osorkon IV and Shabaka pursued policies of conciliation and cooperation, and the Assyrians came no farther. Now Shabataka evidently decided upon a different policy of outright resistance. On a stela from Kawa (IV) of Taharqa, Shabataka's brother and successor, we learn that Shabataka summoned his brothers, including Taharqa as his favorite, to come north to him at Thebes, and that the army went with Taharqa: "Now his majesty had been in Nubia as a goodly youth, a king's brother, pleasant of love, and he came north to Thebes in the company of goodly youths whom his majesty King Shabataka had sent to fetch from Nubia, in order that he might be there with him, since he loved him more than all his brothers. He passed to the nome of Amun of Gematen that he might make obeisance at the temple door, with the army of his majesty which had traveled north together with him."[12]

On another Kawa stela (V), we also learn that Taharqa was himself twenty years of age at the time and that he went on with the king to Lower Egypt.[13] From Sennacherib, we learn that rebellious Ekron asked for help from the kings of Musri (Egypt) and that a large army of the king of Meluhha (Nubia) came out but was defeated by himself at Eltekeh.[14] In 2 Kings 19:9 and Isa. 37:9 we are told that when Jerusalem was under siege by the Assyrians, Tirhakah king of Ethiopia (Kush) came against Sennacherib. The picture provided by these complementary references seems plain: Shabataka joined in the resistance to Sennacherib; the Egyptian army that went to Palestine to fight against Sennacherib was led by Shabataka's brother Taharqa, who later succeeded him as king.[15]

With respect to his assumption of rule, Taharqa says on Kawa stela V: "I received the crown in Memphis after the Falcon had soared to heaven," i.e., Shabataka his brother died, and he was crowned as his successor. Then he also tells how his mother, whom he had not seen since he departed from her as a youth of twenty years (i.e., when Shabataka summoned him and the other brothers and the army to the north), herself came north to see him on the throne. "And she rejoiced exceedingly after beholding the beauty of his majesty [says Taharqa of himself], even as Isis saw her son Horus crowned upon the throne of his father."[16]

In the course of his reign, Taharqa did very considerable building both in Nubia and in Egypt. Most imposing must have been a tremendous colonnade in the first court of the temple of Amun at Karnak, of which one enormous column (twenty-one meters in height) still stands in place.[17]

Before the reign of Taharqa was over, the Assyrian threat to Egypt was renewed. In 701 the youthful future king Taharqa fought against Sennacherib in Palestine, unsuccessfully according to Sennacherib's

FIGURE 121.　Column of Taharqa in the Temple at Karnak. (*Jack Finegan*)

report. In 674/673 the army of Sennacherib's son and successor Esarhaddon was defeated in Egypt, then came again in a successful invasion in 671/670. On the last occasion, according to Esarhaddon's inscriptions, he wounded Taharqa, captured Memphis, carried off Taharqa's family and property, conquered "Egypt, Upper Egypt, and Ethiopia," and appointed local kings, governors, and officers.[18]

Although wounded, Taharqa survived and again instituted resistance to Assyria. Therefore, on his first campaign (667/666), Ashurbanipal marched into Egypt and, according to his own inscriptions, drove Taharqa out of both Memphis and Thebes, and the Egyptian king "was never heard of again." Actually, however, a Serapeum stela notes a Year 26 of Taharqa in which an Apis bull was installed; it died in Year 20 of Psamtik, having lived twenty-one years; thus Taharqa was considered the immediate predecessor of Psamtik I, founder (in 664), of the Twenty-sixth Dynasty. Presumably Taharqa lived until that date (664), then died and was buried in his large pyramid tomb at Nuri near Napata.[19]

In Manetho, Taharqa (Tarcus) appears as the last king of the Twenty-fifth Dynasty. But in the so-called Dream Stela (discovered at Napata along with the Piankhy Stela) we learn of a successor of his named Tanutamun.[20] Tanutamun, it is related, experienced a dream of two serpents, and this was interpreted to him as meaning: "Thine is the Southland, take for thyself also the Northland." Accordingly, after coronation in Napata, he sailed downstream to Lower Egypt, captured Memphis, and received the submission of the Delta princes. Ashurbanipal calls the same king Urdamane, and tells of the same events and more, from the Assyrian point of view.[21] Urdamane, Ashurbanipal says, established himself in Thebes and Heliopolis and attacked the Assyrians in Memphis. Thereupon, Ashurbanipal launched his second campaign against Egypt (664/663). Urdamane forsook Memphis and fled to Thebes. Ashurbanipal marched after him, and Urdamane fled further to Kipkipi, while Ashurbanipal captured Thebes and carried heavy plunder (including two tall obelisks) home to Nineveh. Thebes was "smashed as if by a floodstorm," says Ashurbanipal, and confirmation of the destruction of the city is probably to be seen in the remains of burned houses found in modern excavation at Karnak. Kipkipi, whither Urdamane (Tanutamun) fled, is unidentified; at any rate, he was buried at last in a pyramid tomb at Kurru near Napata.[22]

Twenty-sixth (Saite) Dynasty

The kings of the Twenty-sixth Dynasty are listed, as known from Manetho (Africanus) and (from Psamtik I onward) from relatively numerous

TABLE 37. TWENTY-SIXTH (SAITE) DYNASTY (664–525)

Manetho	Egyptian Name	Years of Reign	Date
Stephinates			
Nechepsos			
Nechao	Menkheperre Necho I	8	672–664
1. Psammetichus	Wahibre Psamtik I	54	664–610
2. Nechao the Second	Wehemibre Necho II	15	610–595
3. Psammuthis the Second	Neferibre Psamtik II	6	595–589
4. Uaphris	Ha'a'ibre Wahibre/Apries	19	589–570
5. Amosis	Khnemibre Ahmose-si-Neit/Amasis	44	570–526
6. Psammecherites	Ankhkaenre Psamtik III	6 months	526–525

Egyptian monuments, in Table 37, with probable lengths of reign and dates.[23] Of these persons, the first several were probably local rulers at Sais who, in one way or another, followed the Twenty-fourth Dynasty, which had been ruling there and was brought to an end when Shabaka killed Bakenranef.[24] Upon the coming of the Assyrians, Necho I was confirmed in his position by Esarhaddon (671/670) and later by Ashurbanipal (667/666).[25] As such a vassal, Necho I was probably killed by Tanutamun when the latter made his attack upon the Assyrians in the Delta (664), a fact to which Herodotus (2. 152) refers when he says that Necho was slain by an Ethiopian king (although Herodotus wrongly thinks that this was Shabaka instead of Tanutamun). Herodotus also says that Necho's son Psammetichus (Psamtik I) fled at the time to Syria (Assyria), then came back to Sais, and there he was presumably at first a vassal of Ashurbanipal. Increasingly, however, the Assyrians were occupied with disturbances at home, relationships with Babylon, and the problems of the decline of their empire. This provided the opportunity for the establishment of Saite rule in freedom from foreign domination, but perhaps still in some measure of alliance with Assyria. Officially, then, Psamtik I was considered the successor of Taharqa (Twenty-fifth Dynasty) and the founder of the Twenty-sixth Dynasty, and it was indeed under him that the dynasty became independent and Egypt again unified.

Sais

Sais, center of this dynasty as also previously of the Twenty-sixth Dynasty, was an ancient city and is mentioned already in the Book of the Dead in connection with Neith (goddess of the waters prior to creation and mother of the sun), who is called "the lady of Sais."[26] Herodotus (2. 59, 163, 170f., 175) visited the city and speaks with admiration of the "great and marvelous palace" of Apries, and of the works of Amasis at "the temple of Athene" (with whom Neith was identified). The temple had a very large outer court with great stone obelisks, huge images, man-headed sphinxes, and, by the temple entrance, a shrine made out of an enormous single block of stone. The royal necropolis was perhaps also in the temple precinct, and Herodotus mentions the tombs of Amasis, Apries, and the latter's ancestors. The festival held at Sais in honor of Athene (Neith), Herodotus also says, was the third greatest festival in Egypt, after only those in honor of Artemis (Bastet) at Bubastis and of Isis at Busiris. In the temple was also a reputed burial place of Osiris, and a lake nearby provided the setting for the performance of the "mysteries" of Osiris. The ruins of Sais are near the present village of Sa el-Hagar ("Sa of stone") on the east bank of the Rosetta branch of the Nile (thirty kilometers northwest of Tanta).

Psamtik I

In the ninth year of Psamtik I, an event took place that evidently signified the acceptance of his authority in Upper Egypt as well as Lower, namely Psamtik I sent his daughter Nitocris to Thebes to be adopted by the "god's wives of Amun" (now Shepenupet II and Amunirdis II) as their successor.[27]

With the renewal of centralized government, peace, prosperity, and strength were restored in considerable measure to Egypt. A revival of the more ancient Egyptian art and culture took place, and in particular, the monuments of the Old Kingdom were copied in the reliefs and sculptures of the time.

As to foreign relations, Herodotus provides several items of information. From Greece, voyaging Ionians and Carians, "men of bronze" (i.e., wearing bronze mail) came to Egypt, assisted Psamtik I in his early efforts to gain the mastery over the other princes of the Delta, were settled in "the Camps" on either side of the Pelusiac branch of the Nile below Bubastis, and finally were removed by King Amasis to Memphis. From these settlers in Egypt, Herodotus says, "we Greeks have exact knowledge of the history of Egypt from the reign of Psammetichus onwards" (2. 152-154). In the direction of Asia, Psamtik I devoted twenty-nine years (2. 157) to the capture of Azotus (Ashdod, sixteen kilometers north of Ashkelon). In Palestine, he also met the oncoming Scythians and persuaded them with gifts and prayers to come no further (1. 103-105); if this required military force as well, the final taking of Ashdod may have had some connection with the matter, for the Scythians passed through nearby Ascalon (Ashkelon) in their withdrawal. On the borders of Egypt proper, Psamtik I had garrisons "at Daphnae of Pelusium on the side of Arabia and Assyria," at Marea on the side of Libya, and at Elephantine on the side of Ethiopia (2. 30). Furthermore, the Babylonian Chronicle (B.M. 21901) records the defeat by Nabopolassar in his tenth year (616/615) of an Assyrian army, assisted by an Egyptian army, near Haran, so Psamtik I was evidently continuing as at least an ally of the Assyrians.

LATE IRON AGE (600-330)

Necho II

Necho II, son and successor of Psamtik I, also tried unsuccessfully to help the Assyrians, for the same Babylonian Chronicle describes the "great Egyptian army" that joined Ashur-uballit II in an effort to recapture Haran, but "retired" in evident defeat in the seventeenth year of Nabopolassar (609).[28] Even though Haran was not retaken, the Egyptian forces evidently remained in Syria for several years, for they were involved in the battles with Nabopolassar at Kimuhu (on the west bank of the Euphrates, south of Carchemish) in the nineteenth and twentieth years (607/606, 606/605) of the Babylonian king, and were only finally and decisively defeated by Nebuchadnezzar II at Carchemish in 605. After that Necho II made no further attempt to challenge the Babylonians. The state of affairs is summarized in 2 Kings 24:7: "And the king of Egypt did not come again out of his land, for the king of Babylon had taken all that belonged to the king of Egypt from the Brook of Egypt to the Euphrates."[29]

Despite the limits he met in his military activities, the seafaring undertakings of Necho II were far-reaching. Herodotus (2. 158f.) says not only that Necho II began the making of the canal into the Red Sea (the canal was finished by Darius the Persian), but also that he had warships (triremes) built both on the northern sea (the Mediterranean) and in the Arabian Gulf. Herodotus (4. 42) also relates that Necho II desired to know whether Libya (Africa) were surrounded on all sides by water and so sent Phoenicians in ships to find out. They were to sail down the Red Sea and come back past the Pillars of Hercules, which they did in a remarkable three-year circumnavigation.[30]

Psamtik II, son and successor of Necho II, evidently continued to avoid military endeavor in Asia, but Herodotus (2. 161) reports an invasion of Ethiopia, probably in this case meaning Lower Nubia.[31] From a sarcophagus of their daughter Ankhnesneferibre, we learn that the queen of Psamtik II was Tahut.[32] At Tell Atrib (Athribis), some fragments of the tomb furniture of Queen Tahut were found, including a tiny pair of exquisitely made gold sandals, characteristic of Saite art, which took delight in works of small scale. On an alabaster stela of Ankhnesneferibre (Cairo Museum), we learn that in the first year of her father's reign, this lady went to Thebes to be officially adopted by Nitocris, then "god's wife of Amun," as Nitocris herself had once been adopted by Shepenupet II at the decree of Psamtik I.[33]

Apries

The stela of Ankhnesneferibre also records the death of Psamtik II and the accession of his son Wahibre, called Apries by Herodotus (2. 161).[34] The new king was soon faced with renewed, heavy Babylonian pressure in Palestine. Nebuchadnezzar II began the long siege of Jerusalem, which resulted in the final capture and burning of the city (probably August 14-17, 586). Reversing the policy of his predecessors since the battle of Carchemish (605), Apries undertook to challenge the Babylonians. Jeremiah uses the name Hophra for Apries (44:30) and must be referring to him when he tells (37:5-11) how pharaoh's army advanced out of Egypt and the Chaldeans raised the siege of Jerusalem to meet them. Since the siege was soon renewed and completed successfully, Apries must have been driven off.[35] Both Jeremiah (43:8-13; 46:13-25) and Ezekiel (29-32) expressed the expectation that Nebuchadnezzar would go on to invade Egypt, but it was only under Apries's successor that this happened.

Amasis

After a later, very disastrous military expedition in Cyrene, a rival king backed by a mutinous army challenged Apries and drove him from the throne. This was Amasis, and Herodotus (2. 161f., 172-174; 4. 159), who tells the story, pictures him as a very common man who came from a town called Siuph in the province of Sais.[36] It was no doubt this time of confusion that provided an especially favorable time for Nebuchadnezzar II to attack Egypt, and a fragmentary cuneiform inscription states that in his thirty-seventh year (568/567), the Babylonian king fought against the troops of "[Ama]su, of Egypt."[37] It does not appear, however, that Nebuchadnezzar II made any effort to hold Egypt, and Amasis evidently returned to the more pacific policies from which Apries had departed, so the Egyptian and Babylonian kingdoms probably continued hereafter in relatively peaceful relations with each other until both were overwhelmed by the Persian empire.[38]

It was in the latter part of his long reign that Amasis witnessed the rise of Cyrus II of Persia. Even as Psamtik I and Necho II vainly took the side of

Assyria against the rising power of Chaldea, so now Amasis entered into an alliance that bound Egypt, Lydia, and Babylonia together against the new Persian threat (Herodotus 1. 77).[39] This was also in vain, however, for, in spite of whatever aid Egypt was able to give,[40] both Croesus of Lydia and Nabonidus of Babylon were swiftly overcome by Cyrus (547/546 and 539). Egypt could presumably expect attack soon, but, as it transpired, Cyrus was occupied with fighting in the vicinity of the Caspian Sea, where he died in 530, and it was his son Cambyses II who accomplished the conquest of Egypt. By that time (Herodotus 3. 10), Amasis was no longer alive, having died after a reign of forty-four years and having been succeeded by his son Psamtik III.

Manetho (Africanus) tells us that Psamtik III (Psammecherites) had a reign of six months and that Cambyses took the Egyptian throne in the fifth year of his own kingship over the Persians. From these and related data, Amasis must have died near the end (say in November/December) of the year 526, and the Persian army must have come against Egypt at about the same time. The defeat of Psamtik III by Cambyses must have ensued in the spring (say in May/June) of 525.[41] The decisive, and for Egypt disastrous, battle was fought at Pelusium (Herodotus 3. 10f.). When it was over, Egypt entered its first period of Persian rule (Twenty-seventh Dynasty).

Twenty-seventh (Persian) Dynasty

Table 38 reproduces the list of Persian rulers of Egypt from Manetho (Africanus) and gives in parentheses the dates of the major kings and notes of identification of the others from Persian history. In the form of Manetho's list preserved in Eusebius, the Magi are inserted for seven months of rule between Cambyses and Darius I, and Artabanus is omitted.

In Egypt, Cambyses at first treated Psamtik III with some consideration, but when Psamtik III tried to revolt, Cambyses caused his death (Herodotus 3. 14f.). The inscription on a statue (Vatican no. 158) of a certain Udjahorresenet, a priest of Neith and physician at Sais, records that Cambyses came to Sais, worshiped Neith, and restored the revenues and festivals of the temple.[42] But Herodotus (3. 16, 27-30, 37, 61) says that Cambyses did many reprehensible things against Egyptian custom and religion and finally, while he still "lingered in Egypt," quite "lost his wits" and "his former want of sense turned . . . to madness."

Darius I

Darius I was in Egypt already as a young man under Cambyses (Herodotus 3. 139) and, when he was king, treated the Egyptians with respect and

TABLE 38. TWENTY-SEVENTH (PERSIAN) DYNASTY (525-405)

1. Cambyses in the fifth year of his kingship over the Persians became king of Egypt, and ruled for six years (525-522).
2. Darius (I the Great), son of Hystaspes, for thirty-six years (521-486).
3. Xerxes (I) the Great, for twenty-one years (485-465).
4. Artabanus, for seven months (vizier and murderer of Xerxes I).
5. Artaxerxes (I Longimanus), for forty-one years (464-424).
6. Xerxes (II), for two months (murdered by his half-brother Sogdianus).
7. Sogdianus, for seven months (defeated and executed by another half-brother Ochus, who became Darius II Nothus).
8. Darius (II Nothus), son of Xerxes (an incorrect statement by Manetho), for nineteen years (423-405).

goodwill (Diodorus 1. 95. 4f.). In an undertaking recorded on the back of the so-called Demotic Chronicle, he called upon the priests and other wise men to set forth in writing the complete Egyptian law down to the end of the reign of Amasis; the collection they made was copied in two languages, demotic, the late form of Egyptian, and Aramaic, the official language of the Persian empire.[43] From the statue of Udjahorresenet, we learn that this personage was with Darius I in the East, but was sent back to Egypt to reestablish the so-called Houses of Life, which probably existed in various cities and had to do both with the copying of sacred texts and with the practice of medicine.[44]

A major undertaking of Darius I in Egypt was the renewal and completion of the canal from the Nile to the Red Sea. Other construction work included expansion of the Serapeum at Saqqara and the erection of a large temple of Amun in the great southwestern oasis of el-Kharga.[45] Administratively, under Darius I, Egypt, Libya, and Cyrenaica were combined in the sixth satrapy of the Persian empire, and the satrap who governed the province had his residence in Memphis (Herodotus 3. 91).

In spite of the benefits of the rule of Darius I in Egypt, the defeat of the Persians in the battle of Marathon (491) showed that the great empire was not invincible, and there was revolt in Egypt in the last years of Darius I, which was put down only in the second year of Xerxes I (484/483). The latter then "laid Egypt under a much harder slavery than in the time of Darius" (Herodotus 7. 1, 7). In fact, however, Xerxes I, Artaxerxes I, and Darius II were largely occupied elsewhere and took little active interest in Egypt, although Darius II did some work on the temple of Amun in the oasis of Kharga. In this time, there were also many other foreigners in Egypt, particularly Greeks and Jews, and it was around 450 that Herodotus came and traveled in the country.

Twenty-eighth (Saite) Dynasty: Last Independence

When Darius II died in the spring of 404, there was renewed revolt in Egypt, and independence was achieved again for a time. At this point, Manetho introduces his Twenty-eighth Dynasty, consisting of one king, Amyrteos (Amyrtaios) of Sais, who reigned for six years (404-399).[46] Like the rulers of the same city of Sais in the Twenty-fourth and Twenty-Sixth dynasties, Amyrtaios may well have been a Libyan. Among the Elephantine Papyri, the latest dated document is a loan contract written in Year 5 of this king (400). This shows that he was recognized in Upper as well as Lower Egypt; therefore, he must have been able to expel the Persians from the whole country.[47]

Twenty-ninth (Mendesian) Dynasty

The four Mendesian kings who, according to Manetho (Africanus), comprised the Twenty-ninth Dynasty are listed in Table 39, with the corresponding names as found on the monuments and with the probable dates.[48]

Mendes

Mendes, center of the Twenty-ninth Dynasty, was the Egyptian Djedi, the city of the sacred Djed pillar of Osiris, the home of the Mendesian goat according to Manetho, and the residence city of Lower Egyptian Nome XVI ("Dolphin"). The site is identified with Tell Ruba (twenty kilometers southeast of Mansura), and the major monument still in place is the granite shrine of a large temple built by Amasis (Twenty-sixth Dynasty). Of the several kings of the Twenty-ninth Dynasty, monuments are found all the way from the Delta to Karnak.[49]

At this time Egypt entered into alliance with Sparta against Persia, and Diodorus (14. 79. 4) tells how Nephereus (Nepherites I) sent the Spartans a gift of equipment for one hundred triremes and 500,000 measures of grain, but lost the grain to the Persians when the ships bringing it from Egypt approached Rhodes without knowing that the Rhodians had in the meantime defected to the Persians.

After Nepherites I, both Achoris and Psammuthis were rival kings at the same time. But Psammuthis was eliminated in the first year, and Achoris continued a relatively long reign. A small temple at Karnak is witness to these happenings, having been begun by Psammuthis and completed by Achoris, with the name of the first king erased and the name of the second king put in its stead. In the reign of Achoris, peace was concluded between Persia and Sparta (386), and Persia was free to move against Egypt once more. Artaxerxes II sent his army, and a three-year war ensued (385-383).

TABLE 39. TWENTY-NINTH (MENDESIAN) DYNASTY (399–380)

Manetho	Egyptian Name	Years of Reign	Date
1. Nepherites (I)	Nef'aurud	6	399–393
2. Achoris	Hakor	13	393–380
3. Psammuthis	Psimut	1	393
4. Nepherites (II)		4 months	380

In contrast with some previous times, Egypt was relatively strong again, and Achoris also found an ally in Evagoras, king of Salamis in Cyprus. Thus Egypt was delivered. Upon the death of Achoris, however, there was unrest in Egypt. His son Nepherites II was able to hold the throne only for four months (the figure given by Manetho) and was then displaced by the founder of the Thirtieth Dynasty.

Thirtieth (Sebennytic) Dynasty

The three Sebennytic kings of the Thirtieth Dynasty are shown in Table 40 as listed by Manetho (Africanus), together with the corresponding names from the monuments and with dates.[50]

Sebennytus

Sebennytus was the Egyptian Tjeb-neter ("Divine Calf") and was the residence city of Lower Egyptian Nome XII, the sign of which was a cow and calf. The reference was to the myth of the birth of the sun god as the calf of the goddess Sekhet-Hathor. In Assyrian, the city was called Zabnuti, and in Arabic Samannud. The ancient ruins are on the west bank of the Damietta branch of the Nile, near the modern town of Samannud. Another arm of the Nile passed not far away, and was the Sebennytic branch. Manetho, born at Sebennytus, probably served in the temple here before going to Heliopolis.[51]

Nectanebo I

Although he had been unsuccessful against Achoris (Twenty-ninth Dynasty), Artaxerxes II renewed the Persian attack upon Egypt in the reign of Nectanebo I (Nectanebes in Manetho, Nectanebos in Diodorus), for Egypt was still regarded as properly a satrapy—although presently fallen away—of the Persian empire. After long preparation, in the spring of 373 the Persian army and fleet came down the coast from Akko (Acre) in

TABLE 40. THIRTIETH (SEBENNYTIC) DYNASTY (380–342)

Manetho	Egyptian Name	Years of Reign	Date
1. Nectanebes	Nakhtnebef (Nectanebo I)	18	380–362
2. Teos	Djeho	2	362–360
3. Nectanebus	Nakhthorhebe (Nectanebo II)	18	360–342

northern Palestine. As Diodorus (15. 41–43) recounts the events, the attackers found Pelusium too strongly defended and moved westward to the Mendesian mouth of the Nile. The forces of Nectanebo I resisted vigorously, two chief Persian commanders disagreed as to strategy, and while time passed, the land itself came to the aid of the defenders. By the end of July/August, the Nile was rising in its annual inundation; soon the Delta was all swamp and sea, and the Persians abandoned their effort and went away. As under Achoris, now a second time—and this time standing all alone—Egypt had turned back the attack of the Persian empire. With peace established, Nectanebo I built and restored many monuments throughout Egypt.[52]

Nectanebo II

Teos, son and successor of Nectanebo I, with mercenaries from Greece to assist his own infantry and warships, ventured a campaign against the Persians in Phoenicia and Syria, but it was a great disaster. The pharaoh's generals disagreed with his leadership, and his own son Nectanebo II rebelled against him. Deserted by both Egyptians and Greeks, Teos fled by way of Arabia and cast himself upon the mercy of his enemy, and Artaxerxes II generously gave him refuge.

Nectanebo II, thereafter, did not risk any further expeditions in Palestine and Syria. In Egypt he left his mark with extensive building activity, and numerous remains of his work, if often fragmentary, have been found throughout the country.[53]

In the reign of Nectanebo II, the Persians, now under Artaxerxes III Ochus, once again undertook to subdue Egypt. This time they were successful. According to a folk tale preserved in Greek translation on a Leiden papyrus, Nakhthorhebe (Nectanebo II) experienced in a dream a premonition of what was to come when the war god Onuris expressed displeasure with the neglect of his temple.[54] As to the actual events, Diodorus (16. 40–51) relates that Cyprus and Phoenicia were also in revolt against Persia, and Nectanebo II sent some assistance to Sidon. Artaxerxes

III destroyed Sidon and proceeded with added Greek troops against Egypt. In the winter months of 343/342, when the fighting took place, the inundation of the Nile, which had proved so disastrous for Artaxerxes II was past and the next flood not yet at hand. The new attack was also made more wisely than on the previous occasion, i.e., not just at Pelusium but at three points simultaneously, and the first penetration was accomplished at a canal near one of the more westerly mouths of the Nile. Nectanebo II withdrew to Memphis, thinking to make a stand. But as city after city capitulated, he saw that he did not dare to risk any further battles. "So," Diodorus concludes the account, "giving up hope of his kingship and taking with him the greater part of his possessions, he fled into Ethiopia."

Thirty-first (Persian) Dynasty

At the point here reached, the Latin version by Jerome of the *Chronicle* of Eusebius states: "Ochus held Egypt, having driven Nectanebo away into Ethiopia. Thereby the kingship of the Egyptians was destroyed. All the way to this point Manetho [i.e., Manetho's *History* extends this far]."[55] The Thirty-first Dynasty recorded in Africanus and Eusebius is therefore a later addition to Manetho. In this addition, the kings listed in the Thirty-first Dynasty are: Ochus (Artaxerxes III), who ruled Egypt for six years (from his conquest in 343 until he was murdered by his own commander Bagoas in the summer of 338); Arses, son of Ochus, who reigned for four years (until he too was killed by Bagoas in 336); and Darius (III Codomannus), who reigned for six years until "he was put to death by Alexander of Macedon" (330).[56]

Coming of Alexander

In 333 Alexander the Great drove Darius III eastward from the battle of Issus and in 332 himself turned southward to Egypt. From the account given by Arrian (*Anabasis* 3. 1-4), we learn that the Persian satrap, Mazaces, surrendered the land without resistance. Alexander proceeded to Memphis and offered sacrifice to Apis and the other gods, then sailed down the Nile. When he had reached Canobus (Canopus) and sailed around Lake Mareotis, he came ashore at what struck him as an admirable place for a city. There he marked out the ground plan of what became the city of Alexandria and ultimately his own place of burial. Having also visited the oracle of Amun in the oasis of Siwa, where he received a favorable word, and having appointed native Egyptians to govern the country, he departed for Phoenicia and Mesopotamia. With the coming of Alexander, Egypt, like the rest of the Middle East, was at the end of the ancient period and on the threshold of a new era.

ABBREVIATIONS

These abbreviations are used throughout the notes section:

AA	*Artibus Asiae*
AAA	*Annals of Archaeology and Anthropology,* issued by the Institute of Archaeology, University of Liverpool
AASOR	*The Annual of the American Schools of Oriental Research*
AfO	*Archiv für Orientforschung*
AICR	*Académie des Inscriptions et Belles-Lettres, Comptes-Rendus*
AJA	*American Journal of Archaeology*
AJBA	*The Australian Journal of Biblical Archaeology*
AJSL	*The American Journal of Semitic Languages and Literatures*
Anatolia	*Anatolia,* University of Ankara
ANEP	James B. Pritchard, *The Ancient Near East in Pictures relating to the Old Testament.* Princeton: Princeton University Press, 1954, Supplement 1969
ANET	James B. Pritchard, ed., *Ancient Near Eastern Texts relating to the Old Testament.* Princeton: Princeton University Press, 2d ed. 1955, Supplement 1969
AnOr	*Analecta Orientalia*
AnS	*Anatolian Studies*
Antiquity	*Antiquity, A Quarterly Review of Archaeology*
AO	*Der Alte Orient, Gemeinverständliche Darstellungen herausgegeben von der vorderasiatisch-ägyptischen Gesellschaft*
AOS	*American Oriental Series*
ARAB	Daniel David Luckenbill, *Ancient Records of Assyria and Babylonia.* Chicago: University of Chicago Press, 2 vols. 1926-27

Archaeology	*Archaeology, A Magazine dealing with the Antiquity of the World*
ARE	James Henry Breasted, *Ancient Records of Egypt.* Chicago: University of Chicago Press, 5 vols. 1906-07
ArOr	*Archiv Orientálni, Journal of the Czechoslovak Oriental Institute*, Prague
AS	*Assyriological Studies*, Oriental Institute
ASAE	*Annales du Service des Antiquitiés de l'Égypte*
BA	*The Biblical Archaeologist*
BABA	*Beiträge zur ägyptischen Bauforschung und Altertums-kunde*, Schweizerisches Institut für ägyptische Bauforschung und Altertumskunde in Kairo
BAR	*The Biblical Archaeology Review*
BASOR	*Bulletin of the American Schools of Oriental Research*
Biblica	*Biblica, Commentarii Periodici Pontifici Instituti Biblici*
BIFAO	*Bulletin de l'Institute français d'archéologie orientale*
BJRL	*Bulletin of the John Rylands Library*, Manchester
BM	*British Museum*
BO	*Bibliotheca Orientalis*
CAH³	*The Cambridge Ancient History.* Cambridge: University Press, 3d ed. 1970ff
CBQ	*The Catholic Biblical Quarterly*
CÉ	*Chronique d'Égypte, Bulletin périodique de la Fondation Egyptologique Reine Élisabeth*, Brussels
DTCFD	*Dil ve Tarih-Coğrafya Fakültesi Dergisi*, University of Ankara
GCS	*Die griechischen christlichen Schriftsteller der ersten drei Jahrhunderte*, herausgegeben von der Kirchenväter-Commission der preussischen Akademie der Wissenschaften. Berlin: Akademie-Verlag
HERE	James Hastings, ed., *Encyclopedia of Religion and Ethics.* New York: Charles Scribner's Sons, 12 vols. 1910-22
Historia	*Historia, Zeitschrift für alte Geschichte, Revue d'histoire ancienne, Journal of Ancient History, Rivista di storia antica*
HUCA	*Hebrew Union College Annual*
IEJ	*Israel Exploration Journal*
Iran	*Iran, Journal of the British Institute of Persian Studies*
Iraq	*Iraq, Published by the British School of Archaeology in Iraq*

JAOS	*Journal of the American Oriental Society*
JANES	*The Journal of the Ancient Near Eastern Society of Columbia University*
JBL	*Journal of Biblical Literature*
JCS	*Journal of Cuneiform Studies*
JE	Isidore Singer, ed., *The Jewish Encyclopedia*. New York: Funk and Wagnalls, 12 vols. 1901-05
JEA	*The Journal of Egyptian Archaeology*
JNES	*Journal of Near Eastern Studies*
JPOS	*The Journal of the Palestine Oriental Society*
JRAS	*The Journal of the Royal Asiatic Society*
JSS	*Journal of Semitic Studies*
JTS	*The Journal of Theological Studies*
KBo	*Keilschrifttexte aus Boghazköi.* 1916ff.
KUB	*Keilschrifturkunden aus Boghazköi.* 1921ff
Kush	*Kush, Journal of the Sudan Antiquities Service*
LÄ	Wolfgang Helck and Eberhard Otto, eds., *Lexikon der Ägyptologie.* Wiesbaden: O. Harrassowitz, 1972ff.
LCL	*The Loeb Classical Library*
LTQ	*Lexington Theological Quarterly*
LXX	The Septuagint
MDAI	*Mémoires de la Délégation Archéologique en Iran*
MDAIK	*Mitteilungen des deutschen archäologischen Instituts Abteilung Kairo*
MDOG	*Mitteilungen der Deutschen Orient-Gesellschaft zu Berlin*
MDP	*Mémoires de la Délégation en Perse, Mémoires de la Mission Archéologique en Iran, Mission de Susiane, etc.*
Mesopotamia	*Mesopotamia, Rivista di Archeologia,* Università di Torino
MJ	*The Museum Journal,* The Museum of the University of Pennsylvania
MMFEP	*Monuments et mémoires publiés par l'Académie des inscriptions et belles-lettres* (Fondation Eugene Piot)
MVÄG	*Mitteilungen der vorderasiatisch-agyptischen Gesellschaft*
MVG	*Mitteilungen der vorderasiatischen Gesellschaft*
NGM	*The National Geographic Magazine*
Numen	*Numen, International Review for the History of Religions issued by the International Association for the History of Religions*
OIC	*Oriental Institute Communications*

OIP	*Oriental Institute Publications*
OLZ	*Orientalistische Literaturzeitung*
OP	*The Oxyrhynchus Papyri.* 1898ff
Orientalia	*Orientalia,* Pontificium Institutum Biblicum
PEQ	*Palestine Exploration Quarterly*
PWRE	Pauly–Wissowa, *Real-Encyclopädie der classischen Altertumswissenschaft.* Munich: Alfred Druckenmüller, 1894ff
RA	Erich Ebeling, Bruno Meissner, D. O. Edzard, eds. *Reallexikon der Assyriologie und vorderasiatischen Archäologie.* Berlin: Walter de Gruyter, 1932ff
RAAO	*Revue d'assyriologie et d'archéologie orientale*
RB	*Revue Biblique*
RHR	*Revue de l'histoire des religions*
RV	*Reallexikon der Vorgeschichte.* Berlin: Walter de Gruyter, 14 vols. 1924–29
SAOC	*Studies in Ancient Oriental Civilization,* Oriental Institute
SBE	F. Max Müller, ed., *The Sacred Books of the East.* Oxford: Clarendon Press, 50 vols. 1885–1910
Scripta Hierosolymitana	*Scripta Hierosolymitana,* Publications of the Hebrew University, Jerusalem
Sumer	*Sumer, A Journal of Archaeology and History in Iraq*
Syria	*Syria, Revue d'art oriental et d'archéologie*
Time	*Time, The Weekly Newsmagazine*
UMB	*The University Museum Bulletin,* University of Pennsylvania
VT	*Vetus Testamentum*
ZA	*Zeitschrift für Assyriologie und verwandte Gebiete*
ZÄS	*Zeitschrift für ägyptische Sprache und Altertumskunde*
ZAW	*Zeitschrift für die alttestamentliche Wissenschaft*
ZDMG	*Zeitschrift der Deutschen Morgenländischen Gesellschaft*
ZDPV	*Zeitschrift des Deutschen Palästina-Vereins*

NOTES

PREFACE

1. Gordon Childe, *What Happened in History* (New York: Penguin Books, 1946), pp. 41, 82. For various factors in the rise of cities, see Samuel Noah Kramer, *Cradle of Civilization* (New York: Time Incorporated, 1967), pp. 32f.; Dora Jane Hamblin, *The First Cities* (New York: Time-Life Books, 1973), pp. 18f. In addition to the works specifically cited in these notes, see throughout *The Cambridge Ancient History,* 3d ed. (Cambridge: University Press, 1970ff.) (abbreviated CAH³), on which work see J. D. Muhly in JAOS 93 (1973):576-578.

2. William W. Hallo and William Kelly Simpson, *The Ancient Near East: A History* (New York: Harcourt Brace Jovanovich, 1971), pp. 27f., 36 (Hallo).

3. Ibid., pp. 188f. (Simpson).

CHAPTER 1. PREHISTORIC AND PROTOHISTORIC PERIODS

1. For this and other archaeological sites in Mesopotamia, see the maps in Martin A. Beek, *Atlas of Mesopotamia* (London: Thomas Nelson and Sons, 1962); and the bibliographical listings in Richard S. Ellis, *A Bibliography of Mesopotamian Archaeological Sites* (Wiesbaden: O. Harrassowitz, 1972). The names of sites are generally spelled in accordance with the usage in the chief publications relating thereto. In addition to the specific citations in Part 1, see also the following general works: A. Leo Oppenheim, *Ancient Mesopotamia* (Chicago: University of Chicago Press, 1964); Georges Roux, *Ancient Iraq* (London: Allen and Unwin, 1964). For specialized topics, see all relevant articles, as far as available, in *Reallexikon der Assyriologie und vorderasiatischen Archäologie,* now ed. D. O. Edzard (Berlin: Walter de Gruyter, 1932ff.).

2. Ralph S. Solecki in *Sumer* 8 (1952):37-48, 127-192; ibid., 9 (1953):60-93; ibid., 11 (1955):14-38 (see pp. 27, 37, pl. 5 for the Carbon 14 date); ibid., 13 (1957):59f., 165-171; ibid., 14 (1958):104-108; ibid., 17 (1961):71-96; T. D. Stewart in ibid., pp. 97-106.

3. Robert J. Braidwood in BASOR 124 (1951):12-18.

4. Robert J. Braidwood in *Sumer* 10 (1954):120-138.

5. Faraj Basmachi in ibid., 4 (1948):134-136; Ann Perkins in AJA 53 (1949):50f.; Robert J. Braidwood in *Sumer* 7 (1951):99-104; Linda S. Braidwood in ibid., pp. 105f.

6. Robert J. Braidwood in *Science* 127 (1958):1419-1430; Robert J. Braidwood and Bruce Howe, *Prehistoric Investigations in Iraqi Kurdistan* (SAOC 31) (Chicago: University of Chicago Press, 1960), pp. 159f.

7. Robert J. Braidwood in *Sumer* 7 (1951):104.

8. Albrecht Goetze in JNES 4 (1950):77f.

9. For the dates in Mesopotamian chronology up to the Third Dynasty of Ur, see Edith Porada in *Chronologies in Old World Archaeology,* ed. Robert W. Ehrich (Chicago: University of Chicago Press, 1965), pp. 133-200, especially the tables on pp. 175-179.

10. Ann Louise Perkins, *The Comparative Archeology of Early Mesopotamia* (SAOC 25) (Chicago: University of Chicago Press, 1949), pp. 15, 37, 64, 155.

11. Ibid., pp. 97, 159; Pinhas Delougaz and Seton Lloyd, *Pre-Sargonid Temples in the Diyala Region* (OIP 58) (Chicago: University of Chicago Press, 1942), p. 8.

12. Stephen B. Luce in AJA 48 (1944):371; Seton Lloyd and Fuad Safar in JNES 4 (1945):255-289; Takey Dabbagh in *Sumer* 21 (1965):93-111.

13. Robert J. Braidwood, Linda Braidwood, James G. Smith, and Charles Leslie in JNES 11 (1952):1-73.

14. Naji al Asil in *Sumer* 12 (1956):87-89; Takahito Mikasa in ibid., 13 (1957):3f.; Namio Egami in ibid., pp. 5-11; ibid., 22 (1966):1-16.

15. R. Campbell Thompson and M. E. L. Mallowan in AAA 20 (1933):127-177; *Proceedings of the First International Congress of Prehistoric and Protohistoric Sciences, London 1932* (London: Oxford University Press, 1934), pp. 165-167.

16. M. E. L. Mallowan and J. Cruikshank Rose in *Iraq* 2 (1935):1-178.

17. Perkins, *The Comparative Archeology of Early Mesopotamia,* p. 11.

18. Robert J. Braidwood, *Mounds in the Plain of Antioch* (OIP 48) (Chicago: University of Chicago Press, 1937), pp. 6f.; C. W. McEwan in AJA 41 (1937):8-16.

19. G. Ernest Wright, *The Pottery of Palestine from the Earliest Times to the End of the Early Bronze Age* (New Haven: American Schools of Oriental Research, 1937), pp. 7-11, 107.

20. Ernst E. Herzfeld, *Die Ausgrabungen von Samarra,* vol. 5, *Die vorgeschichtlichen Töpfereien von Samarra* (Berlin: D. Reimer, 1930).

21. Le Comte du Mesnil du Buisson, *Baghouz, l'ancienne Corsôtê, le tell archaïque et la nécropole de l'âge du bronze* (Leiden: E. J. Brill, 1948), pp. xii, 18f.

22. Harald Ingholt in *Sumer* 13 (1957):214f.; Salim al-Alusi in ibid., 15 (1959):50; Peder Mortensen in ibid., 18 (1962):73-80; ibid., 20 (1964):28-36; and idem, *Tell Shimshara: The Hassuna Period* (Copenhagen: Munksgaard, 1970).

23. Braidwood and Howe, *Prehistoric Investigations in Iraqi Kurdistan,* pp. 161f.

24. Max von Oppenheim, *Der Tell Halaf: Eine neue Kultur im ältesten Mesopotamien* (Leipzig: F. A. Brickhaus, 1931); idem, *Tell Halaf,* 4 vols. (Berlin: Walter de Gruyter, 1943-1962).

25. Perkins, *The Comparative Archeology of Early Mesopotamia,* pp. 16ff.

26. E. A. Speiser in BASOR 66 (1937):2-19; *Excavations at Tepe Gawra,* vol. 2, *Levels IX-XX,* by Arthur J. Tobler (Philadelphia: University of Pennsylvania Press, 1950).

27. M. E. L. Mallowan and J. Cruikshank Rose, *Prehistoric Assyria: The Excavations at Tall Arpachiyah 1933* (London: Oxford University Press, 1935); Takey Dabbagh in *Sumer* 22 (1966):23-43.

28. Beatrice Laura Goff, *Symbols of Prehistoric Mesopotamia* (New Haven: Yale University Press, 1963), pp. 14f., 18f.

29. M. E. L. Mallowan, *Twenty-five Years of Mesopotamian Discovery (1932-1956)* (London: The British School of Archaeology in Iraq, 1956), pp. 3f.

30. Armas Salonen, *Die Ziegeleien im alten Mesopotamien* (Annales Academiae Scientiarum Fennicae, B, 171) (Helsinki, 1972).

31. Perkins, *The Comparative Archeology of Early Mesopotamia,* pp. 46ff., 73ff.

32. *Ur Excavations,* vol. 1, *Al-ʿUbaid,* by H. R. Hall and C. L. Woolley (London: Oxford University Press, 1927).

33. Charlotte Ziegler, *Die Keramik von der Qalʿa des Ḥaǧǧi Mohammed* (Berlin: Verlag Gebr. Mann, 1953).

34. Joan Oates in *Iraq* 22 (1960):32-50.

35. Naji al-Asil in *Sumer* 3 (1947):3; ibid., 6 (1950):3-5; Seton Lloyd and Fuad Safar in ibid., 4 (1948):115-125; Fuad Safar in ibid., 6 (1950):27-33.

36. E. A. Speiser in BASOR 65 (1937):2-8; ibid., 66 (1937):2-19; *Excavations at Tepe Gawra,* vol. 2, Tobler, *Levels IX-XX,* pp. 30-36, 43-47 (for the temples), 131-151 (for the pottery), 175-195 (for the seals).

37. *Vorläufiger Berichte über die von der deutschen Forschungsgemeinschaft in Uruk-Warka unternommenen Ausgrabungen* (Abhandlungen der Preussischen Akademie der Wissenschaften, phil.-hist. Kl.) (Berlin: Akademie der Wissenschaften, 1929ff.); the series Ausgrabungen der deutschen Forschungsgemeinschaft in Uruk-Warka (Leipzig: O. Harrassowitz, 1936ff.); Robert North in *Orientalia* 26 (1957):185-256; Heinrich J. Lenzen in *Sumer* 12 (1956):39-42; ibid., 16 (1960):3-11; ibid., 17 (1961):13-16; ibid., 18 (1962):15-18; ibid., 19 (1963):79-81; and in *Archaeology* 17 (1964):122-131.

38. Seton Lloyd in *Sumer* 4 (1948):39-51; Porada in Ehrich, *Chronologies in Old World Archaeology,* p. 176. To this extent confirmatory of the dating of the Uruk period, there appear to be relationships between the gray ware at Warka and pottery in Palestine there dated 3300-3100. W. F. Albright in AJA 55 (1951):210.

39. Henri de Genouillac, *Premières recherches archéologiques à Kich,* 2 vols. (Paris: E. Champion, 1924-1925); Stephen Langdon et al., *Excavations at Kish,* 4 vols. (Paris: P. Geuthner, 1924-1934).

40. Langdon et al., *Excavations at Kish,* 1:99-101, pl. 31, 1-2; G. R. Driver, *Semitic Writing from Pictograph to Alphabet,* rev. ed. (London: Oxford University Press, 1954), p. 4, pl. 1, no. 2; M. E. L. Mallowan, *Early Mesopotamia and Iran* (New York: McGraw-Hill, 1965), p. 15, figs. 2-3.

41. A. Falkenstein, *Archaische Texte aus Uruk* (Ausgrabungen . . . in Uruk-Warka 2) (Leipzig: O. Harrassowitz, 1940); Henri Frankfort, *The Birth of Civilization in the*

Near East (Bloomington: Indiana University Press, 1951), p. 55.

42. Jean de Mecquenem in *Gazette des Beaux-Arts,* 6ᵉ periode, 18 (1937):201-214; Heinrich J. Lenzen, *Die Entwicklung der Zikkurat* (Ausgrabungen . . . in Uruk-Warka 4) (Leipzig: O. Harrassowitz, 1941); Andre Parrot, *Ziggurats et Tour de Babel* (Paris: Michel, 1949); idem, *The Tower of Babel* (New York: Philosophical Library, 1955); Henri Frankfort, *The Art and Architecture of the Ancient Orient* (Baltimore: Penguin Books, 1955), pp. 5f., fig. 4, pl. 1; Beek, *Atlas of Mesopotamia,* map 21.

43. Henri Frankfort, *Cylinder Seals* (London: Macmillan, 1939), pp. 15-29, pls. 3-4; idem, *Corpus of Ancient Near Eastern Seals in North American Collections,* vol. 1, *The Collection of the Pierpont Morgan Library* (The Bollingen Series 14), 2 vols. (New York: Pantheon Books, 1948), 1:1-4, pls. 1-2.

44. Lenzen in *Sumer* 16 (1960):10f., pl. 1.

45. Henri Frankfort, *Kingship and the Gods* (Chicago: University of Chicago Press, 1948), pp. 313-333; H. A. Groenewegen-Frankfort, *Arrest and Movement* (Chicago: University of Chicago Press, 1951), pp. 150-152; André Parrot, *Sumer, The Dawn of Art* (New York: Golden Press, 1961), pp. 70-72; Thorkild Jacobsen, *The Treasures of Darkness* (New Haven: Yale University Press, 1976), pp. 24, 36f.

46. Perkins, *The Comparative Archeology of Early Mesopotamia,* pp. 194ff.

47. Goff, *Symbols of Prehistoric Mesopotamia,* pp. 128f., 136f., figs. 490-495 (pottery), 513-514 (seals), 565-566 (temples).

48. Ernest Mackay and Stephen Langdon, *Report on Excavations at Jemdet Nasr, Iraq* (Chicago: Field Museum Oxford University Joint Expedition, 1931); Henry Field and Richard A. Martin in AJA 39 (1935):310-320, fig. 1, pls. 30-36.

49. Frankfort, *Cylinder Seals,* pp. 30-38, pls. 6-8; idem, *Corpus of Ancient Near Eastern Seals,* vol. 1, *The Collection of the Pierpont Morgan Library,* pp. 4-8, pls. 3-7.

50. R. J. Forbes, *Studies in Ancient Technology* (Leiden: E. J. Brill, 1955ff.), 9:151.

51. Stephen Langdon, *Pictographic Inscriptions from Jemdet Nasr* (London: Oxford University Press, 1926); Driver, *Semitic Writing from Pictograph to Alphabet,* p. 4, pl. 4.

52. Heinrich J. Lenzen, *Vorläufiger Berichte über die . . . in Uruk-Warka . . . Ausgrabungen* 11 (1940):19-21, pls. 1, 21, 32.

53. Ibid., 5 (1933): pls. 12-13.

54. Ernst Heinrich, *Kleinfunde aus den archaischen Tempelschichten in Uruk* (Ausgrabungen . . . in Uruk-Warka 1) (Leipzig: O. Harrassowitz, 1936), p. 35, pls. 22-23a. For possible astronomical interpretation, cf. below Chapter 10, n. 57.

55. Langdon et al., *Excavations at Kish,* 4:3-5, pl. 7, nos. 3, 4; pl. 8, no. 1.

56. E. Heinrich and W. Andrae, *Fara: Ergebnisse der Ausgrabungen der deutschen Orient-Gesellschaft in Fara und Abu Hatab 1902-1903* (Leipzig: J. C. Hinrichs, n.d.); Erich Schmidt in MJ 22 (1931):192-245.

57. Anton Deimel, *Die Inschriften von Fara* (Wissenschaftliche Veröffentlichungen der deutschen Orient-Gesellschaft 40, 43, 45), 3 vols. (Leipzig: J. C. Hinrichs, 1922-1924).

58. Henri Frankfort et al., *Tell Asmar and Khafaje* (OIC 13) (Chicago: University of Chicago Press, 1932); idem, *Tell Asmar, Khafaje and Khorsabad* (OIC 17) (Chicago: University of Chicago Press, 1934); idem, *Oriental Institute*

Discoveries in Iraq, 1933/34 (OIC 19) (Chicago: University of Chicago Press, 1935); idem, *Progress of the Work of the Oriental Institute in Iraq, 1934/35* (OIC 20) (Chicago: University of Chicago Press, 1936).

59. Perkins, *The Comparative Archeology of Early Mesopotamia*, pp. 163-165, 194, fig. 19; Goff, *Symbols of Prehistoric Mesopotamia*, pp. 140-143, figs. 568-590.

60. Goff, *Symbols of Prehistoric Mesopotamia*, pp. 149-153, 156-158, figs. 650-662, 680; E. Douglas Van Buren, *Symbols of the Gods in Mesopotamian Art* (AO 23) (Rome: Pontificium institutum biblicum, 1945), p. 53; O. G. S. Crawford, *The Eye Goddess* (New York: Macmillan, 1956), pp. 25-28.

61. Samuel Noah Kramer in AJA 52 (1948):156-164; idem, *From the Tablets of Sumer* (Indian Hills, Colorado: Falcon's Wing Press, 1956), pp. 238-248; idem, *The Sumerians: Their History, Culture, and Character* (Chicago: University of Chicago Press, 1963), p. 42; idem, *Sumerian Culture and Society* (Menlo Park, Calif.: Cummings Publishing Co., 1975).

62. Oates in *Iraq* 22 (1960):44-50. For the whole Sumerian question, see Henri Frankfort, *Archaeology and the Sumerian Problem* (SAOC 4) (Chicago: University of Chicago Press, 1932); Tom B. Jones, ed., *The Sumerian Problem* (New York: Wiley, 1969); cf. Robert D. Biggs in JNES 31 (1972):223f.

63. ANET, p. 44.

64. S. N. Kramer in BASOR 96 (1944):18-28; idem, *The Sumerians*, pp. 281-284; P. B. Cornwall in BASOR 103 (1948):3-11.

65. ARAB 2, secs. 41, 43, 70, 81, 92, 99, 185, 970.

66. P. V. Glob and T. G. Bibby in *Scientific American* 203, no. 4 (October 1960):62-71; P. V. Glob, *Al-Bahrain: De danske ekspeditioner til oldtidens Dilmun* (Copenhagen: Gyldendal, 1968).

67. Benno Landsberger in DTCFD 1, no. 5 (1943):97-102; ibid., 2, no. 3 (1944):431-437; ibid., 3, no. 2 (1945):150-158. See especially ibid., 2, no. 3 (1944):433, 435f., for the point here discussed. For the substrate words, see also Armas Salonen, *Zum Aufbau der Substrate im Sumerischen* (Studia Orientalia edidit Societas Orientalis Fennica, 37, 3) (Helsinki, 1968); idem, *Die Fussbekleidung der alten Mesopotamier nach sumerisch-akkadischen Quellen* (Annales Academiae Scientiarum Fennicae, B, 157) (Helsinki, 1969); idem, *Die Ziegeleien im alten Mesopotamien*, pp. 7-9.

68. S. N. Kramer in JAOS 63 (1943):71, no. 4.

69. Thorkild Jacobsen in ibid., 59 (1939):485-495.

70. For a theory concerning the oldest names that corresponded to Sumer and Akkad, see Salonen, *Die Fussbekleidung der alten Mesopotamier*, pp. 99f.

71. A. Falkenstein, *Das Sumerische* (Leiden: E. J. Brill, 1964).

72. Arthur Ungnad and Lubor Matouš, *Grammatik des Akkadischen*, 5th ed. (Munich: Beck, 1969).

73. Falkenstein, *Archaische Texte aus Uruk*, pp. 25, 52, Zeichenliste nos. 44, 45a, 761ff.; pl. 31, no. 339; pl. 4, no. 87, etc.

74. Ibid., pp. 33, 38.

75. Ibid., pp. 37-41, 59f., Zeichenliste nos. 192f., 208f., 892ff.; Langdon,

Pictographic Inscriptions from Jemdet Nasr, pp. viif., nos. 33, 171, 238, 268.

76. Deimel, *Die Inschriften von Fara,* 1:12f.

77. Edward Chiera, *They Wrote on Clay* (Chicago: University of Chicago Press, 1938), pp. 17f., 60f.; I. J. Gelb, *A Study of Writing* (Chicago: University of Chicago Press, 1952), pp. 68, 129, 172.

78. André Parrot, *Tello, vingt campagnes de fouilles (1877-1933)* (Paris: A. Michel, 1948).

79. J. P. Peters, *Nippur, or Explorations on the Euphrates,* 2 vols. (New York: G. P. Putnam's Sons, 1897); H. V. Hilprecht, *The Excavations in Assyria and Babylonia* (Philadelphia: Department of Archaeology of the University of Pennsylvania, 1903); Richard C. Haines in *Sumer* 17 (1961):67-70.

80. S. N. Kramer in BASOR 122 (1951):28-31; Edmund I. Gordon in JAOS 77 (1957):67-79; idem, JCS 12 (1958):1-21, 43-75; and idem, *Sumerian Proverbs: Glimpses of Everyday Life in Ancient Mesopotamia* (Philadelphia: University Museum, 1959).

81. K. A. Kitchen, *Ancient Orient and Old Testament* (London: Tyndale Press, 1966), pp. 41, 88-90.

82. S. N. Kramer, *Sumerian Mythology* (Philadelphia: American Philosophical Society, 1944), pp. 37-40, 51-53, 70; Thorkild Jacobsen in JNES 5 (1946):136-140.

83. For the antediluvian cities, see William W. Hallo in JCS 23 (1971):57-67.

84. S. Langdon, *Semitic Mythology* (Boston: Marshall Jones, 1931), pp. 206-208; Kramer, *Sumerian Mythology,* pp. 97f.; ANET, pp. 42-44; M. Civil, "The Sumerian Flood Story," *Atra-Ḫasīs: The Babylonian Story of the Flood,* ed. W. G. Lambert and A. R. Millard (Oxford: Clarendon Press, 1969), pp. 138-145.

85. S. N. Kramer in *Essays in Memory of E. A. Speiser* (JAOS 88, 1), ed. William W. Hallo, (New Haven: American Oriental Society, 1968), pp. 108-111.

86. Thorkild Jacobsen, *The Sumerian King List* (AS 11) (Chicago: University of Chicago Press, 1939); Kramer, *The Sumerians,* pp. 328-331; ANET, pp. 265-267; M. Civil in JCS 15 (1961):79f.; William W. Hallo in ibid., 17 (1963):52-57; J. J. Finkelstein in ibid., pp. 39-51; cf. Abraham Malamat in Hallo, *Essays in Memory of E. A. Speiser,* pp. 163-173. The original text of the King List is believed to have been written in the time of Utuhegal (around 2120), king of Uruk; the portion covering the earlier period before the flood is not in all the copies and was probably added later. Jacobsen, *The Sumerian King List,* pp. 63f.

87. A. L. Oppenheim in BASOR 97 (1945):26f.

88. Heinrich Zimmern, *Beiträge zur Kenntnis der babylonischen Religion* (Leipzig: J.C. Hinrichs, 1896-1900), vol. 3, *Ritualtafeln,* pp. 116ff.; W. G. Lambert in JCS 21 (1967):126-138. In the biblical record of ten patriarchs from Adam to Noah (Gen. 5), the corresponding seventh name is that of Enoch, and, in Jewish legend, Enoch is the inventor of astronomy as well as of mathematics and writing. In the Book of Jubilees, he was for a long time with the angels of God, "and they showed him everything which is on earth and in the heavens, the rule of the sun, and he wrote down everything" (4:21); in the Book of Enoch, he was shown all the laws of the heavenly luminaries (72-82); and in both books, a solar calendar (of 364 days) is set

forth, the calendar that was used at Qumran. Heinrich Zimmern, *The Babylonians and the Hebrew Genesis* (London: D. Nutt, 1901), pp. 43-45.

89. ANET, pp. 88, 93.

90. Extracts in Josephus (*Against Apion* 1. 19. secs. 128ff.; *Ant.* 1. 3. 6. sec. 93), in Eusebius (*Praeparatio Evangelica* 9. 11. 1f., GCS, ed. Karl Mras, 1954-1956, 1:497; *Chronicle,* Armenian version, GCS, Eusebius 5, ed. Josef Karst, 1911, pp. 4f.), and in the Byzantine chronicler George Syncellus. See Schwartz in PWRE 3, cols. 309-316; Felix Jacoby, *Die Fragmente der griechischen Historiker,* 3 vols., (Berlin: Weidmann, 1926-1963), 3C, no. 680, pp. 364-397; Menahem Stern, *Greek and Latin Authors on Jews and Judaism, Edited with Introductions, Translations and Commentary,* vol. 1, *From Herodotus to Plutarch* (Jerusalem: Israel Academy of Sciences and Humanities, 1974), pp. 55-61.

91. For an ingenious explanation of the figure of 432,000 years, and also of the total of 1,656 years for the ten patriarchs from Adam to Noah in Gen. 5, see Jules Oppert in JE 4:64-68.

92. *Ur Excavations,* vol. 4, *The Early Periods,* by Leonard Woolley (London: Oxford University Press, 1956), pp. 15-19, appendix 6, pp, 165f.; C. L. Woolley, *Ur of the Chaldees* (1929; reprint ed. New York: W. W. Norton, 1965), pp. 22-29; idem, *Excavations at Ur* (London: Ernest Benn, 1955), pp. 26-36; idem, PEQ 88 (1956):14-21; W. F. Albright in BASOR 146 (1957):34f.; Seton Lloyd in *Iraq* 22 (1960):23-31.

93. Julius Jordan in *Vorläufiger Berichte über die . . . in Uruk-Warka . . . Ausgrabungen* 2 (1929):20; V. Christian in AfO 8 (1932):63-65.

94. Schmidt in MJ 22 (1931):201, 217.

95. Stephen Langdon in JRAS (1930):603ff., pl. 8; L. C. Watelin in Langdon et al., *Excavations at Kish* 4:40-44.

96. André Parrot, *The Flood and Noah's Ark* (New York: Philosophical Library, 1955), p. 52, fig. 5; M. E. L. Mallowan in *Iraq* 26 (1964):62-82; R. L. Raikes in ibid., 28 (1966):52-63; William W. Hallo in JCS 23 (1970-1971):61.

CHAPTER 2. EARLY DYNASTIC PERIOD

1. The word *dynasty* is used in the sense of a series of kings (or even one king) in a given place and time, even if it is not known whether the rulers were of the same family. F. R. Kraus in ZA 50 (1952):30 no. 2.

2. William W. Hallo in JCS 23 (1970-1971):60.

3. See the works cited in Chapter 1, n. 58 (Frankfort et al.) and n. 11 (Delougaz and Lloyd).

4. Pinhas Delougaz, *Planoconvex Bricks and the Methods of Their Employment* (SAOC 7) (Chicago: University of Chicago Press, 1933).

5. Ann Louise Perkins, *The Comparative Archeology of Early Mesopotamia,* (SAOC 25) (Chicago: University of Chicago Press, 1949), pp. 132f.

6. Henri Frankfort, *Sculpture of the Third Millennium B.C. From Tell Asmar and Khafaje* (OIP 44) (Chicago: University of Chicago Press, 1939).

7. ANET, pp. 40f.

8. Pinhas Delougaz and Seton Lloyd, *Pre-Sargonid Temples in the Diyala Region* (OIP 58) (Chicago: University of Chicago Press, 1949), pp. 65-69, figs. 61-62; and fig. 205, no. 4 (Kh. IV 126), pp. 6, 8, 70f., 293f. for the Urkisal statue.

9. Pinhas Delougaz, *The Temple Oval at Khafājah* (OIP 53) (Chicago: University of Chicago Press, 1940); Henri Frankfort, *The Art and Architecture of the Ancient Orient* (Baltimore: Penguin Books, 1955), p. 21.

10. Pinhas Delougaz, Harold D. Hill, and Seton Lloyd, *Private Houses and Graves in the Diyala Region* (OIP 88) (Chicago: University of Chicago Press, 1967), pp. 274-278.

11. Henri Frankfort, *Kingship and the Gods,* (Chicago: University of Chicago Press, 1948), pp. 222; 396 n. 23.

12. Henri Frankfort, *Cylinder Seals* (London: MacMillan, 1939), pp. 138f., pl. 24h; Beatrice Laura Goff, *Symbols of Prehistoric Mesopotamia* (New Haven: Yale University Press, 1963), pp. 256f., fig. 721; Rainer M. Boehmer, *Die Entwicklung der Glyptik während der Akkad-Zeit* (Untersuchungen zur Assyriologie und vorderasiatischen Archäologie, Ergänzungsbände zur ZA, Neue Folge, 4) (Berlin: Walter de Gruyter, 1965), pp. 122f., 190, figs. 693-703a.

13. ANET, pp. 114-118.

14. Ultimately this legend was transferred to Alexander the Great, said to have ascended in a basket attached to two hungry birds attracted upward by meat held on a spear above their heads. S. Langdon, *Semitic Mythology* (Boston: Marshall Jones, 1931), pp. 166-174.

15. Delougaz, *The Temple Oval at Khāfajah,* pp. 146f., no. 2 (Kh. III 35), and p. 167.

16. D. O. Edzard in ZA 53 (1959):9-26.

17. S. N. Kramer in *Gilgameš et sa légende: Études recueillies par Paul Garelli à l'occasion de la VIIe Rencontre Assyriologique Internationale (Paris—1958)* (Paris: Imprimerie nationale, 1960), pp. 61, 63.

18. T. Fish in BJRL 19 (1935):362-372; M. Witzel in *Orientalia* 5 (1936):331-346; S. N. Kramer in AJA 53 (1949):1-18; ANET, pp. 44-47.

19. Thorkild Jacobsen in JNES 2 (1943):159-172; Geoffrey Evans in JAOS 78 (1958):1-11.

20. Anshan and Aratta were neighboring city-states on the Iranian plateau. Aratta was probably in the southeast, in the region of the modern province of Kerman. Yousef Majidzadeh in JNES 35 (1975):105-113. For Anshan, see below, Chapter 10, n. 26.

21. Samuel Nash Kramer, *The Sumerians: Their History, Culture, and Character* (Chicago: University of Chicago Press, 1963), pp. 185-205.

22. ANET, pp. 72-99.

23. *Vorläufiger Berichte über die . . . in Uruk-Warka . . . Ausgrabungen* 7:41ff.; 8:5ff.

24. *Ur Excavations,* vol. 2, *The Royal Cemetery,* by C. L. Woolley (Oxford: Oxford University Press, 1934), pls. 270-271; Edith Porada in *Chronologies in Old World Archaeology,* ed. Robert W. Erich (Chicago: University of Chicago Press,

1965), p. 178. Woolley (*Ur Excavations,* 2:223-227) originally dated the royal cemetery between 3500 and 3200, and the First Dynasty of Ur at 3100-3000, but was criticized by E. A. Speiser (*Antiquity* 8 [1934]:451), Valentin Müller (JAOS 55 [1935]:206-208), and H. Frankfort (JRAS [1937]:332-341). A date around 2500 was proposed by W. F. Albright in BASOR 88 (1942):32; idem, AJA 47 (1943):492.

25. *Ur Excavations,* 2:312f., pl. 191 (U. 13607), pl. 207 (U. 8981), and pl. 270 for the strata SIS 1-2; *Ur Excavations, Texts,* vol. 1, *Royal Inscriptions,* by C. J. Gadd and L. Legrain, 2 vols. (London: Harrison and Sons, 1928), p. 71, no. 268.

26. A. Parrot in AICR, 1964, pp. 201f.; Georges Dossin in ibid., 1965, pp. 405f.

27. ANET, p. 165.

28. *Ur Excavations,* vol. 1 *Al-ʿUbaid,* by H.R. Hall and C.L. Woolley (Oxford: Oxford University Press, 1927), pp. 61, 80, 126-128, pls. 35, 40-41, U. 26, TO. 160, TO. 286, TO. 287. For the temple of Ninhursag at Tell al-Ubaid, see ibid., pp. 84ff., 88ff., 141ff., pls. 27-28, 31-33.

29. Sidney Smith in JRAS, 1932, pp. 305-307.

30. *Ur Excavations,* 2:135ff.

31. Ibid., pls. 160-162, 164, U. 10451-10454, from Tomb PG/800 (gold vessels); pls. 128, 131, U. 10933, 10975, from Tomb PG/800 (headdress, jewelry); pls. 150 and Frontispiece, U. 10000, from Tomb PG/755 (helmet); pls. 90c, 91-93, U. 11164, from Tomb PG/779 (the standard); pls. 104, 111, 113-115, U. 12353, U. 12354, from Tomb PG/1237 (lyres, cf. Joan Rimmer, *Ancient Musical Instruments of Western Asia in the Department of Western Asiatic Antiquities,* The British Museum [London: British Museum, 1969], pp. 14f.).

32. *Ur Excavations,* 2:316, pls. 191, 196, no. 55, U. 11751, from Tomb PG/1054 (Meskalamdug); pls. 191, 198, no. 65, U. 11825, from Tomb PG/1050 (Akalamdug); pls. 191, 193, no. 16, U. 10939, from Tomb PG/800 (Shubad); pls. 191, 193, no. 19, U. 10448, from Tomb PG/800 (Abargi); pls. 163, 191, U. 10001, 10002, 10004, from Tomb PG/755 (Meskalamdug, hero of the good land).

33. The less convincing alternate theory is that these were priests and priestesses sacrificed in fertility rites. Sidney Smith in JRAS (1926):862-868; Franz M. Th. Böhl in ZA 39 (1930); H. Frankfort in *Iraq* 1 (1934):12 n. 3; idem, JRAS (1937):341f.; Speiser in *Antiquity* 8 (1934):451.

34. ANET, pp. 50-52; S. N. Kramer in BASOR 94 (1944):6, 10, 12; C. J. Gadd in *Iraq* 22 (1960):51-58.

35. Samuel A. B. Mercer, *Sumero-Babylonian Year-Formulas* (London: Luzac, 1946), p. 5, no. 8.

36. A. Ungnad (with supplements by E. Ebeling) in RA 2:131-196; Taha Baqir in *Sumer* 4 (1948):103-114; and ibid., 5 (1949):34-86, 136-143.

37. Kramer, *The Sumerians,* pp. 53-58, 308-323.

38. Frankfort, *The Art and Architecture of the Ancient Orient,* p. 33, pl. 33B; Faraj Basmachi in *Sumer* 16 (1960):45-47.

39. Edith Porada in *Archaeology* 23 (1970):49f.; Donald P. Hansen in AA 32 (1970):243-258; ibid., 35 (1973):62-78.

40. Edmund I. Gordon in BASOR 132 (1953):27-30.

41. André Parrot, *Tello, vingt campagnes de fouilles (1877-1933)* (Paris: A. Michel, 1948), pp. 95-101; ANEP, figs. 298-302.

42. E. Douglas Van Buren, *Symbols of the Gods in Mesopotamian Art* (AO 23) (Rome: Pontificium institutum biblicum, 1945), pp. 11, 30f.; H. and H. A. Frankfort et al., *The Intellectual Adventure of Ancient Man* (Chicago: University of Chicago Press, 1946), p. 6.

43. André Parrot, *Sumer, The Dawn of Art* (New York: Golden Press, 1961), p. 159, fig. 188F.

44. S. N. Kramer in IEJ 3 (1953):217-232; idem, *Archaeology* 7 (1954):138-148; idem, *From the Tablets of Sumer* (Indian Hills, Colo.: Falcon's Wing Press, 1956), pp. 40-46; idem, *The Sumerians,* pp. 79-83, 317-322; W. von Soden, *Herrscher im alten Orient* (Berlin: Springer, 1954), pp. 8-15.

45. George A. Barton, *The Royal Inscriptions of Sumer and Akkad* (London: Oxford University Press, 1929), p. 91; Kramer in IEJ 3 (1953):232 n. 45.

46. Barton, *The Royal Inscriptions of Sumer and Akkad,* p. 99.

CHAPTER 3. OLD AKKADIAN AND POST-AKKADIAN PERIODS

1. Eckhard Unger in RA 1:62.

2. The East Semitic dialects and their approximate time spans are: Old Akkadian, 2500-2000; Old Babylonian, 2000-1500; Middle Babylonian, 1500-1000; New Babylonian, 1000 to the beginning of the present era; Old Assyrian, 2000-1500; Middle Assyrian, 1500-1000; New Assyrian, 1000-600. Sabatino Moscati, *Ancient Semitic Civilizations* (London: Elek Books, 1957); idem, *An Introduction to the Comparative Grammar of the Semitic Languages* (Porta Linguarum Orientalium) (Weisbaden: O. Harrassowitz, 1964).

3. I. J. Gelb, *Old Akkadian Writing and Grammar,* 2d ed. (Chicago: University of Chicago Press, 1961).

4. Thorkild Jacobsen in JAOS 59 (1939):485-495; E. A. Speiser in JAOS Supplement 17 (1954):14.

5. Brevard S. Childs in JBL 84 (1965):109-122.

6. L. W. King, *Chronicles concerning Early Babylonian Kings,* 2 vols. (London: Luzac, 1907), 2:87-96; ANET, p. 119.

7. A. Falkenstein and L. Matouš in ZA 42 (1934):147, no. 49.

8. From the founder of the dynasty the Old Akkadian period is also called the Sargonic period. In distinction therefrom the period of Sargon II (721-705) of Assyria is called Sargonid.

9. Raymond P. Dougherty, *The Sealand of Ancient Arabia* (New Haven: Yale University Press, 1932), pp. 8f.

10. ANET, p. 267.

11. ANEP, fig. 606.

12. William W. Hallo and J. J. A. van Dijk, *The Exaltation of Inanna* (New Haven: Yale University Press, 1969).

13. I. J. Gelb in AJSL 55 (1938):74f.

14. George A. Barton, *The Royal Inscriptions of Sumer and Akkad* (London: Oxford University Press, 1929), p. 115.

15. Roger T. O'Callaghan, *Aram Naharaim* (AnOr 26) (Rome: Pontificium institutum biblicum, 1948), p. 15. Omen texts embdoy the interpretations and prognostications of the diviners (reputedly the descendants of Enmendur-Anna), but also often contain items of historical interest and importance. Albrecht Goetze in JCS 1 (1947):253-265.

16. André Parrot, *Sumer, The Dawn of Art* (New York: Golden Press, 1961), figs. 206-209.

17. Richard F. S. Starr, *Nuzi*, 2 vols. (Cambridge: Harvard University Press, 1937-1939), 1:21f. Among the business records was an inscribed clay map, prepared perhaps to indicate the location of some real estate, which ranks as the oldest map ever discovered. Ibid., 2, pl. 55, T, U.

18. Barton, *The Royal Inscriptions of Sumer and Akkad*, pp. 119, 131.

19. Ibid., p. 129.

20. I. J. Gelb, *Hurrians and Subarians* (SAOC 22) (Chicago: University of Chicago Press, 1944), p. 36 n. 100.

21. Goetze in JCS 1 (1947):256f., nos. 13, 14.

22. Barton, *The Royal Inscriptions of Sumer and Akkad*, p. 143.

23. Henri Frankfort, *Kingship and the Gods*, (Chicago: University of Chicago Press, 1948), p. 224.

24. *Ur Excavations, Texts*, vol. 1, *Royal Inscriptions*, by C. J. Gadd and L. Legrain, 2 vols. (London: Harrison and Sons, 1928), pp. 74f., no. 275; 2, pl. 56.

25. Other names reportedly found at Ebla and also known later in the Bible are Abraham (*ab-ra-mu*), Israel (*is-ra-ilu*), David (*da-u-dum*), and Saul (*sa-u-lum*). Biblical cities are also mentioned, including Gezer, Hazor, Megiddo, and Jerusalem (*urusalima*). For Ebla (Ibla), see I. J. Gelb in AJSL 55 (1938):77; idem, *The Biblical Archaeology Review* 2 (1976):41f.; Giovanni Pettinato in BA 39 (1976):44-52; G. Pettinato and P. Matthiae in RA 5:8-20; Paolo Matthiae in *Archaeology* 30 (1977):244-253.

26. E. A. Speiser in JAOS 72 (1952):98.

27. M. E. L. Mallowan, *Twenty-five Years of Mesopotamian Discovery, (1932-1956)* (London: The British School of Archaeology in Iraq, 1956), pp. 32f.

28. Gelb, *Hurrians and Subarians*, p. 36, n. 100.

29. Barton, *The Royal Inscriptions of Sumer and Akkad*, p. 143.

30. Christian Zervos, *L'Art de la Mésopotamie de la fin du quatrième millénaire au XVe siècle avant notre ère, Elam, Sumer, Akkad* (Paris: Editions "Cahiers d'art," 1935), p. 165; Parrot, *Sumer, The Dawn of Art*, figs. 212-213.

31. Hans-Gustav Güterbock in ZA 42 (1934):76; Speiser in JAOS 72 (1952):100f.

32. Albrecht Goetze in JNES 12 (1953):118 n. 27.

33. ANET, pp. 646-651.

34. Barton, *The Royal Inscriptions of Sumer and Akkad*, pp. 145f.

35. A. Ungnad in RA 2:133, col. 1, e.

36. Sidney Smith in JRAS, 1932, pp. 295-301; A. Leo Oppenheim, *Letters from Mesopotamia: Official, Business, and Private Letters on Clay Tablets from Two Millennia* (Chicago: University of Chicago Press, 1967), pp. 71f.

37. Ungnad in RA 2:133, col. 1, b.

38. I. J. Gelb in AJSL 55 (1938):73.

39. I. J. Gelb in JCS 15 (1961):27-47; P. Dhorme in RB 37 (1928):63-79, 160-180; ibid., 39 (1930):161-176; ibid., 40 (1931):161-184. The Amorite language is West Semitic (in distinction from Akkadian as East Semitic) and in its later forms becomes Aramaic, Ugaritic, Phoenician, and Hebrew. For Amurru, the eponymous deity of the Amorites (a weather god, with the goddess Ashratum, the lady of the desert plateau, as his wife), see J. -R. Kupper, *L'Iconographie du dieu Amurru dans le glyptique de la Ire dynastie babylonienne* (Brussels: Académie royale de Belgique, 1961).

40. Goetze in JCS 1 (1947):258f., no. 21.

41. Smith in JRAS (1932):301-305.

42. Barton, *The Royal Inscriptions of Sumer and Akkad* p. 143, Seal A; p. 147, Seal B; pp. 172ff.

43. ANET, p. 523.

44. Gaston Cros, *Nouvelles fouilles de Tello,* 3 pts. (Paris: E. Leroux, 1910-1914), 2, pl. 1; Barton, *The Royal Inscriptions of Sumer and Akkad,* p. 181, Statue B; pp. 204-237, Cylinder A; ANEP, figs. 430-431.

45. F. Thureau-Dangin in RAAO 5 (1912):111-120; ibid., 10 (1913):98-100; Güterbock in ZA 42 (1934):14.

46. Goetze in JCS 1 (1947):259.

47. Güterbock in ZA 42 (1934):55.

CHAPTER 4. NEW SUMERIAN PERIOD

1. For the dates in Mesopotamian chronology from the Third Dynasty of Ur onward, see J. A. Brinkman in *Ancient Mesopotamia,* ed. A. Leo Oppenheim (Chicago: University of Chicago Press, 1964), pp. 336-347.

2. *Ur Excavations, Texts,* vol. 1, *Royal Inscriptions,* by C. J. Gadd and L. Legrain, 2 vols. (London: Harrison and Sons, 1928), 1 p. 7, no. 30.

3. William W. Hallo in JCS 20 (1966):133-141.

4. William W. Hallo in HUCA 33 (1962):11f., 25-27.

5. S. N. Kramer in *Gilgameš et sa légende: Études recueillies par Paul Garelli à l'occasion de lat VIIe Rencontre Assyriologique Internationale (Paris—1958)* (Paris: Imprimerie Nationale, 1960), p. 61; Donald McCown in UMB 16 (1951):7-13.

6. George A. Barton, *The Royal Inscriptions of Sumer and Akkad* (London: Oxford University Press, 1929), p. 276, no. 16.

7. H. J. Lenzen in *Iraq* 22 (1960):129f.

8. *Ur Excavations,* vol. 5, *The Ziggurat and Its Surroundings,* by Leonard Woolley (Oxford: Oxford University Press, 1939).

9. For the use of bitumen in antiquity, see R. J. Forbes, *Studies in Ancient*

Technology, (London: E. J. Brill, 1955ff.), 1:1-120.

10. Th. A. Busink, *Sumerische en Babylonische Tempelbouw* (Batavia-Centrum: Noordhoff-Kolft, 1940), p. 69.

11. C. J. Gadd, *History and Monuments of Ur* (New York: E. P. Dutton, 1929), p. 235, pl. 32a.

12. C. Leonard Woolley in MJ 16 (1925):48-55; L. Legrain in ibid., 18 (1927):74-98; C. L. Woolley, *The Development of Sumerian Art* (New York: Scribner's, 1935), p. 112.

13. J. J. Finkelstein in JCS 22 (1968-1969):66-82. For many more scattered legal texts of the time of the Third Dynasty of Ur, see Adam Falkenstein, *Die neusumerischen Gerichtsurkunden* (Bayerische Akademie der Wissinschaften) 3 vols. (Munich: Kommission zur Erschliessung von Keilschrifttexten, 1956-1957); cf. Edmond Sollberger in JCS 12 (1958):105-107.

14. One mina equals sixty shekels.

15. J. J. Finkelstein in JAOS 86 (1966):355-372.

16. Albrecht Alt, *Die Ursprünge des israelitischen Rechts* (Leipzig: S. Hirzel, 1934).

17. Barton, *The Royal Inscriptions of Sumer and Akkad,* pp. 283f., 287f., 292f., 296f.

18. Kramer, *Gilgameš et sa légende,* p. 61.

19. Richard C. Haines in *Sumer* 11 (1955):107-109.

20. T. Fish in BJRL 11 (1927):322-328.

21. C. L. Woolley, *Excavations at Ur* (London: Ernest Benn, 1955), pp. 150-159.

22. Barton, *The Royal Inscriptions of Sumer and Akkad,* p. 287, no. 2, etc.

23. William W. Hallo in JNES 15 (1956):220-225.

24. Albrecht Goetze in JCS 1 (1947):261, nos. 29-31.

25. I. J. Gelb, *Hurrians and Subarians* (SAOC 22) (Chicago: University of Chicago Press, 1944), pp. 25f., 38-40; Thorkild Jacobsen in AJSL 58 (1941):220 n. 4; and in JCS 7 (1953):44.

26. A. Ungnad in RA 2:144, no. 80; J. -R Kupper, *Les nomades en Mesopotamie au temps des rois de Mari* (Paris: Les Belles Lettres, 1957), pp. 156f.

27. *Ur Excavations, Texts,* 1:88, no. 290; vol. 3, *Business Documents of the Third Dynasty of Ur,* by L. Legrain, 2 vols. (London: Harrison and Sons, 1937, 1947), p. 278, no. 13; Ungnad in RA 2:146, nos. 98, 102, 103. For Anshan, see Chapter 10, n. 26.

28. *Ur Excavations, Texts,* 3:278, no. 21.

29. Henri Frankfort, Seton Lloyd, and Thorkild Jacobsen, *The Gimilsin Temple and the Palace of the Rulers at Tell Asmar* (OIP 43) (Chicago: University of Chicago Press, 1940).

30. Vaughn E. Crawford in JCS 2 (1948):14 n. 7.

31. Thorkild Jacobsen in ibid., 7 (1953):39f.

32. ANET, pp. 480f.

33. Jacobsen in JCS 7 (1953):43.

34. André Parrot in RAAO 30 (1933):174-182; and in *Syria* 45 (1968):205-239; Maurice Birot in ibid., pp. 241-247; Jean Margueron in ibid., 47 (1970):261-277; ibid., 48 (1971):271-287.

35. B. Landsberger in ZA 35 (1924):237.

36. Crawford in JCS 2 (1948):14.

37. S. N. Kramer, *Lamentation over the Destruction of Ur* (AS 12) (Chicago: University of Chicago Press, 1940); *Ur Excavations, Texts,* vol. 6, *Literary and Religious Texts,* by C. J. Gadd (London: Harrison and Sons, 1963), pt. 2, nos. 124-134.

38. Woolley, *Excavations at Ur,* p. 163.

CHAPTER 5. OLD BABYLONIAN PERIOD

1. Dietz Otto Edzard, *Die "Zweite Zwischenzeit" Babyloniens* (Wiesbaden: O. Harrassowitz, 1957).

2. F. R. Kraus in JCS 3 (1949):13-16, 26f.

3. Edmond Sollberger in ibid., 8 (1954):135f.

4. Kraus in ibid., 3 (1949):16f., 26f.

5. Henri Frankfort, Seton Lloyd, and Thorkild Jacobsen, *The Gimilsin Temple and the Palace of the Rulers at Tell Asmar,* (OIP 43) (Chicago: University of Chicago Press, 1940), pp. 196-200.

6. A. Ungnad in RA 2:163, no. 232.

7. Taha Baqir in *Sumer* 4 (1948):52f.; Albrecht Goetze in *Sumer* 4 (1948):54, 63-102; idem, *The Laws of Eshnunna* (AASOR 31) (New Haven: American Schools of Oriental Research, 1956).

8. *Ur Excavations, Texts,* vol. 1, *Royal Inscriptions,* by C. J. Gadd and L. Legrain (London: Harrison and Sons, 1928), p. 24, no. 106; p. 62, no. 223.

9. Francis Rue Steele in AJA 52 (1948):425-450; idem, ArOr 18 (1950):489-493.

10. Edzard, *Die "Zweite Zwischenzeit" Babyloniens,* pp. 126-135, 153-156.

11. Eckhard Unger in RA 1:330-369.

12. Ungnad in RA 2:133, col. 1, c.

13. Ibid., pp. 164-192; Samuel A. B. Mercer, *Sumero-Babylonian Year-Formulas* (London: Luzac, 1946), pp. 31-48.

14. ANET, pp. 271f.; A. Poebel in *Miscellaneous Studies* (AS 14) (Chicago: University of Chicago Press, 1947), pp. 110-122.

15. J. J. Finkelstein in JCS 20 (1966):95-118; W. G. Lambert in ibid., 22 (1968):1f.; Abraham Malamat in *Essays in Memory of E. A. Speiser* (JAOS 88, 1), ed. William W. Hallo (New Haven: American Oriental Society, 1968), pp. 163-173.

16. Ungnad in RA 2:175-178.

17. Ibid., pp. 178-182.

18. M. Schorr, *Urkunden des altbabylonischen Zivil- und Prozessrechts* (Leipzig: J. C. Hinrichs, 1913), pp. 403f., no. 284.

19. Ungnad in RA 2:180, nos. 132-134.

20. Ibid., pp. 180f., nos. 135, 137, 139-141.

21. For excavation reports of twenty seasons at Mari, see André Parrot in *Syria,* from 16 (1935):1-28, 117-140, to 49 (1972):281-302; idem, *Mission archéologique de Mari* (Paris: P. Geuthner, 1956–); idem, *Mari, documentation photographique de la mission archéologique de Mari* (Neuchâtel: Ides et calendes, 1953); idem, *Mari, capitale*

fabuleuse (Paris: Payot, 1974); André Parrot, ed., *Studia Mariana* (Leiden: E. J. Brill, 1950); J.-R. Kupper, ed., *La civilisation de Mari* (Paris: Les Belles Lettres, 1967); Abraham Malamat in BA 34, (1971): 1-22 (with select bibliography to 1970).

22. Georges Dossin in *Syria* 32 (1955):1-26.

23. Albrecht Goetze in JCS 11 (1957):63-65.

24. Georges Dossin in Parrot, *Studia Mariana*, pp. 52f.

25. Benno Landsberger in JCS 8 (1954):35 n. 28.

26. Dossin in Parrot, *Studia Mariana*, pp. 53f.

27. Ibid., pp. 54-59.

28. Georges Dossin in *Mélanges syriens offerts a Monsieur Réne Dussaud*, 2 vols. (Paris: P. Geuther, 1939), 2:981-996; Hayim Tadmor in JNES 17 (1958):130 and nn. 12-14.

29. Parrot in *Studia Mariana*, pp. 3-5.

30. Parrot in *Syria* 18 (1937):325-354; idem, *Mari, documentation photographique*, pls. 80ff.

31. Georges Dossin in *Syria* 19 (1938):105-126; ibid., 20 (1939):97-113; André Parrot and Georges Dossin, eds., *Archives royales de Mari* (Paris: Imprimerie nationale, 1950ff.); A. Leo Oppenheim in JNES 11 (1952):129-139.

32. C. Leonard Woolley, *A Forgotten Kingdom* (Baltimore: Penguin Books, 1953); idem, *Alalakh: An Account of the Excavations at Tell Atchana in the Hatay, 1937-1949* (London: Oxford University Press, 1955); Donald J. Wiseman *The Alalakh Tablets* (London: British Institute of Archaeology at Ankara, 1953); and idem, JCS 12 (1958):124-129.

33. Dossin in Parrot, *Studia Mariana*, pp. 41-50.

34. Parrot and Dossin, *Archives royales de Mari*, 2, no. 37. The words are literally "young ass, son of a she-ass," exactly the same as the Hebrew words in Zech. 9:9 (cf. also Gen. 49:11), quoted in Matt. 21:5. The practice of the slaying of animals in the making of covenants is also familiar in biblical examples (Gen. 15:9f.; Jer. 34:18f.).

35. Herbert B. Huffmon in BA 31 (1968):101-124.

36. E.g., ANET, pp. 624 n. 13 and 631, sec. p.

37. According to another Mari letter (ANET, p. 482), this was a place in the region of the *bini iamina*, or "sons of the south."

38. ANET, p. 623.

39. Huffmon in BA 31 (1968):107f.

40. ANET, p. 624, sec. d.

41. Parrot and Dossin, *Archives royales de Mari*, 5, no. 20.

42. Ibid., 10, no. 156.

43. Robert Koldewey, *Das wieder erstehende Babylon*, 4th ed. (Leipzig: J. C. Hinrichs, 1925), p. 88; Oscar Reuther, *Die Innenstadt von Babylon (Merkes)* (Leipzig: J. C. Hinrichs, 1926), pp. 41-49.

44. L. W. King, *The Letters and Inscriptions of Hammurabi, King of Babylon*, 3 vols. (London: Luzac, 1898-1900); A. Leo Oppenheim, *Letters from Mesopotamia: Official, Business, and Private Letters on Clay Tablets from Two Millennia* (Chicago: University

of Chicago Press, 1967), p. 93.

45. G. R. Driver and John C. Miles, *The Babylonian Laws, Edited with Translation and Commentary,* 2 vols. (Oxford: Clarendon Press, 1952-1955).

46. Ibid., 1:92, 95 n. 4. The Akkadian *mushkenum* goes back to the Sumerian *mashenkak,* found already on one of the Jemdet Nasr tablets from around 3000, and in turn has passed into other languages, including Arabic *masqin* ("poor,") and French *mesquin* ("wretched").

47. Albrecht Goetze in JAOS 69 (1949):117f.

48. As in such biblical passages as Exod. 21:15, 23-25, 29; 22:2, Lev. 20:10; Deut. 19:18f., 21; 22:22; 24:1 in comparison with the Hammurabi code.

49. E.g., T. Fish in BJRL 16 (1932):507-528.

50. For Babylonian and also Egyptian (and Hellenistic) mathematics and astronomy, see O. Neugebauer, *The Exact Sciences in Antiquity,* 2d ed. (Providence: Brown University Press, 1962).

51. J. Laessøe in BO 13 (1956):89-102; W. G. Lambert in JSS 5 (1960):113-123; W. G. Lambert, and A. R. Millard, *Atra-Ḫasīs: The Babylonian Story of the Flood* (Oxford: Clarendon Press, 1969); William L. Moran in BASOR 200 (1970):48-56; idem, *Biblica* 52 (1971):51-61; Hope Nash Wolfe in JAOS 93 (1973):75f.; J. Renger in JNES 32 (1973):342-344.

52. ANET, pp. 99f., 104-106, 513f.

53. Bruno Meissner in MVG 7 (1902):1-15.

54. R. Campbell Thompson, *The Epic of Gilgamish* (London: Luzac, 1930); Paul Garelli, ed., *Gilgameš et sa légende* (Paris: Imprimerie nationale, 1960).

55. G. Ernest Wright in BA 18 (1955):44; idem, PEQ, May-October 1955, p. 104.

56. Johannes Friedrich in ZA 39 (1930):1-82.

57. H. Zimmern in ibid., 35 (1923):154-156; S. N. Kramer in JAOS 64 (1944):7-23; Edmond Sollberger, *The Babylonian Legend of the Flood* (London: Trustees of the British Museum, 1962).

58. Alexander Heidel, *The Gilgamesh Epic and Old Testament Parallels,* 2d ed. (Chicago: University of Chicago Press, 1949). In the Gilgamesh Epic, the ark of Utnapishtim grounds on Mount Nisir, a mountain also mentioned in the Annals of Ashurnasirpal II (ARAB 1, secs. 449f.). Perhaps from the details of Ashurnasirpal's itinerary, this mountain is to be identified with Pir Omar Gudrun ("Grandfather Omar"), a 4,000-meter peak in the mountains of Kurdistan south of the Little Zab River, a summit often snow-covered and often visible for more than 160 kilometers. Ephraim A. Speiser in AASOR 8 (1926-1927):7, 17f., and map following p. 420. In the biblical account, the ark of Noah comes to rest upon the mountains of Ararat (Gen. 8:4), a name recognizable as that of the land of Urartu (frequently mentioned by Ashurnasirpal II and other Assyrian kings [ARAB 1, sec. 487, etc.]), corresponding approximately with modern Armenia, north and west of Lake Van, where the lofty peak now known as Mount Ararat is more than 5,000 meters in elevation.

59. Alexander Heidel, *The Babylonian Genesis: The Story of Creation,* 2d ed. (Chicago: University of Chicago Press, 1951).

60. Thorkild Jacobsen in Hallo, *Essays in Memory of E. A. Speiser,* pp. 104-108. The name of Marduk may by interpreted as meaning "Son of the storm."

61. Heidel, *The Babylonian Genesis,* p. 43 nn. 96, 97.

62. Cf. Deut. 6:7; 11:19. For various late Babylonian historical epics, the theme of which is the supremacy of Marduk and the importance of the king's obedience to his will, see A. K. Grayson, *Babylonian Historical-Literary Texts* (Toronto: University of Toronto Press, 1975), pp. 41ff.

63. Chayim Cohen in JANES 2 (1970):106.

64. A common Semitic form may lie back of both the name Tiamat and the Hebrew word (*tehom*) for the "deep" in Gen. 1:2. But the former is a feminine name with mythological connotation and the latter a masculine noun simply designating any large body of water, so the latter is hardly borrowed from the name and concept in the Epic of Marduk. Heidel, *The Babylonian Genesis,* pp. 98-101.

65. In the description of the phases of the moon, the full-moon day at the middle of the month is called *shapattu,* a term that means to "finish" or "complete," and is identical with the Hebrew *sabbath,* so both words may come from a common source although they develop into different meanings. Hildegard and Julius Lewy in HUCA 17 (1942-1943):50f., 66, 77, 84; W. G. Lambert in JTS 16 (1965):297.

66. C. F. Whitley in JNES 17 (1958):32-40.

67. Jean Bottéro, ed., *Le problème des Habiru à la 4ᵉ rencontre assyriologique internationale* (Paris: Imprimerie nationale, 1954), pp. 18f., nos. 16, 18, 19.

68. Ibid., p. 131, nos. 165, 166; Julius Lewy in HUCA 14 (1939):618f.

69. Moshe Greenberg, *The Hab/piru* (New Haven: American Oriental Society, 1955), pp. 11, 53, 78.

70. E. A. Speiser in AASOR 13 (1931-1932):39-41.

71. Mary F. Gray in HUCA 29 (1958):169-172.

72. For Abraham and the other patriarchs, see P. Dhorme in RB 37 (1928):367-385, 481-511; ibid., 40 (1931):365-374, 503-518; R. de Vaux in ibid., 53 (1946):321-348; ibid., 55 (1948):321-347; ibid., 56 (1949):5-36; ibid., 72 (1965):5-28; André Parrot, *Abraham and His Times* (Philadelphia: Fortress Press, 1968). For a different evaluation of the evidence concerning Abraham, see John Van Seters, *Abraham in History and Tradition* (New Haven: Yale University Press, 1975).

73. J. C. L. Gibson in JSS 7 (1962):55. For the theory that the Ur of Abraham was a different city in northwestern Mesopotamia, see Cyrus H. Gordon in JNES 17 (1958):28-31; against this, see H. W. F. Saggs in *Iraq* 22 (1960):200-209. Yet again, see Cyrus H. Gordon in BAR 3 (1977):20ff., for an Ebla tablet that refers to Ur in Haran.

74. Dossin in *Syria* 19 (1938):115; de Vaux in RB 55 (1948):323; Parrot, *Abraham and His Times,* pp. 40f.

75. Dhorme in RB 40 (1931):221.

76. C. J. Gadd in AnS 8 (1958):35-92.

77. Dhorme in RB 37 (1928):487; Roger T. O'Callaghan, *Aram Naharaim* (AnOr 26) (Rome: Pontificium institutum biblicum, 1948), pp. 140f.; J. J. Finkelstein in JNES 21 (1962):84f.

78. Dhorme in RB 37 (1928):487; O'Callaghan, *Aram Naharaim,* p. 96.

79. Albrecht Goetze in JCS 7 (1953):51-72, with map on p. 72; William W. Hallo in ibid., 18 (1964):57-88, with map on p. 87; Albrecht Goetze in BASOR 147 (1957):22-27.

80. Hallo in JCS 18 (1964):86-88.

81. De Vaux in RB 55 (1948):346.

82. John Marshall Holt, *The Patriarchs of Israel* (Nashville: Vanderbilt University Press, 1964), pp. 136-154. For the theory that the patriarchs were adherents of the moon cult, see E. L. Abel in *Numen* 20 (1973):48-59.

83. C. J. Gadd in RAAO 23 (1926):49-161; E. A. Speiser in AASOR 10 (1928-1929):1-73; idem, *Excavations at Nuzi* (Harvard Semitic Series), 8 vols. (Cambridge: Harvard University Press, 1929-1962); Robert H. Pfeiffer and E. A. Speiser in AASOR 16 (1935-1936); Cyrus H. Gordon in *Orientalia* 5 (1936):305-330; Francis R. Steele, *Nuzi Real Estate Transactions* (AOS 25) (New Haven: American Oriental Society, 1943); Ignace J. Gelb, Pierre M. Purves, and Allan A. MacRae, *Nuzi Personal Names* (OIP 57) (Chicago: University of Chicago Press, 1943); and for Nuzi seal impressions, Edith Porada in AASOR 24 (1944-1945).

84. For the spelling of the name, see E. A. Speiser in JAOS 75 (1955):52-55.

85. E. A. Speiser in AASOR 13 (1931-1932):13-54.

86. William F. Albright in *From the Pyramids to Paul,* ed. Lewis G. Leary (New York: Thomas Nelson and Sons, 1935), pp. 9-26.

87. Cyrus H. Gordon in *Orientalia* 7 (1938):32-63.

88. Cyrus H. Gordon in BA 3 (1940):1-12; idem, *The Living Past* (New York: John Day, 1941), pp. 156-178; and idem, JNES 13 (1954):56-59; Charles F. Pfeiffer, *The Patriarchal Age* (Grand Rapids, Mich.: Baker Book House, 1961), pp. 77-79. For the domesticated camel in the patriarchal period (Gen. 24:10f., 64; 31:34, etc.), see E. Douglas Van Buren, *The Fauna of Ancient Mesopotamia as Represented in Art* (Rome: Pontificium institutum biblicum, 1939), p. 36; André Parrot in *Syria* 32 (1955):323; Donald J. Wiseman in JCS 13 (1959):29, text 269, l. 59; Albrecht Goetze in ibid., p. 37; W. G. Lambert in BASOR 160 (1960):42f.; I. J. Gelb in JCS 15 (1961):27 n. 2; A. Leo Oppenheim and Louis F. Hartman in JNES 4 (1945):174f., l. 366; B. S. J. Isserlin in PEQ, 1950, pp. 50-53; Joseph P. Free in JNES 3 (1944): 187-193; D. J. Wiseman in JSS 5 (1960):419; C. H. Gordon in ibid., 8 (1963):90f.

89. Nelson Glueck, *Rivers in the Desert: A History of the Negev* (New York: Farrar, Straus and Cudahy, 1959), pp. 68f.; William F. Albright in BASOR 163 (1961):36-40; idem, BA 36 (1973):16f.

90. In 1 Kings 6:1, the exodus was 480 years before Solomon began to build the temple in the fourth year of his reign (probably 967/966 reckoned from the division of the kingdom in 931/930). Edwin R. Thiele, *The Mysterious Numbers of the Hebrew Kings,* rev. ed. (Grand Rapids, Mich.: Eerdmans, 1965), pp. 52-54; idem, *A Chronology of the Hebrew Kings* (Grand Rapids, Mich.: Zondervan, 1977), p. 31. Therefore, the exodus occurred in 1447. But in Exod. 1:11, Israel builds Raamses, surely the city of Ramses II (1290-1224); therefore, the exodus was more probably in the thirteenth century (and the 480 years is an artificial reckoning of twelve

generations at forty years each. Cf. Chapter 18, n. 45). In Exod. 12:40 (Hebrew text), Israel dwelt in Egypt 430 years—therefore from the late eighteenth or the seventeenth century to the thirteenth. In Gen. 12:4; 21:5; 25:26; and 47:9, the time from Abraham's coming into Canaan to Jacob's going down into Egypt is 215 years; therefore, the time of Abraham is in the late twentieth or early nineteenth century. For a different understanding of the biblical figures but a date for Abraham also between 2000 and 1950, see Heinz Genge in *In memoriam Eckhard Unger: Beiträge zu Geschichte, Kultur und Religion des alten Orients,* (Baden-Baden: V. Koerner, 1971), pp. 89-96. An earlier proposal to identify "Amraphel king of Shinar" (Gen. 14:1) with Hammurabi of Babylon (*Recueil Édouard Dhorme: études bibliques et orientales* [Paris: Imprimerie nationale, 1951], pp. 262, 265) is now considered unlikely.

91. Ungnad in RA 2:183, no. 154 (Samsuiluna); p. 185, no. 187 (Abieshuh); p. 189, no. 248 (Ammiditana).

92. F. R. Kraus, *Ein Edikt des Königs Ammi-saduqa von Babylon* (Leiden: E. J. Brill, 1958); J. J. Finkelstein in JCS 5 (1961):91-104.

93. S. Langdon and J. K. Fotheringham, *The Venus Tablets of Ammizaduga* (London: Humphrey Milford, 1928). Since there are cycles of up to sixty-four years in the recurrence of certain of the Venus phenomena, allowance must be made for possible variations in results up to that magnitude. O. Neugebauer in JAOS 61 (1941):59. The demonstration in the Mari tablets that Hammurabi of Babylon was contemporary with Shamsi-Adad I (1813-1781) of Assyria makes impossible the date for Hammurabi around 2100-2000, which had long been accepted. The material from Alalakh makes probable a date in the nineteenth or eighteenth century. Sidney Smith, *Alalakh and Chronology* (London: Luzac, 1940). At the upper limit of this time span, a date was proposed around 1900 (Landsberger in JCS 8 [1954]:120), but, within the same two centuries, the Venus tablets allow three main solutions, which place the first regnal year of Hammurabi in 1848, 1792, or 1728, respectively. M. B. Rowton in JNES 17 (1958):98. Accepting these figures, a high chronology dates Hammurabi in 1848-1806 (Albrecht Goetze in BASOR 122 [1951]:18-25; idem, JCS 11 [1957]:53-61, 63-73); a middle chronology gives 1792-1750 (Sidney Smith in AJA 47 [1943]:1-24); and a low chronology puts the date at 1728-1686 (Friedrich Cornelius in AfQ 17 [1956]:294-309; idem, JCS 12 [1958]:101-104). In the present book, the middle chronology is followed.

94. Samuel I. Feigin and B. Landsberger in JNES 14 (1955):137-160; J. J. Finkelstein in JCS 13 (1959):39-49.

95. L. W. King, *Chronicles concerning Early Babylonian Kings,* 2 vols. (London: Luzac, 1907), 2:22.

CHAPTER 6. MIDDLE BABYLONIAN PERIOD

1. ANET, pp. 271-274.

2. Raymond P. Dougherty, *The Sealand of Ancient Arabia* (New Haven: Yale University Press, 1932), pp. 11-27.

3. B. Landsberger in JCS 8 (1954):69.

4. Albrecht Goetze, *Hethiter, Churriter und Assyrer* (Oslo: H. Aschehoug, 1936), p. 27; George G. Cameron, *History of Early Iran* (Chicago: University of Chicago Press, 1936), pp. 89-95.

5. Faisal El-Wailly in *Sumer* 10 (1954):43-54; C. Bezold, *Catalogue of the Cuneiform Tablets in the Kouyunjik Collection of the British Museum*, 5 vols. (London: Trustees of the British Museum, 1889-1899), 2:628; A. H. Sayce in *Records of the Past*, 12 vols., ed. S. Birch (London: S. Bagster and Sons, 1874-1881), 3:25-36; Eberhard Schrader, ed., *Keilinschriftliche Bibliothek: Sammlung von assyrischen und babylonishchen Texten*, 6 vols. (Berlin: Reuther and Reichard, 1889-1915), 1:194-203; Friedrich Schmidtke, *Der Aufbau der babylonischen Chronologie* (Münster: Aschendorffsche Verlags-Buchhandlung, 1952), pp. 84-90.

6. J. A. Brinkman in A. Leo Oppenheim, *Ancient Mesopotamia* (Chicago: University of Chicago Press, 1964), pp. 338f., with possible variations in BO 27 (1970):305-307.

7. El-Wailly in *Sumer* 10 (1954):43, no. 9; Albrecht Goetze in JCS 18 (1964):98f.

8. Schrader, *Keilinschriftliche Bibliothek*, 1:194f.; Schmidtke, *Der Aufbau der babylonischen Chronologie*, pp. 84f. For the characteristic Kassite "boundary" (*kudurru*) stones, which most often marked private properties, see L. W. King, *Babylonian Boundary-Stones and Memorial-Tablets in the British Museum*, 2 vols. (London: Trustees of the British Museum, 1912).

9. L. W. King, *Chronicles concerning Early Babylonian Kings*, 2 vols. (London: Luzac, 1907), 2:22f.; El-Wailly in *Sumer* 10 (1954):44, no. 13.

10. King, *Chronicles concerning Early Babylonian Kings*, 2:24.

11. Schrader, *Keilinschriftliche Bibliothek*, 1:194f.

12. El-Wailly in *Sumer* 10 (1954):44f., no. 17; pp. 46-50, no. 22.

13. Taha Baqir in *Iraq*, Supplement 1944, Supplement 1945, 8 (1946):73-93.

14. S. N. Kramer, Taha Baqir, and Selim J. Levy in *Sumer* 4 (1948):1-38.

15. The numbers of the Amarna Letters are the numbers in J. A. Knudtzon, *Die El-Amarna Tafeln*, 2 vols. (Leipzig: J. C. Hinrichs, 1908-1915); Samuel A. B. Mercer, *The Tell El-Amarna Tablets*, 2 vols. (Toronto: Macmillan Co. of Canada, 1939); cf. below, Chapter 17, n. 79.

16. Schrader, *Keilinschriftliche Bibliothek* 1:196f.

17. R. Ghirshman et al., *Tchoga Zanbil (Dur-Untash)*, (MDAI 39-42), 4 vols. (Paris: P. Geuthner, 1960-1968).

18. Jean Vincent Scheil, *Textes elamites-semitiques* (MDP 10) (Paris: E. Leroux, 1908), pp. 85f., pl. 10.

19. ARAB 1, sec. 145.

20. Ibid., sec. 141.

21. Partly owing to this captivity in Assyria, Marduk eventually became a member of the Assyrian royal pantheon. Albert Schott in ZA 43 (1936):318-321.

22. Cameron, *History of Early Iran*, pp. 108-111, with references to the *Mémoires* of the French archeological expedition in Iran.

23. Ungnad in RA 2:132; Edwin R. Thiele, *The Mysterious Numbers of the Hebrew*

Kings, rev. ed. (Grand Rapids, Mich.: Eerdmans, 1965), p. 17; W. F. Albright in JBL 51 (1932):102; Arno Poebel in AJSL 56 (1939):121 n. 3.

24. A. Poebel, *The Second Dynasty of Isin according to a New King-List Tablet* (AS 15) (Chicago: University of Chicago Press, 1955).

25. For accession dates of rulers, and synchronisms, see M. B. Rowton in JCS 13 (1959):6 and table on p. 7. See also John A. Brinkman in ibid., 16 (1962):83-109; and idem, *A Political History of Post-Kassite Babylonia 1158-722 B.C.* (AnOr 43) (Rome: Pontificium institutum biblicum, 1968).

26. King, *Babylonian Boundary-Stones,* pp. 29-36.

27. Sennacherib (704-681) states that in the reign of Tiglath-pileser I, Marduk-nadin-ahhe seized and carried off to Babylon Adad and Shala (consort of Adad), the gods of the city of Ekallate ("the palaces," a royal city a few kilometers south of Ashur), and that he himself brought them back 418 years later, perhaps a few years after his own capture of Babylon in 689 (ARAB 2, sec. 341). Tiglath-pileser I, on the other hand, claims to have burned the palaces of Marduk-nadin-ahhe in Babylon (ARAB 1, sec. 309, cf. secs. 288, 295f.).

28. ARAB 2, sec. 537.

29. King, *Chronicles concerning Early Babylonian Kings,* 1:184f.

30. Ibid., 2:81-83.

31. Karl W. L. Müller, ed., *Fragmenta Historicorum Graecorum,* 5 vols. (Paris: Firmin-Didot, 1868-1884), 2:504; David Sidersky, *Étude sur la chronologie assyro-babylonienne* (Paris: Imprimerie nationale, 1916), p. 1.

32. Samuel Noah Kramer, *The Sumerians: Their History, Culture, and Character* (Chicago: University of Chicago Press, 1963), p. 91. For names of months found on tablets from Telloh and Nippur, see Fr. Hommel in HERE 3:73f.

33. O. Neugebauer in JNES 1 (1942):400f.

34. By modern reckoning, the length of the solar (tropical) year is 365.24219879 days, and the length of the (synodic) month is 29.530588 days. Nineteen solar years, therefore, equal 6939.601777 days, and 235 months equal 6939.688180 days, a difference of 0.086403 days or 2 hours, 4 minutes, 25.22 seconds. For the first steps of astronomy as directed by calendaric and related problems, and for the common assumption of the priority of astrology as unjustified, see O. Neugebauer in JNES 4 (1945):1-38, especially p. 14.

35. Richard A. Parker and Waldo H. Dubberstein, *Babylonian Chronology 626 B.C.-A.D. 75* (Providence: Brown University Press, 1956).

36. E. J. Bickerman, *Chronology of the Ancient World* (London: Thames and Hudson, 1968), pp. 24 f.

37. Ptolemy, *The Almagest,* trans. R. Catesby Taliaferro (Great Books of the Western World, 16) (Chicago: W. Benton, 1952).

38. A. T. Olmstead, *History of Assyria* (Chicago: University of Chicago Press, 1923), p. 178.

39. ARAB 1, secs. 792-806; King, *Chronicles concerning Early Babylonian Kings,* 1:196.

40. Ptolemy calls Merodach-Baladan II Mardokempad, puts the beginning of

his reign in the seventh year of the Era of Nabonassar, and says that in his same first year there was a total eclipse of the moon on the night of Thoth 29/30 (*Almagest* 4. 6. 1. trans. Taliaferro, p. 123). The eclipse is verified astronomically on March 19, 721, and thus the date of the first year of Merodach-Baladan II is established. Karl Manitius, ed., *Des Claudius Ptolemäus Handbuch der Astronomie,* 2 vols. (Leipzig: B. G. Teubner, 1912-1913), 1:219.

41. ARAB 1, sec. 794; 2, secs. 31, 66, 68, 70.

42. ANET, p. 273.

43. King, *Chronicles concerning Early Babylonian Kings,* 1:204; 2:65.

44. ARAB 2, sec. 270.

45. Ibid., secs. 241, 243, 247, 263, 273, 315, 324, 339-341; A. T. Olmstead in AJSL 38 (1922):76, 80f., 83.

46. Esarhaddon explains that Marduk had decreed seventy years as the period of Babylon's desolation (cf. Jer. 25:11f.; 29:10; 2 Chron. 36:21; Dan. 9:2 for the same period for Jerusalem), but the divine anger had lasted only momentarily, and the god had now turned the Book of Fate upside down and ordered the restoration of the city in the eleventh year. The allusion is to the fact that the cuneiform numeral 70 becomes 11 when it is turned upside down or reversed as, for example, the Arabic numeral 9 turned upside down becomes 6. ARAB 2, secs. 643, 650; D. D. Luckenbill in AJSL 41 (1925):166f.

47. ANET, p. 298.

48. Waldo H. Dubberstein in JNES 3 (1944):39f.

CHAPTER 7. HITTITES

1. Enver Y. Bostanci in *Anatolia* 4 (1959):129-178.

2. James Mellaart in AnS 8 (1958):127-156; ibid., 9 (1959):51-65; ibid., 10 (1960):83-104; ibid., 11 (1961):39-75; and *Excavations at Hacilar,* 2 vols. (Edinburgh: Edinburgh University Press, 1970).

3. James Mellaart in AnS 12 (1962):41-65; ibid., 13 (1963):43-103; ibid., 14 (1964):39-119; ibid., 16 (1966):165-191; idem, *Earliest Civilizations of the Near East* (New York: McGraw-Hill, 1965), pp. 81-101; Johannes Lehmann, *Die Hethiter* (Munich: C. Bertelsmann, 1975), pp. 92ff.; idem, *The Hittites* (New York: Viking Press, 1977), pp. 97ff.

4. Hans G. Güterbock in JCS 18 (1964):1-6.

5. Julius Lewy in RV 6:212-219; idem, HUCA 27 (1956):1-79; idem, JAOS 78 (1958):89-101; B. Landsberger, *Assyrische Handelskolonien in Kleinasien aus dem dritten Jahrtausend* (Leipzig: J. C. Hinrichs, 1925); Paul Garelli, *Les Assyriens en Cappadoce* (Paris: Librairie A. Maisonneuve, 1963); Louis L. Orlin, *Assyrian Colonies in Cappadocia* (The Hague: Mouton, 1970); Mogens Trolle Larsen in JAOS 94 (1974):468-475.

6. AnS 1 (1951):10.

7. Lewy in JAOS 78 (1958):99-101.

8. Albrecht Goetze in JCS 8 (1954):74-81.

9. Julius Lewy in HUCA 33 (1962):45–57.

10. Joh. Friedrich in RA 1:109.

11. AnS 5 (1955):19; James Mellaart in ibid., 7 (1957):59.

12. Ibid., 4 (1954):19.

13. Julius Lewy in RHR 110 (1934):41f., 51ff.

14. For the excavation of Boghazköy, see Hugo Winckler, *Die im Sommer 1906 in Kleinasien ausgeführten Ausgrabungen* (Sonderabzug, OLZ December 15, 1906); Kurt Bittel, *Bogazköy-Hattusa* (Stuttgart: Kohlhammer, 1952ff.); idem, *Hattusha, The Capital of the Hittites* (New York: Oxford University Press, 1970). For the rock sanctuary at nearby Yazilikaya, see Kurt Bittel, *Yazilikaya: Architektur, Felsbilder, Inschriften und Kleinfunde* (Leipzig: J. C. Hinrichs, 1941); K. Bittel et al., *Das hethitische Felsenheiligtum von Yazilikaya* (Berlin: Gebr. Mann, 1975); cf. Hans G. Güterbock in JNES 34 (1975):273–277; E. Laroche in JCS 6 (1952):115–123. For Hittite art, including seals, see Ekrem Akurgal in *Neuere Hethiterforschung (Historia, Einzelschriften, 7)*, ed. Gerold Walser (Wiesbaden: F. Steiner, 1964), pp. 74–118; G. Contenau, *La glyptique Syro-Hittite* (Paris: P. Geuthner, 1922); H. G. Güterbock, *Siegel aus Boğazköy* (AfO, Beihefte 5 and 7), 2 vols, 1940.

15. Friedrich Hrozný, *Die Sprache der Hethiter* (Leipzig: J. C. Hinrichs, 1917); Piero Meriggi in ZA 39 (1930):165–212; P. Jensen in ibid., 40 (1931):29–64; Ignace J. Gelb, *Hittite Hieroglyphs* (SAOC 2, 14), 2 vols. (Chicago: University of Chicago Press, 1931–1935); Emil O. Forrer, *Die hethitische Bilderschrift* (SAOC 3) (Chicago: University of Chicago Press, 1932).

16. Edgar H. Sturtevant and George Bechtel, *A Hittite Chrestomathy* (Philadelphia: Linguistic Society of America, University of Pennsylvania, 1935); Albrecht Goetze in BASOR 122 (1951):21; idem, JCS 11 (1957):53–55.

17. Heinrich Otten in MDOG 91 (1958):73–84.

18. Bittel, *Hattusha,* pp. 19f.

19. Albrecht Goetze in BASOR 146 (1957):25.

20. For the Hittite laws, the antecedents of which are presumably even earlier than Telepinush, see Sturtevant and Bechtel, *A Hittite Chrestomathy,* pp. 202–223; E. Neufeld, *The Hittite Laws, Translated into English and Hebrew with Commentary* (London: Luzac, 1951); Johannes Friedrich, *Die hethitischen Gesetze* (Leiden: E. J. Brill, 1959). For correspondences with requirements still prevailing in later Hittite laws in the business dealings of Abraham with "the children of Heth" (i.e., the Hittites) at Hebron (Gen. 23:3ff.), see Manfred R. Lehmann in BASOR 129 (1953):15–18; K. A. Kitchen, *Ancient Orient and Old Testament* (Philadelphia: American Philosophical Society, 1944), pp. 51f., 154–156.

21. I. J. Gelb, *Hurrians and Subarians* (SAOC 22) (Chicago: University of Chicago Press, 1948), pp. 71, 76.

22. Ibid., pp. 70–73.

23. For the offering lists, see K. A. Kitchen, *Suppiluliuma and the Amarna Pharaohs* (Liverpool: Liverpool University Press, 1962), pp. 54f. For the family relationships, sometimes debatable, see CAH³ 2, pt. 1, p. 675; 2 pt. 2, pp. 1040f. Because there was probably a Tudhaliash I prior to Labarnash of the Hittite Old

Kingdom, the first king in the present series is shown as Tudhaliash II (CAH³ 2, pt. 1, p. 820).

24. Kitchen, *Suppiluliuma and the Amarna Pharaohs,* pp. 3, 51f. (K.B. 6:28, obv. 6-25; KUB 19:9).

25. Ernst F. Weidner, *Politische Dokumente aus Kleinasien: Die Staatsverträge in akkadischer Sprache aus dem Archiv von Boghazköi* (Boghazköi-Studien 8) (1923; reprint ed., Hildesheim: G. Olms, 1970), pp. 2-37. On Hittite treaties and comparable biblical forms, see George E. Mendenhall in BA 17 (1954):50-76; Dennis J. McCarthy, *Treaty and Covenant: A Study in Form in Ancient Oriental Documents and in the Old Testament* (Analecta Biblica 21) (Rome: Pontifical Biblical Institute, 1963); idem, *Old Testament Covenant: A Survey of Current Opinions* (Richmond: John Knox, 1972), pp. 10-34.

26. John Garstang and O. R. Gurney, *The Geography of the Hittite Empire* (London: British Institute of Archaeology at Ankara, 1959), pp. 40f.

27. Weidner, *Politische Dokumente aus Kleinasien* (Boghazköi-Studien 8), pp. 70-75.

28. Hans Gustav Güterbock in JCS 10 (1956):41-68, 75-98, 107-130.

29. Elmar Edel in JNES 7 (1948):14f. As written in some of the fragments, the name was previously taken as a corruption of Naphururia, the name of Amunhotep IV (Akhenaten) in the Amarna Letters (no. 9).

30. Walter Federn in JCS 14 (1960):33.

31. ANET, pp. 394-396.

32. Ibid., pp. 400f.

33. Albrecht Goetze, *Die Annalen des Mursilis* (MVÄG 38) (Leipzig: J. C. Hinrichs, 1933).

34. Weidner, *Politische Dokumente aus Kleinasien* (Boghazköi-Studien 8), pp. 76-79; Johannes Friedrich, *Staatsverträge des Ḫatti-Reiches in hethitischer Sprache* (MVÄG 31, 1) (Leipzig: J. C. Hinrichs, 1926), pp. 1-48.

35. Emil Forrer, *Forschungen,* 3 vols. (Berlin: Im Selbstverlag des Verfassers, 1926-1929), 2, pt. 1, pp. 1-9; questioned in Goetze, *Die Annalen des Mursilis,* p. 9 n. 2.

36. R. O. Faulkner in JEA 33 (1947):37.

37. Albrecht Goetze in OLZ 32 (1929), col. 834.

38. ARE 3, sec. 309.

39. Albrecht Goetze, *Ḫattušiliš: Der Bericht über seine Thronbesteigung nebst den Paralleltexten* (MVÄG 29) (Leipzig: J. C. Hinrichs, 1925), pp. 20-23, II 69ff.

40. Goetze in OLZ 32 (1929), col. 837; ANET, p. 319.

41. J. A. Knudtzon, *Die El-Amarna Tafeln,* 2 vols. (Leipzig: J. C. Hinrichs, 1908-1915), pp. 1110-1113.

42. Goetze, *Ḫattušiliš,* pp. 34f.

43. ANET, p. 393. For a statue from Til Barsip of Teshub standing on his bull and brandishing ax and forked lightning, see André Parrot, *Nineveh and Babylon* (London: Thames and Hudson, 1961), fig. 89.

44. Ernst F. Weidner, *Politische Dokumente aus Kleinasien: Die Staatsverträge in*

akkadischer Sprache aus dem Archiv von Boghazköi (Boghazköi-Studien 9) (1923; reprint ed., Hildesheim: G. Olms, 1970), pp. 112-123; S. Langdon and Alan H. Gardiner in JEA 6 (1920):179-205.

45. ARE 3, secs. 415-424.

46. ARAB 1, secs. 72-111.

47. M. B. Rowton in JCS 13 (1959):1-11.

48. ARAB 1, sec. 116.

49. Ibid., secs. 164, 171.

50. ARE 3, sec. 580.

51. Bittle, *Hattusha,* pp. 132f.

52. ARE 4, sec. 64.

53. ARAB 1, secs. 220f., 579f., etc.

54. Ibid, secs. 239, 292, 307.

55. Fr. Thureau-Dangin in *Syria* 10 (1929):185-205.

56. David G. Hogarth, *Kings of the Hittites* (London: Oxford University Press, 1926).

57. Sabatino Moscati, *Geschichte und Kultur der semitischen Völker* (Stuttgart: W. Kohlhammer, 1953), pp. 146f.

58. O. R. Gurney, *The Hittites* (London: Penguin Books, 1952), p. 42.

59. Eckhard Unger in RV 4:579f. For the palace of Kapara, an Aramean ruler of probably the beginning of the ninth century, see Max von Oppenheim, *Tell Halaf,* vol. 2, *Die Bauwerke,* ed. Rudolf Naumann (Berlin: Walter de Gruyter, 1950), pp. 12ff.; vol. 3, *Die Bildwerke,* ed. Anton Moortgat (Berlin: Walter de Gruyter, 1955), p. 19.

60. F. -M. Abel, *Géographie de la Palestine,* 2 vols. (Paris: J. Gabalda, 1933-1938), 1:248-250.

61. Theresa Goell in BASOR 147 (1957):213, 260.

62. Raymond A. Bowman in JNES 7 (1948):65-90.

CHAPTER 8. ASSYRIANS

1. Walter Andrae, *Das wiedererstandene Assur* (Leipzig: J. C. Hinrichs, 1938).

2. E. A. Speiser, *Excavations at Nuzi,* vol. 3, *Old Akkadian, Sumerian, and Cappadocian Texts from Nuzi* (Harvard Semitic Series) (Cambridge, Mass: Harvard University Press, 1935), p. xi.

3. The Istanbul King List in the Archaeological Museum in Istanbul (Essad Nassouhi in AO 4 [1927]:1-11) ends with the reign of Tiglath-pileser II (935). The Khorsabad King List of the Oriental Institute of the University of Chicago (A. Poebel in JNES 1 [1942]:247-306, 460-492; ibid., 2 [1943]:56-90) ends with the reign of Ashur-nirari V (745). The SDAS King List in the Seventh-Day Adventist Theological Seminary in Washington, D.C. (I. J. Gelb in JNES 13 [1954]:209-230) ends with the reign of Shalmaneser V (722). The concluding dates presumably reflect the respective times when the tablets were copied. For the King List and all the other royal inscriptions, see Albert Kirk Grayson, *Assyrian Royal Inscriptions,*

vols. 1-2 (Wiesbaden: O. Harrassowitz, 1972-1976) and following volumes as available in the series Records of the Ancient Near East, ed. Hans Goedicke (Wiesbaden: O. Harrassowitz, 1972ff.).

4. A. Ungnad in RA 2:412-457.

5. Ibid., pp. 430, 432, 447; G. Van der Meer, *The Chronology of Ancient Western Asia and Egypt* (Leiden: E. J. Brill, 1947), p. 5.

6. J. J. Finkelstein in JCS 20 (1966):98, 113f., 116f.

7. ARAB 1, sec. 119; 2, sec. 706.

8. ARAB 1, sec. 51.

9. Ibid., secs. 43-46.

10. Ungnad in RA 2:181, nos. 139, 141.

11. ANET, p. 272.

12. ARAB 2, sec. 576.

13. André Parrot, *Nineveh and Babylon* (London: Thames and Hudson, 1961), p. 4, fig. 7.

14. ARE 2, secs. 408, 444, 446, 449.

15. ARAB 1, sec. 73.

16. G. R. Driver and J. C. Miles, *The Assyrian Laws* (Oxford: Clarendon Press, 1935).

17. A. Leo Oppenheim, *The Interpretation of Dreams in the Ancient Near East, with a Translation of an Assyrian Dream-Book* (Transactions of the American Philosophical Society, New Series 46, 3) (Philadelphia: American Philosophical Society, 1956).

18. A. T. Olmstead, *Assyrian Historiography* (University of Missouri Studies, Social Science Series 3, 1) (Columbia: University of Missouri, 1916), p. 10.

19. ARAB 1, sec. 245.

20. Ibid., sec. 221.

21. Ibid., secs. 268ff. (for the "sea horse," see sec. 302).

22. Ibid., secs. 355-377, 400-417.

23. Ibid., secs. 436-552.

24. Seton Lloyd, *Foundations in the Dust* (Harmondsworth: Penguin Books, 1947), pp. 94-143; M. E. L. Mallowan in *Sumer* 6 (1950):101f.; ibid., 7 (1951):49-54; idem, *Twenty-five Years of Mesopotamian Discovery* (London: The British School of Archaeology in Iraq, 1956), pp. 45-78; idem, *Nimrud and Its Remains,* 2 vols. (New York: Dodd, Mead, 1966).

25. ANEP, fig. 646. Placed generally in pairs at palace, temple, and city entrances, these creatures were intended to ward off evil. In the texts they are called *shedu* and *lamassu,* the former being either good or bad, the latter always good (e.g., ARAB 2, sec. 416). See Eckhard Unger in RV 8:195-216; R. D. Barnett in *Le palais et la royaute (Archéologie et Civilisation),* ed. Paul Garelli (Paris: P. Geuthner, 1974), pp. 441-446.

26. Richard D. Barnett and Werner Forman, *Assyrian Palace Reliefs* (London: Batchworth Press, 1959), pls. 26, 28.

27. Donald J. Wiseman in *Sumer* 6 (1950):103; ibid., 7 (1951):55-57.

28. E. A. Wallis Budge, *Assyrian Sculptures in the British Museum: Reign of*

Ashur-nasir-pal 885-860 B. C. (London: Trustees of the British Museum, 1914), pl. 1.

29. ARAB 1, secs. 487, 504, 516.

30. The first edition of the annals, through the king's sixth year, is the Monolith Inscription, found at Kurkh (in the Upper Tigris region thirty-two kilometers south of Dairbakr). Ibid., secs. 594-611. The second edition, through the ninth year, is on the Bronze Gates from the country palace of Shalmaneser III at Balawat (northeast of Nimrud). Samuel Birch, *Bronze Ornaments of the Palace Gates of Balawat* (London: The Society of Biblical Archaeology, 1880-1881); L. W. King, *Bronze Reliefs from the Gates of Shalmaneser* (London: Trustees of the British Museum, 1915); ARAB 1, secs. 612-625. The third and fourth editions, extending through sixteen and twenty years of reign, respectively, are on a clay tablet and a marble slab in the Iraq Museum, both from Qalat Sharqat. George G. Cameron in *Sumer* 6 (1950):6-26; cf. fragments in ARAB 1, secs. 662f.; Fuad Safar in *Sumer* 7 (1951):3-21. The fifth and latest edition, through the thirty-first regnal year, is on the Black Obelisk, found in the palace of Shalmaneser III at Kalah. Austen Henry Layard, *Nineveh and Its Remains,* 2 vols. (New York: G. P. Putnam, 1849), 1:282; C. J. Gadd, *The Stones of Assyria* (London: Chatto and Windus, 1936), pp. 35, 43, 48. Comparison of the successive editions shows that it was the practice of the scribes to write the original record fully, then in a subsequent edition to abbreviate the part previously covered and go on more fully with the added portions.

31. ARAB 1, secs. 558, 599f.

32. Ibid., secs. 563, 610f.

33. Safar in *Sumer* 7 (1951):18f.

34. Nelson Glueck, *Explorations in Eastern Palestine,* 4 vols. (AASOR 25-28) (Philadelphia: American Schools of Oriental Research, 1945-1949), 4, pt. 1 (text), pp. 153f.

35. Michael C. Astour in JAOS 91 (1971):383-389.

36. ANEP, fig. 355.

37. The mention of Ahab in the sixth year (the summer of 853) of Shalmaneser III and the mention of Jehu in the eighteenth year (probably in the summer of 841) of the same king cohere with biblical data according to the following understanding: Ahab died in 853 after the battle of Qarqar; Ahaz son of Ahab took the throne in the same year and reigned two years (1 Kings 22:51), 853-852; Jehoram son of Ahab took the throne in 852 and reigned twelve years (2 Kings 3:1), 852-841. To allow this result, the reckoning here is according to the nonaccession-year system. For the entire chronology of the kingdoms of Israel and Judah, recognizing both accession-year and nonaccession-year systems all together, and regnal years beginning in Judah in the fall on the first day of Tishri (September/October) but in Israel in the spring on the first day of Nisan (March/April), and with numbered months always counted from Nisan as the first month, see Edwin R. Thiele, *The Mysterious Numbers of the Hebrew Kings,* rev. ed. (Grand Rapids, Mich.: Eerdmans, 1965); cf. William W. Hallo in BA 23 (1960):35.

38. ARAB 1, sec. 602, etc.

39. François Thureau-Dangin and Maurice Dunand, *Til-Barsib* (Paris: P.

Geuthner, 1936); Parrot, *Nineveh and Babylon,* Frontispiece, figs. 109-120, 336-348.

40. ANEP, fig. 819; Parrot, *Nineveh and Babylon,* figs. 19-21.

41. ARAB 1, secs. 584-598.

42. Ibid., secs. 717, 785, 813; 2, sec. 155.

43. In Assyrian, Ishpuini calls himself the king of the land of Nairi, but in Urartian, the king of the land of Biaini; therefore, the latter was the Urartian name of the country. In biblical references the name Urartu is rendered as Ararat (Gen. 8:4; 2 Kings 19:37; Isa. 37:38; Jer. 51:27f.). About the beginning of the sixth century, the kingdom of Urartu was overthrown by the Scythians and came under the rule of the Medes and Persians. Eventually, the Armenians, an Indo-European people probably related to the Phrygians (Herodotus 7. 73), took over the territory as well as much of the culture of the ancient kingdom. Erevan, the capital of Soviet Armenia, preserves the name of Erebuni, an Urartian administrative center, the ruins of which have been found at the mound of Arin-Berd on the northern outskirts of the present city; farther away on the opposite side of the city and looking southward toward Mount Ararat, the mound of Karmir-Blur represents the larger Urartian city of Teishebaini. See Boris B. Piotrovsky, *The Ancient Civilization of Urartu* (New York: Cowles Book Company, 1969); and for Turushpa, see F. Schachermeyr in RV 13:487-498.

44. ARAB 1, secs. 713-726.

45. Ibid., sec. 731.

46. Ibid., sec. 734.

47. The extended stories told by Diodorus about Semiramis may include reminiscences of another famous woman, Nitocris, a queen of Sennacherib. Hildegard Lewy in JNES 11 (1952):264 n. 5.

48. Stephanie Page in *Iraq* 30 (1968):139-153; idem, VT 19 (1969):483f.; Aelred Cody in CBQ 32 (1970):325-340; A. Malamat in BASOR 204 (1971):37-39.

49. ARAB 1, secs. 749-760; Joseph A. Fitzmyer in JAOS 81 (1961):178-222; Wolfram von Soden in OLZ 56 (1961), cols. 578f.; Dennis J. McCarthy, *Treaty and Covenant: A Study in Form in the Ancient Oriental Documents and in the Old Testament* (Analecta Biblica 21) (Rome: Pontifical Biblical Institute), pp. 62-66, 70-72; Jonas C. Greenfield in JSS 11 (1966):98f.

50. Poebel in JNES 2 (1943):89 n. 23.

51. Ungnad in RA 2:424; ARAB 1, secs. 761-779.

52. ARAB 1, secs. 770, 772; Thiele, *The Mysterious Numbers of the Hebrew Kings,* pp. 101, 115; Hayim Tadmor in *Scripta Hierosolymitana,* vol. 8, *Studies in the Bible,* ed. Chaim Rabin (Jerusalem: Magnes Press, Hebrew University, 1961), pp. 232-238, 270; Louis D. Levine in BASOR 206 (1972):40-42.

53. ARAB 1, secs. 779, 801, 816; Thiele, *The Mysterious Numbers of the Hebrew Kings,* p. 131. From Tiglath-pileser III onward, cf. also detailed chronological charts and maps in Mervin Stiles, *Synchronizing Hebrew Originals . . . with Available Records from Assyrian, Babylonian, and Urartian Sources,* 7 vols. (privately printed, 1973).

54. R. D. Barnett and M. Falkner, *The Sculptures of Tiglath-pileser III*

(London: Trustees of the British Museum, 1962).

55. F. Thureau-Dangin, A. Barrois, G. Dossin, and M. Dunand, *Arslan-Tash* (Paris: P. Geuthner, 1931), pp. 135-138 and atlas pl. 47 for the ivory piece with the Aramaic inscription; Parrot, *Nineveh and Babylon,* figs. 27-28, 33, 84, 181, 326. Also from Arslan Tash, but probably of the seventh or sixth century, is an amulet with a magical text in a Canaanite dialect. Le Comte du Mesnil du Buisson in *Mélanges syriens offerts a Monsieur René Dussaud,* 2 vols. (Paris: P. Geuthner, 1939), 1:421-434; W. F. Albright in BASOR 76 (1939):5-11.

56. ARAB 1:297.

57. This document, a cuneiform text in the British Museum, was the first of its kind to be published. H. Winckler in ZA 2 (1887):148-168. The title used for it has also been applied to a whole series of similar texts. See Hugo Winckler, *Keilinschriftliches Textbuch zum Alten Testament,* 2d ed. (Leipzig: J. C. Hinrichs, 1903), pp. 59-68; Robert William Rogers, *Cuneiform Parallels to the Old Testament* (London: Frowde, 1912), pp. 208-219; ANET, pp. 301-303.

58. According to the above text, the latest date for the fall of Samaria would be the fighting season before the death of Shalmaneser V, or sometime between spring and autumn in 722. Since Hoshea was probably put on the throne by Tiglath-pileser III in 732, that was his accession year, and his first full year of reign (as reckoned in Israel from Nisan to Nisan) began in Nisan 731. Thus, his ninth year was from Nisan 723 to Nisan 722. To fulfill these requirements, the fall of Samaria may be dated in the year 723/722. See A. T. Olmstead in AJSL 21 (1904-1905):179-182; and idem, *Western Asia in the Days of Sargon of Assyria, 722-705 B.C.* (New York: Henry Holt, 1908), p. 45 n. 9; Hayim Tadmor in JCS 12 (1943):37; Hallo in BA 23 (1960):51; Thiele, *The Mysterious Numbers of the Hebrew Kings,* pp. 141-147.

59. Poebel in JNES 2 (1943):89 n. 26.

60. Eckhard Unger in RA 2:249-252; *Khorsabad,* vol. 1, *Excavations in the Palace and at a City Gate* (OIP 38), by Gordon Loud (Chicago: University of Chicago Press, 1936); vol. 2, *The Citadel and the Town* (OIP 40), by Gordon Loud and Charles B. Altman (Chicago: University of Chicago Press, 1938).

61. The texts are chiefly inscriptions from his earlier capitals at Ashur (the Ashur Charter [ARAB 2, secs. 132-135] and the Letter to Ashur, father of the gods [ibid., secs. 139-178]), Kalah (the Nimrud Inscription [ibid., secs. 136-138]), and Nineveh (the Prism Inscriptions [ibid., secs. 190-218]), and from his later capital at Dur-Sharrukin (the Khorsabad Texts, notably the Display Inscriptions [ibid., secs. 52-90] and the Annals [ibid., secs. 3-51; A. G. Lie, *The Inscriptions of Sargon II,* pt. 1, *The Annals* (Paris: G. Geuthner, 1929)] from the walls of his great palace). For analysis of the contradictions in the records, see Michael Ford in JCS 22 (1969):83f.

62. ARAB 2, sec. 134. The accession year of Sargon II was from the twelfth day of Tebetu (the date cited just above from the Babylonian Chronicle, corresponding to December 20, 722, or January 18, 721) to the following first day of Nisanu in the spring of 721, the first regnal year was from Nisanu 721 to Nisanu 720, and so on.

63. Ibid., secs. 4, 55.

64. Tadmor in JCS 12 (1943):22-42; Hallo in BA 23 (1960):51.

65. ARAB 2, secs. 5, 55; R. Borger in JNES 19 (1960):49-53. Raphia is described by Strabo (16. 2. 31) as between Gaza and Rhinocolura (Rhinocorura, at the Wadi el-Arish, the Brook of Egypt [Num. 34:5, etc.], the traditional boundary between Canaan and Egypt). Josephus (*War* 4. 11. 5. sec. 662) says the Raphia is where Syria begins, on the way up from Egypt. Sargon II had therefore followed the great military route from Asia to Egypt all the way to the last city of Palestine.

66. ARAB 2, sec. 17.

67. Mahmud El-Amin in *Sumer* 9 (1953):35-59, 214-228; ibid., 10 (1954):23-42; J. E. Reade in JNES 35 (1976):95-104.

68. Daniel David Luckenbill, *The Annals of Sennacherib* (OIP 2) (Chicago: University of Chicago Press, 1924); ARAB 2, secs. 231-496.

69. The site of Nineveh is marked by the two mounds of Quyunjik to the northwest and Nebi Yunus (so called from the reputed tomb of the prophet Jonah) to the southeast, with a small river, the Khoser, flowing between them and into the Tigris. See Austen Henry Layard, *The Monuments of Nineveh from Drawings Made on the Spot,* 2 vols. (London: J. Murray, 1849-1853); idem, *Discoveries among the Ruins of Nineveh and Babylon* (New York: Harper, 1853); R. C. Thompson, *A Century of Exploration at Nineveh* (London: Luzac, 1929); and, for the sculptures, Archibald Paterson, *Assyrian Sculptures: Palace of Sinacherib* (The Hague: M. Nijhoff, 1915); idem, *Assyrian Sculptures in the British Museum: From Shalmaneser III to Sennacherib* (London: Trustees of the British Museum, 1938).

70. ARAB 2, secs. 234, 270.

71. Ibid., secs. 236-238, 277-282.

72. Ibid., secs. 239f., 309-312.

73. Hallo in BA 23 (1960):59; Thiele, *The Mysterious Numbers of the Hebrew Kings,* p. 121. On the withdrawal of the Assyrian army, note William A. Irwin in JNES 9 (1950):123. The biblical account makes prominent mention of the presence of Sennacherib at Lachish (2 Kings, 18:14, 17; 19:8, etc.), and the siege of Lachish is one of the scenes represented in the sculptured wall panels of the palace of Sennacherib at Nineveh. Paterson, *Assyrian Sculptures: Palace of Sinacherib,* pl. 74; R. D. Barnett in IEJ 8 (1958):161-164.

74. ARAB 2, secs. 500-506. The same sequence of events is recorded compactly in 2 Kings 19:37; Isa. 37:38, where the murder of Sennacherib takes place as he is worshiping in the house of Nisroch (Marduk?) his god. The sons involved are named Adrammelech and Sharezer, and they are said to have escaped afterward into the land of Ararat. The assassination of Sennacherib is confirmed by Ashurbanipal, who says later that he has "smashed alive" certain plotters against himself with the very same statues of protective deities with which they had smashed his own grandfather Sennacherib. ANET, p. 288; Emil G. Kraeling in JAOS 53 (1933):335-346.

75. There is a biblical parallel in the action of Bathsheba in making sure that her son, Solomon, should have the throne as David had promised (1

Kings 1:13) after the death of his oldest son, Amnon (2 Sam. 3:2; 13:32), left the matter open for him to choose.

76. Semiramis was probably Sammuramat, queen of Shamshi-Adad V, and that was the first generation. The second generation was that of their son Adad-nirari III, the third that of his son Tiglath-pileser III, the fourth that of Tiglath-pileser's sons Shalmaneser V and Sargon II, and the fifth that of Sennacherib, son of Sargon II. Nitocris must then have been a queen of Sennacherib, and his famous queen was Naqia. See Hildegard Lewy in JNES 11 (1952): 264-286.

77. ARAB 2, secs. 339-341.

78. ANET, pp. 302f.

79. ANEP, fig. 447; ARAB 2, sec. 850. In the carved scene on the stela, Esarhaddon is shown with two captives, and there is an identical scene on another stela found at Tell Ahmar. René Dussaud in *Syria* 8 (1927):366f. One captive is shown in smaller size, kneeling, wears the Egyptian uraeus, and has African features; he must be Ushanahuru. The other captive, larger and standing, is bearded and wears Phoenician/Syrian clothing. He is perhaps to be identified with Abdimilkutti king of Sidon, of whom Esarhaddon says elsewhere (ARAB 2, secs. 511, 513, 527f.) that this king fled into the midst of the sea, whence he pulled him out, like a fish, and cut off his head. In another text (ibid., sec. 690; ANET, p. 291) Esarhaddon names no fewer than twenty-two kings of the Hatti land, seashore, and islands, whom he made to transport timber and stone for his palace at Nineveh. The list begins with Balu (Baal I) king of Tyre, and Manasseh king of Judah, within whose long reign (687/686-643/642) the shorter reign of Esarhaddon fell.

80. ANET, p. 303. A large tablet found at Nimrud and fragments of other copies contain the stipulation of Esarhaddon, imposed upon at least half a dozen rulers, that when he depart from the living, they see to it that Ashurbanipal take the throne of Assyria and become their overlord, and that Shamash-shumukin take the throne of Babylonia and rule over Sumer, Akkad, and Karduniash. The document wishes for the several rulers a great variety of calamities if they be unfaithful. ANET, pp. 534-541.

81. ARAB 2, secs. 762-1129.

82. Ibid., secs. 770-775. On the way to Egypt, Ashurbanipal constrained twenty-two subject kings from the seashore, the islands, and the mainland to accompany him with armed forces on land and on ships by sea. A list of these kings begins, as in the similar list by Esarhaddon, with Baalu of Tyre and Manasseh of Judah (ibid., sec. 876). Later Ashurbanipal besieged Baalu on the island of Tyre (ibid., sec. 779) and also carried Manasseh in fetters to Babylon for a time (2 Chron. 33:10-13).

83. ARAB 2, secs. 775-778. On the sources for the relations of Ashurbanipal and Egypt, see Anthony Spalinger in JAOS 94 (1974):316-328.

84. ARAB 2, sec. 986; Maximilian Streck, *Assurbanipal und die letzten assyrischen Könige bis zum Untergang Ninevehs* (Leipzig: J. C. Hinrichs, 1916), pp. 5, 255, 257.

85. "From Assurbanipal's Library, Studies in Memory of F. W. Geers," in JNES 33 (1974):179-356.

86. Heinrich Schäfer and Walter Andrae, *Die Kunst des alten Orients,* 3rd ed. (Berlin: Porpyläen Verlag, 1925), pp. 566f., pls. 33-34; Parrot, *Nineveh and Babylon,* figs. 63-65, etc.

87. ARAB 2, sec. 1131, Rykle Borger in JCS 19 (1965):75.

88. ANET, p. 566.

89. ARAB 2, secs. 1153, 1160, cf. 1140f., 1145.

90. For the complicated problems and chronology in this obscure period see Waldo H. Dubberstein in JNES 3 (1944):38-42; Joan Oates in *Iraq* 27 (1965):136-159; Julian Reade in JCS 23 (1970):1-9.

CHAPTER 9. NEW BABYLONIAN PERIOD

1. ANET, p. 566.

2. The first published Babylonian chronicle (B.M. 92502), which outlines Babylonian history from Nabonassar of the Dynasty of E to Shamash-shumukin, next to the last king of the Ninth Dynasty of Babylon (Robert William Rogers, *Cuneiform Parallels to the Old Testament* [London: Frowde, 1912], pp. 208-219), and the Esarhaddon Chronicle (B.M. 25091), which extends from the first year of Esarhaddon to the first year of Shamash-shumukin (ANET, p. 303), have already been cited. The further series of New Babylonian Chronicles comprises: the Chronicle of Years (B.M. 86379), which covers the end of the reign of Kandalanu, last king of the Ninth Dynasty of Babylon, and the accession of Nabopolassar, first king of the Chaldean Dynasty (D. J. Wiseman, *Chronicles of Chaldaean Kings [626-556 B.C.]* in the *British Museum* [London: Trustees of the British Museum, 1956], p. 6); the Accession of Nabopolassar Chronicle (B.M. 25127), extending from the accession year to the third year of this king (Wiseman, *Chronicles of Chaldaean Kings,* pp. 50-55); the Earlier Nabopolassar Chronicle (B.M. 21901), covering the tenth to the seventeenth years of Nabopolassar and including an account of the fall of Nineveh (C. J. Gadd, *The Fall of Nineveh* [London: Trustees of the British Museum, 1923]; Wiseman, *Chronicles of Chaldaean Kings,* pp. 54-65); the Later Nabopolassar Chronicle (B.M. 22047), covering the eighteenth to the twentieth years of the same king (Wiseman, *Chronicles of Chaldaean Kings,* pp. 64-67); the Nebuchadnezzar II Chronicle (B.M. 21946), beginning with the twenty-first year of Nabopolassar and extending to the eleventh year of Nebuchadnezzar II, and including the first fall of Jerusalem in the seventh year of the latter king (ibid., pp. 66-75); the Neriglissar Chronicle (B.M. 25124), dealing with the third year of this king (ibid., pp. 74-77); and the Nabonidus Chronicle (B.M. 35382), extending with gaps from the accession year to the seventeenth and last year of this king (ANET, pp. 305-307).

3. ARAB 1, sec. 794; 2, secs. 510, 534, 543; Raymond P. Dougherty, *The Sealand of Ancient Arabia* (New Haven: Yale University Press, 1932), pp. 107-110.

4. Waldo H. Dubberstein in JNES 3 (1944):40; Wiseman, *Chronicles of Chaldaean Kings,* p. 6. Akkad is now evidently the name of the whole of Lower Mesopotamia.

5. Wiseman, *Chronicles of Chaldaean Kings,* pp. 50f. For the regnal years of the kings in Babylon from 626 onward, see Richard A. Parker and Waldo H. Dubberstein, *Babylonian Chronology 626 B.C.–A.D. 75* (Providence: Brown University Press, 1956).

6. Berossos quoted by Alexander Polyhistor and Abydenus in Eusebius (Armenian *Chronicle,* ed., Josef Karst, GCS Eusebius 5, p. 14, ll. 35f., p. 18, ll. 20f.), and by Syncellus (Felis Jacoby, *Die Fragmente der griechischen Historiker,* 3 vols. [Berlin: Weidmann, 1926-1963], 3c, no. 680, pp. 387, 405).

7. Diodorus (2. 26-28) tells of a Bactrian army—perhaps Scythians—that was won over from supporting the Assyrians to joining in the attack against them, but he finally credits the destruction of Assyria to the Medes. See Sidney Smith, *Isaiah Chapters XL-LV* (London: Oxford University Press, 1944), pp. 127f.

8. Wiseman, *Chronicles of Chaldaean Kings,* pp. 12-17, 54-61.

9. The mention in Nah. 1:8 of an "overflowing flood" may reflect the fact stated by Diodorus that a flood of the river contributed to the fall of Nineveh.

10. Wiseman, *Chronicles of Chaldaean Kings,* pp. 18-20, 60-65; W. F. Albright in JBL 51 (1932):87 n. 33.

11. Upon the death of Josiah, the people of Judah put his son Jehoahaz on the throne but after three months, Necho replaced him with Jehoiakim (2 Kings 23:30-34; 2 Chron. 36:1-4). Since the Egyptian army marched north in Duzu (June/July 609), the three months of the reign of Jehoahaz were probably Abu (July/August), Ululu (August/September), and Tashritu (September/October), and Jehoiakim came to the throne after that. Assuming that in Judah accession-year reckoning was used and that the regnal year began in Tishri (Tashritu), the balance of that year was the accession year of Jehoiakim, and his first regnal year began on the first day of Tishri, September 10, 608. Edwin R. Thiele, *The Mysterious Numbers of the Hebrew Kings,* rev. ed. (Grand Rapids, Mich.: Eerdmans, 1965), p. 165.

12. Wiseman, *Chronicles of Chaldaean Kings,* pp. 20-23, 64-67.

13. Ibid., pp. 68-75.

14. Berossos in Josephus, *Against Apion* 1. secs. 135-141; *Ant.* 10. 11. 1. secs. 220-226.

15. Wiseman, *Chronicles of Chaldaean Kings,* pp. 25, 66-69. In Jer. 46:2, the battle of Carchemish is dated in the fourth year of Jehoiakim, and in Jer. 25:1, the accession year (as the unique Hebrew phrase probably means) of Nebuchadnezzar is equated with the fourth year of Jehoiakim. In his own passages (but not in items taken from Kings), Jeremiah probably uses a regnal year beginning in the spring; hence, the fourth year of Jehoiakim began on the first day of Nisan in the year 605, and the equivalences stated are correct. In Dan. 1:1, military action by Nebuchadnezzar against Jerusalem is dated in the third year of Jehoiakim. If this date is stated in terms of the regnal year beginning in Tishri, the third year of Jehoiakim was the year extending from the fall of 606 to the fall of 605 and covered the time of the battle of Carchemish and the subsequent conquest of the whole Hatti country, which included Palestine (as we learn in the seventh year of Nebuchadnezzar, when "the city of Judah" [Jerusalem] is spoken of as in "the Hatti land"). See Hayim Tadmor in JNES 15 (1956):227; Thiele, *The Mysterious*

Numbers of the Hebrew Kings, pp. 161, 163, 166.

16. Bel (Akkadian *belu,* Hebrew *Baal*), "lord," is a title often applied to Marduk (as Belet, "lady," to Ishtar). Cf. Isa. 46:1; Jer. 50:2 (Bel and Merodach, the Hebrew form of Marduk, in apposition); 51:44, and *Bel and the Dragon.*

17. The eleventh and last year of the reign of Jehoiakim (2 Kings 23:36; 2 Chron. 36:5) began on the first day of Tishri, 598. Jehoiachin's three months of reign were from December 598 to the taking of Jerusalem on March 16, 597. Jehoiachin was deported to Babylon after the turn of the year (2 Chron. 36:10), on the tenth day of the first month (Ezek. 40:1) in the eighth year of Nebuchadnezzar (2 Kings 24:12), i.e., on April 22, 597. In Babylon, Jehoiachin's years of captivity were probably reckoned according to the Babylonian system; thus, his first captivity year coincided with the eighth year of Nebuchadnezzar II (597/596) and so on. Some 300 cuneiform tablets found near the Ishtar Gate in Babylon list rations such as barley and oil paid to craftsmen and captives from Egypt, Philistia, Phoenicia, Asia Minor, Elam, Media, Persia, and Judah, then living in and near Babylon; the tablets include various Jewish names, most notably the name of Yaukin, "king of the land of Yehud." Yaukin is an abbreviation of the name of Jehoiachin, Yahud a form of the name of Judah (E. L Sukenik in JPOS 14 [1934]:178-184), so this must be the biblical Jehoiachin, recognized in Babylon as the legitimate claimant to the throne of Judah, although not actually restored to rule. Mentioned with him are his five sons, some of whom no doubt lived to be included in the list of seven sons in 1 Chron. 3:17f. The rations suggest some freedom of movement for Jehoiachin at the time; the imprisonment may have come later, from which he was freed on the twenty-seventh day of the twelfth month in the thirty-seventh year of his imprisonment and in the accession year of Amel-Marduk (Evil-merodach, 2 Kings 25:27-30), or April 2, 561. For the tablets just described, see Ernst F. Weidner in *Mélanges syriens offerts a Monsieur René Dussaud,* 2 vols. (Paris: P. Geuthner, 1939), 2:923-927; W. F. Albright in BA 5 (1942):49-55; D. Winton Thomas in PEQ, 1950, pp. 1-15. For the residence of some of the exiles by the river Chebar (Ezek. 1:1, 3, etc.), see several cuneiform references to a small canal named Kabar (*naru kabari*) near Nippur. E. Vogt in *Biblica* 39 (1958):211-216. For Jewish names in the business records of the non-Jewish Murashu family, found at Nippur, see ANET, pp. 221f.

18. 2 Kings 25:3, 8; Jer. 52:6, 12. This was also the eleventh year of Zedekiah (2 Kings 25:2; Jer. 39:2, 52:5). The accession year of the Zedekiah was from the taking of Jerusalem in the spring of 597 to the fall (the first day of Tishri) of the same year; his first regnal year was from the fall of 597 to the fall of 596; and his ninth and eleventh regnal years were 589/588 and 587/586, respectively. The final siege of Jerusalem began on the tenth day of the tenth month in the ninth year (January 15, 588) and lasted slightly more than two and one-half years (2 Kings 25:1f.; Jer. 39:1f.; 52:4f.) to the final taking of the city on the ninth day of the fourth month in the eleventh year (July 18, 586). The city was burned by Nebuzaradan on the seventh (2 Kings 25:8) or tenth (Jer. 52:12) day of the fifth month (August 14, 17, 586; cf. Josephus, *War* 6. 4, 5 sec. 250; Ta'anith 4. 29a). Word that Jerusalem had fallen reached the exiles in Babylon (Ezek. 33:21) on the fifth day of the tenth

month of the twelfth year of their captivity (January 8, 585), so the messenger took somewhat less than six months for the journey, compared with a full four months required by Ezra for a journey in the reverse direction under peaceful circumstances (Ezra 7:9). Ezekiel (40:1) saw his vision of the temple on the tenth day of the anniversary month (Nisan) in the twenty-fifth year of his and Jehoiachim's captivity, which was also the fourteenth year after Jerusalem was conquered the second time (586), so the date of the vision was April 28, 573. Jewish deportees listed in Jer. 52:28-30 in the seventh (598/597), eighteenth (587/586), and twenty-third (582/581) years of Nebuchadnezzar could be respectively from the first fall of Jerusalem (597), from some event preliminary to the second fall (586), and from the putting down of disturbances at the subsequent assassination of Gedaliah (2 Kings 25:25). For the eighteenth year, cf. Josephus, *Against Apion* 1. sec. 154. For the dates in this note and in the preceding note, see Thiele, *The Mysterious Numbers of the Hebrew Kings*, pp. 156, 167-172; K. S. Freedy and D. B. Redford in JAOS 90 (1970):463, 467, and table 1.

19. Robert Koldewey, *Das Ischtar-Tor in Babylon* (Leipzig: J. C. Hinrichs, 1918); idem, *Das wieder erstehende Babylon*, 4th ed. (Leipzig: J. C. Hinrichs, 1925); Oscar Reuther, *Die Innenstadt von Babylon (Merkes)*, 2 vols. (Leipzig: J. C. Hinrichs, 1926); André Parrot, *Babylon and the Old Testament* (New York: Philosophical Library, 1958); H. W. F. Saggs, *The Greatness That Was Babylon* (New York: Hawthorn Books, 1962).

20. Giorgio Gullini et al. in *Mesopotamia* 1 (1966):3-88; ibid., 2 (1967):7-133; ibid., 3-4 (1968-1969):7-158; ibid., 5-6 (1970-1971):9-104; ibid., 7 (1972):9-41.

21. Henry C. Rawlinson in JRAS 18 (1861):1-34; H. Fox Talbot in ibid., pp. 35-52; Robert Koldewey, *Die Tempel von Babylon und Borsippa* (Leipzig: J. C. Hinrichs, 1911).

22. Perhaps the same unexplained title as appears also in Babylonian texts as *rab mungu* and related forms. Wiseman, *Chronicles of Chaldaean Kings*, p. 94 and n. 3.

23. Ibid., pp. 37-42, 74-77.

24. ANET, p. 566. For chronological purposes, his three months of reign fall within the fourth and last regnal year of Neriglissar (556/555).

25. Raymond P. Dougherty, *Nabonidus and Belshazzar* (London: Oxford University Press, 1929), pp. 17, 72.

26. Herodotus (1. 188) states that Cyrus marched against the son of Nitocris (presumably only meaning a descendant of the famous queen), who inherited the name of his father Labynetus (presumably a corruption of the name Nabonidus). See Smith, *Isaiah Chapters XL-LV*, pp. 32, 116 n. 4; W. F. Albright in BASOR 120 (1950):24. In the cuneiform sources, the father of Nabonidus is a "wise prince" named Nabu-balatsu-iqbi, and the mother is Adad-guppi. Dougherty, *Nabonidus and Belshazzar*, pp. 17f.

27. ANET, pp. 305-307.

28. Raymond P. Dougherty in JAOS 42 (1922):305-316; Julius Lewy in HUCA 19 (1945-1946):405-489. Walls largely buried in the sand show that in ancient times Tema was a very large city, and numerous inscriptions on Jebel Ghunaym (fifteen kilometers to the south) appear to date from the time of Nabonidus. F. W.

Winnett and W. L. Reed, *Ancient Records from North Arabia* (Toronto: University of Toronto Press, 1970), pp. 23, 89ff.

29. C. J. Gadd in AnS 8 (1958):35-92; ANET, pp. 311f., 560-563.

30. ANET, pp. 312-315.

31. Hildegard Lewy in ArOr 17 (1949):33.

32. In an Aramaic fragment from Qumran Cave 4, probably dating from the first century B.C.E. and known as the Prayer of Nabonidus, Nabunai (Nabonidus) is described as in Tema and as suffering for seven years from disease (perhaps reminiscent of the statement in the Haran stela that disease and famine were in Babylon when he left for Tema). But in this fragment, the king confesses his sins and is instructed by a seer who was a Jew of the exiles in Babylonia. The latter writes that in his extremity Nabonidus had prayed to gods of silver and gold, of wood and stone, but that honor should be given instead to the name of the Most High God, and the original intent of the fragment may have been to indicate the conversion of the king to such belief. See J. T. Milik in RB 63 (1956):407-415; David Noel Freedman in BASOR 145 (1957):31f. Rudolf Meyer, *Das Gebet des Nabonid* (Sitzungsberichte der Sächsischen Akademie der Wissenschaften zu Leipzig, phil.-hist. Kl. 107, 3) (Berlin: Akademie-Verlag, 1962); William L. Reed in LTQ 12 (1977):23-30.

33. Bern. Alfrink in *Biblica* 9 (1928):187-205; Raymond P. Dougherty in JAOS 48 (1928):113, 117, 124; idem, *Nabonidus and Belshazzar,* pp. 82f., 97f.

34. For possible explanations of Dan. 5:18, where the father of Belshazzar is Nebuchadnezzar, see Werner Dommershausen, *Nabonid im Buche Daniel* (Mainz: Grünewald, 1964), pp. 36f. The story in Dan. 4 of how Nebuchadnezzar went mad and was driven forth to dwell for seven years with the beasts of the field may reflect the insinuation of insanity and the hostile view of his long absence in Tema which his enemies directed against Nabonidus. Wolfram von Soden in ZAW 53 (1935):81-89.

35. For the problem of "Darius the Mede" in Dan. 5:31; 6:28, etc., and the possibility that this was another name for Cyrus, see D. Winton Thomas, ed., *Documents from Old Testament Times* (London: Thomas Nelson and Sons, 1958), p. 83; H. H. Rowley, *Darius the Mede and the Four World Empires in the Book of Daniel* (Cardiff: University of Wales Press Board, 1959); W. Delcor, *Le livre de Daniel* (Paris: J. Gabalda, 1971), pp. 133f.

36. *A Guide to the Babylonian and Assyrian Antiquities, British Museum,* 3rd ed. (London: Trustees of the British Museum, 1922), p. 144; ANET, pp. 315f.

37. W. F. Albright in BA 9 (1946):7; Kurt Galling in ZDPV 70 (1954):4-32.

CHAPTER 10. PERSIAN PERIOD

1. Dora Jane Hamblin, *The First Cities* (New York: Time-Life Books, 1973), pp. 7, 21-27, 131, 141. For maps locating archeological sites in Iran, see David and Ruth Whitehouse, *Archaeological Atlas of the World* (London: Thames and Hudson, 1975), pp. 78-81.

2. Roman Ghirshman, *Fouilles de Sialk, près de Kashan, 1933, 1934, 1937,* 2 vols. (Paris: P. Geuthner, 1938-1939).

3. Jean Deshayes in *Syria* 40 (1963):85-99.

4. E. F. Schmidt, *Excavations at Tepe Hissar (Damghan)* (Philadelphia: University of Pennsylvania Press, 1937).

5. G. Contenau and R. Ghirshman, *Fouilles du Tépé Giyan, près de Néhavend, 1931 et 1932* (Paris: P. Geuthner, 1935).

6. T. Cuyler Young, Jr., in JNES 25 (1966):231f.

7. C. A. Burney in *Iraq* 23 (1961):138-153; ibid., 24 (1962):134-152; Ruth Amiran in AnS 15 (1965):165-167.

8. Young in JNES 25 (1966):232.

9. M. Pézard and E. Pottier, *Les antiquitiés de la Susiana* (Paris: Musée national de Louvre, 1913); L. Le Breton in *Iraq* 19 (1957):79-124.

10. Pierre Amiet, *Elam* (Auvers-sur-Oise, Archée, 1966).

11. Ghirshman, *Fouilles de Sialk,* 2:26f., 95; idem, *Iran: From the Earliest Times to the Islamic Conquest* (Harmondsworth: Penguin Books, 1954), p. 74; idem, *The Arts of Ancient Iran from Its Origins to the Time of Alexander the Great* (New York: Golden Press, 1964), pp. 10, 277-280, figs. 6-8, 12-14; Jean-Louis Huot, *Persia I: From the Origins to the Achaemenids* (Cleveland: World Publishing Co., 1965), pp. 82, 136f., 179, figs. 114-117; T. C. Young, Jr., in *Iran* 5 (1967):32.

12. Ghirshman, *The Arts of Ancient Iran,* p. 16, figs. 20, 22f., 29-31, 36-38, 40, 43f. For the objects of bronze, silver, and gold from Luristan, usually placed at the end of the second millennium and the first half of the first millennium and hypothetically associated with various peoples of the Zagros region (the Kassites, the Cimmerians, or others), see René Dussaud in *A Survey of Persian Art from Prehistoric Times to the Present,* 12 vols., ed. Arthur Upham Pope (London: Oxford University Press, 1938-1939, reissued 1964-1965), 1:254-277; 7, pls. 25-72; Edith Porada, *The Art of Ancient Iran: Pre-Islamic Cultures* (New York: Crown Publishers, 1965), p. 75; André Godard, *The Art of Iran* (London: G. Allen and Unwin, 1965), pp. 45f., 82, 86, 90; Clare Goff Meade in *Iran* 6 (1968):130-132.

13. ARAB 1, secs. 581, 637.

14. Ernst E. Herzfeld, *Archaeological History of Iran* (London: Oxford University Press, 1935), p. 9; Ghirshman, *Iran: From the Earliest Times to the Islamic Conquest,* p. 90.

15. ARAB 1, sec. 812; 2, sec. 540.

16. Friedrich Wilhelm König, *Älteste Geschichte der Meder un Perser* (AO 33, 3/4) (Leipzig: J. C. Hinrichs, 1934), p. 61. See also the relevant articles in PWRE for the Median kings.

17. ARAB 2, secs. 12, 23, 56.

18. Ibid., sec. 147.

19. D. J. Wiseman, *Chronicles of Chaldaean Kings (626-556 B.C.) in the British Museum* (London: Trustees of the British Museum, 1956), pp. 58f.

20. ANET, p. 305.

21. George G. Cameron, *History of Early Iran* (Chicago: University of Chicago

Press, 1936), pp. 179-181; Young in *Iran* 5 (1967):18f.

22. ANET, p. 316.

23. Roland G. Kent, *Old Persian Grammer, Texts, Lexicon* (AOS 33), 2d ed. (New Haven: American Oriental Society, 1953), pp. 119 (DB I), 124 (DB II), 158f. For the Persian kings, see also the relevant articles in PWRE.

24. Richard A. Parker and Waldo H. Dubberstein, *Babylonian Chronology 626 B.C.-A.D. 75* (Providence: Brown University Press, 1956), p. 14; Weissbach in PWRE, supp. 4, col. 1131.

25. ANET, pp. 305f.

26. The city of Anshan is now identified with Tepe Maliyan (Tall-i-Malyan), forty-six kilometers north of Shiraz, and was probably an earlier summer capital of the Elamites (their winter capital being at Susa). The area of Anshan was here, and Parsa adjacent to the east. See König in RA 1:111f.; Ghirshman, *The Arts of Ancient Iran*, figs. 586, 587, maps; Erica Rainer in RAAO 67 (1973):57-62; Richard N. Frye in JNES 33 (1974):384; Yousef Majidzadeh in ibid., 35 (1976):105-113

27. Weissbach in PWRE, supp. 4, col. 1142.

28. Kent, *Old Persian Grammar*, pp. 107, 116 (AmH, AsH); and idem, JAOS 56 (1936):215; ibid., 66 (1946):207-209, 212.

29. Cameron, *History of Early Iran*, pp. 179-226; A. T. Olmstead, *History of the Persian Empire (Achaemenid Period)* (Chicago: University of Chicago Press, 1948), p. 37.

30. Olmstead, *History of the Persian Empire*, pp. 45-49.

31. King Vishtaspa was of the Naotara family and the son of Kai Lohrasp (*Bundahish*. 31. 28f., SBE 5, p. 137). He is therefore not to be confused with Hystaspes, son of Arsames and father of Darius I, although philologically the names are the same. For the Kayanian dynasty, see Arthur Christensen, *Les Kayanides* (Det. Kgl. Danske Videnskabernes Selskab. hist.-fil. Meddelelser 19, 2) (Copenhagen: E. Munksgaard, 1931).

32. For al-Biruni, see C. Edward Sachau, ed., *The Chronology of Ancient Nations: An English Version of the Athar-ul-Bakiya of Albiruni* (London: W. H. Allen and Co., 1879), p. 17. For the historical importance of the figure of 258 years, cf. Hildegard Lewy in JAOS 64 (1944):197.

33. For Keshmar (south of Nishapur in northeastern Iran) as a possible specific place of the work of Zarathustra in the realm of Vishtaspa, see the Persian *Dabistan*, trans. David Shea and Anthony Troyer, 3 vols. (Washington and London: M. W. Dunne, 1843), 1:306-309; and Walther Hinz, *Zarathustra* (Stuttgart: W. Kohlhammer, 1961), pp. 22-24.

34. Friedrich Wachtsmuth in Pope, *A Survey of Persian Art*, 1:309-320; 7, pl. 81A. For a comparison between Sardis and Pasargadae, supporting the belief that Lydian architects went to Iran and worked there, see George M. A. Hanfmann, *From Croesus to Constantine* (Ann Arbor: University of Michigan Press, 1976), pp. 14f.

35. E. Herzfeld, *Archaelogische Mitteilungen aus Iran*, 2 vols. (Berlin: D. Reimer, 1929-1930), 1:10. All the inscriptions at Pasargadae may have been placed there by

Darius I to mark the significant buildings going back to Cyrus II. R. Borger and W. Hinz in ZDMG 109 (1959):125.

36. Stanley Casson in Pope, *A Survey of Persian Art,* 1:349; 7, pl. 78.

37. Borger and Hinz in ZDMG 109 (1959):126 and fig. 2.

38. See Pope, *A Survey of Persian Art,* 7, pl. 79B; Hinz, *Zarathustra,* pp. 17, 147f., figs. 9, 11; David Stronach in JNES 26 (1967):283, 287; Klaus Schippmann, *Die iranischen Feuerheiligtümer* (Berlin: Walter de Gruyter, 1971), p. 208. If Cyrus II was himself an adherent of the teachings of Zarathustra, he could at the same time attribute his commission to Marduk in the Cyrus Cylinder, and to the Lord the God of heaven in 2 Chron. 36:23; Ezra. 1:2, but this can accord with the description of Cyrus by Aeschylus (*Persae* 770f.) as a gracious man who hated no god.

39. Wachtsmuth in Pope, *A Survey of Persian Art,* 1:310; 7, pl. 80A. For other inscriptions of the monuments at Pasargadae, see Weissbach in PWRE, supp. 4, cols. 1158f.

40. L. W. King and R. Campbell Thompson, *The Sculptures and Inscription of Darius the Great on the Rock of Behistun in Persia* (London: Trustees of the British Museum, 1907); E. Herzfeld, *Am Tor von Asien: Felsendenkmale aus Irans Heldenzeit* (Berlin: D. Reimer, 1920), pl. 9; George G. Cameron in JNES 2 (1943):115f. and pl. 2; idem, JCS 5 (1951):47-54; Roland G. Kent in JNES 2 (1943):105-114; ibid., 3 (1944):232f.; idem, JCS 5 (1951):55-57; idem, JAOS 72 (1952):9-20; idem, *Old Persian Grammar,* pp. 107f., 116-135, and pl. 1; W. C. Benedict and Elizabeth von Voigtlander in JCS 10 (1956):1-10.

41. Bisitun Inscription secs. 11, 13, 16, 18-20, 52, 74, and accompanying inscriptions identifying the individuals. Kent, *Old Persian Grammar,* pp. 120, 128, 135, 161 (DB I, III, Minor Inscriptions). For the dates, see Parker and Dubberstein, *Babylonian Chronology 626 B.C.-A.D. 75,* pp. 14f.

42. Bisitun Inscription sec. 6; Roland G. Kent in JNES 2 (1943):302-306; idem, *Old Persian Grammar,* p. 119 (DB I).

43. As far as is known, the symbol of the winged disk originated in Egypt to represent the sun god. It is also found in Assyria, probably as a symbol of Ashur, by the middle of the second millennium, where the feathered tail also became a characteristic part of the composition. Birger Pering in AfO 8 (1932-1933):281-296.

44. In a very few instances (Kent, *Old Persian Grammar,* pp. 132 [DB V], 136 [DPd], 142 [DSe]), Darius I speaks of "the gods," "the gods of the royal house," or "the other gods who are," along with Ahuramazda, but these few expressions probably signify only a certain tolerance of other deities worshiped by some of his subjects in other parts of his empire. He himself names only Ahuramazda and expresses devotion and gratitude to him as the one god; he was therefore a monotheist according to the teachings of Zarathustra. For the language of Darius I and possibly his own name (Darayavahush, "he who holds firm the good"; cf. *darayat vahishtem mano,* "he held the good thought" [*Yasna* 31. 7, Behramgore Tehmurasp Anklesaria, *The Holy Gathas of Zarathustra* (Bombay: H. T. Anklesaria,

1953), pp. 30f.]), as reminiscent of the teachings of Zarathustra, see Ernst Herzfeld, *Zoroaster and His World,* 2 vols. (Princeton: Princeton University Press, 1947), 1:97; Kent, *Old Persian Grammar,* pp. 164f., 189, 192. Against this explanation of the name of Darius, see R. N. Frye, *The Heritage of Persia* (Cleveland: World Publishing Co., 1962), p. 97. For Darius I as a Zarathustrian or Mazdayasnian monotheist, see Kent in JAOS 56 (1938):214; Ilya Gershevitch, *The Avestan Hymn to Mithra* (Cambridge: University Press, 1959), pp. 15f., 18, 155f., 250f.; and idem, JNES 23 (1964):17.

45. Roland G. Kent in JNES 1 (1942):415-423; idem, *Old Persian Grammar,* pp. 111, 146f. (DZa, b, c).

46. In biblical records the appearance of the prophet Haggai in Jerusalem is dated (Hag. 1:1) on the first day of the sixth month of the second year of Darius (August 29, 520), and the first sermon of Zechariah is placed (Zech. 1:1) in the eighth month of the same year (October/November 520). The completion of the rebuilt Jewish temple is dated (Ezra 6:15) on the third day of the month Adar in the sixth year of Darius (March 12, 515). See also Peter R. Ackroyd in JNES 17 (1958):13-27.

47. E. Herzfeld and F. Sarre, *Iranische Felsreliefs* (Berlin: E. Wasmuth, 1910), pl. 4; Roland G. Kent in JNES 4 (1945):39-52; idem, *Old Persian Grammar,* pp. 109 (DN), 138 (DNa), 140f. (DNb, c, Minor Inscriptions); cf. pp. 131 (DB IV), 145 (DSk). In addition to the tomb of Darius I, there are three other tombs of similar construction in the cliff at Naqsh-i-Rustam. Only the tomb of Darius I bears inscriptions with the name of its owner; therefore, the attribution of the others is provisional. But, including that of Darius I, the four are believed to belong (from left to right as one faces the cliff) to Darius II, Artaxerxes I, Darius I, and Xerxes I. Ghirshman, *The Arts of Ancient Iran,* fig. 275. There are also carvings of the Sassanian kings on the cliff, showing the investiture of Ardashir I (224-241) by Ahuramazda, the triumph of Shapur I (241-272) over the Roman emperors Philip the Arab and Valerian, Bahram II (276-293) on the throne and with his family, the investiture of Narsah (293-302) by Anahita, and a victory of Hormizd II (302-309) over an unnamed enemy. Roman Ghirshman, *Iran, Parthians and Sassanians* (London: Thames and Hudson, 1962), figs. 15, 156, 157, 158, 168, 171, 204-205, 213-214, 218, 219-220, 379; Walther Hinz, *Altiranische Funde und Forschungen mit Beiträgen von Rykle Borger und Gerd Gropp* (Berlin: Walter de Gruyter, 1969), pp. 126-134, 178-182.

48. Two Sassanian inscriptions on the lower part of the tower at Naqsh-i-Rustam suggest that at that later time it was used as a repository for important Zoroastrian documents, perhaps an early copy of the Avesta. But that was hardly the purpose for which the tower was originally erected, nor does it resemble either the tomb of Cyrus or the rock-hewn tombs of the other Achaemenian kings, so it is hardly to be interpreted as a grave monument. See Herzfeld, *Archaeological History of Iran,* pp. 34f., 37; M. Sprengling in AJSL 53 (1936):126-144; Pope, *A Survey of Persian Art,* 7, pl. 79A; Hinz, *Zarathustra,* pp. 16f., 259 n. 5, fig. 8; Stronach in JNES 26 (1967):283; Schippmann, *Die iranischen Feuerheiligtümer,* pp. 185-199.

49. Gobryas the spear bearer and Aspathines the bow bearer appear with Darius I at Naqsh-i-Rustam. Roland G. Kent in JNES 4 (1945):233; idem, *Old Persian Grammar*, p. 140 (DNc, d).

50. Kent, *Old Persian Grammar*, pp. 112, 150 (XPf).

51. Ibid., pp. 112, 150-152 (XPh); and idem, JAOS 56 (1936):214f.

52. Arthur Christensen, *Die Iranier* (Handbuch der Altertumswissenschaft, III, i, 3, 3, 1), (Munich: C. H. Beck, 1933), p. 214; Herman Lommel, *Die Religion Zarathustras nach dem Awesta dargestellt* (Hildesheim: Olms, 1971), pp. 40, 90f.

53. Walther Hinz in PWRE, ser. 2, 9:2, col. 2098. In biblical records Xerxes I is no doubt to be recognized under the name Ahasuerus, corresponding in Hebrew to the Old Persian form of his name, Xshayarshan. In Ezra 4:6 Ahasuerus appears between Darius and Artaxerxes, and in Esther 1:1, etc., he figures in much the same character Herodotus attributes to him in his later years.

54. Nöldeke in PWRE 2, col. 1313.

55. Kent, *Old Persian Grammar*, pp. 113, 153 (A¹Pa, cf. A¹I); and idem, JAOS 58 (1938):327. If the biblical references are to Artaxerxes I, Ezra came to Jerusalem in 458 (Ezra 7:1, 8), and Nehemiah made his request to go there in April/May 445 (Neh. 2:1). On the problem, see Norman H. Snaith in ZAW 63 (1951):53-66; H. H. Rowley, *The Servant of the Lord and Other Essays on the Old Testament* (London: Lutterworth Press, 1952), pp. 131-159.

56. F. H. Weissbach, *Die Keilinschriften der Achämeniden* (Leipzig: J. C. Hinrichs, 1911); Erich F. Schmidt, *The Treasury of Persepolis* (OIC 21) (Chicago: University of Chicago Press, 1939); idem, *Persepolis I* (OIP 68) (Chicago: University of Chicago Press, 1953); idem, *Persepolis II* (OIP 69) (Chicago: University of Chicago Press, 1957); Donald H. Wilber, *Persepolis: The Archaeology of Parsa, Seat of the Persian Kings* (New York: Crowell, 1969); Friedrich Krefter, *Persepolis Rekonstruktionen* (Tejeraner Forschung 3) (Berlin, 1971); cf. Oscar White Muscarella in JNES 33 (1974):423-425.

57. Willy Hartner in JNES 24 (1965):1-16.

58. Kent, *Old Persian Grammar*, pp. 112, 150 (XPg), 153 (A¹Pa).

59. Ghirshman, *The Arts of Ancient Iran*, figs. 280-281.

60. Roland G. Kent in JAOS 51 (1931):229-232; idem, *Old Persian Grammar*, p. 111, 147 (DH), 113, 153 (XH), 114 155 (A²Ha, A²Hb, A²Hc).

61. R. de Mecquenem in Pope, *A Survey of Persian Art*, 1:321-326.

62. J. M. Unvala in ibid., p. 339; Kent, *Old Persian Grammar*, pp. 142-144 (DSf).

63. Pope, *A Survey of Persian Art*, 7, pls. 19B, C, 77; Ghirshman, *The Arts of Ancient Iran*, figs. 190-193.

64. Hinz in PWRE, ser. 2, 9:2, col. 2101; Parker and Dubberstein, *Babylonian Chronology 626 B.C.-A.D. 75*, p. 18.

65. Swoboda in PWRE 4, cols. 2199-2204.

66. Felix Jacoby, *Die Fragmente der griechischen Historiker*, 3 vols. (Berlin: Weidmann, 1926-1963), 3C no. 688, pp. 416-517.

67. Weissbach in PWRE, supp. 4, cols. 1166-1177. The late fifth-century Aramaic papyri from the Jewish military colony on the island of Elephantine in

Egypt provide information about conditions at this time in this outlying part of the Persian empire. They contain dates in the reigns of Darius II and Artaxerxes II and show that Egypt was still under the authority of Persia in the first years of Artaxerxes II. See A. Ungnad, *Aramäische Papyrus aus Elephantine* (Leipzig: J. C. Hinrichs, 1911); E. Sachau, *Aramäische Papyrus und Ostraka aus einer jüdischen Militär-Kolonie zu Elephantine,* 2 vols. (Leipzig: J. C. Hinrichs, 1911); A. Cowley, *Aramaic Papyri of the Fifth Century B.C.* (Oxford: Clarendon Press, 1923); Emil G. Kraeling in BA 15 (1952):50-67; idem, *The Brooklyn Museum Aramaic Papyri: New Documents of the Fifth Century B.C. from the Jewish Colony at Elephantine* (New Haven: Yale University Press, 1953); S. H. Horn and L. H. Wood in JNES 13 (1954):1-20; Bezalel Porten, *Archives from Elephantine: The Life of an Ancient Jewish Military Colony* (Berkeley: University of California Press, 1968).

68. Kent, *Old Persian Grammar,* pp. 154f. (A²Sa, b, d). The appearance of the water goddess Anahita (who probably belongs to an old Iranian background) and of the sun god Mithra (who probably comes from an early Indo-Iranian inheritance) along with Ahuramazda shows the development of a later mixed form of Zoroastrianism, and Berossos (quoted by Clement of Alexandria, *Exhortation to the Greeks* 5) says that Artaxerxes II was the first to make cult statues of Anahita and put them in temples in various parts of the empire. It is also probable that the Magians were by this time assuming a position of religious leadership in Zoroastrianism. Gershevitch, *The Avestan Hymn to Mithra,* pp. 16-22. Strabo (15. 3. 14f.) describes the customs of the Magi in Cappadocia, where, being known as Pyraethi ("fire-kindlers," corresponding with Athravan, literally "fire-man," the proper term for a priest in the Avesta [SBE 4. 51]), they keep an altar fire ever burning and make incantations before it, holding in their hands a bundle of slender myrtle wands (the Barsom [*baresma*] of the Avesta [SBE 4. 22 n. 2])." For other classical references to the Persian religion, see Carl Clemen, *Die griechischen und lateinischen Nachrichten über die persische Religion* (Giessen: Töpelmann, 1920).

69. In Macedonia, with no accession year, reckoning was from the accession of Alexander, and his first year was 336. In Egypt he was probably recognized soon after his invasion late in 332. Parker and Dubberstein, *Babylonian Chronology 626 B.C.-A.D. 75,* p. 19. See also Charles Alexander Robinson, Jr., *Alexander the Great: The Meeting of East and West in World Government and Brotherhood* (New York: E. P. Dutton, 1947); Fritz Schachermeyr, *Alexander in Babylon und die Reichsordnung nach seinem Tode* (Österreichische Akademie der Wissenschaften, phil.-hist. Kl., Sitzungsberichte 268, 3) (Vienna: Hermann Böhlaus Nachf., 1970); A. R. Burn, *Alexander the Great and the Middle East,* rev. ed. (Harmondsworth: Penguin Books, 1973).

CHAPTER 11. PREHISTORIC AND PREDYNASTIC PERIODS

1. For geographical locations in Egypt, see *An Atlas of Ancient Egypt* (Egypt Exploration Society) (London: K. Paul, Trench, Trübner and Co., 1894); Karl Baedeker, *Ägypten und der Sudan,* 8th ed. (Leipzig: Karl Baedeker, 1928); *Baedeker's*

Egypt (1929); reprint ed., London: Newton Abbott, David and Charles (Holdings) Ltd., 1974) (cf. JEA 15 [1929]:277; ibid., 62 [1976]:201); Marcelle Baud and Magdelaine Parisot, *Égypte, le Nil égyptien et soudanais du Delta à Khartoum* (Les Guides Bleus), new ed. (Paris: Librairie Hachette, 1956); Wilhelm Berg and Jürgen von Beckerath, *Historische Karte des alten Ägypten* (Sankt Augustin: Hans Richarz, 1973). In addition to the specific citations in Part 2, see also the following general works: John A. Wilson, *The Burden of Egypt* (Chicago: University of Chicago Press, 1951); Étienne Drioton and Jacques Vandier, *L'Égypte*, 3rd ed. (Paris: Presses universitaires de France, 1952); William C. Hayes, *The Scepter of Egypt*, 2 pts. (New York: Harper and Bros., Metropolitan Museum of Art, 1953–1959); George Steindorff and Keith C. Seele, *When Egypt Ruled the East*, rev. ed. (Chicago: University of Chicago Press, 1957); Alan Gardiner, *Egypt of the Pharaohs* (Oxford: Clarendon Press, 1961); Georges Posener, *A Dictionary of Egyptian Civilization* (London: Methuen, 1962); Pierre Montet, *Eternal Egypt* (New York: New American Library of World Literature, 1964); idem, *Lives of the Pharaohs* (London: Weidenfeld and Nicolson, 1968). For specialized topics, see all relevant articles, as far as available, in Wolfgang Helck and Eberhard Otto, eds., *Lexikon der Ägyptologie* (Weisbaden: O. Harrassowitz, 1972ff.) (abbreviated LÄ).

2. K. S. Sandford and W. J. Arkell, *Paleolithic Man and the Nile-Faiyum Divide* (OIP 10) (Chicago: University of Chicago Press, 1929); idem, *Paleolithic Man and the Nile Valley in Nubia and Upper Egypt* (OIP 17) (Chicago: University of Chicago Press, 1933); idem, *Paleolithic Man and the Nile Valley in Upper and Middle Egypt* (OIP 18) (Chicago: University of Chicago Press, 1934); idem, *Paleolithic Man and the Nile Valley in Lower Egypt* (OIP 46) (Chicago: University of Chicago Press, 1939).

3. Guy Brunton in *Antiquity* 3 (1929):456–467; Gertrude Caton-Thompson and E. W. Gardner, *The Desert Fayum*, 2 vols. (London: The Royal Anthropological Institute of Great Britain and Ireland, 1934); Hermann Ranke in JAOS 59 (1939), supp. 4, pp. 3–16; Helene J. Kantor in *Chronologies in Old World Archaeology*, ed. Robert W. Ehrich (Chicago: University of Chicago Press, 1965), p. 25, "Sketch map of Egypt, showing the distribution of important prehistoric sites."

4. Guy Brunton and Gertrude Caton-Thompson, *The Badarian Civilisation and Predynastic Remains near Badari* (London: British School of Archaeology in Egypt, 1928).

5. W. M. Flinders Petrie and J. E. Quibell, *Naqada and Ballas* (London: B. Quaritch, 1895); D. Randall-MacIver and A. C. Mace, *El Amrah and Abydos 1899-1901* (London: Egypt Exploration Fund, 1902).

6. W. M. Flinders Petrie, G. A. Wainwright, and E. Mackay, *The Labyrinth, Gerzeh, and Mazghuneh* (London: British School of Archaeology in Egypt, 1912).

7. Behnam Abu Al-Soof in *Mesopotamia* 3-4 (1968-1969):178. Also found for the first time in Egypt in the Gerzean period are jars with wavy ledges for handles, a type known already in Palestine in the Late Chalcolithic and Early Bronze periods. Kantor in Ehrich, *Chronologies in Old World Archaeology*, pp. 7f. In Egypt such jars continued in use down into historic times, but the wavy-ledge handholds degenerated progressively into mere decorative marks, and this feature provided

the clue for the establishment of "sequence dates," in which the entire Predynastic period was marked out in fifty stages, identified as S.D. 30-80, with S.D. 1-29 left for earlier cultures if discovered. W. M. Flinders Petrie, *Diospolis Parva: The Cemeteries of Abadiyeh and Hu, 1898-9* (London: Egypt Exploration Fund, 1901), pp. 4-12, 28-30; idem, *Prehistoric Egypt* (London: British School of Archaeology in Egypt, 1920), pp. 3f. More recent revision of the scheme equates S.D. 30-39 with the Amratian period, and S.D. 40-65 with the Gerzean, and puts the beginning of the First Dynasty at S.D. 63. Kantor in Ehrich, *Chronologies in Old World Archaeology,* p. 26; and idem, JNES 11 (1952):250 n. 49.

8. For the nomes throughout the entire discussion of Egypt, see Fritz Hommel, *Ethnologie und Geographie des alten Orients* (Handbuch der Altertumswissenschaft, III, i, 1) (Munich: C. H. Beck, 1926); Pierre Montet, *Géographie de l'Égypte ancienne,* vol. 1, *To-mehou: La Basse Égypte,* vol. 2, *To-Chema: La Haute Égypte* (Paris: Imprimerie nationale, 1957-1961); Wolfgang Helck in LÄ 2, cols. 385-408, 422-426 (with table of nome signs).

9. The pottery found therein points to S.D. 50-60, which is late Gerzean. Helene J. Kantor in JNES 3 (1944):114 n. 24.

10. J. E. Quibell and F. W. Green, *Hierakonpolis,* 2 pts. (London: B. Quaritch, 1900-1902), 2:20f.; Humphrey Case and Joan Crowfoot Payne in JEA 48 (1962):5-18; Joan Crowfoot Payne in ibid., 59 (1973):31-35; Barry J. Kemp in ibid., pp. 36-43.

11. Brunton and Caton-Thompson, *The Badarian Civilization,* pp. 69-79.

12. Al-Soof in *Mesopotamia* 3-4 (1968-1969):176-178.

13. See a cylinder seal from a tomb of late Gerzean (S.D. 48-66) date at Naqada, probably an import, and a cylinder seal from a late Gerzean (S.D. 55-60) grave at Naga ed-Deir (east of the Nile, ninety kilometers south of el-Badari, across the river from modern Girga), probably an Egyptian imitation. Henri Frankfort, *Cylinder Seals* (London: MacMillan, 1939), p. 293, pl. 46a; Kantor in JNES 11 (1952):239, 246f., pl. 35B, figs. 1A, B. After this, cylinder seals remained in general use in Egypt until the Middle Kingdom, when they were replaced by button seals and then by scarabs, i.e., carved forms of the scarab-beetle, used as stamp seals and as amulets and commemorative medals. Percy E. Newberry *Scarabs: An Introduction to the Study of Egyptian Seals and Signet Rings* (London: Archibald Constable, 1906).

14. Georges Bénédite in MMFEP 22 (1916):1-34; idem, JEA 5 (1918):1f.; Wolfgang Decker in LÄ 2, col. 434. The man between the two lions wears a full beard, a turban, and long robe, and looks very much like another personage, perhaps of Semitic character, who is shown shooting a lion, on a Jemdet Nasr period stela from Uruk. René Dussaud in *Syria* 16 (1935):320-323.

15. H. Frankfort in AJSL 58 (1941):358; Kantor in Ehrich, *Chronologies in Old World Archaeology,* pp. 11-14.

16. Quibell and Green, *Hierakonpolis,* 1, pls. 25, 26C.

17. This system of organization of both reliefs and paintings prevailed throughout almost all of ancient Egyptian art. William Stevenson Smith,

Interconnection in the Ancient Near East (New Haven: Yale University Press, 1965), pp. 72, 129, fig. 180.

18. For the eastern desert and the route from Koptos through Wadi Hammamat to Quseir (ancient Leucos Limen) on the Red Sea, and for the Paneion in Wadi Hammamat and the Paneion at El-Boueib, see André Bernand, *De Koptos à Kosseir* (Leiden: E. J. Brill, 1972). Min also became the principal god of the Upper Egyptian Nome IX (known by his name as "Min"), the chief city of which was the Egyptian Ipou, called Chemmis and Panopolis by the Greeks, the modern Akhmim.

19. Ombos (not to be confused with the modern Kom Ombo forty kilometers north of Aswan) was probably at the present Toukh (on the west side of the Nile, a short distance north of Naqada) and, like Koptos on the other side of the river, was in the Upper Egyptian Nome V ("Two Falcons"). The entire immediate region, probably including Ballas a little farther north on the west side of the river, was called Typhonia by the Greeks (Strabo 17. 1. 44), i.e., the region of Typhon (Seth). For the Pyramid Texts, see Samuel A. B. Mercer, *The Pyramid Texts in Translation and Commentary,* 4 vols. (New York: Longmans, Green, 1952); R. O. Faulkner, *The Ancient Egyptian Pyramid Texts* (Oxford: Clarendon Press, 1969). For the Egyptian gods, see E. A. Wallis Budge, *The Gods of the Egyptians, or Studies in Egyptian Mythology,* 2 vols. (London: Methuen, 1904); Adolf Erman, *Die Ägyptische Religion* (Berlin: G. Reimer, 1905); Manfred Lurker, *Götter und Symbole der alten Ägypter,* 2d ed. (Bern: Scherz Verlag für Otto Wilhelm Barth Verlag, 1974).

20. An occurrence of the name of Scorpion in Palestine has been suggested but is doubtful. Ruth Hestrin and Miriam Tadmor in IEJ 13 (1963):265-288; Sh. Yeivin in JNES 27 (1968):37-50; A. Ben-Tor in IEJ 21 (1971):201-206; Trevor F. Watkins in PEQ, January-June 1975, pp. 53-63.

21. From west to east the seven ancient mouths of the Nile were the Canopic, Bolbitine (Rosetta), Sebennytic, Phatnitic (Damietta), Mendesian, Tanitic, and Pelusiac (Strabo 17. 1. 18).

22. W. M. Flinders Petrie, *Ehnasya 1904,* with a chapter by C. T. Currelly (London: Egypt Exploration Fund, 1905); John A. Wilson in JNES 14 (1955):231f.; Dorothy Charlesworth in *Archaeology* 25 (1972):44-47.

23. Kurt Sethe, *Urgeschichte und älteste Religion der Ägypter* (Abhandlungen für die Kunde des Morgenlandes herausgegeben von der Deutschen Morgenländischen Gesellschaft 18, 4) (Leipzig, 1930), pp. 137f., 140-142, 145, 159, 165, secs. 168, 172-175, 178, 193, 201.

CHAPTER 12. EARLY DYNASTIC PERIOD, FIRST AND SECOND DYNASTIES

1. J. E. Quibell and F. W. Green, *Hierakonpolis* 2 pts. (London: B. Quaritch, 1900-1902), 1, pl. 29; 2:41-43; ANEP, figs. 296-297; Sergio Donadoni, *Egyptian Museum Cairo* (New York: Simon and Schuster, 1969), p. 26 (and see this work for many objects in this museum); Kazimierz Michalowski, *The Art of Ancient Egypt* (London: Thames and Hudson, 1969), figs. 57, 178 (and see this work for many objects and sites in Egyptian history).

2. The emblems of kingship shown here are the royal placenta, considered to be the king's stillborn twin brother who had passed immediately into the beyond (Aylward M. Blackman in JEA 3 [1916]:235-246); the wild dog god Wepwawet, "opener of the ways" and "lord of Siut" (i.e., Asyut), a guide of the dead and closely associated with the king and with Nekhen (A. Rosalie David, *Religious Ritual at Abydos (c. 1300 BC)* [Warminster: Aris and Phillips, 1973], p. 353); and two Horus falcons.

3. Henri Frankfort, *Cylinder Seals* (London: Macmillan, 1939), pl. 5, h.

4. Yigael Yadin in IEJ 5 (1955):1-16; idem, *The Art of Warfare in Biblical Lands in the Light of Archaeological Study,* 2 vols. (New York: McGraw-Hill, 1963), 1:50-53, 122-125; S. Yeivin in IEJ 10 (1960):193-203; Ruth Amiran in ibid., 24 (1974):4-12.

5. Alan H. Gardiner, *Egyptian Grammar, Being an Introduction to the Study of Hieroglyphs,* 3rd ed. (London: Oxford University Press, 1957); F. Ll. Griffith in JEA 37 (1951):38-46; Elmar Edel, *Altägyptische Grammatik* (AnOr 34/39), 2 vols. (Rome: Pontificium institutum biblicum, 1955/1964).

6. Hugo Müller, *Die Formale Entwicklung der Titulatur der ägyptischen Könige* (Glückstadt: J. J. Augustin, 1938).

7. Maria Cramer, *Das altägyptische Lebenszeichen* 3rd ed. (Wiesbaden: O. Harrassowitz, 1955).

8. ARE 1, secs. 76-167. The stone was a stela of black diorite. The main fragment, in the Palermo Museum, is now forty-three centimeters high, twenty-five centimeters wide, and six centimeters thick and is inscribed on both sides. Additional fragments are in Cairo and London.

9. Based upon the mean measurement of a number of actual cubits in the Cairo, Turin, and Liverpool museums, the length of the Egyptian royal cubit was 523 millimeters. In its subdivisions, 1 cubit was equal to seven palms or twenty-eight fingers. The small or short cubit was 450 millimeters in length and equal to six palms or twenty-four fingers. An Egyptian unit called the *khet* contained 100 cubits. See W. M. Flinders Petrie, *Measures and Weights* (London: Methuen, 1934), pp. 3f.; Howard Carter in JEA 3 (1916):150; Howard Carter and Alan H. Gardiner in ibid., 4 (1917):136.

10. For the symbol of union, a strange hieroglyphic sign believed to represent a lung and windpipe, and the sign of the Djed column, imitating a bundle of stalks tied together, see Gardiner, *Egyptian Grammar,* pp. 465, 502, F36, R11. For the Sed festival, see Henri Frankfort, *Kingship and the Gods* (Chicago: University of Chicago Press, 1948), pp. 128, 178, 193, 292, 366 n. 2, 387 n. 90.

11. Siegfried Schott,*Altägyptische Festdaten* (Akademie der Wissenschaften und der Literatur in Mainz) (Wiesbaden: F. Steiner, 1950).

12. Richard A. Parker, *The Calendars of Ancient Egypt* (SAOC 26) (Chicago: University of Chicago Press, 1950), pp. 30-50.

13. O. Neugebauer in JNES 1 (1942):397 and n. 3.

14. W. M. O'Neil in AJBA 2 (1973):4, 11f., 13f.

15. Parker, *The Calendars of Ancient Egypt,* p. 34.

16. A temporary reform of the calendar was instituted by Ptolemy III

Euergetes I (237), a lasting reform by Augustus (26), in which the New Year's day (Thoth 1) was stabilized on August 29—except in every fourth year, when it came on August 30. The relative simplicity and accuracy of the Egyptian calendar commended it to the Hellenistic astronomers, and it was used by Ptolemy in the *Almagest* and also, in due time, by Copernicus in *De revolutionibus orbium caelestium*. It was likewise the calendar of early Christian Egypt, and it still provides the structure of the calendar of the Copts. Maria Cramer, *Das christlich-koptische Ägypten einst und Heute* (Wiesbaden: O. Harrassowitz, 1959), p. viii; Walter C. Till, *Koptische Grammatik (Saïdischer Dialekt)*, 2d ed. (Leipzig: VEB Verlag Enzyklopädie, 1961), pp. 87f.; idem, *Datierung und Prosopographie der koptischen Urkunden aus Theben* (Österreichische Akademie der Wissenschaften, phil.-hist. Kl., Sitzungsberichte 240, 1) (Vienna: H. Böhlaus Nachf., 1962), pp. 240-242.

17. Alan H. Gardiner in JEA 31 (1945):11-28; William J. Murnane in JNES 34 (1975):183f.

18. B. Porter and R. L. B. Moss, *Topographical Bibliography of Ancient Egyptian Hieroglyphic Texts, Reliefs, and Paintings,* 7 vols. (Oxford: Clarendon Press, 1927-1951), 6:25, (229)-(230).

19. Ibid., 3:192.

20. Alan H. Gardiner, *The Royal Canon of Turin* (Oxford: University Press, 1959).

21. Excerpts of some length are given by Josephus; lists of dynasties with brief notes on important kings or events are quoted in the *Chronicle* of Sextus Julius Africanus (221), the *Chronicle* of Eusebius (326), and the history of the world by George Syncellus (800); and some additional materials are preserved in a few other ancient sources. W. G. Waddell, *Manetho (LCL)* (Cambridge, Mass.: Harvard University Press, 1940); Felix Jacoby, *Die Fragmente der griechischen Historiker,* 3 vols. (Berlin: Weidmann, 1926-1963), 3C, no. 609, pp. 5-112; Menahem Stern, *Greek and Latin Authors on Jews and Judaism, Edited with Introductions, Translations and Commentary,* vol. 1, *From Herodotus to Plutarch* (Jerusalem: Israel Academy of Sciences and Humanities, 1974), pp. 62-86. In the transmission of Manetho's material, the best form is usually found in Africanus, an often more corrupt form in Eusebius. Omission of kings' names has shortened the entire list, and figures on lengths of reign and summary totals are no longer fully accurate. As far as possible the work must be compared with the data of the king lists and the other monuments. Wolfgang Helck, *Untersuchungen zu Manetho und den ägyptischen Königslisten* (Untersuchungen zur Geschichte und Altertumskunde Ägyptens 18) (Berlin: Akademie-Verlag, 1956).

22. From Coptic equivalents (e.g., *moun*) it is thought that the Egyptian word *mn* means "remain," and Menes can be related to μένω, "remain." Therefore, the Greek name can be a correct rendering of the Egyptian.

23. William F. Edgerton in JNES 1 (1942):307-309; William W. Hallo and William Kelly Simpson, *The Ancient Near East: A History* (New York: Harcourt Brace Jovanovich), pp. 213, 299.

24. E. Amelineau, *Les nouvelles fouilles d'Abydos, 1895-98,* 3 vols. (Angers: A.

Burdin, 1899-1905); W. M. Flinders Petrie, *The Royal Tombs of the First Dynasty* (London: Egypt Exploration Fund, 1900); Edouard Naville, *The Cemeteries of Abydos, Part I—1909-1910, The Mixed Cemetery and Umm el-Ga ʿab* (London: Egypt Exploration Fund, 1914); Harry J. Kemp in LÄ 1, cols. 36f. In the tomb of Djer was found a basalt statue of Osiris on a bier. At a later date, it was evidently thought that this was the tomb of Osiris, and a great many pilgrims came and left at this tomb large quantities of offering pottery (dating from the Eighteenth to the Twenty-sixth dynasties), which led to the Arabic name of "mother of pots" for the whole area.

25. Frankfort, *Kingship and the Gods,* pp. 53f., 360 n. 20; Peter Kaplony in LÄ 1, col. 1110.

26. CAH³ 1, pt. 2, p. 994. For possible equation of Menes with Aha (rather than with Narmer), see Helck, *Untersuchungen zu Manetho,* p. 9; Jürgen von Beckerath, *Abriss der Geschichte des alten Ägypten* (Munich: R. Oldenbourg, 1971), p. 14; Peter Kaplony in LÄ 1, cols. 94-96; but see also Alan Gardiner, *Egypt of the Pharaohs,* (Oxford: Clarendon Press, 1961), p. 407.

27. Henri Frankfort, *The Birth of Civilization in the Near East* (Bloomington: University of Indiana Press, 1951), pp. 103-105.

28. Barry J. Kemp in JEA 52 (1966):13-22.

29. P. M. Fraser in *Opuscula Atheniensis* 3 (Skrifter Utgivna av Svenska Institutet i Athen, Acta Instituti Atheniensis Regni Sueciae, 4°, 7) (Athens, 1950), pp. 1-54; Jean Vercoutter in LÄ 1, cols. 338-350.

30. In its Egyptian form, this name occurs for the first time in the account by the naval officer Ahmose of the war against the Hyksos, when he was in command of a ship called Appearing in Memphis (ANET, p. 233). In Assyrian the name appears as Mempi (e.g., in the inscriptions of Ashurbanipal, ARAB 2, secs. 770f.), and in Hebrew as Noph (Isa. 19:13; Jer. 2:16, etc.).

31. Hermann Kees, *Ancient Egypt: A Cultural Topography* (Chicago: University of Chicago Press, 1961), pp. 147ff.; Mustafa el Amir in JEA 34 (1948):51-56.

32. R. O. Faulkner, *The Ancient Egyptian Pyramid Texts* (Oxford: Clarendon Press, 1969), Index under *Zkr.*

33. Walter B. Emery, *The Tomb of Hemaka* (Cairo: Government Press, 1938); idem, *Great Tombs of the First Dynasty: Excavations at Saqqara,* 3 vols. (Cairo: Government Press, 1949-1958); idem, *Archaeology* 8 (1955):2-9; idem, *Archaic Egypt* (Baltimore: Penguin Books, 1961). The Arabic word *mastaba* designates a platform or bench, and names the rectangular mud benches found in the courtyards of present-day houses in the villages of Egypt.

34. Peter Kaplony, *Die Inschriften der ägyptischen Frühzeit,* 3 vols. (Wiesbaden: O. Harrassowitz, 1963) (with *Supplement,* 1964, and *Kleine Beiträge,* 1966, Ägyptologische Abhandlungen, 8, 9, 15), 1:205; 2:895 n. 1161; I. E. S. Edwards in JEA 52 (1966):183. Radiocarbon determinations from the tombs, corrected by the Suess correlation curve for radiocarbon and calendar dates, give dates of approximately 3300 and 3100 B.C.E., although the curve is uncertain in the range around 3300. Robin M. Derricourt in JNES 30 (1971):272, fig. 1, and p. 289.

35. Edouard Naville, *Bubastis (1887-1889)* (London: K. Paul, Trench, Trübner, 1891).

36. For the transliteration of the name of the city as On in Hebrew and also in Greek, see Gen. 41:45, 50; 46:20; Ezek. 30:17 (where it is vocalized as Aven); Exod. 1:11 LXX; cf. Jer. 43:13, "the obelisks of Beth-shemesh (House of the Sun) and 50:13 LXX, "the obelisks of Heliopolis that are in On."

37. Faulkner, *The Ancient Egyptian Pyramid Texts,* Index under *'Iwnw*.

38. Kurt Sethe, *Urgeschichte und älteste Religion der Ägypter* (Leipzig, 1930), p. 105, sec. 127, n. 6; Alan H. Gardiner in JEA 30 (1944):27 n. 3.

39. ARE 2, secs. 632-636.

40. Ibid., 3, secs. 245, 544-548.

41. Ibid., 4, secs. 151-412, on Heliopolis secs. 247-304.

42. Ibid., 2, secs. 134, 221f.; 4, secs. 806, 870-872.

43. For the Apis of Memphis, the Mnevis of Heliopolis, and the goat of Mendes, see also Diodorus (1. 84f.), and Herodotus (2. 46), who identifies the god of Mendes with the Greek Pan, often represented with the head and legs of a goat.

44. In modern interpretation, one theory understands the root *bn* and its redoubling as *bnbn* to be connected with various outflows, and supposes that the stone stood for a solidified drop of the seed of Atum and thus the first solid matter he created. Frankfort, *Kingship and the Gods,* pp. 153, 380f. n. 26. Another theory surmises an etymological meaning of "the radiant one" for *bnbn* and supposes that the stone symbolized a ray or the rays of the sun. Gardiner, *Egypt of the Pharaohs,* p. 85.

45. This is confirmed in the Pyramid Text (secs. 1653f.) just quoted, since the text is carved in the Saqqara pyramids of Merenre and Pepy II (Sixth Dynasty) and goes on to ask Atum to bless and protect the construction work of the pyramid and the king who was building it, as once he blessed the work he did on the Primeval Hill—to which the pyramid thus plainly corresponds.

46. One Pyramid Text (sec. 1248a-d) states that Atum produced Shu and Tefnut by onanism. Another uses a play on words, in which *ishesh* ("spit") is connected with Shu and *tef* ("sputter") with Tefnut, to say, "Thou didst spit out what was Shu, thou didst sputter out what was Tefnut." After the direct creation of Shu and Tefnut, all the other deities were born naturally, "from the body," in the language of the Bremner-Rhind Papyrus. For this document, see R. O. Faulkner in JEA 22 (1936):121-140; ibid., 23 (1937):10-16, 166-185; ibid., 24 (1938):41-53.

47. James H. Breasted, *The Dawn of Conscience* (New York: Charles Scribner's Sons, 1933), pp. 29-42; Frankfort, *Kingship and the Gods,* pp. 24-35; ANET, pp. 4-6.

48. Cf. Gen. 1:3, etc.

49. Cf. Gen. 2:2.

50. Several terms describe the various aspects of personal existence: (1) *khet* (e.g., Pyramid Texts sec. 474a) is the body, especially the dead body; (2) *'ib* (Pyr. 3c) is the heart, the seat of the intelligence and conscience; (3) *rn* (Pyr. secs. 764a-b, 899b) is the name and the identity; (4) *shut* (Pyr. sec. 413c) is the shadow and seat of procreative power; (5) *ba* (Pyr. sec. 723) is the "soul," the personification of the

vital forces; (6) *ka* (Pyr. secs. 598c, 816d, 1357b) is the "spirit," the ensemble of qualities, and to die is to go to one's *ka*; (7) *akh* (Pyr. secs. 153b, 1469a) is the deceased as a transfigured spirit. See H. Frankfort, *Ancient Egyptian Religion* (New York: Columbia University Press, 1948), pp. 91-101; Eberhard Otto in LÄ 1, cols. 49-52; Louis V. Žabkar in ibid., cols. 588-590.

51. Anubis appears as a wild dog or jackal, or a man with the head of the animal, and his most famous center was at the city the Greeks called Cynopolis (cf. Plutarch, *Isis and Osiris* 72). This city was perhaps at the present el-Kais on the west bank of the Nile three kilometers south of Beni Mazar, or perhaps on an island in the river, with a necropolis on the east bank at Sheikh Fadl, where numerous mummies of dogs have been found. These sites were in Upper Egyptian Nome XVII, known as "Black Dog," in agreement with the usual representation of Anubis.

52. Edfu (on the west side of the Nile about midway between Luxor and Aswan) was the Egyptian Djeba, was named Apollinopolis Magna by the Greeks because of the identification of Horus with Apollo, and was the metropolis of Upper Egyptian Nome II ("Seat of Horus"). The temple was begun in 237 under Ptolemy III Euergetes, with an architect bearing the famous name of Imhotep, and was finally completed in the year 57 B.C.E.

53. A. M. Blackman and H. W. Fairman in JEA 21 (1935):26-36; ibid., 28 (1942):32-38; ibid., 29 (1943):2-36; ibid., 30 (1944):5-22. Behdet, named in this text, was called Diospolis Inferior by the Greeks and is identified with Tell el-Balamun in the Delta, west of the Damietta branch of the Nile and thirty kilometers southwest of the city of Damietta. Gardiner in ibid., pp. 23-60.

54. Blackman and Fairman in ibid., 21 (1935):35.

55. W. M. Flinders Petrie, *The Royal Tombs of the Earliest Dynasties* (London: Egypt Exploration Fund, 1901), pl. 22, no. 181; Jürgen von Beckerath, *Tanis und Theban: historische Grundlagen der Ramessidenzeit in Ägypten* (Ägyptologische Forschungen 16) (Glückstadt: J. J. Augustin, 1951), pp. 34-37.

56. Heinrich Schäfer and Walter Andrae, *Die Kunst des alten Orients,* 3rd ed. (Berlin: Propyläen Verlag, 1925), pp. 182, 201; W. Stevenson Smith, *The Art and Architecture of Ancient Egypt* (Harmondsworth: Penguin Books, 1958), pl. 11A; Cyril Aldred, *The Egyptians* (New York: Praeger, 1961), pls. 3, 4.

CHAPTER 13. OLD KINGDOM, THIRD TO SIXTH DYNASTIES

1. For the end of the Second Dynasty and the transition to the Old Kingdom, radiocarbon analysis of materials from the Saqqara tombs (including the tomb of Djoser) suggests a time 4100 years ago, which, on the Suess curve, corresponds to a calendar date of 2650 B.C.E., remarkably close to the point otherwise indicated by historical considerations. Robin M. Derricourt in JNES 30 (1971):280, 290.

2. For the possibility that Sanakhte/Nebka was a successor of Neterirykhet/Djoser rather than his predecessor, and for other details, see Peter Kaplony, *Die Inschriften der ägyptischen Frühzeit,* 3 vols. (Wiesbaden: O.

Harrassowitz, 1963), 1:170, 536f.; 2:527-529, 702, 875 n. 1089; idem, *Steingefässe mit Inschriften der Frühzeit und des Alten Reichs* (Monumenta Aegyptiaca, 1) (Brussels: Fondation égyptologique Reine Élisabeth, 1968), p. 7 n. 8; and idem, LÄ 1, col. 686. For Sekhemkhet, see Raphael Giveon in BASOR 216 (1974):17-20.

3. Kurt Sethe in *Maḥâsna and Bêt Khallâf,* ed. John Garstang (London: B. Quaritch, 1903), pp. 19-24, pls. 8-10, 19, figs. 5, 7.

4. Alan H. Gardiner, T. Eric Peet, and Jaroslav Černý, *The Inscriptions of Sinai,* 2 vols., 2d ed. (London: Egypt Exploration Society, 1952-1955), 1, pls. 1, 4, 15 (map of Magharah); 2:3, 22, 52-56.

5. Jürgen von Beckerath in LÄ 1, cols. 1111f.

6. Paul Barguet, *La Stèle de la Famine à Séhel* (Cairo: Imprimerie de l'institut français d'archéologie orientale, 1953); ANET, pp. 31f. Whether the text is a late forgery to support the claims of the priests of Khnum and perhaps to defend their god against encroachments of Isis of Philae, or whether it reflects an actual event of the time of Djoser is uncertain. The land grant is defined in the text as between Manu and Bakhu (the western and eastern mountain ranges bordering the Nile), and from Elephantine southward for twelve *iters* to Takompso. Herodotus (2. 29) describes the same territory as extending from Elephantine for twelve *schoeni* to an island in the Nile called Tachompso; accordingly, the Greeks called the region Dodekaschoinos (Adelheid Schwab in LÄ 1, cols. 1112f.) The Egyptian *iter* ("river measure") was a large unit now estimated at 10.5 kilometers. Alan H. Gardiner, *Egyptian Grammar, Being an Introduction to the Study of Hieroglyphs,* 3rd ed. (London: Oxford University Press, 1957), p. 199, sec. 266, 2. The Greek σχοῖνος ("reed"), Latin *schoenus,* English *schene,* was reckoned at thirty or forty stadia or even more, according to Strabo (17. 1. 24), and Pliny (*Nat. Hist.* 12. 30. 53) says that Eratosthenes calculated it at forty stadia. By the Attic standard, the Greek units were 1 foot (πούς) = 0.3086 meters; 1 plethrum (πλέθρον) = 100 Greek feet = 30.86 meters; 1 stadium (στάδιον) = 600 Greek feet = 185.2 meters. Reckoned at forty stadia, the *schoenus* was therefore about 7.5 kilometers, somewhat short of the 10.5 kilometers of the Egyptian *iter.* But, with the variability in the definition of the Greek unit, it and the *iter* were evidently considered substantially equivalent.

7. OP 11:221-234; cf. Thraemer in PWRE 2, cols. 1642-1697; Pietschmann in PWRE 2, col. 1697; Roeder in PWRE 9:2, cols. 1213-1218. In the northwest sector at Saqqara, a veritable labyrinth of subterranean galleries more than 1.5 kilometers in length has been found, containing enormous numbers of mummified ibises. Jean Leclant in *Orientalia* 35 (1966):136. The ibis was both the incarnation of Thoth and also sacred to Imhotep, and some of the mummy wrappings are decorated with images of Thoth or of Imhotep. Ammianus Marcellinus (22. 14. 7) indicates that Memphis was a center of worship of Asklepios (i.e., of Imhotep), and it is a reasonable supposition that his healing sanctuary, an Asklepieion, was in this vicinity, and even that the tomb of Imhotep may be somewhere in the complex.

8. ANET, p. 467.

9. ANET, pp. 431f.

10. W. M. Flinders Petrie, *The Royal Tombs of the Earliest Dynasties*

(London: Egypt Exploration Fund, 1901), p. 13.

11. Ahmed Fakhry, *The Pyramids* (Chicago: University of Chicago Press, 1961), p. 24, and see this work for all the Egyptian pyramids; also I. E. S. Edwards, *The Pyramids of Egypt* (Harmondsworth: Penguin Books, 1947). For the Step Pyramid, see C. M. Firth and J. E. Quibell, *The Step Pyramid,* 2 vols. (Cairo: Imprimerie de l'institut français d'archéologie orientale, 1935-1936).

12. Étienne Drioton and Étienne Sved, *Egyptian Art* (New York: Arts, 1950), pp. 11-17, pls. 1-6.

13. Mohammed Zakaria Goneim, *Excavations at Saqqara,* vol. 1, *Horus Sekhem-khet, The Unfinished Step Pyramid at Saqqara* (Cairo: Imprimerie de l'institut français d'archéologie orientale, 1957).

14. A. J. Arkell in JEA 42 (1956):116.

15. Alan Rowe in MJ 22 (1931):5-84.

16. Alan H. Gardiner in JEA 32 (1946):71-74; Miriam Lichtheim, *Ancient Egyptian Literature: A Book of Readings,* vol. 1, *The Old and Middle Kingdom* (Berkeley: University of California Press, 1973), pp. 59-61.

17. George Andrew Reisner and William Stevenson Smith, *A History of the Giza Necropolis,* vol. 2, *The Tomb of Hetep-heres the Mother of Cheops* (Cambridge, Mass.: Harvard University Press, 1955).

18. Walter B. Emery, *Egypt in Nubia* (London: Hutchinson, 1965), pp. 41, 127. As a general term the Egyptians called Nubia *Ta-kens* ("the land of the bow," written with an upright bow) and named the northern part, between the First and Second cataracts, Wawat, and the southern part, above the Second Cataract and extending to around the Sixth Cataract in what is now Sudan, Kush. The latter name is the Hebrew Cush, which was used in a general sense for the whole known territory south of Egypt proper. Thus in Ezek. 29:10, Migdol (a "tower" somewhere on the northern border of Egypt) and Syene (Aswan) are the northern and southern limits of Egypt, respectively, and at Syene one comes to the border of Cush. The same area was called Ethiopia by the Greeks (e.g., Strabo 1. 2. 24ff.; 3. 8), and in Ezek. 29:10 and elsewhere, the LXX renders Cush as Ethiopia. The name Nubia is now most commonly used for the ancient land. Lower Nubia is equivalent to the Egyptian territory from the First Cataract nearly to Wadi Halfa, and Upper Nubia is approximately the same as the modern Sudan. The name of Nubia is derived from an African people called Nubae (Strabo 17. 1, 2; Pliny, *Nat. Hist.* 6. 35. 192). Up through the period of the Egyptian Middle Kingdom, Nubia was probably inhabited by Hamites rather than blacks. But in the art of the New Kingdom there are numerous representations of genuine black peoples, who may be said to have definitely entered into the circle of historic peoples by that time. Hermann Junker in JEA 7 (1921):121-132.

19. John Pairman Brown, *The Lebanon and Phoenicia: Ancient Texts Illustrating Their Physical Geography and Native Industries,* vol. 1, *The Physical Setting and the Forest* (Beirut: American University of Beirut, 1969), p. 175.

20. For Egyptian seagoing ships, see R. O. Faulkner in JEA 26 (1940):3-9.

21. Gardiner, Peet, and Černý, *The Inscriptions of Sinai,* 1, pls. 2, 4; 2:56f.

22. Ludwig Borchardt in ZÄS 42 (1905):1-11; I. E. S. Edwards in JEA 60 (1974):251f.; Edda Bresciani in LÄ 1, cols. 984-988; K. Mendelssohn in JEA 59 (1973):60-71; ibid., 62 (1976):179-181; Christopher J. Davey in ibid., pp. 178f.

23. A complete pyramid complex consists of (1) valley temple, (2) causeway, (3) wall around the pyramid precinct, (4) subsidiary pyramid(s), (5) main pyramid, (6) mortuary temple on the east side of the main pyramid, (7) chapel on the north side, and (8) boat pits.

24. Jürgen von Beckerath in LÄ 1, cols. 932f.

25. Diodorus (1. 63) states that construction was effected by means of mounds, perhaps meaning such ramps as have been found still in place at the Unfinished Pyramid of Sekhemkhet at Saqqara. Herodotus (2. 125) says that the pyramid was made like a stairway with tiers or steps, then levers made of short wooden logs were used to raise the rest of the stones, i.e., the stones that filled in the angles of the steps and made a final smooth inclined plane.

26. According to the Pyramid Texts, many different boats were used by the gods and the deceased king. Samuel A. B. Mercer, *The Pyramid Texts in Translation and Commentary,* 4 vols. (New York: Longmans, Green, 1952), 4:70-73. Of these, the most famous was the "boat of the morning sun," or the "day-bark," in which the sun crossed the sky from east to west by day, and the "boat of the evening sun," or the "night-bark," in which the sun passed through the underworld from west to east by night (e.g., Pyr. sec. 335b-c). Two of the king's boats were probably "solar barks," in which he would accompany the sun on these eternal journeys. Elizabeth Thomas in JEA 42 (1956):65-79, 117f.; K. A. Kitchen in LÄ 1, col. 619. Since the Pyramid Texts also mention four reed-floats in connection with the gods of the west, east, south, and north (sec. 464a-b), it is possible that four of the king's boats were intended to allow him to journey to the four cardinal points in the sky and to the realms of these four groups of gods. In form, the divine boats were conceived first as reed-floats (as the text just cited shows, and as are still used in Nubia), later as regular Egyptian boats of papyrus, then of wood. James Henry Breasted in JEA 4 (1917):174-176; Warren R. Dawson in ibid., 10 (1924):46; Jaroslav Černý in ibid., 41 (1955):75-79.

27. W. M. Flinders Petrie, *Abydos,* 2 pts. (London: Egyptian Exploration Fund, 1902-1903), 2:30, pl. 13, 2; pl. 14, 284.

28. Gardiner, Peet, and Černý, *The Inscriptions of Sinai,* 1, pls. 2, 3; 2:57f.

29. Jürgen von Beckerath in LÄ 1, cols. 1099f.; Adolf Klasens in ibid., cols. 24f.

30. Hermann Ranke in JEA 70 (1950):65-68.

31. Von Beckerath in LA 1, col. 933.

32. Selim Hassan, *The Sphinx: Its History in the Light of Recent Excavations* (Cairo: Government Press, 1949). A temple of Harmakhis, probably built in the latter part of the reign of Khafre, has been found in front of the Sphinx and beside the valley temple. Herbert Ricke in BABA 10 (1970):1-43; Siegfried Schott in ibid., pp. 49-79. For Thutmose IV as a young prince at the Sphinx, see ARE 2, secs. 810-815.

33. Von Beckerath in LÄ 1, cols. 785f.

34. Uvo Hölscher, *Das Grabdenkmal des Königs Chephren* (Leipzig: J. C. Hinrichs, 1912).

35. G. A. Reisner, *Mycerinus: The Temples of the Third Pyramid at Giza* (Cambridge, Mass.: Harvard University Press, 1931); Drioton and Sved, *Egyptian Art,* pp. 25f., fig. 14; Wendy Wood in JEA 60 (1974):82-93. Three intact triads are in the Cairo Museum, and one in the Boston Museum of Fine Arts.

36. Gustave Jéquier, *Le Mastabat Faraoun* (Cairo: Imprimerie de l'institut français d'archéologie orientale, 1928).

37. Wolfgang Helck, *Untersuchungen zu Manetho und den ägyptischen Königslisten* (Untersuchungen zur Geschichte und Altertumskunde Ägyptens 18) (Berlin: Akademie-Verlag, 1956), p. 25.

38. William Kelly Simpson, ed., *The Literature of Ancient Egypt* (New Haven: Yale University Press, 1972), pp. 15-30. The name *Ruddedet* may be a pseudonym for Queen Khentkaues, who, according to various inscriptions, may have been a daughter of Menkaure and the wife of Userkaf and mother of Sahure and Neferirkare.

39. Werner Kaiser in MDAIK 14 (1956):104-116.

40. Herbert Ricke in BABA 7 (1965):1-54; Elmar Edel, Gerhard Haeny, Wolfgang Helck, Werner Kaiser, Peter Kaplony, Herbert Ricke, and Siegfried Schott in ibid., 8 (1969):1-148.

41. At Saqqara, one of the best known mastabas is that of Ti, who has the title of Overseer of Pyramids and of the Sahure temple. The painted reliefs in the interior depict all kinds of scenes in the life of Ti and on his estates.

42. In Sinai, Sahure is represented in the usual way in the rock carvings of Magharah. Gardiner, Peet, and Černý, *The Inscriptions of Sinai,* 1, pls. 5, 7; 2:58f.

43. Friedrich Wilhelm von Bissing, *Das Re-Heiligtum des Königs Ne-woser-Re (Rathures),* vol. 1, *Der Bau,* with L. Borchardt (Berlin: A. Duncker, 1905); vol. 2, *Die kleine Festdarstellung* (Berlin: A. Duncker, 1923); and vol. 3, *Die grosse Festdarstellung,* with H. Kees (Berlin: A. Duncker, 1928); idem, ASAE 53 (1956):319-338, and see especially pp. 324f. for the seasons, with pl. 9 for Akhet, pl. 10a for Peroyet (?), and pls. 7, 8, for Shomu; Elamr Edel and Steffen Wenig, *Die Jahreszeitenreliefs aus dem Sonnenheiligtum des Königs Ne-user-Re* (Berlin: Akademie-Verlag, 1974).

44. Ludwig Borchardt in *Aegyptiaca: Festschrift für Georg Ebers* (Leipzig: W. Engelmann, 1897), pp. 8-15; and idem, ASAE 38 (1938):210 and pl. 29.

45. Lichtheim, *Ancient Egyptian Literature,* 1:61-80. With the description of old age, cf. Eccles. 12:1ff.; with the maxim on prudent conduct at the table of a greater, cf. Prov. 23:1f. In tomb statues from the Fifth Dynasty mastabas at Saqqara, the deceased is often honored as a man of letters by being shown as a scribe (e.g., the Unknown Scribe in the Cairo Museum, and the Squatting Scribe in the Louvre). See Jean Capart in JEA 7 (1921):186-190.

46. R. O. Faulkner in JEA 21 (1935):180.

47. *The Mastaba of Mereruka,* by the Sakkarah Expedition, 2 vols. (OIP 31, 39) (Chicago: University of Chicago Press, 1938).

48. ARE 1, secs. 292-294, 306-315, 319-324.

49. This was Upper Egypt, defined (ARE 1, sec. 320) as extending to the south to Elephantine and to the north to the Knives Nome (Upper Egyptian Nome XXII, with its residence city at Aphroditopolis, probably at the present Atfih east of the Nile opposite Medum).

50. ARE 1, secs. 316-318.

CHAPTER 14. FIRST INTERMEDIATE PERIOD, SEVENTH TO TENTH DYNASTIES

1. For the First Intermediate period, see Hanns Stock, *Die Erste Zwischenzeit Ägyptens* (Studia Aegyptiaca 1, AnOr 17) (Rome: Pontificium institutum biblicum, 1949). In some outlines of Egyptian history, the Seventh and Eighth dynasties are considered to belong still to the Old Kingdom.

2. Strabo (17. 1. 39) says the people of Herakleopolis also honored the ichneumon, the deadly enemy of the crocodile and the asp.

3. Wolfgang Schenkel in LÄ 1, cols. 945-947.

4. W. M. Flinders Petrie, *A History of Egypt,* 3 vols. (New York: Charles Scribner's Sons, 1899-1905), 1 (4th ed., 1899), pp. 114f.

5. Miriam Lichtheim, *Ancient Egyptian Literature: A Book of Readings,* vol. 1, *The Old and Middle Kingdom* (Berkeley: University of California Press, 1973), 1:149-163. Whether one hopeful passage about an ideal "herdsman" refers to the supreme god or to a future king is not plain.

6. R. O. Faulkner in JEA 42 (1956):21-40; Hans Goedicke, *The Report about the Dispute of a Man with His Ba: Papyrus Berlin 3024* (Baltimore: Johns Hopkins Press, 1970); Lichtheim, *Ancient Egyptian Literature,* 1:163-169.

7. Alan H. Gardiner in JEA 9 (1923):5-25; Lichtheim, *Ancient Egyptian Literature,* 1:169-184.

8. Alan H. Gardiner in JEA 1 (1914):20-36, 100-106; Lichtheim, *Ancient Egyptian Literature,* 1:97-109.

9. Hebenu was the residence city of Upper Egyptian Nome XVI ("Oryx"), probably at Zawiyet el-Meitin across the Nile on the east side about seven kilometers southeast of Minia, with a necropolis four kilometers farther south at Kom el-Ahmar ("Red Mound").

10. The Ways of Horus was almost certainly the name of the northeastern frontier post at Tjel (Sile), the starting point of the main coastal road to Palestine, on which the Horus-king marched triumphantly, hence the name (see below, Chapter 18, n. 9). Kemwey is probably equivalent to Kemwer ("Great Black"), usually the designation of the Bitter Lakes (as in the Story of Sinuhe). But here Kemwey is written with the determinative "bull" and is probably the name of the residence city of Lower Egyptian Nome X ("Black Bull"), the later Athribis. The site is identified with Kom el-Atrib on the east bank of the Damietta branch of the Nile, forty-nine kilometers from Cairo, near modern Benha. Benha is a railroad junction, from which one line runs east to Zagazig and on through Wadi Tumilat to Ismailia and the Suez Canal. In the text a phrase of double import calls this

region, understandably enough, both the "navel-cord" of the bowmen, i.e., their point of entry and center of gravity, and at the same time the "defense" against them.

11. Gardiner in JEA 1 (1914):32-34.

CHAPTER 15. MIDDLE KINGDOM, ELEVENTH AND TWELFTH DYNASTIES

1. Also Diospolis Magna ("great city of Zeus") in distinction from Diospolis Parva ("small city of Zeus"), which was the ancient Hait and now the village of Hou near Chenoboskion.

2. The latter designations are reproduced in the forms of No-Amon in Nah. 3:8 and No in Jer. 46:25 and Ezek. 30:14-16.

3. The great temple of Amun at Thebes was called Ipet-esut ("the [most] esteemed of places"). It is surmised that the first part of this name, with the article, was pronounced something like *taype* and sounded to the Greeks like Thebes (the ancient and important Greek city in Boeotia) and led them to give this name to the city. In this sense the name appears first in Homer, who describes the Egyptian Thebes as "hundred-gated" (*Iliad* 9. 381-383; cf. 4. 406 for the "seven-gated" Greek city, which had an outer wall with seven gates). Diodorus (1. 45. 6f.) quotes the Homeric passage and adds that some explain that it was not one hundred "gates" (*pylaea*) that the Egyptian city had, but rather many great propylaea in front of its temples, and that it was from these that the title "hundred-gated" was given to the city.

4. For Thebes, see Charles F. Nims, *Thebes of the Pharoahs: Pattern for Every City* (London: Elek Books, 1965).

5. G. A. Wainwright in JEA (1964):139-153.

6. Ronald J. Williams in *Studies in Honor of John A. Wilson* (SAOC 35) (Chicago: University of Chicago Press, 1969), p. 95.

7. H. Frankfort, *Ancient Egyptian Religion* (New York: Columbia University Press, 1948), pp. 22f.

8. Papyrus Bulaq 17 in the Cairo Museum, copied in the Eighteenth Dynasty but containing earlier material (ANET, pp. 365-367). With the thought of the unslumbering deity, watchful for his creatures, cf. Ps. 121:3f.

9. For the Middle Kingdom, see H. E. Winlock, *The Rise and Fall of the Middle Kingdom in Thebes* (New York: Macmillan, 1947). A radiocarbon date for the close of the Middle Kingdom, corrected on the Suess curve to 2000 or 1800 B.C.E., agrees well—at least in the latter figure—with the dates given above. Robin M. Derricourt in JNES 30 (1971):290.

10. Alan H. Gardiner in JEA 1 (1914):23.

11. Winlock, *The Rise and Fall of the Middle Kingdom in Thebes,* pp. 22f., 30f.; Hanns Stock, *Die Erste Zwischenzeit Ägyptens* (Studia Aegyptiaca 1, AnOr 17) (Rome: Pontificium institutum biblicum, 1949), pp. 78-86, 92f., 99, 103, and Chronologische Übersicht following p. 110.

12. Alexander Badawy, *A History of Egyptian Architecture,* 4 vols. (Giza: Studio Misr, 1954–), 2:53–59. At a site not far south of Deir el-Bahri, Mentuhotep III also began a tomb-temple similar to that of his predecessor, but did not complete it. In the nearby tomb of his chancellor, Meketre, one chamber was found intact and full of carved wooden models (now in the Egyptian Museum in Cairo and the Metropolitan Museum of Art in New York City), which represent many activities of daily life. H. E. Winlock, *Models of Daily Life in Ancient Egypt: From the Tomb of Meket-Rē ͨ at Thebes* (Cambridge, Mass.: Published for the Metropolitan Museum of Art by Harvard University Press, 1955).

13. ARE 1, secs. 434-453.

14. Gardiner in JEA 1 (1914):100-106; ANET, pp. 444-446; Lichtheim, *Ancient Egyptian Literature: A Book of Readings,* vol. 1, *The Old and Middle Kingdom* (Berkeley: University of California Press, 1973), 1: 139-145.

15. William C. Hayes in JNES 12 (1953):35.

16. ANET, pp. 418f.; Lichtheim, *Ancient Egyptian Literature,* 1:135-139.

17. ANET, pp. 18-22; Lichtheim, *Ancient Egyptian Literature,* 1:222-236. On details, see A. M. Blackman in JEA 22 (1936):35-44; Hans Goedicke in ibid., 43 (1957):77-85; W. V. Davies in ibid., 61 (1975):45-50.

18. In the movement of the civil calendar as compared with the natural and astronomical year, this date has been calculated as equivalent to February 15, 1962.

19. To reach this point from the eastern Delta, Sinuhe's likely route of travel would have been through Wadi Tumilat, a desert-bounded valley, ten kilometers wide at the most, beginning fifteen kilometers east of Zagazig and extending fifty kilometers eastward to Lake Timsah (Crocodile Lake) and the Bitter Lakes. In terms of the Egyptian nomes, Wadi Tumilat corresponded with Lower Egyptian Nome VIII ("Eastern Harpoon"), with Pithom (Tell el-Maskhuta) as its metropolis. Later the western part of the nome became Lower Egyptian Nome XX ("Soped"). See Wolfgang Helck in LÄ 2, cols. 397, 401; for a map of Wadi Tumilat, see Edouard Naville, *The Store-City of Pithom and the Route of the Exodus* (First Memoir of the Egypt Exploration Fund), 3rd ed. (London: Trübner, 1888).

20. Upper Retenu appears in the narrative as a highland country, agricultural, but within reach of desert hunting, yet also close to the main road on which travelers came from Egypt. Therefore, it probably included northern Palestine and southern and central Syria. In language similar to that applied to Palestine in Exod. 3:8, Deut. 8:8, etc., it is described as a good land with an abundance of figs, grapes, wine, honey, olives, and other produce.

21. ARE 1, sec. 510.

22. *Archaeology* 11 (1958):215f.; Walter B. Emery, *Egypt in Nubia* (London: Hutchinson, 1965), pp. 143-152 and map on p. 14, fig. 1.

23. For the dedicatory inscription of the temple, see ARE 1, sec. 498-506.

24. The builder of the pyramid, a certain Meri, describes the work on his stela, now in the Louvre (ARE 1, secs. 507-509). Painted reliefs from the mortuary temple are in the Cairo Museum, the British Museum, and the Metropolitan Museum of Art; life-size limestone statues of Sesostris I from the area are in the

Cairo Museum.

25. In the Fayum, the chief temple was at Shedet, a place mentioned already in the Pyramid Texts (secs. 416c, 1564b) as the center of the crocodile god Sobek, whose cult became especially important in the Twelfth Dynasty. The city was called Krokodilopolis by the Greeks (Strabo 17. 1. 38f., who calls Sobek Suchos), and the ancient ruins are now known as Kiman Faris, just north of Medinet el-Fayum. The temple was probably under construction from the time of Amunemhet I and Sesostris I, and the latter's name has been found at the nearby village of Abgig. Dieter Arnold in LÄ 2, col. 91.

26. P. E. Newberry et al., *Beni Hasan,* 4 vols. (London: K. Paul, Trench, Trübner, 1893-1900), 1, pl. 30; Walter Wreszinski, *Atlas zur altaegyptischen Kulturgeschichte,* 3 pts. (Leipzig: J. C. Hinrichs, 1923-1938), 2, pl. 6.

27. ARE 1, secs. 642-648.

28. Ibid., secs. 651-660.

29. Alan H. Gardiner in JEA 3 (1916):184-192.

30. John A. Wilson in AJSL 58 (1941):232; ANET, p. 230.

31. This was probably the Thuthotep who lived under Amunemhet II, Sesostris II, and Sesostris III. He was governor of Upper Egyptian Nome XV ("Hare"), of which the residence city was Khmunu or Per-Djehuty ("House of Thoth"). The city was called Hermopolis Magna because Thoth was identified with Hermes. It was located at the present el-Ashmunein on the west side of the Nile. Thuthotep's tomb (with fine paintings) is at Deir el-Bersheh across the river on the east side. ARE 1, secs. 688-706; Aylward M. Blackman in JEA 2 (1915):13f.; Edward L. B. Terrace, *Egyptian Paintings of the Middle Kingdom* (London: Allen and Unwin, 1968).

32. Jaroslav Černý in ArOr 7 (1935):384-389.

33. ARE 1, secs. 714f. In Sinai, the moon god Thoth may have been assimilated with the Semitic moon god Sin, and the cow goddess Hathor with Ishtar, the Semitic goddess often represented with crescent-shaped horns. Heinz Skrobucha, *Sinai* (London: Oxford University Press, 1966), p. 5. In Serabit el-Khadem, a temple enlarged by Amunemhet III was dedicated to Hathor as the Lady of the Land of Mefak. W. M. Flinders Petrie, *Researches in Sinai* (London: J. Murray, 1906), pp. 72-108. This was where the Egyptians obtained *mefaket* (turquoise, malachite, and all kinds of green stone), and they called the mountains of Sinai the Terraces of Turquoise.

34. ARE 1, sec. 722.

35. Ibid., sec. 731.

36. Lower Egyptian Nome XX ("Soped") was the western part of the old Lower Egyptian Nome VIII ("Eastern Harpoon"), which extended on through Wadi Tumilat to Lake Timsah (Crocodile Lake). The classical writers called the Soped nome the Nome of Arabia (cf. Strabo 17. 1. 21, where the Egyptian Arabia is the country between the Nile and the Persian Gulf). Ptolemy (*Geography* 4. 5. 53) lists Phacussa (modern Faqus, thirty-seven kilometers northeast of Zagazig) as the metropolis of the Nome of Arabia, evidently a change of the capital from the earlier Per-Soped. See Edouard Naville, *The Shrine of Saft el Henneh and the Land of*

Goshen (London: Egypt Exploration Fund, 1887); Henry G. Fischer in JNES 18 (1959):129-142; Helck in LÄ 2, col. 401.

37. Petrie, *Researches in Sinai,* pp. 113, 118.

38. Perhaps it was St. John's Island, called Zeberged in Arabic, off Ras Benas on the African coast, behind which lay the ancient port of Berenike. G. A. Wainwright in JEA 32 (1946):31-38; ibid., 34 (1948):119; Werner Vycichl in *Kush* 5 (1957):70-72.

39. The pictures are so carefully realistic that it is believed possible to recognize that the fish swimming in the Nile and in the Red Sea are of different varieties, corresponding to the varieties that exist in the river and in the sea, respectively, even today. Evelyn Wells, *Hatshepsut* (Garden City, N.Y.: Doubleday, 1969), p. 238.

40. G. Posener in CÉ 26 (1938):260f.; Pierre Montet, *Everyday Life in Egypt in the Days of Ramesses the Great* (New York: St. Martin's Press, 1958), p. 184.

41. Anne Burton, *Diodorus Siculus, Book I, A Commentary* (Leiden: E. J. Brill, 1972), pp. 130f. For the supposition that the attribution of the canal to Sesostris is only a part of the romantic tendency of the classical writers to connect many things with that name, see Alan B. Lloyd in JEA 61 (1975):289.

42. Herodotus (2. 158) states that the canal left the Nile a little above Bubastis (Tell Basta, two kilometers southeast of Zagazig) and went past the Arabian town of Patumus (probably biblical Pithom, called Heroonpolis in Greek, Tell el-Maskhuta, sixteen kilometers west of Ismailia) and into the Red Sea. Strabo (17. 1. 26) makes the canal start at Phacussa, but the terrain here would not be favorable, and he has probably confused the later capital with the earlier Per-Soped. Alan H. Gardiner in JEA 5 (1915):245 n. 4; ibid., 10 (1924):95.

43. Roland G. Kent in JNES 1 (1942):415-421.

44. "The First Suez Canal?" *Time,* October 20, 1975.

45. Jürgen von Beckerath in LÄ 1, cols. 190f.; Arne Eggebrecht in LÄ 1, cols. 782f.

46. Both Diodorus (1. 61. 2) and Pliny (*Nat. Hist.* 36. 19. 84-89) say that Daedalus adopted the Egyptian Labyrinth as the model for the similar structure he built for King Minos of Crete. A fragmentary manuscript known as the Lake Moeris Papyrus, which has been in the collections of the Egyptian Museum ever since this institution was first housed in Bulaq (a suburb of Cairo) and then in Giza, has been held to be a description of the Hawara labyrinth, but it is more probably a schematic plan of the geography of the whole Fayum. R. V. Lanzone, *Les Papyrus de Lac Moeris* (Turin: Bocca frères, 1896).

47. A. de Buck in JEA 35 (1949):87-97; R. O. Faulkner, *The Ancient Egyptian Coffin Texts,* vol. 1, *Spells 1-354* (Warminster: Aris and Phillips, 1973).

48. James H. Breasted, *Development of Religion and Thought in Ancient Egypt* (New York: Charles Scribner's Sons, 1912), pp. 35, 147, 256.

49. Leonard H. Lesko, *The Ancient Egyptian Book of Two Ways* (Berkeley: University of California Press, 1972); Alexandre Piankoff and Helen Jacquet-Gordon, *The Wandering of the Soul: Texts Translated with Commentary* (Bollingen

Series 40, 6) (Princeton: Princeton University Press, 1974).

50. ANET, pp. 328f.; ANEP, fig. 593. For the date, cf. William F. Edgerton in JAOS 60 (1946):492 n. 44. If Abraham is placed in Middle Bronze I (2100-1800) and perhaps in the late twentieth or early nineteenth century, the account of his visit to Egypt (Gen. 12:10-13:1) will fall in the Middle Kingdom. For Abraham in Egypt, see Pierre Montet, *L'Egypte et la Bible* (Neuchâtel: Éditions Delachaux and Niestlé, 1959), pp. 11-14; idem, *Das alte Ägypten und die Bibel,* trans. Matthis Thurneysen (Zürich: EVZ-Verlag, 1960), pp. 13-19; idem, *Egypt and the Bible,* trans. Leslie R. Keylock (Philadelphia: Fortress Press, 1968), pp. 3-6.

CHAPTER 16. SECOND INTERMEDIATE PERIOD, THIRTEENTH TO SEVENTEENTH DYNASTIES

1. For the Second Intermediate period, see Jürgen von Beckerath, *Untersuchungen zur politischen Geschichte der Zweiten Zwischenzeit in Ägypten* (Ägyptologische Forschungen 23) (Glückstadt: J. J. Augustin, 1964).

2. William C. Hayes in JNES 12 (1953):31-39.

3. A king with the throne name of Userkare and the personal name of Khendjer appears among the Thirteenth Dynasty rulers in the Turin Canon (col. 6, no. 20), and a pyramid excavated in the southern area at Saqqara is identified as his. Another large pyramid a short distance to the southwest, left unfinished and not identified, may belong to the same dynasty. Two more similar ruined pyramids at Mazghuna, between Dahshur and Lisht, may also be from the Thirteenth Dynasty.

4. William C. Hayes, *A Papyrus of the Late Middle Kingdom in the Brooklyn Museum (Papyrus Brooklyn 35.1446)* (Brooklyn: Brooklyn Museum, 1955); cf. W. F. Albright in JAOS 74 (1954):222-223; Georges Posener in *Syria* 34 (1957):145-163; Raphael Giveon in LÄ 1, col. 464.

5. ARE 1, secs. 753-765.

6. Maurice Dunand, *Fouilles de Byblos,* 4 vols. (Paris: P. Geuthner, 1937-1958), 1:197f.; 4, pl. 30.

7. Artapanus, *Concerning the Jews,* quoted by Clement of Alexandria (*Stromata* 1. 23. 154) and by Eusebius (*Praeparatio Evangelica* 9. 27. 3).

8. William C. Hayes in JEA 33 (1947):9.

9. Richard A. Parker in ibid., 28 (1942):68.

10. R. M. Engberg, *The Hyksos Reconsidered* (Chicago: University of Chicago Press, 1939), pp. 9, 49; John van Seters, *The Hyksos: A New Investigation* (New Haven: Yale University Press, 1966), p. 190; Raphael Giveon in LÄ 1, col. 464.

11. T. Säve-Söderbergh in JEA 37 (1951):53-71. Expressive of the later hostility, Hatshepsut, for example, says, "I have restored that which was ruins ... since the Asiatics were in the midst of Avaris of the Northland, and the barbarians were in the midst of them." ARE 2, sec. 303.

12. A heliacal rising of Sothis recorded in the medical Papyrus Ebers on the ninth day of the eleventh month in the ninth year of Amunhotep I (second king of

the Eighteenth Dynasty) would fall in the range 1544-1537 if the place of observation were Memphis or Heliopolis. William F. Edgerton in AJSL 53 (1937). But it would fall in the range of 1526-1519 if observed at Thebes, and the latter may be more likely, since Thebes was the center of administration in the Eighteenth Dynasty. Erik Hornung, *Untersuchungen zur Chronologie und Geschichte des Neuen Reiches* (Ägyptologische Abhandlungen 11) (Wiesbaden: O. Harrassowitz, 1964), pp. 19-21. Therewith the twenty-five year (Manetho) reign of Ahmose (first king of the Eighteenth Dynasty and expeller of the Hyksos) may be placed in 1552-1527, and the 108-year sway of the Hyksos in 1660-1552.

13. Wolfgang Helck, *Untersuchungen zu Manetho und der ägyptischen Königslisten* (Untersuchungen zur Geschichte und Altertumskunde Agyptens 18) (Berlin: Akademie-Verlag, 1956), p. 37. Bnon and Pachnan (Apachnan) who follow, are not otherwise known.

14. Jürgen von Beckerath in LÄ 1, cols. 902f.

15. Ibid., col. 352.

16. Ibid., cols. 903f.

17. Säve-Söderbergh in JEA 37 (1951):65f.; van Seters, *The Hyksos,* p. 159.

18. ANET, p. 231.

19. Säve-Söderbergh in JEA 37 (1951):70f.

20. ARE 2, secs. 4, 8, 14; ANET, p. 233; Jürgen von Beckerath, *Tanis und Theben: Historische Grundlagen der Ramessidenzeit in Ägypten* (Ägyptologishce Forschungen 16) (Glückstadt: J. J. Augustin, 1951), p. 31.

21. *Geography of Claudius Ptolemy,* ed. Edward Luther Stevenson (New York: New York Public Library, 1932), p. 102. The Golénischeff Glossary (a Twenty-first Dynasty geographical papyrus in the Hermitage Museum, Leningrad) names three rivers in the Delta—"the Western River, the Great River, the Waters of the Sun,"—and a Nineteenth Dynasty ostracon, obtained at Thebes by Alan H. Gardiner, speaks of three—"the Great River," one with name missing, and the third "the Waters of Avaris." In each case, the third river can well be the Bubastite/Pelusiac branch of the Nile. If, however, the Bubastite were identified with the Tanite branch (since the latter also flowed not far from Bubastis), this would leave the Pelusiac branch without a known ancient Egyptian name. Alan H. Gardiner in JEA 19 (1933):125.

22. Rainer Stadelmann in LÄ 1, cols. 552-554. A possible more specific location of Avaris in the vicinity of es-Salhiyeh, between Phakusa and Tell Defenneh (ancient Tahpanhes, Daphnae), is suggested by von Beckerath, *Untersuchungen zur politischen Geschichte der Zweiten Zwischenzeit,* pp. 151-157, with map following p. 158. The Sethroite nome (Manetho/Africanus), as the Greeks called it, was Lower Egyptian Nome XIV ("Point of the East"). The metropolis of this nome was at Tjel/Sile, but later at the Egyptian Ninsu, which the Greeks called Herakleopolis Parva or Mikra (in distinction from Herakleopolis Magna, the Ninth and Tenth Dynasty capital in the Fayum). It was the latter city that the Greeks also called Sethroe (probably at Tell es-Serig, at the southeast corner of Lake Menzalah), and the nome therefore Sethroite. Strabo 17. 1. 21, 24; Ptolemy, *Geogr.* 4, 5; Ricardo A. Caminos in JEA 50 (1964):94; W. Helck in LÄ 2, col. 399. The Saite nome

(Manetho/Josephus) would properly be around Sais (residence city of the Twenty-sixth Dynasty), too far west for the Hyksos capital. But it might possibly be the Tanite nome (cf. Strabo 17. 1. 20, the Tanitic mouth of the Nile was sometimes called the Saitic), and some would identify Tanis (at San el-Hagar) with Avaris as well as with Per-Ramses. Pierre Montet in RB 39 (1930):5-28; idem, *Les nouvelles fouilles de Tanis 1929-1932* (Paris: Les Belles Lettres, 1933); idem, *Le Drame d'Avaris* (Paris: P. Geuthner, 1941); idem, *Tanis, douze années de fouilles dans une capitale oubliée du delta égyptien* (Paris: Payot, 1942). Alan H. Gardiner in *Recueil d'etudes égyptologiques dédiées à la mémoire de Jean-François Champollion* (Paris: E. Champion, 1922), p. 215, favored Pelusium for both Avaris and Per-Ramses. In JEA 19 (1933): 122-128, Gardiner accepted Tanis, but in *Egypt of the Pharaohs* (London: Weiden-feld and Nicolson, 1968), p. 258, he regarded this as uncertain because of the rival claims of Khataʿna-Qantir. The god Seth was worshiped at Tanis (as shown by the Steal of the Year 400, see below under Ramses I) and is called "lord of Avaris" on other monuments (e.g., on the statue of King Nehesi from Tell Moqdam, ten kilometers south of Zifta). But Seth was doubtless worshiped at many places in the northeastern Delta. A human foundation sacrifice under the outer enclosure wall of the temple area at Tanis may represent Canaanite custom (cf. 1 Kings 16:34), but the wall may come only from the time of Ramses II. Raymond Weill in JEA 21 (1935):12f., 16-18, 20. Also at Tell ed-Dabaa, near Qantir, burials and pottery have been found of non-Egyptian type, like materials of the Middle Bronze Age in Palestine/Syria. Manfred Bietak in AfO 22 (1968):182-185. But there may have been many such settlements in the northeastern Delta, and again specific proof of identity with Avaris is lacking. The most unambiguous clue remains the statement (Manetho/Josephus) that Avaris was east of the Bubastite branch of the Nile.

23. If the exodus took place in the thirteenth century and the people of Israel were in Egypt for 430 years prior thereto (Exod. 12:40, Hebrew text), they would probably have come there in the late eighteenth or the seventeenth century (cf. Chapter 5, n. 92). Early Christian chronographers, perhaps in dependence upon Jewish sources, put Joseph at this time. Eusebius (in the Armenian version of his *Chronicle,* ed. Josef Karst, *Eusebius Werke* 5, GCS 20, p. 68) lists several of the Fifteenth Dynasty Shepherd Kings (Saites, Bnon, Archles, Aphophis) and says, "It is under these kings that Joseph arises, to rule over Egypt." Syncellus, perhaps in dependence upon Africanus, states that Joseph rose to rule in Egypt in the seventeenth year of Apophis. Adolf Erman in ZÄS 18 (1880):126. See J. Leibovitch in IEJ 3 (1953):99-112; Josef M. A. Janssen, "Egyptological Remarks on *The Story of Joseph in Genesis,*" *Jaarbericht No. 14 van het VoorAziatisch-Egyptisch Genootschap Ex Oriente Lux,* 1955-1956, pp. 63-72; Z. Mayani, *Les Hyksos et le Monde de la Bible* (Paris: Payot, 1956); Pierre Montet, *Egypt and the Bible,* trans. Leslie R. Keylock (Philadelphia: Fortress Press, 1968), pp. 7-15; K. A. Kitchen, *Ancient Orient and Old Testament* (Philadelphia: American Philosophical Society, 1944), pp. 52-55, who notes that the price of twenty shekels of silver paid for Joseph (Gen. 37:28) is the correct average price of a slave in about the eighteenth century, the price being cheaper earlier and afterward steadily higher. In J. Vergote, *Joseph en Égypte* (Louvain: Publications universitaires, 1959), the "Egyptian coloring" of the

Joseph story is held to best fit the Ramesside period in the Nineteenth Dynasty. In Donald B. Redford, *A Study of the Biblical Story of Joseph* (supplements to VT 20) (Leiden: E. J. Brill, 1970), the Saite period is indicated and the composition of the story dated ca. 650-425 (see pp. 242, 250). For a documented famine in Egypt in the Second Intermediate period, see Barbara Bell in AJA 79 (1975):261.

24. In the LXX, Goshen is rendered as Gesem; in Gen. 45:10; 46:34, the name is Gesem of Arabia. Since Egyptian Arabia was the country between the Nile and the Gulf of Suez, and since the Nome of Arabia ("Soped") was in Wadi Tumilat (cf. above, Chapter 15, n. 36), the LXX rendering also points to Wadi Tumilat for the land of Goshen.

25. ANET, p. 259. The Bedouin tribes of Edom are literally "the tribes of the Shasu of the land of Atuma." From other references, the Shasu are known as living in the Sinaitic peninsula, particularly to the south of Palestine. See Edouard Naville, *The Store-City of Pithom and the Route of the Exodus* (First Memoir of the Egypt Exploration Fund), 3rd ed. (London: Trübner, 1888), p. 28; idem, JEA 10 (1924):25; Raphael Giveon, *Les Bédouins Shosou des documents égyptiens* (Documents et Monumenta Orientis Antiqui 18) (Leiden: E. J. Brill, 1971).

26. An inscription of Ramses II, found at Serapeum between Lake Timsah and the large upper Bitter Lake, says, "The king fortifies the mouth of the canal of Tjeku." A possible derivation of the name is from an African word (*thukka*), which means "pastureland" and correctly describes the character of Wadi Tumilat. Naville, *The Store-City of Pithom*, p. 7; idem, JEA 10 (1924):34.

27. In the LXX (Gen. 46:28f.) and in Josephus (*Ant.* 2. 7. 5 sec. 184), Joseph meets his father at Heroonpolis. In the Coptic, the Sahidic version of Upper Egypt retains Heroonpolis; but the Bohairic version of Lower Egypt reads, "to the town of Pethom in the land of Ramasse" and "towards the town of Pethom." Alan H. Gardiner in JEA 5 (1918):262. The identity of Pithom (Per-Atum) and Heroonpolis is perhaps made understandable by an inscription on an Egyptian obelisk from Thebes set up by Augustus in the Circus Maximus at Rome (as translated from the hieroglyphic into Greek by Ammianus Marcellinus [17. 4. 18], following Hermapion, who probably lived in the time of Augustus). In this inscription, the sun god Helios calls King Ramestes both the child of Helios and the son of Heron. Since Helios is of course the Egyptian sun god and can be Atum, and since Helios and Heron seem to be in parallel, Heron can be another name for Atum. Then the original name of the city could have been Heronpolis ("City of Heron-Atum," equivalent to Per-Atum/Pithom), only later understood as Heroonpolis ("City of Heroes"). The names Hero, Eron, and Ero that appear in other authors are probably variants of the same name. Gardiner in JEA 5 (1918):262, 268. In Wadi Tumilat, two excavated sites come into consideration for possible identification with Per-Atum/Pithom, namely, Tell el-Maskhuta (sixteen kilometers west of Ismalia and forty-eight kilometers east of Saft el-Hineh) and Tell er-Retabeh (fourteen kilometers west of Tell el-Maskhuta and thirty-four kilometers east of Saft el-Hineh). Ramses II and later kings built at both places, and at both places there are remains of temples and inscriptional mention of Tum (i.e., Atum) as the chief god of the land of Tjeku. At Tell el-Maskhuta, two Latin inscriptions give

the name of Ero and thus suggest that this site was Heroonpolis/Pithom. For Tell
el-Maskhuta, see Naville, *The Store-City of Pithom;* for Tell er-Retabeh, see W. M.
Flinders Petrie, *Hyksos and Israelite Cities* (London: British School of Archaeology
in Egypt, 1906); for Pithom/Heroonpolis as identified with Tell el-Maskhuta, see
Helck in LÄ 2, col. 406 n. 196.

28. H. E. Winlock in JEA 10 (1924):217-277. The origin of the Seventeenth
Dynasty at Thebes is unknown, but the matriarchal tendency in the family (seen in
the prominent position of several women) and other facts have suggested the
hypothesis that the dynasty was in part or in whole of Nubian origin. Donald B.
Redford, *History and Chronology of the Eighteenth Dynasty in Egypt: Seven Studies*
(Toronto: University of Toronto Press, 1967), pp. 68f.

29. These documents include the Abbott Papyrus (British Museum), the
Amherst Papyrus (Pierpont Morgan Library), and the Papyrus Leopold II (Royal
Museums of Art and History, Brussels), which is the long-missing upper half of the
Amherst Papyrus. See ARE 4, secs. 499-556; T. Eric Peet in JEA 11 (1925):37-55; J.
Capart, A. H. Gardiner, and B. van de Walle in ibid., 22 (1936):169-193.

30. The first tomb visited by the commission was that of Amunhotep I
(Eighteenth Dynasty) on "the High Ascent" (possibly a tomb discovered in
modern times on top of the Dira Abu'n-Naga hill, Erik Hornung in LÄ 1, col. 202).
But from Thutmose I onward, almost all of the kings of the New Kingdom dug
their tombs in the secluded valley behind Deir el-Bahri—now known as the Wadi
el-Biban el-Moluk, i.e., the Valley of the Tombs (literally, Doors) of the Kings—
and erected their mortuary temples on the edge of the cultivated Nile plain, where
they were worshiped as gods alongside the other Theban deities. Even in the more
inaccessible locations, however, most of the royal tombs were found and
despoiled. Accordingly, in the Twenty-first Dynasty, the high priests of Amun at
Thebes made efforts to rescue, transfer, and preserve the endangered royal
remains. In modern times, many of the mummies were found in a cache near Deir
el-Bahri and, in 1881, placed in the Cairo Museum. G. Elliot Smith, *The Royal
Mummies* (Catalogue Général des Antiquities Égyptiennes du Musée de Caire,
Nos. 61051-61100) (Cairo: Imprimerie de l'institut francais d'archéologie orientale, 1912); G. Elliot Smith and Warren R. Dawson, *Egyptian Mummies* (London:
G. Allen and Unwin, 1924).

31. Smith, *The Royal Mummies,* no. 61051, pp. 1-6, pls. 1-3.

32. Winlock in JEA 10 (1924):247-262.

33. Smith, *The Royal Mummies,* no. 61057, pp. 15-18, pls. 11-12.

34. Battiscombe Gunn and Alan H. Gardiner in JEA 5 (1918):40-45; ANET, pp.
231f.

35. Alan H. Gardiner in JEA 3 (1916):95-110; ANET, pp. 232f., 554f.

36. This is the first reference to the horse in Egyptian texts and confirms the use
of this animal by the Asiatics, even as the horse was so important thereafter in the
Asiatic campaigns of the Egyptians themselves.

CHAPTER 17. NEW KINGDOM, EIGHTEENTH DYNASTY

1. Erik Hornung,*Untersuchungen zur Chronologie und Geschichte des Neuen Reiches* (Ägyptologische Abhandlungen II) (Wiesbaden: O. Harrassowitz, 1964), p. 108. See also Edward F. Wente in JNES 34 (1975):265-272.

2. The text is on the walls of the tomb of Ahmose at el-Kab, the Egyptian Nekheb, Greek Eileithyiaspolis, on the east bank of the Nile north of Edfu. Battiscombe Gunn and Alan H. Gardiner in JEA 5 (1918):48-54; ANET, pp. 233f. For details of the war and reign of King Ahmose, see Claude Vandersleyen, *Les guerres d'Amosis, fondateur de la XVIIIe dynastie* (Monographies Reine Élisabeth 1) (Brussels: Fondation Égyptologique Reine Élisabeth, 1971); idem, LÄ 1, cols. 99-101.

3. Yigael Yadin, *The Art of Warfare in Biblical Lands in the Light of Archaeological Study*, 2 vols. (New York: McGraw-Hill, 1963), 1:86f.

4. James Henry Breasted in AJSL 25 (1908):108; George A. Reisner in JEA 6 (1920):28-55. The title designates an important position but does not necessarily mean that the viceroy was an actual son of the king. For copies of a decree addressed to Tjuroy by Thutmose I, see ARE 2, secs. 54-60.

5. ARE 2, sec. 42. The text is in the tomb of Ahmose-Pennekheb at el-Kab, and on certain statues. He himself served under Amunhotep I, Thutmose I, II, and III, and Hatshepsut.

6. William F. Edgerton, *The Thutmosid Succession* (SAOC 8) (Chicago: University of Chicago Press, 1933), p. 41.

7. ANET, p. 234; ARE 2, secs. 84f.

8. ARE 2, secs. 67-73.

9. Ibid., sec. 75.

10. Ibid., sec. 43ff. The text is in the tomb of Ineni in Western Thebes in the hill called el-Qurn ("the Horn") or, with reference to an imaginary Muslim saint, the hill of Sheikh Abd el-Qurna. Ineni served under Amunhotep I, Thutmose I, II, and III, and Hatshepsut.

11. ARE 2, sec. 106; John Romer in JEA 60 (1974):119-127. It is possible that the tomb originally excavated for Thutmose I is no. 20 in the Valley of the Kings and that it was Thutmose III who removed the mummy of Thutmose I to a new tomb, no. 38. The latter tomb is at the very end of the main valley, but was plundered long ago and is badly damaged and now inaccessible, although it still contains the sarcophagus of Thutmose I. Presumably the mortuary temple of Thutmose I was somewhere on the edge of the plain, but it has not been found, although a wooden door panel from the temple is in the Metropolitan Museum of Art.

12. Norman de Garis Davies, *Two Ramesside Tombs at Thebes* (Metropolitan Museum of Art Egyptian Expedition, Robb de Peyster Teytus Memorial Series 5) (New York, 1927), pp. 3-30, pls. 1-19, especially pp. 22-24, pls. 16-17; Nina M. Davies, *La peinture égyptienne ancienne* (Paris: A. Guillot, 1953), see the picture "Le grand-prêtre Userhêt."

13. ARE 2, secs. 108, 116.

14. Ibid., secs. 119-122.

15. Ibid., sec. 125.

16. For his mummy, see G. Elliot Smith, *The Royal Mummies* (Catalogue Général des Antiquités Égyptiennes du Musée du Caire, Nos. 61051-61100) (Cairo: Imprimerie de l'institut français d'archéologie orientale, 1912), no. 61066, pp. 28-31, pls. 23-24.

17. ARE 2, secs. 118, 341.

18. The tomb was in the necropolis area two to three kilometers west of Deir el-Bahri and the Valley of the Kings, and has been found at the extreme inner end of a small, steep-sided valley (Wadi e'Taqa e'Zeide, "the valley of the window of Zeide"), almost two-thirds of the way up an almost vertical cliff 112 meters high. Howard Carter in JEA 4 (1917):107-118, especially pp. 108, 114-118, pls. 19, no. 22, 20).

19. Labib Habachi in JNES 16 (1957):99-104.

20. ARE 2, secs. 290, 359-368.

21. William C. Hayes in JEA 36 (1950):19-23.

22. ARE 2, secs. 391ff.; ANET, pp. 234-241.

23. ARE 2, secs. 408-443, 548f., 554; R. O. Faulkner in JEA 28 (1942):2-15. For the Karnak "map" of the military route from Tjel/Sile to Raphia, see Chapter 18, n. 9.

24. ARE 2, secs. 406, 463-467, 476-487, 528-539.

25. G. A. Reisner and M. B. Reisner in ZÄS 69 (1933):24-39. For the rock of Gebel Barkal, see Breasted in AJSL 25 (1908):30f., figs. 19-20; M. F. Laming Macadam in JEA 32 (1946), pl. 11 bottom, facing p. 64.

26. Hermann Junker in JEA 7 (1921):121-132.

27. Of Thutmose III's four Theban obelisks, none remains at Karnak, but one was taken to Constantinople and erected on the spine of the hippodrome by Theodosius I in 390. The upper portion still stands there in Istanbul (ARE 2, secs. 629-631). A fifth obelisk was brought to Thebes for Thutmose III but only erected and inscribed by his grandson Thutmose IV; in 357 this obelisk was taken to Rome and erected in the Circus Maximus by Constantius II, and is now at the Lateran (ibid., secs. 626-628, 830-838).

28. Kazimierz Michalowski, *The Art of Ancient Egypt* (London: Thames and Hudson, 1969), figs. 90, 91, 100.

29. Smith, *The Royal Mummies,* no. 61068, pp. 32-36, pl. 28.

30. If the fourth year of Solomon was 967/966 (reckoning his forty-year reign to the disruption of the kingdom in 931/930 [Edwin R. Thiele, *The Mysterious Numbers of the Hebrew Kings,* rev. ed. (Grand Rapids, Mich.: Eerdmans, 1965), pp. 52f.]) and if this was the 480th year after the people of Israel came out of Israel (1 Kings 6:1), the date of the exodus would be 1447/1446, in the reign of Thutmose III. J. W. Jack, *The Date of the Exodus* (Edinburgh: T. and T. Clark, 1925), pp. 200-202; Merrill F. Unger, *Archaeology and the Old Testament* (Grand Rapids, Mich.: Zondervan, 1954), p. 141; Siegfried H. Horn in BAR 3 (1977):22ff. But a

different understanding of 1 Kings 6:1 is possible (see Chapter 18, n. 45).

31. P. E. Newberry, *The Life of Rekhmara* (Westminster: A. Constable, 1900); ARE 2, secs. 663-762; Norman de Garis Davies, *Paintings from the Tomb of Rekh-mi-Rē ᶜat Thebes* and *The Tomb of Rekh-mi-Rē ᶜat Thebes* (Metropolitan Museum of Art Egyptian Expedition, 10, 11), 2 vols. (New York: Plantin Press, 1939, 1943). From texts in this tomb and in the tombs of several other persons who occupied the same position, it is evident that the vizier exercised very extensive powers, being administrator, judge, and superintendent of public works.

32. For the making of bricks, see Charles F. Nims in BA 13 (1950):22-28.

33. The coregency has been variously estimated at about four months (Alan H. Gardiner in JEA 31 [1945]:27), one and one-half years (Donald B. Redford in JNES 25 [1966]:124), or two and one-third years (Donald B. Redford in JEA 51 [1965]:107-122; Richard A. Parker in *Studies in Honor of John A. Wilson* [SAOC 35] [Chicago: University of Chicago Press, 1969], pp. 75-82).

34. S. Hassan in ASAE 37 (1937):129-134. On the Egyptian kings in the role of sportsman, see B. Van de Walle in CÉ 26 (1935):234-257.

35. ANET, pp. 245-247.

36. E. Naville, *The XIth Dynasty Temple at Deir el-Bahari*, 3 vols. (London: Egypt Exploration Fund, 1907), 1, pl. 27.

37. Smith, *The Royal Mummies*, no. 61069, pp. 36-38.

38. Davies, *La peinture égyptienne ancienne*, see the picture "Le repas quotidien dans la tombe."

39. Amarna Letters, no. 29, ll. 16-18.

40. ARE 2, sec. 818.

41. Alan W. Shorter in JEA 17 (1931):23-25, pl. 4, figs. 3, 5.

42. James B. Pritchard in BASOR 122 (1951):36-41; Davies, *La peinture égyptienne ancienne*, see the pictures "Porteurs syriens d'offrandes," "Les serviteurs de la maison de Sebkhotpe," "La pêche et la chasse dans les marais," "Jeunes filles offrant des fleurs et des fruits," and "Chasse aux oiseaux sauvages dans les marécages"; idem, *Egyptian Tomb Paintings: From Originals Mainly of the Eighteenth Dynasty in the British Museum and the Bankes Collection* (Faber Gallery of Oriental Art) (London: Faber and Faber, 1958), pls. 3, 4.

43. ARE 2, sec. 862.

44. T. M. Davis, G. Maspero, and P. E. Newberry, *The Tomb of Iouiya and Touiyou* (London: Constable, 1907); John A. Wilson, *Signs and Wonders upon Pharaoh: A History of American Egyptology* (Chicago: University of Chicago Press, 1964), pp. 116f.

45. Christiane Desroches-Noblecourt, *Tutankhamen* (New York: New York Graphic Society, 1963), p. 116 and figs. 56, 57.

46. Ibid., fig. 72; Cyril Aldred, *Akhenaten, Pharaoh of Egypt: A New Study* (New York: McGraw-Hill, 1968), pls. 22, 69; idem, *Akhenaten und Nefertiti* (New York: Brooklyn Museum in association with Viking Press, 1973), p. 105, no. 19.

47. Erik Hornung in LÄ 1, col. 207. On several kohl-tubes of glazed faience (one probably from Malkata, now in the Metropolitan Museum of Art),

Amunhotep III and Sitamun are named together; she is called not only daughter but also wife of the king. Thus the king may have married his daughter. Yet in this and other similar cases *wife* may have been only an honorary title. Schafiq Allam in LÄ 2, cols. 109f.

48. Desroches-Noblecourt, *Tutankhamen,* pp. 120f., fig. 60, table, and p. 133; Aldred, *Akhenaten,* pp. 97-99. Instead of Queen Tiy, it has also been suggested that Sitamun, oldest daughter of Amunhotep III and Queen Tiy, might have been the mother of Smenkhkare and Tutankhamun. Serological study of the mummies of Yuya, Thuyu, and Amunhotep III is held to allow for the latter possibility, but still to favor Queen Tiy for the position of mother. R. C. Connolly, R. G. Harrison, and Soheir Ahmed in JEA 62 (1976):184-186.

49. ARE 2, sec. 896. On an inscribed block originally in a different small temple but now recovered from where it was reused in the Second Pylon of the large Karnak temple, King Ay (who succeeded Tutankhamun) apparently states that he built the temple "as his monument for his son" Tutankhamun. This is basis for the different, but less likely, theory that through otherwise unknown children, Amunhotep III and Queen Tiy and Ay and his wife Tiy (the same name as that of Queen Tiy) were respectively the maternal and paternal grandparents (taking "father" to mean grandfathers, and "son" to mean grandson) of Smenkhkare and Tutankhamun. Keith C. Seele in JNES 14 (1955):168-180. Ay was in fact an important official of Amunhotep IV, was probably a member of a branch of the royal family, and used the title "father of the god," probably meaning, as in the case of Yuya, father-in-law of the pharaoh. In the tomb of Ay at Amarna (no. 25), his wife Tiy is called the nurse of princess Nefertiti, who became the wife of Amunhotep IV, and the circumstances can be reasonably explained by the supposition of the death of a previous wife of Ay, who was the mother of Nefertiti. Aldred, *Akhenaten,* pp. 90-92; idem, *Akhenaten and Nefertiti,* pp. 19f.

50. Desroches-Noblecourt, *Tutankhamen,* pp. 88f., 294, pl. 3a; James E. Harris as reported in the *New York Times,* October 14, 1976, p. 18.

51. An inscription on the rocks of the small island of Konosso at the north end of the island of Philae records a campaign in Kush (ARE 2, sec. 845), a stela speaks of "smiting Naharin" (ibid., sec. 858), and a scarab calls the king the "captor of Shinar" (ibid., sec. 859). But some of this may be boast, and at least in relation to Mesopotamia, the information in the Amarna Letters about his marriages with Asiatic princesses is better evidence about what actually transpired.

52. The name Malkata is from Arabic *el-malkat,* meaning "the place where things are picked up." Medinet Habu, site of the mortuary temple of Ramses III, derives its name from a village of the Christian era, deserted after the Arab invasion (cf. Deir el-Medinah, the "monastery of the city," to the north). For the architecture at Malkata, see Alexander Badawy, *A History of Egyptian Architecture,* 4 vols. (Giza: Studio Misr, 1954ff.), 3, pp. 47-52.

53. ARE 2, secs. 868f.; William C. Hayes in JNES 10 (1951): 35-56, 82-111, 156-183, 231-242.

54. Cf. Strabo 17. 1. 46; Pausanias, *Description of Greece* 1. 42. 3; Philostratus, *Life*

of *Apollonius of Tyana* 6. 4; Alan Gardiner in JEA 47 (1961):91-99.

55. ARE 2, secs. 878-892.

56. Colin Campbell, *The Miraculous Birth of Amon-hotep III and Other Egyptian Studies* (Edinburgh: Oliver and Boyd, 1912); H. R. Hall in JEA 1 (1914):230f.

57. For Thebes at this time, see Elizabeth Riefstahl, *Thebes in the Time of Amunhotep III* (Norman: University of Oklahoma Press, 1964).

58. M. F. Laming Macadam, *The Temples of Kawa*, 4 vols. (Oxford: Oxford University Press, 1949-1955), vol. 2, *History and Archaeology of the Site*, pt. 2, *Text*, pp. 12-14.

59. Smith, *The Royal Mummies*, no. 61074, pp. 46-51, pls. 31-35, 100-103.

60. Wolfgang Helck in LÄ 1, cols. 219-221.

61. ANET, p. 368; cf. Jean Sainte Fare Garnot in JEA 35 (1949):63-68; H. M. Steward in JEA 46 (1960):83-90.

62. Both the name the Book of the Dead and the customary division of the materials into numbered chapters or "spells" derive from the publication by Richard Lepsius in 1842 of a Turin papyrus that contained 165 chapters in his reckoning. Now more than 190 chapters are known. Of the illustrated copies, the finest is the Papyrus of Ani (early Nineteenth Dynasty). See E. A. Wallis Budge, *The Book of the Dead: The Chapters of Coming Forth by Day*, 3 vols. (London: K. Paul, Trench, Trübner, 1898); idem, *The Book of the Dead: An English Translation*, 2d ed. (London: K. Paul, Trench, Trübner, 1938); idem, *The Papyrus of Ani* (New York: Putnam, 1913); idem, *The Book of the Dead* (London: Trustees of the British Museum, 1920); Thomas George Allen, *The Egyptian Book of the Dead: Documents in the Oriental Institute at the University of Chicago* (OIP 82) (Chicago: University of Chicago Press, 1960); Albert Champdor, *The Book of the Dead, Based on the Ani, Hunefer, and Anhaï Papyri in the British Museum* (New York: Garrett Publications 1966); Thomas George Allen and Elizabeth Blaisdell Hauser, *The Book of the Dead or Going Forth by Day* (SAOC 37) (Chicago: University of Chicago Press, 1975).

63. Among the Underworld books of the New Kingdom, the oldest has the Egyptian title—Writing of the Hidden Room—and is known in the sixteenth century. A second has no Egyptian title but is given the modern name the Book of Gates and is known in the fourteenth century. A third is yet later and is now called the Book of Hell. Of these, the Writing of the Hidden Room is itself often simply called the Amduat. The oldest illustration of the Amduat comes from the walls of the burial chamber of Thutmose I (fragments in the Cairo Museum). Relatively complete examples of the work are in the tomb chambers of Thutmose III, Amunhotep II, and Amunhotep III, and later copies are found down into the third century B.C.E. Of the Book of Gates, the oldest example is in the tomb of Horemheb. See Erik Hornung, *Altägyptische Höllenvorstellungen* (Abhandlungen der sächsischen Akademie der Wissenschaften zu Leipzig, phil.-hist. Kl. 59, 3) (Berlin: Akademie-Verlag, 1968); idem, LÄ 2, cols. 184-188, 994f.

64. Hornung, *Untersuchungen zur Chronologie und Geschichte des Neuen Reiches*, p. 81.

65. Steffen Wenig in LÄ 1, col. 214.

66. Such unflattering portrayal could hardly have been executed except with royal approval. In fact, on a stela in the British Museum, a certain Bek is met who was Chief Sculptor to Amunhotep IV—even as his own father had served in the same capacity under Amunhotep III. Bek here calls himself "the apprentice" of the king. In an inscription at Aswan, he says that he was taught by the king himself. Once the naturalistic image of the ruler had been created, however, there was evidently a tendency among the artists to accept the features of this image as a new canon of art and to carry over similar traits in their portrayals of other persons of the same time.

67. The head is sometimes thought to be not of Nefertiti but of one of her daughters, perhaps Meretaten or Ankhesenpaaten. F. J. Giles, *Ikhnaton: Legend and History* (London: Hutchinson, 1970), p. 9, pl. 3.

68. Wilfried Seipel in LÄ 1, cols. 262f.

69. Erik Hornung, *Der Eine und die Vielen: Ägyptische Gottesvorstellungen* (Darmstadt: Wissenschaftliche Buchgesellschaft, 1973), pp. 240-246.

70. R. W. Smith in NGM 138 (1970):634-655; Donald B. Redford in *Archaeology* 28 (1975):16-22. For a similar scene of the king and queen under the radiating Sun Disk in the tomb (no. 55) of the vizier Ramose at Qurna, see ARE 2, secs. 936-948.

71. The often-used longer name of Tell el-Amarna combined the names of et-Till, a village to the north, and of the Beni Amran, a Bedouin tribe in the district. For a remarkable rectangular gap in the otherwise uniform line of the eastern cliffs, a gap that might have contributed to the selection of this site for the "Horizon of the Aten," see Cyril Aldred in JEA 62 (1976):184.

72. ARE 2, sec. 949-972.

73. Wenig in LÄ 1, cols. 213, 218 n. 37. On Stela "S," dated in Year 6, it is stated, "On this day was founded Akhetaten for the living Aten, that favor and love might be received, on behalf of King Akhenaten"; Year 6 therefore evidently marked the anniversary of the founding of the new capital.

74. Nefertiti also added to her name the epithet Neferneferuaten ("Fair is the Goodness of the Aten"). ARE 2, sec. 959.

75. W. M. Flinders Petrie, *Seventy Years in Archaeology* (London: S. Low, Marston and Co., 1931), pp. 134-145; idem, *Tell el Amarna* (1884; reprint ed. Warminster: Aris and Phillips, 1974); T. Eric Peet, C. Leonard Woolley, H. Frankfort, and J. D. S. Pendlebury, *The City of Akhenaten,* 4 vols. (London: Memoirs of the Egypt Exploration Society 38, 40, 44, 1923-1951); J. D. S. Pendlebury, *Tell el-Amarna* (London: L. Dickson and Thompson, 1935); F. von Bissing, *Der Fussboden aus dem Palaste des Königs Amenophis IV zu el Hawata im Museum zu Kairo* (Munich: F. Bruckmann, 1941). The main thoroughfare was a road running along the Nile, probably in use long before Akhenaten. In Arabic, it is known as the Sikket el-Sultan ("Road of the Monarch"); the excavators called it the Royal Road. The three parts of the city were the North Suburb, the Central City, and the South City, the built-up area being nine kilometers in length and one kilometer in width. The plans of buildings were traced by the excavators from the foundation trenches and from the practice of the original architects of covering an

area with lime plaster and marking on it in black the lines of the walls. In the north were a Palace of Nefertiti and the North Palace, thought to have been a royal rest house combined with a zoological garden in which the specimens of animal life were viewed in the Aten cult as symbols of the work of the Creator. In the center of the city, called "the Island," were the Royal Palace and the Great Temple. A bridge over the royal road connected the two parts of the palace and probably contained the "window of appearances," at which the king and queen showed themselves on special occasions. Barry J. Kemp in JEA 62 (1976):81-99. On walls, floors, and columns, frescoes and carvings showed plants, wildlife, and scenes in the life of the king and his family. The Great Temple was no doubt the Per-Aten ("House of Aten") and its first part the Per-Hai ("House of Rejoicing" for the Aten), spoken of in the boundary stelas. E. P. Uphill in JNES 29 (1970):151-166; Jan Assmann in JNES 31 (1972):143-155. The second part was called Gematen ("Finding Aten"), the same name as that of the temple at Kawa. Characteristic of this and of other Aten temples are the facts that there was no place for an image of the deity, that the temple was for the most part open to the sky (hypethral), and that there were many altars upon which the sun's rays fell. Jan Assmann in LÄ 1, col. 541. In the southern part of the city, a religious building called Maru-Aten provided a "Viewing Place of the Aten." Alexander Badawy in JEA 42 (1956):58-64. There also were the residences of various important persons, including the mansion of Nakht, Akhenaten's vizier in Amarna, and the house of the sculptor Thutmose, in which were found the famous head usually thought to be that of Nefertiti, as well as portraits of Amunhotep III, Akhenaten, and many others. Badawy, *A History of Egyptian Architecture* 3:75ff.

76. There was also to be a tomb for Mnevis, the sacred bull of Heliopolis, which, as an incarnation of the sun god, was evidently at the time still acceptable within the Aten cult. There is evidence too (e.g., in the Tomb of Ramose [no. 55] at Qurna in Western Thebes, cf. immediately above n. 70) for the place of Maat, daughter of Re and therefore an emanation of the sun god, in Atenism. Rudolf Anthes, *Die Maat des Echnaton von Amarna* (JAOS 72) (Baltimore: American Oriental Society, 1952, Supplement 14). Apparently, however, the appearance of Maat and of Mnevis in the cult was only early; later these figures are not found, scenes connected with Amun were obliterated, and even the word *gods* (in the plural) was erased on various monuments. Arthur Weigall, *The Life and Times of Akhnaton Pharaoh of Egypt,* rev. ed. (London: Butterworth, 1922), p. 117.

77. Ay later constructed a second tomb for himself (no. 23) in the Valley of the Kings in Western Thebes.

78. James Henry Breasted, *The Dawn of Conscience* (New York: Charles Scribner's Sons, 1933), pp. 281-286; ANET, pp. 369-371. In a number of phrases, the language is comparable to that of Ps. 104. For varying assessments of the religion of Akhenaten, see Leslie A. White in JAOS 68 (1948):91-114; Assmann in JNES 31 (1972):155; John A. Wilson in JNES 32 (1973):235-241. Since biblical tradition attributes monotheistic doctrine (Exod. 20:2f.; Deut. 6:4, etc.) and life in Egypt to Moses, it has been thought that Moses lived in the time of Akhenaten and

was associated with him. Sigmund Freud, *Moses and Monotheism* (New York: A. A. Knopf, 1939), pp. 26-40; Tertius Chandler, *Godly Kings and Early Ethics* (Hicksville, N.Y.: Exposition Press, 1976), pp. 27f. But the antecedents to which Moses himself appealed (Exod. 3:6, etc.) were those of the patriarchal period, and it was presumably from those sources that the distinctive Israelite heritage was most directly derived. William F. Albright, *The Biblical Period* (Pittsburgh: privately distributed, 1950), p. 9, reprinted from Louis Finkelstein, ed., *The Jews, Their History, Culture and Religion* (New York: Harper and Brothers, 1949); idem, *From the Stone Age to Christianity*, 2d ed. (Garden City, N.Y.: Doubleday, 1957), pp. 196-207.

79. The Amarna Letters, some 350 clay tablets inscribed in cuneiform, were found by chance in 1887 in what were established later to be the ruins of the office of palace records at Akhetaten. Now in museums in Berlin, Cairo, London, and Oxford (J. A. Knudtzon, *Die El-Amarna Tafeln*, 2 vols. [Leipzig: J. C. Hinrichs, 1908-1915]; Samuel A. B. Mercer, *The Tell El-Amarna Tablets*, 2 vols. [Toronto: Macmillan Co. of Canada]; ANET, pp. 483-490), the documents are for the most part in Akkadian, the main language of international communication of the time. They consist of originals and copies of correspondence between Babylonian, Hittite, and Mitannian rulers, and vassal princes and governors in Syria, Phoenicia, and Palestine, and Amunhotep III and Amunhotep IV (Akhenaten) in Egypt.

80. In one of the scenes, the two kings bestow gestures of affection upon each other, and in inscriptions Smenkhkare is named the "Beloved of Akhenaten." Percy E. Newberry in JEA 14 (1928):9, pl. 4, 1; Aldred, *Akhenaten*, pp. 243f., pls. 68, 81, 82.

81. The mummy in question was first taken for female and supposed to be that of Queen Tiy. T. M. Davis, G. Maspero et al., *The Tomb of Queen Tïyi* (London: Constable, 1910). But it was later determined to be the remains of a young man less than twenty-five years old. Then it was considered that it might be Akhenaten. Alan Gardiner in JEA 43 (1957):10-25. But it did not exhibit the bodily peculiarities emphasized in the portraits of this king. R. G. Harrison in ibid., 52 (1966):95-119. The skull, however, is similar to that of Tutankhamun, and the mummy is now thought to be that of Smenkhkare. Wenig in LÄ 1, col. 214.

82. Seele in JNES 14 (1955):179 and n. 63.

83. Desroches-Noblecourt, *Tutankhamen*, pp. 136, 181. The name Tutankhaten plainly contains the word *ankh* and the name Aten, but it is explained variously, e.g., "all life is in the hands of the Aten." The name Tutankhamun of course honors the god Amun in similar fashion.

84. John Bennett in JEA 25 (1939):8-15; ANET, pp. 251f.

85. Bennett in JEA 25 (1939):12 n. 25.

86. For the present-day Muslim feast of Abu el-Haggag at Luxor as still reflecting the ancient Feast of Opet, see Charles F. Nims, *Thebes of the Pharaohs: Pattern for Every City* (London: Elek Books, 1965), pp. 122, 127.

87. ARE 2, secs. 1019-1041. Nekhen is identified with el-Kab, north of the First Cataract, and the distance to Napata (equated with Karoy in the text) in the Sudan

is 1,300 kilometers, a considerable territory to administer.

88. Howard Carter, *The tombe of Tut-ankh-Amen,* 2 vols. (New York: George H. Doran, 1923-1927); Charles Breasted, *Pioneer to the Past* (New York: Charles Scribner's Sons, 1943), pp. 327-373; Christine Desroches-Noblecourt, *Toutank-hamon et sons temps* (Musée de Petit Palais), 2d ed. (Paris: Réunion des musées nationaux, 1967); I. E. S. Edwards, *The Treasures of Tutankhamun* (New York: Viking Press, 1972). The tomb is across a narrow valley from the Tomb of Tiy, discovered by Theodore M. Davis in 1907. In 1908, Davis uncovered a cache of materials in the vicinity, left over from the funeral of Tutankhamun, but he did not detect the tomb itself and expressed the opinion that the possibilities of the valley were exhausted.

89. For the ceremony of "the opening of the mouth," performed with an instrument of flint, copper, or iron and intended to restore the deceased to the normal condition of a living person, see Aylward M. Blackman in JEA 10 (1924):47-59; T. J. C. Baly in ibid., 16 (1930):173-186; A. M. Blackman and H. W. Fairman in ibid., 32 (1946):75-91; Champdor, *The Book of the Dead,* pp. 152f.

90. For family relationships, see above in the present chapter n. 49.

91. The stela of the third year was found by the Great Pyramid and is in the Cairo Museum. ARE 2, secs. 1042f.

92. Ibid., 3, secs. 22-32; Alan Gardiner in JEA 39 (1953):13-31; ARE 3, secs. 1-21; ANET, pp. 250f.; H. E. Winlock in JEA 10 (1924):1-5. For the discovery and excavation of the tomb at Saqqara, see Geoffrey T. Martin in ibid., 62 (1976):5-13. For the name of Horemheb, see Keith C. Seele in JNES 4 (1945):234-239.

93. ARE 3, sec. 11. In one case, two Asiatics prostrate themselves, one on his face and the other on his back, literally illustrating the language of the Amarna Letters (no. 232, cf. 233): "At the feet of the king, my lord, the sun of heaven, seven times and seven times I bow down with belly and back."

94. Gardiner in JEA 39 (1953):15f., ll. 14-25; ARE 3, secs. 45-67; Donald B. Redford in BASOR 211 (1973):36-49.

95. Erik Hornung and Frank Teichmann, *Das Grab des Horemhab im Tal der Könige* (Bern: Francke Verlag, 1971), pp. 30f., pls. 23-61.

96. Miriam Lichtheim in JNES 4 (1945):178-212. Tomb no. 50 of Neferhotep at Qurna is not to be confused with Tomb no. 49 at Assasif in Western Thebes, the tomb of another priest named Neferhotep, who also has the same title of "the god's father of Amun." Famous portrayals of the "blind harper" are to be seen in reliefs from the tomb of Paatenemheb at Saqqara in the reign of Akhenaten (in the Leiden Museum) and from the tomb of Tjanefer in Western Thebes in the time of Ramses II (in the Berlin Museum).

CHAPTER 18. NEW KINGDOM (CONTINUED), NINETEENTH AND TWENTIETH DYNASTIES

1. W. F. Albright in JNES 5 (1946):15, no. 25; M. B. Rowton in JEA 34 (1948):71 n. 1; Wolfgang Helck, *Untersuchungen zu Manetho und den ägyptischen*

Königslisten (Untersuchungen zur Geschichte und Altertumskunde Ägyptens 18) (Berlin: Akademie Verlag, 1956), pp. 41-46.

2. ARE 4, sec. 471.

3. Erik Hornung, *Untersuchungen zur Chronologie und Geschichte des Neuen Reiches* (Ägyptologische Abhandlungen 11) (Wiesbaden: O. Harrassowitz, 1964), p. 108; cf. Rowton in JEA 34 (1948):57-74; Richard A. Parker in JNES 16 (1957):42f.; Donald B. Redford, *History and Chronology of the Eighteenth Dynasty in Egypt: Seven Studies* (Toronto: University of Toronto Press), p. 208. For the first year of Ramses II as 1304, see M. B. Rowton in JNES 19 (1960):15-22; for the real choice as being between 1290 and 1279, see K. A. Kitchen in JEA 61 (1975):266.

4. Kurt Sethe in ZÄS 65 (1930):85-89; Jürgen von Beckerath, *Tanis und Theben: Historische Grundlagen der Ramessidenzeit in Ägypten* (Ägyptologische Forschungen 16) (Glückstadt: J. J. Augustin, 1951), pp. 38-41; ANET, pp. 252f.; ANEP, fig. 555, cf. 485, 487.

5. ARE 3, secs. 74-79.

6. Ibid., secs. 88, 103, 111, 141, etc.

7. R. O. Faulkner in JEA 33 (1947):34-39.

8. ARE 3, secs. 132, 134.

9. In the text, the route is described as "starting from the fortress of Tjel, to the Canaan"; in the pictures, a long line of forts and wells or sheets of water is shown. At the boundary between Egypt and the desert, there is a crocodile-infested reed-lined canal called the Dividing Waters and on the desert side, the fortress of Tjel is shown as a large tower. On the further way are such places as the Migdol of Menmare, the Castle of Menmare, watering places called Nakhes and Hebret, and, finally, a town whose name is missing. Several of the same names occur in a passage in Papyrus Anastasi I (B.M. 10247), which begins with the Ways of Horus and extends, after Nekhes and Hebret, to Raphia and Gaza. Therefore, Raphia may be the name missing at the end of the Karnak relief. Tjel is also known as the residence city of Lower Egyptian Nome XIV ("Point of the East"), is called Sile in the Roman itineraries, and is almost certainly to be identified with Tell Abu Seifeh, two kilometers east of modern Qantarah (the starting point, when it was in operation, of the modern railroad to Palestine). Raphia is modern Rafa, thirty-two kilometers short of Gaza, and it was noted above that Thutmose III covered the 200 miles from Qantarah to Gaza in ten days of marching. For this famous coastal road and the Karnak reliefs of Seti I, see ibid., secs. 80-156; ANET, pp. 254f., 477f.; Carl Küthmann, *Die Ostgrenze Ägyptens* (Leipzig: W. Drugulin, 1911), pp. 5, 38-40; Alan H. Gardiner in JEA 6 (1920):99-116, with pl. 13, sketch map of the coast region between Egypt and Palestine; W. F. Albright in JEA 10 (1924):6f.; R. O. Faulkner in ibid., 33 (1947):34f.

10. G. Elliot Smith, *The Royal Mummies* (Catalogue Général des Antiquités Égyptiennes du Musée de Caire, Nos. 61051-61100) (Cairo: Imprimerie de l'institut français d'archéologie orientale, 1912), no. 61077, pp. 57-59, pls. 38, 40, 41, and Frontispiece.

11. Keith C. Seele, *The Coregency of Ramses II with Seti I* (Chicago: University of Chicago Press, 1940); William J. Murnane in JNES 34 (1975):153-190.

12. ARE 3, secs. 251-281.

13. For the dedicatory and building texts of Ramses II in the Luxor temple, see Mahmud Abd el-Razik in JEA 60 (1974):142-160; ibid., 61 (1975):125-136.

14. Diodorus (1. 47-49) calls the king Osymandyas, a name presumably derived from Ramses II's prenomen Usermare, and gives an extended description of this temple, for which he cites Hecataeus of Abdera (early third century B.C.E.). Oswyn Murray in JEA 56 (1970):141-171; M. Stern and Oswyn Murray in ibid., 59 (1973):159-168.

15. Walter B. Emery, *Egypt in Nubia* (London: Hutchinson, 1965), p. 194 and fig. 1, map of the Nile valley, and fig. 2, map of Nubia.

16. ARE 2, sec. 501; Christiane Desroches-Noblecourt and Ch. Kuentz, *Le petit temple d'Abou Simbel,* 2 vols. (Cairo: Centre de documentation et d'étude sur l'ancienne Égypte, 1968).

17. For Memphis, see ARE 3, secs. 260, 412f. For the sites in Wadi Tumilat, see Chapter 16, n. 27.

18. ARE 3, secs. 449-457, 458-477.

19. Alan Rowe in BJRL 36 (1953-1954):128-145, 484-500; G. A. Wainwright in JEA 48 (1962):89-99.

20. ARE 3, sec. 297.

21. Ibid., secs. 305-351; John A. Wilson in AJSL 43 (1927):266-287; ANET, pp. 255f.

22. ARE 3, secs. 352ff.; ANET, p. 256.

23. ARE 3, secs. 367-391; S. Langdon and Alan H. Gardiner in JEA 6 (1920):179-205; ANET, pp. 199-201.

24. The marriage of Ramses II and Maatnefrure is recorded on stelas at Karnak, Elephantine, and Abu Simbel. ARE 3, secs. 415-424; ANET, pp. 257f. At Abu Simbel, the inscription is accompanied by a relief showing the Hittite king and his daughter; at Tanis, there is a small statue of the queen beside the colossus of Ramses II.

25. British Museum Papyrus Anastasi III (no. 10246, from the reign of Ramses II), II (no. 10243, from the reign of Merneptah), and IV (no. 10249, attributed to the first year of Seti II). See Alan H. Gardiner in JEA 5 (1918):184-186; ANET, pp. 470f.

26. In a long geographical inscription at Edfu, the Shi-Hor ("Waters of Horus") is the "river" of Lower Egyptian Nome XIV ("Point of the East"). A king pours out libations, and the legend reads: "These thy libations come forth from Elephantine, they arrive at Waters of Horus, that thou mayest drink of them." This means that the Nile is offered to the god in its full course, from Elephantine in the south to its northernmost reach in the Waters of Horus; the latter must therefore be the Pelusiac branch, or possibly the Tanitic, and the related canals and lakes, from which Per-Ramses could be reached and provided with rushes and salt. Gardiner in JEA 5 (1918):251f.; ibid., 19 (1953):126. In biblical usage, the Shihor is a name of the Nile or a part of it (Isa. 23:3; Jer. 2:18) and represents the border of Egypt on the side toward Israel (Josh. 13:3; 1 Chron. 13:5).

As for the "reed-thicket" mentioned along with the Shi-Hor in the Egyptian text, the word for "reed is _twf,_ and the Hebrew equivalent is _suph,_ which occurs in Exod. 13:18 in _yam suph,_ rendered as "Red Sea" in the LXX, but properly "sea of reeds." W. F. Albright, _The Vocalization of the Egyptian Syllabic Orthography_ (New Haven: American Oriental Society, 1934), p. 65.

27. K. A. Kitchen, _Ancient Orient and Old Testament_ (Philadelphia: American Philosophical Society, 1944), pp. 57-59. The Israelites also labored at Pithom, probably Tell el-Maskhuta in Wadi Tumilat (cf. Chapter 16, n. 27), and (according to the LXX) at On (Heliopolis). Ramses II built at both places.

28. Jürgen von Beckerath, _Untersuchungen zur politischen Geschichte der Zweiten Zwischenzeit in Ägypten_ (Ägyptologische Forschungen 23) (Glückstadt: J. J. Augustin, 1964), map of the eastern Nile Delta, facing p. 158.

29. Inscriptions of Ramses II were found at Qantir by Edouard Naville in 1885 and by F. Ll. Griffith in 1886. Edouard Naville, _The Shrine of Saft el Henneh and the Land of Goshen_ (London: Egypt Exploration Fund, 1887), pp. 21-23; W.M. Flinders Petrie, _Tanis,_ pt. 2 (London: Trübner, 1886); idem, _Nebesheh (Am) and Defenneh (Tahpanhes)_ (London: Trübner, 1888), pp. 45f. Systematic excavations were begun by Mahmud Hamza in 1928. Hamza in ASAE 30 (1930):31-68.

30. Hamza in ASAE 30 (1930):41f. and pl. 3D; William C. Hayes, _Glazed Tiles from a Palace of Ramesses II at Kantīr_ (Metropolitan Museum of Art Papers 3) (New York, 1937).

31. Hamza in ASAE 30 (1930):43-45. One text on the ostraca mentions "wine of the garden"; therefore, the fragments are probably pieces of broken wine jars. It can be objected that the jars might have been brought from elsewhere (Gardiner in JEA 19 [1933]:128), but the probability is rather that they represent the site where they were found, and may even mark the place of wine cellars and storerooms of the royal palace.

32. In 1885 Naville (_The Shrine of Saft el Henneh and the Land of Goshen,_ pp. 21f.) found at Khataᶜna fragmentary monuments with the names of Amunemhet I, Sesostris III, and Queen Sobknofru (Twelfth Dynasty), and a piece of enameled pottery with cartouches of Seti I. In 1942 Labib Habachi (in ASAE 52 [1954]:448-470) found the remains of a large building constructed by Amunemhet I and restored by Sesostris III, and statues of Queen Sobknofru.

33. Manfred Bietak in LÄ 1, col. 913. The ancient name of Khataᶜna may have been Ro-wati, signifying a place where two roads came together, in this case perhaps one from Qantarah along the eastern edge of the Delta, and another that turned off here and went to Tanis or into the center of the Delta. Von Beckerath, _Untersuchungen zur politischen Geschichte der Zweiten Zwischenzeit,_ pp. 155-157.

34. In the Travels of Wenamun, this personage went from Thebes to Djanet and from there by ship "on the great Syrian sea" to ports in Palestine and Syria (ANET, p. 26). At Djanet, a certain Nesubenebded was ruler, and he appears in Manetho as Smendes, the first of the seven kings of Tanis who comprised the Twenty-first Dynasty. Therefore the Egyptian Djanet was the Greek Tanis. The same name is recognizable in Assyrian Saᶜnu (ARAB 2, secs. 771, 844) and Hebrew

Zoan (Num. 13:22; Ps. 78:12, 43; Isa. 19:11, 13; 30:4; Ezek. 30:14; LXX Tanis) and survives in Arabic San, as also in Coptic Ga'ne. For Tanis excavations reports, see above Chapter 16, n. 22; for the history of Tanis, see Hermann Kees, "Tanis," *Nachrichten von der Akademie der Wissenschaften in Göttingen* (phil.-hist. Kl.), 1944, no. 7, pp. 145-182.

35. Since Tanis was the capital of the Twenty-first Dynasty, it has been suggested that the monuments of Ramses II might have been transported thither at that time, but in view of the magnitude of the objects and the relatively weak status of those kings, that is little likely. Von Beckerath, *Untersuchungen zur politischen Geschichte der Zweiten Zwischenzeit,* pp. 158f.

36. Albrecht Alt in *Festschrift für Friedrich Zucker zum 70. Geburtstage* (Berlin: Akademie-Verlag, 1954), pp. 3-13. If Qantir and Tanis were distinctive parts of Ramses II's city, it could explain the fact that Per-Ramses and Djanet are listed separately in some sources, including the Golénischeff Glossary. Gardiner in JEA 5 (1918):198f., no. 38.

37. Smith, *The Royal Mummies,* no. 61078, pp. 59-65, pls. 42-44.

38. ARE 3, sec. 267; W. M. Flinders Petrie, *A History of Egypt,* 3 vols. (New York: Charles Scribner's Sons, 1899-1905), 3:34-38, pls. 42-44. The tomb of Nefertari (no. 66) is probably the finest in the whole Valley of the Queens in the West of Thebes. Gertrud Thausing and Hans Goedicke, *Nofretari: A Documentation of Her Tomb and Its Decoration* (Graz: Akademische Druck- und Verlagsanstalt, 1971).

39. Petrie, *A History of Egypt,* 3:104-106.

40. Smith, *The Royal Mummies,* no. 61079, pp. 65-70, pls. 45-49.

41. Four documents record this event—an inscription in the great temple at Karnak, a text on a granite column, a granite stela from Athribis in the southern Delta, and the "hymn of victory" on the black granite stela appropriated from Amunhotep III. The last three are in the Cairo Museum. ARE 3, secs. 572-617; ANET, pp. 376-378.

42. Per-Berset is presumably Per-Baste or Bubastis (Tell Basta, near Zagazig), and in the great Edfu geographical inscription, Itj is the "river" of the Lower Egyptian Nome XIII ("Hearty Sovereign," of which Heliopolis was the residence city). The *pehu* or "back-lying district" of the Twentieth or Arabian nome, therefore, was probably a well-known canal in this part of the Delta. Gardiner in JEA 5 (1918):249.

43. W. F. Albright in BASOR 74 (1939):22 n. 42.

44. The same determinative of "people" is also used elsewhere on the stela for such unsettled groups as the Madjoi, Nau, and Tekten. The Canaanite cities named (Ashkelon [cf. Josh. 13:3, etc.], Gezer [cf. Josh. 10:33, etc.], and Yenoam [in the far north of Palestine]) may therefore represent the older established culture in Palestine, and Israel may as yet be only tribes occupying the highlands. Von Beckerath, *Tanis und Theben,* p. 67.

45. ARE 3, sec. 606. If the Israelites labored for Ramses II (Exod 1:11; cf. immediately above in the present chapter n. 27) and were in Palestine by the fifth

year of Merneptah, then the general period of the biblical exodus was in the thirteenth century. Kitchen, *Ancient Orient and Old Testament,* pp. 59f. For the less likely theory that the Merneptah stela means that the Israelites were still in Egypt in the fifth year of Merneptah and that the exodus occurred shortly thereafter, see Pierre Montet, *Egypt and the Bible,* trans. Leslie R. Keylock (Philadelphia: Fortress Press, 1968), pp. 25-27. The apparently conflicting date 480 years before Solomon began to build the temple (1 Kings 6:1; cf. above Chapter 17, n. 30), pointing at face value to 1447/1446 in the reign of Thutmose III, may possibly be explained in a different way. The statement in Num. 32:13 that the children of Israel were made to "wander in the wilderness forty years, until all the generation that had done evil in the sight of the Lord was consumed," could suggest that "forty years" (itself a conventional round number) was the normal span of a generation. In 1 Chron. 6 the genealogy of the sons of Levi contains twelve names from Aaron (brother and contemporary of Moses, Exod. 6:20; 7:7) to Ahimaaz (father of Azariah, a priest contemporary with Solomon, 1 Kings 4:2), so twelve generations at forty years each would be 480 years. Alternatively, from Aaron to Zadok (the priest who anointed Solomon, 1 Kings 1:39; who was himself anointed with Solomon, 1 Chron. 29:22; and who became the chief priest of the Jerusalem sanctuary, 1 Kings 2:27, 35) was eleven generations and would give 440 years, the variant figure found in the LXX version of 1 Kings 6:1. Actually, however, a biblical generation (in Hebrew literally a "circle") is the period from the birth of a person to the birth of that person's son and, collectively, the people who live in such a period. A generation would usually be much shorter than forty years, with a correspondingly much shorter period lying back of the statement in 1 Kings 6:1. As to the route of the exodus, Exod. 13:17f. indicates an understandable avoidance of the coastal military road in favor of a wilderness way. See C. Bourdon in RB 37 (1928):232-256; ibid., 41 (1932):370-392, 538-549; H. Cazelles, ibid., 62 (1955):321-364; J. Simons, *The Geographical and Topographical Texts of the Old Testament* (Leiden: E. J. Brill, 1959), pp. 234-253; and for the traditional Mount Sinai, Beno Rothenberg, *God's Wilderness: Discoveries in Sinai* (New York: Thomas Nelson, 1961); Heinz Skrobucha, *Sinai* (London: Oxford University Press, 1966). For the Egyptian derivation of the name of Moses, see J. Gwyn Griffiths in JNES 12 (1953):225-231. For Moses, with a thirteenth-century date and a southern route of the exodus, see also Dewey Beagle, *Moses, the Servant of Yahweh* (Grand Rapids, Mich.: Eerdmans, 1972); Moshe Pearlman, *In the Footsteps of Moses* (New York: Abelard-Schuman, 1973); David Daiches, *Moses: the Man and His Vision* (New York: Praeger, 1975).

46. J. von Beckerath in JEA 48 (1962):70 n. 2; Cyril Aldred in ibid., 49 (1963):43.

47. Cf. Sese as an abbreviation and nickname of the name of Ramses II.

48. Jaroslav Černý in JEA 15 (1929):243-258.

49. Smith, *The Royal Mummies,* no. 61081, pp. 73-81, pls. 64-66.

50. Aldred in JEA 49 (1963):44.

51. ARE 3, secs. 639-651; George A. Reisner in JEA 6 (1920):48f.

52. ARE 3, secs. 642, 646; Alan Gardiner in JEA 44 (1958):12-15.

53. Von Beckerath in JEA 48 (1962):73.

54. Manetho says that the fall of Troy (traditionally dated in 1194) took place in the reign of Thuoris (i.e., Tawosre).

55. Hornung, *Untersuchungen zur Chronologie und Geschichte des Neuen Reiches*, p. 108.

56. ARE 4, secs. 151-412; ANET, pp. 260-262. For the possible identification of the Syrian prince with the chancellor Bay, see Gardiner in JEA 44 (1958):17, 21; von Beckerath in ibid., 48 (1962):73f. Sethnakhte did not finish the tomb (no. 11) he began for himself in the Valley of the Kings and was buried instead in the tomb (no. 14) of Queen Tawosre. Alan Gardiner in ibid., 40 (1954):40-44.

57. ARE 4, sec. 362; Alan R. Schulman in JNES 22 (1963):177-184.

58. *Reliefs and Inscriptions at Karnak*, vols. 1-2 (OIP 25, 35) (Chicago: University of Chicago Press, 1936); *Medinet Habu Communications*, 5 vols. (OIC 5, 7, 10, 15, 18) (Chicago: University of Chicago Press, 1929-1934); *The Excavation of Medinet Habu*, 5 vols. (OIP 21, 41, 54, 55, 66) (Chicago: University of Chicago Press, 1934-1964); *Medinet Habu Publications*, 7 vols. (OIP 8, 9, 23, 51, 83, 84, 93) (Chicago: University of Chicago Press, 1930-1964).

59. G. Bonfante in AJA 50 (1946):251-262.

60. ARE 4, secs. 35-58; *Medinet Habu Publications*, 1 pls. 13-26.

61. ARE 4, secs. 59-82; ANET, pp. 262f.; *Medinet Habu Publications*, 1 pls. 30-41. The foreign confederation consisted of the Peleste, Tjeker (who appear in a Twenty-first Dynasty papyrus—the Travels of Wenamun—as a people then settled at Dor on the north coast of Palestine), Shekelesh (perhaps the Siculi, later of Sicily), Denyen (perhaps the Danaoi of the *Iliad* 1. 56, etc.), and Weshesh (otherwise unknown). They overran Hatti, Carchemish, and other places in the north and came on toward Egypt. Ramses III met them victoriously both on the land ("in Djahi," i.e., probably on the Palestinian coast) and on the water ("at the river-mouths," i.e., probably in the Delta mouth of one or more of the branches of the Nile). The reliefs illustrating the engagement on the water are the earliest known representation of a naval battle. Harold H. Nelson in JNES 2 (1943):40-55.

62. ARE 4, secs. 83-114; *Medinet Habu Publications*, 2, pls. 70, 76A. In Papyrus Harris I, the first and second Libyan wars are treated together as one subject to which one passage is devoted. ARE 4, sec. 405. There are also scenes of warfare in Nubia in the Medinet Habu reliefs (*Medinet Habu Publications*, 1, pls. 9-11), but the name of Ramses III found in a temple at Semna suggests that the region as far as the Second Cataract was firmly under Egyptian administration. There are also scenes of warfare against Hittite and Syrian towns and in Amurru (*Medinet Habu Publications*, 2, pls. 87-98), and Ramses III may have campaigned there. At any rate, Papyrus Harris I (ARE 4, secs. 219, 384) records the building of a temple of Amun in Pekanan ("the Canaan") and lists nine towns of Khuru (Syria/Palestine), so it appears that Palestine and Syria were still under Egyptian control.

63. ARE 4, sec. 407.

64. Ibid., sec. 410.

65. William F. Edgerton in JNES 10 (1951):137-145.

66. The Judicial Papyrus of Turin and the Papyrus Lee and Papyrus Rollin, the latter two papyri being parts of one document. ARE 4, secs. 416-456; ANET, pp. 214-216; A. de Buck in JEA 23 (1937):152-164; Hans Goedicke in ibid., 49 (1963):71-92.

67. ARE 4, secs. 640f.; Smith, *The Royal Mummies,* no. 61083, pp. 84-87, pls. 50-52.

68. These rulers were probably all in some degree related to Ramses III, and there is evidence in particular that Ramses IV, VI, and VIII were sons of Ramses III, and Ramses V the son of Ramses IV. Jaroslav Černý in JEA 44 (1958):31-37; K. A. Kitchen in ibid., 58 (1972):182-194.

69. The tombs are: Ramses IV, no. 2; Ramses V and VI, no. 9; Ramses VII, no. 1; Ramses IX, no. 6; Ramses X, no. 18; Ramses XI, no. 4. Of the tombs, that of Ramses IV (no. 2) is of unusual interest because a plan of it is found on a Turin papyrus. Howard Carter and Alan H. Gardiner in ibid., 4 (1917):130-158. For the mummies, see Smith, *The Royal Mummies,* nos. 61084-61086, pp. 87-94, pls. 50-59. They are judged to indicate that at death Ramses IV was at least fifty years of age, Ramses VI (probably his younger brother) not beyond middle age, and Ramses V (probably the son of Ramses IV) yet much younger. Černý in JEA 44 (1958):36. In addition to his tomb in the Valley of the Kings, Ramses IV began a very large mortuary temple not far from the Ramesseum, on which additional work was probably done by Ramses V and VI.

70. The papyrus was found at el-Hibeh in Middle Egypt, and placed in the Moscow Museum. It dates to the early Twenty-first Dynasty, and the events it narrates took place shortly before, probably in the reign of Ramses XI, last king of the Twentieth Dynasty. See ARE 4, secs. 557-591; ANET, pp. 25-29; Hans Goedicke, *The Report of Wenamun* (Baltimore: Johns Hopkins University Press, 1975).

71. ARE 4, secs. 609ff. In the text, his priestly title, "First prophet of Amun-Re, king of the gods," is treated as his *prenomen* and enclosed in a cartouche; the name Siamun ("son of Amun") is prefixed to his name Herihor, and the composite form is treated as his *nomen* and also enclosed in a cartouche.

72. Charles F. Nims in JNES 7 (1948):157; Petrie, *A History of Egypt,* 3:203, fig. 80. After Herihor and Piankhy, there is only one more occurrence of the title, "king's son of Kush"—this is on a tablet in the Edwards Collection of the University College, London, where it is among the titles of Neskhons, wife of Pinudjem II, a high priest of Amun at Thebes near the end of the Twenty-first Dynasty—and here it must be simply an archaic title used in an honorary sense. Therefore Piankhy, son of Herihor, was the last in the long line of viceroys of Kush. After that, Kush was evidently no longer under Egyptian administration, although Wawat (Lower Nubia) may have continued within the empire. Reisner in JEA 6 (1920):51-53, nos. 22-24. Finally, the relationships were reversed, and Kush conquered Egypt. At that time the leader of the invasion was named Piankhy, and his sons became the pharaohs of the Twenty-fifth Egyptian dynasty. The identity of names even raises the surmise that Piankhy, son of Herihor, might

in some way have been an ancestor of the Kushite royal house. Emery, *Egypt in Nubia*, pp. 206f. For dates at this time both in terms of regnal years of Ramses XI and also in terms of a new era called the Repeating of Births (also used by Amunemhet I at the beginning of the Twelfth Dynasty and Seti I near the beginning of the Nineteenth Dynasty, to express the idea of a new beginning), see Jaroslav Černý in JEA 15 (1929):194-198.

CHAPTER 19. THIRD INTERMEDIATE PERIOD, TWENTY-FIRST TO TWENTY-FOURTH DYNASTIES

1. K. A. Kitchen, *The Third Intermediate Period in Egypt (1100-650 B.C.)* (Warminster: Aris and Phillips, 1972). For this date, see E. P. Uphill in JEA 61 (1975):277-283.

2. The order of the second and third kings is reversed from the order in Manetho on the basis of a tablet in the Berlin Museum (no. 23673), which contains a list of the ancestors of a Twenty-second Dynasty priest together with the kings under whom they served. The tablet names Amunemnisu (Nephercheres) before Akheperre (Psusennes I) instead of after him. L. Borchardt, *Die Mittel zur zeitlichen Festlegung von Punkten der ägyptischen Geschichte und ihre Anwendung* (Cairo: Selbstverlag, 1935), pp. 96-112, pls. 2 and 2a. An inscription on a mummy bandage gives the name of Amunemope (Amenophthis) and a date in "Year 49." This can hardly be a regnal year of Amunemope, to whom Manetho attributes only nine years of rule, but can be plausibly explained as implying a coregency of Amunemope with Psusennes I, and a date in terms of continuing years of reign of Psusennes I. The forty-six years attributed to Psusennes I by Manetho would, then, presumably be his years of sole reign, and his total reign (with Amunemope as a coregent) would have been a few years longer. For Siamun (Psinaches), regnal year dates are known that extend into his seventeenth year, so it is probable that the nine years Manetho attributes to him should be emended to nineteen to correct a presumable scribal error. The dates (Kitchen, *The Third Intermediate Period*, pp. 76, 465, table 1) extend to the relatively well established point of the beginning of the reign of Sheshonq I, first king of the Twenty-second Dynasty, in 945. Erik Hornung, *Untersuchungen zur Chronologie und Geschichte des Neuen Reiches*, (Ägyptologische Abhandlungen 11) (Wiesbaden: O. Harrassowitz, 1964), pp. 101-106, 109, allows 15 years for Psusennes II and 125 years for the entire dynasty, with the inclusive dates of 1070-945.

3. Edward F. Wente in JNES 26 (1967):176.

4. Recognition of Amun and a relationship of some sort with Thebes are reflected in several of the kings' names: Amunemnisu means "Amun is now the king," Psusennes (Psibkhaemne) means "the star which arose in Ne" (i.e., Thebes), Amunemope is "Amun is in Ope" (i.e., Luxor), and Siamun is "son of Amun."

5. Pierre Montet, *La nécropole de Tanis*, vol. 2, *Les constructions et le tombeau de Psousennès à Tanis* (Paris: Centre nationale de la Recherche scientifique, 1951).

6. ARE 4, secs. 636-642; Jaroslav Černý in JEA 32 (1946):24-30.

7. If the forty-year reign of David (2 Sam. 5:4f.) was in 1010-970 and the forty-year reign of Solomon (1 Kings 11:42) in 970-931, David would have become king in the midst of the long reign of Psusennes I (1039-993), and Solomon would have come to the throne in the time of Siamun (978-959). When David conquered Edom (2 Sam. 8:13f.), a young boy of the Edomite royal family named Hadad fled to Egypt and eventually married the sister of the wife of the Egyptian king (2 Kings 11:14-22). For her name, Tahpenes, see W. F. Albright in BASOR 140 (1955):32; Kitchen, *The Third Intermediate Period,* p. 274 n. 183. The record of the marriage of Solomon to the daughter of Pharaoh follows the killing of Shimei "at the end of three years" (1 Kings 2:39) and is prior to the building of the temple, begun in the fourth year (1 Kings 6:1) of Solomon (967/966). Therefore the Egyptian king involved was probably Siamun. The approval of this marriage in Egypt is a testimony to the important position of Solomon, for, at any rate, when the king of Babylon asked for the hand of the daughter of Amunhotep III, he was turned down (according to the Amarna Letters, no. 4) with the words: "From of old, a daughter of the king of Egypt has not been given to anyone." In the case of Solomon, the pharaoh also captured the city of Gezer and gave it to his daughter as a dowry (1 Kings 9:16). Gezer was on the northeastern border of Philistia and the edge of Israelite territory, and had evidently maintained itself as a Canaanite city (Judg. 1:29) against both the Israelites and the Philistines. Two items of archaeological evidence suggest that Siamun made a campaign against Philistine territory and, that on such a campaign, he could well have proceeded to take Gezer. On a fragmentary relief from Tanis, Siamun is smiting an enemy who holds a sort of double ax, probably characteristic of the Sea Peoples; therefore, the defeated enemy may probably be recognized as a Philistine. Pierre Montet, *Le Drame d'Avaris* (Paris: P. Geuthner, 1941), pp. 195f., fig. 58. At Tell Fara, probably ancient Sharuhen, on the road from Egypt to the western Negeb, a scarab was found on which is the name of Siamun. W. M. F. Petrie, *Beth-pelet I (Tell Fara)* (London: British School of Archaeology in Egypt, 1930), p. 10, pl. 29, no. 259. Siamun was, therefore, probably the pharaoh whose daughter was a wife of Solomon. A. Malamat in JNES 22 (1963):11f.

8. ANET, pp. 421-424. Estimates of the date of the work range from the Eighteenth (William Kelly Simpson, *The Literature of Ancient Egypt* [New Haven: Yale University Press, 1972], p. 241) to the Nineteenth to the Twenty-sixth (R. J. Williams in JEA 47 [1961]:106) dynasties. For the date ca. 1000, see Alan H. Gardiner in *The Legacy of Egypt* ed. S. R. K. Glanville (Oxford: Clarendon Press, 1942), pp. 67f.

9. In a number of passages there are parallels with the biblical book of Proverbs, for example, where both say that simple food with happiness is better than riches with strife and sorrow (9:5-8, 16:13f.; cf. Prov. 15:16f., 17:1), where both warn against association with the quick-tempered person (11:13f.; cf. Prov. 22:24), and where both advise circumspection in eating in the presence of a ruler (23:13-18; cf. Prov. 23:1-3).

10. ARE 4, secs. 785-792.

11. Likewise on a stela from Abydos (in the Cairo Museum, ARE 1, secs. 669-687; A. M. Blackman in JEA 27 [1941]:83-95), Sheshonq (I), then only a "great chief of the Me" (an abbreviation of the Meshwesh Libyan tribe), made a request to one of the last kings of the Twenty-first Dynasty, a request that was referred to Pinudjem (II) high priest of Amun at Thebes, for permission to set up in the temple of Osiris at Abydos a statue of his deceased father. The father is named Nimlot, a "great chief of the Meshwesh," and is son of a "great chief of the Meshwesh" named Sheshonq and of his wife Mehtenweskhet.

12. In addition to Bubastis (Tell Basta, near Zagazig), the Twenty-second Dynasty also had main centers at Tanis, where several of the kings did building work (Osorkon II, Sheshonq III, Sheshonq V) and where several were buried (Sheshonq II, Osorkon II, Takelot II, Sheshonq III), and at Memphis, where several kings built (Sheshonq I, Osorkon I, Osorkon II, Sheshonq III). In relation to the preceding dynasty at Tanis, Sheshonq I's first son, the crown prince and his successor as Osorkon I, married Maakare, daughter of Psusennes II, the last king of the Twenty-first Dynasty. In relation to the priesthood in Upper Egypt, Sheshonq's second son, Iuput, was installed as a high priest of Amun at Thebes. Thus continuity was established with the predecessors of the new dynasty.

13. Kitchen, *The Third Intermediate Period,* p. 467, table 3. Note that Sheshonq IV and Osorkon III, missing from the sequence in this dynasty, appear in the Twenty-third Dynasty.

14. Erik Hornung, *Grundzüge der ägyptischen Geschichte* (Darmstdt: Wissenschaftliche Buchgesellschaft, 1965), p. 124.

15. Stone was quarried for these structures at Gebel Silsileh, and a stela was left there to commemorate the undertaking. ARE 4, secs. 701-708. This text dates the project in the twenty-first year of the king, which was presumably the last full year of reign of Sheshonq I, since Manetho attributes to him a reign in round numbers of 21 years. Furthermore, the king's works at Karnak were not fully completed, leading to the supposition that he died not long thereafter. For the Bubastite Gate, see *Reliefs and Inscriptions at Karnak,* vol. 3, *The Bubastite Portal* (OIP 74) (Chicago: University of Chicago Press, 1954).

16. ARE 4, secs. 709-722; ANET, pp. 242f.

17. B. Mazar in VT, Supplement 4, 1957, pp. 57-66. If the division of the kingdom and the accession year of Rehoboam were in 931/930 and Rehoboam's first regnal year in 930/929 (beginning on Tishri 1 in the fall), then his fifth year was 926/925 and the invasion probably in the spring of 925, the spring being the usual time to launch a campaign in Palestine. Since the Silsileh inscription dates the works of Sheshonq I at Karnak in his twenty-first year of reign (see immediately above n. 15), and since the record of the Palestinian campaign was presumably put up soon after that enterprise was completed, the date of the invasion of Palestine was probably in about the twentieth year of the reign of Sheshonq I. This will place the beginning of his reign in approximately 945. Hornung, *Untersuchungen zur Chronologie und Geschichte des Neuen Reiches,* pp. 24-29; Kitchen, *The Third Intermediate Period,* pp. 74-76. Since Sheshonq I attacked Israel as well as Judah, it may be that

Jeroboam I, to whom he had previously given sanctuary from Solomon's attempt
to kill him (1 Kings 11:40), had not proved as subservient in his relations with
Egypt as Sheshonq I might have anticipated. As for the attack upon Judah, the
Karnak list includes places near Jerusalem but not the capital city itself, which
accords with the biblical record that Jerusalem was saved from destruction by
Shishak, but only at the cost of the loss of the sacred and royal treasures (2 Chron.
12:7-9). Confirmatory of the presence of Sheshonq I in northern Palestine is the
discovery at Megiddo of a fragment of a stela with his name. R. S. Lamon and G.
M. Shipton, *Megiddo I, Seasons of 1925-34, Strata I-V* (Chicago: University of
Chicago Press, 1939), p. 61. For the story of the discovery of the stela, see James
Henry Breasted, *The Conquest of Civilization* (New York: Harper and Brothers,
1926), p. xii. Evidences of destruction or decline in a number of excavated sites in
Palestine (e.g., Tell Beit Mirsim, Stratum B, W. F. Albright in *Archaeology and Old
Testament Study*, ed. D. Winton Thomas [Oxford: Clarendon Press, 1967], p. 216)
at the end of the Early Iron Age may also reflect the damage done by Sheshonq I's
campaign.

18. William Stevenson Smith in AJA 44 (1940):145.

19. ARE 4, sec. 743. On the quay at Karnak, records of the levels of the Nile are
dated in the regnal years of a number of kings of the Twenty-second and several
following dynasties. Ibid., secs. 693-698, 793f., 885-888. The record for the third
year of Osorkon II shows that the water would have risen to a depth of sixty-two
centimeters on the pavement of the Luxor temple. Ibid., sec. 696, no. 5.

20. Edouard Naville, *The Festival-Hall of Osorkon II, in the Great Temple of Bubastis
(1887-1889)* (London: K. Paul, Trench, Trübner, 1892). Along with the less well
preserved reliefs in the chapel of the sun temple of King Nyuserre (Fifth Dynasty)
at Abu Gurob, these are the best source for the study of the rites of the Sed festival.
Eric Uphill in JNES 24 (1965):365-383.

21. Kitchen, *The Third Intermediate Period*, pp. 108, 197f., 315f.

22. ARAB 1, sec. 611; ANET, p. 279.

23. Although the reference to the moon has been understood to mean a lunar
eclipse (W. F. Albright in BASOR 130 [1953]:4-11), the words are literally,
"heaven not having devoured the moon." This probably means that although there
was no such event to provide a portent of what was to happen, nevertheless there
was disaster. ARE 4, sec. 764; Kitchen, *The Third Intermediate Period*, pp. 181f.

24. ARE 4, secs. 778-781; W. M. Flinders Petrie, *A History of Egypt* 3 vols. (New
York: Charles Scribner's Sons, 1899-1905), 3:258 and fig. 104.

25. ARE 4, sec. 791.

26. ARAB 2, secs. 5, 55.

27. ANET, p. 286; W. F. Albright in BASOR 141 (1956):24f.; H. Tadmor in JCS
12 (1958):77f.

28. ARE 4, sec. 698, no. 18 (24); Kitchen, *The Third Intermediate Period*, pp. 134f.,
180.

29. Kitchen, *The Third Intermediate Period*, pp. 128, 467, table 3.

30. ARE 4, sec. 878, no. 2.

31. Kitchen, *The Third Intermediate Period*, pp. 129-131, 336f.

32. ARE 4, secs. 818, 838, 859; Kitchen, *The Third Intermediate Period*, pp. 138f.

33. W. Stevenson Smith, *The Art and Architecture of Ancient Egypt* (Harmondsworth: Penguin Books, 1958), p. 242, fig. 76.

34. On a Serapeum stela dated in his Year 6, Bakenranef records the burial of an Apis bull. ARE 4, sec. 884. This was in the same chamber in which the Apis bull was interred that died in the Year 37 of Sheshonq V; the bull that was buried in Year 6 of Bakenranef was therefore probably the one that was installed when the previous sacred animal died. But the same vault also contains an inscription of Year 2 of Shabaka; therefore, before the tomb of the Apis was closed, Shabaka must have taken Memphis and Bakenranef been set aside. Kitchen, *The Third Intermediate Period*, pp. 141, 377, 468, table 4.

35. In Israel the prophet Isaiah was active (Isa. 1:1; 6:1) from the year in which King Uzziah died (740/739) into the reign of Hezekiah (which began in 716/715). He was therefore contemporary with the latter period just described, and he portrays accurately (Isa. 19) the internal disorders and "spirit of confusion" in Egypt at the time.

CHAPTER 20. LATE DYNASTIC PERIOD, TWENTY-FIFTH TO THIRTY-FIRST DYNASTIES

1. G. A. Reisner in JEA 9 (1923):34-77; Dows Dunham in AJA 50 (1946): 376-388; Dows Dunham and M. F. Laming Macadam in JEA 35 (1949):139-149. For Nile-level records at Karnak in the reigns of Shabaka, Shabataka, and Taharqa, see ARE 4, secs. 886-888.

2. K. A. Kitchen, *The Third Intermediate Period in Egypt (1100-650 B.C.)* (Warminster: Aris and Phillips, 1972), p. 468, table 4; closely similar dates in J. Leclant, *Récherches sur les monuments thébains de la XXVe Dynastie dite éthiopienne* (Cairo: Imprimerie de l'institut français d'archéologie orientale, 1965), p. xxv. It is uncertain whether the Kushite kings counted the regnal year from the day of accession as was the custom in the New Kingdom, or whether they equated the regnal year with the calendar year and treated the last unfinished year of the predecessor as the first year of a new king as was done in the Middle Kingdom and again in the Saite period. But the latter may be the more likely because of the Nubian habit of imitating ancient traditions. G. Schmidt in *Kush* 6 (1958):128.

3. Gebel Barkal and the ruins of ancient Napata are on the right bank of the Nile, three kilometers downstream from the modern railway station of Kareima. Napata was a fortified town under Thutmose III, and a temple of Amun was built at the southeast foot of Gebel Barkal by Huy, viceroy of Kush under Tutankhamun. The tombs of the royal family are at two sites, one at Kurru on the right bank of the Nile thirteen kilometers below Kareima, and the other on the other side of the river, three kilometers from Nuri, six kilometers upstream from Kareima. The Napata pyramids are relatively small and very steep. The superstructure is a solid core of earth and stones, with a sandstone casing, either smooth or stepped, sloping upward at an angle of as much as 68 degrees. The burial

chamber is hewn in the natural rock below and is reached by a stairway, which leads down from an entrance outside the pyramid. In the burial chamber a bier was cut out of the rock, and a wooden bed was placed on this structure to receive the mummy and its coffin, such a "bed-burial" being an ancient and long-continued Nubian custom. The identified tombs of Piankhy, Shabaka, Shabataka, and Tanutamun are at Kurru (nos. 17, 15, 18, and 16, respectively), and that of Taharqa at Nuri (no. 1). The Kushites were fine horsemen, and the personal mounts of Piankhy, Shabaka, Shabataka, and Tanutamun were buried beside their pyramids—in each case usually four horses.

4. The fact that the daughter of Kashta, Amunirdis I, was adopted to become a "god's wife of Amun" by the princess and priestess Shepenupet I—herself daughter of Osorkon III and sister of Takelot III (Twenty-third Dynasty) and "god's wife of Amun" at Thebes—may mean that Kashta pushed into Thebes as well. On the other hand, this may have come to pass only in the reign of her brother Piankhy. Kitchen, *The Third Intermediate Period,* pp. 151, 359f., and 478, tables 10 and 11 for the family relationships of Shepenupet I and Amunirdis I.

5. ARE 4, secs. 796-883; Kitchen, *The Third Intermediate Period,* pp. 363-366.

6. For the kings at Herakleopolis and Hermopolis see Kitchen, *The Third Intermediate Period,* p. 485, table 16.

7. Alan H. Gardiner in JEA 21 (1935):220-223.

8. Piankhy's inspection of the conquered city included a visit to the royal stables, and when he found that the horses had suffered hunger during the siege, he rebuked Nemrot severely.

9. Cf. Chapter 19, n. 34. Certain Assyrian data accord well with the date of 715 for the conquest of Egypt by Shabaka. In 716, Osorkon IV (Shilkanni) sent a gift of fine horses to Sargon II at Wadi El-Arish (see Chapter 19), so this last king of the Twenty-second Dynasty had not yet been displaced in that year. In 712 Sargon II suppressed a revolt in Ashdod (Friedrich Karl Kienitz, *Die politische Geschichte Ägyptens vom 7. bis zum 4. Jahrhundert* [Berlin: Akademie Verlag, 1953], pp. 79-84, 92f.) and states in his Display Inscriptions and on Prism A (ARAB 2, secs. 62f., 193-195; ANET, pp. 286f.) that the city had sent in vain for help "to Pir'u king of Musri" (i.e., "to Pharaoh king of Egypt") and that the usurper king in Ashdod, Iamani by name, hearing that the Assyrian expedition was coming, fled "into the territory of Musri [Egypt], which belongs now to Meluhha [Nubia]." The Nubian king, however, sent Iamani back in shackles to the Assyrians. At this time, therefore, a Nubian pharaoh was ruling Egypt. This must mean a member of the Twenty-fifth (Kushite) Dynasty; it cannot be Piankhy, who did not maintain his rule in Egypt, but it fits well with Shabaka. Kitchen, *The Third Intermediate Period,* pp. 143f., 155, 378, 380, and n. 778.

10. ARE 4, sec. 889. It was also Shabaka who (as noted above in Chapter 12) had the text of the Memphite Theology transferred from a worm-eaten roll of papyrus or leather to the stone document on which this document has been preserved.

11. For Amunirdis I and the significance of the role of "god's wife of Amun," see Leclant, *Récherches sur les monuments thébains,* pp. 96-98, 156-158, 358, 369-386, pl.

61. For Amunirdis II and other "god's wives of Amun," see Kitchen, *The Third Intermediate Period,* p. 480, table 13B.

12. M. F. Laming Macadam, *The Temples of Kawa,* 4 vols. (Oxford: Oxford University Press, 1949-1955), 1:15.

13. Ibid., p. 28.

14. ARAB 2, sec. 311; ANET, p. 287.

15. Although Sennacherib defeated the Egyptians, other circumstances dictated his withdrawal from Palestine, and the biblical account concludes (2 Kings 19:36f.; Isa. 37:37f.) with that withdrawal and the eventual death of Sennacherib (681). Since the biblical account is written in the perspective of that later point, it naturally called Tirhakah (Taharqa) king of Kush, as he was at that time, even though in 701 he was as yet only crown prince. In a very comparable way, the Kawa stela (IV) cited above uses the phrase *his majesty*—strictly applicable only to kings and gods—in speaking not only of King Shabataka at the time when he was on the throne, but also of Taharqa himself at the time when he was still only a young man in Nubia and his kingship was yet in the future. Kitchen, *The Third Intermediate Period,* pp. 157-161, 386, and nn. 823, 824; idem, JANES 5 (1973):231.

16. Macadam, *The Temples of Kawa,* 1:28; cf. ARE 4, sec. 895.

17. Leclant, *Récherches sur les monuments thébains,* pp. 8-13, pls. 1, 5. As to works in Nubia, in his first year of reign Taharqa called to mind the Gematen temple, which he had beheld as a youth; he was grieved at its condition, built only of brick and covered over with sand. Accordingly, in his sixth year he sent an architect and craftsmen, and the temple was built again of fine white sandstone. Kawa Stela IV, Macadam, *The Temples of Kawa,* 1:15f.; Jean Leclant and Jean Yoyotte in BIFAO 51 (1952):20f. In the excavation of Kawa, Temple A has sandstone doorways for the first and second courts, which were added by Taharqa and bear inscriptions with his name and the name of "his father Amun-Re of Gematen"; Temple T is a whole new temple built by Taharqa. A processional avenue led to the latter temple, and at the approach to the temple pylon are sandstone bases on two of which were found granite rams (one now in the Sudan Merowe Museum in Khartoum and one in the British Museum), each enclosing between its front paws a small standing figure of King Taharqa. Macadam, *The Temples of Kawa,* 2:28-30, 53-113. At Napata, Taharqa restored a temple of Mut and dedicated an altar in the temple of Amun. ARE 4, secs. 897-900.

18. ARAB 2, secs. 580, 710; ANET, p. 293; Jozef M. A. Janssen in *Biblica* 34 (1953):37f. Of the officials whom Esarhaddon appointed in Egypt, Ashurbanipal later (in connection with his first campaign against Egypt, 667/666) names many and tells how he himself reinstalled them in their offices. ARAB 2, secs. 771-774, 902-905; ANET, pp. 294f. Among them is Necho, king of Memphis and Sais, of whom Ashurbanipal says, "I sent him back to his post in Sais, where my father had set him up as king, and Nabu-shezibanni, his son, I set over Hathariba" (Egyptian Huttahryib, Greek Athribis, in Lower Egyptian Nome X ["Black Bull"]). This Necho is Necho I, one in a line of several local rulers of Sais, who followed

Bakenranef (Twenty-fourth Dynasty) at that place. Nabu-shezibanni is Psamtik I (Psammetichus), who is ordinarily considered the first king of the Twenty-sixth (Saite) Dynasty. It may be noted that Manetho attributes to Taharqa (Tarcus) a reign of eighteen (Africanus) or twenty (Eusebius) years. This span of time, reckoned from accession in 690, would bring Taharqa's reign to 672 or 670, around the time of the Assyrian invasion (671), and could mean that this event was thought of as bringing the Twenty-fifth Dynasty to an end. Or, if one should look for an Egyptian king of another line whose accession marked the dividing point, this could perhaps be found in Necho I (Twenty-sixth Dynasty), coming to the throne of Sais in 672 (in Taharqa's eighteenth year) and confirmed in that position by Esarhaddon in 671. M. B. Rowton in JEA 34 (1948):61; Kitchen *The Third Intermediate Period,* p. 453 and n. 135.

19. ARAB 2, secs. 771, 775; ANET, pp. 294f.; Kitchen, *The Third Intermediate Period,* pp. 161-163. Among the officials whom Ashurbanipal names as having been appointed by Esarhaddon and reinstalled by himself is one Mantimanhe, king of Thebes. This must be Montemhat, a well-known figure under Taharqa and also under Psamtik I. In the temple of Mut at Karnak (constructed by Amunhotep III in place of one built by Hatshepsut, south of the temple of Amun), Montemhat appears in a relief together with Taharqa and has the titles of fourth prophet of Amun, mayor of Thebes, and governor of the Southland. The text says that "the whole land was overturned," speaks of the repelling of rebels in the southern nomes, and tells of Montemhat's many works in Thebes and elsewhere in purifying temples, building temples, and fashioning images, works that may well have been done in repair of the damages caused by the invasion of Ashurbanipal. ARE 4, secs. 901-916.

20. ARE 4, secs. 919-934.

21. ARAB 2, secs. 775, 906; ANET, pp. 295, 297. In one of these two texts, Ashurbanipal called Urdamane the son of Shabaku; in the other, he calls him the son of Taharqa's sister. As a guess, "Shabaku" may be Shabataka, brother of Taharqa, married to his own sister who was also Taharqa's sister. In this case, Urdamane (Tanutamun) was the nephew of Taharqa. Dunham and Macadam in JEA 35 (1949):146f., 149.

22. In the time that followed, the history of Kush is divided into two main periods, the first when the capital was still at Napata, the second when it was moved to Meroe (between the Fifth and Sixth cataracts, in the area often called the Island of Meroe within the fork of the Atbara and Nile rivers). The date of this move is uncertain but may have been connected with a campaign in Kush by Psamtik II in about 591. At the time, the Kushite king was Aspelta, fourth successor of Tanutamun, and he is the first in this line of rulers whose name has been found at Meroe. The kings continued to be buried at Napata (in the necropolis at Nuri), however, down to Nastasen, twentieth successor of Tanutamun in the latter part of the fourth century; Arakamani, early in the third century, was the first king to be buried at Meroe. There the pyramids of the kings and queens are much like those at Napata, with steep sides at an angle

between 65 and 70 degrees. In the last two or three centuries B.C.E., the Meroitic state became an empire that dominated the northern Sudan and Upper Nubia, and the Meroitic culture, blending Egyptian, African, and Hellenistic elements, flourished. Struggles with Rome ensued, however, and by around 350 C.E., Meroe seems to have been under the rule of King Aizana of Aksum. See P. L. Shinnie, *Meroe: A Civilization of the Sudan* (New York: Praeger, 1967).

23. Kitchen, *The Third Intermediate Period,* p. 468, table 4. There are also many references to kings of this dynasty in Greek writers, especially Herodotus (2. 151ff.), who uses the forms Apries and Amasis for their names. In the Saite period (as perhaps in the preceding Kushite period, cf. above in the present chapter n. 2), the regnal year was considered to coincide with the civil year, and the entire calendar year in which a king took the throne was reckoned as the first year of his reign. ARE 4, secs. 959, 975, 984. By the Saite period, the civil calendar had regressed sufficiently that the Egyptian year is calculated to have begun in 664 on February 5, and in 525 on January 2. Richard A. Parker in MDAIK 15 (1957):208-212.

24. In Eusebius, Manetho's list begins with Ammeris the Ethiopian, prior to Stephinathis, and ends with Amosis. Ammeris could be a Nubian governor appointed by Shabaka; Stephinates could be a Tefnakht II (with a Greek sigma added in front of his Egyptian name) and thus a member of Bakenranef's family who renewed the rule of Sais by that line; and Nechepsos can represent an Egyptian name Nekauba, for which there is some evidence. W. M. Flinders Petrie, *A History of Egypt,* 3 vols. (New York: Charles Scribner's Sons, 1899-1905), 3:317-319; Kitchen, *The Third Intermediate Period,* pp. 145f.

25. See above in the present chapter n. 19.

26. Thomas George Allen, *The Egyptian Book of the Dead: Documents in the Oriental Institute at the University of Chicago* (OIP 82) (Chicago: University of Chicago Press, 1975), p. 126.

27. See the so-called Adoption Stela of Nitocris. ARE 4, secs. 935-958; Ricardo A. Caminos in JEA 50 (1964):71-101. The fleet that brought Nitocris set out from the north (presumably Sais or Memphis) in Year 9, the first month of the first season, day 28, and arrived in Thebes in the second month, day 14. There Nitocris was presented to Amun and to the reigning "god's wives," who loved her and accepted her. On a number of relief carvings from the temple of Mut in Karnak, ships are seen arriving, probably at the quay in Karnak; this may be a representation of the flotilla that brought Nitocris to Thebes. In the meantime, Montemhat also continued to occupy a high position at Thebes, as he had under Taharqa, and he prepared for himself a very large tomb (no. 34) in the el-Assasif valley in front of Deir el-Bahri.

28. The statement in 2 Kings 23:29 that "Pharaoh Neco king of Egypt went up to the king of Assyria to the river Euphrates," and the statement in the parallel account in 2 Chron. 35:21 that he went in "haste," must describe this same attempt of Necho II to assist Ashur-uballit II. The disastrous effort of King Josiah to halt Necho on the plain of Megiddo was therefore an endeavor to keep this potential

aid from reaching Assyria, the power that had been such a terrible enemy of Israel and Judah. Perhaps it was upon return from this unsuccessful venture to the Euphrates that Necho II captured Gaza, an event mentioned by Herodotus (2. 159) as taking place after the battle of Megiddo.

29. Thus, although the event took place while he was still on the throne, Necho II did not involve himself when Nebuchadnezzar II came on to accomplish his first conquest of Jerusalem (March 16, 597).

30. For the triremes, see Alan B. Lloyd in JEA 58 (1972):268-279. Upon return from the African circumnavigation, the sailors reported that in sailing round Libya they had the sun on their right hand, which Herodotus disbelieved, but which confirms their story. Later under Xerxes, Herodotus (2. 43) adds, a Persian named Sataspes was sent with an Egyptian ship to make the circumnavigation in the reverse direction, but found the sea so vast that off the west coast of Africa, he turned back to Egypt.

31. There is confirmation of the campaign in a Greek inscription on one of the colossi of Ramses II at Abu Simbel, which states that King Psammetichus (probably Psamtik II) came to Elephantine, that those who sailed with another Psammetichus the son of Theokles went on as far as the river would permit, and that those who spoke foreign tongues (presumably Greek and other foreign soldiers) were led by Amasis. Kienitz, *Die politische Geschichte Ägyptens vom 7. bis zum 4. Jahrhundert,* pp. 41f.

32. Petrie, *A History of Egypt,* 3:337, 341f.

33. ARE 4, sec. 988C-D.

34. Ibid., sec. 988E-F; Herman J. A. de Meulenaere in LÄ 1, cols. 358-360.

35. A. Malamat in IEJ 18 (1968):151-153. Herodotus (2. 161) says that Apries sent an army against Sidon and a sea force against Tyre; therefore, Apries may have made a double move against the Babylonians, by land up the coast of Palestine and by sea to the coast of Phoenicia. K. S. Freedy and D. B. Redford in JAOS 90 (1970):481-483; H. Jacob Katzenstein, *The History of Tyre* (Jerusalem: Schocken Institute for Jewish Research, 1973), pp. 319, 332. In spite of the failure of Apries's outright resistance to Nebuchadnezzar II, Egypt still offered refuge to those who feared the Babylonians, and some time after the fall of Jerusalem, the remnant of Judah fled thither, taking with them the prophet Jeremiah (2 Kings 25:22-26; Jer. 43:4-7).

36. Herman J. A. de Meulenaere in JEA 54 (1968):183-187; idem, LÄ 1, cols. 181f.

37. ANET, p. 308; Kienitz, *Die politische Geschichte Ägyptens vom 7. bis zum 4. Jahrhundert,* pp. 30f.

38. In this period of quiet, Egypt enjoyed a prosperity that Herodotus (2. 177), perhaps with some exaggeration, says was marked by the existence of no fewer than 20,000 inhabited cities in the country.

39. Kienitz, *Die politische Geschichte Agyptens vom. 7. bis zum 4. Jahrhundert,* p. 32.

40. Xenophon (*Cyropaedia* 6. 2, 10) speaks of the coming of 120,000 Egyptians to fight on the side of Croesus, but Herodotus does not mention such actualized assistance.

41. Richard A. Parker in MDAIK 15 (1957):208.

42. Petrie, *A History of Egypt,* 3:360-362.

43. W. Spiegelberg, *Die sogenannte demotische Chronik* (Leipzig: J. C. Hinrichs, 1914).

44. Alan H. Gardiner in JEA 24 (1938):157-179.

45. Petrie, *A History of Egypt,* 3:367f.

46. Kienitz, *Die politische Geschichte Ägyptens vom 7. bis zum 4. Jahrhundert,* pp. 169, 180; Jürgen von Beckerath, *Abriss der Geschichte des alten Agypten* (Munich: R. Oldenbourg, 1971), p. 55.

47. A. Cowley, *Aramaic Papyri of the Fifth Century B.C.* (Oxford: Clarendon Press, 1923), no. 35, pp. 129-131.

48. Kienitz, *Die politische Geschichte Ägyptens vom 7. bis zum 4. Jahrhundert,* pp. 169, 180; von Beckerath, *Abriss der Geschichte des alten Ägypten,* p. 55.

49. Petrie, *A History of Egypt,* 3:373-377.

50. Kienitz, *Die politische Geschichte Ägyptens vom 7. bis zum 4. Jahrhundert,* p. 175; von Beckerath, *Abriss der Geschichte des alten Ägypten,* pp. 55f.

51. The chief temple at Sebennytus was that of Onuris, and the city was also known as the House of Onuris. Onuris, worshiped also at Thinis in Upper Egypt, was a war god, crowned with two feathers; he was considered a form of Horus, particularly in his aggressive aspect, or also of Shu. The Greeks equated him with Ares (Mars). See Kees in PWRE ser. 2, 2:1, cols. 958f.

52. Petrie, *A History of Egypt,* 3:385-388. Fragments of the king's green breccia sarcophagus have also survived and are in the Cairo Museum.

53. Ibid., pp. 378-383. The sarcophagus of Nectanebo II, made of green breccia like that of Nectanebo I, has also survived, although under various vicissitudes. At some point it was removed to Alexandria and put in the mosque of St. Athanasius, where it was venerated as the tomb of Alexander the Great; later it was taken by the French and then by the British and so came to the British Museum.

54. The dream was on the night of Pharmuthi 21/22, on the night of a full moon, in the king's sixteenth year. Astronomical calculation indicates a full moon on the night of July 5/6, corresponding to Pharmuthi 21/22, in the year 343, and not in any other year nearer than 354. Taken with other data, the Persian onslaught can be put in the following months, i.e., in the winter of 343/342. According to the text of Manetho (Africanus), this must have been not in the sixteenth but in the eighteenth year of Nectanebo II. In Greek numerals, however, the difference would be between Iota Vau and Iota Eta, and a mistake in copying between Eta and Vau would not be difficult to conceive. See M. Pieper in PWRE 16:2, cols. 2237f; Kienitz, *Die politische Geschichte Ägyptens vom 7. bis zum 4. Jahrhundert,* pp. 171-173.

55. Rudolf Helm, ed., *Die Chronik des Hieronymus* (GCS Eusebius 7) (Berlin: Akademie Verlag, 1956), p. 121. The notation is placed in the 107th Olympiad (i.e., 352-349), a few years too early according to our chronology.

56. Within this period and perhaps in the time of murders and troubles in Persia between 338 and 336, there may have been one more attempt, temporarily successful, to free Egypt from Persian rule. On a stela of the later Ptolemy I Soter, dated in 311, when he was still only satrap of Egypt under the boy king Alexander

II, the text tells how a certain Khababash went into the marshlands of the Delta "to examine every arm of the Nile which goes into the Great Sea, to keep off the fleet of Asia from Egypt," and how he there restored to the temple of Buto lands that had been taken away by Xerxes, even as he himself (Ptolemy) again in his time guaranteed these lands to the priests. The name of Khababash is not Egyptian, and it is a guess that he might have been a prince of Lower Nubia who asserted himself briefly in Egypt. The time was after the invasion of Egypt by Xerxes (484/483) and before Ptolemy I Soter, and could have been when Persia was weakened by the disorders of 338-336. Two other minor documents are dated in the first and second years of Khababash, and he might have had a brief reign of some such duration. See Edwyn Bevan, *A History of Egypt under the Ptolemaic Dynasty* (New York: Charles Scribner's Sons, 1927), pp. 28-32; Kienitz, *Die politische Geschichte Ägyptens vom 7. bis zum 4. Jahrhundert*, pp. 185-189, 232, nos. 1-2.

INDEX